Epistemic Reasons, Norms and Goals

Epistemic Reasons, Norms and Goals

Edited by
Martin Grajner and Pedro Schmechtig

DE GRUYTER

Printed with financial support from the Deutsche Forschungsgemeinschaft (DFG).

ISBN 978-3-11-061177-9
e-ISBN (PDF) 978-3-11-049676-5
e-ISBN (EPUB) 978-3-11-049363-4

Library of Congress Cataloging-in-Publication Data
A CIP catalog record for this book has been applied for at the Library of Congress.

Bibliographic information published by the Deutsche Nationalbibliothek
The Deutsche Nationalbibliothek lists this publication in the Deutsche Nationalbibliografie; detailed bibliographic data are available on the Internet at http://dnb.dnb.de.

© 2018 Walter de Gruyter GmbH, Berlin/Boston
This volume is text- and page-identical with the hardback published in 2016.
Printing and binding: CPI books GmbH, Leck

♾ Printed on acid-free paper
Printed in Germany

www.degruyter.com

Table of Contents

Acknowledgements —— IX

Martin Grajner and Pedro Schmechtig
Introduction: Epistemic Reasons, Norms and Goals —— 1

I Epistemic Reasons

Martin Grajner
In Defense of Psychologism About Reasons —— 33

Clayton Littlejohn
Learning from Learning from our Mistakes —— 51

Terence Cuneo
Destabilizing the Error Theory —— 71

Andrew Reisner
Peer Disagreement, Rational Requirements, and Evidence of Evidence as Evidence Against —— 95

II Epistemic Norms

Nicholas Unwin
Belief, Truth and Radical Disagreement —— 117

Mona Simion
Assertion, Knowledge and Rational Credibility: The Scoreboard —— 137

Davide Fassio
Commonality Reconsidered: On the Common Source of Epistemic Standards —— 165

Erik Stei
Epistemic Standards: High Hopes and Low Expectations —— 185

Veli Mitova
What do I care About Epistemic Norms? —— 199

III Epistemic Consequentialism

Hamid Vahid
Epistemic Normativity: From Direct to Indirect Epistemic Consequentialism —— 227

Chase Wrenn
Tradeoffs, Self-Promotion, and Epistemic Teleology —— 249

Jochen Briesen
Epistemic Consequentialism: Its Relation to Ethical Consequentialism and the Truth-Indication Principle —— 277

Christian Piller
How to Overstretch the Ethics-Epistemology Analogy: Berker's Critique of Epistemic Consequentialism —— 307

IV Epistemic Goals and Values

Pedro Schmechtig
External Goals and Inherent Norms – A Cluster-Conception of Epistemic Normativity —— 325

Matthew Chrisman
The Aim of Belief and the Goal of Truth: Reflections on Rosenberg —— 357

Christos Kyriacou
Ought to Believe, Evidential Understanding and the Pursuit of Wisdom —— 383

Duncan Pritchard
Epistemic Axiology —— 407

J. Adam Carter and Emma C. Gordon
Objectual Understanding, Factivity and Belief —— 423

Contributors —— 443

Author Index —— 445

Subject Index —— 449

Acknowledgements

There are a number of institutions and people that we would like to thank for their help in the production of this volume. First, we would like to thank the German Research Foundation for providing a printing cost subsidy that made it possible to publish this volume. We also appreciate the financial support that the German Research Foundation provided for a workshop that took place in Dresden in June 2014 where some of the contributions in this volume were presented.

We would also like to thank Gertrud Grünkorn and Johanna Wange at de Gruyter for their help during this project and all the others at de Gruyter who were involved in putting this volume together.

Thanks also goes to all the contributors of this volume for their patience and smooth cooperation throughout the (long) process of completing this volume.

Finally, we would also like to thank Andrej Swindsinski and Johannes Wand for their help in preparing the manuscript.

Dresden, February 2016   Martin Grajner and Pedro Schmechtig

Martin Grajner and Pedro Schmechtig
Introduction: Epistemic Reasons, Norms and Goals

1. Overview of the Main Questions

In contemporary epistemology there are a plethora of normative issues. When, for example, one thinks that we need good reasons for beliefs, or that we should believe something only if it is true, or when one raises the question of whether there is such a thing as a primary goal of our epistemic interest, then one is making direct use of deontic and axiological notions. In recent years questions about the reasons, norms and goals of our epistemic endeavors have been discussed very intensively. The present volume provides further insight into the various aspects of these debates. It brings together a variety of contemporary research that focuses on epistemic normativity. The contributions are arranged into four sections: (1) epistemic reasons, (2) different aspects of epistemic norms, (3) epistemic consequentialism and (4) epistemic goals and values.

1.1 Epistemic Reasons

Reasons play an important role in contemporary epistemology and metaethics.[1] It is common to distinguish between different kinds of reasons.[2] First, there are normative reasons. Normative reasons are reasons that count in favor believing or doing a certain thing. There is some controversy about how to spell out the relation of favoring. Intuitively, however, favoring just amounts to making a doxastic response or course of action in light of the existence of a particular normative reason objectively correct. Second, there is the notion of a motivational reason. Motivational reasons play a role in the psychology of an agent in that they are those mental states which move an agent to do a particular thing. It has been claimed that normative and motivational reasons should be kept apart and that they might not belong to the same ontological categories. However, this claim is controversial. Third, there are explanatory reasons, i.e., reasons that explain why

---

[1] In recent metaethics some regard reasons as the basic building blocks of normativity. This approach goes by the name of the 'reasons-first' program.
[2] See Alvarez (2009, 2010) and Dancy (2000).

an agent believes or does a particular thing. Explanatory reasons differ from normative reasons in that the things explanatory reasons explain or apparently favor might not overall be the right thing to believe or do for this agent.

There are several questions regarding the nature of reasons that have been the focus of current research. The following topics have loomed large in the recent literature: (i) What are reasons—are they mental states, propositions or facts? (ii) How do reasons relate to rationality, normative requirements and peer disagreement? (iii) Should we be anti-realists or realists regarding ascriptions of reasons and epistemic justification?

Ad (i): What are epistemic reasons? In the present literature on the ontology of reasons, the following answers have been given:

Psychologism: epistemic reasons are psychological items, such as mental states or events.

Factualism: epistemic reasons are facts.

Propositionalism/ abstractionism: epistemic reasons are propositions, i.e., the contents of psychological states.

Pluralism: all of the above can be epistemic reasons.

Each of these candidates is usually supported by arguments that highlight one or more roles that epistemic reasons are supposed to play and by the contention that rival candidates fail to fulfill these particular roles.[3] For example, psychologism is often supported by the idea that only a person's psychological states are able to explain why the person believes, disbelieves or withholds believing a particular proposition. Defenders of psychologism stress that entities that are outside a person's ken, such as extra-mental facts or propositions, are not able to fulfill this role in all cases. By contrast, factualism is often considered to account best for the fact that certain reasons are normative. While psychological states or propositions do not seem to possess *per se* any inherent normative force (since they can be inaccurate or false), non-mental facts do seem to favor, in a normative sense, adopting a particular propositional attitude. Propositionalists, by contrast, usually point out that reasons confer a certain probability on a particular

---

[3] See Turri (2009), Mitova (2015), Kelly (2008) and Littlejohn (2012) for a discussion of various desiderata a theory of reasons should accommodate.

propositional content.⁴ But psychological states or facts are in general not the relata of probabilistic relations and thus are not suitable to satisfy this specific role. Finally, pluralism is usually motivated by the thought that the desiderata for a theory of reasons seem to be inconsistent because no single type of entity can satisfy all of the desiderata at the same time. Thus, pluralists urge that we should acknowledge that multiple entities are epistemic reasons.

Martin Grajner (this volume) discusses two challenges to psychologism about reasons. First, linguistic data seem to exist that suggest that facts can be reasons for beliefs. Therefore, it follows that not every reason is a psychological state. Second, several factualists have recently presented solutions to the problem that 'bad cases' pose for their view. Bad cases are cases in which an agent is intuitively in possession of a reason even though the content of the reason does not correspond to a fact. Grajner tries to show that psychologism is not inconsistent with the data that seem to favor factualism and that the recent solutions of the problem that bad cases pose for factualism are not successful.

A further issue closely connected to the nature of epistemic reasons is what it takes to possess or have a reason. Psychologism about reasons provides a straightforward account of possession of a reason. Since reasons are mental states, like experiences or beliefs, an agent is in possession of a reason if that agent is in the mental state, which is her reason. The account of possession of reasons that psychologism can provide is underwritten nicely by the way we attribute a possessed reason to someone. We say, for example, that someone has a reason and, at the same time, we can say that this person has a mental state which is her reason. By contrast, if we conceive of reasons as facts or propositions, it is difficult to reconcile both views with the linguistic data just considered. It is very odd to say that you can have or possess a proposition or a fact, while it is totally okay to say that you can have or possess a reason. In light of this phenomenon, the following argument could thus be presented against propositionalism and factualism about reasons:

(P1) You can have reasons.
(P2) You can't have propositions or facts.
(C) Reasons aren't propositions or facts.

---

4 See Williamson (2000) for this argument. This argument is discussed in McCain (2014), chapter 2.

Despite the initial plausibility of this argument, there are several solutions as to how propositionalism or factualism about reasons can avoid the conclusion of this argument.[5]

Clayton Littlejohn's contribution (this volume) engages the question of what it takes to possess a reason. Littlejohn is of the view that reasons are true propositions and that a particular proposition p is among one's reasons only if one knows p. This view also goes by the name of the 'knowledge-first' approach to reasons and evidence. However, counterexamples exist to the view that possession of reasons requires of an agent that she knows p. One prominent type of counterexample to this view are cases of knowledge from falsehood. These cases illustrate that an agent S can have p as his evidence even though S fails to know p because p is false. Littlejohn presents two arguments that intend to demonstrate that cases of knowledge from falsehood don't undermine the knowledge-first approach to reasons.

Ad (ii): Rationality seems to come, at least initially, in two different varieties.[6] On the one hand, there is what several authors call 'reasons rationality'; on the other, there is what goes by the name of 'structural rationality'. Take reasons rationality first. Reasons rationality is, according to the prevalent view, a matter of correctly responding to reasons. It is, for example, rational for me to believe that I have two hands while it is irrational for me to believe that I am currently president of the United States. Believing that I have two hands is rational for me because this belief is supported by normative reasons available to me. By contrast, believing that I am currently president of the United States is irrational for me because no normative reasons exist that would provide adequate support for this particular belief. Reasons rationality does not only pertain to beliefs but also to actions. Those actions for which I have normative reasons are rational for me to perform while those that are not supported by reasons are irrational for me to perform.

In the structural sense, by contrast, rationality is a matter of coherence and consistency. According to this sense of 'rational', those things are rational for me to believe which are the consequences of other things I believe. So, for example, if I believe that I am currently president of the United States, and given that I further believe that the current president of the United States has a wife whose first name is Michelle, I should also believe that my wife's first name is Michelle. Rationality in the structural sense is determined by the other attitudes I happen to have. If, as in the example just considered, I disbelieve that my

---

5 See Schroeder (2008) and Turri (2012).
6 See, for example, Scanlon (2007).

wife's name is Michelle but at the same time believe that I am currently president of the United States and that the president's wife's name is Michelle, I exhibit a rational failing. But that kind of rational failing is of a different variety than a rational failing that results from incorrectly responding to reasons.

Another notion that is closely linked to the notion of rationality in the structural sense is the notion of a rational requirement.[7] Some philosophers have argued that if I believe or intend to do certain things, rationality requires of me to believe or intend other things as well. For example, if I believe p, it seems that I am rationally required to disbelieve not-p. There is some debate about how to spell out these requirements in more detail. Regarding the particular rational requirement just mentioned, for instance, two readings exist, namely a wide-scope reading on the one hand and a narrow-scope reading on the other:

(Wide Scope) RR(If you believe p → you disbelieve non-p)

(Narrow Scope) If you believe p → RR(you disbelieve non-p)

Rational requirements seem to play an important role in other debates as well. For example, in the debate about the rational significance of peer disagreement, most authors speak about what one is required to do or believe in case one finds out that one disagrees with an epistemic peer. An epistemic peer is usually understood as someone who shares one's reasons or evidence with respect to p and is further on par regarding one's cognitive capacities. The fact that one disagrees with a peer with respect to p is often understood as providing new evidence regarding p—namely, defeating evidence that seems to entail that one should refrain from believing p. However, in the debate about the significance of peer disagreement most authors don't talk explicitly about rational requirements and they further do not specify whether these requirements are of the wide or narrow scope variety. Andrew Reisner (this volume) aims to shed light on the relation between rational requirements and peer disagreement by exploring whether disagreement with a peer affects one's rational requirements with respect to the proposition that is the subject of the disagreement.

Ad (iii): As already alluded to above, many epistemologists assume that there is a close connection between reasons and epistemic justification. According to evidentialism, for example, if an agent S is justified in believing a proposition p, then S is in possession of reasons or evidence which provide adequate support for p. Statements that ascribe reasons to an agent can be referred to as

---

7 See Broome (1999, 2005, 2013).

'epistemic claims'. It is natural to assume that epistemic claims feature the following characteristics: (1) they are genuine assertions with (2) representational contents; (3) the contents of epistemic claims are in principle true or false; and finally, (4) (presumably objective) epistemic facts exist that determine whether particular epistemic claims are true or false. A view that accepts the first three of these theses could be referred to as 'epistemic cognitivism'. If one further endorses the fourth thesis, then the resulting position might be called 'epistemic realism'. It is evident that the core commitments of these views are equivalent to those of their moral counterparts, viz. moral cognitivism and moral realism. However, there are views which deny that epistemic claims possess the characteristics (1) through (4). Views that deny any of the characteristics just mentioned can be considered as versions of epistemic anti-realism. Proponents of classical versions of epistemic expressivism, for example, maintain that epistemic claims serve to express the non-cognitive mental states of the attributor such as their endorsements, valuations or pro-attitudes.[8] Hence, they reject the first three claims characteristic of epistemic cognitivism listed above (and thereby also reject the final claim).

On another anti-realist view, which might be called 'the epistemic error theory', epistemic claims express belief-like states but are uniformly false since there are no facts that make these claims true. One might claim that epistemic facts are 'queer' as their moral counterparts because they should be construed as providing categorical reasons to comply with them. But, as with the moral version of the error theory, there do not seem to be any facts that provide reasons of this particular sort. Terence Cuneo (2007) has argued that the epistemic error theory is subject to a dilemma. Cuneo's central objection to the epistemic error theory is that this view is either (a) self-defeating or (b) entails wholesale epistemological skepticism. Cuneo further claims that there are reasons to adopt the parity principle, which says that if one endorses the moral error theory one is committed to the epistemic error theory as well.[9] Cuneo (this volume) engages with Jonas Olson's recent defense of the moral error theory. Even though Olson accepts the moral error theory, he nonetheless thinks that this view can be combined with a certain version of epistemic reductionism, i.e., the view according to which epistemic facts exist but only in some "lean" sense. Cuneo aims to demonstrate that Olson's commitment to epistemic reductionism destabilizes his commitment to the moral error theory.

---

[8] The term 'classical expressivism' is taken from Cuneo (2007), 124–184.
[9] See Cuneo (2007), Chapter 3.

1.2 Epistemic Norms

1.2.1 Norms of Assertion, Belief and Practical Reasoning

Epistemology has seen a surge of interest in the idea that there are norms governing the propriety of assertion, practical reasoning and belief. Most contributors to this debate assume that asserting, reasoning and believing are activities governed by constitutive norms. They hold that, if someone violates these constitutive norms, then she hasn't properly engaged in the activity in question. With respect to assertion, Timothy Williamson, who speaks of rules instead of norms, says, for instance:

> [...] Someone who knowingly asserts a falsehood has thereby broken a rule of assertion, much as if he had broken a rule of a game; he has cheated. On this view, the speech act, like a game and unlike the act of jumping, is constituted by rules. (Williamson 2000, 238)

Many proposals regarding the precise content of these norms have been made. Regarding assertion, Timothy Williamson has introduced the following schema for any rule or norm of assertion:[10]

(N) You must: Assert p iff. p has C.

(N) specifies necessary and sufficient conditions for the propriety of a particular assertion. The variable 'p' stands for a proposition and C is just some condition that p has to satisfy, like being true, justified, or known. However, it has also been discussed as to which conditions may be sufficient for making a particular assertion. Note that analogous schemata to (N) could also be stated regarding the propriety of belief and practical reasoning, respectively. In the following introduction we wish to focus on the norms governing assertion.

A currently widely discussed proposal is that knowledge is the norm governing assertion – that is, that you should assert p only if you know p.[11] The knowledge norm of assertion is usually thought to provide the simplest explanation of a certain set of data.[12] First, Moorean assertions exist in the form of "Grass is green, but I don't know that grass is green." Even though these assertions

---

[10] See Williamson (2000), 241.
[11] Proponents of this view include Williamson (2000), Hawthorne (2004), DeRose (2002, 2009) and Schaffer (2008).
[12] See Williamson (2000), Chapter 11; Weiner (2007), 187–188; and Benton (2014), 2–5.

may fail to be true, it is nonetheless incoherent to assert them. According to the Knowledge Account of Assertion, Moorean conjunctions are unassertible because the asserter explicitly denies that she is failing to fulfill the norm governing assertion. Second, there are conversational patterns that suggest that knowledge is needed for proper assertion. For example, an assertion of p can be challenged by asking "Do you know p?" or the propriety of the assertion can be flat-out denied by stating "You don't know p!" If the asserter is not in a position to provide an answer to this challenge or concedes that she fails to know p after all, then we usually take this as evidence that her assertion of p was improper. The third phenomenon that speaks in favor of the Knowledge Account of Assertion is that assertions of lottery propositions such as "Ticket t will lose", made before the draw has been announced, seem to be improper from an epistemic perspective. The explanation as to why it is inappropriate to assert lottery propositions is that we fail to know that ticket t will lose before the draw has been announced. The Knowledge Account of Assertion delivers a straightforward explanation of assertions of this particular sort because the lack of knowledge makes the assertion of lottery propositions improper.[13]

Despite the fact that the Knowledge Account of Assertion has been widely endorsed, there are competitors to this view. One competitor to the Knowledge Account of Assertion is the Rational Credibility Account of Assertion proposed by Igor Douven (2006). This account maintains that a speaker should assert those propositions that are rationally credible to her. Douven argues that his account is able to explain most of the data introduced above, but is, in comparison to the Knowledge Account of Assertion, a priori simpler. Mona Simion (this volume) engages with Douven's claim that the Rational Credibility Account of Assertion is superior to the Knowledge Account of Assertion. In particular, Simion attempts to show that the argument for the a priori simplicity of the Rational Credibility Account of Assertion presented by Douven is not sound and that the Knowledge Account of Assertion is preferable to the Rational Credibility Account on a posteriori grounds.

If we assume that knowledge is the norm of assertion, the question of whether this norm governs other types of norm-governed activities becomes pressing.[14]

---

13 Some contextualists about knowledge, such as DeRose (2002, 2009) and Schaffer (2008), subscribe to the Knowledge Norm of Assertion. Erik Stei (this volume) discusses a pivotal issue that contextualists about knowledge need to address, namely how to model the epistemic standards that vary with features of the conversational context.
14 Nicholas Unwin (this volume) engages with the norm of belief. He argues that the possibility of radical disagreement calls into question that we have any genuine beliefs at all, as opposed to

Should we conceive of believing p or taking p as a premise in an agent's practical reasoning as being only permissible if the agent knows p? The claim that there is a common norm governing assertion, belief and practical reasoning has been dubbed "the commonality thesis". Davide Fassio (this volume) presents an argument in favor of the commonality thesis. He maintains that assertions, beliefs and premises figuring in one's practical reasoning are all representations of a particular sort with the same direction of fit, namely a thetic direction of fit. Therefore, it seems to follow, according to Fassio, that activities in which representations of this particular sort figure are governed by the same norm.

1.2.2 Why Follow Epistemic Norms?

Despite the fact that there is wide disagreement regarding many foundational issues in epistemology, there is nonetheless a consensus among epistemologists regarding the epistemic evaluation of certain kinds of beliefs. Beliefs that are not supported by reasons or evidence, such as those based on hunches, wishes or biases, are in general subject to epistemic criticism. By contrast, beliefs that are supported by adequate reasons or evidence (i.e., reasons that speak in favor of the truth of these beliefs), are in general considered as epistemically good or permissible – even though these beliefs might turn out to be false or may be criticized on non-epistemic grounds. In light of the fact that we tend to value beliefs based on adequate evidence or reasons, it has been proposed that believing on adequate evidence or reasons constitutes one of our core epistemic norms.

But why should we follow epistemic norms, such as the norm that one should believe p only if one has adequate evidence or reasons in support of p? And, furthermore, why should we care about following epistemic norms? The question of what grounds epistemic norms has received multiple answers.[15] One strategy to ground epistemic normativity maintains, in short, that since it is constitutive of beliefs that they aim at the truth and believing based upon adequate evidence promotes that this goal will be achieved, it follows that we should follow epistemic norms. Since it might be further claimed that we care about being good believers, we should also care about fulfilling the norm to believe p only upon adequate evidence for p.

---

weaker states, such as acceptances. According to Unwin, this conclusion follows if we conceive of belief as an essentially normative state.

15 See Mitova (this volume), section 2 for a discussion of various answers to the question of what grounds epistemic normativity.

Another strategy assumes that pragmatic considerations provide the key to explaining wherein epistemic norms are grounded. If you follow epistemic norms, so the thought goes, it is much more likely that you will end up with true beliefs and true beliefs are beneficial for survival. If you have true beliefs regarding, say, that the food you perceive in front of you is indeed edible, it is much more likely that you will survive than if you end up with false beliefs regarding which foods are edible and which are poisonous. Since we care about surviving, we also seem to care about following epistemic norms.

On still another view, epistemic normativity is grounded in the constitutive conditions of agency. According to the view outlined in Mitova (this volume), you should follow epistemic norms because, very roughly, you can only exercise conscious control over your actions if the world makes sense to you. Mitova claims that the drive for sense-making can only be satisfied by following epistemic norms, like believing how things appear to you or avoiding being inconsistent. Furthermore, since we care about acting, we also should care about following epistemic norms.

The question of what grounds epistemic normativity is very closely tied to the question of whether epistemic norms are hypothetical or categorical.[16] If the pragmatists' response is right, for example, epistemic norms turn out to be hypothetical. That is, epistemic norms will only command or prescribe to follow them given other goals we happen to have, such as survival. By contrast, if a *sui generis* explanation of epistemic normativity can be given, then epistemic norms will turn out to be categorical. The categorical conception of normativity has it that categorical norms command independently of any goals that we happen to have to comply with these norms. So, providing an explanation of the grounds of epistemic norms will be of major importance for addressing the question what kind of norms epistemic norms are.

1.3 Epistemic Consequentialism

Many epistemologists hold that when we evaluate beliefs as "correct" or "justified", we are making normative judgments about these beliefs. The first question in this context is: How can we generally analyze these normative notions? The best known and most common proposal suggests there is an intimate connection between justification and truth which has a consequentialist structure. From the epistemic point of view, there is an overriding or ultimate external source of epis-

---

16 See Kelly (2003) for a discussion of the nature of epistemic normativity.

temic normativity, namely maximizing truths and minimizing falsehoods in a large body of beliefs. The question of what we should believe is determined by how well our believing conduces with the fulfillment of this binary truth-goal.

The core idea behind this proposal is a teleological interpretation of the epistemic norms that apply to belief. However, Selim Berker (2013 a/b), among others, has recently argued that this approach generates a number of problems. The contributions in the first section of this collection are concerned with this criticism of the consequentialist standard account. At the center of this debate we can locate at least *three* main issues: First of all, we have to ask what is the relationship between epistemic consequentialism and consequentialism in ethics. One of the fundamental questions in normative ethics is: What takes priority when evaluating actions? Should the right be prior to the good or should the good be prior to the right? A similar question arises in the context of epistemic evaluations, and consequentialists claim that the epistemic right (i.e., the justified) is to be understood in terms of conduciveness to the epistemic good (i.e., true belief). But although both variants of consequentialism have many structural similarities, there also seem to be significant differences. For example, epistemic consequentialists seem to be committed to a so-called truth-indication principle, which claims that a belief is justified only if there are factors indicating that the belief itself is true. Such a principle, however, is obviously not relevant for any kind of ethical consequentialism.[17] If we want to hold on to the ethics-epistemology analogy, we therefore need to specify in more detail how to conceive of this analogy.[18]

Another prominent question concerns the different forms of epistemic consequentialism. Very schematically, epistemic consequentialists have to settle three things: They must first identify a certain epistemic goal (e.g., standardly true belief) which structures the norms under consideration; then they need to develop a comparative ranking for each kind of entity that has an epistemic value because it serves or promotes the identified goal; and thirdly, they must also specify the kind of procedure to be used to assign the deontic properties and allocate the production of the final value. Regarding the last aspect, there is an intensive discussion about the right version of epistemic consequentialism. There are at least two dimensions that allow us to distinguish between different versions of epistemic consequentialism.

First, we need to distinguish between act- and rule-consequentialism – a distinction familiar from discussions of consequentialism in ethics. Several versions

---

17 See Briesen (this volume) for the introduction and an extensive discussion of this principle.
18 See Piller (this volume) for a very skeptical response.

of consequentialism *directly* assign the relevant deontic properties (e.g., being right/justified) on the basis of certain properties of a particular belief, namely on the basis of evidence this particular belief is based on. According to this view, if a belief-token is appropriately based on a body of evidence, then this belief is epistemically justified. In contrast, approaches that are of a rule-consequentialist kind, like process-reliabilism, indirectly assign the deontic properties. The indirect view has it that the relevant deontic properties are directly assigned to rules, like types of processes or methods of belief-formation, which, if implemented, tend to produce a greater number of true beliefs than false beliefs. Justification is then *indirectly* attributed to those belief-tokens that are formed in accordance with these rules.

Secondly, we need to distinguish between subjective and objective forms of epistemic consequentialism. In analogy to internalist or externalist conceptions of epistemic justification, consequentialists need to decide whether the identified deontic properties have to enhance the actual ratio of true to false beliefs or whether it is perhaps sufficient for a person to merely believe (reasonably) that the ratio of true to false beliefs will be so enhanced. Note that act- as well as rule-consequentialism can be given a subjective or objective interpretation.[19]

1.3.1 Problems for Epistemic Consequentialism

The consideration that we need to distinguish different versions of consequentialism is closely related to the third main issue. Perhaps the most debated question is the following: Is there a plausible version of the veritistic epistemic consequentialism (i.e., the standard account of epistemic consequentialism) which is capable of avoiding the various objections that can be raised against this position? One objection, possibly the most crucial, centers around the idea that epistemic consequentialism allows for trade-offs. Because all versions of epistemic consequentialism seem to be committed to a diachronic perspective regarding the epistemic evaluation of beliefs, a belief will count as justified if adopting this particular belief will lead to many true beliefs in the future.

Many authors think, however, that the problem of trade-offs can be dismissed because it only applies, if at all, to direct or act-consequentialist versions of epistemic consequentialism. In the case of indirect consequentialist theories like process reliabilism, a central assumption of trade-off cases is not applicable,

---

[19] See Briesen (this volume) for introduction of this second kind of distinction.

namely that adopting a belief is epistemically justified if adopting this belief will lead to many true beliefs in the future. Alvin Goldman stresses that process reliabilism is a backward-looking theory in the sense that the justificational status of a belief-token is dependent on its causal history and not its future effects.[20] In this sense, process reliabilism is a theory that does not assume that the consequences of a particular belief in the future are relevant to its justificational status.

There are even more responses available. Some have argued that it doesn't seem to be clear whether trade-offs really lead to counterintuitive results.[21] Still others (not only in this collection) argue that indirect accounts can handle such counterexamples very easily.[22]

However, Selim Berker has presented instances of trade-offs that also apply to indirect versions of epistemic consequentialism. As Berker highlights, we can distinguish between two different kinds of propositional trade-offs, namely (a) those in which believing one proposition promotes that many other propositions of epistemic value will be believed as well and (b) cases in which epistemic value pertains just to that proposition itself. As a result, he claims (see Berker 2013, 2015) that there is a general recipe for generating counterexamples even for indirect forms of epistemic consequentialism, which deny that you are justified in original trade-off cases. Berker has presented a case involving prime numbers showing that trade-offs do not need to be applied to particular belief-tokens but can also emerge with respect to processes of belief-formation.

Proponents of indirect versions of consequentialism have presented various responses to this kind of counterexample. Some defenders have argued that the proponent of reliabilism must suppose that the relevant beliefs *are* justified even in such cases.[23] Other authors, such as Goldman (2015), have proposed a different strategy of defense. Goldman alleges that the type of belief-forming process specified in such an example is not reliable, and for this reason, the relevant belief is not epistemically justified.[24] Given these competing strategies, it must be clarified in more detail whether indirect consequentialism can reject Berker's general recipe for generating counterexamples, and if so, in what form.[25]

---

20 See Goldman (2015), 135.
21 See Ahlstrom-Vij & Dunn (2014).
22 See Briesen, Piller, Schmechtig, Vahid and Wrenn (all in this volume).
23 See Ahlstrom-Vij & Dunn (2014).
24 Goldman (2015), 141. Goldman mentions that there are two additional responses available to the proponent of process reliabilism. Vahid (this volume) favors the same response as Goldman.
25 See Wrenn (this volume) for an alternative proposal for solving this problem.

Beside these problems for epistemic consequentialism, there are additional problems with this view. It seems that consequentialists are committed to the thesis that true belief is of sole epistemic value. But this assumption is problematic in different ways. For example, trivial or insignificant truths seem to pose a challenge to this view because, at least intuitively, they possess little to no value for us. Furthermore, alternative epistemic standings, such as knowledge, understanding or even wisdom, seem to possess genuine epistemic significance for us as well. Therefore, it is implausible to assume that true belief is the only epistemic standing that possesses epistemic significance for us. For this reason, it is interesting to see whether different versions of epistemic consequentialism can be developed which are not (at least not only) committed to the claim that only true beliefs possess epistemic value.[26]

1.4 Epistemic Goals and Values

Although epistemic consequentialism is the dominant view in epistemology, only very recently fundamental questions about epistemic goals or values have received proper attention. The contributions in the last part of this collection focus on this more general topic. Proponents of epistemic consequentialism assume that truth is the goal of inquiry and this goal has final epistemic value. However, several philosophers are increasingly skeptical of this kind of "veritistic value monism."[27] As Duncan Pritchard notes, there seems to be a "new orthodoxy" in epistemology, according to which truth belief is not the only fundamental epistemic good, and perhaps not even one at all.[28]

1.4.1 A Defense of the old Orthodoxy

Should we reject veritistic value monism? Several authors, such as Pritchard (this volume), argue that we can still adhere to the "old orthodoxy", according to which truth is the fundamental epistemic value. Pritchard claims that most objections which have been leveled against the thesis that truth is of fundamental epistemic value are not convincing if we consider them in light of several plau-

---

26 See Schmechtig (this volume).
27 The phrase 'veritistic value monism' originates first from Alvin Goldman (1999, 5). He labels 'veritistic epistemology' as the form of epistemology concerned with the generation of true belief.
28 See Pritchard (forthcoming).

sible distinctions. Suppose we distinguish more carefully between 'epistemic values' and 'the value of the epistemic', that is, if we distinguish between the question of what is valuable epistemically and the question of what it generally means for a cognitive state to have a value *in epistemic terms* (from the epistemic point of view). Armed with this distinction, it appears plausible that we can solve problems such as the problem posed by trivial truths or the Meno problem ("why is knowledge more valuable than mere true belief?") within the traditional framework of veritistic value monism.[29] Similarly, we can ask whether veritistic value monism is really incompatible with the fact that true belief is in most cases not legitimate to close an inquiry. Plausibly, merely attaining a true belief with respect to some subject matter is not always sufficient to properly finish an inquiry. But perhaps it is possible to retain the traditional account if we keep two things apart: Even though achieving true beliefs is always the main goal of inquiry, sometimes we need other epistemic standings (for example knowledge) to ascertain that the truth-goal has been achieved.

Nevertheless, there are further concerns as to why the "old orthodoxy" seems to be misguided. One of the earliest arguments for the radical conclusion that truth is neither an aim of belief nor a fundamental goal of inquiry comes from Richard Rorty (1995), Donald Davidson (2000) and, in a more detailed form, from Jay Rosenberg (2002). According to these authors, the ordinary teleological strategy of defining what belongs to the domain of epistemic norms and values with regard to the aims of belief or goals of inquiry is in principle misguided. Very shortly, Rorty, Davidson and Rosenberg argue that we are not in a position to recognize whether our beliefs are true, if we conceive of truth as objective or evidence transcendent. Therefore, we can never determine whether we have achieved this fundamental goal. They further hold that truth can only exert a normative force on our belief-forming practices if we can ascertain whether we have achieved this goal. Since there is no epistemically accessible way to detect whether our belief-forming methods result in our having an objectively true belief about the world, the truth goal cannot fulfill the practical function of guiding our actual epistemic policies and practices.

A wide range of philosophers, however, have denied that this argument is convincing. One possible response to this argument maintains that this argument is based on a conflation of practical goals (i.e., goals for actions) and constitutive goals (i.e., goals which constrain or individuate our policies and

---

29 Additionally, Pritchard (this volume) argues, in accordance with Treanor (2013, 2014), that the problem of trivial truths is somewhat confusing since it is based on the dubious requirements of how we should 'weigh' truths.

procedures).³⁰ According to this response, we need to rethink the conception of epistemic ends by distinguishing between "rules of action" and "rules of criticism" (Sellars 1969); i.e., we have to distinguish between practical goals that are connected with norms which prescribe what an agent ought *to do* and epistemic goals that are linked to norms which express how something ought *to be*. This distinction opens up the conceptual space to say that there are at least two ways to how an end can be related to any performance: First, when it is used to evaluate whether a performance is a successful means with regard to achieving the goal, then this end is a regulative goal. Second, if an end is used to define whether or not something *is* an instance of a certain type of performance, then this end is something like a constitutive aim. Chrisman (this volume) responds to the argument outlined above by contending that if we conceive of truth as a constitutive aim of belief, we don't have to assume that we need to recognize whether we have achieved this goal, even though this goal will guide us in forming beliefs. If we treat truth as a constitutive aim of belief, we can therefore reject the guiding assumption of the argument endorsed by Davidson, Rorty and Rosenberg.

1.4.2 Problems with the Priority of the Good over the Right

Epistemic consequentialists maintain that the epistemic good takes priority over the right. But this priority claim seems to generate an additional problem for epistemic consequentialism. While there is a sense in which the good precedes the right, it is not clear whether this supports any sort of consequentialist view in the veritistic standard formulation (i.e., veritistic value monism). Why not? Perhaps the best strategy for rejecting Berker's counterexamples to indirect epistemic consequentialism mentioned above is to concede, on the one hand, that the belief-forming process in Berker's prime number example is indeed reliable. However, it might be suggested that, on the other hand, the particular belief-forming process is still epistemically insignificant. If we use this particular belief-forming process in inquiry, the doxastic output of this process doesn't qualify as a genuine answer to the question we are raising.³¹ If we assume that a process is epistemically significant if this process is conducive to answering a question raised in inquiry, then this seems to entail that we should conceive of the goal of inquiry in different terms than epistemic consequentialists

---

30 See Chrisman (this volume) for this proposal and the corresponding discussion.
31 See Wrenn (this volume) for this proposal.

do. Regarding this view, we are not just interested in obtaining true beliefs, but rather in answering a particular question raised in inquiry. As a result, our epistemic goal seems to be more generic than truth, namely, getting a satisfying answer to a question posed in inquiry.[32] If this approach is on the right track, then epistemic standings other than true belief (such as knowledge or understanding) might also serve as our goals.

The dialectic of this discussion makes it clear that the focus of the veritistic standard explanation of epistemic normativity is too narrow. Epistemic consequentialists just consider the link between truth and justification. But an adequate theory of epistemic normativity should not only answer the question of whether someone is epistemically justified in believing something. The theory should explain, in a broader sense, when a belief is appropriate or correct from the actual epistemic point of view. But if one admits that there are other (external) epistemic goals besides truth, then the focus of the standard explanation must be expanded. A particular external goal is only then leading if it has a "binding sense" within the framework of inquiry. Conversely, the corresponding doxastic norms only have a "normative force" relative to the actual (interrogative) information demands, which generate the leading (external) goal of inquiry. According to this approach, there seems to be no priority of the epistemic good over the epistemic right because the deontic question "What should or may we believe?" cannot be separated from the axiological question "When is a cognitive activity or state good or significant from an epistemic perspective?". If so, a comprehensive characterization of epistemic normativity has to show how the various applications of goals related to both questions are connected.[33]

1.4.3 The Tension Between the Two Sub-Goals of Truth and Alternative Epistemic Goals

As noted above, truth as the goal of inquiry has a binary character, namely maximizing truth and minimizing falsity in a large body of beliefs. A closer look at this binary character reveals another difficulty with the thesis that truth is the primary goal of our epistemic endeavors. It has been argued that both sub-goals are at odds with each other because the conditions for their fulfillment are inversely proportional. The simplest way to maximize truth is to believe as

---

[32] Roughly, we can characterize inquiry as an activity concerned with posing and answering questions.

[33] See Schmechtig (this volume) for a more detailed discussion of these questions and their interrelation.

much as possible. But of course, trying to believe all sorts of things increases the risk of believing something wrong. Conversely, the most effective way to minimize false beliefs is to believe nothing, which entails that we should not try to maximize true beliefs.

Given this polarity, the inverse proportionality makes the normative question of what one ought to believe very puzzling. Moreover, some authors (see Kyriacou in this volume) argue that a 'weighing value dilemma' emerges if we try to resolve this tension. If we assume, on the one hand, that the epistemic value of one sub-goal completely overrides the value of the other, then it is not clear why our epistemic goal is binary. On the other hand, if we try to balance the relative accomplishment of the two sub-goals, then we need an additional external criterion. If we possess a suitable criterion, we can arrive at a decision as to how to balance the two sub-goals.

But what is the nature of the additional external goal that allows for a balance between both sub-goals? Possibly, here we may have to switch from an epistemic goal to a higher "meta-normative" goal as described by the Aristotelian concept of eudaimonia. Nevertheless, this move seems to be highly revisionary because such a moral end is clearly not epistemic. Thus, if the external criterion for evaluating the balance of the binary true goal is supposed to be itself an epistemic criterion, then we cannot resolve this tension by recourse to the concept of eudaimonia. Recently, two alternative candidates, namely understanding and wisdom, have received a particular attention that might provide a more satisfactory resolution of this dilemma.[34]

1.4.4 Understanding as a Goal of Inquiry

Historically, the concepts of knowledge and justification have dominated the field of epistemology. In recent years, however, due to the intense discussion of the value problem, a range of epistemologists have argued that the real focus in epistemology should not be on knowledge or justified belief but on understanding. If the concept of understanding should occupy center stage in epistemology, as some philosophers allege, we need to address at least two questions: First at all, we need to specify the kind of understanding that is of interest to epistemology. Understanding seems to come in different varieties: On the one hand, there is interrogative understanding (e.g., S understands

---

[34] See Kyriacou (this volume) for a position which is based on such alternative goals of inquiry.

why green tea is healthy)³⁵; on the other, there is objectual understanding (e. g., S understand Fermat's last theorem).³⁶

Second, it must be clarified whether understanding is factive; i.e., whether understanding is a species of true belief in the same way as propositional knowledge is. While most cases of understanding suggest that an agent cannot understand why p is the case unless the agent has a true belief that p, there are some examples of understanding that demonstrate that there can be understanding without factivity. For example, cases in which an agent understands false theories seem to demonstrate that there are instances of non-factive understanding.³⁷ These cases further suggest that the object of the understanding is not a proposition but rather a certain phenomena or a body of information.

It might be argued that it is questionable as to whether there is really any disagreement on this point at all. Maybe we can reconcile both positions by representing a more moderate model of factivity. According one possible proposal, an agent S can understand a certain phenomenon φ if all *central* beliefs about φ are true, even though it is conceivable that S possesses some false *peripheral* beliefs about φ (without, of course, this false belief leading to a radical inconsistency of the cognitive behavior).³⁸ However, even a moderate model which allows us to grasp objectual understanding as factive generates a range of further questions. One of these questions concerns *inverse* cases, where the central assumptions of the theory itself are true but the person who understands why this theory fits the world doesn't accept the central claims of this theory. It appears that such inverse cases raise a couple of unexplored questions about how the concept of moderate factivity can be applied to the notion of objectual understanding. Thus,

---

35 It is widely noted in the philosophy of science (e.g., Achinstein 1983, Kitcher 1989, Woodward 2003) that the most salient feature of understanding is that it is closely tied to explanation. But it is disputed whether it is impossible to get understanding-why without any actual explanation (see Lipton 2009). Perhaps it is better to say in a more general way that understanding-why is an umbrella term for grasping information that would answer an explanation-seeking question in whatever form.
36 Such an understanding comprises of a wide variety of phenomena. Sometimes we talk about understanding concrete objects, but often we talk about understanding abstract objects (e.g., theories, processes, models, graphs) as well. See Kalifa (2013) for a more detailed discussion of the distinction between interrogative and objectual understanding.
37 See Elgin (2004), Grimm (2006), Kvanvig (2003), Zagzebski (2001) for this debate.
38 See Carter & Gordon (this volume) and Kvanvig (2003) for such a moderate model of the factivity of understanding.

we need to examine the extent to which objectual understanding is a species of true belief.[39]

2. Synopsis of Chapters

Martin Grajner "In Defense of Psychologism about Reasons"
A popular view shared by many contemporary epistemologists is that epistemic reasons are psychological states. However, several challenges to this view exist. In this paper, I wish to focus on two challenges for psychologism about reasons. The first is that there appears to be linguistic data that speak in favor of factualism, i.e., the view that facts can be reasons for beliefs. If we take these alleged data at face value, we seem forced to accept the claim that not every reason is a psychological state. Second, psychologism is often considered to explain best how a person can be in possession of a reason, and base her belief on it, even when the content of this reason is false or does not correspond to a fact. However, several factualists have recently presented solutions to the problem of 'bad cases' in which apparently no facts are present. My first aim in this paper is to show that psychologism about reasons is not put into jeopardy by the linguistic data that seem to favor factualism. Secondly, I will argue that the solutions that factualists have recently proposed to solve the problem of bad cases for their view are not successful.

Clayton Littlejohn "Learning from Learning from our Mistakes"
What can we learn from cases of knowledge from falsehood? Critics of knowledge-first epistemology have argued that these cases provide us with good reason for rejecting the knowledge accounts of evidence, justification, and the norm of belief. I shall offer a limited defense of the knowledge-first approach to these matters. Knowledge from falsehood cases should undermine our confidence in like-from-like reasoning in epistemology. Just as we should be open to the idea that knowledge can come from non-knowledge, we should be open to the idea that justified beliefs can come from unjustified beliefs.

---

[39] See Carter & Gordon (this volume) for a detailed diagnosis and subsequent solution to this problem.

Terence Cuneo "Destabilizing the Error Theory"
Jonas Olson's recent book *Error Theory: History, Critique, Defense* is a defense of the moral error theory. In the course of responding to an objection to his view, Olson accepts an unusual combination of views, namely, the moral error theory, which implies that there are no moral facts, and a version of epistemic reductionism, which implies the existence of something very close to epistemic facts – so close that many other philosophers hold that they just *are* epistemic facts. My project in this essay is to contend that a commitment to epistemic reductionism of this sort destabilizes a commitment to the moral error theory, providing reasons not to accept it or rendering the position philosophically irrelevant.

Andrew Reisner "Peer Disagreement, Rational Requirements, and Evidence of Evidence as Evidence Against"
This chapter addresses an ambiguity in some of the literature on rational peer disagreement about the use of the term 'rational'. In the literature 'rational' is used to describe a variety of normative statuses related to reasons, justification, and reasoning. This chapter focuses most closely on the upshot of peer disagreement for what is rationally required of parties to a peer disagreement. This follows recent work in theoretical reason which treats rationality as a system of requirements among an agent's mental states. It is argued that peer disagreement has either no, or a very limited, affect on what rationality requires of an agent in a given circumstance. This is in part because of difficulties generated by a novel example of evidence of evidence of p being evidence against p. This example calls into question the mechanisms whereby peer disagreement might affect what is rationally required of an agent. The chapter also reevaluates the importance of actual peer disagreement against the backdrop of prior expectations about whether disagreement is believed to be likely, arguing that peer disagreement is most likely to change what is rationally required of an agent when it is believed to be unlikely.

Nicholas Unwin "Belief, Truth and Radical Disagreement"
The nature of belief, and of the norms that go with it, together with that of the related notion of acceptance, are examined in the context of van Fraassen's constructive empiricism. A generalization of the latter is defended, one which applies to observational sentences as well as narrowly theoretical ones. This is conducted within the context of a general sceptical argument which claims that *all* empirical beliefs, by their very nature (as revealed by the normative constraints which constitute them), are unwarranted. It is claimed that an alternative, weak-

er notion, namely an amplified conception of acceptance, is required in place of belief. Central to this argument, and to its metaphysical consequences, is the notion of alien cognition and the possibility of radical disagreement. The possibility of 'Martians' or 'grue-users' is defended, and it is further shown that the notion of aiming at truth (which is what beliefs are supposed to do) is seriously undermined by this possibility. The distinction between beliefs and believers is examined, and is shown to illuminate the question of why we cannot believe at will. The paper concludes by examining internal realism and transcendental idealism which provide alternative solutions to the problems raised.

Mona Simion "Assertion, Knowledge and Rational Credibility: The Scoreboard"

Recent literature argues that knowledge is not necessary for epistemically proper assertion. The most prominent competing account on the market imposes a weaker, rational credibility norm on assertion (RCNA); it is argued that (1) theoretical considerations, such as a priori simplicity, speak in favor of RCNA, (2) the weaker norm scores equally well when it comes to accommodating linguistic data, and (3) KNA, as opposed to RCNA, has a hard time explaining cases in which assertions on lesser epistemic standings do not render the speakers subject to criticism. This paper tips the balance back in favor of the knowledge norm (KNA). I argue that (1) the argument for the a priori simplicity of RCNA does not go through, (2) KNA scores better when it comes to accommodating linguistic data, (3) KNA and RCNA are shoulder to shoulder when it comes to explaining blamelessness of speakers in breach of the norm, and (4) KNA fares better than RCNA in terms of a posteriori simplicity.

Davide Fassio "Commonality Reconsidered: On the Common Source of Epistemic Standards"

Commonality is the claim that there is a common epistemic standard for assertion, practical reasoning and belief. Assuming that commonality is true, a further issue is whether it is a matter of mere coincidence that different attitudes and practices are governed by the same standard, or whether there is some deeper motivation for it. Attempts have been made in the recent literature to show that epistemic standards of these entities are inter-derivable. However this approach has been the target of some objections. In this paper I suggest an alternative approach avoiding such criticisms. According to this approach, different entities share a common epistemic standard in virtue of some factor independent of reciprocal relations amongst the norms governing these entities. In particular,

I sketch a specific account according to which commonality is due to the fact that beliefs, assertions and premises in practical reasoning share a common representational nature of a peculiar kind. The standard is primarily attached to this feature, and the various entities share it in virtue of all instantiating that feature.

Erik Stei "Epistemic Standards: High Hopes and low Expectations"

The notion of epistemic standards has gained prominence in the literature on the semantics of knowledge ascriptions. Defenders of *Epistemic Contextualism* claim that in certain scenarios the truth value of a knowledge-ascribing sentence of the form "S knows p (at t)"—where S is an epistemic subject and p is a proposition S is said to know at time t—can change even if S, p and t are assigned constant values. This sort of variability, contextualists claim, is due to the epistemic standards governing the context in which the knowledge ascription is uttered. While a specific knowledge ascription may be true when uttered in a context with "low" epistemic standards, it may be false when uttered in a context with "high" epistemic standards. The reason for this, as far as contextualists are concerned, is the context sensitivity of the verb "knows". In standard semantics an expression is said to be context sensitive if and only if it expresses different contents (or intensions) relative to different contexts of utterance. Thus, as epistemic standards influence the content of "knows", they play a crucial role in contextualist semantics. In this paper, I examine different conceptions of epistemic standards and argue that all but one lead to counterintuitive consequences. The conception which avoids these consequences, however, has the downside of seriously restricting the talk of "high" or "low" standards that is so frequent in discussions on the semantics of knowledge ascriptions.

Veli Mitova "What do I care about Epistemic Norms?"

The aim of this paper is to clear space for a novel account of the source of epistemic norms. I argue that there are two constraints on such an account: it must explain both the motivational force of epistemic norms and their normativity. None of the existing accounts I show meets both constraints. So, we should look elsewhere for the source of epistemic norms. A fruitful place to look, I suggest, is David Velleman's proposal that the hallmark of agency is our drive for sense-making. This drive, I argue, plausibly sources both the motivational and normative force of epistemic norms. It does so, moreover, while accommodating what seems plausible about existing accounts without incurring their costs.

Hamid Vahid "Epistemic Normativity: From Direct to Indirect Epistemic Consequentialism"

An important question in epistemology is concerned with whether, in evaluating beliefs, standards of justification should be grounded in facts about values and ends. Epistemic consequentialism is the view that answers this question affirmatively. In this paper, I shall defend a version of epistemic consequentialism against some recent objections to the view. I distinguish between direct and indirect versions of epistemic consequentialism and propose a way of improving on the direct version to make it more plausible and also to safeguard it against some criticisms of that view. This will, however, result in unearthing a more fundamental failing of direct epistemic consequentialism. It will be argued that an indirect version of the view has a better prospect of capturing the motivations behind epistemic consequentialism.

Chase Wrenn "Tradeoffs, Self-Promotion, and Epistemic Teleology"

Epistemic teleology is the view that (a) some states have fundamental epistemic value and (b) all other epistemic value and obligation are to be understood in terms of *promotion of* or *conduciveness to* such fundamentally valuable states. Veritistic reliabilism is a paradigm case: It assigns fundamental value to *true belief*, and it makes all other assessments of epistemic value or justification in terms of the reliable acquisition of beliefs that are true rather than false. Teleology faces potentially serious problems from cases of *cross-propositional tradeoffs* and cases of *epistemic self-promotion*. Both are cases in which committing some intuitive epistemic ill (such as believing against one's evidence) promotes the greater epistemic good. It can seem that epistemic teleologies must incorrectly endorse intuitively unjustified beliefs as justified in such cases. This paper defends epistemic teleology on two fronts. First, I argue that the problems of tradeoffs and self-promotion do not affect minimally plausible epistemic teleologies. Second, I rehearse some of what I take to be the main reasons to prefer epistemic teleology to alternative views. A theme that develops along the way is that plausible teleologies evaluate belief-forming methods by appeal to their promotion of epistemic goals, but they evaluate individual beliefs by appeal to their causal histories. That is the feature that enables them to avoid tradeoff problems, without abandoning teleology and without resorting to ad hoc epicycles.

Jochen Briesen "Epistemic Consequentialism: Its Relation to Ethical Consequentialism and the Truth-Indication Principle"
Consequentialist positions in philosophy spell out normative notions by recourse to certain aims. *Hedonistic* versions of *ethical consequentialism* spell out what is *morally* right/justified via recourse to the aim of increasing pleasure and decreasing pain. *Veritistic* versions of *epistemic consequentialism* spell out what is *epistemically* right/justified via recourse to the aim of increasing the number of true beliefs and decreasing the number of false ones. Even though these theories are in many respects structurally analogous, there are also interesting disanalogies. For example, popular versions of epistemic consequentialism implicitly endorse the truth-indication principle (which claims that a belief is epistemically justified only if there are factors indicating that the belief *itself* is true), whereas popular versions of ethical consequentialism do not subscribe to an analogous pleasure-indicating principle (which claims that an act is morally justified only if there are factors indicating that performing the act *itself* is pleasurable). In a first step I will argue that this difference rests on the fact that plausible versions of *epistemic consequentialism* have to meet certain constraints, which versions of *ethical consequentilialism* do not have to satisfy. As these constraints can be easily met by incorporating the truth-indication principle, epistemic consequentialists tend to subscribe to it. In a second step I will investigate whether the identified constraints can also be met independently of the truth-indication principle. Are there plausible versions of veritistic epistemic consequentialism that reject the principle, thereby allowing that some beliefs can be epistemically justified even though no factors speak in favor of their truth? Building on ideas put forward by Ludwig Wittgenstein, Crispin Wright, and others, I will answer this question affirmatively.

Christian Piller "How to Overstretch the Ethics-Epistemology Analogy: Berker's Critique of Epistemic Consequentialism"
Selim Berker has argued that epistemologists can learn from anti-consequentialism in ethics. He thinks that much of contemporary epistemology is infected by consequentialist ideas. I argue that the anti-consequentialist separateness-of-persons principle, which Berker appeals to, has no clear epistemological analogue and that the normative fact that concerns him most– namely that the epistemic benefits of believing do not determine the justificatory status of such believing–is better explained by general facts about the nature of belief which entail no commitment to any anti-consequentialist doctrine.

Pedro Schmechtig "External Goals and Inherent Norms – A Cluster-Conception of Epistemic Normativity"

Currently, there is a growing debate in epistemology regarding the question of whether the epistemic right should take precedence over the epistemic good or whether the epistemic good should take precedence over the epistemic right. In this paper, I would like to argue for an alternative approach. According to the proposal sketched in this paper, there is no priority because both forms of epistemic normativity are inextricably linked to each other. I will argue for this claim as follows. First, I will examine two versions of epistemic consequentialism, which both assume that the epistemic good is prior to the epistemic right. I will show that both version of consequentialism are misguided due the fact that they mischaracterize the relation between deontic and axiological facts. Secondly, I will examine the reverse approach and I will reveal difficulties of this approach as well. My main argument will be that this approach struggles to explain the regulatory force of epistemic norms. Thirdly, based on the arguments presented previously, I will develop an alternative approach. According to my proposal, epistemic projects can be characterized as *clusters*, which are composed of one or more normative standards and a particular goal of inquiry. As I will try to show in more detail, since the goals constitutive of inquiry vary the norms governing these practices will also correspondingly vary. Finally, I will highlight the advantages of this proposal over rival views.

Matthew Chrisman "The Aim of Belief and the Goal of Truth: Reflections on Rosenberg"

This paper attempts to sympathetically reconstruct an argument due to Rorty, Davidson, and Rosenberg for the conclusion that truth is neither the aim of belief nor the goal of inquiry. Their argument is not an attempt to make the pluralist point that there may be other equally fundamental epistemic aims and goals, but rather a much more radical attempt to undermine the common appeal by epistemologists to an aim or goal of truth as a way of defining what counts as epistemic (e.g., epistemic reasons, norms, values, etc.). I focus on Rosenberg's version of the argument because it is most detailed and convincing. I try to explain why several natural reactions to the argument are misguided in the context of its dialectical purpose in undermining appeal to truth in defining epistemic notions. Ultimately, however, I reject the argument. For I think it trades on a failure to appreciate the socially and diachronically perspectival nature of evaluations of belief-forming methods. Moreover, and more importantly, I think the argument conflates the goals of our actions with the ends capable of constraining our policies and procedures. By understanding belief as partially constituted by its evaluability for truth and, accordingly, belief-forming methods as partially defined by their evaluability relative to an end of truth, we can sustain the practice of appealing to truth as a way of defining what counts as epistemic. By considering a rigorous version of this famous and radical argument against appeals to truth in epistemology, I think we acquire a better understanding of the role appeals to truth can and should play in defining core epistemic notions.

Christos Kyriacou "Ought to Believe, Evidential Understanding and the Pursuit of Wisdom"

It is almost an epistemological platitude that the goal of inquiry is to pursue truth-acquisition and falsity-avoidance. But further reflection on this dual goal of inquiry reveals that the two (sub)goals are in tension because they are inversely proportionate: The more we satisfy the one (sub)goal the less we satisfy the other and vice versa. I elaborate the inverse proportionality point in some detail and bring out its puzzling implications about the normative question of what one ought to believe. As I argue, given the tension between the two (sub)goals, the problem of the correct regulation of belief-fixation pops to the surface. Call this 'the James problem' in tribute to William James who first drew attention to the problem. As a response 'to the James Problem', I sketch the contours of a solution to the problem that involves the rather neglected epistemic concepts of understanding and wisdom and links these concepts with the goal of eudaimonia (or living well). The resultant theory constitutes an approach to epistemic normativity that makes little use of the traditional epistemic concepts of truth and knowledge that have historically dominated the field of epistemology.

Duncan Pritchard "Epistemic Axiology"

An account is offered both of the nature of the epistemic and of the nature of epistemic value. Indeed, it is argued that these topics are tightly interconnected, such that we can offer a unified treatment of both. This unified treatment—what I call the *traditional account*—argues that the nature of the epistemic should be understood in truth-directed terms, such that the fundamental epistemic good is concerned with grasping the truth. While historically popular, the traditional account is now widely rejected. The goal of this paper is to demonstrate that the reasons that have been offered for rejecting this thesis are far from compelling. In particular, it is claimed that: (i) the traditional account can explain how epistemic standings like knowledge can be more valuable than mere true belief (*contra* the so-called *swamping problem*); (ii) the traditional account is not committed to the idea that all true beliefs are of equal epistemic value; and (iii) the traditional account is compatible with the widely-endorsed claim that it is not mere true belief that legitimately closes inquiry, but rather a higher epistemic standing like knowledge. Along the way some important distinctions are introduced and explored, not least an often overlooked distinction between the value of the epistemic and epistemic value.

J. Adam Carter and Emma C. Gordon "Objectual Understanding, Factivity and Belief"

Should we regard Jennifer Lackey's (2007) 'Creationist Teacher' as *understanding* evolution even though she does not, given her religious convictions, *believe* its central claims? We think this question raises a range of important and unexplored questions about the relationship between understanding, factivity, and belief. Our aim will be to diagnose this case in a principled way, and in doing so, to make some progress toward appreciating what *objectual understanding*—i.e., understanding a subject matter or body of information—demands of us. Here is the plan. After some ground clearing in §1, §2 outlines and motivates a plausible working model—*moderate factivity*—for characterizing the sense in which objectual understanding should be regarded as factive. §3 shows how the datum that we can understand false theories can, despite initial suggestions to the contrary, be assimilated straightforwardly within the moderate factivity model. §4 highlights how the *inverse* kind of case to that explored in §3—*viz.*, a variant of Lackey's creationist teacher case—poses special problems for moderate factivity. With reference to recent work on moral understanding by Hills (2009), §5 proposes a solution to the problem, and §6 attempts to diagnose why it is that we might originally have been led to draw the wrong conclusion.

References

Achinstein, P. (1983). *The Nature of Explanation*. New York: Oxford University Press.
Ahlstrom-Vij, K. & Dunn, J. (2014). A Defence of Epistemic Consequentialism. *The Philosophical Quarterly* 64: 541–551.
Alvarez M. (2009). How many Kinds of Reasons? *Philosophical Explorations* 12: 181–193.
Alvarez, M. (2010). *Kinds of Reasons*. Oxford: Oxford University Press.
Benton, M. (2014). Knowledge Norms. *Internet Encyclopedia of Philosophy*, URL= http://www.iep.utm.edu/kn-norms/.
Berker, S. (2013a). Epistemic Teleology and the Separateness of Propositions. *Philosophical Review* 122: 337–392.
Berker, S. (2013b). The Rejection of Epistemic Consequentialism. *Philosophical Issues* 23: 363–387.

Berker, S. (2015). Reply to Goldman: Cutting Up the One to Save the Five in Epistemology. *Episteme* 12: 145–53.
Broome, J. (1999). Normative Requirements. *Ratio* 12: 398–419.
Broome, J. (2005). Does Rationality Give us Reasons? *Philosophical Issues* 15: 321–37.
Broome, J. (2013). *Rationality Through Reasoning*. Oxford: Blackwell.
Cuneo, T. (2007). *The Normative Web: An Argument for Moral Realism*. Oxford: Oxford University Press.
Dancy, J. (2000). *Practical Reality*. Oxford: Oxford University Press.
Davidson, D. (2000). Truth Rehabilitated. In R. Brandom (ed.), *Rorty and His Critics*, Malden, MA: Oxford: Blackwell Publishing.
DeRose, K. (2002). Assertion, Knowledge, and Context. *Philosophical Review* 111: 167–203.
DeRose, K. (2009). *The Case for Contextualism*. Oxford: Oxford University Press.
Douven, I. (2006). Assertion, Knowledge, and Rational Credibility. *Philosophical Review* 115: 449–485.
Elgin, C. (2004). True Enough. *Philosophical Issues* 14, 113–131.
Elgin, C. (2007). Understanding and the Facts. *Philosophical Studies* 132, 33–42.
Goldman, A. (2015). Reliabilism, Veritism, and Epistemic Consequentialism. *Episteme* 12, 131–143.
Grimm, S. (2006). Is Understanding a Species of Knowledge? *British Journal for the Philosophy of Science* 57: 515–535.
Hawthorne, J. (2004). *Knowledge and Lotteries*. Oxford: Oxford University Press.
Kelly, T. (2008). Evidence. In E. N. Zalta (ed.), *The Stanford Encyclopedia of Philosophy*. URL=http://plato.stanford.edu/archives/fall2008/entries/evidence/.
Kelly, T. (2003). Epistemic Rationality as Instrumental Rationality: A Critique. *Philosophy and Phenomenological Research* 66: 612–640.
Khalifa, K. (2013). The Role of Explanation in Understanding. *The British Journal for the Philosophy of Science* 64: 161–187.
Kitcher, P. (1989). Explanatory Unification and the Causal Structure of the World. In P. Kitcher and W. C. Salmon (eds.), *Scientific Explanation*. Minneapolis: University of Minnesota Press.
Kvanvig, J. (2003). *The Value of Knowledge and the Pursuit of Understanding*. Cambridge: Cambridge University Press.
Lipton, P. (2009). Understanding without Explanation. In H. De Regt, S. Leonelli, and K. Eigner (eds.), *Scientific Understanding: Philosophical Perspectives*. Pittsburg/PA: University of Pittsburg Press.
Littlejohn, C. (2012). *Justification and the Truth-Connection*. Cambridge: Cambridge University Press.
McCain, K. (2014). *Evidentialism and Epistemic Justification*. New York, London: Routledge.
Mitova, V. (2015). Truthy Psychologism about Evidence. *Philosophical Studies* 172: 1105–1126.
Pritchard, D. (forthcoming), Veritism and Epistemic Value. In H. Kornblith and B. McLaughlin (eds.), *Alvin Goldman and His Critics*, Blackwell.
Rorty, R. (1995). Is Truth a Goal of Enquiry? Davidson vs. Wright. *Philosophical Quarterly* 45: 281–300.
Rosenberg, J. (2002). *Thinking About Knowing*, Oxford: Oxford University Press.
Sellars, W. (1969). Language as Thought and as Communication. *Philosophy and Phenomenological Research* 29: 506–527.

Scanlon, Th. (2007). Structural Irrationality. In G. Brennan, R. Goodin, F. Jackson, and M. Smith (eds.), *Common Minds: Essays in Honor of Philip Pettit*. Oxford: Oxford University Press.
Schaffer, J. (2008). Knowledge in the Image of Assertion. *Philosophical Issues* 18: 1–19.
Schroeder, M. (2008). Having Reasons. *Philosophical Studies* 139: 57–71.
Turri, J. (2009). The Ontology of Epistemic Reasons. *Noûs* 43: 490–512.
Turri, J. (2012). Reasons, Answers and Goals. *Journal of Moral Philosophy* 9: 491–499.
Treanor, N. (2013). The Measure of Knowledge. *Noûs* 47: 577–601.
Treanor, N. (2014). Trivial Truths and the Aim of Inquiry. *Philosophy and Phenomenological Research* 89: 552–59.
Weiner, M. (2007). Norms of Assertion. *Philosophy Compass* 2: 187–195.
Williamson, T. (2000). *Knowledge and its Limits*. Oxford: Oxford University Press.
Woodward, J. B. (2003). *Making Things Happen: A Theory of Causal Explanation*. Oxford: Oxford University Press.
Zagzebski, L. (2001). Recovering Understanding. In M. Steup (ed.), *Knowledge, Truth, and Duty: Essays on Epistemic Justification, Responsibility, and Virtue*. New York: Oxford University Press.

I Epistemic Reasons

Martin Grajner
In Defense of Psychologism About Reasons

What we belief with justification, we generally believe for a reason. But what are epistemic reasons? The main divide in the current literature on the ontology of epistemic reasons is between psychologists, anti-psychologists, and pluralists. Each of these positions can be defined as follows:[1]

Psychologism: All epistemic reasons are psychological items.

Anti-Psychologism: No reason is a psychological item.

Pluralism: Epistemic reasons can belong to different ontological categories, i.e., they can be psychological as well as non-psychological items.

Most psychologists are statists, that is, they assume that epistemic reasons are psychological states or events.[2] The most popular brand of psychologism maintains that a subject's epistemic reasons are confined to her non-factive mental states. On this view, a subject can possess a reason even though the content of the reason is false.[3] Let's call this view 'Non-Factive Psychologism'.

Non-Factive Psychologism: Only non-factive mental states are epistemic reasons.

There exist at least two alternative versions of psychologism. According to one such alternative version to Non-Factive Psychologism, only factive mental states are reasons; on still another version of psychologism, only tokens of mental states with true contents are reasons. Let's reserve the term 'Factive Psychologism' for the former view and 'Truthy Psychologism' for the latter view.

---

[1] The following taxonomy is inspired by Turri's (2009), 492.
[2] See Turri (2009), 492.
[3] Examples of such non-factive mental states are states that are picked out by phrases like 'It seems to S that p' or 'S seems to see that p.' According to a lot of theorists, states like these are apt to provide epistemic justification because they possess a certain phenomenal character, which is not shared by mental states that don't provide epistemic justification, such as hunches, hopes or guesses. See Huemer (2001), Pryor (2000), Chudnoff (2011, 2012) and Tucker (2010).

Factive Psychologism: Only factive mental states are reasons.

Truthy Psychologism: Only tokens of mental states with true contents are reasons.[4]

The main rivals to psychologism are factualism and propositionalism.

Factualism: All epistemic reasons are facts.

Propositionalism: All epistemic reasons are propositions, i.e., the contents of psychological states.

Non-Factive Psychologism is considered by many to be the most plausible account of epistemic reasons. It has been claimed that this brand of psychologism satisfies the main desiderata a theory of reasons should be able to satisfy.[5] Therefore, many epistemologists subscribe to this view; for examples, Conee and Feldman (1985, 2004), Huemer (2000, 2007), Tucker (2010), and Comesaña (2010), among others. However, there exist several challenges for this view. In the present paper, I wish to focus on two challenges for this view. First, there seem to exist linguistic data that speak against psychologism.[6] When we specify an agent's reasons, we sometimes use locutions that do not seem to make reference to the mental states of the agent, such as 'John believes that he will loose his job *because his secretary plans to expose him*' or 'John believes that he will loose his job *because it is a fact that his secretary plans to expose him.*' If we take these locutions at face value, it seems that we have to acknowledge that reasons are at least sometimes non-psychological items.[7] Consequently, in order to uphold the claim that reasons are mental states, the psychologist needs to show that psychologism is not inconsistent with these linguistic data or that these claims do not make it mandatory to identify the reason with a fact.

---

[4] Mitova (2015) has introduced Truthy Psychologism into the present debate.
[5] See for defenses of psychologism about reasons Turri (2009) and McCain (2014), ch. 2.
[6] An important discussion of linguistic evidence is Pryor (2007). Littlejohn (2012) discusses linguistic evidence in favor of the claim that a proposition is among a subject's evidence only if the subject knows p. The present paper will not engage in a discussion of the conditions necessary for possession of a reason.
[7] Linguistic evidence in favor of Factualism plays a pivotal role in some defenses of Factualism. See for an argument for Factualism that partly relies on linguistic data Schnee (2014). Schnee calls this argument 'the argument from factual reasons'.

Second, Non-Factive Psychologism is often considered to explain best how a person can be in possession of a reason, and base her belief on it, even for cases where the content of the reason is false or does not correspond to a fact.[8] However, several factualists have recently presented solutions to the problem of 'bad cases' in which apparently no facts are present.[9] Ian Schnee (2014), for instance, has suggested that in a bad case the reason should be identified with the nearest determinable fact available of what would have been a subject's reason in a good case. Ernest Sosa and Kurt Sylvan (Forth.) hold that apparent or psychological facts might serve as reasons in bad cases. In case the factualists are able to provide an account as to how beliefs can be based on apparently non-existent facts, then one of the main motivations for Non-Factive Psychologism seems to vanish.

I proceed as follows. In the first section, I shall consider linguistic evidence that seems to suggest that facts can at least sometimes be reasons for beliefs. I will try to show that appearances are misleading, in the sense that they do not force us to adopt the view that those beliefs are indeed based on facts. In the second section, I will consider some recent attempts that factualists have presented to solve the problem of bad cases. The upshot of my discussion will be that these recent attempts by factualists to introduce surrogates for those facts that allegedly serve as reasons in bad cases are not successful.

Before I begin, however, I wish to state two assumptions that are relevant to my discussion. First, the present paper is concerned with reasons that are had.[10] Reasons that are had differ from *reasons to believe* in two important respects. On the one hand, reasons to believe do not affect what a person rationally believes in case the person is not in possession of these reasons. On the other, reasons to believe are always good reasons, while reasons that are had can on closer inspection be bad reasons to adopt a certain doxastic attitude. Second, in the present paper, I'll be mainly concerned with reasons for beliefs. However, I think that the considerations that I will present will carry over to reasons for actions.[11]

---

8 See for a discussion of this problem for factualism Turri (2009, 502–503).
9 Williamson (2000) has introduced the terms 'good cases' and 'bad cases'.
10 Propositionalism and factualism struggle to account for possession of reasons because it is totally okay to say that you can possess a reason, while it is odd to say that you can possess a proposition or a fact. Solutions to this problem for propositionalism about reasons are proposed in Schroeder (2008) and Turri (2012).
11 See Littlejohn (2012) for arguments for the 'unity of reasons'. Littlejohn claims that it counts against a theory of epistemic reasons if this theory does not carry over to reasons for actions.

1. Linguistic Evidence in Favor of Factualism

We use different types of locutions to specify the reasons for which a person believes a particular proposition. We often say things like:

(1) John believes that he will loose his job *because he believes* that his secretary plans to expose him.

(2) Thomas believes that his wife is cheating on him *because he observed* that she often flirted with other men.

Claims like (1) and (2), if taken at face value, state that a person bases her belief in a particular proposition on a certain mental state, such as a belief or a perceptual experience. Locutions of this sort thus seem to favor psychologism. However, we also specify a person's reasons with claims of the following sort:

(1) John's reason for his belief that he will loose his job is the fact that his secretary plans to expose him.

(2) Thomas' reason for his belief that his wife is cheating on him is the fact that his wife is often flirting with other men.

On the face of it, claims (3) and (4) seem to be claims that state an identity between a reason and a particular fact. They thus seem to be claims of the following logical form:

(3') John's reason = the fact that his secretary planned to expose him.

(4') Thomas's reason = the fact that his wife is often flirting with other men.

If (3') and (4') embody the logical form of claims like (3) and (4), then this seems to entail that we are at least sometimes committed to conceive of a subject's reasons as facts.

James Pryor (2007), however, has investigated reasons ascriptions of this sort and has argued that they do not license to identify the subject's reasons with the entities referred to by the singular terms appearing on the right-hand side of (3') and (4'). Pryor urges that the copula that figures in claims like (3) and (4) should not be understood as serving to identify the reason with a particular entity but rather as having a specifying role.[12] Claims like (3) and (4) thus specify the content of the reason, and do not equate the reason in question with a fact. Pryor is of the view that (3) and (4) do not lend support to views like factualism (or propositionalism) because the considerations he has presented do not make it mandatory to identify a subject's reasons with a fact.

Nonetheless, even if Pryor is right, there are still further data that seem to speak against psychologism and that cannot be explained away in the way that Pryor suggests because these claims are of a different logical form. Consider:

(1) John believes that he will loose his job *because his secretary plans to expose him*.

(2) Thomas believes that his wife is cheating on him *because it is a fact that his wife has often flirted with other men*.

(5) and (6) do not apparently state an identity between a subject's reasons and a particular fact, such as in the claims (3) and (4). Nonetheless, due to the factivity of 'because' it can be assumed that both statements (5) and (6) can only be true if their respective conjuncts are true as well. And this might be taken to entail that the statements appearing on the right-hand side of (5) and (6) refer to or denote facts. If we further assume that (5) and (6) serve in these particular instances to specify the basis of the belief in question, we seem to have to acknowledge that facts are at least sometimes reasons for beliefs. Again, this seems to show that not every reason is a mental state.

However, I don't think that it is obligatory to interpret reason-stating claims in the form of (5) and (6) along factualist lines. I am now going to present two considerations that, if taken in conjunction, make an interpretation of these claims equally plausible on which the reason is a mental state, such as a true belief. I will first argue that those reason-stating claims that identify a subject's reason with a fact entail beliefs and are therefore equivalent to claims that identify a subject's reason with a true belief. The second consideration I will present turns on the idea that there are several explanations available as to why we don't tend to *assert* that a subject's reason is a true belief in cases where the content of the reason corresponds to a fact. However, if an explanation can be given as to why we don't specify a subject's reason with locutions that invoke the mental states of the agent, and if reason-stating claims in the form of (5) and (6) are be-

---

12 See Pryor (2007), 236–40. Pryor further maintains that the specificational reading of claims like (3) and (4) does not presuppose that we have to treat that-clauses as non-referential.

lief-entailing, it seems that claims like (5) and (6) do not rule out that a subject's reason can be a mental state.

I now wish to turn to my first claim, viz. that reasons-ascriptions in the form of (5) and (6) entail beliefs. Consider the following claims:

(#5) John believes that he will loose his job because his secretary plans to expose him, *but he doesn't believe that his secretary plans to expose him.*

(#6) Thomas believes that his wife is cheating on him because she often flirted with other men, *but he doesn't believe that she flirted with other men.*

Reason ascriptions in the form of (5) and (6) exhibit a close connection to beliefs in that it seems contradictory to deny that a person that is in possession of a reason thereby does not possess a belief with the same content.

A further feature of reason ascriptions of the sort just considered is that explicitly stating that the person has a belief with a particular content is redundant:

(5′) John believes that he will loose his job because his secretary plans to expose him, and he believes that his secretary plans to expose him.

(6′) Thomas believes that his wife is cheating on him because it is a fact that she is often flirting with other men, and he believes that she is flirting with other men.

Notice that those reason ascriptions that I considered above, and that explicitly identify a reason with a particular fact, exhibit exactly the same properties. To avoid clutter, I'll just focus on the first claim introduced above:

(#3) John's reason is the fact that his secretary plans to expose him, but he doesn't believe that she plans to expose him.

(′3) John's reason is the fact that his secretary plans to expose him, and he believes that his secretary plans to expose him.

I think that both considerations suggest that reason-stating claims indeed entail beliefs. However, it might be suggested that the connection between reason ascriptions under consideration here and beliefs is looser. For instance, it might be maintained that reason ascriptions merely *presuppose* that the person possessing the reason has a particular belief. I don't think that this suggestion is plausible because the examples that I have presented do not satisfy the main tests for presuppositions.[13] The hallmark of presupposition is projection. According to the prevalent tests, presuppositions remain constant under negation, questioning, if embedded in conditionals, and within the scope of modal operators. Now consider:

(PR 1) It is false that John believed that he will loose his job because his secretary plans to expose him.

(PR 1') Did John believe that he will loose his job because his secretary plans to expose him?

(PR 1'') If John believes that he will loose his job because his secretary plans to expose him, someone else is really lucky right now.

(PR 1''') It is possible that John believes that will loose his job because his secretary plans to expose him.

(PR 1) through (PR 1''') do not presuppose that John believes that his secretary planned to expose him. Thus, the entailment view is clearly superior in comparison to this option. Reasons ascriptions in the form under consideration indeed entail beliefs.

Notice that, in the present context, I am just considering reason-ascribing statements that specify the reason by a statement in the form of 'S believes that p because q' and whether these statements indeed commit us to conceive of the reasons specified by them as being facts. When I claim that these locutions entail beliefs, I do not want to commit myself to the view that only beliefs are reasons. The considerations advanced here do not put into jeopardy a view on which also non-doxastic states may confer justification on a given belief and that therefore entails that there are also 'immediately' or non-inferentially justified beliefs. When beliefs are based on non-doxastic states and are non-inferentially justified, we tend to specify the reasons with very different locutions such as those just considered. For example, in case a person is non-inferentially justified in believing a proposition through perception, for example, we tend to specify her reason by locutions that invoke perceptual states or events, such as 'John believes that it is snowing because it perceptually seems to John that it is snowing'.

---

13 See Beaver and Geurts (2011) for an overview of main features of presuppositions.

Now, the consideration that I have presented does not by itself conclusively establish that the beliefs entailed by the claims just considered are indeed those reasons upon which the beliefs are based on. By taking a closer look at the pragmatic effects of reason ascriptions, it will become apparent that an interpretation of claims like those just considered along psychological lines is equally plausible. Consider first the following exchanges:

(JOB 1) A: Why does John believe that he will loose his job?
B: Because he believes that his secretary plans to expose him.

(JOB 2) A: Why does John believe that he will loose his job?
B: Because he truly believes that his secretary plans to expose him.

(JOB 3) A: Why does John believe that he will loose his job?
B_1: Because his secretary plans to expose him.
B_2: Because it is a fact that his secretary plans to expose him.

In the first exchange, B's utterance likely triggers the implicature that John *merely believes* that his secretary plans to expose him, without it being indeed the case that she plans to expose him. In this case, the hearer likely infers that it is not the case that John's secretary in fact plans to expose him. Though B's answer in the second exchange (JOB 2) does not trigger this implicature and the statement by B is not infelicitous, we in general do not tend to use 'truly believes' to specify the reason for which an agent believed a particular proposition. Rather, we just tend to say: 'because his secretary plans to expose him.' If we further bear in mind for what I have argued for above—viz. that reason ascriptions entail beliefs—, it should be evident as to why there is no difference in the claims made by B in (JOB 2) and (JOB 3). Since B's follow up in (JOB 3) entails that John believes that his secretary plans to expose him and the speaker states that she indeed plans to expose him, this further entails that John's belief is true. Thus, in both the second and the third exchange the responses seem to be equivalent, even though the speaker in the third does not use a locution that seems to make reference to a mental state.

However, there also exist examples that show that we specify the reason for which an agent believed a particular proposition by reference to a mental state in case the content of the reason is true. Consider the following exchange:

(JOB 4) A: Why did John believe that he would loose his job?
B: Because he believed that his secretary planned to expose him, and she indeed planned to expose him.

B's response in (JOB 4) is usually used to communicate something different than by the responses figuring in (JOB 2) and (JOB 3). Very roughly, B's utterance in (JOB 4) is used to communicate that John merely thought or suspected that his secretary planned to expose him and that it turned out later that she in fact planned to expose him. It should be evident that this sort of information cannot be conveyed by any of the statements figuring in the above exchanges (JOB 2) and (JOB 3). So, it seems that we tend to use statements that attribute mental states to an agent in case the reason has a true content only if we wish to communicate something like B in (JOB 4).

I think there are several explanations available as to why we tend to specify the reason by a statement that does not invoke the phrase 'truly believes' in case the content of the reason was true or a fact. A very simple explanation might be that the phrase 'because she plans to expose him' is just less cumbersome than 'because he truly believes that his secretary plans to expose him'. It might be suggested that it is therefore much more economical for a speaker to use the former phrase than the latter because the phrase 'because she plans to expose him' is easier to process for a hearer. Another explanation might be that 'believes' triggers on most occasions of use the implicature that the person to whom possession of a reason is ascribed *merely believes* that the content of the reason was true. However, since 'believes' carries this implicature, it could be maintained that this affects the assertibility conditions of statements involving 'believes'. And if a speaker adds 'truly' to 'believes', this seems to call into question that she should use 'believes' in the first place instead of some other expression that doesn't trigger this kind of implicature, such as 'because it is a fact that she plans to expose him.'

If my suggestion is on the right track as to why we don't use 'truly believes' in reason attributions conjoined by 'because', then the alleged data that factualists propose in favor of their view do not make it obligatory to identify the subject's reason with a fact. The above exchanges suggest that we don't specify a subject's reasons by reference to her mental states in cases where the contents of those states are true because locutions that seem to invoke facts are easier to process—at least that was one explanation considered to account for this phenomenon. Moreover, statements that specify a subject's reason by reference to a fact entail beliefs and are therefore equivalent to statements that specify a subject's reason by reference to her mental states. In light of both considerations, it seems that an interpretation of statements like (5) and (6) and those figuring in the exchange (JOB 3) along psychological lines is equally plausible. Hence, the factualist is not in a position to claim that reason-ascribing claims like those figuring in (JOB 3) need to be taken at face value and therefore need to be understood along factualist lines.

It might be even further argued that considerations of simplicity or austerity make the psychologist's interpretation of reason attributions more plausible than the factualist interpretation. If we consider those statements that attribute a reason to an agent that specify the mental states of the agent, such as the claims (1) and (2) introduced above, and if we bear in mind that also those reason-stating claims that seem to identify a subject's reason with a fact are equivalent to claims on which the reason is a true belief, then an ontology of reasons that claims that our reasons belong to the same category in both instances will be more austere than an ontology that claims that reasons belong to different ontological categories. If we want our ontology of epistemic reason to be as austere as possible, then this suggests that we should conceive of the reason in both instances as being mental states.

However, I can think of the following way the factualist might reply to the considerations presented here. The factualist might respond by conceding that reason ascriptions entail beliefs. But these beliefs, the factualist might contend, merely play an *enabling role* to get access to reasons. The reasons themselves, the factualist might urge, can on this view still be identified with facts. Equipped with this idea, the factualist can debunk the interpretation of reason-ascribing statements just given.

However, there are reasons to deny that beliefs merely play an enabling role. John Turri has presented an argument that aims to demonstrate that ascriptions of mental states to a subject, in cases where the subject believes something because of a particular reason, plays a different role to a mere enabling condition. Turri invites us to consider the following exchanges:[14]

(VASE) A: Why did the vase break?
        B: Because it fell off the shelf.
        A: Why was there a shelf?

(WOODS) A: Why do you believe that Tiger Woods will sink the put?
        B: Because Woods excels at putting.
        A: Why do you believe that?

Turri suggests that the second exchange significantly differs from the first. While A's second question in the first exchange is odd, A's follow up in the other case does seem to be perfectly normal. Turri urges that if beliefs would only play an enabling role, then inquiring after them would be odd as in (VASE). But since it

---

14 See Turri (2009, 505–506).

makes perfect sense to ask why someone has a particular belief, this seems to demonstrate that the role of beliefs is different to a mere enabling condition.

2. Reasons and bad Cases

As stated in the introduction to this paper, one of the biggest challenges for the factualist is to provide an account of 'bad cases'—i.e., cases in which a person is in possession of a reason, though the content of the reason does not correspond to a fact. Paradigm examples of this sort are cases of misperception or deception. Say I walk by a store and seem to see that my friend Natalie is inside the store. However, it is not Natalie but someone else who looks very similar to her. In case I go on to form the belief that Natalie is in the store, I cannot base my belief on the fact that Natalie is in the store, since there is no such fact. The famous evil demon case also spells trouble for factualism.[15] Let's say that I am justified in believing that there is a computer screen in front of me right now and this belief is true. My victimized twin, Vic, deceived by an evil demon, is also justified in believing that there is a computer screen in front of him because he happens to be fed with experiences qualitatively identical to mine. Unfortunately, his belief is false and he thus cannot base his belief on the fact that there is indeed a computer screen in front of him, since there is no such fact.[16]

How might the factualist deal with these cases? There are several options available. The most straightforward stance towards this issue is surely to deny that persons in bad cases possess reasons at all. However, this option comes with very high costs. Subjects in bad cases possess justified beliefs. If we further assume that justified beliefs are beliefs based on reasons, we should conclude that subjects in bad cases also possess reasons. If the factualist were to deny that subjects in bad cases do not possess reasons, he either has to give up the claim that subjects in bad cases are justified; or he needs to provide an alternative account as to why their beliefs are justified. Thus, I don't take this option to be a serious contender to solve the problem under consideration.

Another more interesting option that has just been recently proposed maintains that in cases in which no fact is present the subject bases her belief *on the*

---

15 See Lehrer and Cohen (1983) and Cohen (1984). The evil demon case is considered to be a counterexample to reliabilism.
16 Note that the existence of bad cases also poses a problem for defenders of factive psychologism and truthy psychologism. Most of the worries that I will present for the factualist view will carry over to the view of defenders of these versions of psychologism.

nearest determinable fact available. Ian Schnee (2014) has coined the term 'Take-Get Factualism' for this view. He says:

> On this version, in the bad case her reason is the nearest determinable fact of what her reason would have been in the good case. As such her reason is still non-psychological (...). Alice is attending to the world, and the way the world is is her grounds for belief. It just so happens that the world is not exactly as she takes it to be, but her belief is still based on the way the world is inasmuch as it is the way she takes it to be (Schnee (2014), 22).

Schnee suggests that in case of my mistakenly perceiving that my friend Natalie is in the store, I am basing my belief on the fact that *someone qualitatively identical to Natalie* is in the store (see Schnee (2014), 21–22). Schnee contends that someone who holds the belief that Natalie is in the store also dispositionally believes that someone qualitatively identical to Natalie is in the store. On Schnee's view, the case is similar to cases in which we hold beliefs about a determinate (say, that a thing is crimson) and a determinable (say, that the same thing is red). In case someone holds the former belief, she also holds the latter belief, at least dispositionally. So one might claim that I base my belief that Natalie is in the store on the fact that someone identical to Natalie is in the store. Note that in case I base my belief that my friend Natalie is in the store on the fact that someone qualitatively identical to Natalie is in the store, as Schnee suggests, my reason is not about a psychological state of mine. Further, it seems that the existence of this particular fact is not existentially dependent on a psychological state. Schnee's solution thus preserves the main tenets of factualism.

However, I don't think that this solution is ultimately successful. To begin with, is it really true, as Schnee invites us to believe, that in the case described above there exists a fact that someone qualitatively identical to Natalie is in the store? In order for such a fact to exist, there needs to be someone qualitatively identical to Natalie in the store. Note that the existence conditions of facts seem to parallel the truth conditions of statements describing or referring to facts. Thus, in order for the fact <a is F> to exist, for example, the object denoted by 'a' indeed needs to exemplify the property F. Similarly, in order for the fact <someone qualitatively identical to Natalie is in the store> to exist, there indeed needs to be someone in the store who is qualitatively identical to Natalie. But it should be obvious that the person I seem to perceive in the above case does not share all her properties with Natalie, since otherwise she would be identical to Natalie and this case wouldn't qualify as a bad case. I thus take it that, strictly speaking, there is no such fact available as Schnee suggests. Therefore, I cannot base my belief on this particular fact and Schnee's solution does not appear to work.

Nonetheless, even if Schnee's initial proposal does not get off the ground, it could be fixed. There might exist facts in the vicinity of the fact as identified by Schnee. The fact that might be present in the above case is presumably the fact <someone looking like Natalie is in the store> or the fact <someone sharing most of her perceptible properties with Natalie is in the store (when view from a certain angle or perspective)>.

However, I have one major misgiving about this modified proposal. If we identify my reason in the above case with facts of this sort, it seems that these facts, conceived of as reasons for my belief, are not sufficient to explain why I rationally hold the belief that Natalie is in the store. At most, both facts rationalize the beliefs that *someone looking like Natalie* is in the store or that someone *sharing Natalie's perceptible properties is in the store*, respectively. If we further assume that the belief in the above case is a non-inferentially justified belief, then being in possession of the reason in question should be sufficient to rationally hold the belief. However, this does not seem to be the case with respect to the nearest fact available to me in the bad case. If I were to base my belief that Natalie is in the store solely on the fact that someone looking like Natalie is in the store, I would irrationally hold the belief.

Note further that the proposal that reasons in bad cases are facts about how things look does not seem to sit well with the main tenets of factualism. Facts of this particular sort seem to depend existentially on the existence of psychological states. Though most factualists don't say much about how we gain access to reasons, it seems that if facts depend existentially on our psychological states, getting access to them will entail that psychological states are also cognitively more basic. I take this, at least initially, to be a view that undergirds the factualist proposal. If psychological states are cognitively more basic than those facts that serve as our reasons, then why should we introduce facts as reasons in the first place?

How might Schnee deal with the evil demon case? What are the nearest facts that are available to my victimized twin Vic? Schnee acknowledges that there will be no non-psychological fact available to Vic that will serve as his reason for his belief that there is a computer screen in front of him.[17] However, he concedes that we have to introduce psychological facts or facts about how things appear to Vic in order to avoid the conclusion that Vic has no reason at all for his belief. Ernest Sosa and Kurt Sylvan subscribe to a similar view. They hold that apparent facts as well as facts about my psychological states can serve as reasons in bad

---

17 Schnee (2014), 23–24 discusses cases of hallucination. Of course, his solution will carry over to the present case.

cases.[18] My victimized twin Vic could thus base his belief on the fact <it appears to me that there is a computer screen in front of me>.

However, I fear that this solution will also be problematic. For it seems that this particular fact conceived as Vic's reason will not by itself be sufficient to rationalize beliefs concerning worldly propositions such as that there is indeed a computer screen in front of Vic. If we assume that possession of the reason should be sufficient to rationally hold the belief in question, then facts of this particular sort will not be able to explain why Vic rationally believes that there is a computer screen in front of him. At most, facts of this particular sort rationalize beliefs that it appears to Vic as if there is a computer screen in front of Vic.

Further worries for a proposal that introduces appearance facts as reasons in bad cases were raised in the literature on the epistemology of perception.[19] For instance, appearance facts and psychological facts are facts that, in order to be grasped by an agent, seem to require that the possessor be in possession of appearance concepts, expressed by such phrases as 'it seems to me' or 'it appears to me'. However, there might exist epistemic agents who are not in possession of concepts of this sort, though they are nonetheless in possession of reasons. Thus it seems plausible to suppose that they cannot be in possession of facts of this particular sort either.[20] Further, our epistemic reasons seem to be about the external world and seem to reveal to an agent that some extra-mental fact is the case. By introducing appearance facts, we give up this particular feature of epis-

---

18 Timothy Williamson (2000) holds a very similar view concerning bad cases. Williamson assumes, in contrast to Schnee and Sosa and Sylvan, that our reasons in bad cases are propositions. Thus, the propositions that are had in bad cases are appearance propositions of the sort 'it appears to me that p'. This view is subject to similar worries. See for a discussion of Williamson's view Schellenberg (2013).

19 See, for example, Schellenberg (2013). Schellenberg mainly raises some worries for Williamson's (2000) proposal. Williamson thinks that our reasons in bad cases are appearance propositions in the form of <it appears to me that p>. Schellenberg maintains that an agent is in need of the self-concept in order to be in possession of reasons of this sort. However, animals or small children do not seem to possess the concept of a self but still can be possess reasons in bad cases.

20 However, the considerations presented here against this particular brand of factualism do not speak against a view that introduces seemings as justifying states (cf. Huemer (2001, 2007) and Tucker (2010)). The main reason as to why seemings may confer justification on beliefs even though the person might not be in possession of appearance concepts is that it is not part of the propositional content of states that we refer to with statements like 'it appears to me that p' that their content appears to be true. So, seeming internalism is subject to the present objection.

temic reasons since appearance facts tend to be about how things appear to an agent instead of how things are with respect to the external world.

It should be evident that the answer that the Non-Factive Psychologist can give about such cases will fare much better. In cases where I have the perceptual experience or the perceptual seeming with the content that Natalie is in the store, and I base my belief that she is in the store on this reason (and I am not in possession of any defeaters), I rationally hold this belief. By contrast, if I am in possession of a perceptual experience or seeming with a different content—for instance, an experience with the content that someone who looks identical to Natalie is in the store—I don't believe rationally that Natalie is in the store in case I base my belief solely on the experience with this particular content. Only if I possess additional reasons enhancing the justificatory force resulting from this perceptual experience, can I be considered holding rationally the belief in question—say, in case I have reasons to believe that she often visits the store or that she lives in the proximity of the store.

The criticism just canvassed relies on the assumption that the state or entity we introduce as the reason on which a belief is based should be capable of explaining why one rationally places a certain confidence in a particular propositional content. It might be suggested that the beliefs in the examples just discussed are non-inferentially justified beliefs and that the content of the reason presumably should match the content of the belief that is held because of that reason. If the reason does not match the belief's content, then the degree of confidence is not sufficiently explained by the reason in question and we thus have not identified the reason upon which the belief is based on. Since bad cases are cases in which there is no internal difference between both subjects, it can be assumed that both subjects are 'internal twins', i.e., they are identical from their internal perspective. As a consequence, they are equally rational in holding the beliefs they hold.

Note, however, that the argument that I have presented against Schnee's solution only assumes that subjects in ordinary cases and subjects in bad cases do not differ with respect to the rationality in which they hold their beliefs but might probably differ in other respects, such as the kind or degree of justification both possess. On some hybrid views of epistemic justification, which combine internalist and externalist elements, such as Comesaña's (2010) 'Evidentialist Reliabilism', rationality and justification might come apart and subjects in good and in bad cases might thus be equally rational in holding the beliefs they hold, even though they differ with respect to the kind or degree of justification they possess. On Comesaña's view, a subject will, if deceived by an evil demon, have the same reason for her belief as in a good case, but will not possess the same sort of justification as in ordinary cases because the belief-forming process will not be reliable in the same sense. Comesaña's indexical reliabilism has it that a subject's belief-forming process, if exercised in a demon world, is not reliable in this particular world even though the process is reliable in our world. Comesaña's view will thus entail that subjects in good and a bad cases are both rational and justified, but they are not justified in the same sense or degree.

As mentioned above in my argument against Schnee's solution, I do not need to commit myself to stronger claims concerning the epistemic status that both subjects in good and in bad cases share. For instance, one could maintain that both subjects are *justified to the same degree* in case one of them is in a bad case and the other is not.[21] However, I suspect that, at least intuitively, there are reasons to deny the thesis of equal justification. It might be contended, for example, that subjects in bad cases and subjects in ordinary cases differ with respect to the degree of justification they possess because beliefs formed in bad cases are less likely to be true than in good cases. Thus, there are reasons to deny that both subjects are identical in terms of the degree of justification they possess.[22]

Another epistemic status that might be at issue concerning internal twins is that they literally possess the *same reasons*. According to this view, in bad and in ordinary cases the reasons both subjects possess are identical and thus share the same properties.[23] However, I also think that this view is controversial. The reasons that subjects in good cases possess might differ from the reasons they possess in bad cases with respect to their extrinsic properties, such as their distal causes or their reliability. In case I mistakenly seem to see that my friend Natalie is in the store, for example, my reason is not causally connected to the event or fact that my friend Natalie is in the store, but rather to some other event or fact. Thus, I it makes little sense to say that subjects in bad and in good cases literally possess the same reasons. Note further that this assumption would rule out at the outset any attempt of the factualist to introduce a surrogate for those facts that serve as reasons in good cases because subjects in bad cases apparently can never be in possession of the same facts that allegedly serve as reasons on this view in good cases.

---

[21] See for a defense of the thesis of equal justification of internal twins Silins (2005).
[22] I assume that Schnee's solution entails that subjects in bad cases are justified to a lower degree than subjects in good cases because their reasons make it less likely that their beliefs are true.
[23] Turri (2009), 501 seems to subscribe to this view. He states that subjects who are deceived by an evil demon possess the same reasons as when they are not deceived.

3. Conclusion

In this paper, I've argued for two claims. First, I've tried to make it plausible that psychologism is not inconsistent with the linguistic data that factualist might adduce in favor of their view. I've tried to show that ascriptions of reasons that seem to favor factualism do not make it mandatory to identify the reason upon which a belief is based on with a fact. Second, I've argued that recent solutions to the problem of non-existent facts that factualists have presented are not successful.[24]

References

Beaver, D. I. and Geurts, B. (2011). Presupposition. In: E. N. Zalta (ed.), *The Stanford Encyclopedia of Philosophy.* http://plato.stanford.edu/archives/sum2011/entries/presupposition.
Chudnoff, E. (2011). The Nature of Intuitive Justification. *Philosophical Studies* 153: 313–333.
Chudnoff, E. (2012). Presentational Phenomenology. In: S. Miguens and G. Preyer (eds.), *Consciousness and Subjectivity.* Frankfurt: Ontos.
Cohen, S. and K. Lehrer (1983). Justification, Truth, and Knowledge. *Synthese* 55: 191–207.
Cohen, S. (1984). Justification and Truth. *Philosophical Studies* 46: 279–295.
Comesaña, J. (2010). Evidentialist Reliabilism. *Noûs* 44: 571–600.
Conee, E. and Feldman, R. (2001). Internalism Defended. In: Kornblith, H. (ed.), *Epistemology: Internalism and Externalism.* Malden (MA): Blackwell.
Conee, E. and Feldman, R. (2004). *Evidentialism: Essays in Epistemology.* New York: Oxford University Press.
Huemer, M. (2001). *Skepticism and the Veil of Perception.* Lanham: Rowman and Littlefield.
Huemer, M. (2007). Compassionate Phenomenal Conservatism. *Philosophy and Phenomenological Research* 74: 30–55.
King, J. (2002). Designating Propositions. *The Philosophical Review* 101, 341–371.
Littlejohn, C. (2012). *Justification and the Truth-Connection.* Cambridge: Cambridge University Press.
McCain, K. (2014). *Evidentialism and Epistemic Justification.* New York and London: Routledge.
Mitova, V. (2015). Truthy Psychologism about Evidence. *Philosophical Studies* 172: 1105–1126.
Pryor, J. (2000). The Skeptic and the Dogmatist. *Noûs* 34, 517–549.
Pryor, J. (2007). Reasons and That-Clauses. *Philosophical Perspectives* 17, 217–244.
Sosa, E. and Sylvan, K. (Forthcoming). The Place of Reasons in Epistemology. In: Star, D. (ed.), *The Oxford Handbook of Reasons and Normativity.* New York: Oxford University Press.

---

[24] I would like to thank Ian Schnee and an anonymous reviewer for their very helpful comments and suggestions on an earlier version of this paper.

Schellenberg, S. (2013). Experience and Evidence. *Mind* 122, 699–747.
Schnee, I. (2014). Reasoning from the Facts. Manuscript.
Schroeder, M. (2008). Having Reasons. *Philosophical Studies* 139, 57–71.
Silins, N. 2005. Deception and Evidence. *Philosophical Perspectives* 19, 375–404.
Tucker, Ch. (2010). Why Open-Minded People Should Endorse Dogmatism. *Philosophical Perspectives* 24, 529–545.
Turri, J. (2009). The Ontology of Epistemic Reasons. *Noûs* 43, 490–512.
Turri, J. (2012). Reasons, Answers and Goals. *Journal of Moral Philosophy* 9, 491–499.
Williamson, T. (2000). *Knowledge and its Limits*. Oxford: Oxford University Press.

Clayton Littlejohn
Learning from Learning from our Mistakes

Philosophers have long had a soft spot for like-from-like reasoning. Whatever produces a good person must be good. Whenever something is heated it is heated by something hot. The degree of perfection contained in the effect cannot exceed the degree contained in the cause. And so on. We know that there is an intuition that underlies transmission theories of causation, but we also know that the intuition is unreliable. Gin is colourless but it makes you see rainbows. Populations can become increasingly fit over time. And so on. If we were surprised to discover that knowledge can come from mistaken belief, maybe we shouldn't have been. Without some specific reason for thinking that only knowledge can beget knowledge, we should have been open to the possibility of knowledge from falsehood (KFF).

In KFF cases, a subject acquires knowledge by reasoning through a falsehood. Most of the literature on knowledge from falsehood is concerned with the *possibility* of KFF cases.[1] Some of it focuses on the significance of such cases.[2] This is a paper about the significance of the possibility.[3] For various reasons, people think that KFF cases cause trouble for the knowledge-first approach to evidence, justification, and the norm of belief. These arguments all seem to assume that certain like-from-like reasoning fails for knowledge but holds for justification. I think this is a mistake. If it's unreliable for knowledge, it's unreliable for justification.

One kind of like-from-like reasoning in epistemology is reasoning that assumes that knowledge is counter-closed:

---

[1] See Coffman (2008), Fitelson (2010), Klein (2008), and Warfield (2005) for defenses of the possibility. See Schnee (2015) for skepticism.
[2] See Arnold (2013), Littlejohn (2013), and Luzzi (2010).
[3] Comesana and Kantin (2010) and Rizzieri (2011) use cases of reasoning from falsehoods to try to cause trouble for E=K. Their arguments rest on assumptions similar to those at play in this paper, but they do not depend upon the intuitions that suggest that KFF is possible. After writing this paper, I discovered that Murphy (forthcoming) defends the possibility of unjustified beliefs serving as the inferential basis for justified belief. His arguments differ from mine, but he appears to be the first philosopher to criticize counter-closure for justification.

K-Counter-Closure (KCC): Necessarily, if (i) S knows that p entails q and (ii) S comes to believe q solely on the basis of competently deducing it from p, and (iii) S knows q, then S knows p (Luzzi 2010).[4]

Luzzi has argued rather persuasively that we can use KFF cases to show that KCC is mistaken. Let's take this as our starting point. Using these cases, some epistemologists have argued that the cases that undermine KCC also undermine various claims associated with the knowledge-first movement. They have been taken to show that knowledge isn't evidence, it isn't justified belief, and it isn't the norm of belief:

E=K One's evidence includes p iff one knows p (Hyman 2006, Williamson 2000).

KN: One shouldn't believe p unless one knows p (Littlejohn, 2013, Williamson 2000, Sutton 2007).

J=K: One's belief about p is justified iff one knows p (Sutton 2007).[5]

The basic argumentative strategy is something like this. In the KFF cases we will have a pair of beliefs, one that is false and one that constitutes knowledge. The latter will be inferred from the former. For the former to give rise to knowledge, it would have to have *something* going for it. It would have to be justified, have to provide evidence, and have to conform to the norms governing belief. Since, however, the belief doesn't constitute knowledge, E=K, J=K, and KN all must be mistaken.

The strategy only works on the assumption that justification is counter-closed:

---

[4] Reasoning from a false premise is *not* the same thing as reasoning from a false reason. See Alvarez (2010) and Hyman (2011) for discussion of the difference.

[5] In Littlejohn (2012), I argued that doxastic justification should be understood in terms of Sosa's (2007) notion of aptness. Sosa identifies apt belief with knowledge (of a kind). Although he thought that apt beliefs didn't necessarily constitute knowledge, he's changed course. Williamson has also changed course. In his (2000), he allowed that it might be possible to justifiably believe what you don't know, but he has since embraced the view that it's impossible to justifiably believe what you don't know on the grounds that it's impossible to justifiably believe a proposition whilst violating the fundamental norm of belief. See his (2013) for discussion. He allows that there is a sense of 'justification' that is distinct from knowledge, but suggests that this sense really captures the notion of an excuse.

J-Counter-Closure (JCC): Necessarily, if (i) S knows that p entails q and (ii) S comes to justifiably q solely on the basis of competently deducing it from p, and (iii) S justifiably believes q, then S justifiably believes p.

As we will see below, the cases that cause trouble for KCC also cause trouble for JCC. If, as I shall argue below, the KFF cases give us no (new) reason to question E=K, J=K, or KN, the KFF cases are really trouble for JCC. I shall discuss the significance of this below.[6]

1.

Let's consider some representative cases from KFF literature. Three should suffice:

Father Christmas: Virginia's parents tell her that Father Christmas will put presents under the tree for her. Believing what her parents tell her, she infers that there will be presents waiting for her tomorrow under the tree. She knows that there will be presents (Klein 2008).

Meeting Time: Alex has a 7 pm meeting, and extreme (and justified) confidence in my fancy watch's perfect accuracy. Alex makes inferences from what his watch says only if he has extreme confidence that it is perfectly accurate (perhaps he has exacting standards for what constitutes a good watch). Having lost track of the time and wanting to arrive on time for the meeting, Alex looks carefully at his watch. Because of his extreme confidence in his watch's accuracy, he reasons: 'It's exactly 2:58 pm; therefore I am not late for my 7 pm meeting'. Again he knows his conclusion, but as it happens it's exactly 2:56 pm, not 2:58 pm (Warfield 2005; Arnold 2013).

---

6 There are, of course, familiar objections to E=K and J=K. See Coffman (2010) and Kelp (2011), for example. There have also been responses to these criticisms to consider. See Littlejohn (2012), Mitova (2015), and Williamson (2013), for example. I don't want to defend E=K or J=K here. My aim is simply to argue that these cases don't give us any additional reason to think that these theses are mistaken.

Millikan's Experiment: By measuring the electrical charges of many oil drops, Millikan determined both the value of e (i.e., the charge of the electron), and that the charges are all integer multiples of e. Determining a relatively exact value of e involved measuring the following parameters as accurately as possible: temperature, pressure, voltage, the coefficient of viscosity of air, the density of clock oil, the value of the gravitational constant and the times of rise and fall of the oil drops. The important point to note then is that all of Millikan's measurements were—and still are—taken to be evidence for the claim that electrical charge is quantized. But, the measured quantities used to determine the value of e were all approximations due to the measurement errors inherent in determining the values of the relevant parameters ... So, the evidence Millikan used to confirm the claim that electric charge is quantized is only approximately true, due to the inexactness of the various methods of measurement used in the experiment (Shaffer 2013: 31. See also Hilpinen 1988: 164).

If we suppose that the protagonists have inferential knowledge as a result of reasoning from a false proposition, should we say that these cases threaten E=K or J=K?

Let's start with Shaffer's criticism of E=K. Shaffer seems to think that it's obvious that Millikan's evidence includes a falsehood, one that served as the evidential basis for Millikan's inferential knowledge. To deny this, as he sees it, is *immensely* costly:

> Adopting Williamson's or Littlejohn's truther view would then appear to commit us to the totally implausible view that the measurements made in such cases are not really evidence at all, because they are not true, and that the hypotheses that such measurements appear to support are not, in fact, confirmed on the basis of those measurements. This would effectively eliminate the possibility that measured values ever constitute evidence in the conduct of the science and in our more mundane epistemic lives. So, adopting the truther view of evidence with respect to propositions that report measurements undermines the very possibility of conducting rational empirical inquiry involving measurement. But, this is clearly at odds with actual practice and such measurements are evidence in both the sciences and everyday life, often exceptionally good evidence (Shaffer forthcoming: 6).

It is because Millikan's evidence included the false proposition that the value of e was 1.5924(17) X 10^{19}C that Millikan was able to knowingly infer that electric charge is quantized.

Klein criticizes both J=K and E=K. He thinks that the protagonists' relevant false beliefs are justified and apparently thinks that this shows that the protagonists have false evidence. In support of his claim about justificatory status, he says that this is 'an instance of the general requirement that doxastic justification which depends on another belief requires that that belief be doxastically justified' (2008: 50). On this assumption, it is thought to follow that the content of the false belief is part of the protagonists' evidence because it is a consequence of his account of doxastic justification that the content of the false belief propositionally justifies the inferential beliefs that constitute knowledge (2008: 50).[7]

2.

While I can see why someone might describe our KFF cases in ways that would cause trouble for the knowledge-first approach to evidence or justification, the grounds for thinking that this is the best way to describe such cases strikes me as rather weak.

Let's start with Millikan's Experiment. Contrary to what Shaffer thinks, I do not think it is obvious that the right thing to say about Millikan's Experiment is that Millikan came to know by reasoning from false *evidence*. On most views of evidence, the proposition p will not belong to the subject's evidence if the subject knows that p is false or should know that p is false.[8] With this very weak constraint on evidence in place, it seems that Shaffer's case is no threat. Millikan *knew*, or should have known, that the claim that the value of e was 1.5924(17) X 10^{19}C was nothing more than approximately true. If, as Shaffer suggests, something is false if it is merely approximately true, we should expect Millikan to have known this and known this for just the reasons that Shaffer cites. As calculating the value of e required an accurate measure of temperature, pressure, voltage, the coefficient of viscosity of air, the density of clock oil, the value of the

---

[7] Arnold's (2013) criticisms of J=K and E=K are similar.
[8] On the assumption that the subject knows p is false, it is plausible that the subject does not justifiably believe p. On the assumption that one should know that p is false, it is plausible that the subject does not justifiably believe p. Thus, if one thought that having a justified belief in p is necessary for having p as part of one's evidence, the proposed necessary condition on having evidence should be rather plausible.

gravitational constant and the times of rise and fall of the oil drops, it would be *mad* to think that the calculated value of e was anything more than approximately true. If it would be mad to believe p, I don't think p is part of one's evidence.

To make the case plausible as a counterexample to E=K, we have to find a proposition that played some role in Millikan's reasoning that has these three features:

(a) The proposition was one that the protagonist could reasonably have believed;
(b) The proposition would provide adequate support for the protagonist's conclusion in that it would be reasonable for someone who believed the proposition to draw the relevant conclusion;
(c) The proposition was not one that the protagonist knew because the proposition was false.

Since the proposition that Shaffer fixes on was for Millikan either a known unknown or one that Millikan should have known couldn't be known, his proposal does not satisfy (a). The related proposition that the calculated value of e was 1.5924(17) X 10^{19}C satisfies (a) and (b), but does not satisfy (c).

In support of his description of the case, Shaffer writes:

> Millikan's measurements were—and still are—taken to be evidence for the claim that electrical charge is quantized. But, the measured quantities used to determine the value of e were all approximations due to the measurement errors inherent in determining the values of the relevant parameters (2013: 31).

The expression 'Millikan's measurements' seems to me to be a bit of a fudge. It could refer to the value that was later replaced by more careful measurements or a proposition about the measurements that Millikan took (e.g., that Millikan determined the value of e to be such and such). Insofar as Millikan ran the experiment a number of times to calculate e and did not receive the same value for e in each trial, it seems like a rather odd psychological hypothesis to say that Millikan *believed* he got the right value and an odd normative claim to say that that's what he ought to have believed. Moreover, for the purposes of the experiment, getting the precise value would not matter for learning that electric charge is quantized. So long as the charges of the observed oil drops were (roughly) whole integer multiples of e, that would show that electric charge is quantized rather than continuous.

Since Millikan's Experiment does not satisfy (a)-(c), it seems not to be a terribly threatening case to E=K. And insofar as it doesn't threaten E=K, it poses no obvious threat to J=K or KN. Since, however, Father Christmas and Meeting Time do plausibly satisfy these three conditions, a further response is required.

Klein says very little in support of his contention that the protagonists' beliefs in KFF cases are justified beyond saying that there is a general requirement on doxastic justification that doxastically justified beliefs are inferentially justified only if the beliefs they are based upon are themselves doxastically justified. Thus, if he has an argument against E=K and J=K his argument rests on the undefended assumption that justification is counter-closed:

J-Counter-Closure (JCC): Necessarily, if (i) S knows that p entails q and (ii) S comes to believe q solely on the basis of competently deducing it from p, and (iii) S knows q, then S justifiably believes p.

We have to speculate a bit as to why Klein would think that JCC is true because he says little in support of it apart from the fact that he takes it to be an implication of a plausible account of doxastic justification. For my part, I would think that the discovery that KCC is false should lead us to reconsider the status of JCC. Shouldn't the counterexamples to KCC make us sceptical of like-from-like reasoning in general? Perhaps Klein thought that we had no independent grip on what it would be for a belief to be justified apart from a belief that could justify further beliefs. This might explain some of the confidence he had in JCC. To this, I have a response. The beliefs in the useful falsehoods *do not* justify further beliefs in the ways that typical justified beliefs do. Once we see why, we can see why the cases that threaten KCC might threaten JCC.

3.

Are KFF cases any threat to E=K or J=K? Little has been said to justify the claim that they are. Perhaps it's thought that little reason is needed since we already have ample reason to think that beliefs in the useful falsehoods *could* be justified. After all, isn't there ample reason to think that there can be false, justified beliefs? If so, mustn't there be false evidence?

It would be disappointing if this were the only argument that critics of E=K or J=K could muster because then the KFF cases would not be doing much work. If we were independently convinced that J=K or E=K were false, we wouldn't care much about what we could learn from KFF cases in this regard. The interesting question is whether KFF cases put any *additional* pressure on E=K or J=K.

It might seem that Klein has provided us with at least some reason to think that KFF cases present a unique challenge to E=K and J=K. It appears that the standard account of the relationship between doxastic and propositional justification might, if combined with the idea that propositions justifiably believed are evidence (J→E), support this counter-closure principle:

J-Counter-Closure (JCC): Necessarily, if (i) S knows that p entails q and (ii) S comes to believe q solely on the basis of competently deducing it from p, and (iii) S knows q, then S justifiably believes p.

As he sees it, doxastic justification requires propositional justification. Propositional justification, in turn, is either evidence or provided by the evidence. If we assume that the relevant beliefs are justified and accept his account of propositional and doxastic justification, we get some motivation for rejecting E=K:

P1. If the protagonist comes to know q by reasoning from some useful falsehood p, S's belief in q is doxastically justified.
P2. The protagonist comes to know q by reasoning from some useful falsehood p.
C1. Thus, the protagonist's belief in q is doxastically justified.
P3. For the protagonist's inferential belief in q to be doxastically justified, the protagonist must believe q for a good reason.
C2. The protagonist believes q for a good reason.
P4. The protagonist believes q for a good reason only if the protagonist believes q for the reason that p and p is part of the protagonist's evidence.
C3. The protagonist believes q for the reason that p and p is part of the protagonist's evidence.
P5. If p is part of the protagonist's evidence, the protagonist justifiably believes p.
C4. The protagonist justifiably believes p.

If this argument establishes (C3), E=K must be false. If the argument can establish (C4), J=K must be false. If both are false, it looks like KN must be false, too.

The thought behind (P1) is that knowledge requires doxastic justification. I'm happy to grant that this is so. In assuming that KFF cases are possible, we're assuming (P2). It would seem that (P3) and (P4) follow from the standard account of doxastic justification. The standard account says (roughly) that if the protagonist's belief is doxastically justified, it is propositionally justified by virtue of the fact that the subject has adequate reason for having that belief and the subject believes for the relevant justifying reason. The idea behind (P5) might be put this way. If a subject's evidence includes some proposition, the subject has the right to reason from that proposition. If the subject ought not reason from p, the subject must not be justified in believing p in the first place.

While this argument seems initially quite promising, defenders of E=K and J=K have a plausible line of response. Anyone who takes seriously the possibility that J=K might be true would think of proper belief or permissibly held belief as one that conforms to the knowledge norm. In other words, they identify knowing p with permissibly believing p. In discovering that KCC is false, they would reject JCC. If that requires rejecting the standard account of doxastic justification, this might well be a price they'd be willing to pay. They would reject (P3) on the assumption that the good reason that the protagonist must have for believing q is some prior reason that figured in reasoning because they'd deny that p is any reason at all by virtue of the fact that it's false.

How plausible *is* the standard account of the relationship between propositional and doxastic justification? Should we say that doxastic justification is a matter of propositional justification plus basing and that propositional justification is determined by the subject's evidence? We will see that KFF cases cause trouble for the standard story about propositional and doxastic justification, but it is also worth mentioning that there are other sources of difficulty, too. Anyone who accepts E=K will already have to say that the standard story has to be modified for cases of non-inferential belief. Consider the kinds of cases that foundationalists would use to elicit the intuitions that underwrite the isolation objection. You don't know what tonight's dish will be but when the cloche is lifted you see that they're serving fish. Prior to this experience, you had no good reason to believe that it would be fish but now you know that it is fish. If E=K is correct and the case is as I've described it, there was nothing in your possession that could have been evidence for this belief that you possessed independently from the belief. If we think of propositional justification as (a) the whatever-it-is-that-warrants-the-formation-of-a-belief where this can be possessed without the relevant belief and (b) something that supervenes upon the evidence, we would have to reject E=K if we wanted to say that in seeing the fish and coming to believe there was fish for dinner you knew and justifiably believed that it would be fish for dinner. If we accepted E=K, however, we would say that there is nothing that plays both the (a) and (b) roles. There is something that ensures that you're in a position to know that fish is being served and so there is something that ensures that you're entitled to form that belief, but that won't be evidence. So, if propositional justification is understood in terms of (a), we have to reject (b). If it is understood in terms of (b), we have to reject (a). Since we have to give up one of these to understand what happens in cases of knowledge or justified belief not acquired by using independently held evidence, we shouldn't use the standard story about propositional justification and doxastic justification in an argument against E=K. In using it, we're already assuming that E=K is mistaken.

There are two arguments that one might offer in support of the knowledge-first views under attack. The first argument is *the ability argument*. This argument is designed to show that the KFF cases are not cases in which someone believes for a good reason because they are not cases in which the subject's inferring q is a case of believing q for a reason. The second argument is *the generality argument*. The argument is designed to show on independent grounds that the useful falsehoods considered thus far are *not* propositions justifiably believed and plausibly taken to be part of the protagonists' evidence.

3.1

The ability argument requires some set up. We often treat the subject's evidence and the subject's reasons for believing as basically interchangeable. If Alex has evidence to believe that the meeting hasn't started, he has a reason to believe that the meeting hasn't started. The reason isn't idle. It's important to the example that Alex believes that the meeting hasn't started *for* the relevant reason. This of course implies a number of things: that Alex has a certain reason, Alex exercised his capacity for identifying and responding to reasons in the course of forming the relevant belief, and that his believing what he does is a case of believing for a particular reason. The reason for which Alex is said to believe that the meeting has not started is that it is exactly 2:58. Note that the success of the argument against E=K and J=K turns on two things:

(a) Alex believes that the meeting has not started yet for the reason that it is exactly 2:58;
(b) This reason is not just the reason for which Alex believes that the meeting has started, it is a good reason to believe this, a piece of evidence that constitutes a justifying reason.

If one were to deny (a) or (b), one would have to reject one of the assumptions in the argument against E=K or J=K because one would have to deny that doxastic justification requires believing for a reason that's a good reason to so believe.

If Alex can reason from his belief that it is exactly 2:58 to the conclusion that the 7:00 meeting has not yet started, he has exercised a certain capacity to reason and has an ability to respond to things he believes by forming further beliefs. Does he manifest the ability to believe something for the reason that it is exactly 2:58? While one might think that he does if one thinks of reasons as propositions, representations, or propositional attitudes, this is surely not the way that a defender of E=K would think of it. They would say (or should say!) that to believe for the reason that it is exactly 2:58 one must have the overall ability to believe for *that* reason where that reason is a fact, not (just) a proposition, representation, or propositional attitude. Since we've stipulated that the relevant proposition is false, the proponent of E=K will say that Alex's belief about the meeting is not a case of believing something for the reason that it is exactly 2:58. While Alex surely has a general ability to form beliefs in light of things he believes, he surely cannot have the opportunity to respond to the fact that it is 2:58 because it is *not* 2:58.[9] Alex isn't magic. He cannot respond to facts that are not facts.

There is a data point that critics of E=K have ignored or overlooked, one that has to do with the relationship between knowledge and the abilities involved in responding to reasons. Upon seeing that his watch reads 2:58, let's suppose that Alex comes to believe that it is 2:58, is now happy because he believes that it is 2:58, and walks to the bus stop rather than hailing a cab. If asked, he might describe his attitudes and behaviour as follows:

(1) Why do I believe that the meeting will not start for a while? Well, for the reason that it is now 2:58. As you'll recall, the meeting doesn't start until 7:00.

(2) I am happy that it is 2:58. That means that the meeting will not start for hours.

(3) I shall take the bus for the reason that it is 2:58. There is no need to hail a cab. I have plenty of time to get to the office.

We can suppose that Alex is not self-deceived. He does not believe for reasons other than those he reports, does not act for reasons other than those he reports, or feel happy for reasons other than those he would mention. So, taking Alex at his word, we can restate these in the third-person:

(1′) Why does Alex believe that the meeting will not start for a while? Well, for the reason that it is now 2:58. As you'll recall, the meeting doesn't start until 7:00.

---

9 Kenny (1992) distinguishes general ability from overall ability on the grounds that the latter requires opportunity. A subject retains certain general abilities (e.g., the ability to reason) when she is mistaken about the facts, but we cannot say that she has the overall ability to act, believe, or affectively respond to a feature of the circumstance if she's wrong about the relevant features just like one cannot form friendships with ghosts or correctly report events that didn't take place.

(2′) Alex is happy that it is 2:58.

(3′) Alex took the bus for the reason that it is 2:58. There is no need for him to hail a cab because he has plenty of time to get to the office.

If Alex can believe for certain reasons and these beliefs, given how Alex is otherwise, is sufficient for producing a certain affective response or a bit of behaviour, he should be able to act and feel for the very same reasons he believes. If this is right, then the argument against E=K fails. Given the details of the case, it looks like claims about the reasons for which Alex believes that specify his reason as the false proposition that it is 2:58 will be true only if (2), (2′), (3), and (3′) are true. They are false.

It's easiest to see this with the case of emotion, I think. Is Alex happy that it is 2:58? He cannot be happy that it is 2:58 if it is 2:56. As Gordon (1987) and Unger (1975) have argued, Alex can only be happy that p, regret that p, be angry that p, etc. if Alex knows p. The same holds true for acting for the reason that p. Alex cannot act for the reason that p unless he knows p. The linguistic data on this seems to be rather solid. Consider:

(2′a) Although Alex does not know that it is 2:58, he is happy that it is 2:58.

(2′b) Alex is happy that it is 2:58. Not only that, he knows that it is 2:58.

It seems like (2′a) is false. That's some evidence that (2′) is true only if Alex knows that it is 2:58. As for (2′b), it seems like a redundant conjunction. That's some evidence that the information contained in the ascription of emotion contains all of the information contained in the knowledge ascription. Finally, Gordon (1987) reminds us that (2′) seems to be equivalent to the following:

(2′c) It is 2:58. That is why Alex is happy.

(2′d) Alex is happy because it is 2:58.

Clearly, these claims are true only if it is 2:58. If they are indeed equivalent to (2′) and (2), Alex cannot be happy that it is 2:58.

The same points hold true for the cases of acting and believing for reasons. When we try to say that someone acted or believed for the reason that p and then conjoin a knowledge denial, we get the same problematic results we get with (2′a). Of course, people realize this and quickly try to rewrite these claims so that the reasons for which the agent acts or believes will be a fact about the relevant individual's psychology rather than the situation. The case of emotion is helpful here because the psychologized redescription of the subject's reasons come out as clearly false in those cases. We would not say that Alex was happy that he believed it was 2:58. Alex isn't weird, just mistaken. Two points should be stressed here. First, *if* we did want to say that Alex's reason for believing or acting was *that he believed it was 2:58*, then we *would* have to rewrite (2') accordingly. Just as we know that the fact that Alex believes such and such is not what would make him happy, we know that it would not make him act or convince him that the meeting was not going to start for a while. Second, Alex would presumably *know* these facts about his own psychology if there were any plausibility to the idea that he acted or believed for the reason that he believed something. An argument from error against E=K requires that the evidence is some proposition that Alex believes that's false.[10]

The *ability argument* can be summed up as follows. The KFF cases are counterexamples to E=K only if they are cases of believing for a reason where the relevant reason is a falsehood. For these cases to be cases of believing for a reason that's a falsehood, one has to have the ability to believe for the relevant reason. If one had this ability and having the relevant belief was sufficient for producing an affective response or would result in the agent's acting or forming an intention to act, the agent could be happy or angry that the relevant fact obtained or act for the reason that the fact obtains. One doesn't have these abilities, however. The upshot is that 'S believes something for the reason that p' entails that S knows p. While the subject might have the *general* ability to form beliefs on the basis of her belief that p when she doesn't know p, she doesn't have the *overall* ability to believe anything (or feel anything or do anything) for the reason that p because that requires the truth of p and the opportunity to discover it.

3.2

Recall that the success of Klein's argument against E=K and J=K depends upon whether the protagonist in KFF cases believes something for a reason that's a falsehood, the relevant falsehood is part of the protagonist's evidence, and the relevant falsehood is evidence for the protagonist's relevant inferential beliefs

---

10 Does that mean that Alex does not believe or act for any reason when he acts or believes on a false belief? Alvarez (2010) and Littlejohn (2012) say that this is the right way to describe the case. Alvarez helpfully distinguishes psychological explanations of the agent's acts, attitudes, and emotions from reasons explanations. Hornsby (2007) offers a disjunctivist alternative.

(e.g., Virginia's belief that she'll receive presents or Alex's belief that the 7:00 meeting has not started). The ability argument was supposed to show that the protagonists in the KFF cases do not have the ability to believe something for a reason when that reason is a falsehood. The *generality argument*, which I shall discuss in this section, is an argument that's supposed to show that the protagonist's evidence does not include the useful falsehoods that the protagonists reason from in acquiring knowledge.

If we were to suppose, as the argument against E=K and J=K requires, that Alex and Virginia's mistaken beliefs were justified and that the propositions justifiably believed to be true were part of their evidence, it seems that we would have to deny a plausible closure principle for justification:

J-K-Closure (JKC): Necessarily, if (i) S knows that p entails q and (ii) S justifiably believes p, (iii) S can come to justifiably believe q on the basis of competently deducing it from p.

Why is that? It seems that there are a number of obvious consequences of Alex and Virginia's beliefs that they cannot justifiably believe. Consider the following inference:

It is exactly 2:58
If it is exactly 2:58, it is not 2:57: 58.
Thus, it is not 2:57: 58.

Whereas Alex knew that it was not 7:00, it seems rather intuitive that he does not know the conclusion of this inference. Moreover, I don't think he should reason from the premise that it is exactly 2:58 to the conclusion that it is not 2:57:58 in this case. While he's justified in believing that it is not 7:00, I don't think he is justified in believing that it is not two seconds prior to 2:58.

Consider the following inference:

Father Christmas will deliver presents.
If Tim says otherwise, he is either lying or doesn't know what he's talking about.
Thus, if Tim says that Father Christmas will not deliver presents, he is either lying or doesn't know what he's talking about.

I don't think that Virginia should reason in this way *precisely* because I'd object to her reasoning from the first premise to this conclusion.

If the relevant falsehoods really were pieces of evidence justifiably believed, they should serve as a proper basis for the known consequences of those propositions. Intuitively, however, this is not what we find. What seems rather intuitive is that these subjects should not rely on the relevant false premise in inferences like the ones just described. What this suggests is that the intuition that these subjects have knowledge in Meeting Time and Father Christmas is *not* due to the fact that these subjects have a useful premise for reasoning about the world (which they don't). As an alternative conjecture, the reason that we find the reasoning acceptable is *precisely* because we think of the reasoning as a possible source of knowledge.

Speaking just for myself, the reason that I find the intuitions that underwrite treating Meeting Time and Father Christmas as counterexamples to KCC is the thought that by reasoning from the false premise, the subject's are reasoning reasonably and to a conclusion they couldn't easily have been wrong about. One reason that I think the relevant falsehoods aren't genuine pieces of evidence is that they cannot justify drawing conclusions when the subject could have easily been wrong in drawing them. This is what one would expect if the knowledge were something in the neighbourhood of a belief with a safe basis and one subscribed to a kind of knowledge-first approach to these matters. Let the critics of knowledge-first try their hand at explaining why it should be that an alleged piece of evidence is properly included in reasoning to some known logical consequences rather than others and I expect that they will start to see the virtues of the knowledge-first approach.

The *generality argument* can be summed up as follows. The KFF cases considered are not plausible counterexamples to E=K. For these cases to be counterexamples to E=K, the falsehoods have to be part of the protagonists' evidence and generally available to them to serve as the proper basis of inference to the known logical consequences of these propositions. This, however, is not what we find. While it seems proper for Virginia and Alex to believe *some* of the known logical consequences of the relevant falsehoods, it would also be improper for them to believe some of the known consequences of the relevant falsehoods. That suggests that their evidence does *not* include the relevant falsehoods.

4.

In this section, I want to discuss the broader significance of KFF cases if, indeed, the knowledge-first theses I'm interested in (i.e., E=K, J=K, and KN) withstand scrutiny.

Let me begin by offering an argument for J=K, an argument that would show that KCC and JCC are equivalent. Suppose that one justifiably believed p where this was a case of non-inferential justification and then one infers q by means of competent deduction. Might one thereby come to justifiably believe q without knowing q? It would seem that if one subsequently forgot p, one could still justifiably believe q. One couldn't then, however, believe anything for the reason that p. JKC says that if, in this state, one knew that r followed from q, one could justifiably infer r. It seems that one can justifiably infer r only if there's some fact that one has in mind that's the reason for which one believes r. It looks like q is the natural candidate. It looks like q would have to be known.[11]

If we accept J=K, it looks like we should describe our KFF cases as follows:

(a) The protagonist should not believe the premises that she reasons from in the course of learning that p.
(b) The protagonist's belief in the conclusion, p, is justified.

It looks like there's a promising argument for J=K from E=K. Assuming that one can justifiably believe only if one's belief (i.e., what's believed) is itself a reason that can support further beliefs, one's belief about p is justified only if what's believed is known to be true.

If (a) and (b) are both correct, the lesson to take from KFF cases is not that there is something wrong with the knowledge-first approach. The knowledge-first approach can explain why it is sometimes acceptable to conclude that something is so on the basis of a false belief and when it would be wrong to do so. It would be wrong to do so if the inferential belief is not safe. The intuition that it is acceptable to hold the belief based on the inference from a falsehood is probably due to the realization that the inferential belief could not easily be mistaken.

Now, some people might have the following intuition. Virginia, let's say, shouldn't believe that she'll have presents for no reason at all. Moreover, her only available 'reason' seems to be a falsehood. If KFF cases are indeed counterexamples to JCC, how can we vindicate these intuitions? If, in keeping with KN, she abandons her belief that Santa will bring presents, shouldn't she also abandon her belief that she will receive presents? If she should abandon that belief, then either she doesn't know that she'll receive presents or her belief that she will receive presents is not justified in spite of the fact that it constitutes knowledge?

If, in keeping with KN, we identify permissible belief with knowledge and impermissible belief with belief that doesn't constitute knowledge, we can vindi-

---

[11] The crucial step here is the idea that evidence can be acquired via inductive inference. For discussion, see Bird (2004).

cate these intuitions. It is true that she should not form the inferential belief that she'll receive presents without believing that Santa will bring them. If she didn't do that, she wouldn't have come to know that she'd get presents. KN says that you shouldn't infer that something is so unless you'd therein come to know that it's so. (It's *not* true that Virginia shouldn't believe she'll receive presents unless she believes that Santa will bring them. If she knows that she'll receive presents and then forgets why she believes this, she can retain knowledge and the right to believe this.) KN vindicates the intuition that if she hadn't believed Santa would bring presents, she shouldn't believe she'd receive presents.

If KFF cases are indeed counterexamples to KCC, they would seem to show that a certain evidentialist view must be mistaken. The core commitment of Conee and Feldman's (2004) evidentialist approach to justification is that justified beliefs get that status by virtue of being supported by the subject's evidence. If the evidentialist view is combined with a factualist treatment of evidence, a view on which all evidence consists of facts or true propositions, it's easy to see that this version of the evidentialist view is in serious trouble:

FE: Every justified belief is justified because it is supported by some piece of evidence the subject has that consists of a true proposition that is distinct from the proposition believed and part of the subject's evidence.[12]

If we dispense with JCC along with KCC, there will be cases where a subject's belief gets to be justified in spite of the fact that the subject doesn't hold that belief on the basis of further facts that support that belief. Since FE insists that the only way that a justified belief gets to be justified is by virtue of being supported by a body of evidence that consists of facts, FE must be mistaken if there are indeed counterexamples to JCC.

Of course, the evidentialists like Conee and Feldman might not be bothered by this result because they don't subscribe to FE. They don't (currently) think that a subject's evidence consists of facts or true propositions (Conee and Feldman 2011: 321–4). If the evidentialists are forced to abandon FE, it seems that they must either embrace a view that allows for 'false evidence' or a view that identifies a subject's evidence with something that isn't a proposition.[13]

---

12 Cases of non-inferential justification seem to constitute a problem for this view. Even if FE is restricted to cases of inferential justification, the view seems to be problematic because there can be cases in which a false non-inferential belief is the sole basis for an inferential belief that appears to constitute knowledge.
13 For defenses of 'false evidence' (i.e., evidence that consists of falsehoods), see Arnold (2013), Fantl and McGrath (2009), and Rizzieri (2011). For arguments that all propositional evi-

There are two problems with these evidentialist views. The first problem is the obvious problem. There are powerful arguments in the literature for thinking that some evidence, at least, consists of propositions and for thinking that all such evidence must be true. These arguments suggest that evidentialists ought to embrace FE rather than try to fend off objections by embracing an objectionable treatment of what our evidence consists in. The second is less obvious. Evidentialists often present their views as if they are intuitive or as if they provide the obviously correct treatment of a case. Once we see that the evidentialist position is untenable if it is combined with an independently plausible account of what evidence consists in, we should see that the core evidentialist commitment isn't really the truism its defenders often present it as being.

If we reject the evidentialist view, we have to reject the idea that justified beliefs get to be justified by virtue of the support they receive from the subject's evidence. Sometimes that's why they're justified, but there's no essential connection between the status of being justified and the property of being supported by evidence. I'm not the first to question this picture. Externalists have long argued that it's a mistake to try to think of all justification as being grounded in relations between reasons and beliefs. Here we see that there is an independent reason to take the externalist worries seriously.[14]

By denying JCC, I'm denying the following conditional: If one shouldn't believe the premises, one shouldn't believe the conclusion. The lesson is an anti-evidentialist lesson that's in keeping with knowledge-first epistemology. Pedigree matters only to the extent that it matters to acquiring knowledge. When evidence is needed for acquiring knowledge, only knowledge will fulfil one's needs. Sometimes one can come to have a safe belief by reasoning through falsehoods and thereby acquire knowledge. This just shows that there are normatively significant relations that don't obtain by virtue of relations between beliefs and prior evidence.

The assumption that pedigree must matter to justification figures prominently in the literature on foundationalism. In discussions of the regress argument for foundationalism, for example, it's not uncommon to see the argument formulated in such a way that all justified beliefs either are non-inferentially justified or derive their justification from another justified belief. Fumerton appeals to his principle of inferential justification, for example, to generate a regress argument for foundationalism and his principle clearly requires that any justified inferen-

---

dence must consist of truths, see Leite (2013), Littlejohn (2011), and Unger (1975). For arguments that evidence is indeed propositional, see Dougherty (2011) and Williamson (2000).
14 See Greco (2004), for example.

tial belief must derive from some further justified belief that supports it (1995: 36). If JCC is false, these options are not exhaustive. Some beliefs might be justified by virtue of support they receive from further beliefs that are not themselves justified. Thus, it looks like a common version of the regress argument for foundationalism is unsound.

Of course, the foundationalist might well admit that the argument is unsound and embrace the possibility that there are counterexamples to JCC. If anything, the counterexamples to JCC might alleviate some of the pressures that the foundationalists have to contend with. It is exceptionally difficult, for example, to say what it is about properly basic beliefs by virtue of which these beliefs to stop regresses. If there are counterexamples to JCC, the power to stop a regress has to be distinguished from the possibility of being justified on the basis of something that isn't a belief. Thus, the critics of foundationalism cannot argue that an infinite chain of reasons or some web of mutually supporting belief is necessary for justification simply by arguing against the possibility of non-inferentially justified belief. For even if there is no non-inferentially justified belief in some chain of belief, the fact that JCC is false means that it might be possible for there to be beliefs 'upstream' based on an unjustified belief that are nevertheless justified. There are interesting issues to be explored here if, indeed, JCC is false and the standard platitudes about pedigree prove to be mistaken.

Conclusion

The thought that KFF cases provide us with new reasons to reject knowledge-first approaches to evidence, justification, or the norm of belief assume that like-from-like reasoning fails when it's reasoning about knowledge but succeeds when it's reasoning about justification. This faith in like-from-like reasoning is unwarranted. Knowledge does beget knowledge, but it need not be begotten by knowledge. This is true for justification, too.

References

Alvarez, M. (2010). *Kinds of Reasons*. Oxford University Press.
Arnold, A. (2013). Some Evidence is False. *Australasian Journal of Philosophy* 91: 165–72.
Bird, A. (2004). Is Evidence Non-Inferential? *Philosophical Quarterly* 54: 252–65.
Coffman, E. J. (2008). Warrant without Truth? *Synthese* 162: 173–94.
Coffman, E. J. (2010). Is Justified Belief Knowledge? *Philosophical Books* 51: 1–21.
Comesaña, J. and H. Kantin (2010). Is Evidence Knowledge? *Philosophy and Phenomenological Research* 80: 447–454.

Conee, E. and R. Feldman (2004). *Evidentialism*. Oxford University Press.
Conee, E. and R. Feldman (2011). Replies. In T. Dougherty (ed.), *Evidentialism and its Discontents*. Oxford University Press, pp. 283–324.
Dougherty, T. (2011). In Defense of Propositionalism about Evidence. In T. Dougherty (ed.), *Evidentialism and its Discontents*. Oxford University Press, pp. 226–33.
Fantl, J. and M. McGrath (2009). *Knowledge in an Uncertain World*. Oxford University Press.
Fitelson, B. (2010). Strengthening the Case for Knowledge from Falsehood. *Analysis* 70: 666–69.
Fumerton, R. (1995). *Metaepistemology and Skepticism*. Rowman and Littlefield.
Gordon, R. (1987). *The Structure of Emotions*. Cambridge University Press.
Greco, J. (2004). *Putting Skeptics in their Place*. Cambridge University Press.
Hilpinen, R. (1988). Knowledge and Conditionals. *Philosophical Perspectives* 2: 157–82.
Hornsby, J. (2007). A Disjunctive Conception of Acting for Reasons. In A. Haddock and F. MacPherson (ed.), *Disjunctivism: Perception, Action, and Knowledge*. Oxford University Press.
Hyman, J. (2006). Knowledge and Evidence. *Mind* 115: 891–916.
Hyman, J. (2011). Acting for Reasons: Reply to Dancy. *Frontiers of Philosophy in China* 6: 358–68.
Kelp, C. (2011). Not Without Justification. *Dialectica* 65: 581–95.
Kenny, A. (1992). *The Metaphysics of Mind*. Oxford University Press.
Klein, P. (2004). Useful Falsehoods. In Q. Smith (ed.), *New Essays in Epistemology*. Oxford University Press.
Leite, A. (2013). But That's not Evidence; It's not Even True! *Philosophical Quarterly* 63: 81–104.
Littlejohn, C. (2011). Knowledge and Evidence. *Erkenntnis* 74: 241–62.
Littlejohn, C. (2012). *Justification and the Truth-Connection*. Cambridge University Press.
Littlejohn, C. (2013a). No Evidence is False. *Acta Analytica* 28: 145–59.
Littlejohn, C. (2013b). The Russellian Retreat. *Proceedings of the Aristotelian Society* 113: 293–320.
Luzzi, F. (2010). Counter-Closure. *Australasian Journal of Philosophy* 88: 673–83.
McCain, K. (2014). *Evidentialism and Epistemic Justification*. Routledge.
Mantel, S. (Forth.). Acting for Reasons, Apt Action, and Knowledge. *Synthese*.
Marcus, E. 2012. *Rational Causation*. Harvard University Press.
Mitova, V. (2015). Truthy Psychologism about Evidence. *Philosophical Studies* 172: 1105–1126.
Murphy, P. (forthcoming). Justified Belief from Unjustified Belief. Pacific Philosophical Quarterly.
Rizzieri, A. (2011). Evidence Does not Equal Knowledge. *Philosophical Studies* 153: 235–242.
Schnee, I. (2015). There is no Knowledge from Falsehood. *Episteme* 12: 53–74.
Shaffer, M. (2013). E Does not Equal K. *The Reasoner* 7: 30–31.
Shaffer, M. (Forth.). Approximate Truth, Quasi-Factivity, and Evidence. *Acta Analytica*.
Sutton, J. (2007). *Without Justification*. MIT Press.
Unger, P. (1975). *Ignorance*. Oxford University Press.
Warfield, T. (2005). Knowledge from Falsehood. *Philosophical Perspectives* 19: 405–16.
Williamson, T. (2000). *Knowledge and its Limits*. Oxford University Press.
Williamson, T. (2013). Gettier Cases in Epistemic Logic. *Inquiry* 56: 1–14.

Terence Cuneo
Destabilizing the Error Theory

Philosophers sometimes defend unusual combinations of positions. Bertrand Russell, for example, appears to have defended both phenomenalism regarding perception and Platonism regarding abstract objects, holding that we have knowledge of only sense-data and universals.[1] More recently, Peter van Inwagen has defended the view that there are no material objects such as toasters and planets but that sentences such as "Saturn has several moons" are literally true (and not in some deflationary sense).[2] Combinations such as these can be not only unusual but also problematic when commitment to one member of a combination destabilizes one's commitment to the other. By saying that commitment to one member of a combination "destabilizes" commitment to the other, I mean that accepting one member provides reasons not to accept the other or renders that member of the combination theoretically irrelevant. I would say, for example, that van Inwagen's commitment to there being no planets destabilizes his commitment to the claim that sentences such as that mentioned above are literally true.

Jonas Olson's recent book *Error Theory: History, Critique, Defense* is a defense of the moral error theory.[3] In the course of responding to an objection to his view, Olson also accepts an unusual combination of views, namely, the moral error theory, which implies that there are no moral facts, and a version of epistemic reductionism, which implies the existence of something very close to epistemic facts – so close that many other philosophers hold that they just *are* epistemic facts.

My project in this essay is to contend that a commitment to epistemic reductionism of this sort destabilizes a commitment to the moral error theory, providing reasons not to accept it or rendering the position philosophically irrelevant. To formulate this argument, however, I need to first offer and defend an interpretation of Olson's view. Having done that, I turn to the task of explaining why a commitment to epistemic reductionism destabilizes a commitment to the moral error theory.

---

1 Russell (1912) and (1914).
2 van Inwagen (1990) and (2014), Introduction.
3 Olson (2014). I will insert page references to this book parenthetically in the body of this essay.

1. Error Theories: Moral and Epistemic

Call sentences that incorporate moral terms such as "wrong," "required," and "just" in the predicate position *moral sentences*. Call the use of these sentences in our day-to-day lives *ordinary moral discourse* and the mental states that these sentences express *moral thoughts*. Moral realists and moral error theorists agree that ordinary moral thought and discourse represent moral facts, such as the fact *that it is wrong to physically abuse others*.[4] While realists believe that some of these thoughts accurately represent the moral facts, error theorists deny this, holding that:

Ordinary moral thought and discourse, by and large, represent moral facts. But they fail to do so accurately, since there are no such facts. In this respect, ordinary moral thought and discourse are deeply and systemically mistaken.

In *The Normative Web*, I suggested that we could model a view in metaepistemology on the moral error theory by engaging in a series of moves parallel to those made above. Start by calling sentences that incorporate terms such as "justified," "rational," and "warranted" in the predicate position *epistemic sentences*. Call the use of these sentences in our day-to-day lives *ordinary epistemic discourse* and the mental states that these sentences express *epistemic thoughts*. Epistemic realists and epistemic error theorists agree that ordinary epistemic thoughts represent epistemic facts, such as the fact *that beliefs formed on the basis of mere wishful thinking are unjustified*. While epistemic realists believe that some of these epistemic thoughts accurately represent the epistemic facts, epistemic error theorists do not, claiming that:

Ordinary epistemic thought and discourse, by and large, represent epistemic facts. But they fail to do so accurately, since there are no such facts. In this respect, ordinary epistemic thought and discourse are deeply and systemically mistaken

There are some metanormative views – such as versions of moral naturalism and constructivism – that affirm the existence of moral and epistemic facts but understand their nature differently from realists. Error theorists are unwilling to set-

---

[4] In this essay, I'll mean by moral realism so-called robust realism of the sort defended by Fitz-Patrick (2008) and Enoch (2011). When I use the term "represent," I will not use it as a success term; to say that x represents y does not imply that x accurately represents y.

tle for such views, maintaining that if there were moral or epistemic facts, then they would be exactly as realists describe them. Moreover, there are other metanormative views – such as versions of expressivism and fictionalism – that accept the error theorists' ontology but are unwilling to conclude that ordinary moral and epistemic thought and discourse are massively in error.[5] Proponents of these views defend them by denying that moral and epistemic thought and discourse represent moral and epistemic reality. Error theorists also reject these views; they do not flinch at drawing the conclusion that moral and epistemic thought and discourse are deeply mistaken. In both these respects, the error theory is resolutely uncompromising.

What, though, is the understanding of moral and epistemic facts that realists and error theorists both accept? In *The Normative Web*, I suggested that this understanding is captured by our *commonsensical conceptions* of these facts. Our commonsensical conceptions of moral and epistemic facts, in turn, are constituted by platitudes of two sorts – what I called the *substance* and *authority* platitudes.[6]

Roughly put, the substance platitudes with regard to the moral domain tell us that any standard (i.e., non-deviant) moral system would have to incorporate substantive propositions such as:

It is wrong to recreationally slaughter fellow persons.
And:
It is wrong to physically abuse another merely for pleasure.

The account adds that actions such as these are wrong (at least in part) because they are aimed at undercutting or destroying the victim's ability to enjoy goods that constitute human wellbeing, such as enjoying adequate health and bonds of trust.

The epistemic domain is similar. According to the substance platitudes with regard to the epistemic domain, a standard epistemic system would have to incorporate propositions such as:

It is irrational to believe a proposition simply on the basis of wish-fulfillment.

---

[5] Blackburn (1993) and (1998) develop expressivist views and Kalderon (2008) defends fictionalist ones.
[6] Cuneo (2007), chs. 1 and 2. The account I offer here expands a bit on what I say in that discussion, drawing on Cuneo and Shafer-Landau (2014).

And:

It is justified to believe a proposition on the basis of one's best evidence.

Propositional attitudes have epistemic merits such as *being justified*, the account adds, in virtue of their being such as to represent reality aright, being likely to represent reality aright, or being such that an agent has done what she ought to in attempting to represent reality aright.[7]

The *authority platitudes* with regard to the moral and epistemic domains concern the normative force or authority of the facts (if there are any) that correspond to propositions such as those stated above. According to these platitudes, moral and epistemic facts are or imply excellent reasons for us to behave in certain ways, regardless of our desires, goals, or the social roles we may occupy. In terminology that has become popular, these facts are or imply "robust reasons." (I shall have more to say about the character of these reasons in a moment.)

Some philosophers reject our commonsensical conception of moral and epistemic facts. For example, in epistemology, those I term reductionists often reject the authority platitudes, holding that there are epistemic facts but denying that they are or imply robust reasons. Some reductionists, for example, claim that epistemic facts generate only hypothetical reasons, which are determined by the (contingent) desires or goals an agent has.[8] Under one version of this view, one has a reason to believe a proposition only if one cares about believing the truth (with respect to propositions of its kind). Other reductionists, in contrast, deny that epistemic facts are or generate any reasons whatsoever – at least when reasons are understood to consist in irreducible favoring relations that facts bear to agents such as us (or facts that stand in such relations). According to these philosophers, while it is possible to legitimately say that we have reasons to believe propositions, doing so would be only to claim that there are norms that direct one to believe propositions because these propositions are true or appear to be true.

Thus understood, advocates of reductionism take an approach toward the moral and epistemic domains that is both more liberal and conservative than error theory. The reductionist approach is more liberal because it does not insist that moral and epistemic facts must satisfy the two dimensions of our common-

---

[7] In my (2007), 79, I explore explanatory relations that might hold between both sets of platitudes.

[8] Or would have under more idealized conditions. In what follows, I'll understand the qualification to be understood.

sensical conception of moral and epistemic facts. Instead, reductionism maintains that moral and epistemic facts (as it understands them) are "imperfect but good enough" satisfiers of our commonsensical conception of the moral and epistemic domains.[9] The reductionist approach is more conservative because, unlike error theory, reductionism holds (with realism) that moral and epistemic thought and discourse are not radically and systemically mistaken, since our thoughts sometimes accurately represent moral and epistemic facts (as reductionists understand them). In this respect, reductionism preserves the appearance that in the moral and epistemic domains we sometimes get it right. (By saying that a theory "preserves the appearances," I mean simply that it is likely that things are as they appear if the theory were true.)

Later in our discussion, I will be returning to this last point because it proves important. Before I do, I need to emphasize that the authority platitudes play a pivotal role in the way that error theorists think of moral and epistemic facts. For error theorists hold not simply that the authority platitudes are deeply embedded in (non-defective) ordinary thinking about moral and epistemic reality. As Olson points out, error theorists also accept the stronger:

Conceptual Claim: It is conceptually necessary that, if there are moral or epistemic facts, then there are robust (or categorical) reasons.[10]

It is because they deny that there could be robust (or categorical) reasons that error theorists deny that there are moral facts. In fact, when Richard Joyce and Olson defend the error theory, they do so only on the basis of this rejection.[11]

So far I have claimed that it is possible to model the epistemic error theory on the moral error theory, pointing out that advocates of these views reject the existence of moral and epistemic facts because they hold that nothing satisfies the authority platitudes. It is now widely accepted, however, that if one ought to accept the moral error theory, then one ought also to accept the epistemic error theory.[12] Let me call this widely accepted claim the *parity principle*. In

---

9 I borrow the phrase in quotes from Lewis (1995).
10 See Olson (2014), 124–25.
11 See Joyce (2001). Joyce offers an additional line of argument in his (2006).
12 See the references in Olson (2014), ch. 8. The more nuanced way to state the point made above would be as follows: it is widely accepted that, if one ought to accept the moral error theory for the reasons adduced by its primary defenders in the Anglo-American tradition (as opposed to, say, the Nietzschean tradition), then one ought also to accept the epistemic error theory. The version of the error theory I have in mind is of the variety one finds in the Anglo-American tradition.

his discussion, Olson accepts the parity principle, agreeing that if one ought to accept the moral error theory, then one should also accept the epistemic error theory (156). Yet Olson also contends that accepting the epistemic error theory is compatible with accepting a version of epistemic reductionism. In the next section, I want to explore why Olson says this and how we should understand his view.

2. Epistemic Reductionism

There is a perfectly respectable sense in which the game of hockey is normative. For like most games, hockey is governed by rules or norms for how to play it. The rules or standards that govern the game of hockey tell us, for example, that a standard game is divided into three periods, at most only six players on each team can play at once, a player is not allowed to enter the opponents' zone before the puck does, the puck is considered "dead" during play if it leaves the perimeter of the rink, and so on. Along with these standards are rights, responsibilities, and obligations that attach to participants in the game, namely, players, coaches, and officials. Players, for example, have a right to take a shot on goal but they do not have the right to determine whether a shot counts as a goal (officials do); officials have the right to determine whether a player is off-side but coaches do not; officials have the responsibility of tracking how many penalties a player might have but players do not, and so on. These rights, responsibilities, and obligations are enforced in various ways. If a player, for example, fails to comply with them, he or she may be penalized, assessed a fee, or suspended. If this is right, the standards that govern the game of hockey play at least two roles: they determine not only whether someone is playing the game correctly or incorrectly but also whether an activity counts as hockey at all. For were some activity that had the trappings of hockey – a game played on a rink with sticks, a puck, and so forth – not to sufficiently conform to the standards of the game, this activity would not count as a game of hockey.

Although the game of hockey is normative, it is common for philosophers to characterize the game's normativity as being thin. Stating why the normativity in question is thin is not easy but the explanation typically goes something like this. Let's say that a system of putative rights, responsibilities, and obligations is *normative in the lean sense* just in case it does not necessarily imply reasons such that an agent ought, on the whole, to conform to the rights, responsibilities, and obligations that constitute that system. The rights, responsibilities, and obligations that constitute the game of hockey seem to satisfy this description. We do not hold that the responsibilities that attach to participants in the National

Hockey League (qua participants) necessarily provide reasons on the whole for them to act in certain ways. In fact, we can think of cases – such as when a hockey player no longer cares about playing the game because he has better things to do – in which these responsibilities provide no reason to act at all. By contrast, a system of putative rights, responsibilities, and obligations is *normative in the robust sense* just in case it necessarily implies (possibly defeasible) reasons such that an agent ought, on the whole, to conform to the rights, responsibilities, and obligations that constitute that system. These reasons are, to use Olson's terminology, *irreducibly normative* (116–17). Although there are no uncontroversial examples of systems that are robustly normative, many philosophers hold that the moral domain is the most vivid example we have of a system that is normative in the robust sense.

Lean normativity attaches to activities that are goal-directed or involve agents occupying roles of various kinds.[13] Everything from hockey and Gregorian chant to etiquette are systems that are normative in the lean sense. It is worth stressing that while all the examples I've offered of systems that are normative in the lean sense are conventional, there might be systems that are normative in the lean sense but are not conventional. Some have suggested that the rights, responsibilities, and obligations of rationality, for example, constitute such a system. According to these philosophers, there are rights, responsibilities, and obligations that attach to those who can regulate their beliefs and actions in various ways. Still, these philosophers suggest, we may not have reason to be rational.[14] However that may be, we can now connect the distinction between lean and robust normativity with our discussion in the last section regarding the authority platitudes. What the authority platitude tells us, in effect, is that the moral and epistemic systems are normative in the robust sense; at least some of the reasons that these systems generate are robust. Those who reject the authority platitudes with regard to the moral domain – holding that moral facts exist but are not characterized by this platitude – believe that morality is normative but only in the lean sense.

I am emphasizing the distinction between lean and robust normativity because it is central to not only Olson's understanding of the moral and epistemic domains, but also his response to an objection I have elsewhere posed to the epistemic error theory.[15] According to what I'll call the *central dilemma*, epistemic error theory is either (i) self-defeating insofar as it presupposes the very

---

13 See Olson (2014), 159.
14 See Kolodny (2005) and Broome (2007) and, for a response, Way (2009).
15 Cuneo (2007), ch. 4 presents the dilemma in a slightly different form.

sorts of entities it says do not exist or (ii) implies wholesale epistemological skepticism, according to which we have no epistemic reason to believe anything, including the error theory itself. An implication of this second horn is that epistemic error theory would be polemically toothless if true, as no one could make a rational mistake in rejecting the position. Since neither of these options is palatable – or so the challenge runs – we have powerful reason to reject the epistemic error theory. Given the parity principle that, if one ought to accept the moral error theory, then one also ought to reject the epistemic error theory, it follows that one ought not to accept the moral error theory.

Olson contends that the error theory can escape the central dilemma. In response to the dilemma's first horn, Olson points out that epistemic error theorists needn't presuppose the very entities that they reject, namely, epistemic facts that are or imply robust reasons. In response to the dilemma's second horn, Olson maintains that rejecting the existence of epistemic facts needn't imply wholesale epistemic skepticism according to which we could not have reason to believe anything.

The key to avoiding the second horn of the dilemma, Olson suggests, is to make two moves. The first is to point out that the term "reason" as it is used in the epistemic domain is multiply ambiguous. Understood in one way, the term is supposed to designate an irreducibly favoring relation (or a fact that stands in such a relation). Understood in another way, it purports only to designate the evidence relation (or a fact that stands in such a relation). Olson does not say much about how he understands the evidence relation, simply pointing out that for something to be evidence for a proposition is for that thing to indicate that that proposition is true or likely to be true (162). The details regarding what the evidence relation consists in, however, are secondary to Olson's project. What matters is that the central dilemma has bite only if we understand "reason" in the robust sense. Epistemic error theorists, however, can plausibly maintain that while reasons do not exist in the first sense, they exist in the second sense. Epistemic error theorists can claim this, Olson says, because there is nothing "queer" about reasons so understood.

The second move Olson makes is to note that the practice of forming and assessing beliefs is a goal-oriented and role-involving activity. Because it is, this practice is governed by norms that are normative in the lean sense. Speaking of responsible believing, Olson writes:

> The error theorist can maintain that she uses 'responsible' (and 'irresponsible') in a purely descriptive fashion that indicates that the agent meets (or fails to meet) the standard for being a responsible believer, where the standard for being a responsible believer can be cashed out in purely descriptive terms.... According to this purely descriptive use of the

term 'responsibility', the norms associated with epistemic responsibility are comparable to those of etiquette and chess.[16]

Olson continues:

> Error theory, then does not rule out the possibility of standards of epistemic merit and demerit. It says that in order for claims about epistemic merit and demerit to be true, they must be understood as purely descriptive claims. (165)

To advert to the terminology that I've introduced, error theorists can say that there are normative facts such as the fact *that a belief is justified* just so long as we understand justification as being normative in only the lean sense.

At this point, however, Olson exegesis becomes a little tricky. On the one hand, Olson explicitly says that he will assume that epistemic facts would imply the existence of robust reasons and, hence, would be robustly normative (see p. 156). Since the error theory implies that there are no such reasons, it implies that there are no epistemic facts, including facts that consist in some belief's having an epistemic merit such as *being justified* or *being entitled* (i.e., responsibly formed). On the other hand, in the passage just quoted, Olson states that, according to the error theory, claims regarding epistemic merits and demerits can be true, provided they concern these merits and demerits understood in a lean sense. On the face of things, then, Olson seems to grant both that:

Epistemic facts must be robustly normative and there are no such facts.
And also:
There are epistemic facts but they are not robustly normative.

Olson seems to want to embrace both the epistemic error theory and a version of epistemic reductionism, which would render his view incoherent.

Before I attempt to relieve this apparent tension in Olson's view, let me canvass two attempts to relieve it that seem to me unhelpful. The first would be to embrace the second option stated above, advocating epistemic reductionism. This option would require Olson to surrender the epistemic error theory. It would also have unattractive ramifications. For consider the parity principle, which states:

---

16 At various points, Olson says that entities that are normative in the lean sense are "descriptive." I find this terminology infelicitous since "descriptive" is often used interchangeably with "natural." Entities that are normative in the lean sense, however, needn't be natural or reducible to the natural.

if one ought to accept the moral error theory, then one ought also to accept the epistemic error theory.

Now suppose one ought to reject the epistemic error theory because epistemic reductionism is true. It would follow that:

it is false that one ought to accept the moral error theory,

which is an implication that Olson would not accept (at least when the ought in play is of the non-robust variety).

A second unsatisfactory option would be for Olson to propose that, when he uses epistemic terms such as "justified" and "rational," they designate facts but not epistemic facts as either realists or reductionists think of them (or anything close to how realists or reductionists think of them). According to this view, epistemic terms would characterize facts that do not satisfy even the substance platitudes with regard to the epistemic domain (or anything like them).

The problem with this proposal is that it would not address the central dilemma posed to the error theory. The dilemma's second horn, recall, charges epistemic error theorists with being committed to radical epistemological skepticism according to which there is no reason to believe anything and that no beliefs could be justified or rational. Responding to this dilemma by pointing out that we can use *terms* such as "reason," "justified" or "rational" to designate facts that have little to do with the epistemic domain as we ordinarily understand it would fail to address the objection. (Berkeley silenced none of his critics by proposing that we could use terms such as "chair" and "lake" to designate objects that are radically different from chairs and lakes as we ordinarily think of them.) If so, a satisfactory response to the dilemma's second horn requires that under what Olson calls their "purely descriptive use," these epistemic terms designate entities that at least come close enough to satisfying our commonsensical conceptions of the moral and epistemic domains. This guarantees that in responding to the central dilemma error theorists would not switch the subject.

Having considered two options that I believe Olson should reject, let me present an option that I think he should accept.[17] This option requires us to distinguish two types of reductionist views regarding the epistemic domain. The first reductionist view I shall call:

---

17 Olson has indicated to me in correspondence that this is the position that he intends to defend.

Weakly revisionist: epistemic facts exist but do not satisfy the authority platitudes. These facts are good enough but imperfect satisfiers of our commonsensical conception of epistemic facts.

This position is a variant of what (to this point) I've simply called *reductionism*. The second reductionist view, I'll term:

Strongly revisionist: nothing answers to our concept of an epistemic fact (since some such facts would have to satisfy the authority platitudes regarding the epistemic domain). But there are concepts that are closely related to ordinary epistemic concepts. Although the facts that these "successor" concepts characterize are not epistemic facts, these facts satisfy more or less exact analogues to the substance platitudes with respect to epistemic facts.

Let us, for ease of expression, refer to epistemic successor concepts and the properties and facts for which they stand by the use of expressions in small caps, such as RATIONAL, JUSTIFIED, and REASON. The proposal I wish to advance is that Olson accept strongly revisionist reductionism with regard to the epistemic domain.

The benefits of doing so are multiple. One benefit is that it would allow Olson to be an epistemic error theorist, since this position is compatible with all of our epistemic beliefs being untrue. Another benefit is that accepting this view would provide the materials for responding to the central dilemma. The response would be to concede that, strictly speaking, epistemic error theory implies wholesale epistemic skepticism; there is no epistemic reason to believe anything. But there are concepts – the epistemic successor concepts – that error theorists and others could employ to guide the formation, revision, and evaluation of our propositional attitudes. These concepts could play nearly all the same practical roles as epistemic concepts for all practical purposes: they are practically employable. In principle, we could substitute them for ordinary epistemic concepts.

The reason we could substitute them for ordinary epistemic concepts is that the application conditions for these successor concepts mirror those of epistemic concepts. As I am thinking of them, the application conditions for epistemic concepts are given by claims such as these:

Necessarily, if a belief falls under the concept <u>being based on one's best evidence</u>, then it falls under the concept <u>justified</u>.
Necessarily, if a belief falls under the concept <u>being formed on the basis of</u>

wish-fulfilment, then it falls under the concept <u>unjustified</u>.
And so on.

If the application conditions of a concept tell us what it is to be that concept, then these conditionals (which correspond to the substance platitudes for the epistemic domain) give us insight into the essence of epistemic concepts.

We can formulate application conditions for EPISTEMIC concepts that mirror those given above, such as:

> Necessarily, if a belief falls under the concept <u>being based on one's best evidence</u>, then it falls under the concept JUSTIFIED.
> Necessarily, if a belief falls under the concept <u>being formed on the basis of wish-fulfilment</u>, then it also falls under the concept UNJUSTIFIED.
> And so on.

Once again, if the application conditions of a concept tell us what it is to be that concept, then these conditionals (which more or less exactly mirror the substance platitudes with regard to the epistemic domain) give us insight into the essence of these EPISTEMIC concepts.

My suggestion, then, is that the best way to reconcile Olson's commitment to the epistemic error theory with his claim that epistemic terms admit of a purely descriptive use is to interpret him as embracing Strongly revisionist epistemic reductionism. Doing so would enable Olson to reply to the central dilemma in the following way. Olson could concede that while nothing satisfies the concepts <u>rational</u> or <u>justified</u>, our beliefs often satisfy concepts such as RATIONAL and JUSTIFIED. When they do, they have properties such as BEING RATIONAL and BEING JUSTIFIED. Because they do, the epistemic error theory is not polemically toothless, for there are REASONS to believe the view that error theorists can offer to others and that others can accept. Others could accept and employ these reasons because they satisfy exact analogues to the substance platitudes for epistemic concepts. Moreover, when offering these reasons, epistemic error theorists would not be vulnerable to the charge that in responding to the central dilemma they had switched the subject, giving us EPISTEMIC stones for epistemic bread.

We can summarize the difference between Weakly and Strongly revisionist views by identifying the ways in which their proponents would answer two questions.

(A) Do the two views share the same ontological commitments?

Yes, by all appearances, they share the same ontological commitments, at least with regard to those properties and facts characterized by our epistemic or EPISTEMIC concepts. For both views maintain that there are facts that satisfy the substance platitudes with regard to the epistemic domain, or platitudes that exactly mirror the substance platitudes with respect to the epistemic domain. Moreover, both views agree that there are no facts that satisfy the authority platitudes.

(B) Does each view imply that ordinary epistemic thought and discourse is massively and systemically mistaken?

They do not.

Weak revisionists maintain that ordinary epistemic thought and discourse is not massively and systemically mistaken. For in their view there are epistemic facts that answer to our epistemic concepts.

Strong revisionists hold that ordinary epistemic thought and discourse is massively and systemically mistaken. For in their view there are no epistemic facts that answer to our epistemic concepts. Still, there are EPISTEMIC concepts and EPISTEMIC properties and facts that answer to EPISTEMIC concepts. Error theorists can appeal to these concepts, properties, and facts when replying to objections, such as the central dilemma.[18]

One could think of the primary difference between these views like this: Weak revisionists hold that there are (perhaps imperfect but good enough) *satisfiers* of ordinary epistemic concepts. These are epistemic properties and facts, reductively understood. Strong revisionists maintain that there are (perhaps imperfect but good enough) *substitutes* for our epistemic concepts. These successor concepts characterize the very same facts that weak revisionists claim satisfy ordinary epistemic concepts.

---

18 I am assuming that, since concepts are fine-grained entities, epistemic and EPISTEMIC concepts are different, since they have non-equivalent conditions for their competent application. Someone with reasonable mastery of the concept (epistemically) justified, for example, could rightly claim that it fails to apply to facts that are normative in only in the lean sense. In contrast, someone with reasonable mastery of the concept JUSTIFIED could not do the same.

In what follows, I'll interpret Olson as defending the combination of epistemic error theory and Strongly revisionist reductionism with respect to the epistemic domain. We can refer to this pairing of positions as the *epistemic combination*.

3. From the Epistemic to the Moral Domain

J. L. Mackie is well-known as being the first prominent philosopher to articulate and defend the moral error theory in Anglo-American analytic philosophy.[19] In a memorable passage, Gilbert Harman expressed mystification regarding Mackie's approach to ethical theorizing in *Ethics: Inventing Right and Wrong*, writing: "Mackie (1977) argues in Chapter 1 that ethics rests on a false presupposition, but then he goes on in later chapters to discuss particular moral issues. It is almost as if he had first demonstrated that God does not exist and had then gone on to consider whether He is wise and loving."[20]

I believe that there is something to Harman's worries regarding Mackie, although locating the problematic features of Mackie's view proves to be not entirely straightforward. In the next section, I will attempt to articulate what I find puzzling about Mackie's approach. In the meanwhile, let me note that Olson finds nothing puzzling about Mackie's approach to ethical theorizing, writing:

> there is no deep puzzle here... Since most social life presupposes something like a system of morality... we need, according to Mackie, 'to find some set of principles which [are] themselves fairly acceptable to us and with which ... our "intuitive" (but really subjective) detailed moral judgments are in "reflective equilibrium."'

Moral error theorists can without tongues-in-cheek engage in the pursuit of theories that meet these criteria. The one criterion that cannot be met is of course that of truth. (197)

Before I attempt to substantiate Harman's worries, let me try to articulate what I find puzzling about Olson's own attempt to follow Mackie.

Consider two reductionist positions regarding the moral domain that mirror those we formulated regarding the epistemic domain. The first view is:

---

[19] Mackie (1977). As Olson notes (pp. 56–60), Mackie was not the first in this tradition to defend the error theory;
[20] Harman (1984), 30.

Weakly revisionist: moral facts exist but do not satisfy the authority platitudes. These facts are good enough but imperfect satisfiers of our commonsensical conception of moral facts.

Weakly revisionist positions are very close to and perhaps identical with some naturalist views in metaethics, such as that defended by David Copp.[21]

The second reductionist view is:

Strongly revisionist: nothing answers to our concept of a moral fact (since some such facts would have to satisfy the authority platitudes regarding the moral domain). But there are "successor" concepts that are closely related to ordinary moral concepts. Although the facts that these concepts characterize are not moral facts, these facts satisfy more or less exact analogues to the substance platitudes with respect to moral facts.

Let us refer to those facts that satisfy the more or less exact analogues to the substance platitudes as the MORAL facts and the concepts that characterize them, MORAL concepts. While it is not possible to coherently combine the moral error theory with Weakly revisionist reductionism, it is possible to combine the moral error theory with Strongly revisionist reductionism. Not only is it possible to combine these views, I take it that Olson has compelling reasons to combine them, given his commitment in the epistemic domain to a similar combination.

The justification for embracing each view, after all, would be the same: we need practical guidance when it comes to our believings. EPISTEMIC principles provide such guidance in the form of principles for the formation, revision, and evaluation of our doxastic attitudes. But we also need practical guidance when it comes to our action-plans and their implementations. MORAL principles provide such guidance in the form of principles for the formation, revision, implementation, and evaluation of action-plans.[22] Moreover, while the concepts that compose MORAL principles are successors to ordinary moral concepts, they could play nearly all the same practical roles as moral concepts for all practical purposes: they are practically employable. In principle, we could substitute them for our ordinary moral concepts.

---

21 See Copp (2007). As Olson states in the Introduction to his book, he has very little to say about positions such as these, focusing on nonnaturalist versions of realism.
22 Here I simplify. EPISTEMIC principles would, presumably, apply to a wider array of entities than our doxastic attitudes and MORAL principles would apply to a wider array of entities than our action-plans and their implementations. See Cuneo (2007), ch. 2.

The reason is that the application conditions for these successor concepts mirror those of moral concepts. As I think of them, the application conditions for moral concepts are given by claims such as these:

> Necessarily, if an action falls under the concept <u>being a case of recreational slaughter of a fellow person</u>, then it falls under the concept <u>wrong</u>.
> Necessarily, if an action falls under the concept <u>being a case of physically abusing another for pleasure</u>, then it falls under the concept <u>wrong</u>.
> And so on.

We can identify application conditions for MORAL concepts that exactly mirror these, such as:

> Necessarily, if an action falls under the concept <u>being a case of recreational slaughter of a fellow person</u>, then it falls under the concept WRONG.
> Necessarily, if an action falls under the concept <u>being a case of physically abusing another for pleasure</u>, then it falls under the concept WRONG.

If the application conditions of a concept tell us what it is to be that concept, then these conditionals (which more or less exactly mirror the substance platitudes with regard to the moral domain) give us insight into the essence of these MORAL concepts.

Let's call the combination of the moral error theory and Strongly revisionist reductionism with respect to the moral domain the *moral combination*. My contention is that Olson should accept both the epistemic combination and the moral combination, combining the error theory with Strongly revisionist reductionism with regard to both the epistemic and moral domains. Doing so would allow Olson to claim both that the moral error theory is true but also that moral terms also admit of a purely descriptive use that parallels the use of epistemic terms.

Having offered reasons for Olson to accept the moral combination, let me now explain why I find the characterization that Olson offers of his own position puzzling. When defending Mackie's approach to moral theorizing, Olson explains how error theorists can engage in normative theorizing, positively contributing to this project and reaping its fruits.[23] But, Olson cautions, error theorists cannot say that the results of their efforts are true. I am not sure why Olson

---

23 See Olson (2014), ch. 9.

would say this, however.[24] The reason is this: if normative theorizing were to consist in reporting ordinary moral or epistemic beliefs, then one could see why Olson says what he does. For if his view were correct, such theorizing would consist in reporting false moral and epistemic beliefs. But normative theorizing needn't consist in simply reporting ordinary moral or epistemic beliefs. It could consist in formulating and advocating MORAL and EPISTEMIC principles. Error theorists could, moreover, maintain that the theories that they construct on the basis of these principles are *true*, enjoying properties such as being JUSTIFIED. For the theories they advocate may be constituted by no other normative propositions than those that represent EPISTEMIC and MORAL facts. What is more, error theorists needn't claim, as Mackie does, that we somehow "invent" these facts or that they are "subjective." So long as these facts do not satisfy the authority platitudes, trafficking in "queer" normative relations, they can be as objective as you like. Indeed, if what I argued earlier regarding the epistemic domain is correct, Olson has good reason to hold that MORAL facts would be objective in the sense of satisfying more or less exact analogues to the substance platitudes with regard to this domain.

Call the conjunction of the epistemic and moral combinations *the error theorist's positive view*. My suggestion has been that Olson accept this view. What we've learned when articulating this view's commitments is that there is substantial common ground between the error theorist's positive view and epistemic and moral reductionism: both views agree that there are facts that are normative in the lean sense and that satisfy the substance platitudes with regard to the epistemic and moral domains, or more or less exact analogues to these platitudes. Moreover, both views agree that there are no facts that satisfy the authority platitudes. While there is this shared ground, these views disagree about the character of epistemic and moral concepts. Reductionists hold that epistemic and moral concepts accurately represent epistemic and moral facts. Error theorists deny this.

4. Destabilizing the ET

My project in the previous two sections has been to argue for a pair of claims. First, we should interpret Olson as defending the epistemic combination. And, second, Olson should accept the moral combination given his commitment to

---

[24] Unless Olson were assuming that normative theorizing must involve the use of moral and epistemic concepts. But the passage quoted above seems to indicate that he is not assuming this.

the epistemic combination. In this section, I want to argue that commitment to the epistemic and moral combinations – what I've called *the error theorist's positive view* – destabilizes commitment to the error theory. The argument for destabilization runs as follows: the error theorist's positive view is not identical with certain versions of moral reductionism such as Weakly revisionist reductionism. But the two positions are *very* close cousins because of their shared positive ontological commitments. (In what remains, when I use the term "reductionism," I shall have in mind Weakly revisionist reductionism.) When we bring to light other methodological claims to which error theorists are committed, however, powerful reasons surface for holding that error theorists should either not accept their own view, or continue to accept their view but concede that it is philosophically irrelevant.

In the previous two sections, I've argued that the core of the disagreement between reductionism and error theory concerns the nature, role, and implications of moral and epistemic concepts. Error theory maintains that any fact that falls under moral concepts must satisfy the authority platitudes, while reductionism denies this. The question to ask is whether this difference is theoretically significant, signifying a difference between these positions that is deep or one that is superficial.

The answer to this question, I believe, depends on what one thinks a metanormative theory should accomplish. On this matter, I see two options. One option is to maintain that a satisfactory metanormative theory should offer us not only an accurate account of what sorts of normative facts there are but also an account that preserves deeply entrenched features of ordinary epistemic and moral thought and discourse. A second option is to say that metanormative theorizing needn't concern itself with preserving deeply entrenched features of ordinary epistemic and moral thought and discourse but should accurately state what the ontology of the normative domains is like. Were normative theorizing to accomplish this, the folk may ultimately have to surrender their deeply entrenched views to bring them into line with our best theories of what there is.

Both options present challenges to the error theory. Begin with the first. Suppose it is true that a satisfactory metanormative theory should preserve the deeply entrenched features of ordinary moral thought and discourse in at least this sense: if theories A and B are otherwise identical (or nearly so) but A preserves the deeply entrenched features of ordinary moral thought and discourse better than B, then (all else being equal) one ought to accept A. And suppose, further, that reductionism and the error theorist's positive view are otherwise on par insofar as they have the same ontological commitments: both maintain that there are normative facts in the lean sense but not in the robust sense and that these facts satisfy the substance platitudes with regard to the epistemic and moral domains, or exact analogues to them. Given these two assumptions, I contend that error theorists should not accept their positive view.

For among the deeply held convictions that we have is that, when it comes to moral and epistemic matters, we sometimes get it right. Indeed, it belongs to the broadly Moorean appearances that we not only sometimes get it right, but also that we have knowledge regarding moral and epistemic matters. By all appearances, for example, we appear to know moral propositions such as:

It is wrong to recreationally slaughter fellow persons;
and:
It is wrong to physically abuse others for pleasure.

And epistemic propositions such as:

It is irrational to believe a proposition simply on the basis of wish-fulfillment; and:
It is justified to believe a proposition on the basis of one's best evidence.

While error theorists cannot preserve these commitments – since they would not be true if the error theory were correct – reductionist positions can. Reductionists can even help themselves to the claim that we know what we have reason to do, provided that we understand "reason" in the lean sense. Moreover, reductionists have at their disposal resources to explain why properties such as *being wrong* and *being justified* answer to our moral and epistemic concepts even though these properties do not satisfy the authority platitudes.

This last claim might seem surprising. If reductionists agree that it belongs to our commonsensical conceptions of the moral and epistemic domains that moral and epistemic facts satisfy both the substance and authority platitudes, how could they plausibly maintain that these facts satisfy the substance but not the authority platitudes?

In principle, they could do so in several ways. Let me sketch one strategy that they might use. This strategy operates with a distinction between *concepts*, on the one hand, and *conceptions*, on the other. According to this distinction, concepts are referential devices that are the constituents of propositions, which often give us insight into the nature of the objects for which they stand. Conceptions, in contrast, are not referential devices or constituents of propositions. Rather, they are descriptive thoughts – often widely held and implicit – that a thinker associates with a concept or the object thereof. Of course "from the inside," it may be difficult to distinguish the two; extensive theorizing might be the only way to mark the distinction.

To take a familiar example, suppose the concept being solid characterizes composite material objects in terms of the cohesion of their parts or the relative impenetrability of these objects. Still, those of us who possess this concept might also harbor a variety of conceptions about objects that are solid. Among these conceptions, for example, might be the belief that solid objects have no space between their constituent parts. While widespread, we know that this conception is false. But since it does not belong to the concept being solid – as it does not belong to the application conditions of the concept – it would not prevent this concept as it is used in ordinary thought and discourse from characterizing objects that are solid.

In a similar fashion, ordinary moral and epistemic concepts might incorporate or be given by the substance platitudes with regard to these domains. If they do, then their application conditions would include propositions such as:

> Necessarily, if an action falls under the concept being a case of recreational slaughter of a fellow person, then it falls under the concept wrong.

But we might also harbor conceptions that attend possession of the concept wrong. One such conception might be the belief that a divine being will ultimately punish people who perform many wrong actions. Another conception might be that the concept wrong applies only to those objects that satisfy the authority platitudes. Reductionists hold not only that these conceptions do not belong to the concept wrong, but also that some, such as the authority platitudes, are false. However, even if the authority platitudes were false, as reductionists believe, our moral and epistemic concepts could still refer to epistemic and moral features. So, while we might ordinarily suppose that reasons are robustly normative, the falsity of this supposition would not prevent our concept reason from referring to reasons.

I have argued that reductionists can accept:

(C) our commonsensical conception of moral and epistemic facts incorporates a commitment to both the substance and authority platitudes with regard to the moral and epistemic domains,

but reject:

(B) it belongs to the nature of moral and epistemic concepts that moral and epistemic facts must satisfy the authority platitudes.

Because reductionists accept (C), they can offer a characterization of ordinary moral and epistemic thought and discourse that is very close to that accepted by error theorists'. But because they reject (B), they needn't agree with error theorists that the contents of this thought and discourse are systematically untrue. If this is right, however, then reductionists can claim that their position preserves the deeply entrenched commitments of ordinary epistemic and moral thought and discourse *at least* as well as the error theorists' positive view. On the assumption that this is what a satisfactory metanormative theory should accomplish, it follows that error theorists ought not to accept their positive view.

We can summarize the argument as follows:

(1) The error theorists' positive view and reductionism are (or are nearly) identical except with regard to their understanding of the nature, role, and implications of moral and epistemic concepts.
(2) The reductionists' understanding of the nature, role, and implications of moral and epistemic concepts preserves the deeply entrenched commitments of ordinary epistemic and moral thought and discourse *at least* as well as the error theorists' understanding of the nature, role, and implications of moral and epistemic concepts does.
(3) A satisfactory metanormative theory should preserve the deeply entrenched commitments of ordinary epistemic and moral thought and discourse: all else being equal, if two metanormative theories are otherwise identical (or nearly so), one ought to accept whatever theory that better preserves these commitments (if any).
(4) So, all else being equal, there is no reason to accept the error theorists' positive view rather than reductionism.
(5) All else being equal, if there is no reason to accept the error theorists' positive view rather than reductionism, then those who accept the error theorists' positive view ought not to accept their own view.
(6) So, all else being equal, those who accept the error theorists' positive view ought not to accept their own view.

Let's review this argument's premises. (1) is simply an implication of the error theorist's positive view, which implies that the fundamental difference between this view and reductionism is how advocates of each position understand the nature, role, and implications of moral and epistemic concepts. (3) is true by hypothesis, since we are assuming that a satisfactory metanormative theory should preserve the appearances. Although, it may be worth reminding ourselves that (3) does not say that a theory ought to preserve our commonsense commitments full stop. It says only that if two theories are otherwise identical (or nearly so), we should accept whatever view that better preserves these commitments (if any). I have, moreover, contended that the error theorist's positive view and reductionism are otherwise identical (or nearly so): both accept the same ontology of the normative domains and very similar characterizations of ordinary moral and epistemic thought and discourse. Both theories hold, for example, that a commitment to the substance and authority platitudes is constitutive of ordinary moral and epistemic thought and discourse. As for (5), this premise is an application of the very plausible principle that, for any two mutually incompatible theories, A and B, if one has no more reason to accept A than B, then one ought not to accept A.

This leaves only premise (2), which looks true. Indeed, this premise probably understates how the error theory and reductionism compare. Both views, after all, agree that we commonly assume that we can know propositions such as *it is wrong to recreationally slaughter fellow persons* or *it is irrational to believe a proposition merely on the basis of wish-fulfillment*. If the error theorists' positive view were correct, however, then we could not know any such propositions. In contrast, if reductionism is correct, we know these propositions and many more like them. On the face of things, reductionism seems not only to save the appearances as well as but much better than the error theory.

The argument just offered hinges on the assumption that a satisfactory metanormative theory should preserve the deeply entrenched features of ordinary epistemic and moral thought in the sense specified by premise (3). In principle, error theorists could reject this premise. But doing so would, I believe, be costly.

Error theorists maintain that ordinary moral and epistemic thought and discourse are in deep and systematic error; none of it is true. But there would be no error if competent participants in ordinary moral and epistemic discourse did not suppose that moral and epistemic reality must satisfy the authority platitudes (or our moral and epistemic concepts did not imply the truth of these platitudes). Why think, then, that participants in ordinary moral and epistemic thought and discourse hold that the authority platitudes are true of moral and epistemic reality (or that our moral and epistemic concepts imply the truth of these platitudes)?

According to error theorists such as Joyce, it is because it is difficult to make sense of our practices of blaming and praising if they did not.[25] If Joyce's views are representative – and I believe they are – it follows that error theorists are committed to preserving at least this deeply entrenched feature of ordinary epistemic and moral thought and discourse:

---

25 Joyce (2001), ch. 2.

Competent participants in ordinary moral and epistemic discourse suppose that moral and epistemic reality must satisfy the authority platitudes.

But error theorists could not in one breath deny that a satisfactory metanormative theory should preserve the deeply entrenched features of ordinary epistemic and moral thought and discourse and recommend their view on the basis of this claim. If so, it is not really an option for error theorists to surrender this claim, since doing so would undercut what looks like an indispensable premise in the case that they offer for their view.

Suppose, however, error theorists could plausibly reject the claim that a satisfactory metanormative theory should preserve the deeply entrenched commitments of ordinary epistemic and moral thought and discourse in the sense specified by (3). The implication of doing so would be that the sole remaining difference between reductionism and the error theorists' positive view becomes theoretically irrelevant. After all, if a metanormative theory needn't preserve the deeply entrenched commitments of ordinary epistemic and moral thought and discourse, it wouldn't matter (at least as normative theorizing goes) whether ordinary agents employ moral and epistemic concepts or whether these concepts characterize moral and epistemic reality. In fact, it wouldn't matter if reductionists were to *agree* that moral and epistemic concepts fail to characterize moral and epistemic facts, joining error theorists by employing MORAL and EPISTEMIC concepts when theorizing. What would matter is what error theorists and reductionists say about normative reality. And on this matter, we've seen, they say the same thing. Of course none of this would establish that the error theory is false or that error theorists should surrender their view. It would only establish that what renders the error theory a distinctive view is theoretically irrelevant (so far as metanormative theorizing goes). As far as normative theorizing goes, the fact that the moral and epistemic beliefs of ordinary people are massively mistaken is neither here nor there.

Here is the conclusion I reach. It is possible for error theorists to escape the central dilemma by grasping the dilemma's second horn. Doing so commits them to the error theorists' positive view, which is a blend of the epistemic and moral combinations. However, when error theorists advocate their positive view, they thereby destabilize commitment to their own position. If this is right, the strategy that Olson advocates for avoiding the central dilemma is one that error theorists should not embrace. This conclusion is compatible with there being other strategies for resisting the central dilemma. One such strategy, for example, might be to reject the parity principle on which the central dilemma is predicated.[26]

References

Blackburn, S. (1993). *Essays in Quasi-Realism*. Oxford: Oxford University Press.
Blackburn, S. (1998). *Ruling Passions*. Oxford: Oxford University Press.
Broome, J. (2005). Does Rationality Give Us Reasons? *Philosophical Issues* 15: 321–37.
Copp, D. (2007). *Morality in a Natural World*. Oxford: Oxford University Press.
Cuneo, T. 2007. *The Normative Web*. Oxford: Oxford University Press.
Cuneo, T. and R. Shafer-Landau (2014). The Moral Fixed Points: New Directions for Nonnaturalism. *Philosophical Studies* 171: 399–443
Enoch, D. (2011). *Taking Morality Seriously*. Oxford: Oxford University Press.
FitzPatrick, W. (2008). Robust Ethical Realism, Non-Naturalism, and Normativity. In R. Shafer-Landau (ed.), *Oxford Studies in Metaethics*, vol. 3. Oxford: Oxford University Press.
Harman, G. (1984). Is There A Single True Morality? In D. Copp and D. Zimmerman (eds.), *Morality, Reason, Truth*. Lanham: Rowman & Allanhead.
Joyce, R. (2001). *The Myth of Morality*. Cambridge (MA): Cambridge University Press.
Joyce, R. (2006). *The Evolution of Morality*. Cambridge (MA): MIT Press.
Kalderon, M. (2005). *Moral Fictionalism*. Oxford: Oxford University Press.
Kolodny, N. (2005). Why Be Rational? *Mind* 114: 509–63
Lewis, D. (1995). Should a Materialist Believe in Qualia? *Faith and Philosophy* 12: 467–71.
Olson, J. (2014). *Moral Error Theory: History, Critique, Defence*. Oxford: Oxford University Press.
Russell, B. (1912). *The Problems of Philosophy*. London: Williams and Norgate.
Russell, B. (1914). *Our Knowledge of the External World*. London: Open Court.
Inwagen, P. (1990). *Material Beings*. Ithaca (NY): Cornell University Press.
van Inwagen, P. (2014). *Existence*. Cambridge (MA): Cambridge University Press.
Way, J. (2009). Two Accounts of the Normativity of Rationality. *Journal of Ethics and Social Philosophy*. December. Available at: http://www.jesp.org/

---

[26] Thanks to audiences as the University of Vermont, York University, and Southampton University for their feedback. Thanks, also, to Chris Cowie, Tyler Doggett, Susanne Mantel, Jonas Olson, Timothy Rosenkoetter, and Daniel Whiting for comments or discussion on an earlier version of this essay.

Andrew Reisner
Peer Disagreement, Rational Requirements, and Evidence of Evidence as Evidence Against

1. Introduction

Worries about the significance of disagreement amongst actual, or perceived (perhaps with a good reason), peers has in recent years prompted a substantial body of work by epistemologists.[1] It is common in this literature to discuss a variety of normative issues that may arise from peer disagreement in terms of 'rationality'. This is regrettable. For roughly the last fifteen years, philosophers working on normativity have been growing ever more sensitive to the important differences between normative reasons, rational requirements, and requirements of reasoning. The term 'rationality', as used by epistemologists in this debate, can be used to make claims about any or any combination of normative reasons, rational requirements, and requirements of reasoning.[2] 'Rationality', in the broader literature on theoretical reason, typically denotes requirements or permissions that appertain to relations amongst mental states, as opposed to considerations generally that count in favour of having particular beliefs or other mental states. Those fall under the rubric of 'normative reasons'.

Despite the terminological difficulties, it seems clear that the main focus of the peer disagreement literature in epistemology is best understood as being on normative reasons for belief.[3] Consequently, in this chapter I shall consider the possible import of peer disagreement with respect to rationality in its more regimented use and as distinct from the importance of peer disagreement with respect to the normative reasons it may provide or its import for the requirements of reasoning. My suggestion is that there is little upshot rationally to peer disagreement. A possible exception are cases in which peer disagreement is believed to be antecedently unlikely or in which it is assigned a low credence. At present,

---

[1] See De Ridder (2014) as an example of work on disagreement between idealised peers. For disagreement between agents who regard each other with reason as peers, see Enoch (2010).
[2] Cases of ambiguous usage include Ballantyne and Coffman (2011), Kelly (2010) and White (2005). This is often the result of an uneasy slide from traditional talk of justification in epistemology to the use of reasons talk in concert with justification. For a brief discussion of the incorporation of reasons into epistemology, see Reisner and Steglich-Petersen (2011).
[3] I thank Michele Palmira for suggesting this reading of the literature to me.

the question of the rational significance of peer disagreement has received little attention, and I hope to provide at least a starting point for a more thorough investigation of the topic.

The paper proceeds as follows. In §1, I introduce the distinction among normative reasons (just 'reasons' from here forward), rationality, and reasoning. In §2, I consider two views about the nature of evidence itself. In §3, I introduce an example of how evidence of evidence of p can be evidence against p. In §4, I discuss how this example limits the ways in which peer disagreement might affect what rationality requires of the respective peers. In §5, I discuss some ways in which improbable peer disagreements might affect what rationality requires of an agent. I offer some concluding thoughts about the limited importance of peer disagreement for theoretical rational requirements in §6.

2. Reasons, Rational Requirements, and Reasoning

Reading through the literature on peer disagreement in the early part of the now decade long boom in research on the topic reveals some surprises. At the start of this period, then recent work by John Broome, Derek Parfit, and Ralph Wedgwood had already begun to mark important differences between normative reasons and the requirements of rationality.[4] My own work on the distinction already dated back several years in the form of the beginnings of my doctoral thesis,[5] although it would not appear in published form for some time to come.[6] Niko Kolodny's now famous paper, 'Why Be Rational',[7] which argues for the distinction, had been in wide circulation for not a short period prior to its 2005 publication in *Mind*. Attentive readers may have noticed a quite different pair of earnests in work by Christopher Cherniak and Logi Gunnarsson.[8] Yet this important distinction does not appear in a careful or systematic way in the early – and some of the later – literature on peer disagreement, even as interest in the relation and distinction between normativity and rationality has grown steadily.

---

4 Broome (1999), Parfit (2001), and Wedgwood (2003).
5 Reisner (2004).
6 Reisner (2011). The original paper that formed the basis of my docto'ral work was 'Why Rational Requirements Are not Normative Requirements'. The main argument from this paper was folded into a book chapter, 'Is there Reason to Be Theoretically Rational?'.
7 Kolodny (2005).
8 Cherniak (1986) and Gunnarsson (2000).

As a consequence, before considering the importance of peer disagreement to rationality in its current more carefully specified sense, it will be useful to keep careful track of the respective domains for which peer disagreement may pose a puzzle. I shall discuss each of reasons and oughts, rationality, and reasoning briefly to explain the differences amongst them.

2.1 Oughts and Reasons

Ought is the final normative operator. In this way, it is distinguished from there being a reason, which is non-final normative operator. If one ought to believe x, then the matter is normatively settled, absent relevant changes in how things are. If one has a reason to believe x, it is still possible that one ought not to believe x. What one ought (or ought not) to believe will depend on whether and which other reasons bear on believing x.

There are competing views about the relationship between oughts and reasons. Some philosophers believe that reasons can be analysed in terms of oughts.[9] Some believe that oughts may be analysed in terms of reasons.[10] My own view is that neither can be analysed in terms of the other. Whatever the relation in which they stand, they share an important feature: they are robustly normative.

It is difficult to give an illuminating account of what it is for something to be robustly normative.[11] Happily, an illuminating account is not necessary for present purposes. Robust normativity is the kind of normativity that is thought to be associated with moral requirements, the requirements of prudence, and epistemic requirements by philosophers who are realists – perhaps non-deflationary realists – about such requirements. It is different from the kind of normativity associated with systems or collections of rules, such as chess, etiquette, and doctoral thesis formatting.

Put another way, oughts and reasons, and any elaborations thereon (*prima facie* oughts, for example) are the currency of robust normativity. There are many

---

[9] See Broome (2013), Brunero (2013a) and Kearns and Star (2009) for a discussion of these analyses.
[10] This is the view expressed in Parfit (2001) and Skorupski (2011). However, they do not themselves call oughts 'oughts'. Nonetheless, it is perfectly clear that oughts are what they are discussing.
[11] Although his principal work on the subject is unpublished, Nicholas Shackel deserves the most credit for exploring different forces of normativity, distinguishing between 'correctness' and 'directivity'. See Shackel (MS).

other uses of 'ought' and 'reason' in English, and of their appropriate translations in other languages, but our concern is not with natural language usage.

Regrettably, remarks on the natural language usage of the word 'reason' from time to time exert a strong pull on theorising about reasons in particular. Would that it were not so. As it is, we must guard against a particular kind of quick move. This is the association, principally on grounds of linguistic commonality, of three conceptually distinct concepts that go by the name 'reason', such that they eventually merge into one.

The kind of reasons that are of interest here are normative reasons. A normative reason can be glossed as a consideration that counts in favour of something. A reason for belief is a consideration that counts in favour of believing something. There is a substantive issue as to what is required for one thing to count in favour of another, and indeed there is controversy even about the correct ontology for the relata in the counting-in-favour-of relation. The details of these controversies fortunately need not detain us here. We may understand the notion of counting in favour, and therefore of a normative reason, as what is being gestured at by the claim that seeing dark clouds counts in favour of believing that it will soon rain.

Separately, there is the notion of an operative or motivational reason. These are reasons that are thought to play some kind of psychological role for an agent, often in an actual or idealised reasoning process. Sometimes motivational or operative reasons are thought to be mental states themselves, other times something else that figures in reasons for explanations of belief or behaviour.[12] However they are understood, they are conceptually distinct from normative reasons. This must be pointed out, because it is often claimed that to be a normative reason, something must be able to be an operative or motivating reason. I am sceptical that there is any interesting relation between normative and motivational reasons. If there is, however, it is one that must be explained; it is not true in virtue of their being one and the same thing in a non-obvious way.

A final use of 'reason' is to mean 'explanation'. This use is generally not conflated with the normative use. Broome claims that normative reasons are weighing explanations of oughts. In this sense, he is a reductivist about normative reasons. Broome's view should be treated as a substantive metaphysical or conceptual claim that requires support.

---

[12] I can make little sense of what philosophers are trying to get at in discussions of reasons for. Given that the role of claims about reasons for is normally to limit what can count as normative reasons, the two are clearly intended to be conceptually or metaphysically distinct.

2.2 Rationality

Much of the discussion of peer disagreement is presented in terms of 'rationality'. It can be difficult to tell what the sense of 'rationality' is that is being used. I shall introduce the current popular regimentation here. It is how I shall use 'rationality', and it would be sensible for philosophers writing on peer disagreement to adopt the now common convention, as it is a great aid to clarity.

It is sometimes said that the rational supervenes on the mental.[13] It is more accurate to say that the requirements of rationality take as their object mental states, or relations amongst mental states. The supervenience formulation is introduced to avoid a confusion with reasons. What mental states it is rational for me to have depends primarily on what my other mental states are. One could imagine, as fitting attitudes theorists sometimes seem to, that all normative claims are fundamentally claims about what reasons there are for one to be in particular mental states. However, it is still open to say that the reasons are themselves exclusively, or primarily, non-mental facts. Thus, one could have reasons to be in mental state M, whilst one is rationally required not to be in mental state M.

An example will be useful. Take the rational requirement that if you believe p, then do not also believe not p. This requirement may be expressed in a wide-scope formulation:

NCW: $RR(Bp \rightarrow B\neg p)$

Or it may be expressed in a narrow-scope formulation:

NCN: $Bp \rightarrow RR\neg B\neg p$

Whichever formulation is correct, each is thought to hold on account of a feature of an agent's mental life, namely that the contents of his beliefs are logically inconsistent, when he at once believes p and also believes not p. A typical rational requirement, whether wide or narrow in scope, has only mental states within the scope of the requirement, and in the case of narrow scope requirements, there are only mental states in the antecedents to the conditional.

What is being excluded are requirements of a form like this one: you are required to bring an umbrella, whenever it rains, even if you neither know nor believe that it is raining. I have deliberately been ambiguous about the scope of the

---

[13] Broome (2013), who follows Wedgwood (2003).

requirement, because the point stands in both the wide-scope and narrow-scope versions; rationality does not include requirements like this one. This requirement is an ought, or perhaps a prima facie ought. It arises out of the reasons one has for not getting wet, when out in the rain.

The relation between rational requirements and reasons or oughts remains controversial. Fortunately, the correct answer to the debate about the normativity of rationality does not matter for the discussion in this paper, and thus it suffices to note that there is a distinction between reasons and oughts on the one hand and rationality on the other.[14]

2.3 Reasoning

Reasoning is a process. We commonly describe reasoning, or at least explicit reasoning, as a series of mental states. In the case of belief reasoning, both the states containing the premises and that which contains the conclusion are beliefs. When describing one's own theoretical reasoning, the mention of beliefs is typically omitted.[15]

These are the easy things to say about reasoning. The rest is more difficult. To say that reasoning is a process is to say that it is more than just a sequence of disconnected propositional attitudes. Reasoning, as opposed to just having a series of attitudes, is distinguished by those attitudes with their contents having some sort of relation to each other. One arrives at the conclusion on account of the premises. Just how to understand on account of is unclear.

I shall not try to shed any light on the matter. There is something that makes the occurence of a series of mental states in an agent's pscyhology an instance of reasoning rather than an instance of having a series of disconnected mental states, such that it is possible to have the same series of mental states on two different occassions and have one count as reasoning and the other not. What that something is remains controversial.[16]

---

14 In saying this, I assume that whether there are reasons to be rational, rationality is not reducible to reasons. I find the arguments in chapters 5 and 6 of Broome (2013) convincing on this point.
15 This notion of reasoning, specifically within the context of belief revision, appears in Harman (1984 and 1986), where he helpfully distinguishes it from arguments that are used in reasoning.
16 This is the source of an interesting dialogue between Paul Boghossian and Broome. The outlines of the discussion may be found in Broome (2013). Boghossian's view is set out in detail in Boghossian (2012).

In ordinary speech and in philosophy we make a further distinction between good reasoning and bad reasoning. It is important not to define reasoning in such a way that bad reasoning is impossible. As with the requirements of rationality, I shall not assume that the requirements (or permissions) of reasoning are robustly normative. This leaves open the possibility that how one ought to reason may be at times contrary to the requirements of reasoning.

3. Evidence and Evidential Parity

In debates about epistemic peer disagreement, one needs a notion of epistemic peerdom. Typically, two necessary conditions are assigned to epistemic peers:

Evidential parity: Two individuals are epistemic peers with respect to p only if they share the same evidence with respect to p.

Shared capacities: Two individuals are epistemic peers with respect to p only if they are equally cognitively capable with respect to assessing whether p.

These conditions are not precise, and how they are made precise is significant for understanding what follows from the fact, or possibility, of epistemic disagreement. Some particularly interesting issues arise in the case of evidential parity.

The evidential parity condition is typically intended as a claim about agents' actual evidence, rather than what they take their evidence to be. Evidential parity will therefore look different depending on one's substantive theory of evidence. For illustrative purposes, I have chosen two extreme views about the nature of evidence, which I call 'strong evidential externalism' or just 'evidential externalism' and 'strong evidential internalism' or just 'evidential internalism'. Both are views that can be found in recent literature, although neither is especially popular in their strong forms. I use them as an illustrative example because they are easy to work with, and the relevantly external and internal characteristics of evidence on each view apply to the full spectrum of more nuanced theories of evidence.

Strong evidential externalism is a view that one finds primarily in the literature on theoretical reason. Although externalist views differ with respect to details, they typically share three features. The first is that the evidential relation is between facts (or true propositions) and propositions (either true or false). The second is that these facts need not be known or believed by agents for whom they are evidence. The third is that, although the agent need not know or believe the facts that constitute evidence for a particular proposition, there is some restriction on the accessibility of the facts that is stricter than that which applies to those facts that constitute practical reasons.[17]

As a consequence, for two individuals to be evidential peers with respect to p, they need not share the same mental states with respect to p. They do, however, need to be similarly situated such that they have the same epistemic access, however defined, to the same facts about or pertaining to p.

By way of contrast, strong internalists about evidence think that an agent's beliefs, or credences, constitute his evidence. It is not always clear whether they think that the evidential relation is between doxastic states and propositions or doxastic states and other doxastic states, but the identity of the second relatum is not important in this context. We may note, then, that two individuals are evidential peers, according to strong internalism, just in case they share the same relevant doxastic states.[18]

One consequence of strong evidential externalism is that there are no rational requirements concerning first order evidence. That is because evidence is not a mental state, and rational requirements only govern relations among mental states. We cannot assume any principle of the sort that says: if there is a change in an agent's evidence, there is a change in what is rationally required of him.

Strong externalism about evidence does not preclude the possibility of there being second order rational requirements concerning evidence. One such requirement might be a version of *belief enkrasia*:

Belief enkrasia (BE): You are rationally required that if you believe that your total evidence supports proposition p to degree d, then you believe p.[19]

BEF: $RR(BE_d p \rightarrow Bp)$.

The general plausibility of BE is much debated.[20] I shall return to BE and its more general role in rational disagreement in §3.

---

[17] Dancy (2002) and Skourpski (2011) offer versions of this form of strong externalism, and the position is perhaps implied in Parfit (2001).
[18] With some modifications, notably from working with beliefs to working with credences, evidential internalism is the account of evidence in classical Bayesianism.
[19] I have used all out belief in the consequent to avoid some complications arising from the use of credences.
[20] See Brunero (2013b) and Reisner (2013) for discussions of its status as a rational requirement.

Strong internalism about evidence is in a quite different position. The strong evidential internalist may accept that there are rational requirements on evidence, because evidence is itself a mental state.[21] An example of such a requirement is the *direct evidential requirement*:

Direct evidential requirement (DE): You are rationally required that if your total evidence supports proposition p to degree d, then you believe p.[22]

DEF: $RR(E_d p \to Bp)$.

The DE schema does not apply to all accounts of evidence. There is an asymmetry between BE and DE in this way; unlike DE, BE in principle could apply to any account of evidence. If externalist theories of evidence are correct, then there are no first order evidential requirements of rationality.

This point is significant for claims that there are rational requirements that arise from peer disagreement. If there are no DE-like rational requirements that apply to externalist accounts of evidence, then there are none to violate. Evidential externalism does not affect rationality through DE-like requirements.[23]

What may be less obvious is that if externalism is true, then the fact of peer disagreement also does not bear on second order theoretical rational requirements like BE. According to the externalist account of evidence, my beliefs do not figure as direct evidence either for their own contents or for other propositions.[24] If you are my epistemic peer, then presumably your beliefs have the same epistemic status as my own, which is to say that they do not constitute direct evidence for the proposition about which we are in disagreement. If I (correctly, according to strong externalism) do not take your belief that not p as evidence for not p, then it is difficult to see why it would exert any pressure on my second order belief about whether there is sufficiently strong evidence for p.

Of course, I might believe that your belief is evidence that there is evidence that not p, perhaps because you are equally as good as I am at detecting external

---

21 Note that on this way of classifying theories of evidence, so-called 'knowledge first' theories of evidence will come out as internalist. See Williamson (2000).
22 It may be more natural to have a credence rather than a belief in the consequent of this conditional.
23 De Ridder (2014) offers an extensive discussion on important of evidential externalism for peer disagreement.
24 This way of putting things is not meant to exclude my having a particular belief's standing as evidence for propositions concerning my belief states and other cases in which my having a particular belief or beliefs is an evidentially salient fact.

evidence. In this case, our disagreement is a sign that one of us erred either in appreciating the evidence we have or in reasoning with it. In the next section, I shall raise some doubts about whether this second order approach provides a way in which peer disagreement could change what we are rationally required to believe.

4. Evidence of Evidence as Evidence Against and Higher Order Evidential Requirements

It is by now well known that evidence of evidence is not necessarily evidence, due to Brandon Fitelson's playing card example.[25] Things can be worse than mere failure: evidence of evidence can be evidence against. It may be useful to consider briefly an example in which that is the case.

4.1 The Polaroid murder

Sometime in the future, there are only two functioning Polaroid cameras left on earth. Each has a single remaining cartridge, which cannot be removed before it is used. Due to their scarcity, they have been rigged with a sophisticated biometric scanner that only allows them to be used by their respective owners, Paul and Brian. We should assume that these facts are known to all parties in the example.

A murder has been committed. The detective on the scene notices that there is what looks to him like a recently taken Polaroid lying on the body. He manages a quick but clear look at it as he approaches, but then the wind blows the picture away. If he saw the image correctly, it was a picture of the murderer's hand stabbing the victim. Given the angle and location of the body, only the murderer could have taken the photograph. Although neither have a (known) motive and neither are (known to be) violent, the detective knows that only Paul and Brian own a functioning Polaroid camera. To start the investigation, he pays Paul a visit.

The detective tells Paul that he is confident that there is evidence that Paul committed the murder and explains that he has likely seen a photograph that implicated either Paul or Brian. Paul pulls from his pocket a recently taken Po-

---

[25] Fitelson (2012). This is the example. That the card is black is evidence that the card is the ace of spades. That the card is the ace of spades is evidence that the card is an ace. But, that the card is black is not evidence that it is an ace.

laroid photograph. It is not the one that the detective saw, but rather it appears to be a photograph of the photograph that the detective saw. Brian could have taken the second photograph and Paul could have stolen it, but the logistics are such that it is very much more likely that Paul would have taken the second photograph himself.[26]

Let us call the proposition that Paul committed the murder 'M'. We can see that Paul's being in possession of the second photograph is evidence that he did not commit the murder, so it is evidence for ¬M. But the original photograph, for which the second is evidence, is itself evidence for M.[27] The second photograph is in the epistemologists' lingo a rebutting defeater. That is to say that it drives down the probability of a proposition by driving up the probability of its contrary. Importantly, however, there is still evidence that Paul committed the murder, it is just lower than it would have been, had Paul not been in possession of the second photograph. The second photograph is not an undermining defeater of the first.

5. Peer Disagreement, Evidence of Evidence, and Rational Requirements on Belief

The lesson of the Polaroid Murder example is that peer disagreement will not change what one is rationally required to believe by serving as evidence that there is evidence for the contrary of one's own belief.[28] The general problem is that there is no free entailment from believing that there is evidence of evidence of p to believing that there is evidence of p. It is worth looking in more detail at why this is so with respect to particular rational requirements. We may return to

---

26 A simpler example of radical EE failure is this: Somebody said x; an anti-reliable person said x. For reasons that will become apparent, I prefer my example, because it does not rely on treating testimony as *prima facie* evidence. Stewart Cohen for drew my attention to the example in this footnote.
27 This assumes that the only evidence that Paul committed the murder was the photograph, and so the probability that Paul committed the murder is higher conditional on the detective's having seen the photograph (or on his believing that he saw it) than it is conditional on his not having seen it (or on his believing that he did not see the photograph). If one prefers, the example can be altered slightly so that Paul is more likely to have committed the murder than Brian.
28 Christensen (2010) and Kelly (2010) seem to treat peer disagreement as an undermining rather than a rebutting defeater. This is significant for the construction of their arguments and others related to how, or whether, to revise one's credences in the face of peer disagreement. The argument in this chapter is not substantively changed by treating disagreement as an undermining defeater rather than a rebutting defeater.

two requirements that I have already mentioned: BEF and DEF. Let us consider BEF first:

BEF: $RR(BE_t p \to Bp)$

BEF says that your are required that if you believe the total strength of the evidence for p is sufficiently strong, then you believe p. BEF is likely false, for reasons I set out elsewhere,[29] but it is a good approximation of the kind of higher-order belief principle that features in discussions about rational disagreement.

Even if we are strong evidential internalists, the belief that there is peer disagreement has no direct bearing on this principle. BEF is just a rational requirement concerning beliefs about the sufficiency of one's total evidence. The belief that there is peer disagreement would have to connect to BEF indirectly, as it is itself not a belief about the sufficiency of one's total evidence.

The most obvious route to this is through what I shall call 'belief enkrasia aggregation':

Belief enkrasia aggregation (BEag): Where the strength of your total evidence (TE) constituting beliefs concerning p, $TE_{dt}\{B\alpha...B\omega\}$, is sufficient for believing p, you are rationally required that if you believe that α is evidence for p to degree d_1 and you believe that β is evidence for p to degree d_2 ... and that ω is evidence for p to degree d_n, then believe that there is sufficient total evidence for p.

BEagF: $(TE_{dt}\{B\alpha...B\omega\} \to BE_s p) \to RR\{[(BE_{d1}\alpha p) \& (BE_{d2}\beta p) ... \& (BE_{dn}\omega p)] \to BE_t p\}$

BEag links your individual beliefs about the evidential support relations between individual pieces of evidence and p with your belief about the sufficiency of the total evidential support for p. The requirement should be read with enough latitude to treat the relations amongst the evidence and the total sufficiency as being non-monotonic, when appropriate.

BEag provides a place where changed beliefs about evidence can change the contents of one's rational requirements. Adding or subtracting a belief on the lefthand side of the conditional contained within the scope of the requirement, or changing the degree of evidential support for one or more of the beliefs on the lefthand side of the conditional contained within the scope of the requirement, in principle can change what belief, if any, belongs on the righthand side of the conditional contained within the scope of the requirement. Yet BEag does not

---

[29] Reisner (2009 and 2014).

apply to beliefs of the form: my peer believes not p, while I believe p. This belief, whether read *de dicto* or *de re*, does not have evidence as part of its content.

We need not consider other similar rational requirements. The problem with BEag for bringing beliefs about disagreement to bear on theoretical rational requirements is that the lefthand side of the conditional contained within the scope of the requirement only contains beliefs about evidence. We would thus need a rational requirement, the lefthand side of which does not contain beliefs about evidence and the righthand side of which does contain beliefs about evidence. The beliefs on the righthand side may be either about individual evidential relations or whether there is sufficient total evidence.

It is easy enough to produce a sample of such a requirement. We may call this one the 'interlevel belief requirement':[30]

Inter-level belief requirement (IB): Where your total evidence concerning p is {Bx, By, Bz}, and it is sufficietly strong for believing p, you are rationally required that if you believe x, believe y, and believe z, then you believe that there is sufficient evidence for p.[31]

IBF: $(E_d\{Bx, By, Bz\} \to E_t p) \to RR[(Bx \& By \& Bz) \to BEtp]$

It contrasts with the direct or first order analogue of BEagF:

DEagF: $(E_d\{Bx, By, Bz\} \to E_t p) \to RR[(Bx \& By \& Bz) \to Bp]$

DEagF is just DEF with the individual pieces of internalist evidence, which are beliefs, written out individually and with the fact that they are beliefs made explicit. The beliefs Bx through Bz are just an example of a total set of beliefs that constitute sufficient evidence for p in DEagF. In this sense, we may treat DEagF as a fully unpacked version of DEF.

Rational requirements like DEagF are presumably explained as having the status of rational requirement on the grounds that they enforce a consistency relation on our doxastic states. In this case, the consistency relation is some kind of evidential or probabilistic consistency.

If we were to explain IBF in exactly the same way, we would be claiming that there is an evidential relation between the having of the beliefs in the antecedent

---

30 I borrow the name, and the general idea, from Worsnip (MS).
31 This principle could be rewritten with credences rather than outright beliefs.

of the conditional and the content of the belief in the consequent. The content of the belief in the consequent is a proposition about the strength of evidence for p.

To be precise, IBF relies on evidence for p being evidence of evidence for p. If evidence for p is not evidence of evidence for p, then it is difficult to see how IBF could be explained. So much the worse for IBF. For the same reason that evidence of evidence of p is not necessarily evidence for p, evidence for p is not necessarily evidence of evidence of p. If M is evidence of evidence for p and also evidence for not p, as in the Polaroid murder example, then it follows that M is evidence for not p and not evidence of evidence for not p. The inter-level belief requirement is not a rational requirement.

This leaves us with DEF. When I form the belief that I disagree with a peer, that belief could feature as direct evidence in one of two ways (on the assumption of strong evidential internalism), at least in principle. The first is that it could be direct evidence for a belief such as the belief that Paul committed the murder.

It is difficult to explain on internalist accounts of evidence how this would work. My evidence consists of my beliefs or credences, or some restricted subset thereof. If we accept that peers have the same evidence, then we accept that they have the same set of doxastic states. The new information that comes from peer disagreement is that given the same doxastic states and the same degree of reasoning competence, my peer and I have arrived at different conclusions. Although I shall revisit this assumption presently, let us for the moment assume peer disagreement indicates that in some way I may have mishandled the evidence that I have.[32] This is evidence about my evidence. Given that we cannot assume that evidence of evidence for p is evidence for p, there is no simple way to make the fact of peer disagreement matter evidentially for an ordinary first order belief, such as that Paul committed the murder.

We have already noted that DEF is a rational requirement relating first order evidence in the form of beliefs (on the assumption of evidential internalism) to another belief. There is no restriction special restriction on the content of the belief in the condition's consequent. Thus it is possible to have a belief about the sufficiency of one's total evidence feature in DEF as the consequent. This is the second way in which my belief that I disagree with a peer could change what is rationally required of me. The belief that I disagree with a peer could feature in the antecedent of DEF, when the belief that there is sufficient evidence for p is in the consequent.

---

[32] At least, this is what is sometimes claimed. I think this claim is probably wrong on the merits, at least for any simple version of it, but I concede the point for the sake of argument.

6. The Direct Evidential Requirement, Actual Peer Disagreement, and Improbable Disagreement

The strategy suggested at the end of the last section is to relate a belief about there being peer disagreement with respect to p to the belief that I have sufficient evidence for p. To do this, we would have to show that actual peer disagreement, or my belief that there is actual peer disagreement, is new evidence that I have missed some evidence concerning p and thus cannot assume that there is still sufficient evidence for p.

It is important to notice that I have said 'new evidence' in the preceding paragraph. It is normally the case that I shall take myself to have missed some evidence for p, when I am considering whether p. The importance of uncertainty about whether I have all the available evidence, if rationally significant at all to whether there is sufficient evidence for p, is already priced into the strength that I assign to the total evidence for p, provided that I am rational in the relevant way. The question, then, is whether discovering that there is actual peer disagreement raises or lowers the probability that I have missed, or mishandled, some of the evidence for p.

One way in which my belief that there is actual peer disagreement may raise the probability that I have missed or mishandled some evidence concerning p is by that disagreement being unexpected. To see why the probability that I have assigned to there being peer disagreement, prior to its occurrence, is significant for whether it is rational to believe I have missed or mishandled some evidence, it will help to look at the two cases. The first is of improbable disagreement, the second is of probable disagreement.

6.1 Probable and Improbable Disagreement

Electronic computers, although not flawless, are rather good at following instructions. People are less good at it, and even when doing our best, we quite often reason incorrectly. This makes certain kinds of conversations between two or more computers and two or more humans quite different in character, especially when the computers disagree amongst themselves and the humans disagree amongst themselves.

We can think of two or more computers as being epistemic peers, or the appropriate analogue of that if you do not like the idea of computers having an epistemic status, just in case they meet three conditions. 1) They have the same hardware. 2) They have the same software. 3) They are in the same initial information state and receive the same new instructions and data in the same sequence. If we make the further assumption that the software and hardware are both well implemented, computer epistemic peers will almost never disagree with each other.[33]

The extraordinary reliability of computers at executing their programmes, at least under favourable conditions, is such that the chance that two computers will make an error at the same time for the same operations is minuscule. It is this fact that led NASA to use a voting protocol for its computer systems used on the space shuttle fleet.[34] Three computers simultaneously performed critical calculations during the space shuttle missions. Because disagreement between peer computers was highly improbable, if two of the three computers agreed, the outlying computer's results were discarded.[35]

We can describe an alternative scenario in which a space shuttle only had two computers. In this case, disagreement between the computers would be regarded with great concern. Absent evidence about which computer made the mistake, mission control would no doubt recommend some sort of recalculation procedure, perhaps after checking the computers for damaged hardware or corrupted software.

If we imagine a human agent with computer-like reliability and accuracy disagreeing with a peer about a matter that was computationally tractable, he would be in the same position as mission control would be in with respect to the two computer disagreement case. That there is disagreement indicates that one of the two peers has mishandled the evidence. Assuming that there is no further evidence as to which peer has done so, one peer's belief that there is actual peer disagreement stands as new evidence that he has missed or mishandled his evidence.

6.2 Probable Evidence

In other cases, when disagreement is, or is thought to be, very likely, the fact of actual disagreement has little impact on the probability that we have missed, or

---

[33] In fact, we will need some further assumptions about the set-up of the computers. Two important assumptions are that their programmes are computationally tractable and that the programmes do not employ randomisers.

[34] It is well worth looking at Tomayko (1988), which records the history of NASA's experience with computers in Spaceflight. I thank Paul Niles for directing me to this resource and for numerous invaluable discussions about this and other topics.

[35] Assuming that one computer is not undergoing some kind of systematic failure.

mishandled, our evidence. As the probability of error increases, it becomes increasingly surprising that two peers agree rather than that they do not. Peer disagreement ratifies the prior expectation in cases where non-systematic error is likely.[36] Indeed, in some cases it may have no impact at all.[37]

Examples of this situation abound in philosophy. I know that it is highly likely that I disagree with someone whom I regard as an epistemic peer about a variety of substantial philosophical positions that I currently believe. I may or may not have updated my philosophical beliefs appropriately, given the high probability that I assign to peer disagreement. However, discovering that there is an actual peer disagreement, when I have already assigned a high probability to one's occurring, does not raise by very much the probability that I have erred in my reasoning.

6.3 A Rational Requirement?

The preceding discussion suggests that the rational importance of actual peer disagreement, if it has any at all, may depend on the antecedent probability assigned to the proposition that there will be peer disagreement. It has done so without having given a concrete rational requirement for linking beliefs about actual peer disagreement to beliefs about the sufficiency of an agent's evidence.

Before giving the precise rational requirement, I shall offer the actual disagreement schema:

Actual disagreement schema (ADS): The degree to which actual peer disagreement about p constitutes evidence that a peer's credence towards p is incorrect partially depends on the credence that that peer has antecedently assigned to the probability that there will be peer disagreement about p. The relation is such that actual disagreement about p counts for more when the antecedent probability assigned to there being disagreement is low than when it is high.

---

[36] Systematic errors should be understood as those that are likely to produce common judgements by those who share in them, as opposed to non-systematic errors, which should be assumed to produce common judgements infrequently.

[37] Predicates of taste may be one such case. According to relativists, disagreement is expected and in many circumstances devoid of normative or rational significance. See MacFarlane (2014) for a complete discussion of the current state of the art.

ADS is a way of giving shape to the thought that actual peer disagreement can sometimes make us less confident that we have got the right conclusion, because we may have missed or mishandled our evidence.

What ADS does not do is tell us how to complete the story of how believed actual peer disagreement will change our rational requirements concerning what to believe about the proposition that is the subject of the disagreement. It may be possible to formulate a rational requirement in which there is a link between uncertainty about the state of one's total evidence for p and whether there is sufficient evidence to believe p. If this can be done, and if we accept the higher order belief requirement, belief enkrasia,[38] then we may establish some rational link between believing that there is actual peer disagreement about p and whether to believe p.

7. Conclusion

This chapter has been about a narrow question concerning peer disagreement: namely whether peer disagreement affects an agent's theoretical rational requirements concerning beliefs about the proposition that is the subject of the disagreement. This is a separate question from that of whether it changes an agent's reasons for belief or affects how an agent ought to reason about a particular proposition. The debate on epistemic peer disagreement would benefit from a greater regimentation of the use of the term 'rational'. At present, it is unclear whether authors are using the term to refer to normative reasons, requirements of reasoning, or requirements of rationality in the more regimented sense of 'rationality'.

The contention in this chapter is that disagreement between epistemic peers does not clearly have an influence on what an agent is rationally required to believe, or on which collections of beliefs he is rationally required to have. This is so mainly on account of two considerations. The first is that evidence of evidence of p can be evidence against p. A natural belief to form on account of peer disagreement that is that the disagreement constitutes evidence that there is evidence for the contrary of one's belief. Because this does not entail that there is evidence for the contrary of one's belief, or that there is some other sort of evidence against one's belief, there is no direct rational upshot for one's first order belief.

---

[38] You are rationally required that if you believe that your total evidence supports proposition *p* to degree *d*, then you believe *p*.

The second consideration is that rational requirements govern mental states. Whatever the evidential situation is when there is peer disagreement, it only has a bearing on one's rational requirements when there is a relevant belief associated with it. There mere fact that there is disagreement is not relevant to one's rational requirement. That one believes that there is disagreement could in principle be important. The difficulty is in explaining how.

I have suggested that the belief that there is actual peer disagreement may play a role in determining what rationality requires of us, when we also believe that peer disagreement about a particular proposition is improbable. However, it remains to be seen whether this is really so. One would need to accept an internalist theory of evidence and to defend both something like belief enkrasia and also a principle linking uncertainty about the state of one's evidence for p with beliefs about the sufficiency of one's evidence for p. I have not attempted either task in this paper. Until they are both discharged, it remains unclear as to whether there is any rational upshot to believing that there is actual peer disagreement. [39]

References

Ballantyne, N. and Coffmann, E. J. (2011). Uniqueness, Evidence, and Rationality. *Philosophers' Imprint* 11: 1–13
Boghossian, P. (2012). What Is Inference? *Philosophical Studies* 169: 1–18.
Broome, J. (1999). Normative Requirements. *Ratio* 12: 398–419.
Broome, J. (2013). *Rationality through Reasoning*. London: Wiley Blackwell.
Brunero, J. (2013a). Reasons as Explanations. *Philosophical Studies* 165: 805–824.
Brunero, J. (2013b). Rational Akrasia. *Organon F* 4: 546–566.
Cherniak, C. (1986). *Minimal Rationality*. Cambridge: MIT Press.
Christensen, D. (2010). Higher-Order Evidence. *Philosophy and Phenomenological Research* 81: 185–215.
Dancy, J. (2002). *Practical Reality*. Oxford: Oxford University Press.
de Ridder, J. (2014). Why Only Externalists Can Be Steadfast. *Erkenntnis* 79: 185–199.
Fitelson, B. (2012). Why Evidence of Evidence Is not (Necessarily) Evidence. *Analysis* 72: 85–88.
Gunnarsson, L. (2000). *Making Moral Sense: Beyond Habermas and Gauthier*. Cambridge: Cambridge University Press.
Harman, G. (1986). *Change in View*. Cambridge: MIT Press.

---

[39] I would like to thank Stewart Cohen for sparking my interest in peer disagreement over the course of several conversations about the subject. And I would especially like to thank Michele Palmira, who patiently discussed many of the topics in this chapter with me and provided invaluable comments on an earlier draft.

Harman, G. (1984). Logic and Reasoning. *Synthese* 60: 107–127.
Kearns, S. and Star, D. (2009). Reasons as Evidence. *Oxford Studies in Metaethics* 4: 215–242.
Kelly, T. (2010). Peer Disagreement and Higher Order Evidence. In A.I. Goldman and D. Whitcomb (eds.), *Social Epistemology: Essential Readings*. Oxford: Oxford University Press.
Kolodny, N. (2005). Why Be Rational? *Mind* 114: 509–563.
MacFarlane, J. (2014). *Assessment Sensitivity: Relative Truth and its Applications*. Oxford: Oxford University Press.
Parfit, D. (2001). Reasons and Rationality. In D. Egonsson, J. Josefsson, B. Petersson, and T. Rønnow-Rasmussen (eds.), *Exploring Practical Rationality*. Aldershot: Ashgate.
Reisner, A. (2004). *Conflicts of Normativity*. DPhil Thesis. University of Oxford.
Reisner, A. (2009). The Possibility of Pragmatic Reasons for Belief and the Wrong Kind of Reasons Problem. *Philosophical Studies* 145: 157–172.
Reisner, A. (2014). A Short Refutation of Strict Normative Evidentialism. *Inquiry* 5: 1–9.
Reisner, A. (2013). Is the Enkratic Principle a Requirement of Rationality? *Organon F* 20: 436–462.
Reisner, A. & Steglich-Petereson, A. (2011). Introduction. In A. Reisner and A. Steglich-Petersen (eds.), *Reasons for Belief*. Cambridge: Cambridge University Press.
Shackel, N. (Manuscript). Two Kinds of Normativity.
Skorupski, J. (2011). *The Domain of Reasons*. Oxford: Oxford University Press.
Tomayko, J. E. (1988). The History of Computers in Spaceflight: The NASA Experience. NASA Contractor Report 182505. Available at http://history.nasa.gov/computers/Compspace.html.
Wedgwood, R. (2003). Choosing Rationally and Choosing Correctly. In S. Stroud and C. Tappolet (eds.), *Weakness of Will and Practical Irrationality*. Oxford: Oxford University Press.
Williamson, T. (2000). *Knowledge and its Limits*. Oxford: Oxford University Press.
White, R. (2005). Epistemic Permissiveness. *Philosophical Perspectives* 19: 445–459.
Worsnip, A. (Manuscript). The Conflict of Evidence and Coherence.

II Epistemic Norms

Nicholas Unwin
Belief, Truth and Radical Disagreement

1. Introduction

It is now widely accepted that belief is an essentially normative concept, but there is considerable dispute as to the details. In particular, it is widely held that beliefs aim at truth, but there is no consensus as to what 'aiming at truth' is supposed to mean. Thus it may be thought that beliefs have a kind of inbuilt function of truth-directedness. Alternatively, it may be thought that it is not so much beliefs as believers that need examining. There are also many related issues. For example, belief is often contrasted with allied notions such as acceptance, and there is a lively debate in the philosophy of science as to whether theoretical claims are suitable subjects for belief as opposed to mere acceptance, as is whether a viable distinction can be drawn between the theoretical and the non-theoretical. Also, there is the question of why belief is involuntary in a way in which acceptance is not, and how it is possible for there to be a divergence here. It will be argued that, underlying all these issues is a more general sceptical worry about how to handle the possibility of radical disagreement. The challenge here is whether it is appropriate to have any genuine beliefs at all, as opposed to weaker states such as acceptances, or acceptances which have been amplified in various ways. This question is shown to have profound metaphysical consequences.

2. Motivations for Scepticism

The chief motivation for scepticism that is relevant here concerns the underdetermination of theories by data. I shall not attempt to justify this principle here in any detail, but merely to outline a few essential points.[1] Firstly, we are creatures with two-dimensional boundaries that inhabit a three-dimensional world. It follows, from basic geometrical considerations, that a huge amount of information is lost when the world impinges on our sensory surfaces. There are many different ways that the world could be and yet still yield the same perceptual cues that we actually have. We do not worry about this in practice be-

---

[1] A fuller defence of underdetermination and its sceptical consequences can be found in Unwin 2007, chapter 2.

cause the alternative theories of the world are either minor variations on the original, or else too bizarre to be psychologically available to us. For example, we do not take seriously the theory that physical objects go out of existence when not perceived, since it lacks a good many desirable heuristic features, such as simplicity, fecundity and so on. The problem remains, however, that there could be alien creatures psychologically very different from ourselves—Martians, 'grue-users' and so forth—for whom these alternative theories are more appropriate.[2] Such alternative theories, although bizarre, are internally consistent and empirically adequate, so these aliens can claim as well as we can that they have both reason and experience on their side. Given that reason and experience are our only sources of knowledge, this seems to lead to a massive scepticism.

How much should we worry about this? It may be thought that we should not be concerned at all. If these alternative theories are simply unbelievable for us, then they can present no significant challenge to our ordinary beliefs. We should therefore carry on believing what we do. And why, it may be asked, should we care about what Martians and grue-users think in the first place? There is much to be said for this view, and we should not expect our ordinary intellectual practices to be overly influenced by such exotica. But are we entitled to actually *believe* our theory of the world, bearing in mind that there are alternative states, such as acceptance, which might be more appropriate here? Some, notably Bas van Fraassen (1980), insist that, in order for a scientific theory to be acceptable, it is sufficient that it be empirically adequate, that is to say, consistent with all actual and possible experimental evidence. Should a theory be shown to be adequate in this way, then we have fulfilled our epistemic duty. We do not need to show, in addition, that our preferred theory is actually *true*, and we are, in any event, unable to do this. This is not to say that any empirically adequate theory is acceptable, for there are important heuristic constraints, notably simplicity, which will limit our choices. But there is no reason for thinking that simpler theories are more likely to be true than more complex ones. This is not to deny that it is rational to *prefer* simpler theories over more complex ones, for it is always rational to avoid unnecessary hard work. But this is a maxim of practical reason, and has nothing to do with truth. Martians and grue-users may have quite different views from us as to which of two theories is the simpler, if only because the question of whether one theory is simpler than another depends largely on what is regarded as conceptually basic, and grue-users will dif-

---

2 Nelson Goodman's (1983) (in)famous concept of *grue* may be too absurdly artificial to be usable even by an alien intelligence. But I shall treat the term 'grue' simply as a place-holder for any exotic concept that is so usable.

fer from us in this respect. Moreover, there is no neutral vantage point from which such disagreements can be assessed. The upshot seems to be that actual *belief* in our theory of the world is inappropriate. This is van Fraassen's 'constructive empiricism', to be contrasted with scientific realism (about which, more later).

Van Fraassen's scepticism extends only to scientific theories themselves, and not to the observations that support or confute them. However, there are familiar reasons for doubting whether a sharp distinction can be drawn between theoretical and observational sentences. When Quine (1960), for example, talks about our world view, or our theory of the world, he is not talking about a scientific 'theory' in the ordinary sense of the word, such as the theory of gravitation or the theory of evolution, but rather our total belief-system, a system which is seriously underdetermined by the surface irritations that constitute our perceptual cues. A thoroughly holistic model is defended, one which dispenses with the traditional theory/observation distinction, and such a view is quite plausible. It seems to follow, therefore, that the sort of scepticism being defended here has a much wider application, namely all of our empirical beliefs, not just our narrowly theoretical ones.

Of course, it must also be shown that we can make sense of this sort of alien cognition, and need, at some point, to say more about the 'Martians' and 'grue-users', as I call them. But not too much needs to be said at this stage. We shall see that all that is required is that such alien beings are a logical possibility, a very weak requirement. We do not need to show that there really are such beings, or even that they are biologically (as opposed to logically) possible. We do not even need to show how such possible beings could ever be identified as such (though it would certainly improve the overall credibility of the position I am defending if we could show how an alien language could be interpreted as yielding assent to sentences which genuinely contradict those to which we assent).[3] On the contrary, it does not even matter all that much if the actual existence of aliens is an entirely unverifiable hypothesis. Rather, mere logical possibility will be shown to be enough, and this is a *prima facie* plausible requirement if only because it seems very far-fetched to suppose that it is *logically* necessary that there is only a human form of advanced intelligence. Given this (mere) logical possibility, radical disagreement enters the debate, and with it a serious threat to the legitimacy of all empirical beliefs.

---

3 See Unwin 2007, chapter 3, for an account of how such interpretation might work.

3. Norms of Belief

But what is it specifically about *belief*, as opposed to weaker attitudes such as acceptance, that causes the problem? Evidently, it is because beliefs have a very special relationship with truth, one which acceptances (perhaps) do not have. But what is this relationship? Bernard Williams, who was, I think, the first to use the phrase 'beliefs aim at truth' (in his seminal paper, 'Deciding to Believe'), says that to believe something is specifically to believe that it is *true:* this is (part of) what is actually constitutive of belief.[4] But this cannot explain what it is for beliefs to aim at truth. As David Velleman (2000, 245) points out, it is equally the case that to consider a proposition is to consider whether it is *true*, even though consideration, in this sense, does not aim at truth (there is no harm in merely *considering* false propositions, and it can on occasion be thoroughly desirable to do so). We might add likewise that to accept a proposition is to accept that it is *true*, to imagine that p is to imagine that <p> is *true*, to wish that p is to wish that <p> is *true*, and so on. The point, simply, is that 'p' and '<p> is true' express logically equivalent propositions (this is the 'Equivalence Schema' (ES), which is generally accepted), and regardless of what attitude we have towards them; so adding 'is true' in this manner fails to make the kind of difference needed—even if we utter the word 'true' in a peculiarly emphatic sort of way. It does not distinguish one sort of propositional attitude from another, as is required.

What we appear to need, rather, is a truth norm for belief, that is to say, a principle along the lines of

(TN_1) It is permissible to believe that p, only if <p> is true

Given (ES), this can be rephrased more economically *as*

(TN_2) It is permissible to believe that p, only if p

Analogous principles, where 'believe' is replaced by 'consider', 'imagine', 'accept' (perhaps), 'wish', and so on, are, by contrast, not true. But notice that we get an immediate dire consequence, namely what I shall call the 'Unrestricted Universality Principle'

---

[4] Williams 1973, 136–51.

(UUP) If it is permissible for S_1 to believe that *p*, then it is not permissible for S_2 to believe that not-*p*

Given that the (TN) principles are meant to be *analytic* truths, something constitutive of the meaning of 'believe', it follows that (UUP) is also an analytic truth. There can therefore be no restriction as to the nature of the believers S1 and S2; so there is no reason why S1 should not be a Martian or grue-user, and S2 you or me. It is enough that it be analytically possible for subjects such as S1 to exist, and we argued in the previous section that it is so possible. But if S1 and S2 are directed towards mutually inconsistent theories of the world, then this causes havoc. If, for example, it is rational for S1 to believe that emeralds will stay grue after midnight, then it cannot be rational for us to believe (as we do) that emeralds will not stay grue after midnight. Yet it is rational for S_1 to go for alien theories, so it follows that we are not entitled to believe the opposite non-alien theory: we might be allowed to 'go for it', in some weaker sense, but we cannot *believe* it, given the symmetry between S_1 and S_2 (why should only one of them be entitled to have genuine beliefs?). Generalizing this, we see that genuine beliefs are rendered unwarranted across the board.

This is an extreme form of scepticism, much stronger than the Cartesian variety, which concerns only the possibility of knowledge (about which we have said nothing), but which does not forbid belief. It is even stronger than the Pyrrhonian variety which only forbids beliefs about the reality of things, and does not forbid us to make 'avowals', or *apangeliai*, which in this context mean something like the expressions of subjective states. Thus my scepticism not only forbids me to believe that honey is sweet in itself (for example); it also forbids me to believe, *pace* Sextus Empiricus, that honey tastes sweet to me, for an alien theory of the world might have an alternative view about my psychology. Moreover, what is distinctive and original about this scepticism is that it does not stem primarily from an argument about the poverty of our *justifications* or epistemic capabilities. It is simply the nature of belief itself that makes it a self-forbidding state (together with some ancillary claims about the logical possibility of alien intelligences). Of course, in another respect it is much weaker than either Cartesian or Pyrrhonian scepticism, since we hold out for the possibility of something slightly more noncommittal than belief which satisfies most of our epistemological needs, and which is something to which we are entitled; but it is still a highly unsettling conclusion.

So what, if anything, has gone wrong? It would seem that it must be the (TN) principles that give rise to the problem, so maybe we need an alternative kind of normative constraint on belief. How would this work? The way forward, I think, is to examine more carefully the notion of *aiming* at something, and focus not so much on beliefs as believers. This makes some sense if only because it is unclear how beliefs themselves, or indeed any psychological states, can have 'aims'. We know what it is for a person to aim at some outcome, but to treat that person's mental states as having some sort of intrinsic function or Aristotelian *ergon* is mysterious, unless it is just an alternative way of talking about the person's aims. Thus instead of asking what it is for a belief to aim at truth, we ask what it is for a person to aim at truth; and instead of asking what is involved in saying that beliefs 'ought' to be true, we ask what is involved in saying that a believer *qua* believer ought to think only what is true.

To see why this strategy leads to dividends, notice that the notion of *aiming* has both intensional and extensional senses, to invoke an important mediæval distinction. Thus suppose that, with J.L. Austin, I point my gun at your donkey thinking that it is mine. Am I 'aiming' to shoot your donkey or mine? Mine, I think, even though it is your donkey that I am aiming to shoot. This is potentially confusing, but the matter can be resolved by invoking the intensional/extensional distinction: it is my donkey that I am intensionally aiming at, but your donkey that I am extensionally aiming at. Now, it may seem as though the (TN) principles say nothing more than that we should all adopt the maxim, 'Believe only what is true'. However, this is to ignore the subtle difference between the intensional 'We should aim for believing only what is true' and the extensional 'Only if something is true should we aim to believe it'. More formally, we have the distinction between:

(ITN) We should aim that (we believe that p only if <p> is true)
and
(ETN) (We should *aim* that we believe that p) only if <p> is true.

(ETN) reads the aim extensionally: the object of the aim, namely the truth of <p>, is referred to outside the intensional context yielded by 'We should aim that ...'. However (ITN), the intensional reading, is significantly weaker. Crucially, it does not imply (UUP). This is because we can extend (ITN) to Martians without demanding their agreement (more accurately, their non-disagreement) with us. The sentence 'We believe only the truth' is one that everyone, including Martians, should want to be realized. However, this does not mean, concerning the truth, that everyone, including Martians, want to believe only it; which is to read the aim extensionally.

This is a subtle point, but it provides us with a way forward. It suggests a (possibly revisionary) conception of belief which is now apparently free of its viciously sceptical implications. Both the Martians and we are entitled to our (incompatible) 'beliefs', but we are not neglecting the fact that 'believers' should aim at truth—albeit only in an intensional sense. But can we really dispense with principles such as (TN$_2$)? (UUP), which follows immediately from it, may have undesirable consequences, but it looks plausible all the same. It seems very strange for us to say that the aliens believe what they ought to believe if what they believe is (according to us) false. Possibly we can diminish the strangeness by appealing to justificatory norms as well as purely alethic ones, and say that the aliens are right according to the former but not the latter. This is to take into account the fact that, thanks to our different psychologies and methods of theory-construction, what is justified for us need not be justified for aliens, and vice versa. But if we go down this road, it becomes more plausible to say that the aliens really are breaching the alethic norms (though not the justificatory norms), as is prescribed by (ETN), which suggests that (ETN) is genuinely constitutive of our ordinary conception of belief after all.

We should also remember that it is not only beliefs that are expected to be truth-directed, but also the intellectual practices that generate them. If our cognitive methodologies—our research programmes and so forth—fail to lead to increasing verisimilitude, then we naturally feel that they must be seriously defective. Moreover, it should make no difference whether we are talking about humans, Martians or anyone else. It is also clear that if the beliefs generated by two such methodologies A and B were to diverge—not just every now and then, but massively and even when taken to their respective ideal limits (in something like Peirce's sense)—then A and B cannot both lead to increasing verisimilitude (there cannot be incompatible truths), and therefore cannot both be said to be 'truth-directed'—in an extensional, and yet quite ordinary, defensible sense. So if we were to relax the constraint that they ought to be so directed, as we are apparently saying, then we are evidently claiming something very radical. In particular, we are denying that truth *per se* has the kind of intrinsic normative pull usually attributed to it.

My position is that it is indeed constitutive of our ordinary concept of belief that it satisfy (ETN) as well as (ITN), and that we should therefore abandon all our empirical beliefs. However, this should immediately be qualified by insisting that we adopt instead a modified concept of belief, one which satisfies only (ITN) though not (ETN), and which implies only a restricted universality principle (RUP), which demands non-disagreement only from creatures cognitively similar to ourselves. So modified, our 'beliefs' (for want of a better name) are now mostly justified: at least, we no longer face the earlier argument that says otherwise. Justification is regained by making some concessions, but not in the conventional idealist or anti-realist manner, whereby the *contents* of our cognitive states are reduced, either by prefixing them with (something like) 'It appears to us as if __' or by introducing an anti-realist semantics. On my view, by contrast, it is not content but the attitude towards it that is reduced. We shall later see that this has metaphysical as well as epistemological advantages. For the moment, it is sufficient to note that the actual change in our ordinary intellectual practices required by this sort of attitude-reduction is fairly minimal, if only because we are seldom actually confronted by Martians or grue-users; so my position is not as extreme as it might initially seem.

4. Belief and Acceptance

It still needs to be shown, however, that our concept of belief can be so modified, and that a viable alternative can be created. I have already discussed in §2 van Fraassen's view that scientific theories need only be accepted rather than believed. But van Fraassen himself says surprisingly little about what the concept of acceptance really is, and how it is supposed to differ from belief. However, others, notably Michael Bratman, have explored the matter further. He writes:

> Belief has four characteristic features: (a) it is ... context-independent; (b) it aims at the truth of what is believed; (c) it is not normally in our direct voluntary control; and (d) it is subject to an ideal of agglomeration. In contrast, what one accepts/takes for granted (a) can reasonably vary ... across contexts; (b) can be influenced by practical considerations that are not themselves evidence for the truth of what is accepted; (c) can be subject to our direct voluntary control; and (d) is not subject to the same ideal of agglomeration across contexts. So acceptance in a context is not belief.[5]

The fourth criterion is closely related to the first if only because contexts tend to be individuated precisely according to whether agglomeration is possible. We have already talked about the second criterion, and shall say something about the third in the next section. What about the first? It seems true that what we merely accept can vary across contexts, even if we are talking about scientific theories. Notoriously, quantum mechanics (QM) and the general theory of relativity (GTR) do not mix, and indeed seem to be mutually inconsistent. Yet we are happy to accept QM (but not GTR) in some contexts, and vice versa. This seems quite consistent with our ordinary scientific practices (and it works); and although it is not entirely satisfactory (we usually suppose that the inconsistency here will need, at some stage, to be resolved), we do not have the imme-

---

5 Bratman 1991, 9. Jonathan Cohen 1992 defends the distinction as well, and in even more detail, though in a slightly different way.

diate problem that we would have if these theories were to be believed and not merely accepted.

Does this point underlie van Fraassen's preference for acceptance over belief? Oddly enough, not. His view, it will be recalled, is that our epistemic duty will be fulfilled if, but only if, we show that our theory is empirically adequate: which means, on van Fraassen's definition, that it is consistent with *all* (actual and possible) observations. So defined, it follows that empirical adequacy cannot be relativized into contexts, any more than truth can. He thus does not allow theories to be context-dependent, which is strange since they would still 'save the phenomena' even if they were so contextualized, and this is all that is supposed to matter.

This gives us a worry about whether van Fraassen's conception of acceptance is sufficiently different from belief to yield the desired results. Indeed, more urgently, there are many who doubt whether belief and acceptance differ at all.[6] But there are good grounds for thinking that we have a distinction here. After all, when we ask 'What are scientists doing when they accept T in context C?', we answer by appealing to which equations they actually *use*, which assumptions they *adopt*, which measurements they *choose* to make, which alternatives they *select*, and so forth. These italicized terms, which are central to the notion of acceptance, may be explicated without mention of belief, if only because they have a much wider range of application (we may use, adopt, choose and select all sorts of things, not all of which have propositional content). Moreover, the mere fact that we can accept a theory in only some contexts and not others is sufficient to show that we are dealing with an attitude that is significantly weaker than that of belief.

Nevertheless, it is plainly too weak to count as the revised notion of belief that we are looking for, since such a contextualizable notion will not satisfy (ITN) or (RUP). What we need to do is to strengthen acceptance in such a way that it yields our desired notion. In particular, we want it to be context-independent, involuntary—and also truth-directed, but only in a weaker sense than full-blown belief. Is this possible?

It ought to be possible, even if this amplified acceptance resembles belief rather more than original acceptance, according to Bratman's four criteria. For example, although the truth-aiming criterion entails the non-contextualism criterion (we cannot relativize truth into contexts if it is to satisfy (ES)), the converse does not seem to hold. For suppose we define a new notion, 'accept*' as follows:

---

6 See, for example, Horwich 1991.

(A*) S accepts* that p $=_{df}$ S accepts that p in all *contexts*

If acceptance* turns out to be the same as belief, *then* the truth-norm schema

(TN) We may φ that p, only if <p> is *true*

must hold when we substitute 'accept*' for 'φ', but not when we substitute 'accept'. Since the only difference between these attitudes comes from A*, there must somehow be an inference from A* to the substituted (TN) (perhaps with some innocuous background premises added). It is hard to see what could underlie such an inference, enthymematic or otherwise, since the premise and the conclusion look wholly unrelated. It seems to follow that acceptance* falls some way short of full belief, as is required. It may aim at empirical adequacy, but it does not aim at truth in the original sense.

5. Voluntariness

This leaves us with the issue of voluntariness, the fact that we can (usually) choose what to accept (and also what to accept*), but cannot choose what to believe. Do we want our revised notion of belief also to be involuntary? To determine this, we need to examine why full beliefs are required to be involuntary, and in what sense.

The *locus classicus* of this investigation is, again, Williams's paper, 'Deciding to Believe'. He argues that voluntary belief is a conceptual impossibility, that is to say, rests on more than just a contingent fact, such as the fact that I am unable to blush at will. Moreover, it is precisely the fact that beliefs aim at truth which demonstrates this:

> If I could acquire a belief at will, I could acquire it whether it was true or not; moreover I would know that I could acquire it whether it was true or not. If in full consciousness I could will to acquire a 'belief' irrespective of its truth, it is unclear that before the event I could seriously think of it as a belief, i.e. as something purporting to represent reality. At the very least, there must be a restriction on what is the case after the event; since I could not then, in full consciousness, regard this as a belief of mine, i.e. something I take to be true, and also know that I acquired it at will. With regard to no belief could I know—or, if all this is to be done in full consciousness, even suspect—that I had acquired it at will. But if I can acquire beliefs at will, I must know that I am able to do this; and could

I know that I was capable of this feat, if with regard to every feat of this kind which I had performed I necessarily had to believe that it had not taken place?[7]

As Williams goes on to say, we may quibble about the details, for I could come to acquire a belief by devious means, for example by voluntarily undergoing hypnosis, or brain-washing or some such thing (though even this is hard to maintain if I remember that this is how the belief was acquired). But what does seem to be the case is the fact that I cannot acquire a belief 'just like that', as we say, i.e. in the same immediate sort of way as I can just raise my arm.[8]

But is it just the fact that beliefs aim at truth that secures this result, and if so, in what sense of 'aiming at truth' are we to be concerned with here? This is where the earlier point about the difference between beliefs aiming at truth and believers aiming at truth comes back into play. Thus, it is often said that beliefs have a world-to-mind 'direction of fit', meaning that if there is a mismatch between belief and world, then the mistake is in the belief, not the world. This contrasts with the case of desires, which have a mind-to-world direction of fit. This is often thought to imply some kind of intrinsic functional capacity of beliefs, a capacity with essentially normative implications, and therefore relevant to our primary concern, namely what it is for beliefs to aim at truth. However, the risk of treating this sort of fact as explanatory of why belief is involuntary is precisely the fact that it hinges on normativeness, on the way that beliefs *ought* to be. This makes it sound as if voluntary belief just involves some kind of normative failure, but this is not so. The whole point is that believing at will is not merely normatively forbidden, an epistemically vicious activity to be ruled out by good cognitive behaviour. It is, rather, just downright *impossible*! Talk of directions of fit does not explain this. There is also the related point, raised by Paul Noordhof, that any system, no matter how well designed, can always malfunction, and we need to explain why even a malfunctioning person cannot believe at will.[9] Beliefs do not aim at truth in the same sort of way as the eye aims at vision, or even as perceptions aim at representing the environment, and the notion of a biological function (or malfunction), or of an Aristotelian *ergon*, cannot usefully be

---

7 Williams 1973, 148.
8 However, Jonathan Bennett (1990) argues that Williams's argument fails to make adequate use of this distinction between mediate and immediate volition, and so, if sound, would prove far more than it should. *Ergo*, it is not sound. Many others have entered the debate.
9 Noordhof 2001, 249. His own view is that we are just psychologically unable to believe what we see to be false. However, although that may be true of what is right in front of us, relatively few of our beliefs are of this type.

cited in order to explain the truth-directedness of belief. In short, talk about the functional properties of belief-states does not get us very far.

If we focus instead on believers, rather than belief-states, however, matters improve. Williams's basic point is that if a person manipulates her judgement whether p at will and is conscious of so doing, and also knows that the truth or falsity of <p> is independent of her will, then she is plainly not interested in whether her judgement that p is true or not. In short, she is ignoring the truth-norms with respect to <p>. Therefore, her attitude here, whatever else it may be, is not one of belief. So understood, the matter is very straightforward. Clearly, it is now the aims of the believer that are paramount in the discussion, and it is here that a more useful discussion of the truth-directedness of belief is to be found.

However, our primary concern is to reform the concept of belief, and this requires us to add to our conception of acceptance* (i.e. acceptance in all contexts) an involuntariness condition without its collapsing into full-blown belief as originally understood. What we therefore need to do now is to investigate not whether there could be voluntary belief, but rather its converse, whether there could be involuntary acceptance. Bratman suggests not, but this is *prima facie* implausible, even if most acceptances are voluntary. After all, suppose that we continue my earlier strategy and define a new attitude 'acceptance**' as follows:

(A**) S accepts** that p $=_{df}$ S involuntarily *accepts** that p

Must 'accept**', so understood, be substitutable for 'φ' in the truth-norm schema

(TN) We may ϕ that p, only if <p> is *true*

even though neither 'accept' nor 'accept*' is? If so, we must ask *once* again what could underlie the inference, enthymematic or otherwise, from (A**) to (TN), so substituted. And if the inference is rejected, then it evidently follows that acceptance** is not the same as belief, as is required.

The idea may still seem odd, but it makes sense when we remember that my starting point is a generalization of van Fraassen's constructive empiricism, one which extends it from narrowly theoretical claims to all of science. My position is that there is no sharp distinction to be drawn between theoretical and observational sentences, and that at best we have here a continuum with degrees of theoreticity, where even sentences standardly described as 'observational' are theory-laden to some extent. Now, I may be able to decide voluntarily which theory (as ordinarily understood) to go for, but I cannot voluntarily influence what I observe (I can decide what to look at, of course, but cannot decide what I see when I do so). If I see a tree in the quad, then I have no relevant choice but to do so, even though the observational sentence 'I see a tree in the quad' is theory-laden in so far as it implies that the tree I see would still exist even if I were not to look at it (the latter claim goes beyond what I 'observe' in the strictest sense, as the classical empiricists have stressed). This is why we have a sceptical problem about the external world, one which is reinforced when we remember that Martians and grue-users might not rationally be bound to make the same inferences. Given (UUP), this means that we are not entitled to *believe* in the external world in the ordinary sense, but it is still perfectly rational to *accept* its existence. Yet this is something that we are forced to do by our very natures: it is just psychologically impossible for us to adopt an alternative claim. Does this rule out acceptance as such since acceptances are (it is alleged) necessarily voluntary? It does not seem so, so it seems to follow that acceptance** is a legitimate state in its own right, and is not the same as full belief.

It may be protested that it is not just psychologically impossible for us not to *accept* such claims: it is equally impossible for us not to *believe* them, in the full sense of 'believe', and this undermines my whole picture of what is rational for us to claim. It may be that such belief is unwarranted but it is unavoidable all the same, it may be insisted. Now, the philosopher who we most associate with the view that sceptical scenarios are simply unbelievable even if they are rationally required is, of course, Hume. In his conclusion to Book I of the *Treatise*, he agonizes over the dilemmas forced on his mind by the conflict between Reason and Nature. His deeply pessimistic conclusion is that we survive these problems simply because Reason has only minimal influence in our lives: intellectual effort is powerless to override such forces as carelessness, inattention and backgammon. Yet he, like most other people, does not consider the possibility of attitude-reduction, of weakening the notion of belief in such a way that it becomes consistent with both Reason and Nature. It may be feared that he was right to do so, and that my whole position is psychologically impossible either to accept or to believe—and in every sense. But this is too hasty. It is an unfamiliar position, and we have not yet tried to adopt it, or even to consider it. And it should be remembered that the changes required here are not that drastic.

But how can we amplify acceptance** so that the resulting attitude satisfies (ITN) and (RUP), and in such a way that it does not collapse into full-blown belief? Our earlier strategy which led us from acceptance to acceptance*, and thence to acceptance**, will not obviously work here, since norms cannot just be 'bolted on' in the sort of way that the other conditions can. The solution, I think, is to focus on extensional aiming, in the first instance. We do not want our revised beliefs to aim extensionally at truth, for reasons already explained, but what then should they extensionally aim at? I suggest *pragmatically conditioned empirical adequacy*. The pragmatic conditions (simplicity and so forth) limit the alternatives to what is psychologically available to us, and we agree with van Fraassen that they are not themselves truth-directed: they primarily concern our own contingent psychology, not the nature of the world outside, which is why (ETN) fails to apply to such states. Ostensibly, truth no longer enters into the matter even though such a revised attitude is eminently achievable given the credibility of constructive empiricism. But how can we aim extensionally instead at pragmatically conditioned empirical adequacy, as I require? I suggest that it is simply: *by intensionally aiming at truth*. This is just what we should actually *do*. There is no other way that is psychologically available to us of getting at empirical adequacy, at least at the more observational end of the continuum, which is where our interests primarily lie. The same is true of the aliens. Thus there is no need to prefix our target sentences by 'It is empirically adequate that__', or 'Our best theory of the world implies that __', or some such thing, when we investigate the world. The relevant constraints are already built into the attitudes themselves. And conversely, there is nothing other than pragmatically conditioned empirical adequacy that we are going in fact to end up with if we aim intensionally at truth. Of course, we might also end up aiming extensionally at truth as well, but that is just a matter of fortune which is not required by our legitimate cognitive practices. Nor should we want it to be otherwise.

My position rests heavily on the question of what is psychologically available to us, and it might be feared that this will undermine Williams's argument, which I endorse, that beliefs are involuntary as a matter of simple conceptual necessity. Specifically, it might be feared that it will turn out instead that it is no more than a deep psychological fact that we cannot simply choose what to believe, especially if 'belief' is modified in the way recommended, a result with various dire consequences (perhaps). But this is not so. For imagine that I was able, through some strenuous act of will, to entertain some proposition which I had hitherto believed to be false. What could make us suppose that my new attitude towards it is one of belief, in my revised sense? The argument discussed earlier to show that (original) belief cannot be the attitude in question only concerned what the subject intensionally aims at, so the same point ought to apply to my revised conception of belief. Such revised beliefs remain involuntary, and for the same immediate sort of reason. It ought nevertheless to be possible for us to relinquish all our genuine beliefs in favour of revised beliefs, as we demand, to address a slightly different objection, for it is not required that such relinquishing be due to bare acts of will: rather, it is required to be in response to argument; so Williams's objection does not apply here.

6. Some Metaphysical Consequences

My position has important metaphysical as well as epistemological implications, particularly concerning the question of whether reality is mind-independent. To see why, we need to look not only at van Fraassen's constructive empiricism (again), but also at some of its alternatives.

The terms 'realism' and 'anti-realism' are often used in this context, but as David Papineau (1996, 2–6), for example, has pointed out, such terms can be used in almost exactly opposite senses in the philosophy of science. Originally, the notion of anti-realism was used in Michael Dummett's sense, and was contrasted with a Platonist conception of the world, or of some portion of the world, that is completely independent of the mind.[10] It is in this sort of sense that Frege was a 'realist' about arithmetic and Berkeley an 'anti-realist' about physical objects: arithmetical truths were claimed by Frege (unlike Dummett) to hold quite independently of thought, language or any other human institution; whereas Berkeley (unlike Locke) held that the physical world is essentially dependent on our perception of it. In this same sense, van Fraassen's constructive empiricism is also robustly realist, as it holds that the world of theoretical entities, although unknowable, is definitely 'out there', and is entirely independent of the human mind.

But in a more recent sense, van Fraassen's position is described as (paradigmatically) 'anti-realist', since theoretical truth is not what is aimed at. Likewise, some scientific 'realists', in this new sense, are anti-realists in Dummett's sense. For example, Hilary Putnam (1981) and Brian Ellis (1988) talk of 'internal realism'. This view reforms our ordinary conception of truth, and maintains that theoretical claims thereby become knowable and that their truth is what we should aim to discover; but that truth, when properly understood, is shaped by how we cognize it (this is largely how scientific knowledge becomes possible). Likewise pragmatists such as Peirce define truth itself in terms of the ideal limit of inquiry, and this forms a crucial part of his defence of the (in my view, over-optimistic) claim that our inquiries are bound to aim (extensionally) at truth: that is to say, that we really do get closer to the truth as our inquiries progress, and as a matter of necessity.

All this is potentially confusing, but the basic problem is quite old. It was Kant who first insisted that the notion of realism is ambiguous, namely between 'empirical' and 'transcendental' senses; and further that 'realism' in the first sense becomes defensible only if we abandon 'realism' in the second sense.

---

10 See, for example, Dummett 1978.

We thus have a trade-off; and this, again, is how empirical knowledge becomes possible. I shall say more about the metaphysical implications of transcendental idealism shortly, but firstly will investigate further some aspects of internal realism.

Putnam writes:

> 'Truth', in an internalist view, is some sort of (idealized) rational acceptability—some sort of ideal coherence of our beliefs with each other and with our experiences *as those experiences are themselves represented in our belief system*—and not correspondence with mind-independent or discourse-independent 'states of affairs'.[11]

Immediately afterwards, he writes:

> There is no God's Eye point of view that we can know or usefully imagine; there are only the various points of view of actual persons reflecting various interests and purposes that their descriptions and theories subserve.

He evidently believes that these two theses go together. My position, however, is that his first thesis is wrong, but that his second thesis is right; and moreover, that holding the second thesis, when appropriately understood and defended, is exactly what obviates the need for us to hold the first.

Do we ordinarily think that there is a God's Eye point of view, and that we can attain it? It is not immediately obvious what is at stake here, but if we allow for the possibility of alternative lines of inquiry, for example, those adopted by Martians and grue-users, then we can see why such a point of view becomes unattainable in at least one, fairly straightforward sense. The point is that we cannot tell, from a neutral perspective, which line of inquiry is (extensionally) pointing in the right direction. We have one theory of the world, the aliens have another, and there is no accessible unbiased vantage-point from which they can be compared. Of course, we can, and should, still 'assert', in some sense, that it is our theory, not theirs, that is true, but only if our concept of assertion is modified in a parallel way to the way in which our ordinary concept of belief needs to be modified. This modification ensures that our 'assertions' are not made *ex cathedra*. This enables us to continue with our ordinary inquiries, albeit with a subtle adjustment. This is not to rule out a God's Eye point of view as such —perhaps God has one—but our whole strategy is geared towards making it unnecessary (as well as undesirable) for *us* to attempt to adopt one, which is what really matters here.

---

[11] Putnam 1981, 49–50 (original emphasis).

Notice, however, that I am not required to manipulate the notion of truth itself. My view is that truth is a fairly minimal notion. It satisfies (ES), and therefore involves correspondence to reality in a fairly basic, uncontentious sort of way, but should not be strengthened by introducing epistemic constraints of any kind. Such constraints are better put elsewhere, notably within the notion of assertoric force and the revised conception of belief that goes with it. Is my view preferable to that of the internal realists when it comes to explaining what is meant by a 'God's Eye point of view?' I think so. An Olympian standpoint (or God's Eye point of view, if you prefer) involves commitment to a kind of universal legislation. It involves supposing it to be superior to other standpoints, to be one over which *all* other standpoints should be preferred in the final analysis. Now, this sort of universal legislation is precisely what the unrestricted universality principle (UUP) involves, a principle accepted by most people—including, of course, the internal realists. We are allowed, on this view, to think or say something only if *everyone* (including God) is forbidden to think or say otherwise. Consider, moreover, what happens when we abandon (UUP) and retreat instead to a restricted universality principle, as I recommend. We cease to legislate for all, and instead concentrate only on what people who share our own limited perspective should think or say. Is that not the most natural way of understanding what the descent from Mount Olympus involves?

There are other drawbacks with internal realism as well, in that it is hard to see how it can avoid a rather undesirable form of idealism or mind-dependence. After all, if truth is epistemically constrained, then how can reality also fail to be, given that truth involves correspondence to reality in at least the minimal sense demanded by (ES) (though perhaps not in a deeper sense)?[12] The same is more obviously true of Kant's transcendental idealism, to which internal realism is a natural successor. Kant thought that we can only know of how things appear to us, and not of how they are in themselves. Indeed, he thought that there were two different branches of reality, the world of appearances (or 'phenomena') and the world of things in themselves (or 'noumena'). Their natures, and how they are supposed to interact, are mysterious and controversial. Things become even more mysterious and controversial if we pluralize matters by bringing the Martians and grue-users back into play. For now we require there to be several worlds of appearances as well as an inaccessible world of things in themselves somehow holding things together. Since the alien theories genuinely contradict

---

[12] I develop this point, together with my account of the nature of truth itself, in Unwin 2013. I also argue there that pragmatist theories of truth have unwanted idealist implications, contrary to what Peirce and many of his contemporary followers maintain.

ours, we must conclude that our world of appearances is ontologically separate from theirs (incompatible propositions cannot be true of the same world), and hence, by symmetry, ontologically separate from the world of things in themselves.[13] This rules out some of the more anodyne interpretations of what transcendental idealism actually involves. Perhaps, following Fichte, we can dispense with the noumena altogether, but that still leaves us with the problem of how different phenomenal worlds are supposed to relate to each other. An alien *Erscheinungswelt* needs to be in some way accessible to ours, otherwise the aliens could never have entered the story—our story—to begin with. So what sort of ontology does that leave us with? It is very hard to say.

An important virtue of my alternative approach is that we do not have to go down this road. My ontology is the ordinary familiar one, namely a single world which exists independently of our minds, but which contains (perhaps) many different kinds of cognitive being. Moreover, these beings (both us and them) interact with the rest of reality in an ordinary contingent sort of way, and do not view it from an external vantage-point (or God's Eye point of view). This position is fundamentally non-paradoxical. True, it involves a sort of cognitive relativism, but one which is free from the problems usually associated with such doctrines. The fact that it is attitude not content, and force rather than sense, that is reduced ensures this, for I can claim that all our beliefs (and assertions) should be reduced in the appropriate way—*including this one*—without undermining my own doctrine. It does not happen that my position can only be formulated from a standpoint ruled out by the position itself, as Quine (1975), for example (following a famous line of reasoning in Plato's *Theætetus*), has argued happens with cognitive relativism of the more usual type, and as P.F. Strawson (1966) has argued happens with transcendental idealism even when not pluralized.

The possibility of radical disagreement has been argued here to be fundamental in many ways, and this is certainly an unusual position. Most philosophers, I suspect, will still have misgivings as to whether my Martians and grue-users, as I call them, are even conceivable, and will certainly doubt, even if they are, whether they are of any real importance. My thesis, that they are not only conceivable and important, but also lie at the very heart of epistemology and metaphysics, will, I dare say, be generally met with flat incredulity. It is therefore worthwhile summarizing just how and why they enter the argument.

---

[13] Kant does not consider the possibility of alien intelligences in my sense, and indeed seems temperamentally opposed to the idea. He does, however, claim in his earlier writings that the outer planets are inhabited, and by creatures cognitively superior to ourselves. See, for example, Kant 1981, 189. See also David Lamb 2001, 8–9. He never seemed to waver from his view that other planets are inhabited: see, for example, Kant 1996, A828/B853.

The first and fundamental point is that our cognitive system is essentially contingent. Our brains are constructed in such a way as to generate beliefs from incoming data, but there is no reason to think that they are the only possible sort of brains. This cognitive contingency ensures that there is no metaphysical guarantee that there is a resemblance between such beliefs and the original reality. This gives us a powerful argument for an all-embracing scepticism. But contingency requires alternatives, and talk about Martians and grue-users enters the matter as a way of fleshing out what these alternatives amount to. However, they are only limiting notions, and we are not required to say in any detail what they are like, or how we could ever identify them as such. Secondly, they play a vital role in explaining what sort of concession we need to make to the sceptic if we are to recover most of what we require. In talking of a restricted universality principle, we need to say who is outside the restricted area, for without Martians and grue-users, or other outsiders of some kind, such boundaries become meaningless. Thirdly, and relatedly, they help to explain just what is meant by a God's Eye point of view, and why we should not try to attain it, an issue of fundamental metaphysical importance in its own right. And fourthly, they help to explain why transcendental idealism (and also, perhaps, internal realism) has dire consequences in so far as a pluralized mind-dependence is especially hard to make sense of.

These are all issues of substance which are very difficult to address without making the possibility of alien cognition central to the discussion. Furthermore, it is hard to deal with our original topic, namely what the normativity of belief amounts to, without addressing these issues if only because the most natural way of understanding the claim that belief aims at truth leads directly to an unrestricted universality principle which is hard if not impossible to defend, given the bare logical possibility of alien cognition.[14]

References

Bennett, J. (1990). Why is Belief Involuntary? *Analysis* 50, 87–107.
Bratman, M. E. (1991). Practical Reasoning and Acceptance in a Context. *Mind* 101, 1–15.
Cohen, L. J. (1992). *An Essay on Belief and Acceptance*. Oxford: Clarendon Press.
Dummett, M. (1978). *Truth and Other Enigmas*. London: Duckworth.
Ellis, B. (1988). Internal Realism. *Synthese* 76, 409–434.

---

[14] Many of the issues discussed in this paper are also examined, albeit from a slightly different perspective, in Unwin 2007, which in turn develops issues first introduced in Unwin 1987 and Unwin 2003.

Goodman, N. (1983). The New Riddle of Induction. In *Fact, Fiction and Forecast*. Cambridge MA: Harvard University Press.

Horwich, P. (1991). On the Nature and Norms of Theoretical Commitment. *Philosophy of Science* 58, 61–77.

Hume, D. (1978). *A Treatise of Human Nature*, 2nd edn, (eds) L.A. Selby-Bigge and P.H. Nidditch. Oxford: Clarendon Press.

Kant, I. (1981). *Universal Natural History and Theory of the Heavens*, tr. S.L. Jaki. Edinburgh: Edinburgh University Press.

Kant, I. (1996). *Critique of Pure Reason*, tr. Werner S. Pluhar. Indianapolis IN: Hackett.

Lamb, D. (2001). *The Search for Extraterrestrial Intelligence: A Philosophical Inquiry*. London and New York: Routledge.

Noordhof, P. (2001). Believe What You Want, *Proceedings of the Aristotelian Society*, 247–265.

Papineau, D. (ed.) (1996). *The Philosophy of Science*. Oxford: Oxford University Press.

Peirce, C.S. (1966). *Charles S. Peirce: Selected Writings*. New York NY: Dover Publications.

Putnam, H. (1981). *Reason, Truth and History*. Cambridge: Cambridge University Press.

Quine, W.V. (1960). *Word and Object*. Cambridge MA: MIT Press.

Quine, W.V. (1975). On Empirically Equivalent Systems of the World, *Erkenntnis* 9, 313–328.

Strawson, P.F. (1966). *The Bounds of Sense*. London: Methuen.

Unwin, N. (1987). Beyond Truth: Towards a New Conception of Knowledge and Communication. *Mind* 96, 299–317.

Unwin, N. (2003). What Does It Mean to Aim at Truth?. *American Philosophical Quarterly* 40, 91–104.

Unwin, N. (2007). *Aiming at Truth*. Basingstoke: Palgrave Macmillan.

Unwin, N. (2013). Deflationist Truth is Substantial. *Acta Analytica* 28, 257–266.

Van Fraassen, B. C. (1980). *The Scientific Image*. Oxford: Oxford University Press.

Velleman, J. D. (2000). *The Possibility of Practical Reason*. Oxford: Oxford University Press.

Williams, B. (1973). *Problems of the Self*. Cambridge: Cambridge University Press.

Mona Simion
Assertion, Knowledge and Rational Credibility: The Scoreboard

1. Introduction

One must: assert p only if one knows that p. Or at least that is what a very popular view on the epistemic normativity of assertion states. This has become known in the literature as the Knowledge Norm of Assertion (KNA).[1]

The *locus classicus* for the defence of KNA is Williamson (2000).[2] At a first glance, the view has quite a lot going for it; namely, linguistic data concerning the paradoxical nature of assertions of the form 'p but I don't know that p', the fact that assertions can be challenged by the question 'How do you know that p?', and the intuitive impropriety of asserting lottery propositions.

However, in recent literature, KNA is taken by many to be too strong of a requirement. The most prominent competing account on the market[3] imposes a weaker norm on assertion, and has been most notably defended, among others, by Douven (2006) and Lackey (2008). Roughly, the thought is that one should only assert p if p is rationally credible to one (henceforth, RCNA), where the epistemic status at stake is taken to be equivalent to knowledge-level justification – that is, whatever turns un-gettiered true belief into knowledge.

---

[1] This paper is only concerned with the necessity claim involved in the knowledge account of assertion. For a defence of the sufficiency claim, see e.g. Simion (2015), DeRose (2002).

[2] Among its main defenders also figure Hawthorne (2004), Turri (2011). Williamson also holds that knowledge requires probability one on one's evidence and that knowledge is the single constitutive norm for assertion. This paper stays neutral on these matters.
To be clear, though: by not committing to the constitutivity claim I do not mean to suggest that there might be instances of assertion that are not governed by KNA. On the account defended in this paper, there are none. I take it, though, that the constitutivity claim is stronger than that. That is, it looks as if the following is true of constitutive norms: if activity *A* is constituted by only a single constitutive norm, *n*, and if one violates *n* with near maximal systematicity, then one does not count as engaging in *A*. Given, though, that it seems that one can lie – and thus beak KNA – with near maximal systematicity and still count as asserting, this paper does not commit to the constitutivity claim.

[3] The truth norm of assertion, according to which one's assertion is epistemically permissible only if true, is the other main competitor on the market. This paper does not engage with this account. See e.g. Williamson (2000) for some related worries, and Weiner (2005) for a rejoinder on behalf of the truth account.

Defenders of RCNA argue that (1) theoretical considerations, such as a priori simplicity, speak in favour of RCNA, (2) the weaker norm will do just as fine in accommodating the above linguistic data too, and (3) KNA, as opposed to RCNA, has a hard time explaining cases in which assertions on some lesser epistemic standings do not render the speakers subject to criticism. As such, it is argued, RCNA scores better overall.

In response to (3), defenders of KNA have largely employed one incarnation or another of what has become known as 'the excuse manoeuvre'. That is, they have maintained that the cases put forth by JNA defenders feature speakers who, although non-knowledgeable, and therefore performing an impermissible speech-act, have a good excuse for it. However, due to its lack of value-theoretic backing, this strategy has been charged with ad-hoc-ness by the main proponents of RCNA.

Thus, at the end of the day, it looks as if things are not looking very good for KNA anymore. What we are being offered by its contenders is a fairly attractive counter-candidate norm that 1) imposes less stringent epistemic constraints on the speaker and 2) offers an a priori simpler explanation of the empirical data.

This paper's main ambition is to tip the balance back in favour of KNA. To this effect, I will first argue that the argument for the a priori simplicity of RCNA does not go through (§2). Furthermore, I will show that KNA scores better on the second front – that is, accommodating linguistic data (§3). Secondly, I will provide a unitary defence of KNA on the third front, sourced in the normativity of action in general, so as to avoid charges with ad-hoc-ness (§4). Finally, in the fifth section, I will provide more reasons to believe that knowledge is the norm of assertion, reasons pertaining to the epistemic function plausibly associated with this speech act. In the last section I will conclude.

2. Assertion and the 'Zeroth Law of Rationality'

Igor Douven first introduced the 'scoreboard approach' to the debate. In his 2006 paper, he goes through a series of data and argues that, on balance, RCNA scores better in accommodating them than KNA. According to Douven, while both KNA and RCNA do an equally good job in explaining the empirical data, RCNA is to be preferred due to considerations pertaining to a priori simplicity (2006, 451). That is, Douven argues, RCNA is but an extension of what he dubs 'the zeroth law of rationality':

LR: Only ϕ if it is rational for you to ϕ.

From this, Douven derives the equivalent principle for assertion (henceforth LRA):

LRA: Only assert p if it is rational for you to assert p.

Furthermore, Douven goes along with Jonathan Adler (2002) in supporting the belief-assertion parallel – that is, the claim that belief is nothing but assertion to oneself. In the light of this, and by the plausible assumption that if it is rational for one to assert that p, then it is rational for one to assert p to oneself, he derives:

RCNA: Only assert p if it is rational for you to believe p,

As such, Douven argues, we are faced with the following situation: RCNA seems to be a mere extension to a fundamental principle of rationality, to wit, LR – to which, he argues, we are committed anyway (2006, 456). Furthermore, the extension is obtained by an application of a principle that is equally endorsed by Williamson (2000) – that is, the belief-assertion parallel.

Now, say that it turns out that RCNA deals with the linguistic data as well as KNA does. If that is the case, in absence of similar support for KNA – that is, support coming from things that we endorse on independent grounds – RCNA will just provide an a priori simpler explanation of the data, and will thus turn out to be the preferable account.

Let us, though, take a closer look at Douven's LR. Recall that what we are interested in is the epistemic norm governing assertion. Douven (2012, 293) points out that the rationality at stake is going to be epistemic rationality, concerned with the purpose of maximizing epistemic utility. As such, on a first approximation, we can restate the principle as follows:

LR*: You must (epistemically): φ only if it is epistemically rational for you to φ.

Further on, for the particular case of assertion, we get:

LRA*: You must (epistemically): assert p only if it is epistemically rational for you to assert p.

By the belief-assertion parallel, we get:

RCNA*: You must (epistemically): assert p only if it is epistemically rational for you to believe p.

However, there are two major problems with this move. First, Kelp and Simion (2016) identify cases in which it looks as if it is epistemically rational for me to assert p in spite of the fact that I have no justification whatsoever to believe p. If that is the case, there is reason to believe that either the epistemic status at stake in RCNA is not knowledge-level justification, or the belief-assertion parallel does not hold. Here is why:

> Consider a case in which I am offered a million true beliefs for asserting that two plus two equals five. Given, as Douven (2008) himself accepts, that attaining a large body of beliefs with a favourable truth to falsity ratio is our epistemic goal, it would seem highly epistemically rational for me to make this assertion. After all, I will make great progress towards attaining my epistemic goal. At the same time, [...] I do not have justification for believing what I assert (Kelp and Simion 2016, 12).

Furthermore, what I will argue next is that, even if we leave these worries aside,[4] Douven's argument still fails to go through. That is, in what follows, I will point towards a missing link in Douven's argument which renders it incapable to offer support to his favourite account of assertion.

Let us first grant Douven, for the sake of the argument, that his derivation of RCNA* is fine. Recall, however, that Douven also wants rational credibility to stand for knowledge-level justification. Therefore, the claim Douven is making is actually stronger than RCNA*:

RCNA**: You must (epistemically): assert p only if you have knowledge-level justification to believe p.

As such, the argument seems to go along the following lines:

---

4 Notice that, arguably, this argument, at least in its present form, only goes through on an act consequentialist value theoretic assumption. Notice, also, that this assumption would create a similar problem for any norm of assertion, including KNA; after all, we can always bring cases in which on a particular occasion one gains more epistemically by breaking the norm. This problem parallels the classical 'scapegoat' objection to act utilitarianism in ethics.
That is not to say, however, that, as things stand, the argument does not go through. After all, Douven does commit himself to a combination of RCNA and epistemic act consequentialism in several places, so it looks as if it is on his shoulders to refine his view in order to escape these worries. One way for him to escape this issue is by going for a milder value theoretic schema, say, a rule consequentialist one. That is, by arguing that respecting RCNA brings more epistemic gain overall, even though it fails to do so on some particular occasions. Of course, though, this might also open a bunch of rejoinder options. Thus, given the complexity of this discussion, this paper limits itself to mentioning these worries and then setting them aside. Nothing in what follows rests on this.

(1) You must (epistemically): only ϕ if it is epistemically rational for you to ϕ.
(2) You must (epistemically): assert p only if it is epistemically rational for you to assert p (from (1)).
(3) Belief is assertion to oneself.
(4) If it is epistemically rational for one to assert that p, then it is epistemically rational for one to assert p to oneself.
(5) You must (epistemically): assert p only if it is epistemically rational for you to believe p (from (2), (3) and (4)).
(6) You must (epistemically): assert p only if you have knowledge-level justification to believe p. (from (5))

It becomes clear then that Douven misses an argument from (5) to (6); that is, an argument to establish the equivalence between rational credibility and knowledge-level justification.

Note, though, that when first presented, the argument was not supposed to establish more than (5). That is because Douven (2006) does not take much of a stance with regard to what the notion of rational credibility in RCNA is supposed to stand for. Douven (2006, 459) does, though, gesture in the direction of Keith Lehrer's (1990) coherentist theory of justification, and in later personal communication with several authors he acknowledges that he has knowledge-level justification in mind (see e.g. Kelp and Simion (2016) for discussion). In contrast, Lackey (2008, 128) explicitly states that knowledge-level justification is the epistemic status at stake.

Notice, however, that, at the end of the day, this does not help Douven much. Here is why: even if Douven were to not stand behind any particular account of rational credibility, his argument would end up equally supporting whatever norm of assertion that also comes with a well-defended norm for rational belief, including KNA. Inasmuch as rational credibility is supposed to stand for knowledge-level justification, both the KNA and RCNA defender need a further argument for their preferred account of normativity of belief in order to get support from Douven's 'zeroth law of rationality'. If that is the case, as things stand, Douven's argument offers as much support to KNA as to RCNA. To see this, let us have a look at the epistemic extensions of Douven's LR for belief:

LRB*: You must (epistemically): believe p only if it is epistemically rational for you to believe p.

Given that Douven wants rational credibility to stand for knowledge-level justification, we get:

LRB**: You must (epistemically): believe p only if you have knowledge-level justification for p.

Both of these principles state epistemic norms for belief. However, only the first is a direct instance of LR*. The second presupposes that it is epistemically rational for you to believe p if and only if you have knowledge-level justification for p.

However, why shall we buy without further argument that epistemically rational credibility is knowledge-level justification and not some other epistemic standard? Many people in the literature argue for different epistemic norms for belief: truth and knowledge are the most common counter-candidates.[5] Williamson himself, for instance, takes it that the epistemic norm for belief is knowledge – that is, one should only believe p if one knows p.

As such, for Williamson, it is only epistemically rational to believe p if one knows that p.[6] Therefore, Williamson's position is perfectly compatible with RCNA*: one must, indeed, only assert p if p is rationally credible to one, where p is rationally credible to one only if one knows that p. Therefore, one should only assert p if one knows p. Thus, insofar as we are missing an argument for a knowledge-level justification norm for epistemically rational belief, Douven's derivation fails to offer support for his preferred norm over KNA.

To sum up: we have seen that, against Douven, RCNA, at least in the shape envisaged by its main proponents, misses independent theoretical support over KNA. If that is the case, all we are left with for our scoreboard are empirical data. This still does not mean much for KNA, though; after all, if the RCNA supporters are right, and the two norms do deal equally well with these data, there is still an argument to be made that one should go for the weaker norm on grounds of user-friendliness.

Thus, let us have a look at how the two fare when it comes to a posteriori adequacy and simplicity.

3. Linguistic Data

I have mentioned that KNA is strongly supported by linguistic data concerning: 1) The intuitive impropriety of asserting 'My ticket lost' before knowing the results of the lottery draw; according to the vast majority of the literature, lottery prop-

---

[5] See Gibbons (2013) for discussion.
[6] While Williamson (2000) is unclear on whether rational belief is governed by a knowledge norm, in more recent work he openly stands behind this claim (e.g. his 2013 exchange with Comesana and Cohen).

ositions are not knowable and therefore, by KNA, unassertable. 2) The fact that assertions can be challenged by the question 'How do you know that p?'; if knowledge is the norm of assertion, it makes sense that the hearer expects the speaker to know what he asserted. 3) The paradoxical soundingness of Moorean statements of the form 'p but I don't know that p' (see below).

Now, defenders of RCNA would have it that their favourite norm does not fall far behind in these respects. Douven (2006, 2009) argues that, in terms of empirical adequacy, RCNA does as good as KNA in explaining all of the above. Here is how: by Douven's lights, the intuitive unassertability of lottery propositions is triggered by the fact that not only are they not knowable, but, in accordance with the most recent solutions to the lottery paradox[7], they are not even rationally credible to one. Therefore, they are also unassertable by RCNA (2006, 459).

When it comes to explaining the 'How do you know?' challenge, Douven argues that, even if KNA is false, due to the mostly friendly epistemic environment we inhabit, we typically know what we assert; as such, it makes sense that hearers would assume it to be the case (2006, 469).[8]

This paper will not take issue with Douven's case in either of these two respects; that is mostly because I agree with Douven on the former and I find the latter fairly plausible. What I will, though, discuss in more detail is the RCNA explanation of the paradoxical soundingness of Moorean statements. I will argue below that not only does RCNA not fare as well as KNA in this respect, but it does not even come close to giving a satisfactory account.

3.1 Moorean Statements

It is widely acknowledged that KNA offers a very straightforward explanation of why sentences such as 'It is Wednesday but I don't know that it is Wednesday' and 'It is Wednesday but I don't believe that it is Wednesday' sound paradoxical to us. If knowledge is the norm of assertion, on the plausible assumption that knowledge distributes across conjunctions, one is in a good enough epistemic position to assert 'p but I don't know that p' only if one knows both conjuncts. However, since knowledge is factive, one only knows the second conjunct if it is true that one does not know that p. But that contradicts knowing the first conjunct. Thus, according to KNA, one cannot meet the conditions for making a

---

7 See Douven (2006) section (2) for a brief overview.
8 Douven does acknowledge that the RCNA explanation falls short of the simplicity of that of KNA here.

proper assertion of the form 'p but I don't know that p' (Williamson 2000, 253). Furthermore, if KNA is true, it is plausible that when the speaker asserts that p, the hearer is led to believe that she knows that p;[9] therefore, when one asserts the second conjunct of a Moorean statement, one denies what one has led one's hearer to believe by asserting the first conjunct (Moore 1962, 277). Thus, KNA explains why the conjunction 'p but I don't know that p' is not only unassertable, but it also sounds paradoxical.

It is easy to see that, by similar reasoning, KNA scores equally well when it comes to Moorean statements with belief. If, by KNA, one is supposed to know both conjuncts of the Moorean statement, given that knowledge implies belief, it follows that one has to 1) believe that p and 2) know that one does not believe that p. Given, again, factivity of knowledge, one needs to 1) believe that p and 2) not believe that p. Thus, the conditions for proper assertability of Moorean propositions with belief cannot be met and, again, on similar grounds as above, it makes sense that such statements sound paradoxical to the hearer.

At a first glance, RCNA does not seem to be able to give as good an explanation of the phenomenon, given that rational credibility is not factive. In his 2006 paper, Douven himself acknowledges the superiority of KNA on this front; thus, he argues that, while RCNA can also make sense of why Moorean statements come with a paradoxical flavour, KNA scores better in terms of simplicity. Douven's early explanation goes, roughly, along the following lines: first of all, notice that the champion of RCNA need not hold that Moorean statements are not assertable. All she needs is a good explanation of the fact that they sound paradoxical. Now, it is a fact that we do not encounter Moorean statements every day. If that is the case, it also makes sense that they sound odd to us, due to lack of exposure. Why is it, though, that we do not hear Moorean statements every day? Well, according to Douven, although KNA is strictly speaking false, it is the case that we typically know what we assert. That is, in normal, friendly environmental conditions, if p is rationally credible to me, I also know that p. Given this, Moorean sentences are extremey rarely uttered, therefore extremely rarely heard, which explains their odd-soundingness. As such, according to Douven, although RCNA does not offer an equally straightforward explanation

---

[9] In what sense does asserting p lead the hearer to believe that the asserter knows p? The received view is that it is a matter of 'presenting oneself' as knowing; however, people do not usually go to much into detail about this. One thing: if it is an implicature that is at stake here, it will probably not be a mere conversational implicature, since it is clearly not cancellable. Most likely, what we are dealing with is a conventional implicature (non-cancellable); for more on this distinction, see Grice (1989, 25–39).

as KNA for the oddity of Moorean statements, it is able to accommodate the data in a perfectly plausible way (2006, 474).

In later work, though, Douven (2009) comes back to the issue and concedes that his early explanation of the odd-soundingness of Mooreean sentences is vulnerable to charges with lack of empirical adequacy; after all, many expressions we do not often encounter do not seem to share the odd-soundingness of Moorean statements. Consider, for instance, 'John seeks a unicorn'; surely we do not hear this every day. Still, it seems clear enough that whatever is happening when one hears a Moorean sentence pertains to a completely different category of oddness than that of other sentences to which we have little exposure (2009, 363).

However, Douven (2009) argues that, on the bright side, on more careful examination, RCNA is able to do as good a job as the knowledge norm in accommodating the odd-soundingness of Moorean statements. That is because, according to him, not only are the latter statements not knowable, but, on a Bayesian analysis, they are also not rationally credible, and, therefore, unassertable. Roughly, the argument goes as follows: first, Douven assumes that one plausible and fairly weak requirement on rational credibility is that a person believes p rationally only if it does not readily follow strictly on the basis of the assumption of her rationally believing p plus some fairly uncontroversial doxastic principles[10] that her degrees of belief are not probabilities. Second, Douven proves that, if one assumes, towards a *reductio*, that one rationally believes Moorean sentences, it does follow that one's degrees of belief are not probabilities. Thus, Douven argues, Moorean sentences are not rationally credible and therefore not assertable.

Even if we accept Douven's unassertability diagnosis, though, there are still two major problems for his account. First, even if RCNA is the norm of assertion, it is not immediately clear that laymen would immediately 'feel' that Moorean statements are unassertable by RCNA. After all, by Douven's own lights, Moorean statements are, at first glance, rationally credible to one – Douven himself granted their assertability by RCNA in his 2006. Furthermore, proving that Moorean statements are not rationally credible, as we have seen, required quite some amount of work: "it is not immediately clear that it could never happen that, for some ϕ, ϕ is rationally credible to a person and at the same time it is rationally credible to this person that she does not know ϕ" (2009, 363). But if it is not immediately clear to philosophers that this is the case, how can it be that it is as clear to laymen as to trigger such feeling of paradox?

---

10 (1) if you rationally believe p and q you also rationally believe p; (2) rationally believing some p requires believing that p is more likely than not, and (3) if you rationally believe some p, then your degree of belief that you believe p is at least as great as your degree of belief that you don't believe p.

Second, crucially, even if we put this problem aside, mere unassertability will not suffice for doing the intended work here. Recall that the KNA explanation of the paradoxical soundingness of Moorean statements had two essential components: first, there was the unassertability; second, the heard contradiction triggered by it. Notice, also, that the former without the latter would do quite a poor job in what empirical adequacy is concerned. After all, there are many sentences for which one cannot ever meet the conditions for assertability imposed by KNA; take, for instance, necessary falsehoods. By KNA, and given factivity of knowledge, '2+2=5' is unassertable, due to it being necessarily false and, therefore, unknowable. However, just like in the case of 'John seeks a unicorn', the oddity involved in hearing someone assert '2+2=5', if any, is definitely of a completely different sort than the paradoxical soundingness of Moorean statements. As such, it looks as if what completes the work for empirical adequacy for KNA's explanation of the latter is the heard contradiction triggered by what the hearer is led to believe by the assertion of the first conjunct, together with the assertion of the second.

We have seen that, according to Douven, Moorean statements are not rationally credible to one, and, therefore, by RCNA, not assertable. Now, similarly to the case of KNA, this result, on its own, will not do the intended work in accounting for the paradoxical soundingness at stake. To see this, consider the case of lottery propositions; we have seen that according to Douven, they are not rationally credible, and therefore, by RCNA, not assertable. However, again, if I assert 'My ticket did not win' in absence of any inside information about the draw, although I am criticisable for making an improper assertion, there is not much feeling of oddity there to be experienced by the hearer. Again, while merely unassertable propositions do trigger a feeling of impropriety, this still does not come close to the paradoxical soundingness of Moorean statements. To see this, consider, in contrast: 'My ticket did not win but I don't believe my ticket did not win'.

If that is the case, Douven needs more for his argument to work. What needs to be the case is not only that Moorean statements are unassertable by RCNA, but also that this triggers their paradoxical soundingness. Recall the KNA explanation of the latter: knowledge is the norm of assertion, therefore when one asserts that p one leads one's hearer to believe that one knows that p, which is contradicted by the second conjunct; therefore, the heard contradiction. Let us try to construct an RCNA account along similar lines: when I assert that p I lead my hearer to believe that p is rationally credible to me. Notice, however, this does not contradict the second conjunct in any of the two Moorean schemas that we have been looking at. Take, for instance, the case of someone who is (irrationally) afraid of flying and consider his relationship to the proposition 'Flying is the least dangerous mode of transportation'. Even if the corresponding Moorean sentences are not rationally credible to her, it is certainly not contradictory for that person to say that p is rationally credible to her but she doesn't know or believe it. As such, it looks as if Douven is still missing an explanation of the paradoxical soundingness of Moorean sentences.

4. The 'Blameless Asserter' Objection

Recall that, according to its objectors, KNA-Nec has a hard time explaining cases of assertions on lesser epistemic standings which intuitively do not render the speaker subject to blame. Furthermore, according to the same objectors, the several lines of the defence employed by KNA champions suffer from some degree or another of ad hoc-ness. That is, the KNA-friendly responses available in the literature employ one variety or another of what has become known as 'the excuse manoeuvre'; roughly, the latter consists in arguing that, although in breach of the norm, the speakers in the problem cases have a good excuse for having broken it.[11] Surprisingly enough, however, no general account of excusability is being offered; furthermore, in several cases, the claim seems to be tailor-made to fit the KNA defence against one charge or another, as the manoeuvre does not seem to work similarly well when it comes to the normativity of action in general.[12] As such, the epistemological literature suffers greatly from the lack of a detailed account of blame attribution:[13] many of the charges with ad hoc-ness brought by opponents of KNA are sourced in the fact that a clear and complete account of blame attribution is not being offered. What I will do next is try to fill this gap. Assertion is a type of action; thus, in what follows, I will put forth a framework for the normativity of assertion in line with what I take to be a fairly uncontroversial framework for the normativity of action in general, so as to escape charges with ad-hoc-ness. Also, to the same purpose, I will put forth a fairly detailed and wide picture of blame attribution, although I will not need to appeal to it in its entirety for the purposes of this paper.

---

[11] For several incarnations of the excuse manoeuver, see, e.g., Williamson (2009), De Rose (2002) and Turri (2011). For charges with ad hoc-ness, see, e.g. Lackey (2007) and Douven (2006).

[12] See, e.g., De Rose's (2002) distinction between primary and secondary propriety, and Lackey's (2007) reply, dismissing the respective distinction on grounds of lack of fit with the normativity of action in general.

[13] Only very recently, people like Tim Williamson and Clayton Littlejohn have started taking steps in this direction (see their forthcoming papers on the issue).

4.1 Blame and Action

Let us begin by making some necessary distinctions, in order to clear the normative air a bit. In the literature concerned with the relationship between an agent's blameworthiness and the impropriety of her action according to a particular norm governing its type – call it norm X – one can identify (at least) four fairly uncontroversial ways in which the two can come apart:[14]

Blame-Action1: An agent is blameless for performing a token act which is improper according to norm X if it is an all-things-considered proper act, unless she believes[15] it to be all-things considered improper;

Blame-Action2: An agent is blameworthy for performing a token act which is proper according to norm X, but is all-things-considered improper, with the following exceptions:

Blame-Action2.1: An agent is blameless if she performs an all-things-considered improper act due to her performance not being under her control, provided that it is not the case that it should have been under her control.

Blame-Action2.2: An agent is blameless for performing an all-things-considered improper act if she conformed to her epistemic duties and she had good reasons to believe she was respecting the norm.

To see how this goes, notice, first, that actions are governed by several norms in virtue of their being actions as such (prudential, moral etc.). But also, actions are subject to norms specific to the particular type they belong to: chess moves to rules of chess, driving to traffic norms etc. As such, it might be that your act is proper[16] in one sense, but improper in another. Also, an act can be subject to an all-things-considered evaluation. Requirements according to a particular norm are defeasible: they can be overridden by the requirements of other norms stepping in. For instance, promising your friend Ted that you are going

---

[14] I am not aiming to offer an exhaustive account regarding blame attribution, but only to identify those instances which are fairly uncontroversial. For discussion, see e.g. Haji (1998), Zimmerman (1997).

[15] See footnote 19.

[16] I follow the literature on norms of assertion (e.g. DeRose 2002) in using propriety and permissibility interchangeably. Some philosophers would disagree with this, due to phenomena related to suberogation. However, nothing here hinges on this.

to meet him for lunch and not showing up is improper according to the norms of social commitment, which essentially govern promise keeping. If you meet an injured stranger on the way to lunch, though, and you're the only one around to help him get to the hospital, then this further state of affairs overrides your *prima facie* obligation to meet Ted for lunch. Thus, blameworthiness will not necessarily be attached to acts which are improper according to a particular norm X, as they might be all-things-considered proper. If you do decide to help the injured stranger instead of joining Ted for lunch, your breaking your promise remains improper according to the norms of social commitment; however, your act is, all-things-considered, perfectly fine, due to moral considerations stepping in. Also, you are not worthy of blame for performing it.

Secondly, it might be that your act is improper on all grounds, as there's no requirement keeping you from conforming to norm X, but you are still blameless for breaking it. The classical case is one in which you violate the norm because[17] your action is not under your control, say, because you have been brainwashed into performing it. Second, according to a fairly uncontroversial view in the literature[18] that has been with us since Aristotle, one is an apt candidate for blame for violating a norm only if one is aware of what it is one is doing or bringing about (*NE*, 1110a-1111b4). As such, one may reasonably do something impermissible because one reasonably but falsely believes it to be permissible. If you fail to keep your promise to Ted because your (otherwise highly reliable) secretary misinforms you about the time at which you're supposed to meet him, you're blameless for not showing up. However, breaking your promise remains an improper act according to the norms of social commitment.

With regard to this, some qualifications are needed. The literature (e.g Zimmerman (1997)) distinguishes between direct and indirect blameworthiness for performing an action. One is indirectly blameworthy for something x, if and only if one is blameworthy for it by way of being blameworthy for something else, y, of which x is the consequence.

One could be indirectly blameworthy for performing an action out of ignorance, by being directly blameworthy for being ignorant.[19] Notice, though, that

---

17 The 'because' here is crucial to blamelessness. See Harry Frankfurt (1969).
18 See e.g. Haji (1998), Zimmerman (1997). People working in this field disagree whether a belief or a knowledge condition is appropriate for blameworthiness. Although not much in this paper hinges on this, I here go with the stronger view – supporting the belief condition – in order to stay on the safe side by attributing blameworthiness more generously.
19 Similarly, even if an action was not under your control, it might be that the action *should* have been under your control (e.g. you lack control of your driving for having been drinking before getting behind the wheel).

in the above case, although the agent ends up with a false belief that his action is in accordance with the relevant norms, this seems to happen through no fault of his own. That is, he seems to have conformed to his epistemic duties: asking your secretary about your schedule for the day is quite a reliable way to go about it. Surely, if our agent were to be late for lunch due to his trusting his three years old son's testimony about his schedule, we would tend to find him blameworthy for his breaking the norms of social commitment.[20]

4.2 Bad Assertions, Good Asserters

To sum up: assertion is a type of action. Given that we have identified at least four instances in which the propriety of the action and the blamelessness of the agent can come apart, it follows that we will not be able to trace whether a particular norm X governs assertion or not by merely identifying instances of blamelessness/blameworthiness of the speaker. However, most cases put forth by KNA objectors are not intended to do more than this in the first place. Lackey, for one, purports to "show that there are cases in which a speaker asserts that p in the absence of knowing that p without being subject to criticism [...], thereby showing that knowledge cannot be what is required for proper assertion" (2007, 594). On a similar line, Douven argues that "if breaching a rule makes one blameworthy, which typically it does, then, [in these cases], on the knowledge account, the asserter comes out as being blameworthy, contrary to intuition" (2006, 477).

There are three types of cases put forth in the literature to this aim: assertion on (i) rational credibility in absence of belief, (ii) justified false belief, and (iii) justified true belief that falls short of knowledge.

(i) Assertion on rational credibility in absence of belief:

CREATIONIST TEACHER: Stella is a devoutly Christian fourth-grade teacher; as such, she strongly believes in the truth of creationism and, accordingly, in the falsity of evolutionary theory. Despite this, Stella fully recognizes that there is an overwhelming amount of scientific evidence against both of these beliefs. Stella regards her duty as a teacher to include presenting material that is best

---

[20] It might also be that your belief is unjustified yet blameless—say because you have been brainwashed into believing your 3-year-old son on this. Notice that this case falls under the 'control' condition.

supported by the available evidence. As a result, while presenting her biology lesson today, Stella asserts to her students, "Modern day Homo sapiens evolved from Homo erectus," though she herself neither believes nor knows this proposition (adapted form Lackey (2007, 548)).

Lackey argues that Stella "offers an assertion in the absence of knowledge and is not properly subject to criticism" (2007, 549).

I agree with Lackey that Stella is hardly blameworthy for her assertion. However, it looks as if the prudential constraint is the one dictating this intuition. To see this, consider: if I believe in witches, for instance, prudentially it would be best to not disclose that to my group of friends, as it might seriously affect my public image. Thus, when asked, I will go with the scientific view point and assert: 'Witches do not exist'. Surely, I can hardly be subject to blame for this. Recall, also, that in line with action in general (*Blame-Action1*), a speaker is not blameworthy for making an assertion which is improper according to norm X governing its type if it is all-things-considered proper. Again, by Lackey's own lights, "Stella regards her duty *as a teacher* to include presenting material that is best supported by the available evidence" (my emphasis). Plausibly enough, given the usual norms governing the activity of teaching – that is, "presenting students with material that is best supported by the available evidence" – Stella is all-things-considered blameless, as more stringent requirements are overriding the epistemic norm governing her assertion. This, however, in no way implies that her assertion is proper according to the latter. To see this, imagine how Stella's KNA-proper assertion would have looked like:

CREATIONIST TEACHER – KNA: I don't know how our species came into being. Evolutionary theory says that Homo sapiens evolved from Homo erectus, but I don't believe that's true. I believe that men were created by God, but I have no scientific evidence that this is so.

Would we really want this to be what our children get from their biology course? Certainly not. Prudentially, Stella's assertion is surely impermissible. In fact, I trust that Stella would soon lose her job if she were to keep this kind of assertions coming. Which is nicely explained by *Blame-Action2*. To see this, let us change the structure of the audience: imagine that Stella would make the KNA-proper assertion in a conversation with her mother. Surely, we will no longer think she deserves criticism in this case.

(ii) Assertion on justified false belief:

FAKE SNOW: [...] it is winter, and it looks exactly as it would if there were snow outside, but in fact that white stuff is not snow but foam put there by a film crew of whose existence I have no idea. I do not know that there is snow outside, because there is no snow outside, but it is quite reasonable for me to believe not just that there is snow outside but that I know that there is; for me, it is to all appearances a banal case of perceptual knowledge. Surely it is then reasonable for me to assert that there is snow outside (Williamson 2000, 257).

And

(iii) Assertion on justified true belief that falls short of knowledge:

FAKE BARNS: [...] suppose that Wendy correctly sees the only real barn that, unbeknownst to her, is completely surrounded by barn facades and asserts to me "There was a barn in the field we just passed" on this basis (Lackey 2007, 544).

In both the cases above, speakers assert from what they mistakenly take to be knowledge. And, intuitively, and according to RCNA champions, they can hardly be subject to blame. Also, notice that no further normative constraints seem to be active in these cases. As such, according to Douven, "someone who [...] on the basis of what seems to be excellent evidence, reports about the issue, [...] appears not to have done anything for which she would need an excuse – even if what, to the best of her knowledge, is true is in fact false" (2006, 480).

Notice, though, that even if Douven is right, the fact that the speaker is in no need of an excuse need not imply that her action was proper. The speaker in FAKE SNOW walks free (by *Blame-Action2.2*), for he has broken the relevant norm blamelessly; this does not mean, however, that this assertion must therefore be proper also. Similarly to your blamelessly breaking your promise to meet Ted for lunch due to being misinformed by your secretary, the speaker in FAKE SNOW blamelessly breaks KNA, since he had good reasons to believe he was respecting the norm. Perception is a pretty reliable way to come to believe it is snowing outside, just as testimony from a reliable secretary is a good source for beliefs regarding one's schedule.

To see that what we have here is a blameless speaker performing an improper speech act, think about what the attitude of the speaker should be towards her assertion after finding out that she was mistaken or gettiered: it looks as if one should take back the initial speech act and not stand by the commitments implied by it anymore. Thus, rather than presenting excuses as such, an appropriate reaction would go along the lines of "Oh, I take that back. I was not aware of there being a film crew producing fake snow outside", or "Oh, I take that back, I had no idea we were in Fake Barn County". This suggests that what we are dealing with is a speaker having blamelessly performed an improper speech act.

In reply to this line of defence, Jonathan Kvanvig (2009), however, argues that "in some cases of correction, we take back the content of our speech act, and in other cases we apologize for, and regret, the very act itself".[21] For instance, if we assert p and then are shown that p is false or that we have been gettiered, we take back the content of our speech act, but we needn't apologize for or regret the very act itself. In contrast, Kvanvig argues, when you don't have justification for what you say, apologizing and taking back the speech act itself is the right thing to do. Kvanvig argues that, given that norms of assertion are norms governing a certain type of human activity, they relate to the speech act itself, not to its content.

I have defended KNA against Kvanvig's 'two ways of taking back' argument in more detail in previous work (Simion forthcoming), thus I will only give a sketch of a reply here and, further on, attempt to accommodate some worries about it: speech act literature distinguishes between the content of a speech act and the illocutionary force by which the content is being put forward. One can perform various speech acts upon p: one can ask whether p, promise that p, threaten that p etc. In the case of assertion, by uttering p the speaker presents p as true. Given this, however, a *proposition* is itself communicatively inert;[22] that is to say that to actually perform a speech act, one has to put forth a proposition with an *illocutionary force*, such as assertion, promise, command, etc.

But if the propositional content is inert in isolation, it is less clear how one can take it back in isolation. To see this, notice that assertion, as opposed to other types of actions – say, vacationing in Hawaii – can be 'taken back'. Not by changing the past, of course, but by no longer standing behind the commitments implied by asserting that p. Now, p itself, in isolation, does not imply any commitments whatsoever. That is, depending on which illocutionary force we will act upon it with, different commitments will follow. If I promise that p, I commit myself to a future course of action; if I assert that p, I commit myself to it being the case that p.

But if that is the case, in order to take an assertion back, that is, to be released from the commitments implied by it, it has to be the case that I take back everything, force and content. I cannot only take back the content p, be-

---

21 Kvanvig (2009) defends a Justified Belief Norm of Assertion.
22 For more on this, see Green (2009).

cause p in isolation does not commit me to anything, inasmuch as I do not present it as true, or command p, or promise p, etc. Also, on similar gorunds, I cannot only take the action back either.

Something is, indeed, different between the two cases presented by Kvanvig, though. By *Blame-Action2.2*, the speakers in FAKE SNOW and FAKE BARNS, asserting on justified belief, are epistemically blameless. As opposed to that, asserters missing any justification whatsoever are indirectly blameworthy, as they failed to conform to their epistemic duties before proceeding.

To sum up: we have seen that Kvanvig's distinction did not manage to stand tall in the face of close speech-act-theoretic scrutiny. We have also seen that the normative framework put forth by this paper is perfectly able to accommodate the target phenomena in a KNA friendly way. However, the KNA objector might still maintain that that's not all there is to it; that is, that all this does not go all the way in showing that the phenomenon of taking back one's speech act when finding out one has been mistaken or gettiered supports KNA. The thought would go along the following lines: there seems to still be sense to the thought that some of the acts we take back were perfectly proper. Imagine I promise to come to your party. Plausibly enough, there's some norm of promising to the effect that you should only promise to do something you have good reason to think you will be able to do. Now say I can't come to your party, because of an entirely unforeseen event. It makes sense to say that, even though I ask to be released from the commitment to come, my original act of promising was perfectly proper. I need not apologise for having promised, or regret having promised. Why? Because I didn't do anything wrong. Why can't we say something parallel about assertion? When it turns out I was gettiered, I 'take back' my assertion (act and content), but I need not apologise for having asserted, or feel any regret. Why? Because I didn't do anything wrong.[23]

Notice, though, that the claim made by this paper is not a biconditional: all I claim is that taking back of speech acts is sufficient for asking to be released from the relevant commitments, not that it is necessary. That is, it is perfectly compatible with the claim made here that there will be instances of commitment release demand that do not amount to taking back the relevant speech act. What I will try to briefly argue next is that this is what is going on in the case above.

To see this, note there is a clear disanalogy between the party case and the gettiered assertion case. That is, by stipulation, in the party case my reason for

---

[23] Thanks to an anonymous referee for pressing me on this point.

promising to come, while still standing, gets overridden[24] by unforeseen, more pressing considerations; in contrast, Wendy's reason to assert in the first place gets undercut by the information that she is in Fake Barn County.

To see how this makes a difference, consider another speech act, that of agreeing to marry someone. If I agree to marry you because I think you love me, and it turns out you don't, I will most likely take my speech act back and thereby ask to be released from my commitment. In contrast, if after twenty happy years of marriage we are not getting along very well anymore, and I ask for a divorce, I am asking to be released from my commitments without taking my initial speech act back; surely, if we had a perfectly fine marriage for twenty years, it is hardly appropriate or necessary for me to take back my having agreed to marry you to begin with, rather than merely ask to be released from my commitments now.

Returning to the assertion/party cases, say my reason to promise to come to the party was a known fact: I knew that my partner wanted to go. Say that later on, however, something unforeseen came up at my office, and it turns out I have to work late and finish a project that evening. As such, while my initial reason is still in good standing, it has just been overridden by more pressing considerations. It looks as if, in this case, there is no reason for me to take back my initial speech act, rather than merely demand to be released from the commitment implied by it. That is, it would sound inappropriate if I were to tell you something along the lines of 'I take it back, I should not have promised to come when I did'. Rather, merely letting you know that I will not be coming after all, due to unforeseen events, seems more suited to the situation.

In contrast, in the Gettier case, when I point out to Wendy that there is no way in which she can know that there is a barn over there, since we are in Fake Barn County, her initial reason to believe the asserted proposition gets undercut, which makes taking back the speech act the appropriate move. To see this, here is how an assertion case analogous to the party case would look like: I know there is an opening in my department, therefore I tell you: 'There is an opening in my department. I therefore commit myself to this being the case. Now say that the very next day the position gets filled. Plausibly enough, when I tell you that there is no opening in my department anymore, I am not taking my initial assertion back – there was nothing wrong with it – but rather I am

---

[24] Again, I am not claiming that overriding is necessary for cases of commitment release demand without taking back the initial speech act; in general, it is beyond the ambition of this section to give a full account thereof. Rather, the thought is more to argue that KNA, through the normative picture put forth by this paper, can accommodate the target phenomena.

merely releasing myself from the commitment to there being an opening in my department, since that is not the case anymore.

5. The Scoreboard

Let us take stock and revisit the scoreboard: we have seen that, against Douven, RCNA does not immediately follow from principles that we are committed to on independent a priori grounds. As it turns out, for all Douven has proven, both the KNA and RCNA defender need a further argument for their preferred account of normativity of belief in order to get support from Douven's 'zeroth law of rationality'. So no advantage here on either side.

Further on, I have conceded that RCNA does a fair job in accounting for the unassertability of lottery propositions and for the practice of challenging assertions by means of 'How do you know?' questions. However, when it comes to Moorean statements, I have argued that, even if we accept Douven's argument for their unassertability, RCNA still fails to account for their paradoxical soundingness. So there's an advantage on KNA's part on this front.

Last but not least, I have also offered a unified defence of KNA against 'blameless speakers' objections, by putting forth a framework for the normativity of assertion in line with the normativity of action in general, so as to escape charges with ad-hoc-ness.

5.1 Objections

Now, the RCNA defender might still want to argue that her preferred account offers a simpler explanation of the cases put forth. Douven gives it a go. He argues that it seems simpler, and thus methodologically preferable, to explain our intuitions about false but reasonable assertions without having to appeal to an extra story about how one can breach rules blamelessly (2006, 478).

As much as one might value simplicity, however, the illustrations in the previous section stand as pretty solid proof to the fact that, in this case, it might get us in trouble when it comes to empirical adequacy. Unless Douven provides us with a principled explanation regarding how assertion differs from other actions, simplicity would lead us to conclude that traffic norms are not, in fact, governing driving, just because I'm blameless for violating them due to my broken speedometer. Similarly, the simpler explanation for my not being blameworthy for breaking my promise to Ted, that is, that there is no rule obliging me to keep my promises, would not do either.

Here are two more reasons to resist this objection; first, it is not clear that the fact that KNA needs to account for the relationship between propriety of action and blamelessness in order to explain the above cases speaks towards its lack of a posteriori simplicity. After all, recall that Douven himself tried to account for the a priori simplicity of RCNA by attempting to show that it follows from principles to which we are committed on independent grounds. Similarly, the defence put forth above follows from principles about the normativity of action to which we are committed on independent grounds. So, rather than speaking against KNA, the fact that it is coheres with an account of the normativity of assertion that follows from the normativity of action in general seems to speak in its favour.

Furthermore, one can easily imagine parallel cases against RCNA which will render the latter in need of a similar line of defence. Take, for instance, Williamson's (2000) famous train case: suppose that I, knowing that it is urgent for you to get to your destination, shout 'That is your train!' upon seeing a train approach the station. That looks like the right thing to do, even though I do not know that it is your train, nor do I have knowledge-level justification for believing it; I merely believe that there's a fair chance that it is your train, and it's prudentially better for you to check it out. This is a case in which the prudential norm overrides whatever the epistemic norm says and renders me blameless and my assertion all-things-considered proper. Also, even if my assertion is both in breach of RCNA and improper on all other grounds, I might still be blameless for it, if, for instance, the reason why I assert without having any justification whatsoever is because I have been hit over the head with a bat. In fact, Douven (2006) himself acknowledges that "we will need a story about breaching rules blamelessly anyway, regardless of what we are going to say is the rule of assertion". Thus, it does not look like RCNA fares better in what a posteriori simplicity is concerned either.

On the other hand, for all I have shown in section §4, neither does KNA. Insofar as both norms are compatible with a normative account that explains breaching rules blamelessly by starting from the wider framework of the normativity of action, the two seem to be shoulder to shoulder in this respect.

Thus, up to now, the scoreboard[25] seems to only feature one extra point on the part of KNA due to its ability to explain the paradoxical flavour of Moorean statements. Now, as things stand, this will do. Say, however, that the RCNA defender will find a way to account for Moorean statements too. In this case, again,

---

25 To be clear, neither Douven nor I mean to attach much theoretical weight to the scorekeeping business (see Douven 2006, 481); rather, its use is merely illustrative.

RCNA would gain precedence due to its being the weaker and, thus, more user-friendly norm. For this very reason, what I am going to do below is offer the sketch of an argument for the superiority of KNA in terms of a posteriori simplicity. That is, following Douven's strategy, I will try to argue that KNA follows from a posteriori principles that we are independently committed to.

5.2 Epistemic Goals and A Posteriori Simplicity

If there's such a thing as an epistemic norm for assertion in the first place, it is plausibly somehow associated with an epistemic goal;[26] roughly put, it is there to insure that assertion delivers the epistemic goods we are using it for.

Now, first, notice that I can tell you that p with many purposes in mind: I might tell you that the weather is nice to the aim of making polite conversation; I can tell you that you have ugly shoes in order to offend you etc. What we are concerned with, however, are the epistemic purposes associated with the practice of assertion: what epistemic goods is assertion meant to deliver?

Second, speech-act theoreticians[27] distinguish between two types of goals associated with speech acts: essential goals – accompanying every token of the type – and characteristic goals – often attached to tokens of that type.[28] In what assertion is concerned, presenting p as true is an essential goal associated with this particular speech act: one cannot assert that p without presenting p as true. When it comes to its characteristic aim, generating true belief/knowledge in the hearer are taken to be obvious candidates; most assertions will be directed at

---

[26] Note that Douven (2012) himself argues that the epistemic norm of assertion is concerned with maximizing epistemic utility. Importantly, though the claim made here – and needed for this argument – is weaker. It is a claim of mere association between epistemic norms and epistemic goals; as such, it does not, in any way, imply any value theoretic commitments. The teleologist will explain the 'ought' in terms of the 'good'; he will say that the norm is there to guide us in reaching the goal. The deontologist reverses the order of explanation; he would have it that the goal is only valuable in virtue of the fact that the norm gives us reasons to favour it. Anyhow, the mere association claim holds. Thus, the argument that follows can be construed in both consequentialist and deontological terms.
[27] See e.g. Austin (1962), Green (2009).
[28] Which is not to say that what defines a characteristic goal need be frequency. To the contrary, the fact that this particular goal will often be attached to tokens of that type of action suggests an underlying functional explanation, i.e., that is the kind of good that this particular type of action is meant to deliver. For an account along these lines, see, e.g. Graham (2010). Thus, for the purposes of this paper, I use function and characteristic aim interchangeably; nothing hinges on it.

this aim. Although not essentially – I can, say, make assertions in a diary, which are plausibly not intended to affect no audience in any way –, characteristically, assertions will aim at generating true belief/knowledge in the audience. Furthermore, plausibly enough, this is the main social function of assertion to begin with.

Now, crucially, notice that, for actions in general, norms governing them tend to be associated with their characteristic rather than their essential purposes. Consider any action governed by norms, say for instance chess; plausibly, similarly to any game, the characteristic aim of chess playing is enjoying oneself. As such, like all other games, chess playing is governed by a set of rules that are there to insure a high probability of that happening. That is not to say, however, that enjoying oneself is an essential aim of chess; surely one can play chess for several other purposes, like, for instance, teaching someone else how to do it. That, however, again, does not imply that separate norms will be in place in this situation. Thus, it looks as if, when it comes to other types of action, the characteristic goal dictates the content of the relevant norm.[29]

Assertion is a type of action. In line with other types of action, then, we should expect the norms regulating it to be concerned with its characteristic aim. Furthermore, we should expect the *epistemic* norms governing it to be concerned with its characteristic *epistemic* aim.

Now, on one hand, several people take the main epistemic function of assertion to be transmission of true belief (e.g. Graham (2010)). The competing camp (e.g. Kelp and Simion (2016), Reynolds (2002)) defends a knowledge goal; accordingly, the characteristic purpose of assertion is generating testimonial knowledge in the hearer. Due to our physical and cognitive limitations, most of the knowledge we have is testimonial; thus, assertion is one of our main epistemic vehicles.[30]

For our purposes here, we need not decide this issue; on both these accounts, KNA fares better than RCNA. Here is why: all the epistemic aims we have identified so far are factive. If that is the case, however, mere rational credibility on the part of the speaker is not very likely to deliver the epistemic goods: first, uncontroversially, no matter how much justification I have to believe that p

---

[29] Note that the case of chess is hardly isolated. Similar examples can be construed with many norm-governed activities: driving, speaking a language, studying at the university...

[30] Is all knowledge/true belief on a par in this respect? Some items thereof seem entirely useless (e.g. about the number of blades of grass on my lawn). Perhaps it is more plausible to think that the epistemic goal of assertion is generating interesting true belief/knowledge (see, e.g., Alston 2005 for discussion). For the purposes of this paper, I will take any such restriction on the relevant epistemic goal as read.

is the case, if p is false and I assert that p, my hearer will not get a testimonial true belief that p.

Furthermore, on the knowledge-goal view, KNA looks even more promising. First, given that knowledge is factive, the objection to RCNA above applies, mutatis mutandis, here too. Second, on most if not all accounts of testimony in the literature,[31] in the vast majority of cases, the speaker needs to know in order to be able to generate knowledge in the hearer. Exceptions are few, and they roughly boil down to two types of cases: first, we have, again, 'selfless asserters' like Stella. Notice, though, that Stella's case will not help the RCNA defender here: after all, Stella is able to generate knowledge in her students because, as it so happens, on top of its being justified, her assertion is true. Secondly, we have 'Compulsive Liar' cases (Lackey 2008). Roughly, what happens in these cases is that, although the speaker intends to lie on a regular basis, some external intervention makes it so that she safely asserts the truth. Again, though, these cases will not help the rational credibility account, given that compulsive liars also violate RCNA.

Also, notice that both of these cases describe fairly unusual scenarios, thus they are highly unlikely to affect the argument from testimony to the knowledge norm in any way. After all, if the characteristic purpose of assertion is generating testimonial knowledge, and in the vast majority of the cases knowledge on the part of the speaker is needed for generating testimonial knowledge in the hearer, it makes sense to have a knowledge norm governing assertion. To see this, consider driving: norms regulating speed limit within city bounds are presumably there to make it so that we arrive safely at our destination. Surely, though, driving 50 km/h within city bounds is not *always* the ideal speed; there are instances when, for instance, overtaking at 80 km/h will avoid a major accident. However, presumably, the reason why the norm says 'Drive at most 50 km/h within city bounds!' is because, most of the time, that is the ideal speed for safety purposes.

In sum, things seem to stand as follows: on one hand, in the vast majority of cases, assertions need be knowledgeable in order to deliver the epistemic goods they are meant to deliver; also, by Douven's own lights, in the friendly epistemic environment we inhabit, knowledge is readily available. Furthermore, unlike rational credibility, the concept of knowledge is widely mastered and used. If that is the case, it looks as if simplicity speaks in favour of KNA. Given that "the prac-

---

[31] See Lackey (2008) for a nice overview.

tice of assertion is, in an incontrovertible sense, a part of reality of our making" (Douven 2006, 451), we should expect ourselves to have kept it simple.³²

6. Conclusion

This paper has argued that the knowledge norm of assertion scores better than the main competing account on the market when it comes to both empirical adequacy and simplicity. To this aim, I have first shown that Igor Douven's argument for the superiority of the rational credibility norm in terms of a priori simplicity does not go through. Further on, I have argued that RCNA, as opposed to KNA, is unable to explain the paradoxical flavour of Moorean statements.

I have also put forth a framework for the normativity of assertion as part of a fairly uncontroversial normative framework for action in general, and argued that it helps to defuse several notable objections to KNA.

And, last but not least, I have brought new reasons to believe that KNA fares better than RCNA when it comes to a posteriori simplicity. That is because, I have argued, KNA is compatible with some fairly uncontroversial assumptions about 1) the characteristic function of assertion and 2) the necessary conditions for generating knowledge/true belief in one's hearer.

---

32 Here is how RCNA might accommodate all this: recall that, according to Douven, due to knowledge being readily available, in most cases, if p is rationally credible to one, then one also knows that p. In virtue of this, Douven might argue, RCNA-permissible assertions will also generate testimonial true belief/knowledge in the hearer in the vast majority of cases. Notice, though, that this explanation falls quite significantly behind the KNA one when it comes to a posteriori simplicity. Secondly, it looks as if RCNA is not even exceptionally well positioned to offer it, as many norms on the market could just as plausibly help themselves to this explanation: the defender of a truth norm will argue that, when we truly believe that p, we usually know that p, the defender of a belief norm will say that when we believe that p, we usually know that p etc. And, last but not least, again, given that we are talking about a part of reality of our making, and given the readily availability of knowledge and the wide mastering of the concept, in absence of independent grounds to favor RCNA, it is not clear why we should buy this explanation in the first place. Consider the case of driving again: the norm is not: 'Try your best to drive at most 50 km/h!', because if you do that, most of the time you are going to actually drive 50 km/h, and therefore be safe. The norm just says 'Drive at most 50 km/h!'.

References

Adler, J. (2002). *Belief's Own Ethics*. Cambridge (MA): MIT Press.
Alston, W. (2005). *Beyond 'Justification': Dimensions of Epistemic Evaluation*. Ithaca NY: Cornell University Press.
Aristotle. (1985). *The Nicomachean Ethics*. (T. Irwin, Trans.) Indianapolis: Hackett Publishing Co.
Austin, J. L. (1962). *How to Do Things with Words* (2nd ed.). (J. U. Sbisá, Ed.) Cambridge, MA: Harvard University Press.
Brown, J. (2010). Knowledge and Assertion. *Philosophy and Phenomenological Research* 81, 549–566.
Chisholm, R. (1964). The Ethics of Requirement. *American Philosophical Quarterly* 1, 147–153.
De Rose, K. (2002). Assertion, Knowledge and Context. *Philosophical Review* 111, 167–203
Douven, I. (2006). Assertion, Knowledge and Rational Credibility. *Philosophical Review* 115, 449–485.
Frankfurt, H. (1969). Alternate Possibilities and Moral Responsibility. *The Journal of Philosophy* 66, 829–839.
Green, M. (2009). Speech Acts. In E. Zalta (ed.), *The Stanford Encyclopedia of Philosophy*, URL = <http://plato.stanford.edu/archives/spr2009/entries/speech-acts/>.
Grice, P. (1989). *Studies in the Way of Words*. Cambridge, MA: Harvard University Press.
Haji, I. (1998). *Moral Appraisability*. Oxford: Oxford University Press.
Hawthorne, J. (2004). *Knowledge and Lotteries*. Oxford: Oxford University Press.
Heyd, D. (2012). Supererogation. In E. Zalta (ed.), *The Stanford Encyclopedia of Philosophy*. <http://plato.stanford.edu/archives/spr2012/entries/supererogation/>
Kelp and Simion (2016). Assertion: A Function First Account. Unpublished Manuscript.
Kvanvig, J. (2009). Assertion, Knowledge and Lotteries. In P Greenough and D. Pritchard (eds.), *Williamson on Knowledge*. Oxford: Oxford University Press.
Lackey, J. (2007). Norms of Assertion. *Noûs* 41, 594–626.
Lackey, J. (2011). Assertion and Isolated Secondhand Knowledge. In J. A. Brown and H. Cappelen (eds.), *Assertion: New Philosophical Essays*. Oxford: Oxford University Press.
Littlejohn, C. (Forthcoming). A Plea for Epistemic Excuses. In F. Dorsch and J. Dutant (eds.) *The New Evil Demon Problem*. Oxford: Oxford University Press.
Pagin, P. (2011). Information and Assertoric Force. In J. A. Brown and H. Cappelen (eds.), *Assertion: New Philosophical Essays*. Oxford: Oxford University Press.
Reynolds, S. (2002). Testimony, Knowledge, and Epistemic Goals. *Philosophical Studies* 110, 139–61.
Simion (forthcoming). Assertion: Just One Way to Take It Back. *Logos and Episteme*.
Simion (2015) Assertion: Knowledge is Enough. *Synthese*. Online First.
Turri, J. (2011). The Express Knowledge Account of Assertion. *Australasian Journal of Philosophy* 89, 37–45.
Turri, J. (Forthcoming). You Gotta Believe. In J. Turri and C. Littlejohn (eds.), *Epistemic Norms*. Oxford: Oxford University Press.
Williamson, T. (2000). *Knowledge and its Limits*. Oxford: Oxford University Press.
Williamson, T. (2009). Replies to Critics. In P. Greenough and D. Pritchard (eds.), *Williamson on Knowledge*. Oxford: Oxford University Press.

Williamson, Y (2013). Gettier Cases in Epistemic logic. *Inquiry* 56, 1–14.
Williamson, T. (Forthcoming). Justifications, Excuses and Sceptical Scenarios. In F. Dorsch and J. Dutant (eds.) The New Evil Demon Problem. Oxford: Oxford University Press.
Zimmerman, M. (1997). Moral Responsibility and Ignorance. *Ethics* 107, 410–426.

Davide Fassio
Commonality Reconsidered: On the Common Source of Epistemic Standards

Commonality is the claim that there is a common epistemic standard for assertion, practical reasoning and belief.[1] The most popular version of this view holds that this epistemic standard requires knowledge: it is appropriate to assert that *p*, believe that *p* and rely on *p* in one's practical reasoning only if it is known that *p* (e.g., Hawthorne (2004), Hawthorne and Stanley (2008), Williamson (2000), (2005)). According to other versions of commonality, this standard requires other epistemic conditions such as justified belief that one knows (Smithies (2012)) or warrant (Gerken (2011)).

Philosophers interested in commonality are mainly concerned with two kinds of question. The first kind (which we may call 'Validity questions') includes questions such as whether commonality is true, and if yes, which type of similarity occurs amongst the various standards – whether standards require the very same conditions in all circumstances, or their similarity is at a more abstract, structural level, allowing contextually variable and divergent requirements. Those engaging with these questions provide arguments in support of or against specific variants of commonality, or try to challenge these arguments. Assuming that some form of commonality is true, one can then ask how commonality can be motivated or explained, whether it is a matter of mere coincidence that different attitudes and practices are governed by the same epistemic standard or whether there is some deeper motivation for it, and if yes, what it is. We can regroup these various questions under the label 'Motivation questions'.[2] The two kinds of questions are obviously related: on the one hand, if arguments against commonality succeed, Motivation questions don't make much sense, since they presuppose the truth of the commonality thesis; furthermore, different versions of commonality may suggest alternative answers to Motivation questions. On the other hand, a plausible explanation of commonality could provide

---
[1] See in particular Brown (2012) and Gerken (2014). Brown and Gerken refer only to the standards of assertion and practical reasoning. However, since many have also argued that the same standard governs belief on similar bases and using similar arguments, I don't see why the claim shouldn't be extended to belief.
[2] Brown first introduced this order of questions. In Brown 2012, she writes: 'My interest in this paper is not primarily in whether commonality is true but, whether, if it is, there is a deeper theoretical motivation for it.' (Brown 2012: 124). See also id., 123–124 and Gerken 2014 for discussion.

further grounds for thinking that commonality is true; and *vice versa*, the failure to find a deep motivation for commonality may be taken as a *prima facie* argument against commonality.

This paper is primarily concerned with Motivation questions. In particular, I will investigate what type of motivation or explanation can be given for commonality. Two types of answer to this question are available: epistemic norms governing belief, assertion and practical reasoning could be the same either because these norms are inter-derivable, or because there is some common factor independent of the reciprocal relations amongst these norms determining the common standard. Let's call these two options *horizontal* and *vertical approaches* to an explanation of commonality. In this paper I will sketch a specific version of the vertical approach. According to my account, there is a common reason why beliefs, assertions and premises in practical reasoning end up sharing a common epistemic standard. Roughly, the idea is that these entities share a common representational nature of a peculiar kind; the standard is primarily attached to this feature and the various entities share the common standard in virtue of all instantiating that feature.

This is the plan of the paper. In §1 I introduce commonality and provide an overview of the debate surrounding the two kinds of question considered above. In §2 I introduce my account. In §3 I draw some final conclusions.

1. Epistemic Norms and Commonality

My aims in this section are, first, to provide a more rigorous characterization of commonality, and second, to briefly introduce the contemporary debate surrounding the two kinds of question considered above. In §1.1, I provide a general introduction to commonality and distinguish between two main versions of this thesis: Equivalence and Structural commonality; in §1.2, I provide an overview of the main arguments for and against commonality; in §1.3, I briefly review some strategies to motivate and explain commonality and mention some objections to them.

1.1 Introducing Commonality

Many philosophers have argued recently that belief, assertion and practical reasoning are governed by epistemic norms.[3] Usually philosophers characterize such norms in terms of conditional or bi-conditional claims having the following form:

(EN assertion) It is appropriate for S to assert p iff (if/only if) C^A.

(EN practical reasoning) It is appropriate for S to use p as a premise in one's practical reasoning iff (if/only if) C^{PR}.[4]

(EN belief) It is appropriate for S to believe p iff (if/only if) C^B.

Here C^A, C^{PR} and C^B are epistemic conditions such as 'S knows that p', 'S justifiably believes that p' or 'S is warranted to believe that p'. Which epistemic conditions is a debated matter. Some argue that this condition is knowledge (Hawthorne (2004); Hawthorne & Stanley (2008); Stanley (2005); Williamson (2000)). Others suggest that weaker conditions like justified or warranted belief are better candidates (Fantl & McGrath (2009), Littlejohn (2009) and (2012)). Still others argue that the epistemic condition is contextually variable (Brown (2008), Gerken (2011) and (2014)). While in some cases it is appropriate to assert, believe and act on epistemic positions weaker than knowledge, in other cases, such as

---

[3] A terminological remark: as is common in the literature on the topic, the terms 'norm' and 'normative standard' are sometimes used as synonyms, while at other times 'standard' refers to the epistemic condition conformity to which is required in order to appropriately believe, assert and rely on p. In the present article I will primarily use these two terms as synonyms. When this is not the case, the specific sense of 'standard' will be sufficiently clear from the context.
[4] A couple of remarks about (EN practical reasoning) are in order: First, alternative formulations substitute "to use p as a premise in her practical reasoning" with "to rely on p in one's practical reasoning" or "to treat p as a reason for action" (on the difference between these formulations see for example Gerken (2011), fn2). The formulation in the main text is significantly similar to those discussed by, e.g., Hawthorne (2004); Hawthorne and Stanley (2008); Locke (2015); Williamson (2005). Second, those defending the right-to-left direction of the norm usually add a restriction of the norm to cases in which one's choice is p-dependent, where a choice between options is p-dependent iff the most preferable option conditional on the proposition that p is not the same as the most preferable one conditional on the proposition that not-p (Hawthorne and Stanley (2008), 578). This restriction is needed in order to avoid cases in which whether p is irrelevant to the issue considered in the practical reasoning. In such cases intuitively the agent is not required to use it as a premise in her deliberation even if she has a strong epistemic position with respect to it.

when it is very important to be right about whether *p*, only a level of warrant sufficient for certainty would make rational one's asserting, believing and acting on *p*. The debate on the relevant epistemic conditions is ongoing. In this article I will remain neutral on this issue.

Some further remarks on the formulation of the norms are in order here. First, we assess actions, assertions and beliefs according to very different standards: prudence, morality, etiquette, and so on. The standard of assessment relevant in the various norms considered above is an epistemic one, concerning the goodness of one's epistemic position with respect to a given proposition. Second, as is apparent from the above formulations, the norms can take the form of biconditionals, or necessary or sufficient conditionals. Third, while I formulated the norms in terms of standards of appropriateness, some philosophers suggest slightly different formulations: some use "rational", "permissible" or "warranted" instead of "appropriate". Since I want to remain as neutral as possible on these specific features of the standards, I am open to revising the above formulations as may be thought appropriate. Further discussions in the paper don't depend on such details.

Usually commonality is defined as the claim that the epistemic standard for assertion and practical reasoning is the same (Brown (2012), Gerken (2014)). However, many philosophers discussing the relations between common epistemic standards consider the norm of belief as strictly related to those governing assertion and practical reasoning (e.g., Williamson (2000), Smithies (2012)). Therefore I don't see any reason not to extend commonality to epistemic standards of belief. In this paper I will use 'commonality' in this wider sense.

Gerken distinguishes between two forms of commonality: Equivalence and Structural commonality (2014: 729). According to Equivalence commonality, C^A, C^{PR} and C^B designate the same, context-invariant epistemic condition (e.g., knowledge, justified belief...).[5] According to Structural commonality, while epistemic standards of belief, assertion and practical reasoning have relevantly similar structures, the epistemic condition required by these standards may diverge and be different in different situations. For instance, according to the specific version of Structural commonality developed by Gerken, the epistemic condition required by these standards can vary across contexts depending on features such as stakes, urgency and availability of further evidence. In contexts in which stakes are very high, there is no urgency of acting, asserting or forming a belief, and there is further available evidence, a very strong epistemic position (say,

---

[5] Arguments have been provided against Equivalence commonality (Brown, 2012; Gerken, 2014). I will consider these arguments and possible ways of addressing them in §1.2.

knowledge or certainty) is required to believe, act or assert, while in contexts in which not too much is at stake, it is urgent to act, assert or form a belief, and there is no further evidence available, a weaker epistemic position may do. The structural similarity consists in the fact that when the deliberative, conversational and doxastic contexts are relevantly similar (with respect to the features considered above), the epistemic condition required by the various standards will be the same.[6] Another way of describing this version of Structural commonality is that, while according to this view it is still true that $C^A = C^{PR} = C^B$, here C doesn't denote a specific epistemic condition, but a function from contexts to specific epistemic conditions.

In this paper I want to remain neutral on the specific account of commonality. For simplicity of exposition, in what follows I will normally refer to epistemic standards requiring context-invariant conditions – unless it is differently specified. However the same ideas can be easily reformulated in ways compatible with versions of Structural commonality.

1.2 Arguments for and Against Commonality

Philosophers have provided several arguments in favour of and against commonality. These arguments are primarily directed toward answering the Validity question concerning whether commonality is true, i.e., whether belief, assertion and practical reasoning share the same epistemic standard. Though this question is not the central focus of this paper, as I said in the introduction, the Validity and the Motivation questions are strictly related: on the one hand, if the criticisms to commonality were to the point, the very project of finding a deeper explanation for commonality would be a non-starter. On the other hand, a plausible explanation of commonality could provide further grounds for thinking that commonality is true, and *vice versa*, the failure to find a deep motivation for commonality

---

6 Two clarifications are in order here. First, with the phrase 'deliberative context', Gerken denotes "the configuration of factors that determines the epistemic position vis-à-vis p one must be in to act on p or rely on p in practical reasoning". Similarly, 'conversational context' denotes the configuration of factors that determines the epistemic position vis-à-vis p one must be in to assert that p (2014: 10). We may define the 'doxastic context' as the configuration of factors that determines the epistemic position vis-à-vis p one must be in to believe that p. Second, as we will see below (§1.2), some philosophers have argued that the deliberative, conversational and doxastic contexts may differ also in the same situation (for example, because stakes are much higher in asserting p than in believing that p and acting on p). In such cases, the specific conditions required by the epistemic standards of belief, practical reasoning and assertion may be different, even though these standards remain structurally identical at a more abstract level.

may be taken as a *prima facie* argument against commonality. It is thus helpful to consider some arguments supporting commonality, as well as to examine objections to this thesis and how they could be addressed.

The main rationale in support of commonality relies on the common ways of assessing (criticizing, justifying and judging) assertions, beliefs and practical reasoning according to epistemic standards. If Mary doesn't know that her friend Jane will arrive at the airport at around 5pm, it seems inappropriate for her to go at the airport at that time to pick her up without first checking the time of arrival. Similarly, if Mary's mother asks her at what time Jane will arrive at the airport, provided she has no reasons to lie to her mother, it seems inappropriate for her to answer that Jane will arrive at 5pm. Furthermore Mary's epistemic position seems not sufficiently good to endorse an outright belief that Jane will arrive at 5pm. In general we tend to consider outright beliefs falling short of knowledge as defective. These considerations are intended merely to provide an example of the general line of argument used by philosophers to defend commonality. Though they *prima facie* support the claim that knowledge is the common standard, analogous ordinary intuitions have been used to support other common standards. The general point is that strong similarities in the ways we assess beliefs, assertions and actions suggest that the corresponding epistemic standards are also the same.

Another consideration in support of commonality comes from certain views and principles recently defended by prominent epistemologists. For example, so-called "knowledge first" theorists tend to see commonality as an expected consequence of the explanatory centrality of knowledge amongst epistemic notions.[7] Other philosophers have defended Unity of Reasons principles according to which good reasons to believe are also good reasons to act and *vice versa* (e.g., Fantl & McGrath (2009); Littlejohn (2014)).

Philosophers have always remarked on the strict relation between assertion and belief, for example by identifying assertions as linguistic expressions of beliefs, or by considering beliefs as inner assertions. Similarly, many have considered beliefs as attitudes ideally suited to provide premises in reasoning; and conversely many have tried to partially define beliefs in terms of their role in deliberation. Moreover, assertions are supposed to convey actionable information, information that can be used in deliberative practices, such as premises in practical reasoning. If beliefs, assertions and practical reasoning ended up

---

[7] For this kind of approach see, for example, Hawthorne (2004); Hawthorne and Stanley (2008); Stanley (2005); Williamson (2000).

sharing the same epistemic standard, this wouldn't be surprising given these strict relations amongst them.

Arguments against commonality consist of counterexamples. In particular, Brown (2012) considers cases in which epistemic standards of belief, assertion and action seem to diverge.[8] Consider the following case to the effect that it is epistemically appropriate for a subject to believe that p and act on it, but not to assert that p:

> [S]uppose that Sally is standing on the train platform waiting for a train to Edinburgh. Both express and non express trains frequently pass the platform. She has consulted the timetable and so comes to truly believe that the next train is an express to Edinburgh. She has a mild preference for taking an express train, but it will not be a disaster if she happens to take a non-express. This would merely result in her getting home 10 minutes later than need be. In such circumstances, it seems that she is in a good enough epistemic position to believe that the next train is an express and act on this assumption, say by taking the next train. Despite this, it need not be the case that she is in a good enough epistemic position to assert that the next train is an express. Imagine that a stranger approaches her on the platform and explains that it is crucial to him whether the next train is an express or not. Given how high the stakes are for the stranger, it seems that Sally is not in a good enough epistemic position to assert that the next train is an express. This is so even though it continues to be the case that, given her own much lower stakes, she is in a good enough epistemic position to believe that the next train is an express and act on it herself. Indeed, she may well tell the stranger that he should check at the very same time as she steps on to the train herself (Brown 2012, 140).

This example is supposed to show that it is epistemically appropriate for Sally to believe and act on the proposition that the next train is an express, but not to assert it. Brown also offers an analogue case in which it seems epistemically appropriate to assert a certain proposition, but not to rely on it in practical reasoning (ibid., 141).

Let me stress that, since the target of the paper is not to address the Validity question, providing a reply to these arguments is beyond the scope of this paper.[9] However, as noted above, the Validity and Motivation questions are strictly related. It would make little sense to consider the possible explanations of why a certain thesis is true while leaving completely aside objections to that thesis. In what follows, I suggest three possible strategies for addressing Brown's counterexamples:

---

8 For a discussion of Brown's arguments see also Gerken (2014).
9 My interest in Brown's article rather concern her other more general arguments against the possibility of providing a general motivation or explanation for why commonality is true. See §1.3.

(i) A defender of commonality may argue that the examples do not constitute cases in which the propriety of acting on *p*, believing that *p* and asserting that *p* come apart. For example, it may be suggested that while in Brown's Train case it seems inappropriate for Sally to assert that the next train is an express, this is due to a lack of prudential or conversational propriety; prudence, convention, and other practical standards may impose certain supplementary epistemic constraints on what it is proper (according to these standards) to assert in a certain situation. However, this is compatible with it being fully *epistemically* appropriate for Sally to assert that the next train is an express.[10] Alternatively, one may argue that the putative counterexamples ignore the distinction between violating a norm and being to blame for violating a norm (see, e.g., Hawthorne and Stanley (2008); Littlejohn (forthcoming, 2014); Williamson (forthcoming, 2005)). The thought is that while it is equally epistemically inappropriate for Sally to believe, assert and rely on the proposition that the next train is an express (because, for example, she doesn't know it), her violation of the norms of belief and practical reasoning are blameless; since the consequences for Sally of being wrong about whether the next train is an express are not particularly serious, Sally is excusable for these infractions. In contrast, the violation of the norm of assertion is seriously blameworthy given how important it is for the stranger to take an express train.

(ii) A more direct reply consists in directly challenging the persuasiveness of Brown's counterexamples. There is plenty of room to disagree with Brown's interpretation of the described cases. Let's assume, as Brown suggests, that when the stranger approaches Sally and asks her whether the next train is an express or not, it is inappropriate for Sally to assert that the next train is an express (hereafter, *p*). However, in the same circumstance it seems also inappropriate for Sally to self-ascribe knowledge that *p*, and thus to possess a degree of confidence sufficient for an outright belief that *p*. A charitable interpretation of the case is that Sally knows that it's very likely that *p*. This knowledge makes it appropriate for her to believe that it's very likely that *p*, to possess a quite high degree of credence that *p*, but not to outright believe that *p*. Furthermore, knowledge that it's very likely that *p* makes it rational for Sally to act as if *p* (i.e., to step on the train) given that not

---

10 Here it may be useful to compare this strategy to other well-known similar ones. For example, some philosophers explain certain judgements that it is wrong to assert things you know in certain situations on the basis of moral and prudential considerations (e.g., Williamson 2000).

too much is at stake for her, but not to unqualifiedly assert that p in a conversation with an interlocutor whose stakes on whether p are significantly higher.

(iii) My last suggestion doesn't involve directly challenging Brown's examples; rather, it maintains that these cases are compatible with a certain interpretation of commonality. As Gerken (2014) persuasively argued, these cases can have some force only against equivalence commonality, since they show that, for example, the very same epistemic condition can be sufficient to believe a proposition and act on it, but not to assert it. However, these cases are compatible with a qualified version of structural commonality. In particular, they are compatible with an account such as that developed by Gerken (2011, 2012), according to which the epistemic position required by epistemic norms of belief, assertion and practical reasoning can vary depending on features of the context such as stakes, urgency and availability of further evidence. In some contexts a very strong epistemic position is required. In others, a weaker epistemic position may do. This account can easily accommodate Brown's examples. In the Train case, Sally's deliberative and doxastic contexts are importantly different from her conversational context (while stakes in believing p and acting on p are low, they are high in asserting p). This explains why the same epistemic position is sufficient to warrant Sally's belief and action, but not her assertion.

Though I remain neutral on the strategy one should adopt to counter Brown's counterexamples to commonality, I consider the third suggestion the most promising, since it avoids problems without directly challenging Brown's interpretation of the examples.

1.3 The Motivation Questions

Motivation questions can be summarized as follows: assuming that commonality is true, is there some deep motivation or explanation for why it is true? If yes, what is this motivation? Philosophers usually agree that a positive answer should be given to the former question. Assume that commonality is true. This (alleged) fact could be due to a mere coincidence, in the same way in which laws in different countries could require the same thing even if enforced for completely different and unrelated reasons. However this would be quite surprising given the strict relations occurring between belief, assertion and premises in reasoning. If there is some plausible way of explaining why these different attitudes and practices share a common standard, this motivation would also constitute an argument to the best explanation for thinking that commonality isn't merely a matter of chance.

Assuming that commonality is not a mere coincidence, there should be some motivation or explanation for why assertion, belief and practical reasoning share the same epistemic standard. What could this motivation or explanation be? There are two types of answer one can give to such a question: first, the epistemic norms governing belief, assertion and practical reasoning are the same because one of these norms is more fundamental and allows a derivation of the others in conjunction with relatively uncontroversial principles. Pursuing a similar strategy in answering the question is what I call a *horizontal approach* to commonality. Alternatively the common standard could be determined by some common source or factor independent of reciprocal relations amongst the different epistemic norms. Let's call an approach pursuing the latter strategy a *vertical approach* to commonality.

Attempts to defend commonality in the literature have focused on horizontal approaches. Examples are Montminy, Smithies and McKenna.[11] Montminy (2013) argues that the epistemic norm of assertion derives from the norm of practical reasoning together with a rule of assertion according to which assertion must manifest belief.[12] Smithies (2012) and McKenna (forthcoming) explain the standards of assertion and practical reasoning in terms of the standard of belief[13]

Horizontal approaches have been the target of criticisms. In particular, Brown (2012) provides objections to two types of derivation, from the norm of practical reasoning to that of assertion, and from the norm of belief to the norms of assertion and practical reasoning.[14] It is not my intention here to introduce and assess these criticisms. This would lead us too far from the target of this paper. I will simply assume the validity of these criticisms for the sake of argument. With a note of scepticism Brown observes that the various objections to the main strategies attempting to explain commonality, though not decisive in

---

[11] See also McKinnon (2012).

[12] For a criticism see McKenna (2013).

[13] I will not be concerned here with the specific arguments provided by these philosophers. Notice also that these philosophers disagree on the epistemic condition constituting the common standards of assertion, practical reasoning and belief. For example, for Montminy this condition is knowledge, while for Smithies it is having a justification to believe that one is in a position to know. These differences are immaterial for the present discussion.

[14] Notice that I am talking here of Brown's arguments specifically directed to the possibility of providing a general motivation or explanation for why commonality is true. Brown's other criticisms to the truth of commonality have been discussed already in §1.2.

showing the falsity of the thesis, illustrate the difficulty of providing a theoretical motivation for commonality. The failure to find a deep motivation for commonality may be taken as weakening the claim that similar epistemic norms actually govern such attitudes and practices – at least by the critics of these norms.

In my view Brown's above-mentioned conclusions are partially unjustified. The debate on commonality is still at its beginning and much more has to be said and written before we can reach similar conclusions. Furthermore some versions of commonality seem able to avoid Brown's challenges.[15] Most importantly, Brown's criticisms to a theoretical motivation of commonality focus exclusively on what I called horizontal approaches. Vertical approaches are untouched by such criticisms. In the next section, I will sketch a specific version of a vertical approach to commonality.

2. A Vertical Approach to Commonality

My vertical approach to commonality aims to explain why different entities like beliefs, assertions and premises of practical reasoning have a common standard by looking at some further factor these entities have in common. We can illustrate this approach with an analogy: imagine that different communities that cannot communicate with each other enforce a certain social rule for the same reason. For example, before the discovery of America, both Europeans and Native Americans enforced social rules preventing suicide. Suppose that these societies introduced such a rule for a common reason (e.g., suicide is a socially destabilizing practice). This common reason explains the adoption of a social rule in two separated communities. Importantly, the rule is not adopted by a community because of some relation with the other community and its rules (e.g., by imposition or imitation).[16]

My explanation of commonality relies on the assumption that beliefs, assertions and premises of practical reasoning involve a representational component: all represent possible states of affairs, i.e., possible ways in which the world can

---

15 See in particular the approach suggested by Gerken (2014).
16 Curiously, Brown suggests a similar example when she presents the issue of whether a deeper theoretical motivation is possible for commonality. She considers the case of two local tennis clubs having the same membership rules. She writes "one possible deeper explanation of the commonality is that both local clubs are members of a national association, where membership of that association requires adopting a given membership rule" (2012, 124). However in her article she doesn't consider the strategy for explaining commonality implied in this example.

be.[17] Furthermore, all these representational entities have a *thetic direction of fit:*[18] if the representation doesn't fit what is supposed to be represented, what is wrong and should be changed is the representation, not the thing to be represented. So, for example, if what is believed is not the case, the belief is wrong and should be revised to fit the world, and not *vice versa*. The representational nature of these entities differs from others having a *telic* direction of fit, like desires: if what is desired is not the case, the world should be changed in order to fit what is desired, and not *vice versa*. Another popular way of describing entities with a thetic direction of fit is to say that they are supposed to represent the world *as it is* rather than *as it should be*.[19]

The specific focus here is on entities having a thetic direction of fit. These are, for example, beliefs, maps, conjectures, hypotheses, guesses, assertions, presuppositions, descriptions, and so on.[20] We can group these entities into more general types. For example, beliefs and conjectures are mental attitudes, guesses and assertions are speech acts, maps are artefacts, and so on. In

---

17 I merely note here that the unqualified claim that beliefs involve a representational component is quite undisputed and is compatible with different accounts of the nature of belief, including dispositionalist and functionalist accounts. Here I don't want to take a position on issues about the specific nature of beliefs, though elsewhere I have provided a criticism of dispositionalist and functionalist accounts (see Fassio (2014)).

18 Though some philosophers apply the distinction between thetic and thelic direction of fit only to mental attitudes, the general distinction is not restricted to this type of entity. One of the classical presentations of the direction of fit, that of Anscombe (1957), relies on an example not involving mental attitudes, that of the buyer's shopping list and the investigator's list. For a discussion of how the distinction can be extended to speech acts see, for example, Searle (1983). Philosophers use different terminologies for directions of fit, such as "mind-to-world" vs "world-to-mind" and "cognitive" vs "conative". The present terminology was first introduced by Humberstone (1992). I find it particularly appropriate in the present context for it is neutral on the type of entity under consideration (mental attitude, speech act, artifact, and so on). For similar terminological remarks see Humberstone (1992), fn2.

19 Philosophers have offered very different accounts of direction of fit. The present statement is similar to the one introduced in Platts (1997), 257. For other accounts see, for example, Anscombe (1957); Humberstone (1992); Searle (1983); Velleman (2000); Zangwill (1998). There is disagreement on how to interpret the direction of fit: as a literal aim, a goal, a norm, or a function. Here I remain neutral on this issue.

20 Some terminological remarks: the term "guess" is sometimes used to express a type of mental state or act. Here, however, with this term I mean a specific type of speech act expressing a partial belief or a conjecture. Similarly, I will use "conjecture" to refer to a specific mental attitude requiring a degree of confidence weaker than that needed for a belief, but stronger than one sufficient to justify a suspension of judgment; I will not use this term to refer to speech acts manifesting this type of attitude. I will use "presupposition" to refer to the mental attitude, not to the act of premising.

order to avoid terminological confusions, I will call these general types of representational entities (mental attitudes, speech acts...) *species*.

Here we are particularly interested in three types of entities: beliefs, assertions and premises in deliberative practical reasoning. These are of different species: beliefs are mental attitudes; assertions are speech acts; premises of deliberative practical reasoning are of the same species as other entities including, for example, premises of conjectural reasoning, hypotheses and assumptions per absurdum. Unfortunately we lack a name for this species; let me call these entities *modes of premising*. It is important to note here that the distinction amongst species is completely orthogonal to that between thetic and telic representational entities. The latter concerns entities in virtue of their representational nature, while differences in species concern other aspects of these entities (their being mental items, linguistic acts...).

Representational entities having a thetic direction of fit can be assessed according to several *epistemic standards*. For example we assess all these entities according to how accurately they represent the things they are supposed to represent. Other standards of assessment concern psychological confidence, reliability, warrant, rationality, safety, epistemic justification, and so on. We can conceive ideals to which each species of entity with a thetic direction of fit tries to approximate by satisfying all these standards: speech acts aim at a fully grounded and informed assertion; mental attitudes ideally aim at knowledge with psychological certainty, excellent justificatory grounds, reflective access, and so on; premises of reasoning about whether to *F* plausibly aim at being well known and grounded reasons for or against *F*-ing.

One specific epistemic standard is particularly interesting for our present discussion: this is the standard that each entity is supposed to meet *qua* that type of entity (*qua* belief, conjecture, assertion, guess, and so on). This standard differs from others in the facts that (i) it is *constitutive* of a type of entity, and (ii) it is *individuative* of that type of entity amongst the types of entities of its own species. More schematically, where E^1, E^2, ... E^n are types of entities involving a thetic direction of fit, E^1 is a certain type of entity in virtue of the fact that it can be assessed according to epistemic standard N^1, and it is distinguishable from other types of entities of the same species E^2, E^3, E^4... in virtue of being the only type of entity of that species constitutively governed by N^1.

For example, a mental state is a belief partially in virtue of the fact that it should meet a certain epistemic standard (it should amount to knowledge, be warranted, or whatever else one takes the standard to be). This standard is what distinguishes beliefs from other mental attitudes possessing a thetic direction of fit, such as conjectures and presuppositions. Beliefs are governed by a more demanding standard than these other attitudes: one believing *p* on flimsy evidential grounds doesn't meet a minimal threshold required for appropriately believing and can be criticized for her epistemic position. On the contrary, it is perfectly appropriate to conjecture that *p* on relatively weak evidence supporting *p* over not-*p*. The constitutive standard for appropriate conjecture is less demanding than that for appropriate belief, even if more demanding than that for mere presupposition.

Similarly, amongst speech acts, weak evidential grounds may be sufficient for an appropriate guess that *p*, but not for an appropriate assertion that *p*. In this respect, a guess can be seen as that type of speech act that should represent a truth as accurately as possible given a limited amount of evidential support, while a full assertion involves a higher epistemic commitment such as knowledge or fully justified belief.[21] Amongst modes of premising, weak evidence for *p* may be sufficient for using *p* as a premise in a reasoning resulting in a conjecture about whether *p* (a conjectural reasoning); but the same amount of evidence may be insufficient to use *p* as a reason in a full deliberation about what to do.[22]

Different constitutive epistemic standards distinguish different types of entities of the same species. However types of entities of different species can possess the same constitutive standard. Indeed, this seems to be the case for several types of entities that have a thetic direction of fit and belong to different species: beliefs, assertions and premises of deliberative reasoning are types of entities of different species (mental attitudes, speech acts, modes of premising), but share a common epistemic standard – the most demanding, be it knowledge, warranted belief or whatever other condition one take it to be; similarly conjectures, guesses and premises of conjectural reasoning seem to be constitutively governed by a common, less demanding epistemic standard; presuppositions, hypotheses per

---

21 The idea that different 'assertives' (e.g., asserting, guessing, hypothesizing...) can be distinguished on the basis of their respective epistemic requirements is not new in the literature. It was already implicit in the works of Searle on speech acts (e.g., 1969, 1975). More recently, this idea has been defended by, for example, McKenna (2015) and Turri (2010). Arguments in favor of this idea can indirectly support the view that representational mental attitudes and modes of premising also share a similar structure – at least if we assume structural similarities in the way in which types of entities of each species can be distinguished from each other.
22 Notice that these distinctions amongst mental attitudes, speech acts and modes of premising are not exhaustive. I have omitted other entities whose constitutive epistemic standards are placed in between the exemplified entities. We could also think that there are no neat gaps between entities of the same species; such entities would be placed on a continuum. Indeed the borders between, for example, a conjecture and a partial belief are vague, as are the epistemic standards constitutive of borderline entities. Still, in order to introduce the present framework it is useful to simplify a bit by presupposing neat gaps between these entities and their standards.

absurdum and assumptions in reasoning per absurdum seem to share a very low epistemic standard; and so on.[23]

One may disagree on some details about the above considerations. I am open to revising such details as one may think opportune. This is intended to be merely an illustration of how I conceive the general framework relating different types of entities, species and constitutive epistemic standards. We can imagine a full spectrum of types of entities distinguished from others of the same species by standards of different strength. The following schema can help to illustrate the general framework I've in mind:

Constitutive standards	Species		
	Cognitive attitudes	*Speech acts*	*Modes of premising*
Very demanding (Knowledge, Warranted belief...)	Belief	Full assertion	Premise of deliberative reasoning
Less demanding (Weak evidential support...)	Conjecture	Guess	Premise of conjectural reasoning
Minimally demanding (Coherence, consistency...)	Presupposition	Hypothesis per absurdum	Assumption in reasoning per absurdum

As I conceive this framework, constitutive standards directly shape distinctions amongst types of representational entities having a thetic direction of fit, regardless of whether they belong to one species or another. These standards end up producing distinctions amongst types of entities of the same species as a consequence of their dividing the conceptual space internal to each species. However the latter intra-species distinctions are only indirect products of the more general distinctions amongst thetic representational entities determined by constitutive epistemic standards. So these epistemic standards are primarily constitutive of

---

23 This account is fully compatible with the idea that the condition required by the epistemic norms governing these entities is context sensitive (e.g., Gerken (2011, 2012, 2014)). Though involving a contextually variable conformity condition, N^1 would still be common to belief, assertion and practical reasoning and different from another standard governing weaker attitudes (which eventually also would be context sensitive). For example, the common standard of guesses and conjectures could require that p be more probable than not-p to a higher degree in high stakes than in low stakes contexts. Still, this standard would be weaker than the one of assertion, belief and practical reasoning, the latter requiring, for example, fully justified belief in low stakes contexts and certainty in high stakes contexts.

entities *qua* thetic representations, and only indirectly *qua* types of entities of this or that species.²⁴

If so, we can conceive beliefs, assertions and premises of deliberative reasoning as the same type of thetic representation, involving a quite demanding constitutive epistemic standard.²⁵ The three are reciprocally distinguishable according to conditions unrelated to their thetic representational nature, and in particular to the fact that they belong to different species (mental attitudes, speech acts, modes of premising). For instance, a belief is constitutively governed by a certain epistemic standard N, not in virtue of being a certain mental attitude, but in virtue of being a certain type of thetic representation; and it is distinct from an assertion not because of some feature related to their representational nature, but because one is a mental state and the other a speech act.

The claim that beliefs, assertions and premises in reasoning are 'the same type of thetic representation' can but must not be read as the metaphysically substantive claim that they are the very same kind of entity under a certain respect – as for example Mercedes, Audi and Fiat are all models of the same kind of thing, i.e., cars. Different representations governed by a common standard must not necessarily fix a kind. We could interpret it as the claim that beliefs, assertions and premises in deliberative reasoning are different kinds of things essentially having a common representational role or function constitutively constrained by a certain epistemic standard – as in the case of cars, bicycles and trains, different kinds of things all sharing the function of being means of transportation. Alternatively the common standard could be a contingent consequence of the fact that for each species including thetic representational entities (mental attitudes, speech acts, modes of premising...) we need a concept referring to a type of entity constitutively governed by that standard. In the latter case the standard would still be a property of the entity *qua* thetic representa-

---

24 Here I introduced only three species of entities with thetic direction of fit, those relevant in the debate about commonality. However there can be others. Consider for example objectual perception, which is perception aimed at representing a certain object. We can eventually individuate perceptual concepts constitutively governed by more or less demanding epistemic standards. Accordingly we can distinguish different forms of perceiving: (non-factive) seeing, appearance, mere seeming, and so on. In an analogous way, we can distinguish between types of maps supposed to be more or less accurate and precise. For example, the degree of accuracy required in military maps is not required for an atlas in a tourist guide.

25 I leave open here the question whether the common standard of beliefs, assertions and premises of deliberative reasoning is the most demanding constitutive standard, or there are other types of entities sharing an even more demanding one (e.g., knowledge with certainty, understanding...).

tion, even though entities of different species would have this property for a contingent common reason. I remain neutral on these alternative interpretations.

This sketched framework provides a straightforward explanation of commonality. Different types of entities of different species share the same constitutive standard in virtue of all instantiating a type of thetic representation constitutively governed by a given epistemic standard. Beliefs, assertions and premises in reasoning all instantiate a certain representational type involving a quite demanding epistemic standard.[26] We can individuate other groups of entities instantiating representational types constitutively governed by weaker standards, such as conjectures, guesses and premises in conjectural reasoning.[27] In considering commonality we tend to focus on beliefs, assertions and premises in practical reasoning because these notions (i) are more commonly used in ordinary thinking and talks and (ii) they play more important roles in our lives.[28] About (i), normally we have or we take to have a good grasp of how things are, and thus we tend to use more regularly concepts involving quite high epistemic standards, and only more rarely concepts governed by less demanding standards. About (ii), these concepts have a higher practical utility: we need them

---

26 Let me reiterate once again that this epistemic standard could require different epistemic conditions in different contexts. This will be the case if, for example, someone adopts an account of commonality similar to that introduced by Gerken (2014), which is a version of Structural commonality. According to such an account, there may also be contextual variance in the required epistemic conditions amongst entities instantiating the same type of thetic representation (and thus governed by the same standard). This contextual variance may eventually occur in the very same situation, as in the examples discussed by Brown (2012), Gerken (2014) and McKinnon (2012). On this point, see the discussion of structural commonality in §1.1 and footnote 6. See also reply (iii) to Brown's counterexamples in §1.2 and footnote 23. Thanks to an anonymous reviewer for inviting me to clarify this important point.

27 Why do we end up with entities of different species governed by the same standard? Providing an answer to this question is beyond the purpose of the present paper. However this is a possible suggestion: we have concepts for cognitive attitudes, speech acts and modes of premising with different standards because we need such concepts, for these concepts do important jobs for us. For example, in certain contexts we want to express the thought that we have a mental attitude supported by a strong degree of evidence and confidence. In these cases we can deploy the concept of full belief. In other contexts we want to stress that our mental attitude is only weakly supported by evidence: for such cases we have the concept of conjecture. Similarly, we need a concept for a speech act meant to communicate information and we want to flag that our information is grounded on solid evidential bases. For this we have the concept of assertion. For weaker standards we have the notion of hypothesis (as type of speech act). A similar need for different concepts distinguishing modes of premising on the base of different epistemic standards could motivate the distinctions between different modes of premising.

28 See Gerken (2015) for an explanation of the prominence of knowledge in ordinary epistemic assessments.

to signal the full possession of reasons and the communication and use of them. Only fully possessed information allows us to appropriately assert, believe and rely on it even in situations in which it is relatively important not to get things wrong.[29]

The present account differs from horizontal approaches to commonality in that it doesn't require any relation of derivation between standards of different attitudes (for example of the standards of assertion and practical reasoning from that of belief). Rather, the account is an instance of what I called a vertical approach. It explains the common standard of beliefs, assertions and premises in practical reasoning by looking at some common factor independent of their reciprocal relations. This factor is that these different types of entities all instantiate a thetic representation of a common kind characterized by the fact of being constitutively governed by a certain epistemic standard.

3. Conclusion

Commonality is the claim that there is a common epistemic standard for assertion, practical reasoning and belief. Assuming that commonality is true and that it is not a mere coincidence that the epistemic standards of these entities are the same, philosophers have tried to provide some deeper motivation and explanation for it. Attempts in the recent literature focus on what I called horizontal approaches, which try to argue that epistemic norms governing belief, assertion and practical reasoning are inter-derivable. This type of approach has been the target of some objections. In this paper I suggested an alternative approach, that I called vertical, according to which epistemic norms governing different items share a common standard in virtue of some common source or factor independent of reciprocal dependence relations amongst these norms.

In particular I sketched a specific account according to which the common standard is due to the fact that beliefs, assertions and premises of practical rea-

---

[29] Another argument for the special focus on assertion, belief and premises of reasoning can be that attitudes and acts governed by these high epistemic standards are more useful than all the others in achieving the constitutive aim of thetic representations. These standards would satisfy this aim in the best possible way by granting a full contact between representation and what should be represented. However this line of argument is problematic: assuming that the common standard of these entities is knowledge or something just weaker than knowledge, there may be much better epistemic positions than this, such as absolute certainty and the highest level of justification. Thus the satisfaction of the standard wouldn't grant the best possible realization of the aim of thetic representations.

soning share a common representational nature of a peculiar kind. The standard is primarily attached to this feature, and the various entities share it in virtue of instantiating that feature. Notice that this sketched account is only a tentative suggestion of what an explanation following a vertical approach would look like. There may be other better explanations based on this approach. A virtue of my specific account is that it reveals several levels of commonality amongst other types of entity. We can identify weaker epistemic standards each constitutively governing triples of entities including a mental attitude, a speech act and a mode of premising.

I conclude with an analogy that may help in understanding the approach advanced in this paper. Anne, Mikkel and Robert are three lecturers in philosophy. They are different in several respects: they are affiliated to different institutions, they come from different countries, they have different specializations, and so on. However, they share a common normative standard: all of them have a commitment to teach classes this term. The fact that one of them must teach doesn't explain and isn't explained by the fact that the others have to teach. Rather, they must all teach in virtue of a common reason, one independent of their reciprocal relations: the fact that all them are lecturers. They must teach this term not *qua* affiliated to such or such university or *qua* human beings, but *qua* lecturers. Similarly, beliefs, assertions and premises of practical reasoning have a common epistemic standard, not in virtue of their reciprocal relations, but in virtue of a specific feature they share: their being all instances of thetic representations constitutively governed by that specific epistemic standard.[30]

References

Anscombe, G. E. M. (1957). *Intention*. Harvard University Press.
Brown, J. (2008). Knowledge and Practical Reason. *Philosophy Compass* 3, 1135–1152.
Brown, J. (2012). Assertion and Practical Reasoning: Common or Divergent Epistemic Standards? *Philosophy and Phenomenological Research* 84, 123–157.
Fantl, J., and McGrath, M. (2009). *Knowledge in an Uncertain World*. Oxford University Press.
Fassio, D. (2014). A Blind-Spot Argument Against Dispositionalist Accounts of Belief. *Acta Analytica* 29(1), 71–81.
Gerken, M. (2011). Warrant and Action. *Synthese* 178, 529–547.
Gerken, M. (2012). Discursive Justification and Skepticism. *Synthese* 189, 373–394.

---

[30] I would like to thank Jie Gao, Jacques Vollet and an anonymous reviewer for helpful comments on earlier versions of this paper. The work on this paper was supported by the SNSF research project 'Knowledge-Based Accounts of Rationality' (grant number: 100018_144403 / 1).

Gerken, M. (2014). Same, Same but Different: the Epistemic Norms of Assertion, Action and Practical Reasoning. *Philosophical Studies* 168, 725–744.

Gerken, M. (2015). The Roles of Knowledge Ascriptions in Epistemic Assessment. *European Journal of Philosophy* 23, 141–161.

Hawthorne, J. (2004). *Knowledge and Lotteries*. Oxford University Press.

Hawthorne, J., and Stanley, J. (2008). Knowledge and Action. *Journal of Philosophy* 105, 571–590.

Humberstone, I. L. (1992). Direction of Fit. *Mind* 101, 59–83.

Littlejohn, C. (2009). Must We Act Only on What We Know? *Journal of Philosophy* 106, 463–473.

Littlejohn, C. (2012). *Justification and the Truth-Connection*. Cambridge University Press.

Littlejohn, C. (2014). The Unity of Reason. In C. L. John and J. Turri (eds.), *Epistemic Norms: New Essays on Action, Belief, and Assertion*. Oxford University Press.

Littlejohn, C. (Forthcoming). A Plea for Epistemic Excuses. In F. Dorsch and J. Dutant (eds.), *The New Evil Demon Problem*. Oxford University Press.

Locke, D. (2015). Practical Certainty. *Philosophy and Phenomenological Research* 90, 72–95.

McKenna, R. (2013). Why Assertion and Practical Reasoning are Possibly not Governed by the Same Epistemic Norm. *Logos and Episteme* 4, 457–464.

McKenna, R. (2015). Assertion, Complexity and Sincerity. *Australasian Journal of Philosophy* 93 (4): 782–798.

McKenna, R. (Forthcoming). Clifford and the Common Epistemic Norm. *American Philosophical Quarterly*.

McKinnon, R. (2012). What I Learned in the Lunch Room About Assertion and Practical Reasoning. *Logos and Episteme* 3, 565–569.

Montminy, M. (2013). Why Assertion and Practical Reasoning Must be Governed By the Same Epistemic Norm. *Pacific Philosophical Quarterly* 94, 57–68.

Platts, M. (1997). *Ways of Meaning: An Introduction to a Philosophy of Language*. MIT Press.

Searle, J. R. (1969). *Speech Acts: An Essay in the Philosophy of Language*. Cambridge University Press.

Searle, J. R. (1975). A Taxonomy of Illocutionary Acts. In *Language, Mind and Knowledge: Minnesota Studies in the Philosophy of Science*. Keith Gunderson.

Searle, J. R. (1983). *Intentionality: An Essay in the Philosophy of Mind*. Cambridge University Press.

Smithies, D. (2012). The Normative Role of Knowledge. *Noûs* 46, 265–288.

Stanley, J. (2005). *Knowledge and Practical Interests*. Oxford University Press.

Turri, J. (2010). Epistemic Invariantism and Speech Act Contextualism. *Philosophical Review* 119(1), 77–95.

Velleman, D. (2000). On the Aim of Belief. In D. Velleman, *The Possibility of Practical Reason*. Oxford University Press.

Williamson, T. (2000). *Knowledge and its Limits*. Oxford University Press.

Williamson, T. (2005). Contextualism, Subject-Sensitive Invariantism and Knowledge of Knowledge. *Philosophical Quarterly* 55, 213–235.

Williamson, T. (Forthcoming). Justifications, Excuses, and Sceptical Scenarios. In J. Dutant and F. Dorsch (Eds.), *The New Evil Demon*. Oxford University Press.

Zangwill, N. (1998). Direction of Fit and Normative Functionalism. *Philosophical Studies* 91, 173–203.

Erik Stei
Epistemic Standards: High Hopes and Low Expectations

1. Epistemic Standards

Epistemic standards play an important role in many discussions about knowledge ascriptions: consider, for instance, the recent debate about the "factivity problem" for contextualism,[1] where Peter Baumann (2008) and Anthony Brueckner & Christopher Buford (2009) speak freely of contexts with "ordinary" standards and contexts with more demanding "sceptical" standards; Wolfgang Freitag (2011, 277), meanwhile, explicitly classifies epistemic standards, speaking of a "set of high-standard contexts" and a "set of low-standard contexts", such that the union of both sets is the set of all contexts.[2] Of course, there may be a far greater variety of standards, but no matter how many different epistemic standards there are—two or indefinitely many—the question of what exactly it is that makes low standards low and high standards high needs to be addressed. We need a story about what it means to order contexts according to the strength of their respective epistemic standards. Given the importance of the notion for contextualism, subject-sensitive invariantism or epistemic relativism, it is surprising how few detailed and systematic accounts have been proposed given concerning how epistemic standards work. I discuss the most important ones in section 2.

In what follows, I presuppose a few things about epistemic standards that I take to be fairly uncontentious: First, epistemic standards can be raised. Maybe they can be lowered, too (Lewis 1996, 560), but this does not matter for my purposes here. Secondly, in the cases relevant to my discussion, the factors responsible for a rise in standards are "error-possibilities", possibly but not necessarily accompanied by an increase in the practical importance of the proposition p of which the speaker is attributed or denied knowledge. Something along those lines is endorsed by all contextualists. Take, for instance, Keith DeRose: "The mentioning of alternatives like painted mules, or barn facades, or changes in banking hours [...] can be seen as raising the strength and changing the content

---
[1] Variants of the factivity problem are developed by Brendel (2005), Williamson (2001), and Wright (2005).
[2] The latter is a simplifying assumption. As far as I can tell, Freitag is happy to allow more than two standards.

of 'know'" (DeRose 1992, 992). Similarly, Michael Williams claims that "raising and lowering of standards consists in the expansion and contraction of the range of error-possibilities in play" (Williams 2001, 2). Related characterisations can be found in Cohen 1999 or Lewis 1996. Thirdly, in stereotypical contextualist cases, contexts in which a given knowledge ascription comes out true have lower standards than contexts in which the same ascription comes out false.[3] Any contextualist should happily subscribe to these assumptions.

Little work has been done on the details of epistemic standards. Exceptions are the views discussed in section 2, some critical comments on those views (e.g. Hawthorne 2004, Stanley 2005) and a paper by Jonathan Schaffer (2005) in which he argues that a "point-like" conception of epistemic standards in terms of relevant alternatives is plausible, whereas conceptions that rely on "thresholds" or "standards" are problematic.[4] I agree with a lot of what he says, but I modify some of his results and generalize others. The general claims I defend in this paper are as follows: First, where the above assumptions are combined with a view that links epistemic standards to a measure on alternatives (including a contextually determined threshold) that allows the relevant set of contexts to be totally ordered, the resulting view leads to highly implausible results. Secondly, a theory that avoids these kinds of measures as well as a total ordering of contexts according to their epistemic standards has no resources to make sense of low or high standards. The conclusion I draw is that, as things stand, talk of low or high standards is ill-founded.

2. Three Models of Epistemic Standards

I discuss three ways of modeling epistemic standards that have been proposed by the most prominent defenders of contextualism (cf. Cohen 1988, DeRose 1995, Lewis 1979, 1996). According to those views, standards are associated either with modality, or with probabilities, or with quantifier domains. I briefly sketch each view in turn.

---

[3] Note that this is not the same as presupposing that contexts have low and high epistemic standards *simpliciter*, i.e. standards that are just low or just high, as opposed to low or high compared to the standards of some other context.

[4] Schaffer's terminology differs from mine. My use of "standards" includes all of the conceptions Schaffer discusses. He uses "standards" to refer to what I call the "truth tracking" model or the "spheres" model, which is one way to model epistemic "standards" (in the sense in which I use the word).

Keith DeRose (1995, 33–38) links epistemic standards to modal considerations underlying his externalist view on the strength of the "epistemic position" of a subject. A subject S is in a strong epistemic position with respect to her belief p if her belief is not only true at the actual world, "but also at the worlds sufficiently close to the actual world" (DeRose 1995, 34), where closeness is measured in terms of similarity to the actual world.[5] Now, generally, S knows p just in case her epistemic position is strong enough. Just how strong it needs to be in order to be strong enough for knowledge is determined by the epistemic standards of the context of ascription. Accordingly, DeRose invites us to picture his view of epistemic standards "as a contextually determined sphere of possible worlds, centered on the actual world within which a subject's belief as to whether p is true must match the fact of the matter in order for the subject to count as knowing" (DeRose 1995, 36). A belief that is true in all worlds of a relatively small sphere may turn out to be a false belief in some worlds of a larger sphere. Thus the sphere symbolizes the epistemically relevant worlds and its extent is determined by the context in which the knowledge ascription is uttered. The mechanism of raising standards is given by the Rule of Sensitivity (DeRose 1995, 37): "When it's asserted that S knows (or doesn't know) that P, then, if necessary, enlarge the sphere of epistemically relevant worlds so that it at least includes the closest worlds in which P is false." Accordingly, what counts as epistemically relevant depends on the contextually determined sphere. With the standards for knowledge linked to the extent of the sphere via epistemic relevance of alternatives, we get the following connection: The higher the epistemic standards, the larger the sphere of epistemically relevant worlds. Interestingly, as a belief that is true in all worlds of some sphere cannot be a belief that is false in some worlds of a smaller sphere, another result is that if the sphere associated with context c_1 is bigger than or as big as the sphere associated with c_2, and if S "knows" p in c_1, then S "knows" p in c_2.[6]

Stewart Cohen (1988) agrees that context determines which alternatives are epistemically relevant, but he links relevance to an internalist probabilistic picture. Some not-p alternative h "is relevant, if the probability of h conditional on reason r and certain features of the circumstances is sufficiently high (where the

---

[5] It is not plain overall similarity that is at issue here, but similarity with respect to the methods of belief formation. This takes care of scenarios like Nozick's *grandmother case* (Nozick 1981, 179; DeRose 1995, 20).

[6] As contextualism is in part a metalinguistic position about "knows", I use quotation marks to indicate the dependence of the semantic value of "knows" on context. More precisely the phrase "S 'knows' p in c" is to be understood as "the utterance of the sentence 'S knows p' if made in c is true". Thanks to an anonymous reviewer for pressing that point.

level of probability that is sufficient is *determined by context*)" (Cohen 1988, 103). In case the subject has sufficient reason to deny the alternatives with a probability above this contextually determined level, there are no relevant alternatives precluding her from knowing *p*. Accordingly, alternatives with a probability below a certain threshold are irrelevant for *S*'s knowledge of *p* in that context, even if they are compatible with the subject's reasons *r*. The connection we get on this picture is as follows: The higher the epistemic standards, the lower the probability of not-*p* alternatives (conditional on *r*) needs to be in order for those alternatives to be relevant. Like in DeRose's case, we also get a further result. As no not-*p* possibility that is below the threshold of some context can be relevant in less demanding contexts with higher thresholds, it follows that if the threshold associated with c_1 is lower than or equal to the threshold associated with c_2, and if *S* "knows" *p* in c_1, then *S* "knows" *p* in c_2.

Finally, David Lewis prominently discusses epistemic standards on two occasions: the first when applying his conception of conversational score to relative modality (Lewis 1979), the second when developing his theory of knowledge ascriptions (Lewis 1996). In the first paper, Lewis classifies the dynamics of knowledge ascriptions as an instance of the more general connection between conversational score and modal expressions (see Lewis 1979, 354–355). He speaks of a "boundary between the relevant possibilities and the ignored ones", which enters into the truth conditions of sentences containing expressions like "must", "can", and also "knows". This boundary can be formally modelled by an accessibility relation between possible worlds, which may change in the course of conversation—that is, in the terminology adopted here, from context to context. Depending on the constraints on the accessibility relation, there are a number of ways to understand the workings of that boundary: for instance, if one relies on similarity between possible worlds (with respect to actual methods of belief formation), the view resembles DeRose's picture. Lewis's talk of attending to and (proper) ignoring of not-*p* possibilities, however, points to a view developed in more detail in his *Elusive Knowledge* (1996). In the definition of knowledge developed there, context-dependent standards enter in terms of properly ignored not-*p* possibilities. As *every* not-*p* possibility not properly ignored must be eliminated by the subject's evidence and what is properly ignored depends on context, the account can be linked to the context-dependency of quantifier domain restrictions (see also Ichikawa 2011). Here is the definition: "*S* knows that *p iff S*'s evidence eliminates every possibility in which not-*p* [...] except for those possibilities that we are properly ignoring" (Lewis 1996, 554). So every not-*p* possibility that is not properly ignored is epistemically relevant.

Proper ignoring is tied to several rules which, among other things, are meant to take care of the factivity of knowledge (Lewis 1996, 554) and various epistemological problems like the lottery paradox and Gettier cases (Lewis 1996, 556). Most important for the purpose of this paper, however, are the Rule of Belief and the Rule of Attention as they reflect the contextual influence on epistemic relevance and, therefore, on epistemic standards. According to the Rule of Belief, no possibility is properly ignored "if the subject gives it, or ought to give it, a degree of belief that is sufficiently high" (Lewis 1996, 555), where what is sufficiently high may depend on how much is at stake. Lewis's definition, as well as his examples (1996, 556), suggest that it is the stakes of the epistemic subject as well as objective stakes that matter. The rule may become sensitive to the context of ascription in case the ascribers know that the subject ought to give a higher degree of belief to a given not-p possibility than she actually does. The Rule of Attention is explicitly focused on the context of ascription (see Lewis 1996, 561). A not-p possibility attended to in the context of ascription may not be properly ignored. By attending to a possibility, ascribers make it relevant for a knowledge ascription in that context. If the subject's evidence does not eliminate that possibility, the subject cannot be said to "know" that p in that context. The rule does not require a certain threshold, probability or degree. Attendance is an all-or-nothing affair.

It seems the Rule of Attention is more powerful with respect to ascriber sensitivity than the Rule of Belief. The cases in which ascribers know that the epistemic subject should give a higher degree of belief to a given not-p possibility are cases in which the ascribers attend to that possibility. This is sufficient to make that possibility epistemically relevant. Cases in which the ascribers or the subject fail to give a sufficiently high degree of belief to a possibility are cases in which S does not know that p for reasons independent of the context of ascription. So, in order to capture the contextualist cases at issue here, we need to focus on the Rule of Attention. As attendance is an all-or-nothing affair, there is no measure of relevance connected to alternatives on Lewis's view. Thus, the only correlation we get on his picture is this: Given two contexts c_1 and c_2, the epistemic standards of c_2 are higher than the epistemic standards of c_1 just in case the set of relevant alternatives of c_1 is a proper subset of the relevant alternatives of c_2. We are not able to say that, generally, some not-p possibility q_1 is to be ranked higher, epistemically speaking, than some other not-p possibility q_2. Given a context in which q_1 is salient but not q_2, and another context in which q_2 is salient but not q_1, we simply cannot tell whether the standards in the first context are higher than or equal to the other. On Lewis's account, there is nothing that would allow us to speak of higher or lower standards in case the sets of possibilities relevant in c_1 and c_2 are disjoint or even in case they intersect without one being a subset of the other. But we do get the result that if the relevant alternatives of c_2 are a subset (proper or improper) of the relevant alternatives of c_1, and if S "knows" p

in c_1, then S "knows" p in c_2. If S's evidence is incompatible with every element of a given set of alternatives, it is also incompatible with every element of a subset of that set.

It is worth noting that although some of the views discussed here allow for a general notion of epistemic strength (in terms of modal closeness or probabilities), none of the views offers any kind of general (i.e. context-independent) threshold, such that all contexts with epistemic standards above that threshold count as high standards contexts and all others as low standards contexts. So, except for the limiting cases in which either all alternatives are relevant or else no alternatives at all are relevant, it seems to make little sense to speak of absolutely high or absolutely low standards. Some views, however, do allow the notion of *relatively* high or *relatively* low standards, thereby enabling a comparative reading of epistemic standards: DeRose's and Cohen's views generally admit comparisons of contexts with respect to their epistemic standards (either in terms of modal distance or in terms of probabilities), while Lewis's analysis only allows a rather restricted form of comparison.

3. Orderings of Epistemic Standards and Some Problematic Results

We are now in a position to take a closer look at the way contexts may be ordered according to their epistemic standards. Assume a set M_c containing contexts of utterance. As we will see, there may or may not be restrictions as to which contexts may be elements of M_c. The comparative reading of epistemic standards in the spirit of Cohen's and DeRose's views requires a binary relation "$\leq$" on the elements of M_c (such that $\leq\, \subseteq M_c \times M_c$) that allows at least a partial ordering. If "$c_1 \leq c_2$" is to represent the intuitive notion that the standards of c_1 are lower than or equal to the standards of c_2, "$\leq$" needs to be reflexive, transitive and antisymmetric.[7]

It was shown that DeRose's sphere model links epistemic standards to the extent of a sphere of possible worlds. As the worlds are centred on the actual world and ordered by a similarity measure, we can interpret "$c_1 \leq_S c_2$" as "the sphere of possible worlds of c_1 is smaller than or equal to the one of c_2".[8] As

---

[7] Thus, for any $a, b, c \in M_c$: $a \leq a$; if $a \leq b$ and $b \leq c$, then $a \leq c$; and if $a \leq b$ and $b \leq a$, then $a = b$.
[8] The additional restriction on the method of belief formation—only worlds in which S forms her belief that p in the same way she does in actuality are to be considered—leads to a constraint on M_c. Worlds in which S forms her belief in different ways are not epistemically relevant, as they

we have seen in the previous section, contexts are ordered according to how far the sphere of epistemically relevant worlds reaches into modal space. According to this reading, M_c appears to be totally ordered, as it meets the additional constraint that for any $a, b \in M_c$: $a \leq b$ or $b \leq a$.[9] The reason for this is that (with the similarity ordering of possible worlds remaining fixed) the only thing that varies with context is the extent of the sphere. Given a contextually determined sphere s_1 encompassing all worlds up to distance d_1, any other contextually determined sphere s_2 encompassing all worlds up to distance d_2 will either be as large as s_1 or smaller than s_1 or larger than s_1. For every pair of members of M_c, one is smaller than or equal to the other. This allows for a contextually determined value, such that if S "knows" p in c_1, then S "knows" p in all contexts c_n for which $c_n \leq_S c_1$.

This leads us to the first counterintuitive result: the problem with this picture is that shifts in epistemic standards "globally infect" other propositions believed by the epistemic subject (see Schaffer 2005, 124). Given DeRose's conception of the closeness relation between possible worlds, it is an immediate consequence that even propositions unrelated to p and known in a low-stakes context may not be known in a high-stakes context. The reason is that modal closeness is measured by similarity to the actual world and the actual method of how S's belief that p is formed. If standards are raised, the sphere of epistemically relevant worlds includes *all* worlds up to the contextually determined similarity value. In some of those worlds, propositions other than p which are truly believed by the subject in actuality will turn out to be falsely believed by the subject. Thus, the epistemic subject does not know those propositions in the high-stakes context, as her epistemic position is not strong enough: her belief is not true in all worlds sufficiently close to the actual world. This may be a suitable position with respect to radical scepticism—the problem DeRose is dealing with when developing his view. Should the possibility of S being a brain in a vat be uttered, S loses "knowledge" of a considerable number of propositions, at least according to the contextualist view. It is far less convincing with respect to more moderate kinds of epistemic doubt. Consider, for instance, Cohen's airport case. Passenger

---

cannot be pictured as being inside or outside of any sphere centred on actuality including S's method of belief formation.

9 Schaffer (2005, 124) proposes a different view according to which the conversational context not only determines the size of the sphere but also the way in which the possible worlds are ordered (Schaffer's metric m). This results in a very powerful conception of context. My impression is that the above reconstruction, where the objective features of the world of the subject's context determine the ordering (but not the sphere), is closer to DeRose's view. Nothing of importance for the present paper depends on this, however, as the cases considered here are such that in both contexts the way in which possible worlds are ordered remains fixed.

Smith is asked whether the plane stops in Chicago. After looking at his flight itinerary, he responds "Yes, I know it stops in Chicago". Assume that in this context the sphere of possible worlds is of size n. After the possibility of a misprint in Smith's itinerary is brought up, context is changed by a rise in epistemic standards and the sphere becomes larger, now measuring $n + 1$. It is not only Smith's belief that the plane stops in Chicago that is false in some worlds in the modal space between n and $n + 1$, but many other beliefs as well. So Smith not only loses "knowledge" of the proposition that the plane stops in Chicago; "knowledge" of propositions completely unrelated to p may be lost too, namely all those propositions that Smith believes truly in n, but that he falsely believes in some worlds between n and $n + 1$.

I take this to be a highly implausible result. Suppose that the gate for the flight in question is not mentioned in the itinerary, but Smith reads it on the destination board. Given that worlds in which the itinerary contains a misprint are at least as far off in terms of similarity to actuality as worlds in which the gate of the flight is changed (a plausible assumption, I think), why should mentioning the possibility of a misprint exclude Smith's "knowledge" that the flight leaves at gate 46? If we suppose that it is both true that the plane stops in Chicago and that the departure is at gate 46, and that Smith is in a reasonably good epistemic position with respect to those propositions, such that he knows both of them in the lower-standards context, it seems false to say that Smith loses "knowledge" that the departure is at gate 46 just because an error-possibility as to whether the itinerary might have been changed is raised. However, this is exactly what the sphere model predicts.

A similar problem can be constructed for Cohen's conception of epistemic standards. We saw in the last section that, on Cohen's view, the higher the epistemic standards, the lower the probability of not-p alternatives needs to be in order for those alternatives to be relevant. Thus, we can read the relation "$c_1 \leq_T c_2$" as "the (probability) threshold of c_1 is lower than the threshold of c_2", resulting in a total ordering on M_c with decreasing strictness of epistemic standards. On this view, M_c is totally ordered, just like in DeRose's sphere model. For every pair of members of M_c, the threshold of one is smaller than or equal to the other's. This allows for a contextually determined value such that if S "knows" p in c_1, then S "knows" p in all contexts c_n for which $c_1 \leq_T c_n$.

One way of interpreting Cohen's suggestion is that context influences the threshold for how probable (conditional on S's reason r) an alternative to any of S's belief must be to count as a relevant alternative. On this reading, discussed by Schaffer (2005, 118–121), the probability model is just as globally infectious as the sphere model. Mentioning error-possibilities with respect to the belief that p or raising the practical importance of p would globally lower the probability for alternatives to S's beliefs, stripping her of "knowledge" of all propositions with alternatives relevant according to the new probability threshold. Thus, counterexamples like the gate/misprint case discussed above would arise just as easily.

But there is another way to reconstruct the position. Unlike the sphere model, the probability model explicitly refers to not-p alternatives. So a sensible option may be to suppose that only the threshold value for the probability of not-p alternatives (conditional on r) shifts, while the threshold for possibilities unrelated to p may remain untouched. This may affect the actual ordering, but not the structure of the relation "≤" on M_c, however. According to this picture "$c_1 \leq_T c_2$" would have to be read as "the threshold for not-p possibilities in c_1 is lower than the threshold for not-p possibilities in c_2", still resulting in a total ordering of the contexts of M_c according to the probability of the alternatives relevant in a context. But it would render the model less infectious than the sphere model. In case Smith cannot deny the alternative that the itinerary contains a misprint, this may prevent him from "knowing" that the plane stops in Chicago, but it need not prevent him from "knowing" that the departure gate is 46 even if the probability of the latter possibility is equal to or higher than the first. Possibilities in which the gate is changed are epistemically independent of possibilities in which the flight does not stop in Chicago. A change of the probability threshold for not-p possibilities need not affect all of S's other beliefs.

This may be an improvement, but the position is problematic nonetheless. The focus on not-p possibilities is still too broad, as it leads to other counterintuitive cases. Imagine two possibilities: Smith's itinerary contains a misprint (q_1), and the plane in question suffers an engine defect when steering out to the manoeuvring area, resulting in the cancellation of the flight (q_2). Let us suppose for the sake of argument that both possibilities have the same probability 0.n (conditional on r). Let us assume, further, that both q_1 and q_2 are not-p possibilities. Now imagine, as before, that the plane really stops in Chicago, but that the possibility of a misprint in Smith's itinerary is raised. Thus, the probability threshold for not-p alternatives is lowered accordingly to value 0.n. Now, Smith decides to check back at the counter of the flight company and has his itinerary confirmed. He cannot, however, deny the possibility that the flight is cancelled because of an engine defect, which also takes value 0.n. Now, given that the possibility of a defective engine is as probable as the possibility of a misprint, he cannot be said to "know" that the plane stops in Chicago (in that context), because the probability threshold on not-p possibilities is too low (in that context). Again, this is a highly counterintuitive result.[10]

One might object that an error-possibility, in that case q_2, needs to be salient in order to be relevant in the first place, but we have seen that, given $\leq_T$, and irrespective of the specific not-p possibilities of a context, if S "knows" p in c_1, then S "knows" p in all contexts c_n, such that $c_1 \leq_T c_n$. Besides, the insistence on salience immediately leads to further problems. One I will not address here is how to avoid knowledge ascriptions coming out as true far too easily in contexts of ignorant subjects and/or ascribers. More important for my purposes is this: the only sensible use the probability of an alternative (conditional on r) as an additional criterion to salience could have is that some salient alternatives may be ignored, namely those that are irrelevant in that context according to the probability threshold. The problem is that on practically all contextualist accounts (and certainly on the ones discussed so far), salience is usually sufficient to raise epistemic standards. So what would be needed is an account of how salience sometimes does and sometimes does not raise the standards. It is not at all clear what this account would look like.[11] Besides, why should an ordering be introduced in the first place, if salience does all the important work?

In the last section, it was shown that the only cases in which we can speak of higher or lower standards on Lewis's picture is if the set of relevant not-p possibilities of one context is a proper subset of the set of relevant not-p possibilities of another context. It is not possible, however, to compare the epistemic standards of contexts in which this subset requirement is not fulfilled. So there are pairs of contexts for which we cannot say which one has the higher standards or, more precisely, it is not the case that for any element a, b of M_c, $a \leq b$ or $b \leq a$. So, although it also holds on Lewis's view that, for all contexts, if $c_n \leq c_1$, and if S "knows" p in c_1, then S "knows" p in c_n, it is impossible for c_n to contain relevant alternatives that are not also in c_1, due to the restrictions on the relation "$\leq$". This seems to be exactly the feature that avoids the counterexamples

---

10 Note that Cohen's analysis of the lottery case (Cohen 1988: 106–108) does not help to avoid the problem: as the chance of error is the same for both q_1 and q_2, it does not matter whether it is salient or not. Further, it is one and the same context we are considering, so Smith's reasons for his belief that the plane stops in Chicago remain unchanged. Besides, it is not a radically skeptical result: possibilities that are less probable (conditional on r) than q_1 and q_2 remain epistemically irrelevant.

11 Cohen notes (1999, 85 n. 27) that salience does not necessarily raise the standards, but he does not offer a systematic analysis of the phenomenon. To be sure, there are accounts that deal with this problem (see, e.g., Blome Tillmann 2009), but those are typically ones that do not picture contexts as totally ordered according to their epistemic standards.

against DeRose's and Cohen's conceptions of epistemic standards. As there is no measure on not-p possibilities, the only context-dependent feature affecting their epistemic relevance is *being attended to*. So there is no context-dependent way a not-p possibility not attended to could become relevant.[12] Just because a misprint in Smith's itinerary is relevant (because of its salience), there is nothing in Lewis's account that automatically makes other possibilities relevant. The above counterexamples can be avoided.

But this comes at a cost. In the absence of a measure that would allow us to order contexts according to their epistemic standards, it seems that we cannot speak of high and low standards or of "everyday" and "sceptical" standards in an absolute sense. Even talk about standards of one context being higher or lower than the ones of another context is quite limited with a Lewis-style partial ordering. Even if we know, for instance, $c_1 \leq c_2$ and $c_3 \leq c_4$, it may be impossible to say anything about the relation of the epistemic standards of c_1 and c_4. Take, for instance, $M_x = \{c_1, c_2, c_3, c_4\}$ and the partial ordering $\leq_x = \{<c_1, c_1>, <c_2, c_2>, <c_3, c_3>, <c_4, c_4>, <c_1, c_2>, <c_3, c_4>\}$. Given $\leq_x$, it is not only impossible to tell which contexts have low epistemic standards and which have high epistemic standards: there are also contexts for which we cannot even say whether their standards are higher or lower than those of other contexts. To make this point more vivid, imagine that $\leq$ in the example above orders individuals according to their height. If for all we know c_1 is smaller than or as tall as c_2 and c_3 is smaller than or as tall as c_4, then we are at a loss when asked whether e.g. c_1 is smaller than or as tall as c_4. There is a consistent extension of $\leq$ according to which c_1 is smaller than or as tall as c_2 but taller than both c_3 and c_4, but there is also one according to which c_4 is taller than c_1. The situation is similar with respect to Lewis's conception of epistemic standards. While avoiding the counterexamples, it severely limits talk of high or low epistemic standards.

4. Diagnosis and Conclusion

Abstracting a bit from the modified airport case, the counterexamples seem to build on a simple recipe: Take some not-p possibility q_1 that is incompatible with S's epistemic situation (e.g. the possibility that Smith's itinerary contains a misprint, which turns out to be incompatible with Smith's evidence after he has checked back with the airline agent in the example above). Assume a meas-

---

12 Of course, a possibility not attended to may be relevant due to other rules, but those are of no use when analysing the contextualist cases, so we need not worry about them here.

ure F assigning values to alternatives, such that q_1 takes value n. Take another not-p possibility q_2 with the same or a lower value as q_1 on F that is compatible with S's epistemic situation (e. g. the possibility that the plane in question suffers an engine defect when steering out to the manoeuvring area, resulting in the cancellation of the flight). Describe a context c_1 where the epistemic standards are at level n at which neither q_1 nor q_2 are relevant and S "knows" p. Then describe a context c_2 resulting from c_1 where q_1 is brought to the ascriber's attention (e. g. the mentioning of the misprint possibility resulting in Smith's checking with the airline). This leads to a rise in epistemic standards to level $n + 1$, making q_2 relevant too (both q_1 and q_2 take the same value on F). Then, although S's evidence is incompatible with the not-p possibilities salient in context c_1 (including q_1), she still does not know p, because her evidence is not inconsistent with every alternative relevant in c_1 according to F. After all, q_2 is consistent with her evidence by hypothesis.

Now, what is the fundamental problem this recipe takes advantage of? We have seen that, in the case of DeRose and Cohen, a measure of epistemic strength formulated in terms of the epistemic relevance of alternatives resulting in a total ordering of contexts according to their epistemic standards leads to counterexamples. Is it enough to reject one of those two characteristics, that is, either the measure on epistemic strength or the total ordering, in order to avoid the problematic cases? As far as I can see, the dependencies are as follows: First, if contexts are totally ordered, even absent any measure for epistemic standards it will be possible to construct counterexamples—at least if the ordering respects the intuitively plausible constraint that if $c_n \leq c_1$, and if S "knows" p in c_1, then S "knows" p in c_n.[13] The recipe will have to be rephrased such that it does not refer to values on F, but this is only a change in detail, not in spirit. Describe contexts c_1 and c_2 in the way outlined above with the modification that the epistemic standards of c_2 are lower than or equal to c_1 given the relevant relation "$\leq$" on the set of contexts (instead of the measure F).

Further, we have seen that Lewis's account is not affected by the counterexamples as it dispenses with a measure on epistemic strength and imposes only a partial order (in combination with the constraint that if $c_n \leq c_1$, and if S "knows" p in c_1, then S "knows" p in c_n). But this comes at the cost of seriously restricting the discourse about epistemic standards. Is it possible to improve on this? It seems that Lewis's account could only allow a more extensive discourse about standards if the subset requirement were dropped and an independent measure

---

[13] This constraint immediately followed from Cohen's and DeRose's accounts, but it might have to be stipulated as an additional constraint on alternative conceptions.

for the strictness of epistemic standards added. What would be needed, in other words, is some F_x that assigns values to the alternatives relevant in a context, such that, irrespective of the details of those values, the resulting ordering on the class of contexts M_x will not be total. In light of the results above it seems unlikely that this will be helpful. Assume, for the sake of an example, that M_x contains four contexts c_1, c_2, c_3, and c_4 with F assigning the values $\{1, 2, 4, a\}$ to contexts in view of the epistemic strength needed for the subject's evidence to be strong enough for "knowledge" (with $1 < 2 < 4$ and "a" symbolizing something like "unsettled" standards[14]): $c_1 = 1$, $c_2 = 2$, $c_3 = a$, $c_4 = 4$. The resulting ordering relation would be as follows: $\leq_x = \{<c_1, c_1>, <c_2, c_2>, <c_3, c_3>, <c_4, c_4>, <c_1, c_2>, <c_1, c_4>, <c_2, c_4>\}$. This would allow us to say, for instance, that standards in c_4 are higher than in both c_1 and c_2, but the ordering would not be total because no context except c_3 itself stands in relation "$\leq_x$" to c_3. But it would also allow for counterexamples following the recipe above. Let q_1 and q_2 be not-p-possibilities with value 4. Assume that q_1 is incompatible with S's epistemic situation while q_2 is compatible with it. Imagine the ascribers are in c_1 so neither q_1 nor q_2 are relevant. Assume further that S "knows" p in c_1. Now assume that q_1 is uttered, causing the epistemic standards to rise to value 4. Will q_2 (and any other not-p-possibility with value $n \leq 4$) be relevant in the resulting context? If one wants to keep the constraint that if $c_n \leq c_1$, and if S "knows" p in c_1, then S "knows" p in c_n, one is compelled to say "yes", but then S does not "know" p in c_4, as there is an alternative, namely q_2, compatible with her evidence. If one refuses to make every alternative with a value $n \leq 4$ relevant, one will have to give up on the constraint: S may be said to "know" in c_4 but not in a different context c_{4^*} which differs from c_4 only insofar as q_2 (and all other not-p-possibilities with value $n \leq 4$) is relevant as well. As both contexts will be "value 4"-contexts, the fact that S "knows" p in c_4 but S does not "know" p in c_{4^*} violates the constraint.

If these considerations are correct, then in order to avoid the counterexamples it is necessary to avoid both a total ordering of contexts according to their epistemic standards and an independent measure F that assigns values to alternatives. A further option may be to give up the constraint that if $c_n \leq c_1$, and if S "knows" p in c_1, then S "knows" p in c_n, but this means giving up a lot of the initial attraction of contextualism. If knowing in high standards, like for instance sceptical standards, has no consequences whatsoever for knowledge in lower standards, like everyday standards, then the notion of standards loses its pull. The result is that either the intuitively plausible talk of (relatively) low- and (rel-

---

[14] For the notion of "unsettled standards" see, e.g., Montminy and Skolits 2014.

atively) high-standard contexts must be abandoned, or its defenders must find another way to block the counterexamples.[15]

References

Blome-Tillmann, M. (2009) Knowledge and Presuppositions. In: *Mind* 118, 241–294.
Brendel, E. (2005). Why Contextualists Cannot Know They Are Right: Self-Refuting Implications of Contextualism. In: *Acta Analytica* 20(2), 38–55.
Cohen, S. (1988). How to be a Fallibilist. In: *Philosophical Perspectives* 2, 91–123.
Cohen, S. (1999). Contextualism, Skepticism, and the Structure of Reason. In: *Noûs* 33, 57–89.
DeRose, K. (1992). Contextualism and Knowledge Attributions. In: *Philosophy and Phenomenological Research* 52(4), 913–929.
DeRose, K. (1995). Solving the Skeptical Problem. In: *The Philosophical Review* 104(1), 1–52.
DeRose, K. (2004). Single Scoreboard Semantics. In: *Philosophical Studies* 119, 1–21.
Freitag, W. (2011). Epistemic Contextualism and the Knowability Problem. In: *Acta Analytica* 26, 273–284.
Hawthorne, J. (2004). *Knowledge and Lotteries*. Oxford: Oxford University Press.
Ichikawa, J. (2011). Quantifiers and Epistemic Contextualism, In: *Philosophical Studies* 155, 383–398.
Lewis, D. (1979). Scorekeeping in a Language Game. In: *Journal of Philosophical Logic* 8(3), 339–359.
Lewis, D. (1996). Elusive Knowledge. In: *Australasian Journal of Philosophy* 74(4), 549–567.
Montminy. M. and Skolits, W. (2014). Defending the Coherence of Contextualism. In: *Episteme* 11, 319–333.
Nozick, R. (1981). *Philosophical Explanations*. Cambridge.
Schaffer, J. (2005). What Shifts? Thresholds, Standards, or Alternatives? In: Preyer, P. and Peter, G. (eds.), *Contextualism in Philosophy*. Knowledge, Meaning, and Truth. Oxford, 115–130.
Stanley, J. (2005). *Knowledge and Practical Interest*. Oxford: Oxford University Press.
Williams, M. (2001). Contextualism, Externalism and Epistemic Standards, In: *Philosophical Studies* 103: 1–23.
Williamson, T. (2001). Comments on Michael Williams' "Contextualism, Externalism and Epistemic Standards". In: *Philosophical Studies* 103, 25–33.
Wright, C. (2005). Contextualism and Scepticism: Even-Handedness, Factivity and Surreptitiously Raising Standards. In: *Philosophical Quarterly* 55, 236–262.

---

[15] I would like to thank the audience of the workshop "Neue Perspektiven in der Erkenntnistheorie II" at TU Dresden for discussion and comments on the material presented in this paper. Thank you also to an anonymous referee and especially to Martin Grajner and Pedro Schmechtig for their patience and for their helpful reactions to an earlier draft of this paper.

Veli Mitova
What do I care About Epistemic Norms?

Suppose you found out that a bunch of your beliefs was ill-supported by your evidence, or that it was inconsistent with other beliefs you held. Maybe the bunch is a lofty one – it concerns, say, the rocket you are launching into space; or maybe it is a homely one – it's about the cake you are baking. Either way, why should you care? To answer this question is to tell us why epistemic norms have normative authority over us. As Hilary Kornblith puts it:

> If you tell me that a belief of mine is unjustified, this gives me reason to give up that belief. The epistemic claim is something about which I should care, *and an account of the source of epistemic norms must explain why it is that I should care about such things* (Kornblith (1993), 363, my italics).

Pragmatists think that you should care, to put it crudely, because otherwise the rocket or cake would flop (Stich (1990), Heil (1992)). Moralists say that you should care because otherwise you'd be a lousy believer and that would vitiate your moral integrity (Clifford (1877), Zagzebski (1996)). Constitutivists think that you should care as 'the price of admission' to the 'belief business' (Railton (1997), 57; Wedgwood (2002)).

Who is right? The stakes are high. To begin with, epistemic norms prescribe procedures for believing in a way that gets us the cardinal epistemic blessings – justification, truth, and knowledge. So, different accounts of why we should care about these norms would give us different reasons to care about the blessings themselves[1]. But there are also broader theoretical stakes here: different accounts of the source of epistemic norms yield drastically differing views on two issues of central concerns to the present collection – the nature of epistemic norms and their relationship to other kinds of normativity (e. g., Kelly (2003)). To get the rough idea, suppose the source of epistemic norms lay in the practical domain as pragmatists insist, or in the moral domain, as moralists urge. Suppose, that is, that the only reason for caring about these norms was that following them would gain us other things we value, such as moral integrity or simply

---

[1] This would have implications, for instance, for the debate on the value of knowledge (e. g., Pritchard 2007, 2011). If the source of epistemic norms came from anywhere outside epistemology, this would turn their value instrumental. This would preclude knowledge itself from being intrinsically more valuable than true belief, since its normative dimension – the one governed by epistemic norms – would be just instrumentally valuable.

the attainment of our more mundane goals (the rocket and the cake). Then all epistemic norms would be hypothetical: they would be premised on our having the moral or practical goal which gives them authority over us. The norms themselves would, consequently, be a subcategory of moral or prudential norms.

If, by contrast, it turned out that the source of epistemic norms was sui generis, as the constitutivist supposes, then things would look dramatically different: epistemic norms would be categorical, since they wouldn't be premised on our goals; and, consequently, epistemic normativity itself would constitute a sui generis, autonomous normative domain, since its authority would not derive from morality or prudence.

In this paper I propose a new sui generis account of the source of epistemic norms. I argue that the normative authority of these norms is constitutive of the hallmark of our agency – our drive for sense-making.

I proceed as follows. First, I argue for two constraints on any account of normative authority: it must explain both the motivational and normative force of the thing whose authority is in question (§ 1). I then briefly argue that none of the existing accounts of the source of epistemic norms meets both of these constraints: pragmatic and moral accounts run afoul of both, while constitutive accounts violate the normative (§ 2). This takes the shine off existing accounts and makes it attractive to look elsewhere for the source of epistemic norms. I then sketch the account which meets both of these constraints: the source of epistemic norms flows from our drive for sense-making (§ 4), which, according to David Velleman, is the hallmark of agency (§ 3). Finally, I clarify and strengthen the proposal by forestalling two objections to it (§ 5).

I should stress that the paper is meant to provide neither knockdown negative arguments nor a full-blown positive account of the source of epistemic norms. It is, rather, intended to open up a certain overlooked space for thinking about this source, and to show that this is, at present, our only hope for finding out why we should care about epistemic norms.

1. Two Constraints on Accounts of Normative Authority

What are epistemic norms? As already mentioned, understood substantively, the question is a barbed one. But according to a more neutral understanding, epistemic norms are norms prescribing epistemically good procedures for belief formation, maintenance and revision. They are norms, in other words, that tell you how to hold (or not hold) your beliefs for good reasons. Two uncontroversial exemplars are the ones with which I opened the paper: the evidence norm (proportion your belief to the evidence) and the consistency norm (do not hold inconsistent beliefs).

What are we asking when we ask after the source of epistemic norms, so understood? There are three candidates:

The should-question: Why *should* believers follow epistemic norms?
The care-question: Why *do* believers *care* about following epistemic norms?
The should-care question: Why *should* believers *care* about following epistemic norms?

As evident from the Kornblith quote above, I understand the question about the source of epistemic norms as the should-care question. I now show why the question is best understood in this way.

1.1 Two Constraints

An account of the source of epistemic norms must, at a minimum, explain how the fact that a belief of mine complies with, or contravenes, epistemic norms gives me a reason to hold or abandon it. It is an account, to use Scanlon's (1998) phrase, of the reason-giving force of epistemic norms. There are two constraints on such an account, which are widely accepted in metaethics, and onto which epistemologists are slowly cottoning (e.g., Jones (2009), Shah (2006)):

The Motivation Constraint: An account of the reason-giving force of x must explain how x can *motivate* agents.

The Normative Constraint: An account of the reason-giving force of x must explain the *normative authority* of x.

If we accept these constraints, it would be obvious that a satisfactory account of the source of epistemic norms must answer the third, should-care question. An answer only to the should-question would violate the motivation constraint: it wouldn't tell us how the fact that my belief is held against the evidence, say, could move me to abandon it. An answer only to the care-question would violate the normative constraint: it would leave us in the dark as to why being moved by epistemic norms is appropriate or required in the first place. I find these constraints obvious, but it is not clear that other epistemologists do, so let me briefly argue for them.

1.2 The Argument for the Motivation Constraint

Both constraints flow directly from the concept of a reason. A reason for an action, as Williams taught us, must be able to motivate the action. Here is Williams's argument in outline (Williams (1981), 106–7)[2]:

(P1) A reason for an action must be able to be someone's reason for the action on a particular occasion, and so must be able to explain the action.
(P2) But a reason could not explain an action if it could not motivate it.
(C) So a reason for an action must be able to motivate the action.

The intuition behind this argument is simple enough. If I don't enjoy jogging, my jogging can hardly be explained by appeal to my wanting to do something pleasurable. Rather, the explanation must appeal to something that could have in fact moved me to go jogging – concern for my health, say. A reason, that is, has *a motivational* aspect. (See also Dancy (2000)). We should expect, likewise, reasons for belief to be the sorts of considerations that can move agents to adopt or abandon beliefs. Otherwise, they could never explain *this* agent's holding *this* belief. Hence, the motivation constraint: an account of the reason-giving force of epistemic norms must explain how these norms can motivate agents[3].

1.3 The Argument for the Normative Constraint

Here is a little story from metaethics to show that an account of the reason-giving force of epistemic norms must meet the normative constraint. Suppose we ask how the fact that an action is right or wrong gives me a reason to perform or not perform it. And suppose someone answered that we as a matter of fact

---

[2] For a defence of this way of hearing Williams's argument as well as a more extensive defence of the argument itself, see Mitova (2015).
[3] Notice that this requirement does not amount to endorsing metaethical internalism, according to which the judgement that I have a reason to act necessarily motivates me to act. (Some add, 'insofar as I am rational', e.g., Korsgaard (1986)). Although Williams's larger argument aims to establish internalism, these are just its first premises and only require that a reason must be *able to* motivate not that every reason motivates, let alone that it does so necessarily.

care for rightness. Such an explanation construes our concern for rightness as fetishistic, to borrow Michael Smith's phrase (Smith (1994), Chapter 3)[4]. This is how Wallace explains the fetishism problem:

> the charge of fetishism is in place when a source of moral motivation is posited that cannot be understood as a proper response to its object, *a response that is rendered appropriate by independent facts about what one has reason to do* (Wallace (2006), 333, my italics).

Sexual fetishism, Wallace explains, involves an unmerited response – that of erotic arousal – to something that is not (at least conventionally perceived as) erotic. Analogously, our caring about rightness would be inappropriate if rightness did not merit the response of caring. To avoid fetishism, we must show that it is appropriate to be concerned with rightness in the first place (*ibid.*, 337).

An account which explains the reason-giving force of epistemic norms, then, must likewise show how epistemic norms are something that *merits* concern, lest it turn out fetishistic. Hence, the normative constraint on such an account. So, we should understand the question about the source of epistemic norms as the question of why we *should care* about following these norms. The 'should' points to the normative constraint; the 'care', to the motivational constraint.

1.4 Two Ways of Breaching the Normative Constraint

Two ways of breaching the normative constraint should be distinguished, as they will become relevant in what follows. They are neatly captured by what Scanlon ((1998), 149 – 50) calls 'Prichard's dilemma'. Questions about the reason-giving force of right and wrong, he argues, usually receive either no answer or the wrong answer. The first happens when the answer to the question 'Why do the right thing?' is 'Because morality requires it'. Such an answer presupposes the very reason-giving force of moral requirements that it is supposed to explain. But, on the other horn, if we gave non-moral reasons for heeding right and wrong, such as, say, that it's in our interest,

> [t]his account might supply a reason for doing the right thing, but it would not be the kind of reason that we suppose a moral person first and foremost to be moved by (*ibid.*).

---

[4] Smith's fetishism argument targets metaethical externalism about moral reasons. I use here Wallace's version of the argument, because it conveys my point more vividly, without getting bogged down with the metaethical internalism-externalism debate.

The dilemma is dramatized by analogy with friendship. Suppose we ask, 'Why be loyal?':

> The answer, "Because friendship requires it," seems to be no response at all to the question that is being asked. But if, on the other hand, we cite some value other than friendship—if, for example, we appeal to the benefits of having friends—then this seems the wrong kind of response. A person who was "loyal" for that kind of reason would not be a good friend at all (*ibid.*, 161).

If an account of the source of epistemic norms is to meet the normative constraint, then, it must walk the tricky tightrope between these two horns. The answer to the should-care question must be neither empty nor wrong-headed.

2. Four Accounts of the Source of Epistemic Norms

I now introduce the four main existing views of the source of epistemic norms and briefly argue that none of them meets both the normative and motivational constraints. I should stress again that my aim is neither to cover each version of these views, nor to provide knockdown arguments against them. (I take myself to have done at least the latter in Mitova (2008a), (2008b).) The point of this section is simply to create a prima facie presumption against these views, by way of motivating a search for the source of epistemic norms in a different place. I will therefore be fairly brief in my treatment of the existing positions.

2.1 The Accounts

Four main views of the source of epistemic norms are floated in the literature: (call them) the soft-pragmatic, the moral, the normative, and the teleological[5].

---

[5] There are three more positions in the literature: (1) pragmatism proper (e.g., Stich (1990)), (2) communitarianism (e.g., Kusch (2002)), (3) a view which attaches intrinsic value to true belief (e.g., Lynch (2004)). I do not consider these views because none of them is susceptible to the quick assessment I give other existing positions: (1) and (2) involve too many revisions, and all three presuppose an account of truth. My aim here, recall, is merely to drum up some prima facie support for my proposal. So, it is enough to create a presumption against the prima facie plausible views.

According to soft-pragmatic positions, the source of epistemic norms derives from the pragmatic value of true beliefs. We need true beliefs, the thought goes, in order to survive (Lycan (1988)), and/or to attain our goals (Heil (1992)), and/or for practical reasoning (Kornblith (1993)). This value is inherited by epistemic norms, since following these norms is our best shot at getting true beliefs. We should care about following epistemic norms, in other words, because doing so promotes other things we care about.

Moral positions locate the source of epistemic norms in the moral realm. W.K. Clifford (1877), for example, thought that violating the evidence norm threatens the very moral and social fabric of humanity. And according to some virtue epistemologists (so called responsibilists), we should follow epistemic norms because doing so is constitutive of being intellectually virtuous (Zagzebski (1994)). Since the intellectual virtues are, on some of these views, simply a subset of the moral virtues, the authority of epistemic norms is, as for Clifford, grounded in the moral realm[6].

Constitutive positions locate the reason-giving force of epistemic norms in belief's aim. There are two interpretations of this aim – a normative and a teleological. According to the normative view, the *concept* of belief is constituted by belief's correctness norm – a belief is correct if and only if the believed proposition is true. The reason-giving force of other epistemic norms derives from the normativity of the belief-concept itself (Shah (2003), Wedgwood (2002)).

According to the teleological view, to say that belief aims at truth is to say that believing that p is accepting p with the aim of thereby accepting a truth. The reason-giving force of truth, and hence of epistemic norms, flows from belief itself (Velleman (2000), Chapter 11; Steglich-Petersen (2006)).

2.2 The Moral and Soft Pragmatic Accounts Breach Both Constraints

These superficial sketches should do for the purposes of creating a presumption against these positions. It is obvious even from them that both the pragmatic and moral accounts plunge straight against the second horn of Prichard's dilemma. Saying that what is wrong with violating epistemic norms is that doing so undermines one's goals or moral integrity, is to ascribe the wrong kind of normativity to epistemic norms. The test, as in the moral and friendship cases, is whether

---

6 The other camp of virtue epistemologists, 'reliabilists', do not endorse this subsumption of intellectual to moral virtues, e.g. Sosa (2009). Nor do all responsibilists, e.g., Baehr (2011).

such considerations are what would primarily move a good believer. And, of course, they are not. Indeed, they cannot so much as explicitly feature in his reasoning about what to believe[7]. They cannot, therefore, be reasons – let alone *good* reasons – for her to believe anything[8].

Once we appreciate this, though, it becomes clear that soft pragmatic and moral accounts also fail the motivation constraint: for how could something that cannot explicitly move me to adopt a belief account for how my beliefs are moved by epistemic norms? Reasons, we suppose, are the paradigmatic sorts of things which can move me through deliberation[9].

The moral and soft pragmatic accounts, then, breach both the normative- (through the second horn of Prichard's dilemma) and the motivation constraints.

2.3 The Normative Constitutive Account

We are asking why we should care about following epistemic norms. The normativist answer is that such caring is constitutive of applying the belief concept. That is, I cannot ask 'Should I *believe* that p?' without already caring about the truth of p and, thereby, caring about epistemic norms. If I did not care, I wouldn't be asking about *believing* p. On this view, then, the motivational force of epistemic norms comes for free with using the belief-concept. The motivation constraint is honoured.

What of the normative constraint? Since belief is the epistemic notion par excellence, the account is not offering the wrong sorts of reasons for caring for epistemic norms. So, it is not prone to the second horn of Prichard's dilemma. But since the account is not just saying 'otherwise you would be violating epistemic requirements', it seems that it is immune to the first horn, too.

---

[7] This is just a psychological, and widely accepted, claim, e.g., Williams (1973).

[8] Objection: it begs the question against the pragmatist to assume that epistemic reasons are sufficiently like moral reasons for Prichard's dilemma to be applicable to them. (Thanks to Martin Grajner and Pedro Schmechtig.) Reply: I must confess that I don't have a knockdown reply here. But I think that the objection would only be a genuine problem if I were aiming at giving conclusive arguments against existing views. Since my aim is merely to provide a prima facie presumption against these views by way of clearing space for mine, I think it is enough that many others share the intuition that the reason-giving force of epistemic norms is sufficiently like the one of moral considerations (e.g., Grimm (2009), Kornblith (1994)).

[9] A further reason why these cannot be the right accounts of the source of epistemic norms is that motivation by epistemic considerations is non-inferential and hegemonic (Shah (2006), 490–2), but if the moral and soft pragmatic views were right, epistemic reasons would be neither.

So it seems, anyhow, until we ask 'Why should I care about using the belief concept?' We could perhaps say: well, you just cannot help it by virtue of being a believer. But that won't do if by 'believer' we meant any old creature representing how things are, for animals and young children do that cheerfully without having the concept of belief. If, on the other hand, we mean a higher sort of believer, then we fall straight against the first horn of Prichard's dilemma. For what is a higher sort of believer? One with the concept of belief. Why should I care about the concept of belief? So that I can be a creature which has the concept of belief. The normative account in this garb, then, would take for granted, instead of explaining, the normativity of epistemic considerations.

To avoid this problem, one might modify[10] a move Railton (1997) makes: we could say that without having the concept of belief, I wouldn't be an agent, since being a higher order believer is constitutive of agency. Now, this is true, but (unhappily for the normativist) results in a strange account of the source of epistemic norms: we source their reason-giving force in agency, *but not through a distinguishing mark of agency.*

How so? Six-year olds, who manage the false-belief task, have, and can use, the concept of belief (Wimmer and Perner (1983)). But they are by no means full-blown agents, the sort of creatures which deliberate and guide their actions by the conclusions of deliberation. (This conception of agency will be defended in section 3.) So, even if having the concept of belief is necessary for full-blown agency, it is not its distinguishing mark. The normative account, then, either faces the first horn of Prichard's dilemma, or avoids it at the price of weirdness.

2.4 The Teleological Account

How about the teleological account? According to this account, we should care about epistemic norms because we should care for truth; and we should care for truth because otherwise we wouldn't *have beliefs*. Here is, for instance, Velleman:

> Reasons for belief are recognized...as considerations that appear to guarantee or probabilify the truth of the belief. And these considerations influence a person's belief by virtue of an inclination to believe what seems true...If someone is not inclined to believe what seems

---

10 I say 'modify' because Railton seems to think that caring for truth is the price not of having the concept of belief but of having beliefs. This forces him into the corner that I argue Velleman is forced into (§ 2.4, below).

true on a topic, he is no longer subject to reasons for believing things about it...He is no longer a believer at all (Velleman (2000a), 181).

Four things to notice about this account. First, it obviously clears the motivation constraint: the inclination to believe what is true is what automatically moves me to abandon a belief if I take it to have breached epistemic norms. Second, the account clears the second horn of Prichard's dilemma, since no non-epistemic considerations are invoked to ground the authority of these norms.

Third, though, the account plainly faces the first horn of Prichard's dilemma as much as the normative account did, and for the same reason. Why should I care about having beliefs? Because you are a creature with beliefs. But what is so amazing about being a creature with beliefs? We need to answer this question, else the account breaches the normative constraint.

The fourth thing to notice is that the teleological account will not even yield the tenuous link to agency that the normative account could. For according to the teleologist, the sort of aiming at truth involved in belief can be a sub-personal affair (Velleman (2000a), 186; Steglich-Petersen (2006)). So, while it is true that having beliefs is *necessary* for being an agent, the ability to believe will not even distinguish an agent from an out-and-out non-agent, since animals can have beliefs in this sense of 'belief'. So, having beliefs is merely an enabling, rather than a constitutive, condition of agency. But in that case, the teleological account falls even harder against the first horn of Prichard's dilemma, since it does not even have the weird route out of it.

2.5 Taking Stock

So, it looks like none of the existing positions is likely to yield a satisfactory account of the source of epistemic norms. There are two constraints on such an account: the motivational and the normative. The normative can be breached in two ways, captured by Prichard's dilemma. The normative and teleological positions fall against the first horn of the dilemma: they give either no answer or a strange answer to the question why we should care about epistemic norms. The soft pragmatic and moral positions, on the other horn, give the wrong answer, by citing considerations of the wrong sort to move a good believer. To add insult to injury, these latter positions breach the motivation constraint, too.

None of this is to deny that following epistemic norms might be practically useful or morally felicitous. Nor is it to take sides in the debate on what constitutes the belief-concept. It is just to say that however our bread is buttered on these issues, they won't give us the right answer to the question why we should care about epistemic norms.

Of course, I have hardly mustered conclusive arguments against these positions. My sketches of them are much too rough, and it may be that once they are refined, they can honour both constraints. Be that as it may, I think that these considerations are enough to establish at least a prima facie presumption against the accounts and kindle an interest in looking for a different approach. If that approach is not bedevilled by their problems, then the effort will pay.

3. An Account of Agency

In the next section I ground the source of epistemic norms in agency. But we need to get to agency by the right route. In this section, I introduce what seems to me the most promising candidate – Velleman's account of agency. On this account, what makes one an agent is the drive to understand what one is doing and to do what makes sense. Call this 'the drive to sense-making'. Velleman develops several arguments for this claim throughout his work, but I will here reconstruct the two that strike me as the most compelling.

3.1 The Argument from Metaethics

The first argument is that an agent-constituting drive *of some sort* would open up a space between two positions in metaethics whose fight has reached an impasse of legendary proportions – metaethical internalism and externalism (Velleman (2000a), Chap 8; (2009), Chapter 5). Metaethical internalism holds that something is a reason only if it necessarily motivates (rational) agents. The attraction of the view is that it accounts for the motivational force of reasons by hooking them up to our goals. But this is also its weakness: the account has no room for categorical reasons, reasons which apply to us regardless of our goals. The externalist makes room for these reasons by denying the necessary link between a reason and motivation. But he then has the problem of explaining how such reasons could motivate us, given that they are intrinsically unmoored from our motivations.

These fairly standard objections to internalism and externalism are enough to make attractive any position which avoids them. Positing a single agency-constituting drive is just such a position. It accounts for the motivational force of reasons: they move us through our drive for sense-making, since acting in light of reasons is making our actions intelligible. But it does so without turning all of our reasons hypothetical. Since the drive is something which we share qua agents, to say that our reasons are conditional on it, is just to say that they are reasons for agents. But that just means that they are reasons for action (Velleman (2000a), 180; (2009), 120).

3.2 The Argument from the Nature of Action

The second argument is more complicated. In a nutshell, it shows that thinking of the drive to sense-making as the hallmark of agency is our only naturalistic hope for capturing the involvement of the agent in his own actions. I will break down the argument into three steps, to keep things clearer[11]:

Step 1: Accounts which do not posit this drive leave the agent out of his own actions.
Step 2: Conscious control over what one does is constitutive of full-blown action.
Step 3: The drive to sense-making is constitutive of conscious control.
So, the drive to sense-making is the hallmark of agency.

I now look at each step in more detail.

3.2.1 Step 1: Accounts which do not Posit This Drive Leave the Agent out of his Own Actions

Suppose I reached for a glass of beer. How was I involved in this? The standard naturalistic story, after Davidson (1980), is that I had a certain desire and certain beliefs about how to satisfy this desire[12]. But this story, Velleman argues, leaves the agent out of the picture, by construing his action as the product of a bunch of unauthored occurrences. One way to see this is to look at addiction and compulsion (Frankfurt (2007)). In such cases, the action, even though a product of the

---

[11] I piece together these steps from Velleman's various writings. I take it this is OK, given that my aim here is not exegesis, but making the account plausible enough to ground the authority of epistemic norms.

[12] The non-naturalistic answer is so called agent-causation: it posits the agent as a primitive sui generis causal force, which interferes in an inherently 'gappy' natural causal order (e.g., Chisholm (1976)). This position indeed makes room for the agent's involvement in his own actions, but at such a heady price, that few take it seriously nowadays.

agent's desires and beliefs, is performed despite the agent rather than by him: if I were an unwilling alcoholic, say, I would reach for the beer out of the same desires and beliefs, *despite* myself. So, *I* cannot just be a matter of these desires and beliefs.

Frankfurt's solution to this problem was to locate the agent's involvement in his actions at the level of his identification with his first-order desires. He thought of this identification initially in terms of second-order desires and later in terms of decisions to go with this motive rather than another. But both construals, Velleman argues, still leave the agent out of his action. The agent is someone who mediates between his first- and second-order mental states, on the one hand, and action, on the other:

> His role is to intervene between reasons and intention, and between intention and bodily movements, in each case guided by the one to produce the other (2000a, 125).

But once we see that, it becomes plain that the agent cannot be reduced to his own states, be they first- or second-order, for the simple reason that 'intervening between these items is not something that the items themselves can do' (*ibid.*).

Now, Velleman does not want to say that the agent ultimately will be something mysterious. Recall that he is after a naturalistic account of agency. So, he looks for a single mental state that is 'functionally identical with the agent' (*ibid.*, 137), a state that is not reducible to other mental states, but underpins both their role as reasons and the agent's 'intervention' between them and action. The one he settles on is the drive to understand what one is doing, and to do only what makes sense.

This sort of drive is different in kind from all other mental states: it is eligible for arbitrating amongst them and, hence, does not face the problem faced by attempts to reduce the agent to his particular bunch of mental states. The difference is made vivid when we think of the impossibility of rejecting the drive:

> To ask 'why should I have the aim of making sense?' is to reveal that you already have it. If you do not seek to do what makes sense, then you are not in the business of practical reasoning, and so you cannot demand reasons for acting or aiming (2009, 137).

One cannot, in other words, reject the drive to sense-making while remaining an agent.

3.2.2 Step 2: Conscious Control over what one does is Constitutive of Full-Blown Action

So far, the argument shows that we need something like this drive to capture our involvement in our actions. But why should we think of this as functionally identical with the agent[13]?

The drive is the hallmark of agency, Velleman argues, because it is what distinguishes full-blown action from lower forms of intentional activity. What characterises full-blown action, the argument goes, cannot be that it is goal-directed, for reflexively catching a falling glass, say, is goal-directed, but is not a full-blown action (2000a, Chapter 8). It cannot be that it aims at the good either, because this rules out perverse action (2000a, Chapter 5). What distinguishes full-blown action from merely goal-directed activity is that in the case in which I reflexively catch the glass I am not in *conscious control* of my action, I am not, that is, controlling what I am doing through consciousness of what I am doing.

3.2.3 Step 3: The Drive to Sense-Making is Constitutive of Conscious Control

So, conscious control is the hallmark of full-blown action and, therefore, of agency. But I have this type of control only when what I am doing makes sense to me. This is made vivid by cases in which we lack control precisely through not being able to make sense of what we are doing. Suppose, Velleman urges, you catch yourself absentmindedly walking down the street. As soon as you catch yourself, you stop and try to make sense of what you are doing. Until you work it out, you do not walk again. When you do, you have assumed control of your walking by doing something that now makes sense.

How so? When you wonder what you are doing in the middle of the street, you already know one description of what you are doing – walking down the street. Even so, you are puzzled about what you are doing. What is missing is a description of the action which includes *why* you are doing it[14]. When you wonder what you are doing, in other words, you are after the sort of description of the action that *makes sense* of the action in light of your motives for it (Velleman (2007), 27–8). This drive can be gratified in two ways: 'by understanding any-

---

[13] A further question is whether we in fact have such a drive. Velleman (2000b) makes a persuasive case that we do, based on empirical research.
[14] For independent support of this thought, see Wallace (2006, Chapter 2) who argues that the content of intentions – the locus of our control – includes one's reason for performing the action.

thing that you are up to and by not being up to anything that you do not understand' (*ibid.*, 28). It is this latter, which explains your control over your actions as well as why you stopped in the middle of the street.

If you are not impressed with this – admittedly rather quirky – argument, think of more homely cases, such as dementia, in which we lack agency precisely because we do not understand what we are doing and we keep doing things that do not make sense to us. Or think, again, how often we absolve ourselves and each other from responsibility for an action by simply saying 'I didn't know what I was doing'.

This is, of course, a broad-brushstroke sketch of long and sophisticated arguments, but I hope to have at least given a taste for the attractiveness of this picture: it solves *the* central problem of philosophy of action (§ 3.2) and one of the central ones of metaethics (§ 3.1).

4. The Drive for Sense-Making is the Source of Epistemic Norms

4.1 The Proposal

What does all this have to do with epistemic norms? Velleman understands practical deliberation as a species of theoretical deliberation. The conclusion of an episode of practical deliberation is an intention to ϕ which, according to him, just is a belief that I will ϕ. This automatically turns the norms governing practical sense-making into epistemic norms. But it is enough for present purposes to make the more modest assumption that intention is *partly constituted* by a belief (that one will perform the intended action)[15]. The drive to sense-making is, hence, partly the drive to have this belief make sense to the agent in light of other beliefs about his motives, means to attaining his goals, and how the world is. But such beliefs making sense just amounts to their being the product of following things like the evidence- and consistency norms. Since following these norms is constitutive of things making sense, the drive to sense-making is partly constituted by our accepting the normative force of these norms. By caring about sense-making, I already care about following epistemic norms.

---

15 Naturally, this assumption has its opponents (e. g., Bratman (1991), 117 – 128). But at least they are fewer than those of the identification of intention with belief.

4.2 The Proposal Meets the Motivation Constraint

It is easy to see how both the motivating force of epistemic norms and their normativity fall out of our drive for sense-making. The motivating force first: how does the consideration that this belief is formed against the evidence move me to abandon the belief? On the present proposal, I am the sort of creature which is driven to act in a way that makes sense. But sense-making happens through reflection on how the world is and on my motives for doing things in it. The outputs of reflection are beliefs. So, for reflection to be conducted in a way that would genuinely make sense of what I am about, it must be governed by epistemic norms. Consider: could what I am doing make sense if my beliefs about what I am doing and the world were systematically inconsistent or held against the evidence? Plainly, no. They must be at least largely consistent with one another. (More on this in § 5.)

So, the drive for sense-making is in part a drive to be moved by epistemic norms. But since the drive to sense-making is constitutive of agency, as long as I am an agent I am moved by epistemic norms. This is not to say, of course, that I will always succeed at *following* these norms and that my beliefs will be always impeccable. Nor is it to say that I can't wilfully violate these norms. After all, the odd violation will not undermine my agency (more of this in § 5.1). It is just to say that epistemic norms have normative force for me. I care for them in virtue of being driven to sense-making.

4.3 The Proposal Meets the Normative Constraint

What about the normativity of epistemic norms? What makes the fact that my belief has violated epistemic norms a reason not to hold it is, on this view, precisely what makes any consideration a reason. Why should I care about epistemic norms? Because agency requires caring. Stop caring and you lose the very thing that is prompting you to ask such questions in the first place – your drive to make sense of what is going on with you and the world. This was the moral of trying to imagine what it would be like to reject the drive to sense-making (§ 3.2). It cannot be done by an agent.

This view of the normativity of epistemic norms clears the first horn of Prichard's dilemma. It does not ring with the hollowness of the answer 'Because epistemic normativity requires it'. It cites no epistemic reason, and so cannot presuppose the force of such reasons. It just presupposes that agency is something which merits the response of caring, a reasonable assumption, surely.

Nor does the answer invest epistemic norms with the wrong kind of normativity. For on this account, epistemic norms move me through my drive for sense-making. Given that intention is partly constituted by belief, sense-making is partly an epistemic matter. So, the account clears the second horn of Prichard's dilemma.

The proposal, then, meets both the motivation and the normative constraints, something that none of the discussed existing accounts did.

5. Two Objections

In this section I clarify and strengthen the proposal by forestalling the two most pressing objections to it. I first develop the objections and a reply to each (§§ 5.1–5.2); I then bolster both replies with a case study from literature by way of putting more flesh on the proposal (§ 5.3).

5.1 What About Intention-Unrelated Beliefs?

The first objection is that the above arguments secure, at best, the authority of epistemic norms only over beliefs about the things we intend to do. It would seem that not caring about these norms when it comes to many beliefs about matters unconnected to our actions is perfectly compatible with being a creature driven to doing only what makes sense. Here the objector might cite highly theoretical, or abstractly aesthetic, beliefs, say. If so, I have failed to give an account of the source of epistemic norms, since these norms are supposed to have authority over us for all of our beliefs, regardless of their content (e.g., Grimm (2009)).

Here is my reply. To begin with, for any belief about my intentions to make sense and so to have complied with epistemic norms, its inferential neighbours need to have likewise complied with these norms, since justificatory status transmits over inference-neighbourhoods. As it happens, a belief about what I will do and why I will do it has many kinds of inferential neighbours, more perhaps than any other type of belief. To oversimplify, these neighbours include first, beliefs about my goals and about possible means to attaining these goals; second, beliefs about the desirability of, and my relative suitability for, pursuing certain goals and taking certain means over others; third, beliefs about the moral status of the envisaged goals and means; fourth, beliefs about how the world is.

If I did not have the first set of beliefs, I wouldn't be an agent, since I wouldn't be an actor. If I did not have the other three sets, the drive to sense-making would be continuously frustrated. For, how could my intentions make sense to me if I had no views on my own nature, and on the moral and descriptive contours of the world which I am trying to negotiate? But since the beliefs in all four sets are *inferential* neighbours of my intention-beliefs, and justificatory status transmits, the intention-beliefs cannot comply with epistemic norms without the neighbours having likewise complied. So, caring for epistemic norms concerning intention-beliefs just is caring for these norms with regard to all four sets of inferentially neighbouring beliefs.

But since these four groups of neighbours have multitudes of inferential neighbours themselves, these multitudes must have, in turn, complied with epistemic norms. In this way, the drive to sense-making constitutively extends to all of our beliefs. Thus this drive can non-instrumentally ground the normative authority of epistemic norms for all of our beliefs.

5.2 What Happened to Truth?

The second potential objection is that my proposal fails to accommodate the stock-in-trade idea that epistemic norms are our best shot at getting true belief. One might worry that the notion of sense-making at play here is not enough to yield the robust connection to truth required by epistemic norms. There can be several incompatible belief-systems, which are equally coherent and would, thus, equally make sense, but which cannot all be true (e.g., Kvanvig (2012), 21). And so, the worry goes, the notion of sense-making at play cannot ground the source of epistemic norms, since epistemic norms bear a much stronger kinship to truth. Another way of putting the objection: while the current proposal may explain the normative authority of the consistency-norm, it fails to explain that of the evidence-norm.

My reply is this. The drive to sense-making is not the drive to make up any old coherent narrative about yourself; it is a drive to do what makes sense in light of your *real* motives and in light of *how the world actually is*. Sourcing the reason-giving force of epistemic norms in this drive, therefore, preserves the intuition that truth-directedness is central to epistemic norms. The account just says that the attraction of truth lies in agency itself: we need true beliefs because otherwise the world would keep tripping up our beliefs and actions into not making sense. Concern for both truth and consistency, in other words, falls out of the drive for sense-making. Thus, the drive grounds both the evidence- and consistency norms.

5.3 Supporting the two Replies

Thinking about self-deception bolsters my replies to both objections. Start with a toy example, to fix ideas. (In a moment I will offer a grown up one.) All the evidence points to her infidelity. Yet he believes her faithful in order to preserve his marriage, dignity, or whatever. His belief has two features:

(1) it violates the evidence-norm;

(2) yet it must be made consistent with – to make sense in the context of – his other beliefs (this is just a psychological fact about belief).

Since (as mentioned in § 5.1) beliefs are not isolated mental items, but come in mutually supportive networks, in order for him to maintain the self-deceptive belief he must manufacture a whole *coherent* network of beliefs which aren't supported by the evidence. It is only within this network that the self-deceptive belief makes sense and can be sustained.

Call the case in which both the consistency and evidence norms have been observed, a case of 'veridical coherence'; and call the case in which the consistency norm is observed but the evidence-norm violated, 'sham-coherence'. (The labels are just shorthand. They are not meant to imply that all of one's beliefs are true in the first case or false in the second; just that they are largely true or false.) The case of self-deception involves the tension between these two types of coherence: the fact that things need to make sense to us, compels us to make up coherent stories when the real thing is, for whatever reason, beyond our reach. But the world keeps intruding into our sham-coherent stories and destabilises the coherence we seek. When the story becomes long (and tall) enough, things stop making sense. If this is right, then the drive to sense-making is shown both to be the drive to veridical coherence, that is the drive for both evidence-following and consistency (bolstering my reply to the second objection), and to involve vast tracts of one's belief system (bolstering my reply to the first objection).

W. G. Sebald's novel *Austerlitz* neatly dramatizes both of these points. Austerlitz's case has the following two features:

(5.3.1) Austerlitz's life stops making sense, due to the fact that his beliefs do not veridically-cohere, even though

(5.3.2) they do sham-cohere.

I now adduce some textual support for each of these claims. (The less literarily inclined reader who just wishes to see how these features bolster my replies to the two objections, may wish to skip to § 5.3.3.)

5.3.1 Austerlitz's Life Stops Making Sense due to his Beliefs not Veridically-Cohering

Austerlitz is a historian of architecture and an extremely erudite and prolific thinker. There is just one thing he does not think about: he was on the Kindertransport in 1939. In his fifties, he has a complete nervous breakdown, as a result of endless dreams and hallucinations which hint at the past. The break-down is due, that is, to things not veridically cohering – to the overwhelming force of things no longer fitting together and his 'ever greater efforts' to make them fit together without recalling the *evidence* of his past (Sebald (2001), 198). The breakdown culminates in endless walking through the streets of London without knowing or caring why he is doing it (in neat counterpoise to Velleman's walker, who stops until he works out why he is walking) and, significantly, a complete loss of language, our vital tool for sense-making. Austerlitz himself makes it amply clear that the breakdown is precisely one in sense-making:

> The entire structure of language, the syntactical arrangement of parts of speech, punctuation, conjunctions, and finally even the nouns denoting ordinary objects were all enveloped in impenetrable fog...*I could see no connections any more*, the sentences resolved themselves into a series of separate words, the words into random sets of letters, the letters into disjointed signs, and those signs into a blue-grey trail gleaming silver here and there, excreted and left behind it by some *crawling creature*, and *the sight of it increasingly filled me with feelings of horror and shame* (175–6, my italics).

Notice especially the last line, where the revulsion and horror are simultaneously directed at language not making sense and at himself ('shame'), as though one is identical with things making sense.

5.3.2 Austerlitz's Beliefs, however, Perfectly Sham-Cohere

Yet, Austerlitz has spent his entire life producing a perfectly sham-coherent story about himself. Although a historian of architecture and a highly educated man, he:

knew nothing about the conquest of Europe by the Germans and the slave state they set up, and nothing about the persecution I had escaped (197).

How is this possible for a historian? Just avoid the evidence:

> I did not read newspapers because, as I now know, I *feared* unwelcome revelations, I turned on the radio only at certain hours of the day, I was always refining my *defensive reactions, creating a kind of quarantine or immune system which as I maintained my existence in a smaller and smaller space, protected me* from anything that could be connected in any way, however distant, with my own early history...And if some *dangerous* piece of information came my way despite all my precautions, as it inevitably did, I was clearly capable of closing my eyes and ears to it, of simply forgetting it like any other unpleasantness (197–8, my italics).

Crucially, Austerlitz himself makes it clear that this continuous violation of the evidence norm is what causes the break-down in sense-making:

> Today I know why I felt obliged to turn away when anyone came too close to me, I know that I thought this turning away *made me safe*, and at the same time *I saw myself transformed into a frightful and hideous creature, a man beyond the pale* (304, my italics).

The 'frightful and hideous creature' here neatly echoes the earlier 'crawling creature' which symbolized the breakdown in sense-making (end of first quote). By connecting this image to the desire to 'be safe' from the real story about himself in the present passage, Austerlitz and Sebald make it clear that it is the urge to maintain the sham-coherent story (to be 'safe' and 'protected') that undermines the intelligibility of things, turns Austerlitz into a 'crawling creature', 'a man beyond the pale'.

5.3.3 How Austerlitz Bolsters my Replies

What we have here, in other words, is the maintenance of a perfectly sham-coherent belief system, yet things not *really* making sense. Why? The obvious explanation is that it is veridical coherence – the observation of *both* the evidence- and consistency norms – that is required for genuine sense-making. This sounds plausible. The drive to understand what I am doing and to do only what makes sense is, after all, the drive of a creature negotiating a world. If the sense-making in question is fantasy, if it is sufficiently divorced from the world which this creature is negotiating, the creature will be a confused one: he will be telling himself a story, whose intelligibility will be continuously tripped up by the world.

Austerlitz ratifies my replies to both objections above. To start with the second: his case demonstrates that the relevant drive for sense-making constitutive of agency is the veridical one, not the drive to make up any old coherent story about what we are doing. This veridical sense-making drive, therefore, bears a sufficiently robust connection to truth to be an eligible candidate for grounding the evidence- as well as the consistency norms. So, the drive to sense making is constituted by caring for both of these norms. Hence, the second objection is misguided. To reiterate, I don't mean to suggest that for things to make sense, one's every belief needs to be true, or that a false belief can't make sense. Rather, the thought is that unless one's beliefs *as a whole* were *largely* true, the world and one's actions in it wouldn't make sense. But this is enough to guarantee that aiming at sense-making is aiming at truth-aiming epistemic norms[16].

But Austerlitz's story also makes vivid how entangled one's intention-related beliefs are with the rest of one's belief system. Austerlitz must shrink his sphere of activity, must (as he tells us) 'maintain [his] existence in a smaller and smaller space', in order to be able to continue to violate the evidence norm. One cannot violate epistemic norms when it comes to a bunch of beliefs about the world, without the rot spreading to one's beliefs about what one is doing. Austerlitz must doctor vast swaths of his beliefs in order to maintain the single belief that he is just an ordinary adopted child, and to see his goals, motives and actions as those of an historian of integrity and of a Holocaust-undamaged person. This ultimately results in things no longer making sense. The drive to sense-making, in other words, will be frustrated not only because the evidence norm is violated for the one belief (as per the second reply), but also because shamming requires that one cultivate swarms of further beliefs against the evidence. The result is that while the deception lasts, one's actorship shrinks; the only way out is a breakdown in sense-making. Hence, the first objector was wrong to insist that my account secures the authority of epistemic norms solely for beliefs which directly bear on our intentions. The drive for sense-making is far more pervasive than that, simply in virtue of the inferential interdependence of our beliefs.

---

16 This observation helps dispel a potential worry. The whole distinction between sham- and genuine sense-making, the worry goes, is ad hoc (Thanks to Martin Grajner and Pedro Schmechtig for this objection as well as the following way of supporting it.) Two points may be thought to kindle this suspicion – the New Evil Demon scenario and research on various kinds of bias (e. g., the fact that we regularly overestimate our own attractiveness and intelligence). Both, the thought goes, show that the world can make sense when one doesn't just have true beliefs. Both of these instances of sense-making despite false beliefs are compatible with the current proposal, since all that the latter requires is that one's beliefs are largely true.

Conclusion

If these thoughts are on the right track, the drive to sense-making is an eminently plausible candidate for grounding the source of epistemic norms. No doubt much more needs to be said to fill out this sketch. But instead of saying it, I wish to conclude by showing how the proposal does justice to what seems right about existing accounts of the source of epistemic norms without inheriting their problems.

The soft pragmatist and the moral accounts were right to insist that the source of epistemic norms is connected to our being actors in the world. They just went wrong in doing so instrumentally through our practical and moral goals. The temptation is understandable, though, on the current proposal: what gives a grip to all normative considerations is our agency.

Caring about epistemic norms is, however, not instrumental to, but constitutive of, caring about coherent actions and beliefs. The constitutive accounts got right the thought that the reason-giving force of epistemic norms must be located constitutively, rather than instrumentally. They just did it through the wrong feature of agency – belief. Being a believer is not a source of ultimate normative authority; being an agent is.

Once we see things this way, we can also address the two issues of interest to this collection with which I started. I said that if we have a sui generis account of the source of epistemic norms, then these norms turn out to be categorical, and that hence, epistemic normativity is assured autonomy from other normative domains. We can now see how the present proposal makes good on this. Since caring about epistemic norms is simply premised on our agency, the norms apply to all agents regardless of their particular goals. But for a norm to apply to all agents in this way is just for it to be categorical. Concerning the second issue, since the feature of agency through which we connect epistemic norms and agency is at bottom an epistemic one – sense-making – the authority of epistemic norms over us does not depend any form of normativity other than the epistemic. Epistemic normativity thus is shown to constitute an autonomous normative realm.

Clearly, this sketch needs to be worked out in much more detail. But I hope to have at least shown here that if we are ever to find out why we should care about epistemic norms, the most auspicious place to look for an answer is the hallmark of agency, our drive to make sense[17].

---

[17] Many thanks to Alexandra Couto, Martin Grajner, Christoph Hanisch, Martin Kusch, Herlinde Pauer-Studer, Pedro Schmechtig, David Velleman, and the participants in the workshop 'Justifi-

References

Baehr, J. (2011). *The Inquiring Mind: On Intellectual Virtues and Virtue Epistemology*. New York: Oxford University Press.

BonJour, L. (1985). *The Structure of Empirical Knowledge*. Cambridge, MA: Harvard University Press.

Bratman, M. (1991). Cognitivism about Practical Reason. *Ethics, 102*(1), 117–128.

Chisholm, R. (1976). *Person and Object*. London: Allen and Unwin.

Clifford, W. K. (2001). The Ethics of Belief. In A. Burger (ed.), *The Ethics of Belief*. Roseville: Dry Bones.

Dancy, J. (2000). *Practical Reality*. Oxford: Oxford University Press.

Davidson, D. (1980). *Essays on Actions and Events*. Oxford: Clarendon.

Frankfurt, H. (2007). *The Importance of What we Care About*. Cambridge: Cambridge University Press.

Grimm, S. (2009). Epistemic Normativity. In A. M. Haddock, A. Millar, and D. Pritchard (eds.), *Epistemic Value*. Oxford: Oxford University Press.

Harman, G. (1976). Practical Reasoning. *The Review of Metaphysics, 29*(3), 431–463.

Heil, J. (1992). Believing Reasonably. *Noûs, 26*(1), 47–62.

Jones, W. (2009). The Goods and Motivation of Believing. In A. M. Haddock, A. Millar, and D. Pritchard (eds.), *Epistemic Value*. Oxford: Oxford University Press.

Kelly, T. (2003). Epistemic Rationality as Instrumental Rationality: A Critique. *Philosophy and Phenomenological Research, 66*(3), 612–640.

Kornblith, H. (1993). Epistemic Normativity. *Synthèse, 94*(3), 357–378.

Korsgaard, C. M. (1986). Skepticism about Practical Reason. *The Journal of Philosophy, 83*(1), 5–25.

Kusch, M. (2002). *Knowledge by Agreement*. Oxford: Oxford University Press.

Kvanvig, J. (2012). Coherentism and Justified Inconsistent Beliefs: A Solution. *Southern Journal of Philosophy, 50*(1), 21–41.

Lycan, W. G. (1988). Epistemic Value. In W. G. Lycan (ed.), *Judgement and Justification*. Cambrige: Cambrige University Press.

Lynch, M. (2004). *True to Life*. MIT Press.

Mitova, V. (2008a). Why W. K. Clifford was a Closet Pragmatist. *Philosophical Papers, 37*(3), 471–489.

Mitova, V. (2008b). Why Pragmatic Justifications of Epistemic Norms Don't Work. *South African Journal of Philosophy, 27*(2), 141–152.

Mitova, V. (2015). Truthy Psychologism about Evidence. *Philosophical Studies, 172*(4), 1105–1126.

Pritchard, D. (2007). Recent Work on Epistemic Value. *American Philosophical Quarterly, 44*(2), 85–110.

---

cation: Normality and Normativity' (Paris, March 2012), for invaluable comments on earlier drafts. Thanks also to the organizers of that workshop, Benoit Gaultier and Claudine Tiercelin, for their invitation and for the opportunity to work on this topic. Thanks to the Institute for Philosophy and the Chair for Epistemology and Philosophy of Science at Vienna University for their financial support.

Pritchard, D. (2011). The Value of Knowledge. *Stanford Encyclopedia of Philosophy*.
Railton, P. (1997). On the Hypothetical and Non-Hypothetical in Reasoning about Belief and Action. In *Cullity and Gaut (1997)*.
Scanlon, T. M. (1998). *What We Owe to Each Other*. Harvard University Press.
Sebald, W. (2001). *Austerlitz*. (A. Bell, Transl.) London: Penguin.
Shah, N. (2002). Clearing Space for Doxastic Voluntarism. *The Monist, 85*(3), 436–445.
Shah, N. (2003). How Truth Governs Belief. *The Philosophical Review, 112*(4), 447–482.
Shah, N. (2006). A New Argument for Evidentialism. *The Philosophical Quarterly, 56*(225), 481–498.
Shah, N. (2008). How Action Governs Intention. *Philosophers' Imprint, 8*(5), 1–19.
Shah, N. (2005). Doxastic Deliberation. *The Philosophical Review, 114*(4), 497–534.
Smith, M. (1994). *The Moral Problem*. Oxford: Blackwell.
Sosa, E. (2009). *Reflective Knowledge*. Oxford University Press.
Steglich-Petersen, A. (2006). No Norm Needed: On the Aim of Belief. *The Philosophical Quarterly, 56*(225), 499–516.
Stich, S. (1990). *The Fragmentation of Reason*. Cambridge, MA: MIT Press.
Stout, R. (2005). *Action*. Acumen.
Turri, J. (2010). On the Relationship between Propositional and Doxastic Justification. *Philosophy and Phenomenological Research, 80*(2), 312–326.
Velleman, D. (2000). From self psychology to moral philosophy. *Philosophical Perspectives, 14*, 349–77.
Velleman, D. J. (1985). Practical Reflection. *The Philosophical Review, 94*(1), 33–61.
Velleman, D. J. (2000). *The Possibility of Practical Reason*. Oxford: Clarendon.
Velleman, D. J. (2005). The self as narrator. In J. A. Christman (ed.), *Autonomy and the Challenges to Liberalism*. New York: Cambridge University Press.
Velleman, J. D. (2009). *How We Get Along*. New York: Cambridge University Press.
Wallace, R. J. (2006). *Normativity and the Will: Selected Papers on Moral Psychology and Practical Reason*. Oxford: Clarendon Press.
Wedgwood, R. (2002). The aim of belief. *Philosophical Perspectives, 16*, 267–297.
Williams, B. (1973). Deciding to believe. In B. Williams, *Problems of the Self*. Cambridge: Cambridge University Press.
Williams, B. (1981). Internal and External Reasons. In B. Williams, *Moral Luck*. Cambridge: Cambridge University Press.
Zagzebski, L. (2004). Epistemic Value and the Primacy of What we Care About. *Philosophical Papers, 33*(3), 353–377.
Zagzebski, L. T. (1996). *Virtues of the mind: An inquiry into the nature of virtue and the ethical foundations of knowledge*. Cambridge: Cambridge University Press.

III Epistemic Consequentialism

Hamid Vahid
Epistemic Normativity: From Direct to Indirect Epistemic Consequentialism

1. Introduction

Beliefs can be evaluated from a number of perspectives. Depending on our choice of the standards and goals (moral, practical, etc.) the evaluation will yield different results. Epistemic evaluation, however, involves epistemic standards and appropriate epistemic goals. A theory of epistemic justification must, thus, address the question of the aim and objective of epistemic justification, i.e., what is the point of epistemic justification and why we value it. It is generally thought that there is an intimate connection between justification and truth. This is usually construed along the lines that epistemic justification aims at maximizing true belief and minimizing false belief, or, more simply, believing truths and not believing falsehoods (call this, following Foley[1], the 'truth-directed' goal or the 'truth goal').

A view that naturally incorporates the aforementioned ingredients of justification, namely, epistemic consequentialism, takes our concept of epistemic justification to have a consequentialist or teleological structure in the sense that what makes a belief worth having from the epistemic point of view is whether it helps promote things with intrinsic epistemic value. Thus, on such a view the source of epistemic normativity lies in the value of appropriate epistemic goals that characterize our epistemic endeavors. Epistemic reasons, in other words, acquire their normative force in virtue of serving the goals in question.

In general, as Wayne Riggs[2] has put it, the normative structure of any domain can be characterized by a theory of final value, the kinds of objects that are valuable in that domain and a set of value-transmitting relations. One prominent consequentialist or teleological approach to epistemic normativity identifies the fundamental end or value with having true beliefs and avoiding false beliefs or with ends that have true belief as a necessary component. This means that any feature of beliefs that is probably correlated with truth, counts towards the original aim of maximizing true and minimizing false beliefs. These factors

---
1 Foley (1993).
2 Riggs (2008).

include reliable belief formation, being the best explanation of certain phenomenon and so on. On the other hand, the set of objects that are valuable include beliefs, belief-forming processes, the subject's cognitive behavior or intellectual character, and so on. Finally, there are the ways through which an epistemically valuable object (x) derives its value from the fundamental value or end (y). Different consequentialist theories suggest different accounts of the transmission of value depending on how they conceive of the relation between x and y. We can, for example, say of x that it promotes a state of affairs y that has value if it is a causal means to y in the sense that x's occurrence brings about y, or that it contributes to the obtaining of y in virtue of, say, being part of y, and so on.

It is a measure of the strength and plausibility of epistemic consequentialism that many epistemologists of various stripes in the justification debate take epistemic value to have a teleological structure. Thus, many internalists and externalists about epistemic justification seem to think of the concept of justification as an evaluative concept whose attachment to a belief makes the belief worth having from the epistemic point of view, in turn, characterized in terms of the truth goal. BonJour, for example, says that the

> basic role of justification is that of a *means* to truth… The distinguishing characteristic of epistemic justification is thus its essential or internal relation to the cognitive goal of truth. It follows that one's cognitive endeavors are epistemically justified only if and to the extent that they are aimed at this goal.[3]

Alston is also equally explicit.

> Beliefs can be evaluated in different ways. One may be more or less prudent, fortunate, or faithful in holding a certain belief. Epistemic justification is different from all that. Epistemic evaluation is undertaken from what we might call the "epistemic point of view". That point of view is defined by the aim of maximizing truth and minimizing falsity in a large body of beliefs.[4]

So, according to epistemic consequentialism, the epistemic value of a belief derives entirely from the value of its consequences. But not all consequences of a belief are epistemically relevant. After all, some of those consequences are non-epistemic. And even when the consequences are epistemic, it is not clear whether, by themselves, they are sufficient to render a belief justified. Accordingly, to single out those consequences of a belief that are epistemically relevant, we need to do two things. First, we need to have a strategy to deal with the question

---

3 BonJour (1985, 7–8).
4 Alston (1989, 83).

whether the non-epistemic consequences of a belief can epistemize the belief in question. In fact, this turns out to be an instance of a more general problem known as the 'wrong kind of reason' (WKR) problem. It is important to have a response to this problem because, as we shall see, some of the implausible claims made on behalf of (or against) epistemic consequentialism can be shown to have their roots in their failure to take note of the fact that sometimes an agent's reasons for a belief are not epistemic reasons but reasons to do something. This issue will be discussed in Section 2.

Secondly, turning now to the epistemic consequences of a belief, we need to specify the conditions under which such consequences count as the promotion of the truth goal, thus, conferring justification on that belief. This is, in effect, a request for an adequate formulation of the thesis of epistemic consequentialism. I deal with this issue in Section 3 where I distinguish between direct and indirect versions of epistemic consequentialism. Having argued against the direct version, I subsequently seek to qualify it in order to make it immune against the objections raised earlier on. I try various strategies, but eventually come down in favor of, what I call, a 'sensitivity' constraint on such an account. The idea roughly is that the production of true beliefs by a particular belief p must be sensitive to the content of p if it is to count as the promotion of the truth goal. In Section 4, I show how the qualified account can deflect some of the recent objections raised against epistemic consequentialism by Selim Berker. It will be argued, however, that the appending of direct epistemic consequentialism with the sensitivity requirement actually shows that the direct version of the thesis should be abandoned in favor of its indirect version. The rest of Section 4 will be devoted to spelling out the virtues of indirect epistemic consequentialism.

2. The Conceptual Ingredients of Epistemic Consequentialism

In the absence of an adequate account of epistemic consequentialism, one can choose to proceed in two opposite directions: Either deny that the epistemic consequences of a belief are, in any way, relevant to its epistemic status, or take the mere fact that a belief has valuable, truth-related consequences as providing epistemic reason to hold that belief. The latter attitude can be illustrated by considering the following well-known example.[5] Suppose an atheist scientist is trying to secure a grant from a religious organization which gives the grant only to

---

5 Adapted from Fumerton (2001).

believers. Realizing that he is a bad liar, the scientist's only chance of getting the grant is to bring herself to believe that God exists. Having secured the grant, the scientist would then be able to further her research and accumulate a large number of true beliefs and also revise a large number of previously held false beliefs. The question which such a case highlights is whether the scientist is epistemically permitted to hold the belief that God exists under the envisaged circumstances. Some consequentialists[6] are inclined to answer the questions in the positive while other consequentialists would regard the belief as epistemically unjustified.[7] An adequate formulation of epistemic consequentialism is precisely what is needed in order to properly adjudicate between the two views.

To this purpose, I begin with the question of how to single out those consequences of a belief that are epistemically relevant. For, as it turns out, an answer to this question would be highly pertinent to finding an adequate formulation of the thesis of epistemic consequentialism. Let us start with the question of whether the non-epistemic consequences of a belief can constitute reasons for that belief. As noted earlier, this is an instance of a more general problem known as the 'wrong kind of reason' (WKR) problem.[8] The problem arises because it seems that reasons for valuing an object do not always reflect that object's value. For example, if an evil demon threatens to kill us unless we admire cruel actions, then it seems that we have good reason to admire those actions even though they are not admirable. Similar cases also arise for cognitive attitudes like beliefs, the best known of which is typified, perhaps, by Pascal's wager. Pascal pointed out that we should believe in God because, in case he exists, the consequences of believing that he exists (going to heaven) are far superior to not believing that he exists (ending up in hell) whereas, in case God does not exist, the costs of believing that he exists are negligible when compared to the expected gain. It has seemed to many, however, that the desirable consequences of a belief should not be taken as being relevant to the epistemic status of that belief. The claim is that such reasons are the wrong kind of reasons. Accordingly, a distinction is made between the right kind of reasons and the wrong kind of reasons for attitudes. Finding a principled way of drawing the distinction is what constitutes the WKR problem.

There have been a number of attempts to solve this problem. I shall mention some of them that are particularly relevant to the case of propositional attitudes

---

6 See, for example, Talbot (2014).
7 See, for example, Goldman (forthcoming).
8 See, for example, Rabinowicz and Rønnow-Rasmussen (2004), Olson (2004) and Lang (2008).

and, in particular, beliefs. A long standing solution to this problem has been to distinguish between two kinds of reasons for attitudes: object-given reasons and state-given reasons.[9] Object-given reasons for an attitude are said to be grounded in the properties of the object of that attitude whereas state-given reasons are provided by the properties of the attitude itself. State-given reasons are then identified as the wrong kind of reasons. This strategy is thought to fall prey to the objection[10] that one can always pair every property of the object of an attitude with a corresponding property of the attitude itself. It is nevertheless acknowledged that any solution to the WKR problem must be drawn along the lines suggested by the aforementioned distinction.

One such attempt involves a distinction made by Joseph Raz between standard and non-standard reason.[11] In drawing this distinction, Raz exploits a general mark of the right kind of reasons, namely, the fact that one can seem to follow such reasons directly. For example, while it is difficult to see how one could believe in God on grounds of the expected utility of such a belief, it seems that one could directly form the belief in case one found, say, the argument from design convincing. To inculcate belief in God on the basis of its expected utility, however, requires some indirect strategy which, as Pascal suggested, may include regularly attending church, hanging out with believers, etc. Accordingly, Raz distinguishes between reasons that one can follow directly (i.e. the 'standard' reasons) and reasons that one cannot follow directly (viz. the 'non-standard' reasons). Furthermore, he takes standard reasons to be those that relate to the standard that determines the appropriateness of the kind of the relevant attitude. In the case of belief, for example, the standard is truth. Thus, non-standard reasons (i.e., the wrong kind of reasons) for a belief are those that are unrelated to the truth of the belief. But this seems too quick. In the absence of having a proper account of the notion of truth-relatedness, it seems rather rash to identify the wrong kind of reasons with those that are not truth-related for some such reasons may also involve truth in a rather more roundabout way. For example, in the case of Pascal's wager itself, the sort of expected utility of believing in God that Pascal refers to requires that the proposition 'God exists' be true. So it is not true that all wrong kind of reasons are unrelated to truth.

The strategy that I wish to adopt in this paper (another offshoot of the distinction between object-given and state-given reasons) is one that denies that the wrong kind of reasons are reasons for attitudes at all. Rather, they are reasons to

---

9 See, for example, Parfit (2001) and Piller (2006).
10 See, for example, Rabinowicz and Rønnow-Rasmussen (2004).
11 Raz (2009). See also Heuer (2011).

do something, namely, to bring about that you have those attitudes.¹² Thus, in the case of Pascal's wager, the incentives for believing in God are not reasons to believe that God exists. Rather, they are reasons to bring it about that we have this belief. The bringing-it-about strategy (henceforth, BIAS) is by no means novel. It was suggested as early as 1993 by Nozick who made a distinction between (1) a proposition that p being the rational thing to believe and (2) believing p being the rational thing to *do*.¹³ We may then say that only the right kind of reasons (or evidential reasons) are relevant to (1) whereas the wrong kind of reasons are actually reasons for action and bear on (2). Accordingly, we may say that the situation envisaged by Pascal does not actually speak to the rationality of belief in God. Rather, under such circumstances, forming the belief that God exists is a rational thing to *do*. As we shall see later BIAS is explanatorily very powerful. So it is worth seeing how it fares in comparison with those approaches to the WKR problem which deny that evidential reasons exhaust epistemic reasons.

One such approach (due to Schroeder¹⁴) holds that there are non-evidential, state-given reasons which bear on distinctively epistemic rationality. Schroeder specifically holds that there are right-kind reasons against beliefs that are not object-given and, in fact, are intuitively state-given. So it is not the case that right kind of reasons consist exclusively of evidential reasons. The novelty of Schroeder's position is that the reasons he discusses concern the attitude of withholding rather than belief. Let us consider a typical example that Schroeder invokes in support of his claim.

Suppose I have been having spots on my skin in the past and that each time my doctor has ordered a biopsy to make sure that they are not cancerous. So far, however, biopsy has ruled that they are benign. Suppose now that my doctor has again found suspicious spots on my skin. A tissue sample is once again sent to the lab. Based on the past evidence (e), it would be reasonable to assume that the tissue is benign. However, the fact that the lab is soon going to report its findings, says Schroeder, is a reason to withhold with respect to the proposition that my skin spot is benign. This reason, according to Schroeder, is a right kind of reason because it possesses one of the marks of such reasons, namely, that no indirect strategy is needed in order not to make up one's mind (i.e., to withhold) on the basis of such reason. But it is also not an object-given reason as it is neither evidence for nor against the proposition (p) that my skin spot is benign.

---

12 See, for example, Parfit (2001) and Skorupski (2007). See also Reisner (2009).
13 Nozick (1993, 70).
14 Schroeder (2012).

But this example does not support Schroeder's claim. Given that the context of the example is one in which one's survival is at stake, there are two ways of reading p as either p_1 ('this spot is certainly benign'), or p_2 ('This spot is likely to be benign'). If we read p as p_1 then it would be rational and indeed no indirect strategy is needed in order to withhold with respect to p_1. But in that case our reason consists, not of the fact that the lab is going to report its results soon but, of my inductive evidence (e). My evidence, e, is such that it is not strong enough to support either p_1 or its negation. e is, however, an evidential, object-given reason. One might, however, still find some plausibility in Schroeder's suggestion that the fact that the lab is soon going to report its results is a reason to withhold. But BIAS can explain where this plausibility comes from. The thought is that, under the circumstances described, withholding with respect to p_1 is a rational thing to do, in the sense that if one wants to get more evidence in order to make up one's mind about whether or not the spot is definitely benign, then, given that the lab is soon going to report its findings, waiting for more evidence before making up one's mind about p_1 is a rational thing to do. On the other hand, if p is read as p_2, then to withhold with respect to p_2 requires an indirect strategy since my inductive evidence is strong enough to support the belief that the skin spot is likely to be benign. Schroeder's example, thus, fails to support his claim that the right kind of reasons are sometimes state-given reasons. A similar strategy can be employed against Schroeder's other examples.

We have thus far briefly discussed the question of what kind of consequences of a belief bear on its epistemic status. With BIAS in place, we can now proceed to address the main concern of this paper which is to spell out the conditions under which the epistemic consequences of a belief can render it justified.

3. Varieties of Epistemic Consequentialism

It was pointed out that, according to epistemic consequentialism, beliefs acquire their epistemic status by virtue of bringing about or promoting the goal of maximizing truth and minimizing falsity. An initial problem with this formulation of epistemic consequentialism is that it is extremely vague. We are not told under what conditions the promotion of the truth goal confers justification on a belief and how epistemic value is transmitted from the final value to the belief. To inject some precision into this crude formulation of epistemic consequentialism, it would be wise to, once again, look at its moral analogue.

According to moral consequentialism, moral rightness depends only on consequences of an act, motive, etc., that is, whether an act is morally right depends on nothing other than its consequences. Thus, utilitarianism, a consequentialist theory *par excellence*, takes an act to be morally right if and only if it maximizes the good. But there are two ways to conceive of the consequences of an act. One can either take them to be the direct consequences of the act itself in which case we will have a direct version of moral consequentialism (as in 'act utilitarianism'). Or, we might focus on the consequences of something else, such as a motive or a rule, in which case we have an indirect version of consequentialism (as in 'rule utilitarianism'). Thus, on indirect moral consequentialism, whether an act is good depends on, say, moral rules which are, in turn, evaluated on the basis of their consequences.

Now, we can likewise distinguish between direct and indirect versions of epistemic consequentialism. In the direct version, the epistemic status of a belief is determined by what it brings about whereas in the indirect version beliefs achieve their epistemic status in virtue of the consequences of something else. Both versions of epistemic consequentialism have had adherents. In what follows, I will first discuss the direct version and suggest a way of strengthening it in order to deflect some of the objections raised against it. This will however unearth a more fundamental problem with the view, forcing us to move in the direction of indirect epistemic consequentialism. As it turns out, it is the indirect version of epistemic conservatism that best captures its underlying motivations.

A version of direct epistemic consequentialism has been recently defended by Brian Talbot who argues that, in addition to evidential reasons, there are also, what he calls, 'truth promoting non-evidential' reasons (henceforth, TPR) that (objectively) support a belief that p iff having the belief that p would promote having other true beliefs i.e., the truth goal.[15] The thought is that the fact that one's belief p results in other true beliefs is sufficient, on its own, to confer epistemic justification on that belief (even when one lacks evidence to otherwise justify the belief that p). Thus, going back to the example of the atheist scientist, Talbot would say that the scientist's belief that God exists is epistemically justified on the ground that holding that belief yields lots of true beliefs.[16] Many would however be unhappy with this verdict. Indeed, they would take this example to show that it is, at best, controversial that a belief's mere presence in the causal chain leading to the production of true beliefs is sufficient to confer justification on that belief.

---

[15] Talbot (2014).
[16] Talbot considers a similar example where someone is threatened with death if he does not believe some proposition p whose truth he has no information about. If he survives, however, he will form lots of true beliefs and comes to have lots of knowledge.

To defend his claim, Talbot also suggests an argument consisting of the following premises: (T_1) Epistemic oughts have a source; (T_2) The source of epistemic oughts is an end in which true belief plays an essential role, and (T_3) Epistemic oughts are normative. There are a number of ways in which this argument can be criticized. One might, for example, suggest views which, while incorporating (T_1)-(T_3), categorically deny that a TPR can ever justify a belief.[17] I wish, however, to pursue a different line of criticism. It seems to me that, as it stands, premise T_2 is inadequate. T_2 merely says that being epistemically right should be construed in terms of conducivity to the epistemic good (e.g., true belief). This obviously concerns the third level of the normative structures indicated earlier, namely, the level which concerns the transmission of value from the final goal to the objects of value. But T_2 is silent on how value is being transmitted to beliefs and, thus, on how beliefs acquire their justification in virtue of promoting the final (truth) goal.

The atheist scientist example, however, suggests that we should understand the transmission relation as causal. But this is inadequate as it stands. To begin with, it does not seem that a belief's mere presence in the causal chain leading to true beliefs is sufficient to confer justification on that belief. This is presumably why many would find the verdict about the scientist's belief's being justified to be intuitively implausible. Moreover, if one is willing to countenance the scientist's belief as justified merely on the ground that it results in true beliefs, there is no reason why one should not also take the extra, but absurd, step of claiming that her continued breathing is also backed by epistemic reasons. After all, breathing is also a necessary condition of the scientist's continued existence which is, in turn, necessary if she is to put her grant to good use and acquire lots of true beliefs in her life time. However, rather than being dismayed by this consequence of his account of TPRs, Talbot thinks that we should be open to the possibility of having epistemic reasons to engage in behaviors like breathing as long as epistemic oughts can be applied to behaviors like reasoning, inquiry and scientific investigation.[18]

There are, however, other problems that explain why T_2 cannot provide epistemic consequentialism with a secure foundation. For example, by emphasizing true belief as a necessary component of the epistemic end, T_2, it seems, is intended to rule out practical considerations as the right kind of reasons. But it is clear that, thus understood, T_2 is not strong enough to discharge this function for, as noted before, not all practical considerations are truth-independent. For exam-

---

[17] See Littlejohn (ms.) for this line of criticism.
[18] Talbot (2014).

ple, it was noted that, in the case of Pascal's wager, the expected practical utilities of believing that God exists obtain only if that belief is true. Without the truth of this belief none of its expected consequences, as highlighted by Pascal, would ensue. These considerations all point in the direction of the need to qualify T_2. The question then is how T_2 should be qualified if it is to adequately reflect the thought behind epistemic consequentialism.

It is best to address this question by considering what it is for a belief p to promote the truth goal if it is to be justified. Presumably, this requires the belief p to result in a set of beliefs the majority of which are true. For the sake of concreteness, we may pick up certain of our beliefs where it is easy to see how they could give rise to true beliefs. These would include 'My cognitive faculties are functioning properly', 'There is an external world', and 'I am not a brain in a vat (BIV)'. It is easy to see how the belief in, say, 'My cognitive faculties are functioning properly', would result in mostly true beliefs. For if we lack such a belief we would stop trusting perception, memory, etc., culminating in a situation of cognitive poverty where only few beliefs would be formed. The same is true about failing to hold the beliefs that 'There is an external world', and 'I am not a brain in a vat (BIV)'.

Accordingly, if I hold the belief p that 'My cognitive faculties are functioning properly' in a normal world like ours, it would result in lots of true beliefs. On the other hand, if the belief p is held in a vat world (where it is false) the resulting beliefs would be mostly false. It does not however follow that whenever such a belief is false, the resulting beliefs are also false. Consider a recently envatted agent who has previously lived a normal life but, unaware of his predicament, still holds that his cognitive faculties are functioning properly. This leads him to form lots of beliefs which will be mostly true because his environment is normal. Although the beliefs resulting from the belief about one's cognitive faculties have different truth values in different scenarios, what all those scenarios have in common is that the holding of the belief that one's cognitive faculties are functioning properly leads to further beliefs. Whether those beliefs are true or false depends entirely on whether the world cooperates. It seems then that what is directly brought about by the belief about one's cognitive faculties is the state of affairs of having lots of beliefs. Whether these beliefs are true or false depends on whether or not there are facts that correspond to them. In the light of preceding remarks we can formulate our question thus: When the world cooperates, what is it that makes the production of true beliefs count as the promotion of the truth goal? To put it differently, how are we to cash out the notion of 'serving the truth goal'? Here are some possible responses.

One might opt for a weak notion of 'serving the truth goal' along the following lines. Belief p serves the truth goal (in a given scenario) and is therefore teleogically valuable as long as the goal in question can be realized in some other possible scenario (even if it fails to obtain in that scenario).[19] But this is too weak to be able to give content to the epistemic consequentialist thesis. The reason is that, by parallel reasoning, one can also take a belief that yields lots of true beliefs in a particular scenario as epistemically unjustified on the ground that it would yield lots of false beliefs in some other possible scenario (like a vat world). This is how the argument would proceed. Assuming, plausibly enough, that a belief is epistemically worthless if it serves the falsity goal (viz., the goal of maximizing falsehood and minimizing truth), one can equally claim that the belief p (which yields lots of true beliefs in the actual world) is worthless because it serves the falsity goal where to serve the falsity goal it is enough that the goal is realized in some other possible scenario (even if it fails to obtain in the actual scenario). If the possible realization of the truth goal is sufficient for the serving of the truth goal, then so is the possible realization of the falsity goal for the serving of the falsity goal.

Another construal of 'serving the truth goal' focuses specifically on the goal of having lots of knowledge.[20] It then notes that having lots of beliefs is required for having lots of knowledge. On the other hand, since having a belief like the belief p is, by hypothesis, necessary for having lots of beliefs, it therefore follows that belief p is teleologically valuable, thus, justified. Whether this account of 'serving the knowledge (truth) goal' is successful depends on how one is to understand its seemingly plausible claim that "having lots of beliefs is *required* for having lots of knowledge". Here are some possible suggestions to cash out the sense of 'being required' in the context of this claim. One possible suggestion is that beliefs are required for knowledge in the sense that knowledge that p entails believing that p (we may call this the 'entailment' sense of 'being required). But this cannot be right in the context of our discussion. For not only knowledge entails having beliefs but also having false beliefs entails having beliefs. So if the belief p is to be justified because it serves the truth goal by yielding lots of beliefs that are required (in the sense just described) for having lots of knowledge, it should also be regarded as unjustified because, by parity of reasoning, the resulting beliefs are also required for having lots of false beliefs. Thus, for the belief p to serve the truth goal, the link between the beliefs it yields and the truth goal must be stronger than a mere logical relation.

Another way of giving content to the notion of 'being required' might be to say that belief is required for knowledge in the very sense that, say, wood is re-

---

19 Something like this has been defended by Pedersen (2009).
20 See, for example, Hazlett (2006).

quired for building boats, tables and so on (we may call this the 'constitution' sense of 'being required'). The idea is that we first get some quantity of wood and then mould it into whatever shape we want. But there is an asymmetry here. Wood has no determinate shape whereas beliefs are born true or false (just as people are born male and female – barring exceptional cases). So if belief p is to serve the knowledge goal by virtue of providing beliefs that are required (in the constitution sense) for knowledge, we had better make sure that those beliefs are true. But then, by requiring true beliefs at an earlier stage, the truth goal has already been served at that stage rendering the strategy involving the constitution sense of 'being required' superfluous.

This brings us to a final sense in which belief can be said to be 'required' for knowledge. This is, perhaps, the more intuitive sense of 'being required' in which having lots of beliefs can be said to be required for having lots of knowledge. The claim is simply that if we want lots of knowledge our best bet is to produce as many beliefs as we can, on the basis of holding the belief p, and hope for the best. The idea is that if one wishes to maximize the epistemic good (knowledge or true belief) then one ought to epistemically accept p because accepting p is a priori more likely to generate more of the epistemic good than not accepting p. That is to say, while holding belief p will not guarantee lots of true beliefs, not holding it will guarantee that one does not get lots of true beliefs (since no beliefs will subsequently be made).

This understanding of the belief requirement, however, renders the claim that the belief p is epistemically justified in virtue of serving the truth goal suspect. For, on this account of what serving the truth goal consists in, the situation looks increasingly like one in which the subject is faced with a forced option. As in the Jamsean example of the Alpine hiker whose only chance to escape death, by either avalanche or the cold, is to believe that he can jump the chasm he is facing, our truth-seeking subject has to hold the belief p for by so doing he will not lose anything and may in fact acquire lots of true beliefs. I have no objection to this line of thought except that, in line with our Nozickean BIAS, I am more inclined to take this as showing, not that the belief p is epistemically rational but, that believing p, under the envisaged circumstances, is the rational thing to do.

It seems to me, however, that an adequate account of epistemic consequentialism must, at least, require that the production of true beliefs by a belief p be sensitive to the obtaining of that belief if it is to count as the promotion of the truth goal (we may call this the 'sensitivity requirement'). In other words, the belief p must be reliably correlated with the promotion of the truth goal if epistemic value is to transmit form the goal to that belief. The sensitivity requirement is best seen as reflecting the fact that, if the production of true beliefs is to count as the promotion of the truth goal, thus, conferring justification on the belief from which they result, the belief must be seen as making a difference to the production of those beliefs. And the difference it makes must be a difference from what would have happened without it. Compare: for a belief p to count as knowledge, the content of p (what the world is like) must be making a difference to the holding of that belief (thus, the Nozickean tracking conditions). The thought then is that only if belief p is reliably correlated with the promotion of the truth goal does epistemic value transmit from the final goal to the belief in question. The sensitivity requirement can be cashed out in terms of the following subjunctives to reflect the required reliable correlation.

(a) If the belief p were held lots of true beliefs (knowledge) would ensue.
(b) If the contrary of the belief p (or no such belief) were held, true beliefs (knowledge) would fail to ensue.

Condition (a) says that true beliefs result in virtue of the belief p having a particular content (p), while (b) says that if a belief with a different content (~p) (or no such belief) were held, true beliefs would fail to result. (a) and (b) together ensure the transmission of value from the fundamental value to the objects of value. The inclusion of condition (b) does not, on its own, warrant the claim that belief p promotes the truth goal. (b) indicates that the belief p merely plays a casual role in the production of true beliefs. Rather, if the true beliefs resulting from the belief p are to signal that the truth (knowledge) goal is served, (a) should also be true of that belief. (a) and (b) together entail that if the production of true beliefs is to count as the promotion of the truth goal by belief p, the production of true beliefs must 'track' the content of the belief p not only in the actual world but also in the nearby possible worlds.

4. From Direct to Indirect Epistemic Consequentialism

Having spelled out the conditions under which the production of true beliefs counts as serving the truth goal, we can now engage with some of the arguments that both the proponents and opponents of epistemological consequentialism have suggested in favor of their views. Let us start with the views of those, like Talbot, who advocate a direct version of epistemic consequentialism. It is best to begin with the atheist scientist example. According to Talbot, the scientist's belief that God exists is justified because it facilitates the obtaining of the grant that will subsequently lead to the obtaining of true beliefs and the revising of previously held false beliefs. As noted earlier, many would find such a verdict implausible and it is now easy to see why. On the current thinking of epistemic consequentialism, the reason why the scientist's belief is unjustified is because the production of true beliefs does not count as the promotion of the truth goal since the sensitivity requirement is violated.

The belief that God exists merely plays a causal role in the production of true beliefs. All it does is to facilitate the obtaining of the grant that, in turn, kicks off scientific research which eventually leads to true beliefs. Here it is the grant that is doing all the work in the production of true beliefs. No matter how it is secured, it would still yield the same set of true beliefs. However, by thus intervening, the grant 'screens off', as it were, the content of the scientist's belief to play the role required by (a). Although the scientist's belief secures the grant (and the subsequent beliefs) in the actual world, it fails to do so in the nearby possible worlds where the obtaining of grant is made conditional on the applicants' being atheists or having no beliefs at all about God's existence.

The sensitivity requirement can also avoid further implausible consequences of Talbot's TPR account. For example, his account seems to commit him to the view that believing obvious falsehoods can be epistemically justified under certain circumstances. For instances, he says that one might be justified in believing that five is not prime if one would otherwise die.[21] However, we can avoid this conclusion by noting that condition (a) is once again violated in this example. There are nearby possible worlds where believing falsehoods fails to yield true beliefs because survival is made conditional on believing truths in those worlds. Furthermore, we can also save any remaining intuitions of rationality in this case by appealing to BIAS and say that what is rational here is not the belief that 5 is not prime but that believing such a proposition is, under the envisaged circumstances, a rational thing to do.

The sensitivity requirement can also deflect some of the objections leveled against (direct) epistemic consequentialism by its opponents. Selim Berker, for example, has recently advanced some trenchant objections against consequentialism.[22] Berker's main concern is to argue against the view that epistemic theories have a teleological structure. He thinks that, unlike consequentialism in normative ethics, consequentialism in epistemology is not an attractive option. To explain, he highlights the problem of trade-offs in ethics which arises whenever we are forced to determine what we should do under various circum-

---

21 Talbot (2014).
22 Berker (2013).

stances, as when, say, a situation calls for sacrificing the life of one person in order to save the lives of a number of other people. The need for trade-offs arises because ethical consequentialist theories build a theory of overall value out of a theory of final value. Sometimes allowing such trade-offs seems intuitively correct. Nevertheless, it has been objected that in allowing such trade-offs, ethical consequentialist theories become susceptible to the charge of ignoring "people's separateness"[23].

Berker likewise thinks that by allowing the epistemic status of a belief in a given proposition to depend on whether it tends to promote true belief and avoid false belief in other propositions, epistemic consequentialist theories also become vulnerable to the charge of ignoring "the epistemic separateness of propositions". Furthermore, he thinks that while it is not altogether normatively incorrect to ignore the separateness of persons in the ethical case, the epistemic separateness of propositions is nonnegotiable in the epistemic case. Although Berker presents his case against epistemic consequentialist in terms of the preceding argument, he actually proceeds by offering counterexamples which, he thinks, undermine consequentialism. So, to evaluate Berker's case against epistemic consequentialism, it would be best to examine his counterexamples. I think, however, that the sensitivity requirement has the resources to accommodate Berker's counterexamples.

Berker's first case is our familiar atheist scientist's example where, he claims, from the consequentialist's perspective, the scientist's coming to believe in God's existence would be a sacrifice for the greater epistemic good of forming a lot of true beliefs. I have already explained how our qualified consequentialist theory can explain why this counterexample fails. In this particular example, the grant screens off the content of the scientist's belief from playing the required role (a) in the promotion of the truth goal.

Berker's other example involves items of self-knowledge. Let us begin by supposing that higher-order beliefs are partially constituted by the lower-order beliefs that they are about. Suppose further that, due to a psychological glitch, whenever I come to believe p (where p is a claim about the external world), I also, at the same time, form second-order beliefs about the nature of first-order beliefs and how they are formed: 'I believe p', 'I formed my belief in p on such-and- such day', 'I formed my belief in p using so-and-so method', etc. Suppose the same pattern holds for my second-order, third-order beliefs and so on. Finally, let us assume that although I am not particularly reliable in forming first-order beliefs about the world, I am very good at introspection and, thus,

---

[23] See, for example, Rawls (1971) and Nagel (1970).

all my higher-order beliefs about my lower-order beliefs are accurate. Now, suppose that, one day, I come to believe that 'she loves me' by picking petals from a daisy while reciting 'she loves me, she loves me not,...'. Then, given the stated facts about my psychology, I form various higher-order beliefs like 'I believe she loves me', 'I came to believe 'she loves me' by picking petals from a daisy' and so on. All my higher-order beliefs are, by hypothesis, true. But my first-order belief is clearly unjustified even though it was this first-order belief that led to all those true, higher-order beliefs. If n is the number of higher-order beliefs that I form about each belief of one lower-order, then, says Berker, my first-order belief has resulted in $(n + n^2 + n^3)$ number of true, higher-order beliefs.

Although it took us some time to explain this example, our response to it, on behalf of our qualified epistemic consequentialism, can be relatively brief. This case is not a counterexample because it violates the sensitively requirement. Earlier, we said that if a belief p is to be justified on the ground of promoting the truth goal, it should not only be the case that the belief p results in the promotion of the truth goal, but also that the holding of the contrary belief would fail to promote the goal. The promotion of the truth goal must, in other words, be sensitive to the content of the belief p. Suppose, however, that when picking the petals, we had instead arrived at the belief ~p ('she loves me not'). This first-order belief would still have resulted in the promotion of the truth goal by promoting the same number of true beliefs $(n + n^2 + n^3)$. The sensitivity requirement can thus easily accommodate this example.

Another example by Berker concerns a brilliant set-theorist, John Doe, who is on the verge of proving an important hypothesis from which a large number of set-theoretic results follows. John is also suffering from a fatal illness that will kill him in less than two months. However, it so happens that if he believes he will recover from the illness, that would prolong his life enough to let him prove the set-theoretic hypothesis. On a direct epistemic consequentialist account, John's belief that he will recover from his illness is justified because it promotes the truth goal but intuitively it is not. But, once again, on our qualified direct consequentialism, John's belief is not justified because condition (a) fails to be satisfied. There are nearby possible worlds where believing that one will survive fails to prolong one's life.

Judging by its impact, our sensitivity requirement has turned out to be explanatorily powerful.[24] Does this mean that the qualified version of direct conse-

---

24 Here is another counterexample. Consider a particular paradox consisting of three (equally plausible) propositions, and let us assume that I have excellent evidence (say, my teacher's tes-

quentialism fully captures the intents behind epistemic consequentialism? The answer is no because the failure of the sensitivity condition in the aforementioned counterexamples is actually reminiscent of a more fundamental failing that eventually undermines direct epistemic consequentialism.

To see this, let us begin by noting that all counterexamples to direct epistemic consequentialism share, among other things, the following important feature: all such scenarios contain, at least, one unreliable belief forming process (or method). In the atheist scientist example, the process that results in the belief about God is driven by a desire to discover many scientific truths. It is, thus, an instance of a process type, wishful thinking, which is obviously unreliable. The scenario also involves a reliable process, scientific reasoning, which is responsible for producing true scientific beliefs, but the scientist's belief about God is not an input to this process which is why the epistemic status of scientific beliefs is independent of the epistemic status of the scientist's belief about God. As noted earlier, the grant screens off the scientist's belief about God form making an epistemic contribution to the epistemic status of output scientific beliefs. In the daisy example, there are two processes involved, namely, the process of forming beliefs by picking petals from a daisy and the process of introspection. The former process is clearly unreliable. The sick mathematician's example also involves two belief forming processes, namely, the process of 'stubbornly clinging to a belief about one's recovery in the face of contrary medical evidence' and the process of

---

timony) that only one of the three propositions is false. Suppose, after failing to identify the culprit, I reason that I had better believe all three propositions rather than suspending judgment on all three. The epistemic consequentialist, says Berker, would approve of this reasoning because by believing all three propositions, as against suspending judgment on all of them, I have maximized the number of my true beliefs. It is, however, obvious that my beliefs are unjustified. But an epistemic consequentialist can avoid this conclusion by adopting a diachronic conception of the truth goal according to which the truth goal is not just a function of truth-ratio in a body of beliefs at a particular time but involves the overall maximization of truth and minimization of falsity in one's belief repertoire in the long run. Now, since having an inconsistent set of beliefs is the source of great many false beliefs in the long run, the epistemic consequentialist can effectively rule out the option of believing the inconsistent triad. Moreover, as an argument against direct epistemic consequentialism, this example seems hardly relevant. For it is not even clear which proposition it is whose belief it is supposed to promote the truth goal. It is not *because* we believe either of these propositions that we end up maximizing true beliefs. Neither the false proposition, nor the two true propositions play such a role. We are simply faced with three propositions which we know one of them is false. We also have two options: either believe all three or believe none. Now, if our goal is to maximize the number of true beliefs at a particular time slice, then, again in line with BIAS, believing the three propositions would be a more rational thing to do than suspending judgment on all three. This has no consequence for the rationality of beliefs in those propositions.

mathematical reasoning. Again, the former process is clearly unreliable. Moreover, the mathematician's belief about his recovery is not an input to the process of mathematical reasoning which is why the epistemic status of the resulting mathematical beliefs is not affected by the status of the mathematician's recovery belief.

It would, thus, be fair to conclude that an adequate account of epistemic consequentialism must recognize reliability as an essential ingredient in explaining how the consequences of a belief can be epistemically relevant. Our chief complaint about direct epistemic consequentialism, however, was that it fails to secure a reliable connection or correlation between a belief and the promotion of the truth goal by that belief. Reliabilism (in particular, process reliabilism) is able to secure such a correlation. According to process reliabilism, a belief is justified if and only if it is produced by a process that is a token of a reliable process type viz., a process which tends to produce mostly true beliefs. So reliabilism is not concerned with the consequences of a belief or with what the belief brings about.

What *is* consequentialist about process reliabilism is that process types are evaluated for their reliability in terms of the truth ratios of the beliefs produced by them. A reliable process is one which tends to produce more true beliefs than false beliefs i.e., one that can be put at the service of promoting the truth goal. In this respect, process reliabilism is akin to rule utilitarianism in that they are both indirectly consequentialist. Just as, in determining whether an action is moral, rule utilitarianism considers, not the direct consequences of the action but, the consequences that result from following a pertinent rule of conduct, process reliabilism also considers, not the direct consequences of holding a belief but, its causal history to see whether it is justified. And, in so doing, it looks to the process type, whose token has yielded the belief in question, to see if it directly results in beliefs with high truth ratio. Process reliabilism can therefore be classified as an indirect consequentialist theory because it secures the reliable correlation between a belief and the promotion of the truth goal by virtue of the belief being produced by a process that is a token of a reliable process type. Process reliabilism is at odds with direct consequentialist theories, because it does not evaluate beliefs in terms of their consequences, but rather in terms of whether they result from the operation of processes which are themselves evaluated in terms of their consequences: they are good if they are reliable i.e., if they have normally good consequences.

In a more recent article, Berker concedes that an indirect epistemic consequentialist theory, like process reliabilism, is immune to the aforementioned counterexamples but still thinks that it is not off the hook.[25] Those counterexamples, he thinks, can be reproduced in the case of indirect epistemic consequentialism because what they involve is to forgo the promotion of true belief with regard to one proposition in order to promote truth with respect to many other propositions. He thinks, however, that the "same underlying structure can also apply to cases in which something else, such as a process type, is sacrificing its performance with regard to one proposition in order to promote its performance with regard to many other propositions"[26].

But Berker's perceived similarity between direct and indirect epistemic consequentialism with regard to their corresponding trade-offs is misplaced. What allows trade-off in the case of direct epistemic consequentialism is the fact that on such a theory the justified status of a belief is determined by what the belief brings about. And, since justification is a matter of promoting the truth goal, it would only be natural to sacrifice one proposition for the greater benefit of promoting truth with respect to many other propositions. Not so in the case of an indirect consequentialist theory such as process reliabilism where the justified status of belief is determined by what causes the belief. Here, if the process type is seen as sacrificing its performance with respect to one proposition in order to promote it with respect to many other propositions, this is because (1) what is crucial for justification is that it is the process type, not the process token, that must be reliable and (2) that justified belief can be false. So, on a reliabilist justificational architecture, it would be quite legitimate for a process type to sacrifice its performance with regard to one proposition in order to promote its performance with regard to many others without undermining the consequentialist motives.[27]

---

25 Berker (forthcoming).
26 Ibid., 5.
27 Berker offers another example which, he claims, also works against process reliabilism. He asks us to consider the following belief-forming process: suppose that whenever I consider whether a given national number (n) is prime, I immediately form the belief that 'n is not prime'. Given that the density of primes less than x approaches 0 as x approaches ∞, this processes is extremely reliable resulting in great many true beliefs. By the consequentialist's light, beliefs resulting from this process are justified but, intuitively, when I form the belief that '7 is not prime', this belief is not justified. The lesson, says Berker is that "even veritists of a process-reliabilist persuasion allow illicit cross-propositional trade-offs between our epistemic goals" (2013, p. 375). But if the process is really reliable, there is no reason why a process reliabilist should not take the relevant beliefs as justified especially if he can also offer an explanation of why they might appear otherwise (for a response along these lines see Ahlstrom-Vij and Dunn (forthcoming). If so, then, like the well-known clairvoyance case, Berker's example can, at best, be regarded as calling into question the sufficiency of reliability for justification. But the

Finally, an indirect consequentialst theory such as process reliabilism can naturally accommodate the sensitivity constraint and its associated subjunctive conditionals (a) and (b). This is because reliability itself is a modal notion. This can be brought out by considering a case such as Plantinga's brain-lesion example where an agent's brain lesion just happens to produce the true belief that he has a brain lesion. The belief is clearly unjustified though it is produced by a seemingly reliable process. In response, reliabilists point out that for a process to be reliable, it must not only produce true beliefs in the actual world but also in the nearby possible worlds.[28] So a reliabilist version of indirect epistemic consequentialism can quite naturally respect the subjunctive requirements of the sensitivity requirement.

To conclude, we started by identifying two questions regarding which an adequate account of epistemic consequentialism must provide some answers. These included an explanation of why only the epistemic consequences of a belief are epistemically relevant and an account of the conditions under which the production of true beliefs would count as the promotion of the truth goal, thus, conferring justification on the belief from which they result. It was argued that only when the production of true beliefs is reliably correlated with the belief that produces them does it count as the promotion of the truth goal. This led to the distinction between direct and indirect versions of epistemic consequentialism. While direct consequentialist theories evaluate beliefs directly in terms of their epistemically valuable consequences, indirect consequentialist theories evaluate beliefs indirectly in terms of their connection with some other items which are themselves directly evaluated in terms of their epistemically valuable consequences. It turned out, however, that only an indirect consequentialist theory (such as process reliabilism) has any chance of saving our intuitions in various test cases. Thus understood, an indirect version of epistemic consequentialism can avoid the excesses of both its direct version as well as its total dismissal.

---

novelty of Berker's critique is supposed to stem from the process reliabilism's consequentialist character rather than whether reliability is sufficient for justification. I prefer, however, another line of response that has been offered by Goldman (forthcoming) which focuses on the issue of how the process involved in this example is supposed to be typed. His first point that within the class of relatively small integers (where this process is actually applied), the process is unreliable. Secondly, he notes that process types should be general and not content-neutral. So what Berker calls a 'process' in this example is regarded as illegitimate by this criterion. It is, at best, a rule or method, and the use of a reliable method does not necessarily confer justification on its output beliefs.

28 See, for example, Kornblith (2009). See also Becker (2013).

References

Ahlstrom-Vij, K. and J. Dunn (Forthcoming). A Defence of Epistemic Consequentialism. *The Philosophical Quarterly.*
Alston, W. (1989). *Epistemic Justification.* Ithaca (NY): Cornell University Press.
Becker, K. (2013). Why Reliabilism Does not Permit Easy Knowledge. *Synthese* 190: 3751–3775.
Berker, S. (2013). Epistemic Teleology and the Separateness of Propositions. *Philosophical Review* 122(3): 337–393.
Berker, S. (Forthcoming). Reply to Goldman: Cutting Up the One to Save the Five in Epistemology. *Episteme.*
BonJour, L. (1985). *The Structure of Empirical Knowledge*, Harvard University Press.
Fantl, J. and McGrath, M. (2002). Evidence, Pragmatics, and Justification. *The Philosophical Review*, 111, 67–94.
Foley, R. (1993). *Working Without a Net.* Oxford: Oxford University Press.
Fumerton, R. (2001). Epistemic Justification and Normativity. In M. Steup (ed.), *Knowledge, Truth, and Duty: Essays on Epistemic Justification, Responsibility, and Virtue.* Oxford: Oxford University Press.
Goldman, A. (Forthcoming). Reliabilism, Veritism, and Epistemic Consequentialism. *Episteme.*
Hazlett, A. (2006). How to Defeat Belief in the External World? *Pacific Philosophical Quarterly* 87: 198–212.
Heuer, U. (2010). Beyond Wrong Reasons: The Buck-Passing Account of Value. In M. Brady (ed.), *New Waves in Metaethics.* New York: Palgrave.
Klausen, S. (2009). Two Notions of Epistemic Normativity. *Theoria* 75: 161–178.
Kornblith, H. (2009). A Reliabilist Solution to the Problem of Promiscuous Bootstrapping. *Analysis* 69: 263–267.
Lang, G. (2008). The Right Kind of Solution to the Wrong Kind of Reason Problem. *Utilitas* 20: 472–489.
Littlejohn, C. (MS). Are Epistemic Reasons Reasons to Promote?
Nagel, T.: (1970). *The Possibility of Altruism*, Princeton: Princeton University Press.
Nozick, R. (1993). *The Nature of Rationality.* Princeton: Princeton University Press.
Olson, J.: (2004). Buck-Passing and the Wrong Kind of Reasons. *Philosophical Quarterly* 54: 295–300.
Parfit, D. (2001). Reasons and Rationality. In D. Egonsson, D. Josefsson, B. Petersson and T. Rønnow-Rasmussen (eds.), *Exploring Practical Philosophy.* Farnham: Ashgaten Press.
Pedersen, N. (2009). Entitlement, Value and Rationality. *Synthese* 171: 443–457.
Piller, C. (2006). Content-Related and Attitude-Related Reasons for Preference. *Philosophy* 59: 115–218.
Rabinowicz. D. and Rønnow-Rasmussen, T. (2004). The Strike of the Demon: On Fitting Pro-Attitudes and Value. *Ethics* 114: 391–423.
Raz, J. (2009). Reasons: Practical and Adaptive. In D. Sobel and S. Wall (eds.), *Reasons for Actions.* Cambridge: Cambridge University Press.
Rawls, J. (1971). *A Theory of Justice.* Cambridge (MA): Harvard University Press.
Reisner, A. (2009). The Possibility of Pragmatic Reasons for Belief and the Wrong Kind of Reasons Problem. *Philosophical Studies* 145: 257–272.

Riggs, W. (2008). The Value Turn in Epistemology. In V. Hendricks and D. Pritchard (eds.), *New Waves in Epistemology*. New York: Palgrave Macmillan.
Skorupski, J. (2007). Buck-Passing about Goodness. In: T. Rønnow-Rasmussen, B. Petersson, J. Josefsson and D. Egonsson (eds.), *Hommage à Wlodek*.
http://www.fil.lu.se/hommageawlodek/site/papper/SkorupskiJohn.pdf
Schroeder, M. (2012). The Ubiquity of State-Given Reasons. *Ethics*122: 457–88.
Talbot, B. (2014). Truth Promoting Non-Evidential Reasons for Belief. *Philosophical Studies* 168: 599–618.

Chase Wrenn
Tradeoffs, Self-Promotion, and Epistemic Teleology

1.

Here is one way to address issues of value and obligation in epistemology. First, presuppose the value of some characteristically epistemic goal states, such as believing the truth and avoiding error. Then, explain all other epistemic value and all epistemic obligation derivatively, in terms of promoting or conducing to those goals. We can fairly call such an approach "teleological" or "epistemic teleology."[1]

Reliabilism may be the most obvious instance of epistemic teleology. It treats true belief as the fundamental epistemic goal, and it counts beliefs as justified or not depending on whether they are formed in ways that sufficiently reliably accomplish the goal. But even evidentialists can be teleologists. They can hold that the characteristic epistemic goal is to believe what fits one's evidence, and they can count beliefs as justified or not insofar as they constitute realizations of that goal. Or, they can hold that one ought to believe what fits one's evidence because that is what maximizes one's chances of achieving the goal of truth.

I borrow the term 'teleology', of course, from ethics. Teleological moral theories assess actions, motives, policies, etc. in relation to the promotion of some ultimate moral good. Likewise, epistemic teleology assesses beliefs, methods of inquiry, belief-forming processes, habits of mind, etc. in relation to the promotion of the ultimate epistemic good. Epistemic teleology is, perhaps, even more attractive than its ethical counterpart, but it also appears to face a significant challenge.

---

[1] On one use of 'teleology', "epistemic teleology" would involve studying the purposes our cognitive faculties are meant to fulfill, either by evolution or by a conscious designer. I wish to remain uncommitted as to whether it is the *purpose* of our faculties to achieve the cognitive good, so I am not using the word in that sense. On another use, 'teleology' is a synonym for 'consequentialism', the idea that the value of something is a function of the value of its effects. That is not my sense of it either. As I am using the word, teleology is the view that value and obligation are to be understood in terms of promoting or conducing toward the realization of fundamentally valuable goal states. Since *causing* a valuable state is a way of promoting it, consequentialism turns out to be one species of teleology, but perhaps not the only one.

The problem, which Selim Berker has articulated most fully in a pair of recent papers (2013a, 2013b), concerns what I will call *cross-propositional tradeoffs* and *epistemic self-promotion*. The general phenomenon in both cases is that of *epistemic tradeoffs:* sometimes, a lesser epistemic ill is conducive to a greater epistemic good. In such cases, epistemic teleology can seem committed to wrong answers about what one is justified in believing.

To see how the problem can manifest, consider *veritism*, the version of epistemic teleology that says true belief has fundamental epistemic value and false belief has fundamental epistemic disvalue.[2] If we understand epistemic justification as a matter of promoting or conducing to that goal, there are apparent problems. What if I could put myself into a position to acquire many new true beliefs, if only I form one belief unsupported by my evidence right now? Veritism can seem committed to calling that unsupported belief *epistemically justified*, but that assessment seems wrong. Or, what if the very fact that I believe p somehow increases the probability that p? Veritism might seem committed to counting such a belief that p epistemically justified, since the belief appears to be "conducive" to its own truth. Again, though, that assessment seems wrong.

The problems are not specific to veritism. We could construct similar cases for any proposed epistemic end at all—truth, empirical adequacy, coherence, acceptability under ideal scrutiny, fit with one's evidence, whatever. Any theory that treats epistemic value and obligation in terms of the promotion of an epistemic end seems saddled with cases in which beliefs that are most conducive to the epistemic greater good are also intuitively unjustified, unwarranted, unreasonable, or irrational. The cases can come in either of two forms. *Cross-propositional tradeoff* cases occur when believing one proposition promotes the achievement of the epistemic good with respect to many other propositions. *Epistemic self-promotion* cases occur when believing a proposition promotes the achievement of the epistemic good with respect to that proposition itself.

In response to such concerns, one might be tempted to give up epistemic teleology altogether and find an alternative way of understanding epistemic value. As I argue toward the end of this paper, such a move is not as easy as it might initially appear. Epistemic teleology has significant advantages, and so it's worth

---

[2] There are possible views, aptly called "veritism," that assign fundamental epistemic value and disvalue to true and false belief, but that aren't teleological because they do not treat other epistemic value as derived from the *promotion of* or *conduciveness to* them. As I will use the term, though, 'veritism' combines the view true and false belief have fundamental epistemic value and disvalue, respectively, with the view that non-fundamental epistemic value/disvalue derives from promotion of or conduciveness to what has fundamental epistemic value/disvalue.

considering whether it can avoid the problems of cross-propositional tradeoffs and epistemic self-promotion.

I will defend epistemic teleology on two fronts. First, I argue that cross-propositional tradeoffs and epistemic self-promotion are problematic for only the least plausible forms of epistemic teleology. Minimally plausible versions of the approach avoid the problems easily. Second, I describe some of what I think are the best reasons to understand epistemic value and obligation teleologically. Along the way, an important theme will develop. The best forms of epistemic teleology take their central issue to be the evaluation of *methods of inquiry* and *belief-forming processes*, rather than the direct evaluation of beliefs themselves. Plausible epistemic teleologies address the question of what one ought to believe only by first addressing questions about how one ought to make up one's mind.

2.

Some writers think of the "epistemic" domain as what is left when we have bracketed all our moral, practical, aesthetic, and other interests that are not purely intellectual. Still others identify the epistemic with that realm of value and obligation applicable to believers and beliefs *merely as such*. And some take an explicitly teleological tack: the epistemic domain is defined by characteristically epistemic goals, such as believing what is true rather than what is false.

It could appear that epistemic teleologists and non-teleologists are quibbling over the definition of 'epistemic'. Sometimes, perhaps, they are. But there is also a substantive disagreement in the neighborhood. Are we bound by obligations pertaining to our beliefs, or to our reasoning, that aren't ultimately dependent on the promotion of valuable states of affairs? Teleologists will say we are not; non-teleologists say we are. Even if both sides agree that we ought to proportion our belief to the evidence, they disagree about *why* that is so. Teleologists will ground that obligation in the promotion of a valuable cognitive end, such as believing the truth. Non-teleologists will ground it in something else, such as our nature as believers, irrespective of any valuable goals, epistemic or otherwise.

The teleological outlook has been popular in epistemology. Descartes opens his *Rules for the Direction of the Mind* saying, "The aim of our studies should be to direct the mind with a view to forming true and sound judgments about whatever comes before it"(1984, 9). William James (1896) claimed we should evaluate our beliefs in terms of the dual aims of believing what is true and avoiding error, bearing in mind that those are distinct goals to be weighed against one another. Roderick Chisholm says, in the second edition of *Theory of Knowledge* (1977), that our basic intellectual obligation is to do our best, for each proposition we consider, to believe it if and only if it is true. Laurence BonJour (1985) and Richard Feldman (2003) distinguish epistemic normativity from other sorts by reference to distinctive epistemic goals. W. V. Quine compares normative epistemology to engineering and calls it the "technology of truth-seeking" (1998; see also Wrenn (2006)). Alvin Goldman (1986) explicitly compares the reliabilism of *Epistemology and Cognition* with consequentialist (and therefore teleological) moral theories, and Hilary Kornblith (1993) contends we should understand epistemic value and epistemic obligation in relation to the intellectual goal of true belief.

Teleological theories, in ethics, epistemology, or elsewhere, start from the idea that certain kinds of things have *fundamental* or *ultimate* value and disvalue. Non-teleological theories can (but need not) do the same. The distinctively teleological moves, though, are these: (1) Teleologists think of ultimate value as something to be *pursued* or *promoted* (and correlatively for ultimate disvalue). (2) Teleologists account for all other value, and all obligation, in terms of the promotion and pursuit of what is ultimately valuable. Kantian ethics, at least as elaborated in the opening pages of the *Groundwork*, starts from the idea that only the *good will* has ultimate or fundamental value, but it does not treat that as a kind of value to be pursued or promoted, but rather as a kind of value to be *respected* or *honored*. It isn't teleological.[3]

The teleological structure is evident in straightforward, unsophisticated, act utilitarianism. Pleasure is fundamentally good; pain is fundamentally bad. Acts are better or worse depending on how great a surplus of pleasure over pain they produce, all things considered. One morally ought to take, in any given circumstance, whatever available action would be best (or tied for best) by that metric, and one morally ought not to take any other action. This view starts with fundamental value, and it analyzes other value and obligation in terms of that value's promotion.

Any teleological theory starts with a specification of states that, so far as the theory is concerned, are primitively valuable (or primitively disvaluable). We should not put too much metaphysical weight on that fact, though. A theory might treat a state as primitively valuable, when in fact its value derives from considerations external to the theory. To accept a teleological theory is to accept a theory of how other value or obligation derives from a given source, but not to take any particular view of where that source gets its value. Consider, for example, this normative theory of chess:

---

[3] Berker (2013a, p. 343) makes a similar point.

I. Checkmating your opponent has primitive value; being checkmated has primitive disvalue, and ending the game in a draw is primitively neutral.

II. Where P(W|m) is the probability that you will eventually checkmate your opponent or your opponent will resign, given the board position after move m, P(L|m) is the probability that you will eventually be checkmated or resign given the board position after move m, and P(D|m) is the probability that the game will be drawn given the board position after move m, the expected value of m is E(m) = P(W|m) + P(D|m)/2 − P(L|m). Move m is better than move n if E(m) > E(n), worse if E(m) < E(n), and equally good if E(m) = E(n).

III. In any given situation, a move is justified if it is no worse than any other available move.

It is implausible to think checkmate is primitively valuable in any deep sense, outside the context of chess strategy. In doing chess strategy, though, it is irrelevant *why* checkmate is good. Rather, it is taken for granted that checkmate is a worthwhile goal, and strategy distinguishes better from worse moves in terms of their promotion of that end. If we want to know why checkmating Anand is a suitable goal for Carlson, or vice versa, we need to step outside chess and consider other things.

Straightforward, unsophisticated, act utilitarianism and the above theory of chess strategy are both specimens of teleology. They exhibit the structure Berker claims is definitive of teleological theories. That structure involves three components (Berker 2013a, 344–7, 2013b, 365–6):

I. A "theory of final value," which either "specifies a set of states of affairs that have value or disvalue as ends in themselves" (i.e., which have primitive value or disvalue to be pursued or avoided) or "identifies a certain list of goals or aims that structure the norms under consideration. ... [T]hese must be ultimate goals or aims, not goals or aims that serve other, more basic goals or aims" (2013a, 345).

II. A "theory of overall value," that specifies, for each kind of entity that might "conduce toward or promote" the states affairs identified in the theory of final value, "a comparative ranking" of everything of that kind "in terms of how well, all things considered, it conduces toward or promotes the various states of affairs that, according to the teleologist's theory of final value, have value or disvalue as ends in themselves" (2013a, p. 346). Berker calls the sorts of entities addressed by the theory of overall value "evaluative focal points," following Kagan (2000).

III. A "deontic theory that assigns deontic properties such as being obligatory or permissible, being right or wrong, being justified or unjustified, on the basis of the theory of overall value" (Berker 2013a, 347).

This structure allows for a wide variety of teleological theories. It does not stipulate *which* states of affairs the theory of final value must accord primitive value to.[4] It accommodates the idea that "[d]ifferent teleological theories will interpret what it takes for an entity X to promote or conduce toward a state of affairs S ... in different ways" (Berker 2013a, 345). Berker mentions that the theory of overall value might treat X's "conducing to" S as some or all of: causation (X partially or entirely causes S), instantiation (X's occurrence just is the obtaining of S), or constitution (X's occurrence wholly or partly constitutes or is constituted by S's obtaining) (2013a, 345). He even allows for a theory to be teleological if it is missing the deontic component altogether, as in scalar theories that confine themselves to comparative assessments of value without saying anything about duty or "deontic status" (2013a, 344).

When present, the deontic theory might concern itself with *maximizing* overall value, with *satisficing*, or it could depend on the theory of overall value in some other way. What matters is that the theory of overall value depends on the theory of final value, and the deontic theory depends on the theory of overall value (2013a, 344).

We can formulate any number of normative theories that share the structure Berker describes. As much as they might differ in their contents and substantive commitments, all would represent a teleological approach to their subject matter. It will be helpful for us to consider the following specimen of epistemic teleology, formulated to make the structure evident:

---

[4] I follow Berker in calling the part of a teleological theory specifying the valuable ends to be promoted or avoided a "theory of final value," but I am reluctant to describe those ends as "finally valuable" or as bearers of "final value" in the sense of Korsgaard (1983). So, I will generally refer to the value of a teleological theory's specified ends as "ultimate," "fundamental," or "primitive," to emphasize that the theory takes their value to be underived from the value of anything else.

Toy Process Reliabilism (TPR)[5]
I. Theory of Final Value
    a. *True belief* has fundamental epistemic value.
    b. *False belief* has fundamental epistemic disvalue.
    c. Nothing else has fundamental epistemic value or disvalue.

II. Theory of Overall Value
    a. Belief-forming process *P1* is epistemically superior to belief-forming process *P2* if and only if *P1* has a stronger propensity to output true beliefs than process *P2*.
    b. Belief-forming process *P1* is epistemically inferior to belief-forming process *P2* if and only if *P1* has a weaker propensity to output true beliefs than process *P2*.
    c. The *reliability* of a belief-forming process is its propensity to output true beliefs.

III. Deontic Theory
    a. A belief-forming process is *reliable* for S with respect to the question whether p if and only if its reliability is greater than 0.5 and no less than the reliability of any other process available to S for acquiring a belief as to whether p.
    b. S's belief that p is *ex post justified* if and only if it is the output of a process that is reliable with respect to the question whether p.
    c. S's belief that p is *ex ante justified* at time t if and only if it would be the output of a process that is reliable for S with respect to the question whether p.

I mean TPR to be an example of an initially plausible teleological theory. It has obvious deficiencies that should prevent us from endorsing it without modifica-

---

[5] TPR bears some similarities to Berker's (2013a, 349–50) "(Simplified) Process Reliabilism" exemplar of epistemic teleology, which we can call SPR. There are also important differences between TPR and SPR. First, SPR calculates truth-ratios as ratios of true beliefs produced to false ones. TPR, like most reliabilist theories, calculates them as the proportion of true beliefs among total outputs. Second, SPR counts any process as reliable if its truth ratio meets a certain threshold. TPR, in contrast, counts processes as reliable only if there are no other, available processes whose reliability is greater. Third, SPR's deontic theory does not distinguish *ex ante* and *ex post* justification (Goldman 1979), while TPR does. Though I suspect TPR and SPR both avoid the problem of epistemic tradeoffs, I focus my discussion on TPR because I find it to be *prima facie* more plausible.

tion. For example, TPR lacks a solution to the Generality Problem; it simply takes for granted the individuation of cognitive processes. It also focuses on belief *production* to the exclusion of belief *preservation*, and it lacks the usual provisos to handle cases in which reliable process *P* outputs a false belief to the effect that process *Q* is unreliable in one's circumstances. Further, it leaves it completely unspecified what makes an alternative process qualify as "available" to S.[6]

Despite its problems, TPR exemplifies the structure of epistemic teleology quite well. Its most obvious problems are to be solved by repairing or expanding its theory of overall value or its deontic theory, not by making deep structural changes.

We can think of TPR as a simplified, idealized teleological theory – a frictionless plane for meta-epistemology. If epistemic tradeoffs are a problem for epistemic teleology, they are a problem derived from the structure of teleological theories, rather than their specific contents. If they aren't a problem for TPR, then I am confident they are not a serious problem for any minimally plausible version of epistemic teleology.

3.

To see how the problem of epistemic tradeoffs can affect epistemic teleology, let us consider these cases, all of which are based on cases Berker discusses (Berker 2013a, 2013b):[7]

---

[6] As one reader has pointed out, if all processes one could possibly engage count as "available," then TPR will count beliefs as justified only if formed by the most reliable process possible, which is almost certainly too demanding. So, TPR needs to restrict the range of alternative processes that count as "available." There are several ways of doing that. For example, one might count alternative processes as "available" only if they are not too expensive to be worth employing, given the importance of getting a true belief as to *p*. Such a move would allow for "pragmatic encroachment" on justification (Fantl & McGrath, 2002), and it might be a departure from a purely veritistic conception of epistemic value. It would not, however, be a departure from epistemic teleology. Even if it turns out that a process can be *reliable enough* to provide justification without being the *most reliable available*, the required changes to TPR would not involve giving up teleology, but rather altering its way of setting the threshold of reliability for the output beliefs of a process to be justified.

[7] Berker discusses a series of different cases, each built in response to moves he takes to be required to avoid the problems raised by earlier ones. It would be impractical to address all those cases in this space, but doing so is also unnecessary. Berker (2013a; 2013b) only indirectly considers the response to the problem of epistemic tradeoffs I consider, by way of the cases like the **Doxastic Abundance** case discussed in Section 6, below.

EPISTEMIC OPPORTUNITY: Carrie the chemist is an atheist, but she needs a grant to do her research. The only group interested in funding her has said she must believe in God to receive anything. Carrie knows she is a terrible liar, and she knows the group is very good at rooting out false faith. If she gets the funding, she will discover many new truths of chemistry, but not otherwise. Epistemically, ought Carrie to acquire a belief in God? If she did, would her belief be justified?[8]

ANTINOMY: Bruce has long believed (a) that all his actions have sufficient physiological causes, (b) that he is morally responsible for some of his actions, and (c) that he is not morally responsible for actions with sufficient physiological causes. Yesterday, his friend Abbie, an expert on issues of free will and moral responsibility, showed Bruce the inconsistency of (a), (b), and (c), and she assured him convincingly that exactly one of them is false. He spent several hours trying, unsuccessfully, to figure out which was the false one. Bruce then gave up and continued believing (a), (b), and (c), despite knowing they are inconsistent with one another. Is Bruce thereby believing as he epistemically ought? Are his beliefs justified?[9]

SELF-PROMOTION: Jane suffers from a disease that is almost always fatal, and her doctors have given her only a few weeks to live. As it happens, Jane is more likely to recover if she sincerely believes she will recover, irrespective of what the doctors say. Jane's belief that she will recover thus increases the likelihood that, in believing it, Jane has a *true* belief. Is it thus epistemically right for Jane to believe that she will recover, irrespective of what the doctors say? Is such a belief justified?[10]

Berker thinks it is clear that, if one were to form a belief in God in order to get research funding, the belief would not be epistemically rational/reasonable/warranted. Yet, he says, a veritist would have to grant that, in Carrie's case, forming such a belief would maximize overall epistemic value. "And," he writes,

> this would seem to be so regardless of whether the veritist's theory of overall epistemic value is applied to [beliefs] or to [belief-forming processes or methods]: a belief-forming process that yields a belief in God's existence in the given circumstance would, surely,

---

[8] This case is based on Berker's scientist case (2013a, 363–4). See also Firth (1981) and Fumerton (2001).
[9] This case is based on Berker's paradox case (Berker 2013a, 370).
[10] This case is based on Berker's Jane Doe case (2013b, 376).

tend to promote veritism's ultimate epistemic ends better than one that doesn't.... So, regardless of how we fill in the veritist's epistemic theory, it appears that the veritist is committed to the highly implausible claim that [Carrie's] coming to believe in God's existence in order to get the grant is epistemically rational/reasonable/justified. (2013a, 365).

Berker applies similar reasoning to a case like **Antinomy** (2013a, 370). If Bruce were to withhold belief in the three propositions, he would lose two true beliefs and one false one. By continuing to believe the propositions, he is believing in a way that produces a surplus of true over false beliefs. So, it seems Bruce best promotes the aim of believing what is true rather than false by believing as he does. Berker thinks veritists are thus committed to counting Bruce's continued belief in the three propositions as epistemically justified, reasonable, or rational, even though that is clearly the wrong judgment (according to Berker).

Both **Epistemic Opportunity** and **Antinomy** are addressed against veritism, the family of teleological theories that assign ultimate value to true belief and ultimate disvalue to false belief. It is clear, though, that they could be modified for use against forms of teleology with different theories of final value. What matters is that they are *cross-propositional tradeoff* cases. In **Epistemic Opportunity**, the great epistemic good of all Carrie's new true beliefs about chemistry outweighs whatever epistemic ill there is in her mercenary theism. In **Antinomy**, the epistemic ill of Bruce's one false belief is outweighed by the epistemic good of his two true beliefs.

A teleologist might try to avoid the problems posed by cases such as **Epistemic Opportunity** and **Antinomy** by ruling out cross-propositional tradeoffs from the outset. Berker considers one way of doing that, which involves two steps. First, the teleologist would formulate her theory of overall value not in terms of evaluative focal points such as *beliefs* and *belief-forming processes* but, instead, in terms of focal points such as *beliefs-that-p* and *belief-that-p-forming-processes*. For example, Berker mentions that the theory might address not the broad process, "forming a belief about the external world via visual perception," but the much narrower one, "forming a belief that there is a computer in front of one via visual perception" (2013b, 375). Second, the teleologist would "restrict the conducing relation in [her] theory of overall value so that an item in an evaluative focal point with a given propositional content only counts as conducing toward an epistemically valuable end if that epistemically valuable end *has the same propositional content*" (2013b, 375).[11]

---

[11] See Ahlstrom-Vij & Dunn (2014) and Goldman (forthcoming) for criticisms of the liberties Berker takes in identifying processes here.

Even if those moves enable a teleologist to avoid problems from cross-propositional tradeoffs, Berker thinks the teleologist is still on the hook for cases along the lines of **Self-Promotion**. In those cases, a belief conduces to *its own* truth (or another epistemically valuable end with respect to that very belief). Here is what Berker says about these cases:

> [B]y stipulation, Jane's belief that she will recover raises the chances that she will in fact recover. Or in other words: Jane's belief that she will recover raises the chances that she will thereby have a true belief. Or in other words: Jane's belief that she will recover promotes her being in a cognitive state which (according to advocates of veritism) has final epistemic value, where this cognitive state has the same propositional content as the state that promotes it. But, I insist, Jane's belief is not for that reason epistemically justified. (2013b, 376)

Berker endorses a doctrine of "the epistemic separateness of propositions." According to that doctrine,

> When it comes to the evaluation of individual beliefs, it is never epistemically defensible to sacrifice the furtherance of our epistemic aims with regard to one proposition in order to benefit our epistemic aims with regard to other propositions (even if we grant to the teleologist that there are such things as distinctively epistemic aims and that all epistemic appraisal should be explicated in terms of how well the objects of appraisal conduce toward the furtherance of those aims). (2013a, 365)

A teleological theory that violates "the separateness of propositions" is bound to face counterexamples from cases such as **Epistemic Opportunity** and **Antinomy**. But a teleological theory that does *not* violate the separateness of propositions is bound to face counterexamples such as **Self-Promotion**. Either way, Berker thinks, counterexamples are inevitable, and they derive from the teleological structure of the theory (2013b, 378).

4.

There is no doubt that there are possible teleological theories that would suffer precisely the problems Berker describes, but he himself allows that some logically possible theories might wriggle past the problem of epistemic tradeoffs (Berker 2013a, 380, 2013b, 379). Such theories, he thinks, would be hopelessly baroque (2013a, 380) or else they would have to incorporate a non-teleological component (2013b, 379).

This section aims to show that **Epistemic Opportunity**, **Antinomy**, and **Self-promotion** are not counterexamples to TPR.[12] Section 5 discusses how epistemic teleology can avoid the general problem of epistemic tradeoffs—no baroque codicils or non-teleological components required.

According to TPR, a process is reliable with respect to the question whether p if and only if its propensity to produce true outputs is at least 0.5 and no less than that of any other available process for deciding whether p. TPR also says that a belief is *ex post* justified iff it is the output of a reliable process and *ex ante* justified iff it would be the output of such a process. TPR does not say that a belief-forming process is reliable iff its use at time t would cause one, in the long run, to believe more truths than one would believe if one did not use it at t. Nor does it say that a belief is justified iff having it would cause one, in the long run, to believe more truths than one would if one did not have it. By TPR's lights, the fact that Carrie would gain many true beliefs about chemistry, if only she formed a belief in God, is irrelevant to both the *ex post* and *ex ante* justification of her belief. The justification of the belief depends on its causal history, not its downstream effects.

Epistemic Opportunity could work out in either of two ways. Perhaps Carrie's need for funding motivates her to revisit the arguments for and against the existence of God, taking care to approach them with an open mind and to guard against bias. She might then become convinced of God's existence, as a result of using reliable belief-forming processes. In that case, TPR would count her belief justified, as would our intuitions.

On the other hand, Carrie could start attending the local megachurch, tuning in to evangelical radio stations, and listening to moving Christian pop music, because she knows she is liable to believe almost anything she hears often enough from enthusiastic people. Such a process might make her a believer. Then intuition says her belief would be unjustified, but so does TPR. The belief is not the output of a reliable belief-forming process.

In **Antinomy**, TPR will again focus on the processes of which Bruce's beliefs are outputs. It need not count Bruce's beliefs as justified, unless they are the outputs of reliable processes. If they are not, TPR is not committed to calling them justified, even if having them would realize more overall epistemic value in the long run than withholding judgment would.

---

12 See Ahlstrom-Vij & Dunn (2014) and Goldman (forthcoming) for additional defenses of different versions of reliabilism. Like me, they argue that Berker errs in assuming reliabilists must assess the justification of beliefs in terms of the consequences of holding or forming them, rather than in terms of the reliability of the processes that produce or sustain the beliefs, and they argue that Berker underspecifies the belief-forming processes in the cases he discusses.

Bruce's beliefs could be sustained by ordinary memory or by the usual processes whereby we keep on believing what we used to believe. Then TPR (or a version that addresses belief-sustaining as well as belief-forming processes) might have to count them justified, but there is nothing implausible about that. The mere knowledge that a set of beliefs is inconsistent does not undermine its justification. After all, you probably know the totality of your beliefs *right now* is inconsistent (or at least contains some falsehoods), but that doesn't mean you are not justified in holding any of them. To the contrary, we tend to think of beliefs as justified when they are formed and sustained in a reliable way, despite our acknowledgement of our own inconsistency and fallibility.

It is also worth pointing out that we often do find ourselves in situations not very different from Bruce's, and we count the resulting beliefs as justified. Suppose I have given a medical test to 1,000 people and believed its results in every case. Later, I learn the test results are correct only 99% of the time, and so there is nearly a 100% chance that at least one of the test results is wrong. I do not then give up my 1,000 beliefs, nor do any of them become unjustified. Bruce's situation is similar to mine, except that he is dealing with three beliefs instead of 1,000.

That difference might matter. Bruce is sure one of the three beliefs is false, and so each of them appears to have only a two-in-three chance of truth, which is much worse than each medical belief's 99% chance of truth. Maybe a two-in-three chance is just too low. And in that case TPR might be giving a wrong answer. But note that it isn't TPR's *teleology* that produces this wrong answer; it is TPR's over-tolerance of epistemic risk-taking. If teleology were at fault, then we should count all 1,000 beliefs about the medical test results as unjustified, because it is practically certain that they are not all true.

TPR is not committed the view that Bruce's beliefs are formed by a reliable process, and so it is not committed to the view that they are justified. On TPR, Bruce might or might not be justified in believing as he does, depending on the reliability of the processes that produce and sustain his beliefs.

According to Berker, the only way to avoid cross-propositional tradeoffs is to honor the separateness of propositions. Maybe TPR does that. But then, if Berker is right, it should face the tradeoff problem in cases such as **Self-Promotion.** It should have counterexamples from cases in which holding a belief promotes the achievement of the epistemic good with respect to that belief itself.

TPR appears to escape that problem as well. According to TPR, what would make Jane's belief justified would be that it is the output of a process whose reliability is more than 0.5 and not less than any other available process for deciding whether she will recover. So, for Jane to be justified in believing she will recover, her belief must come from a process that is *at least as reliable as* deferring to her doctors regarding her prognosis (assuming that qualifies as an available alternative process). The mere fact that believing in her recovery boosts her chances is insufficient to justify her belief. After all, Jane's chance of recovering given that she believes might be 2 in a million, while she has only a 1 in a million chance of recovering if she does not believe. Believing *doubles* the chance that the proposition believed is true, but it still doesn't promote epistemic value in the way TPR requires for epistemic justification.

Berker imagines a version of this case in which Jane's failure to believe she will recover would (without her knowing it) *cause* her to have only a 10% chance of recovery, but her believing she will recover would (again, without her knowing it) cause her to have a 90% chance of recovery (Berker 2013b, 376). We are now guaranteed that, whatever process Jane uses to arrive at her belief, she has a 90% chance of believing the truth. According to Berker, this commits the teleologist to counting Jane's belief as justified (2013b, 376–7).

I disagree. As Ahlstrom-Vij & Dunn (2014) point out, we must consider what process outputs Jane's belief. If the process is *wishful thinking*, then TPR counts it as unjustified because it is the output of an unreliable process (even if it has a 90% chance of correctness in this case). On the other hand, if her belief is the output of a specialized *belief-about-my-prospects-of-recovery-forming process*, then it might turn out to be reliable in these circumstances. The mere fact that the belief helps to cause its own truth is no barrier to its being justified. Ahlstrom-Vij & Dunn mention that a judge's belief that a prisoner will be sentenced and a priest's belief that a couple will be wed can help to cause the relevant states of affairs as well. The main intuitive obstacle to counting Jane's belief unjustified appears to be her ignorance of the causal connection between her belief and her chances of survival. In that case, though, the problem would not be that TPR is *teleological*, but rather that it is *externalist* (Ahlstrom-Vij & Dunn, 2014, 549).

5.

Epistemic teleology might appear bound to count unjustified beliefs as justified when it serves the greater epistemic good to hold an intuitively unjustified belief. There are logically possible epistemic teleologies with that feature. They treat the 'ought' of 'Epistemically, what ought I to believe?' as an all-things-considered practical 'ought' aimed at a characteristic epistemic goal, such as the veritist's goal of believing what is true rather than false. On these theories, just as what one ought to *do*, as a lover of truth, is whatever best conduces to the goal of believing a large surplus of truths over falsehoods, what one epistemically ought to *believe* is whatever, in the believing it, best conduces to that same goal. And when one believes as one epistemically ought, one's belief is epistemically justified.

Such a theory, unlike TPR or anything as plausible as it, conflates epistemic justification with prudential justification relative to the epistemic goal. It thereby treats the question of what one ought to *believe* too much on the model of the practical question of what one ought to *do*. We can decide what to do on the basis of consequences of doing it, but we generally can't decide what to *believe* by considering the consequences of *believing it*. Carrie can't take note that it would promote the epistemic good for her to become a theist, and on that basis decide that God exists. Even Bruce doesn't *decide*, on the basis of consequences, to believe rather than withhold judgment. Rather, he decides to stop his inquiry. He makes that decision just as we make any practical decisions about inquiry: by considering whether continued investigation is likely enough to improve his position with respect to the truth goal. Bruce decides it isn't, so he calls it off.

A plausible epistemic teleology would acknowledge the distinction between practical deliberation about what to do and theoretical deliberation about what is so. It would not evaluate their products in the same way. Such a theory would still be teleological, though. It would explain epistemic normativity in terms of the value of our epistemic goals. Those goals play different roles in theoretical deliberation than they play in practical deliberation.

A minimally plausible teleology, such as TPR, addresses its theory of overall value to processes, methods, or strategies of inquiry in the first instance. If individual beliefs are evaluated at all (either in the theory of overall value or in the deontic theory), they are evaluated *in relation to* those processes/methods/strategies. The theory's evaluation of a particular belief is based on (a) what process output it, and (b) the propensity of that process to output beliefs that constitute realizations of our epistemic goals.

A similar theoretical structure occurs outside epistemology. A teleological account of benevolence could say that acting from benevolent motives is good because it tends to make people better off, while acting from malevolent motives is bad because it tends to make them worse off. A particular malevolent action might happen to have the overall consequence of improving everyone's lot. Such an action would have the good feature of making everyone better off and also the bad feature of being malevolent. If we ask whether one ought, morally, to have taken the action, the answer can depend on why we are asking. Are we interested in laying blame? Then the right answer might be that one should not have done it, as there are sound reasons to assign blame on the basis of motives. On the other hand, if our interest is not in blame but in overall welfare, we might care less about motives than results and allow that one did as one should, albeit from a deplorable motive. And if we ask whether the act was good or bad all things considered, we might have to settle for an equivocal answer: it was good in one way, bad in another.

It is rare to ask what one ought to believe in a context where our main concern is our overall best interest, and rarer still to ask in the practical sense of "What belief will give me the greatest surplus of true over false beliefs, on the whole and in the long run?" Instead, we ask it in the sense of "What is the case?", or with an eye to figuring out what method to apply to a problem. A plausible epistemic teleology will treat the justification of beliefs *etiologically*. Beliefs are justified in virtue of their origins in epistemically good kinds or methods of reasoning.

Berker supposes that, in order to honor the separateness of propositions, a teleology must restrict its theory of overall value to evaluative focal points with fixed propositional content: *beliefs-that-p*, and *belief-that-p-forming processes*. That is not the teleologist's only option. TPR avoids cross-propositional tradeoffs by evaluating beliefs in terms of their histories, rather than their effects.

That same feature also allows TPR to avoid tradeoff problems based on epistemic self-promotion. The theory does not imply that a belief is justified when holding it increases its likelihood of truth, nor does it imply that it even counts in favor of a belief that holding it increases its probability. The consequences of *believing* a proposition are irrelevant to TPR; what matters is how strongly the process generating the belief tends to achieve the epistemic goal.

Such an approach differs from what Berker typically assumes teleologists must do. To generate counterexamples to most teleological epistemologies, he thinks it suffices to follow a simple recipe. If the theory does not honor the "separateness of propositions," then construct a cross-propositional tradeoff case for it. If it does, then construct a problematic case of epistemic self-promotion. "I believe," he writes,

> it is possible to use my recipe to construct problem cases for all varieties of epistemic consequentialism that do not go so far as to restrict the conducing relation to the instantiation relation, or (even more radically) to give up on the epistemic evaluation of individual beliefs all together. (Berker 2013b, 379)

What he says against consequentialism, he means to go for teleology more generally as well (2013b, 379). Berker underestimates the prospects of what we might call *etiological epistemic teleology*, which is precisely what TPR represents. The approach is teleological in that it ties all value to the value of a goal state, but it allows for uses of 'ought', 'justified', 'reasonable', etc. that concern history and not just consequences. It neither restricts "the conducing relation to the instantiation relation" nor gives "up on the evaluation of individual beliefs altogether." Instead, it emphasizes the evaluation of belief-forming processes in the first instance, but it has the resources to build evaluations of individual beliefs out of those prior evaluations.

6.

Promising as it is, the etiological move, which I think any plausible epistemic teleology will make, does not solve all tradeoff problems. Berker considers some cross-propositional tradeoff cases that might still be trouble for etiological teleology. Consider, for example, the following case:

DOXASTIC ABUNDANCE: Debbie's mind includes a strange module, implementing a process we'll call NOPE. Whenever she considers the question whether a given number x is prime, NOPE outputs 100 beliefs. One is the belief that x is not prime (irrespective of x's primeness). Each of the others is a belief to the effect that some random composite number is not prime. *At worst*, this process's ratio of true outputs to all its outputs will be .99. So, when Debbie considers whether 11 is prime and comes to believe it is not, is her belief justified?[13]

TPR can seem committed to counting Debbie's belief that 11 is not prime as justified. After all, it is output by a process that is extremely reliable. But one might have the intuition that Debbie's belief should not count as justified. How can a teleologist avoid this kind of case?

One response would be akin to the one Berker considers for teleologists. The teleologist might focus on the reliability Debbie's *belief-that-11-is-not-prime-forming process,* instead of her *belief-forming process.* While the latter is quite reliable, the former is not. That move, though, is implausible. No *belief-that-11-is-not-prime-forming process* is reliable, but surely it is possible to believe, with justification, that 11 is not prime. (Maybe the International Congress of Number Theo-

---

13 This case is a relative of Berker's prime number cases (2013a, 375, 2013b, 374–5), modified to incorporate features of his self-knowledge case (2013b, 373), which make things even harder for reliabilism. In Berker's prime number case, the process simply delivers a negative answer to the question that a given number is prime, whatever number it is asked about; it does not also output the 99 other true beliefs. The inclusion of those beliefs guarantees that the ratio of true outputs to total outputs of this process will be quite high, *regardless* of how reliable its "just say no" heuristic is at deciding whether a given number is prime.

rists announces a surprising discovery of the non-primeness of 11, and it is much more likely that one has been mistaken about what prime numbers are than that the ICNT would make a false announcement of a non-prime number so small.)

A better response would be to move in a similar direction, but not quite as far. Michael Bishop and J. D. Trout (Bishop & Trout, 2008, 2005) argue for a view they call "strategic reliabilism." A key feature of that view is that the reliability of a problem-solving strategy is always relativized to a range of problems the strategy is intended to solve. We do not ask whether the strategy is reliable *full stop*, but whether it is reliable *over range R*.

Bishop and Trout's idea can be adapted to other teleological views. Consider this amended version of TPR:

TPR2
I. Theory of Final Value
   a. *True belief* has fundamental epistemic value.
   b. *False belief* has fundamental epistemic disvalue.
   c. Nothing else has fundamental epistemic value or disvalue.

II. Theory of Overall Value
   a. The *reliability* of a given belief-forming process, over its intended range of problems, R, is the propensity of that process to output true answers to questions in R.
      i. Belief-forming process $P1$ is epistemically superior to process $P2$ over problem range R if and only if:
         1. R is part of both P1 and P2's intended ranges of problems, **and**
         2. Either:
            a. $P1$ is more reliable in R than process $P2$,
            b. $P1$ and $P2$ are equally reliable but, whenever their outputs in answer to a given question differ, $P1$'s answer is correct and $P2$'s answer is incorrect.
   b. Belief-forming process $P1$ is epistemically inferior to process $P2$ over problem range R if and only if $P2$ is epistemically superior to $P1$ in R.

III. Deontic Theory
   a. A belief-forming process is *reliable* for S with respect to problem range R if and only if its reliability is at least 0.5 and it is not epistemically inferior to any other process available to S for answering questions in R.
   b. S's belief that p is *justified* relative to problem range R if and only if the belief has been output as the answer to a question in R by a belief-forming process that is reliable over R.

We can think of the input to a belief-forming process as including both questions and relevant background data. A process outputs *answers* to the questions it takes as input, even if it might output some other beliefs as well. The reliability of the process depends on its tendency to give true answers to the questions it addresses, not just its tendency to produce true beliefs.

The relativization of reliability to problem-ranges is not an ad hoc codicil, needlessly complicating TPR to honor the separateness of propositions. It is, to the contrary, a well-motivated amendment we would want to make on independent grounds. First, when we engage in inquiry, we can decide what to believe only indirectly. We decide among candidate problem-solving strategies, and then we wind up believing the result of the strategy we chose. So, the question we ask ourselves is, "How can I best *solve this problem?*", and we answer it by considering the available ways of solving problems in the relevant domain. That alone can motivate the relativization of reliability to problem-ranges. As it happens, that relativization also provides means for dealing with the so-called generality problem for reliabilism (Bishop & Trout 2005, 178–82).

Consider some questions Debbie might pose to herself. She might ask herself whether 11 is prime. The fact that NOPE outputs true beliefs that are not answers to her question is irrelevant. Only two things matter. First, how strong is NOPE's propensity to output true answers *to questions it is applied to answer?* Second, is there a more reliable alternative process available to Debbie for answering her question?

There is a further problem, though. NOPE doesn't just have a high ratio of truths among its outputs, but it also might appear to be quite reliable *at answering questions about whether numbers are prime.* That appearance is due to the fact that the prime numbers are pretty spread out among the natural numbers on their usual ordering, and so the chance that a randomly selected number is prime can seem to be vanishingly small. Nevertheless, isn't Debbie unjustified in believing that 11 is not prime, having come to that belief by employing NOPE?

Suppose there is no better alternative available. Then the most reliable method available to Debbie for deciding about the primeness of a number is NOPE, and her resulting belief could well be justified. Now suppose Debbie does have another method available. She knows how to test a number n for primeness by checking its divisibility by every positive integer from 2 to $n / 2$. This algorithm is epistemically superior to NOPE. If it is available, Debbie should not rely on NOPE, and her belief formed via NOPE is not justified. These are the intuitively correct conclusions—at least, they satisfy *my* intuitions.

When Ahlstrom-Vij & Dunn (2014) address Berker's cases, they emphasize that reliabilism avoids giving the wrong conclusions because it evaluates the reliability of processes with respect to their "direct outputs."[14] That is, it rates processes as better or worse in terms of the ratio of truths among the beliefs they output directly. To see why it is important *also* to take into account what questions the process is engaged to answer, consider a case similar to **Doxastic Abundance.** Suppose Peggy employs a process, YEP, that always gives an *affirmative* answer when queried about whether a given number is prime, but also always outputs 99 other, true beliefs to the effect that some other, random, nonprime numbers are not prime. YEP's reliability with respect to its direct outputs is no less than 99%, but it is still quite *unreliable* with respect to the questions actually put to it. If reliability is measured in terms of direct outputs, without taking into account a process's intended range of application, we can be forced to count unreliable processes as reliable. On the other hand, measuring reliability in terms of the ratio of *true answers* a process outputs to questions in its range avoids the problem.

We can now describe some general features of teleological theories that can enable them to avoid counterexamples from epistemic tradeoffs. First, and crucially, they should evaluate beliefs on the basis of their causal *histories*, not the beliefs' own consequences. Doing so is consistent with teleology, because what makes a way of arriving at beliefs good or bad is still a matter of how well it promotes ultimate epistemic value.

The second important feature is an orientation *away* from the evaluation of individual beliefs and *toward* the comparative evaluation of cognitive processes themselves, considered as strategies for answering related sets of questions. That move maintains the emphasis on cognitive goals. We want true answers to our questions, or well-supported ones. When worked out well, the move avoids counterexamples from cases like self-promotion as well as cross-propositional tradeoffs. Even if believing that p somehow increases the probability of p, that does not mean the process outputting a belief that p is automatically the most reliable available for answering questions in its intended range of problems. That is how it avoids self-promotion cases. It avoids cross-propositional tradeoffs by evaluating processes in terms of their answers to questions, rather than all their outputs or all the effects of engaging the processes.

---

14 In response to Berker's prime number cases, which involve processes that always answer "No" to the question whether a given number is prime, Ahlstrom-Vij and Dunn agree with Berker that reliabilists should say the output beliefs are justified, but they also insist that is the right answer to give. It is likely they would contend that, if a more reliable alternative process is available to Debbie, that might be a *defeater* of her justification, but the possibility of such defeat does not count against epistemic teleology at all.

When Berker entertains the possibility of a teleology that gives "up on the epistemic evaluation of individual beliefs altogether," he considers such a teleology to be extremely radical, presumably so radical that it might constitute giving up on epistemology altogether. Nothing as radical as that is necessary for teleologists, though. They do not need to *give up* on the evaluation of individual beliefs. It suffices for them simply to recognize that those evaluations depend on a more fundamental evaluation of ways of getting answers to our questions.

7.

Even if plausible epistemic teleologies avoid epistemic tradeoff problems, there might be other reasons to prefer a non-teleological understanding of epistemic value and obligation. It is thus worth considering what advantages the teleological approach has over alternative views.

Berker describes two examples of non-teleological epistemology. One is a form of evidentialism, according to which one epistemically ought to fit one's belief to one's evidence, with the notion of "fit" understood in an unspecified, non-teleological way. Another is a view on which rationality overall is a matter of conforming to certain rules, the subset of which that govern theoretical reasoning qualify as "epistemic." The rules are to be understood as fundamental and constitutive of rationality, not as derived from the value of anything (Berker 2013a, 380–3).

It may be possible to shoehorn these views into the teleological framework, especially if we treat *instantiating* an end as a way of conducing toward it. Still, there is a difference in spirit between these sorts of views, which focus on the requirements of reason as such, and paradigmatic teleology, which focuses on the effective pursuit of valuable intellectual goals. Perhaps it is best to think of non-teleological epistemology more along the lines of what is often called "deontology" in ethics (while turning a blind eye to uses of 'deontology' inspired by Alston's (1988) discussion of a quite different set of issues). It can be hard to pin down just what ethical deontology amounts to, but one way comes from Thomas Nagel's (1986) "side constraint" approach. On Nagel's view, there are some moral constraints on how we pursue whatever ends we happen to have. They are rules it is wrong to break, even for the sake of preventing further violations of the rules. If lying is wrong in that way, then it is wrong for me to lie, even if lying once right now would prevent me or someone else from lying five times tomorrow.

The epistemological analog would be the idea that there are constraints on our believing that we epistemically ought not to violate, even if doing so would prevent further violations later. Don't believe one proposition on inadequate evidence today, even if doing so would keep you from believing five propositions on inadequate evidence tomorrow.

Whatever utility the distinction between deontology and teleology has in ethics, the analogous distinction in epistemology looks misguided, especially given that the distinction between practical and theoretical reasoning is already in place.

A plausible epistemic teleology treats the justification of beliefs etiologically. Such a theory can allow for the possibility that what is practically best to believe, from the standpoint of maximizing epistemic value, might not be epistemically justified. Suppose beliefs based on wishful thinking are unjustified, and suppose I could avoid forming five wishful beliefs tomorrow by forming one today. Today's wishful belief would be unjustified because it would have the wrong sort of causal history; it would be output by a process that is relatively unreliable over its range. Its effects are irrelevant to its justification. Unjustifiedness is a form of wrongness, and so there is a way in which, even on TPR, it is wrong for one to think wishfully, even in order to avoid more wishful thinking later.

Even the Nagel-inspired characterization of non-teleological normative epistemology seems not to provide the clear distinction between teleological and non-teleological epistemology that we want. Worries about exactly how to draw the distinction aside, teleology does enjoy some important advantages. I will describe three.

First, the teleological approach does justice to the fact that, in tradeoff cases, the belief in question is good in one way and bad in another. Suppose my unjustified belief causes me to acquire many other, justified beliefs. The former belief is unjustified; that's a way of being bad. But there is also a way in which it is good: it is helpful in the achievement of my epistemic ends. The same could even be said for cases in which the most epistemically prudent strategy is epistemically inferior to other available strategies. The use of such a strategy is good in that it puts one into a position to acquire more true beliefs, but it is bad in that it is less likely output true beliefs than an alternative strategy.

It is not clear that a non-teleological approach can do justice to such nuances. While it might have room to allow that there is something, in some sense, good about the promotion of valuable cognitive goals, it also appears forced to insist that the non-teleological constraints of rationality trump that goodness. Those constraints govern our *pursuit* of cognitive goals, but they have no basis in the value of our *achieving* them. Even if a belief that violates those constraints is good in some way, for the non-teleologist it isn't good in a way that matters for the purposes of normative epistemology.

The second advantage of epistemic teleology is a close relative of the first. The teleological approach provides a unified account of two arenas of goodness in inquiry. On the one hand, there is the forward-looking, practical goodness involved in conduciveness to the goals of inquiry. On the other, there is the backward-looking, theoretical goodness of beliefs originating from good methods of inquiry, where "good methods" are those of a type that tends to be good in the first, practical sense. Ultimately, both sorts of value derive from the value of the same goal. It will thus be no surprise that, on the teleological approach, choosing methods that promote the aims of inquiry is also likely to result in the acquisition of justified beliefs. On a non-teleological approach, though, one might be left to wonder what connection there is between believing as one epistemically ought and accomplishing one's cognitive goals, or even if there is any connection at all. If what I want is truth, why should I believe rationally? Teleologists have a more direct answer, because they understand epistemic rationality by reference to the truth goal in the first place.

A final advantage for teleology is more aptly described as a disadvantage for epistemic non-teleology. The latter view is susceptible to objections very much like common objections to non-teleological *ethics*. For example, imagine a normative ethic without a welfare component at all. This is a theory that ignores the welfare consequences of actions in evaluating them. On such a theory, the fact that an act would do great harm to many people does not count morally against it. Likewise, the fact that an act would benefit many people greatly does not count in its favor. There will be cases in which the right thing to do, according to the theory, is something that makes everyone worse off, and is known to do so. Now suppose a non-teleological theory has a welfare component, but it can be trumped by other considerations. So long as that welfare component can be trumped by deontological considerations, there will be cases in which the theory forbids what would make the world better, or requires what would make the world worse. Though some philosophers are happy to go that way, my moral compass points elsewhere.

In the case of non-teleological epistemology, similar objections apply, and may be even more forceful. There will be cases in which one knows the best way to pursue the cognitive good is by doing something the non-teleologist's rules forbid. In those cases, it turns out to be unequivocally *epistemically irrational* to do what best promotes the epistemic good. That, it seems to me, is a mistake.

To see why it is a mistake, consider the ongoing debates concerning cognitive heuristics and ecological rationality. A recurring theme in those debates is that there are families of cases in which people naturally employ decision-making strategies that violate *a priori* canons of reasoning. Commonly, the strategies involve ignoring relevant information. Nevertheless, in the problem-solving environments where the strategies are normally employed, the counter-normative strategies can be faster and more reliable than their *a priori* counterparts. Some of this has to do with features of the environment, and some is due to our own psychological imperfection. Just as preventing teen pregnancy through contraception turns out to be more reliable in the field than the *a priori* better method of abstinence, heuristic reasoning in the field can turn out to bring us to the truth more reliably than taking into account all the relevant information would (Gigerenzer & Goldstein, 1996).

From a teleologist's perspective, it is a mistake to demand that people abide by canons of reasoning that are either unreliable in their circumstances or that they can't reliably implement. Decision-making strategies that will reliably produce better outcomes, from the standpoint of our cognitive goals, are epistemically better strategies, and one ought to use good strategies in the pursuit of those goals. When one does, one's beliefs are justified. That is the fundamental insight of epistemic teleology, and it is difficult at best for a non-teleological approach to accommodate it.

Even for a teleologist, there will be cases in which one might best promote the overall epistemic good by employing unreliable processes. Carrie the chemist may be in such a case. She can go to the megachurch and listen to the evangelical radio station and, ultimately, induce herself to embrace theism, with the consequence that she gains a lot of new true beliefs about chemistry. The teleologist can give a nuanced assessment of the case. Carrie's mercenary theism is *good* in at least one way; it is helpful in her achievement of further epistemic goals and so, all things considered, epistemically prudent. But it is also *bad* in at least one way; it is unjustified by virtue of being the output of an unreliable process.

8.

One way to do normative epistemology is to focus on the appraisal of particular beliefs. This approach, which I have called "belief-centered epistemology" (Wrenn 2008), emphasizes such questions as "Epistemically, what ought I to believe?" over methodological questions, such as "What is the best way for me to find out the answer to this question?"

If we take the belief-centered approach, a number of problems might arise for us. One of the most obvious is the problem of doxastic voluntarism. Do we have the right sort of control over our beliefs for talk about what we *ought* to believe, epistemically or otherwise, to make any sense?

We do not have to think about normative epistemology in that way. We can instead emphasize *methods* over *beliefs*. Even if we don't have the sort of control over our beliefs presupposed by epistemic duties to believe (or not to believe), we often do have considerable control over how we find answers to our questions. We could start with questions about *how we ought to inquire.* We might even give a trivial answer to the question what one ought to believe. What ought you to believe as to *p?* You ought to believe whatever properly conducted inquiry leads you to believe. This shift from belief-centered normative epistemology to an epistemology that is more methodologically oriented is, to my mind, a good idea.

Once we see the possibility of normative epistemology as something other than a discipline dedicated to passing judgment on the justification of beliefs, we can also see how epistemic teleology can avoid tradeoff problems. Cross-propositional tradeoffs and epistemic self-promotion are problematic only so long as we think of *beliefs themselves* as means to our cognitive ends. On plausible epistemic teleologies, they are not. Rather, the means to our cognitive ends are the belief-forming processes we engage, and beliefs are evaluated, if at all, only in relation to the processes of which they are outputs.

If we put our emphasis in the first instance on evaluating methods of inquiry, rather than beliefs, we can also begin to address such issues as *which* outputs of a process matter to its epistemic evaluation. I have suggested that the outputs that matter are the process's answers to questions posed to it. Such an approach enables teleology to avoid the kinds of tradeoffs involved in cases such as **Epistemic Abundance.** There might be other ways to avoid those problems, some of which may be better than my suggestion.

Until recently, epistemic teleology has received little direct scrutiny. Many who have endorsed it have seen little reason to argue for it, perhaps thinking it was just a trivial matter of the definition of 'epistemic'. I have sought to remedy that situation in two ways. I have argued that there are plausible epistemic teleologies that do not suffer counterexamples from cross-propositional tradeoffs or self-promotion. Epistemic teleology is not committed to identifying our justified beliefs with the beliefs that are practically best, all things considered, with respect to our epistemic goals. I have also argued that epistemic teleology has important advantages over a non-teleological approach to epistemology. It makes sense of the fact that, in tradeoff cases, there is something epistemically good *and* something epistemically bad about the target beliefs. It gives a unified account of how those two forms of value are legitimately *epistemic*, and it does not condemn as unjustified or irrational beliefs or decision-making strategies that are better suited to one's situation than those recommended by *a priori* norms. Those are advantages that non-teleological epistemology seems to lack.[15]

References

Ahlstrom-Vij, K., & Dunn, J. (2014). A defence of epistemic consequentialism. *The Philosophical Quarterly*, *64*(257), 541–551.
Alston, W. P. (1988). The deontological conception of epistemic justification. *Philosophical Perspectives*, *2*, 257–299.
Berker, S. (2013a). Epistemic teleology and the separateness of propositions. *Philosophical Review*, *122*(3), 337–393.
Berker, S. (2013b). The rejection of epistemic consequentialism. *Philosophical Issues*, *23*(1), 363–387.
Bishop, M. A., and Trout, J. D. (2008). Strategic reliabilism: A naturalistic approach to epistemology. *Philosophy Compass*, *3*(5), 1049–1065.
Bishop, M. A., and Trout, J. D. (2005). *Epistemology and the psychology of human judgment*. New York: Oxford University Press.
BonJour, L. (1985). *The structure of empirical knowledge*. Cambridge, Mass.: Harvard University Press.
Chisholm, R. M. (1977). *Theory of knowledge*. Englewood Cliffs, N.J.: Prentice-Hall.
Descartes, R. (1984). Rules for the direction of the mind. In *The philosophical writings of Descartes* (Vol. 1). Cambridge; New York: Cambridge University Press, 7–78.
Fantl, J. and McGrath, M. (2002). Evidence, pragmatics, and justification. *Philosophical Review*, *111*(1), 67–94.
Feldman, R. (2003). *Epistemology*. Upper Saddle River, N.J.: Prentice Hall.
Firth, R. (1981). Epistemic merit, intrinsic and instrumental. *Proceedings and Addresses of the American Philosophical Association*, *55*, 5–23.
Fumerton, R. (2001). Epistemic justification and normativity. In M. Steup (ed.), *Knowledge, truth, and duty: Essays on epistemic justification, responsibility and virtue*. Oxford, UK: Oxford University Press, 49–61.
Gigerenzer, G., & Goldstein, D. G. (1996). Reasoning the fast and frugal way: Models of bounded rationality. *Psychological Review*, *103*(4), 650.
Goldman, A. I. (forthcoming). Reliabilism, veritism, and epistemic consequentialism. *Episteme*.
Goldman, A. I. (1979). What is justified belief? In G. Pappas (ed.), *Justification and knowledge*. Springer Netherlands, 1–23.
Goldman, A. I. (1986). *Epistemology and cognition*. Cambridge, Mass.: Harvard University Press.

---

[15] Previous versions of this paper were presented at the 2013 Southeastern Epistemology Conference and the 2014 meeting of the Southern Society for Philosophy and Psychology. I am grateful to the audiences at both conferences for their helpful discussion. I am also grateful to Stuart Rachels, Susanna Siegel, and an anonymous reviewer for this volume for the valuable feedback and suggestions they gave me on earlier versions of this paper.

James, W. (1896). *The will to believe, and other essays in popular philosophy.* Longmans.
Kagan, S. (2000). Evaluative focal points. In E. Mason, B. Hooker, and D. E. Miller (eds.), *Morality, rules, and consequences: A critical reader.* Rowman & Littlefield, 134–55.
Kornblith, H. (1993). Epistemic normativity. *Synthese, 94*(3), 357–376.
Korsgaard, C. M. (1983). Two distinctions in goodness. *The Philosophical Review, 92*(2), 169–195.
Nagel, T. (1986). *The view from nowhere.* New York: Oxford University Press.
Quine, W. V. (1998). Reply to Morton White. In L. E. Hahn and P. A. Schilpp (eds.), *The philosophy of W. V. Quine* (Expanded ed.). La Salle, IL: Open Court, 663–5.
Wrenn, C. B. (2006). Epistemology as engineering? *Theoria, 72*(1), 60–79.
Wrenn, C. B. (2008). Naturalism and belief-centered epistemology. In C. B. Wrenn (ed.), *Naturalism, reference, and ontology: Essays in honor of Roger F. Gibson.* New York: Peter Lang, 77–92.

Jochen Briesen
Epistemic Consequentialism: Its Relation to Ethical Consequentialism and the Truth-Indication Principle

1. Introduction

The terms "justification" and "rationality" refer to many different relations and phenomena. Many epistemologists agree that the best way to specify epistemic justification/rationality and thereby differentiate it from other forms of justification/rationality is the following: Epistemic justification/rationality, unlike moral or pragmatic justification/rationality, is directed at an epistemic aim, whereas other forms of justification/rationality are directed at other aims. Thereby, many epistemologists adopt a consequentialist position in the sense that they spell out the normative notions of "justification" or "rationality" by recourse to certain epistemic aims.[1]

The main motivation for adopting such a consequentialist position in epistemology is its explanatory strength. Consider the following case:

Criminal child. The child of person S is accused of a terrible crime based on very good evidence. Even though S knows about all the evidence and can neither undermine nor override it in any way, S nonetheless holds onto the belief that the child is innocent.

From a pretheoretical perspective, it seems plausible that S's belief can be justified/rational in a certain sense, whereas in another sense the belief seems clearly unjustified/irrational. This can be easily explained within the above-mentioned epistemic consequentialist framework: S's belief might be *pragmatically* justified because entertaining the belief that one's child is innocent might be conducive to a person's practical aim; maybe the person aims at living a happy life and would not be able to achieve that aim if she gave up the belief. However, S's belief is

---

[1] One might claim that the given characteriziation only specifies what we might call a "teleological" and not necessarily a consequentialist position. However, in the context of this paper I will not differentiate between the two. I will use the term "consequentialism" to refer to all positions that spell out normative notions via recourse to the aim of achieving something of final value.

obviously not *epistemically* justified/rational because entertaining the belief that the child is innocent does not seem to be conducive to an epistemic aim, for example the aim of increasing the number of true beliefs and decreasing the number of false ones. In the light of cases such as this, many epistemologists take truth-conduciveness to be a defining feature of epistemic justification/rationality and thereby adopt an epistemic consequentialist position.

Even though the whole epistemic consequentialist framework has been recently attacked by Selim Berker (2013a, 2013b), I will accept the general framework in what follows. Berker's considerations do not seem to constitute devastating objections to the general framework, and the necessity of explaining the differences among various forms of justification/rationality gives us very good reason to adopt such a framework.[2]

Moreover, even though I agree that different important epistemic values have to be distinguished, for the purpose of this paper, I accept that one very important epistemic value is truth, and one very important epistemic disvalue is falsity.[3] Thus, I will accept that increasing the number of true beliefs while avoiding false beliefs can be considered an important epistemic goal by recourse to which some important epistemic notions can be specified. (I will mostly concentrate on the notion of epistemic justification.) Hence, I will accept a *veritistic* consequentialist framework.

What I am interested in is the question of how such a framework should be spelled out in more detail. What are the constraints for a convincing veritistic consequentialist position? In what way can these constraints be met? To answer these questions, it is helpful first to consider the putative analogy between epistemic and ethical consequentialism. Even though epistemic and ethical variants of consequentialism are in many respects structurally analogous, there are also important disanalogies. Some of these disanalogies will eventually help to identify constraints that epistemic versions of consequentialism have to meet. Identifying these constraints will in turn allow consideration of different ways in which the constraints might be satisfied. In following this general strategy, the paper is organized as follows:

In section 2, I will first specify structural analogies between epistemic and ethical variants of consequentialism. After highlighting the analogies, I will, in section 3, identify an important disanalogy with respect to these positions. In

---

[2] I will hint at some reasons why Berker's objections do not seriously undermine the epistemic consequentialist framework below (see fn. 22). It should also be noted that Berker does not take the reasons that speak *in favor* of such a framework seriously into account.
[3] For interesting discussions of various epistemic values, see, e.g., Haddock et. al 2009; Grimm 2008; Kvanvig 2005.

this context, I will introduce the following "truth-indication principle" (henceforth (TI)).

(TI) For all subjects S and propositions p: S's belief that p is epistemically justified only if there are factors indicating that the belief *itself* is true.

Even though this principle is rarely explicitly mentioned, I will argue that popular consequentialist positions in epistemology (internalist and externalist versions alike) implicitly endorse (TI). However, no analogue principle (for example, a pleasure-indication principle) can be found within ethical consequentialist positions. Thus, from a certain perspective, an important difference between epistemic and ethical consequentialism amounts to the fact that epistemic versions of consequentialism seem to be committed to (TI), whereas no analogous principle is warranted in the ethical domain. The reason epistemic consequentialists tend to incorporate (TI) into their framework is that, by incorporating (TI), they can meet certain constraints that every plausible version of epistemic consequentialism has to satisfy. In the course of section 3, I will identify these constraints in detail.

In section 4, I will consider whether the identified constraints can only be met by accepting (TI) or also be met differently. In other words: Are there plausible versions of epistemic consequentialism that reject the truth-indication principle (TI)? If there were, then the analogy between epistemic and ethical consequentialism would, in a certain sense, be even stronger than it seems at first. By specifying and modifying some ideas famously introduced by Ludwig Wittgenstein (1969) and further developed by Crispin Wright (2004, 2014) and others, I will spell out a promising epistemic consequentialist position that meets the identified constraints but is nevertheless not committed to (TI).

2. The Analogy Between Ethical and Epistemic Consequentialism

Consequentialist positions in philosophy spell out normative notions by making recourse to the goal of achieving states of affairs that have final value. A state of affairs has final value if and only if it has value as end in itself (in contrast to having instrumental value as a means to some other valuable end). To keep things simple in terms of theories of value, I will concentrate on a simple version of hedonism in ethics, which claims that experiencing pleasure has final value and experiencing pain has final disvalue, and a simple version of veritism in epistemology, which claims that having true beliefs has final epistemic value and having false beliefs has final epistemic disvalue. [4]

By accepting these final values, consequentialists in ethics and epistemology can formulate important aims, namely the aims of achieving the states of affairs of final value in their respective domains. In what follows, I will call these aims "ultimate aims". For hedonistic consequentialists, the ultimate aim in the ethical domain consists in improving the overall balance of pleasurable versus painful experiences (by increasing the number of pleasurable experiences and decreasing the number of painful ones). For veritistic consequentialists, the ultimate aim in the epistemic domain consists in improving the overall balance of (interesting) true beliefs over false ones (by inreasing the number of true and decreasing the number of false beliefs).[5] [6]

By making recourse to these aims, those taking consequentialist positions in ethics and epistemology can put forward normative evaluations. For example, by referring to the specified aims, hedonistic consequentialists in ethics can evaluate acts as being morally justified, and veritistic consequentialists in epistemology can evaluate beliefs as being epistemically justified:

(MJ) Moral Justification of Acts. For all subjects S and acts A: S's action A is morally justified only if performing A is conducive to the ultimate aim of improving the overall balance of pleasurable experiences over painful experiences (to a certain degree).[7]

---

[4] Note that according to this characterization veritists claim that true beliefs have *final epistemic* value and not *epistemic final* value. Thus, veritist consequentialists merely claim that true beliefs have final value in the *epistemic domain*. I will follow the common practice of taking this formulation to be indifferent with respect to the question whether true beliefs have this value only in virtue of being conducive to some other value outside the epistemic domain.

[5] It seems plausible to formulate the epistemic aim as improving the balance of *interesting* true beliefs over false ones. Otherwise, it would be epistemically appropriate to concentrate exclusively on beliefs that can be easily verified. Examples include beliefs concerning the number of grains of sand in our shoes and beliefs concerning the number of coffee beans in jars. By specifying the epistemic aim as being directed at *interesting* true beliefs, epistemic consequentialists can explain why this kind of behaviour would be epistemically inappropriate. Why I nonetheless put the term "interesting" in parentheses in the formulation of the ultimate epistemic aim in the main body of the text will be explained below (see. fn. 8).

[6] Note the double character of this aim, it can be achieved either by increasing the number of (interesting) true beliefs or by decreasing the number of false ones. That the epistemic truth-aim has this kind of double character rests on insights by William James (cf. James 1897:18).

[7] These kinds of evaluations in the context of ethical consequentialism are variable with respect to two important parameters. First, both acts and other things can be morally evaluated: e. g. motives, maxims, institutions, and even beliefs. Second, acts and other things can be evaluated

(EJ) Epistemic Justification of Belief. For all subjects S and propositions p: S's belief that p is epistemically justified only if having the belief that p is conducive to the ultimate epistemic aim of improving the overall balance of (interesting)[8] true beliefs over false beliefs (to a certain degree).[9]

Different versions of these positions can be characterized by further specifying what it means to be "conducive" to the respective aims.

Let us first consider some important variations within ethical hedonistic consequentialism.[10] Hedonistic consequentialists agree that, for an act A to be conducive to the specified aim, there must be some feature of A that will be accountable for a greater balance of pleasurable over painful experiences. However, different views take different features of A to be relevant. Act-consequentialists, for example, claim that the relevant feature is the causal chain of events set off by A. If this chain of events leads to a certain improvement of the balance of pleasure over pain, then the act is morally justified. Motive- or rule-consequentialists, on the other hand, think that the relevant feature is not the causal chain of events set off by A, but rather the motive-set M or the set of rules R according to which S performed A. If acting according to M (when possessed in appropriate circumstances) or according to R (when properly internalized by a sufficiently large group of the population) leads in the long run to a certain improvement in the balance of pleasure over pain, then the act in accordance with M or R is morally justified.

---

as being morally justified as well as being morally right, being morally required, being morally permitted, etc. For more variable parameters, see fn. 11.

8 Even though the epistemic aim should be specified as being directed at *interesting* true beliefs, we should allow that uninteresting beliefs can be justified as well. Take the belief, for example, that there are 321 grains of sand in my shoe. Let us suppose that holding this uninteresting belief cannot have any positive consequences with respect to increasing the number of *interesting* true beliefs. Nevertheless, we should allow that this belief could be justified. This is why I put the term "interesting" in parentheses in the formulation of (EJ). Even though the ultimate epistemic aim should be spelled out as being directed at increasing the number of *interesting* true beliefs, in our epistemic evaluation of beliefs sometimes the more general aim of increasing the number of true beliefs *simpliciter* seems relevant.

9 Just as evaluations in the context of *ethical* consequentialism are variable, so are the evaluations in the context of *epistemic* consequentialism. First, not only beliefs but also other things can be epistemically evaluated: e.g. belief-sets, theories, belief-forming processes, and even acts. Second, beliefs or other things can not only be evaluated as being epistemically justified, they can also be evaluated as being epistemically rational, epistemically correct, epistemically required, epistemically permitted, etc. See also fn. 11.

10 For a general overview of different versions of consequentialism in ethics, see Sinnot-Armstrong 2014.

It is important to note that, in the light of motive- or rule-consequentialism, act A is conducive to the specified aim in an indirect way. This is why these variants of consequentialism are sometimes subsumed under the term "indirect consequentialism". In a certain sense, the act itself is not supposed to be conducive to the specified aim in order to be morally justified, but rather the motive set M or the rules R on which act A is based. This allows that, in individual cases, acting in accordance to M or R can even have negative effects with respect to the specified aim without thereby necessarily being unjustified. As long as acting in accordance to M or R will lead to a greater balance of pleasure over pain in the long run, an individual act can even have negative consequences with respect to the specified aim and still be morally justified.

Besides identifying the feature of act A that is accountable for the act's conduciveness towards the specified aim and thereby specifying in which way the act has to be conducive to the aim, hedonistic consequentialists have to decide whether the identified features of A have to improve the actual balance of pleasure over pain or whether it is enough that subject S reasonably believes that the ratio is improved. In other words: Are the features such that they improve the balance of pleasure over pain from a third- or a first-person perspective? Objective act-consequentialists hold that what is morally relevant is whether the actual chain of events set off by A leads to a greater balance of pleasure over pain. Subjective act-consequentialists, on the other hand, claim that what is morally relevant is not the actual chain of events, but rather the chain of events intended or expected by the agent. A similar distinction can be drawn within motive- or rule-consequentialism in ethics. Is it morally relevant whether acting according to motive-set M or rules R actually improves the balance of pleasure over pain in the long run, or is it relevant whether the subject intends or reasonably expects that this is the case?

Even though there are more variable parameters within hedonistic consequentialism, the parameters introduced so far will suffice to spell out the analogies and disanalogies between ethical and epistemic consequentialist theories in which I am interested. So I will turn to epistemic variants of consequentialism.[11]

---

[11] There are two more variable parameters within hedonistic consequentialism that should at least be mentioned. The first concerns the question of to what degree the balance of pleasure over pain has to be improved, i.e. is a satisficing or a maximizing version of hedonistic consequentialism preferred? Even though an analogous question could be raised in the epistemological realm, for the purposes of this paper this analogy is negligible. The second parameter concerns whether an egoistic or a non-egoistic form of hedonistic consequentialism should be preferred. In egoistic versions, only the ratio of the *subject's* pleasurable over painful experien-

Veritistic consequentialists in epistemology agree that, for a belief B to be conducive to the epistemic aim of increasing the number of true beliefs and decreasing the number of false ones, there must be some feature of B that will be accountable for a greater balance of true over false beliefs. However, as different ethical theories disagree with respect to the relevant features of act A, different versions of veritistic consequentialism in epistemology take different features of belief B to be relevant. Evidentialist versions of consequentialism, for example, think that the relevant feature is the body of evidence E on which B is based. If believing in accordance with E leads to a greater balance of true over false beliefs, then the belief appropriately based on E is justified.[12] Conversely, process-reliabilists think that the relevant feature is not the body of evidence available to S, but rather the belief-forming process P that caused S to entertain the belief B (where this process does not have to include evidence). If P is sufficiently reliable—if it leads to true beliefs most of the time—then the belief based on P is epistemically justified.[13]

Furthermore, veritistic consequentialists in epistemology not only disagree about the features accountable for a better ratio of true over false beliefs, they also disagree whether the identified features have to actually improve the balance in question or whether it is enough that the subject S thinks or believes that the balance is improved. In other words: Are the features such that they improve the balance of true over false beliefs from a third- or a first-person perspective or both? Pure objective epistemic consequentialists vote for the first option, pure subjective epistemic consequentialists vote for the second option, and mixed positions claim that the balance has to be improved both from a first- and third-person perspective.[14] [15]

---

ces is relevant, whereas in non-egoistic versions the experiences of *other people* have to be taken into account. For obvious reasons, epistemic versions of consequentialism are more closely related to egoistic versions of ethical consequentialism than to non-egoistic versions.

12 For views coming close to such a position, see Alston 1989; BonJour 1985, 2003; Conee 1992; Feldman 2000; Foley 1987, 1993. These philosophers agree that in order for a belief to be justified it has to be conducive to the epistemic truth-aim, where what is accountable for the conduciveness to the specified aim is the subject's available body of evidence on which she is basing the belief. (Please note, however, that all these philosophers spell out the epistemic truth-aim slightly differently.)

13 This very influential view has been suggested, developed, and defended by Alvin Goldman. He thinks that in order for a belief to be justified it has to be conducive to the epistemic truth-aim, where what is accountable for the conduciveness to the specified aim is the process leading to the belief (cf. Goldman 1979, 1986, 2001).

14 For a view coming close to a *pure* subjective position, see Lehrer 1974; a good example of a mixed position can be found in Alston 1989, 2005.

Please note that evidentialist and process-reliabilist versions of veritistic consequentialism can both be classified as forms of indirect consequentialism. In a certain sense, not the belief itself is supposed to be conducive to the epistemic aim in order to be justified but rather the body of evidence E or the belief-forming process P on which B is based.

This is not an accident. Epistemic consequentialism tends to be spelled out as an instance of indirect consequentialism because it is pretheoretically plausible to assume that false beliefs can be epistemically justified. It seems plausible to suppose that, for example, in certain circumstances, my belief that my bike has been stolen is justified, without that belief's being true. Perhaps, maybe unbeknownst to me, my neighbour borrowed the bike.[16]

Subjective epistemic consequentialists can easily account for this possibility. However, if objective epistemic consequentialists want to allow that a false belief can be epistemically justified, then they have to claim that, in a certain sense, it is not the justified belief itself that has to be conducive to the specified epistemic aim but rather something else, such as the belief-forming process P or the body of evidence E on which B is based. This allows for the possibility that, in individual cases, a belief that is caused by a reliable process P or that is appropriately based on evidence E can be false and can thereby have negative effects with respect to the specified epistemic aim, without that belief's thereby necessarily being unjustified. As long as believing in accordance to P or E will lead to a greater balance of true over false beliefs in the long run, the false belief in question can still be epistemically justified. It is interesting to note that, as indirect versions of consequentialism, epistemic consequentialist theories are more closely related to ethical motive- or rule-consequentialism than to ethical act-consequentialism.

Up to this point, the similarities between ethical and epistemic forms of consequentialism are pretty straightforward. Both have to specify due to which features and in what way a morally/epistemically justified act/belief is conducive to the respective aims. This decision will settle whether a direct or an indirect variant of consequentialism is accepted. Consequentialists of both camps also have to specify whether the identified features are supposed to be conducive to the

---

15 In a certain usage of the terms "epistemic internalism" and "epistemic externalism", the distinction between *subjective* and *objective* consequentialism amounts to the difference between epistemic *internalism* and epistemic *externalism*. However, because the latter terms are used differently in the literature it is better to stick to the terms "subjective epistemic consequentialism" and "objective epistemic consequentialism" with their stipulated meanings.

16 Even though most epistemologists think that there can be justified false beliefs, not everyone agrees. For a defense of the opposite view that justification is factive, see Littlejohn 2012.

respective aims from a first- or third-person perspective or both. This decision will settle whether a subjective or an objective form of consequentialism (or a mixed position) is accepted.

3. An Important Disanalogy Between Ethical and Epistemic Consequentialism

There is a difference in the way we set things up between ethical and epistemic variants of consequentialism that catches one's eye. The versions of epistemic consequentialism characterized above are all committed to the view that a belief is epistemically justified partially in virtue of factors speaking in favor of the truth of the justified belief itself, be it from a first- or a third-person perspective or both. Thus, the characterized positions are all committed to the following truth-indication principle (hereafter, (TI)):

(TI) For all subjects S and propositions p: S's belief that p is justified only if there are factors indicating that the belief *itself* is true.[17]

The epistemic consequentialist positions characterized in section 2 claim that the justified belief is conducive to the global epistemic aim of improving the balance of true over false beliefs because there are some factors—either the body of available evidence E or the reliability of the belief-forming process P, etc.—that (to a certain extent) indicate—either from a first- or third-person perspective or both—that the belief itself is true. This is why holding justified beliefs will ultimately lead to a greater balance of true over false beliefs either from a first- or third-person perspective or both. Thus, in a certain sense, holding justified beliefs has positive epistemic consequences globally only because a justified belief has positive epistemic consequences locally. Holding justified beliefs has the positive global consequence that a greater balance of true over false beliefs is achieved in the long run. However, this positive global consequence is due to the positive

---

[17] It is not easy to spell out in detail what it means to say that X partially in virtue of Y. I assume it implies that whenever X is present, Y is present. Thus, it implies that X only if Y. This is why a position that claims that a belief is epistemically justified partially in virtue of factors indicating the truth of the justified belief itself is committed to (TI).

local consequence that the justified belief itself is likely to be true—again, either from a first-person perspective, a third person perspective or both.[18][19]

In contrast, the characterized versions of hedonistic consequentialism are not committed to an analogous pleasure-indication principle. What would such a principle look like? If we simply substitute "epistemically justified" in (TI) by "morally justified" and any instance of "belief" by "act" and "truth/true" by "pleasure/pleasurable", we yield the following pleasure-indication principle (PI):

(PI) For all subjects S and acts A: S's act A is morally justified only if there are some factors indicating that the act *itself* is pleasurable.

In contrast to (TI), (PI) is quite implausible. First of all, in the way (PI) is formulated, it is not even intelligible because, although a belief itself can be true or false, an act itself cannot be pleasurable or painful. Only the experiences a subject has in performing an act can be pleasurable or painful. Thus, the pleasure-indication principle has to be formulated slightly differently:

(PI)* For all subjects S and acts A: S's act A is morally justified only if there are some factors indicating that S's *experiences in performing* act A *itself* are pleasurable.

In this form, the pleasure-indication principle is intelligible, but none of the versions of hedonistic consequentialism characterized in section 2 is committed to (PI)*. Hedonistic consequentialists do not subscribe to (PI)* because the principle seems clearly false. It is obviously not a necessary condition for an action to

---

18 In a certain strand of Bayesian epistemology, known as epistemic utility theory, global and local epistemic aims are standardly differentiated (cf., e.g., Leitgeb and Pettigrew 2010). I am suggesting that an analogous distinction should be drawn within a binary model of belief as well. The global aim concerns our whole belief-set and consists in improving the balance of true over false beliefs within this set. The local aim concerns individual beliefs and can roughly be characterized as: Believe that *p* if and only if *p* is true. The idea is that by subscribing to (TI), achievements with respect to the global aim are in a certain sense mediated by achievements with respect to the local aim.

19 In the following quote, Carrie Ichikawa Jenkins claims that mediating positive global consequences via positive local consequences should be considered a constraint for plausible versions of epistemic consequentialism: "The basic thought is roughly that we shouldn't be able to establish that accepting S is epistemically rational just by establishing that such acceptance has optimal epistemic consequences *overall*, and without needing to make reference to *particular* epistemic goals we have with respect to S" (Jenkins 2007: 36).

count as morally justified that the agent experiences pleasure during the performance of this very action. Assume I am an incredibly penurious person, so that in donating money I literally experience pain. Is my action of donating money thereby condemned to be morally unjustified? Surely not. Thus, ethical consequentialists have very good reason to reject (PI)*.[20]

In contrast, incorporating (TI) into the epistemic consequentialist framework seems like an attractive move because, by subscribing to (TI), consequentialists can handle certain well-known and obvious counter-examples to crude versions of epistemic consequentialism.

Grant-Seeking. Person X, a brilliant virologist and an agnostic, is seeking to obtain a research grant from a religious organization. If she receives the funding, she will be able to continue her research, which will eventually allow her to form a great many true beliefs and to revise many previously held false beliefs about matters of great importance. However, the funding organization will only give grants to persons who believe in the existence of God. Given these circumstances, should X form the belief that God exists? Would such a belief be epistemically justified (cf. Fumerton 2001: 55)?

Prima facie, this case seems to be a counter-example to epistemic consequentialism. After all, X's belief in the existence of God would clearly be conducive to the aim of improving the balance of interesting true beliefs over false ones. However, pretheoretically it is quite implausible to judge the belief in question as justified.

By incorporating (TI) into the consequentialist framework, epistemic consequentialists can easily dismiss this case. Even though X's belief concerning the existence of God is in a certain sense conducive to the epistemic aim, it is not conducive to that aim in the right kind of way, i.e. in the way specified by (TI). There are no factors indicating that the proposition in question is true – in the example, X neither has available evidence for the existence of God, nor would X's belief forming method be particularly reliable. Thus, even though the belief is in a certain sense conducive to the epistemic aim, it is nevertheless epistemically unjustified.

---

20 One might think that (PI)* is only unattractive for someone rejecting egoistic versions of hedonistic consequentialism. However, that's not true. As long as S's act A will eventually lead to a greater balance of S's pleasurable experiences over her painful experiences, even egoist versions of consequentialism will usually allow that A might very well be justified, even though performing A is accompanied by some pain for S.

Counter-examples like these can be found in various places in the literature.[21] Before I localize the general lessons to be learned from these cases, let me introduce another very drastic one:

Truth-Fairy. Suppose a truth-fairy exists who guarantees that, if I believe that Lake Constance is filled with milk—a proposition I have many good reasons to think is false and that is, in fact, false—then she will arrange things in a way that all the other (and logically independent) beliefs I entertain now and in the future will be true. Given these circumstances, should I believe that Lake Constance is filled with milk? Would that belief be epistemically justified (cf. Jenkins 2007: 37)?

Again, my belief that Lake Constance is filled with milk is clearly conducive to the epistemic aim. However, pretheoretically it is overwhelmingly plausible to think that this belief would be epistemically unjustified. By incorporating (TI) into the consequentialist framework, epistemic consequentialists can dismiss this case. My belief that Lake Constance is filled with milk is not truth-conducive in the right kind of way, i.e. in the way specified by (TI). [22]

---

[21] For a list of references with similar uses of similar cases, see Berker 2013a: fn. 38.

[22] It should be noted that by incorporation of (TI) not all counter-examples to epistemic consequentialism can be dismissed. Two examples discussed by Berker still pose problems, namely the prime-number case (Berker 2013a: 375) and the John-Doe case (cf. Berker 2013b: 369; for a slightly modified version of the case, see p. 376). It could be argued that in both cases, beliefs are characterized that are not only conducive to the general epistemic goal; there are also certain factors indicating that the beliefs *themselves* are true. Nonetheless, in these cases we pretheoretically judge the beliefs in question as not being epistemically justified. Thus, consequentialists have to handle these cases differently. Simply incorporating (TI) into their framework will not allow resisting the pretheoretically implausible result with respect to these cases.

However, I am unsure whether this poses an insurmountable problem for consequentialists. In the context of this paper I can only hint at ways in which consequentialists could react to these cases. First, a general remark: By incorporating (TI) into the consequentialist framework, most counter-examples put forward in the literature can be dismissed, and the remaining counter-examples do not show that there is some deep structural problem with epistemic consequentialism. Rather, they show that some specific formulations of epistemic consequentialism are problematic.

The prime-number case (Berker 2013a: 375; 2013b: 374–375), for example, only establishes a problem for *reliabilist versions* of consequentialism. And in the face of other well-known problems and counter-examples, reliabilists have to enhance and modify their accounts anyway. As far as I can see, some of these modifications will allow them to get to grips with the prime-number case as well. Berker himself mentions one such modification: The reliabilist theory could be modified such that what matters with respect to the justificatory status of a belief is not just whether it is formed by a reliable process, but also whether there is an alternative reliable be-

There are two general lessons to be learned from considering these two counter-examples. Epistemic consequentialists claim that the epistemic evaluation of a belief that p depends on positive consequences of entertaining that belief with respect to the specified epistemic end. However, plausible versions of epistemic consequentialism have to satisfy the following constraints.

(a) *The Means-End Constraint.* The means-end relation of holding the justified belief that p and the specified epistemic aim of achieving a greater balance of true over false beliefs should be as close and direct as possible. It should not be remote (in the sense that it holds only due to many intermediary steps) or arbitrary.

(b) *The No-Trade-Off Constraint.* Trade-offs between epistemic goods with respect to different propositions that involve guaranteed epistemic sacrifices (however small they might be) should not be allowed. It should not be allowed that one knowingly makes epistemic sacrifices with respect to a belief that p to achieve a greater epistemic good with respect to beliefs in other propositions.[23]

---

lief-forming process available to the subject S that, had it been used, would have resulted in that belief's not being held (cf., Berker 2013a: fn. 55). Berker quickly dismisses this strategy for the simple reason that we can just stipulate that in the prime-number case at hand such an alternative process is *not* available to S. However, I am not sure whether this can really be reasonably stipulated. It seems right to suppose that as soon as S entertains the beliefs that n is a prime number for various n and thereby grasps the concept PRIME NUMBER, an alternative belief-forming method than the one described by Berker in his example is available to S that, had it been used, would have resulted in S's *not* believing that 7 is not a prime number.

As for the John-Doe-case, it has the same kind of structure: A person holds the belief that p, where this belief has positive epistemic consequences and there are also some factors indicating that the belief itself is true. Nevertheless, in considering the John-Doe-case we pretheoretically judge that the belief in question is unjustified. However, Berker admits that the person's belief is only obviously unjustified as long as we think that the person is *not aware* of the truth-indicative factors with respect to that belief. As soon as we suppose that she is aware of these factors, it is pretheoretically not so obvious anymore that the belief is unjustified. Thus, the case seems to rest on familiar internalistic intuitions. The case does not show that there is a general problem with the consequentialist framework, but rather that externalistic versions of such a framework are problematic.

23 Berker 2013a argues that the most pressing problem of epistemic consequentialism is its countenance of this kind of trade-off.

The importance of the first constraint is vividly illustrated by the grant-seeking case and the importance of the second by the truth-fairy example. The latter illustrates that, even in drastic cases where we only have knowingly to trade in one insignificant and uninteresting false belief to guarantee the truth of all other beliefs we have—beliefs that might be very important and interesting to us—we pretheoretically do not countenance these kind of epistemic trade-offs.

An epistemic consequentialist can easily meet these two constraints by incorporating (TI) in the consequentialist framework. First, incorporating (TI) ensures that the positive epistemic consequence of holding a justified belief with respect to the general epistemic aim is mediated by local positive epistemic consequences with respect to the justified belief itself. According to (TI), there have to be some factors that speak in favor of the truth of the justified belief either from a first- or a third-person perspective or both. The means-end relation between holding the belief and the epistemic aim of reaching a greater balance of true over false beliefs—either from a first- or a third-person perspective or both—is thereby not arbitrary and remote. Second, by incorporating (TI) into the epistemic consequentialist framework, the specified epistemic trade-offs are prevented.[24] (TI) prevents an epistemically inferior belief from counting as epistemically justified just because many other epistemically excellent beliefs are gained by holding this epistemically inferior belief. Thus, recourse to constraints (a) and (b) helps explain why (TI) is quite plausible within the framework of epistemic consequentialism.

We can also identify additional reasons based on this explanation, besides the one already given, as to why the analogue principle (PI)* in the ethical domain is implausible. Plausible versions of ethical consequentialism do not have to meet the ethical analogues to the epistemic constraints (a) and (b). First, it is implausible to think that the means-end relation between undertaking act A and the general aim of achieving a greater balance of pleasure over pain has to be spelled out so as to rule out many intermediary steps (cf., constraint (a)). My act of donating money is obviously not condemned to be morally unjustified just because this act leads to a greater balance of pleasure over pain only via many intermediary steps. Second, it is also implausible to suppose that every kind of trade-off in the ethical domain has to be prevented (cf. constraint (b)). On the contrary, it seems plausible to think that, in certain circumstances, painful experiences can be compensated for by many other pleasurable experiences. For example, if I could heal every suffering patient by pinching myself and my

---

[24] Other suggestions to prevent these trade-offs are discussed in Berker 2013b: 375–376 and Jenkins 2007: 36–40.

friend in the arm, this act of pinching could very well be morally justified. At least in drastic scenarios like this, where the sacrifice with respect to the specified aim is very small (a little pain for my friend and me) and the benefits gained very high (no actual and future pain for anybody else), it seems overwhelmingly plausible that trade-offs should not be prevented.[25]

So far we have seen that an important disanalogy between ethical and epistemic consequentialism lies in the fact that the latter position has to satisfy constraints (a) and (b), the former does not have to meet analogous constraints. We have also seen that epistemic consequentialists can meet these constraints by incorporating (TI) into their framework, whereas ethical consequentialists are well advised not to incorporate the analogous principle (PI)*. In the next section, I will consider the question of whether constraints (a) and (b) could also be met independent of (TI). Are epistemic consequentialists committed to (TI) or are there plausible versions of epistemic consequentialism that reject (TI), but nevertheless satisfy constraints (a) and (b)? If there were such a position, then the analogy between epistemic and ethical consequentialism would in a certain sense be stronger than one might think. It is true that, in contrast to ethical consequentialism, epistemic consequentialism has to satisfy constraints (a) and (b). However, if these constraints could be met independent of (TI), then just as hedonistic consequentialism in ethics is not committed to the pleasure-indication principle (PI)*, so veritistic consequentialism in epistemology would not be committed to the truth-indication principle (TI).

4. Epistemic Consequentialism Without the Truth-Indication Principle

With respect to many beliefs the truth-indication principle (TI) seems plausible. If, for example, my belief that it is raining right now is justified, then it seems plausible that this belief is justified through factors speaking in favor of its

---

[25] However, it is well known that countenancing trade-offs is also a source of serious problems of ethical consequentialism. After all, there are many cases where such trade-offs seem implausible (cf. Thomson 1976). This leads to one of the most serious challenges for consequentialist theories in ethics, namely restricting the aggregative element in the theory, so as to allow for some trade-offs but not for others. It should be clear, however, that this restriction cannot be achieved by incorporating (PI)* into the theory, because by incorporating (PI)* all trade-offs would be prevented across the board.

truth either from a first- or a third-person perspective or both. However, are there any exceptions to the principle? Is (TI) as a general principle correct?

If one rejects (TI), then one allows that there are at least some beliefs that are non-truth-indicatively justified, i.e. beliefs that are justified independently of factors speaking in favor of their truth. If veritistic consequentialists want to allow for such beliefs (thereby allowing for exceptions to the general principle (TI)) then they have to give satisfying answers to the following questions:[26]

(1) Which beliefs have a chance of being non-truth-indicatively justified?

(2) In which sense are non-truth-indicatively justified beliefs *epistemically* justified, i.e. in which sense are they conducive to our epistemic aim of improving the balance of (interesting) true beliefs over false ones?

(3) Is there a way to spell out the conduciveness of non-truth-indicatively justified beliefs towards the specified truth-aim that respects constraints (a) and (b)?

I will try to answer these questions based on some some ideas put forward by Ludwig Wittgenstein (1969), Michael Williams (1996: 121–134; 2001: 146–172), and most explicitly Crispin Wright (2004). These philosophers agree that beliefs in certain propositions have a special epistemic status, namely beliefs in presuppositions of scientific inquiries or cognitive projects.[27] I take this to be a promis-

---

[26] Note that non-veritistic epistemic consequentialists obviously have more resources to account for the existence of non-truth-indicatively justified beliefs than veritistic versions of consequentialism.

[27] Each of these philosophers can be interpreted as claiming that the special status of beliefs in presupposition of cognitive projects consists precisely in being candidates for beliefs that are justified independently of truth-indicative factors. However, in the context of this paper I will not defend this exegetical claim. It should be noted, though, that Wright's theory of entitlements is most explicit with respect to this point, even though he does not use the term "presuppositon" for the propositions in question anymore (Wright 2014, fn. 3). Wright specifies entitlement as a form of epistemic warrant that is independent of truth-indicative factors (cf. Wright 2004; 2014). However, it is unclear according to Wright's view whether the propositional attitude of *belief* is conceptually tied to truth-indicative factors, namely to reasons/evidence. Maybe it is conceptually impossible to believe that p without having any kind of evidence (broadly construed) in favor of p. Therefore, Wright only claims that one can be entitled to *accept* or *trust* p where the propositional attitudes of *acceptance* and *trust* are supposed to be not as closely tied to evidence as the attitude of belief (cf. Wright 2004: 175–178). In what follows, I will ignore this complication. I will assume that it is possible to entertain the propositional attitude of belief, even though there are no truth-indicative factors that speak in favor of the truth of the belief.

ing starting point to answer questions (1)–(3) satisfactorily. Beliefs in presuppositions of cognitive projects are candidates of non-truth-indicatively justified beliefs. However, questions (2) and (3) especially can only be answered satisfactorily if it is specified what cognitive projects are and what kind of presuppositions they make.

It is widely agreed that scientific inquiries and cognitive projects in general can be understood as attempts to formulate and answer questions (cf., Dewey 1938: 105; Hookway 1996: 7; Wright 2014: 215; etc.). If we accept that there is a close connection between cognitive projects and questions, then we might try to analyze the structure of cognitive projects by recourse to the semantics of questions. Perhaps the structure and presuppositions of a cognitive project can be clarified by analyzing the meaning of the question that in a certain sense constitutes the project. One approach to the semantics of questions is especially helpful in this respect, namely, a certain variant of the proposition-set theory. In subsection 4.1. I will introduce this theory. Fortunately for our purposes, introducing the basics of this theory will suffice. In subsection 4.2. I will then analyze the structure of cognitive projects via recourse to the introduced theory. Finally, in subsection 4.3 I will specify a version of consequentialism that allows for non-truth-indicatively justified beliefs and answer questions (1)–(3) on the basis of the results in 4.1. and 4.2.

4.1 The proposition-set theory of questions

Within truth-functional or possible-worlds semantics the meaning of a declarative sentence p is considered to be a function from possible worlds into the set of truth-values {true, false}. Because these functions are equivalent to sets of possible worlds in which p is true, the meaning of a declarative sentence p (i.e. the proposition expressed by the sentence p) is simply considered to be the set of worlds in which p is true.

Can this general idea be transferred to interrogative sentences?[28] Obviously, an interrogative sentence ?p is neither true nor false. Thus, its meaning cannot be identified with the set of worlds in which it is true. The basic idea guiding the proposition-set approach to interrogatives is: understanding the meaning of an interrogative sentence ?p amounts to knowing what counts as a possible answer to it. Thus, the meaning of ?p cannot be identified with a set of worlds in which

---

28 In what follows I will concentrate on direct questions and will not consider issues concerning embedded interrogatives.

?p is true but with a set of possible answers to ?p or, more precisely, with the set of meanings of possible and congruent answers. Because answers are taken to be the meanings of declarative sentences, the meaning of a question amounts to a set of propositions, i.e. a set of sets of worlds (cf., Hamblin 1958, 1973; Karttunen 1977; Gronendijk & Stokhof 1982, 1984, 1997).[29]

Take a look at the following interrogative sentence: "Who left the party?" For simplicity's sake, let us suppose that there is no possible world with more than two people, Maria and Joseph. Proposition-set theorists specify the meaning of "Who left the party?" as the set of congruent answer-propositions, i.e. the set of propositions expressed by the sentences: "Maria left the party", "Joseph left the party", "Maria and Joseph left the party", and "Nobody left the party". [30]

Note that the proposition expressed by the sentence "Maria left the party" does not exclude that Joseph left as well. However, the answer "Maria left the party" is in a certain sense incomplete if Joseph also left and the speaker knows that. This observation can be incorporated into the semantic framework by following Gronendijk and Stokhof's suggestion that answer-propositions form a mutually exclusive and complete partition of possible worlds (cf. Gronendijk & Stokhof 1984; 1997).[31] In such a system the meaning of "Who left the party?" divides a certain subspace of the space of possible worlds into non-overlapping cells that correspond to the propositions that only Maria left, that only Joseph left, that Maria and Joseph left, and that nobody left.

A complete answer to the question, "Who left the party?" corresponds to one cell of this partition and thereby excludes all the other cells. An incomplete or partial answer, however, does not exclude all cells except for one, but it does exclude at least one cell. In this sense, "Either Maria or Joseph left the party" con-

---

29 Please note that these authors spell out the specified general idea very differently.
30 An answer is not congruent if its meaning is not an element of the meaning of ?p. Take a look at our example: "Who left the party?" First, there are many sentences that would not even count as possible answers: e.g. "Berlin is the capital of Germany", "It's raining". To react to the question by uttering these sentences would be completely off the mark or would introduce some kind of implicature. Thus, the meanings of these sentences are obviously not elements of the meaning of the question. Second, there are other sentences that might constitute acceptable reactions to the question but still cannot be considered answers: e.g. "I do not know"; "I won't tell you". Thus, the meanings of these sentences are also not an element of the meaning of the question. Third, there are some sentences that can be considered answers, but not *congruent* answers: e.g. "Joseph left without his shoes"; "Either Joseph or Maria left". The first sentence constitutes an over-informative and the second an under-informative or incomplete answer to the question. I will come back to over-informative and incomplete answers in the main body of the text.
31 In his seminal paper on questions, Hamblin already suggested this option (cf., Hamblin 1958).

stitutes a partial answer insofar as it excludes that nobody left. Besides complete and partial answers, we can also specify over-informative answers, answers that are not complete though they imply a complete answer. Thus, the sentence, "Joseph left the party without his shoes" constitutes an over-informative answer.

Within such a framework, two kinds of presuppositions of questions can be differentiated, namely semantic and pragmatic presuppositions. By "semantic presupposition of a question" I mean a proposition that is implied by every complete answer-proposition (cf. Higginbotham 1996: 375). In our example, the proposition that there is a party taking place is a semantic presupposition of the question, "Who left the party?" Every complete answer-proposition implies that there is a party taking place. Thus, all worlds in which no party is taking place are excluded. This can be illustrated by the following figure (Fig.1). (Please note that square brackets are used to refer to the proposition that is expressed by the sentence inside the brackets.)

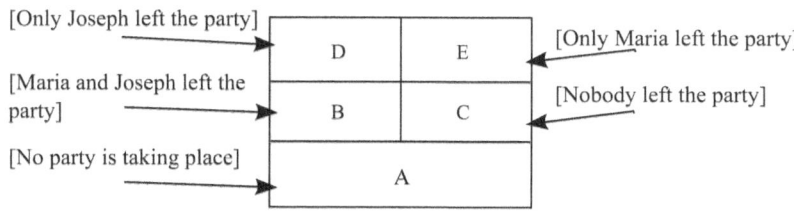

Fig. 1

The big rectangle that incorporates compartments A–E (each of which represents a set of worlds) symbolizes the space of all logically possible worlds. In a certain sense, the meaning of the question, "Who left the party?" divides this space into an answer-space and a presupposition-space. The answer-space is the exhaustive set of answer-propositions. It is divided into non-overlapping cells B–E, which together fill the whole answer-space. The presupposition space A includes all worlds that are excluded by the semantic presuppositions of the question, i.e. it includes all worlds in which no party is taking place. In more general terms, the presupposition-space can be characterized as the union of all propositions incompatible with the semantic presuppositions of the question.

Besides semantic presuppositions, we also need to introduce pragmatic presuppositions. Note that in some situations the sentence, "Maria's husband left the party", is just as good an answer as, "Joseph left the party". However, the propositions (the sets of worlds) that correspond to these two sentences are not identical. After all, there are some possible worlds in which Maria and Joseph are not married. Even though "Maria's husband left the party" and "Joseph left the party" are not equivalent, in the sense that these sentences do not express the same proposition, the sentences can nevertheless in certain circumstances constitute equally good answers to the given question. How is that possible?

Building on insights by Robert Stalnaker (1970, 1973), this can be explained by recourse to beliefs taken for granted by the participants of the conversation. Assume that all participants of a conversation take for granted that Maria and Joseph are married. Thus, all possible worlds in which they are not married are excluded in the sense that they are not an element of the sets of possible worlds that represent the doxastic sets of the participants. In this case the conversational impact of the answers, "Joseph left the party", and, "Maria's husband left the party", will be identical. This can be illustrated by the following figure (Fig. 2).

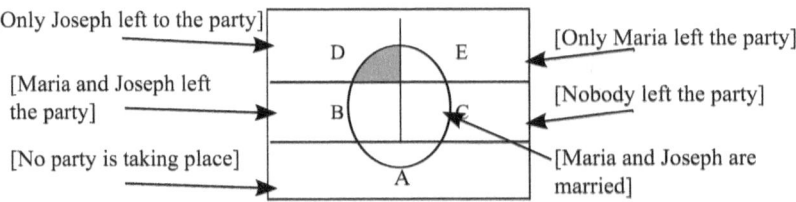

Fig. 2

The circle in the middle symbolizes the set of worlds in which Maria and Joseph are married, and thereby it symbolizes a belief taken for granted by the participants—i.e. all worlds in which they are not married (all worlds outside the circle) are excluded. Fig. 2 represents that the set of worlds in which Maria and Joseph are married contains elements of the sets A, B, C, D, and E. In some worlds in which Maria and Joseph are married, no party is taking place; in others a party is taking place and both left the party; still in others, nobody left, etc. If the participants of the conversation take for granted that Maria and Joseph are married, then the answers, "Joseph left the party", and, "Maria's husband left the party", will both correspond to the same set of worlds, namely, the set of worlds represented in Fig. 2 by the grey-tinted compartment representing the intersection of the propositions [Only Joseph left the party] and [Maria and Joseph are married]. Thus, by introducing pragmatic presuppositions and characterizing them as the set of beliefs taken for granted by the participants it can be explained why the answers, "Joseph left the party", and, "Maria's husband left the party", can in certain circumstances constitute equally complete and satisfying answers.

Gronendijk and Stokhof, therefore, relativize the meaning of questions on the set of beliefs taken for granted by the participants of a conversation (Gronendijk & Stokhoff 1984: 147–148). Let us call the union of the sets of possible worlds corresponding to the beliefs all participants take for granted the "context set". The meaning of an interrogative sentence ?p can then be specified as the partition of the context set into an exhaustive set of answer-propositions on the one hand and the union of all propositions incompatible with the semantic presuppositions of ?p on the other.

This characterization of questions and their semantic and pragmatic presuppositions will help us to specify the structure and presuppositions of cognitive projects, which in turn will allow us to spell out the idea that beliefs regarding the presuppositions of cognitive projects are promising candidates of non-truth-indicatively justified beliefs.

4.2 The Characterization of Cognitive Projects

Based on the proposition-set theory, we can spell out the idea that cognitive projects are closely related to questions in more detail.

What is a cognitive project? A cognitive project is an attempt to formulate and answer a question. The meaning of a question in the context of a cognitive project can be understood as a partition of the set of possible worlds along the lines of the proposition-set theory.[32] The meaning of the question gives the cognitive project its direction and goal. The goal of a cognitive project consists in identifying the complete and true answer to the question, thereby excluding all other possible answers.[33] [34]

---

[32] Please note that this does not presuppose that the proposition-set theory is correct as a semantic theory of interrogative sentences. Even if one thinks that the proposition-set theory is unconvincing as a semantic theory of everyday interrogative sentences, the theory could nevertheless be used as a tool to analyze the questions in the background of cognitive projects.

[33] This specification of the goal of a cognitive project is given from a veritistic perspective. After all, the given characterization of cognitive projects is supposed to lead to an interesting version of *veritistic* epistemic consequentialism that is not committed to (TI). All philosophers claiming that truth (or more precisely improving the balance of true over false beliefs) is not the only and not even the most important epistemic value will probably dismiss this specification of the goal of cognitive projects.

[34] Note that two cognitive projects described by interrogative sentences with the same wording might still be very different projects. This is because two interrogative sentences with the same

What does it mean to make progress within a cognitive project? One has made progress in a cognitive project if one (or more) of the following conditions are met: (i) the set of possible answers is identified (or at least some possible answers are identified); (ii) a true but incomplete answer is identified, i.e. at least one possible answer is excluded; or (iii) the true and complete answer is identified, i.e. all other possible answers are excluded.

Meeting condition (i) in a certain sense constitutes minimal progress within a project because by meeting (i) only the meaning of the question (i.e. the set of possible congruent answers) that constitutes the project in the first place is clarified. Meeting condition (iii) constitutes maximal progress within a cognitive project because by meeting (iii) the project is successfully concluded.

The given characterization of a cognitive project makes it reasonable to regard such a project as a systematic attempt to achieve the epistemic aim of improving the balance of interesting true beliefs over false ones. Particularly in light of the double character of this aim, performing a cognitive project seems to be one of the most attractive means available to achieve this aim. In light of the double character of the epistemic goal, we are supposed to strive for increasing the number of interesting true beliefs (beliefs in the truth of which we are interested), but we have to strive for them in a way that simultaneously avoids false beliefs. This is exactly what we do during the performance of a cognitive project. First, we ask for something of interest to us. Second, we try to clarify the meaning of the question by clarifying what would count as a possible answer to it. Third, we systematically check each possible answer and dismiss it if it is false. In the best case, we will conclude such a project by having identified the one and only true and complete answer to the question we are interested in.

What are presuppositions of a cognitive project? The presuppositions of a cognitive project are the semantic and pragmatic presuppositions of the question constituting the project. Semantic presuppositions are the propositions implied by all complete answers to the question constituting the project. Pragmatic presuppositions are the beliefs taken for granted by all people engaged in the project, or more precisely: the propositions the truth of which is taken for granted by the participants of a project.

The latter presuppositions have two important functions. First, remember that the meaning of a question is specified as the partition of the context set. Thus, the propositions the truth of which is taken for granted by the participants of a cognitive project in part determine the meaning of the question that defines

---

wording can have a very different meaning, i.e. they can partition the set of possible worlds very differently.

the structure and direction of the project. Second, pragmatic presuppositions of a cognitive project will specify in which circumstances a possible answer qualifies as being excluded. It will thereby in part determine in what circumstances progress within a project is achieved. Suppose Sherlock Holmes and Dr. Watson are engaged in a cognitive project specified by the question, "Who committed the murder?" They systematically check the possibly correct answers: "the gardener committed the murder", "the chauffeur committed the murder", etc. Let us suppose that both believe that, if a person has been a thousand miles away from the crime scene at the time of the murder, then that person did not commit the murder. The content of this conditional belief is part of the context set i.e. it is a pragmatic presupposition of the question that defines the project. It is obvious that this pragmatic presupposition will determine under which circumstances Holmes and Watson are in a position to exclude a possible answer, thereby making progress in their project.

When is a cognitive project hopeless or irrational? If the presuppositions of a cognitive project imply that no progress within a project can be made or if the presuppositions are contradictory, then the cognitive project is hopeless or irrational.

4.3 Cognitive Projects and Non-Truth-Indicatively Justified Beliefs

Based on the characterization of cognitive projects given in subsection 4.2, we can spell out a version of veritistic epistemic consequentialism that allows for non-truth-indicatively justified beliefs and is therefore not committed to (TI) in its general form. At the beginning of section 4, we saw that veritistic consequentialists who want to allow for non-truth-indicatively justified beliefs have to give satisfying answers to questions (1)–(3).

Question (1): Which beliefs have a chance of being non-truth-indicatively justified?
The beliefs in presuppositions of cognitive projects that are neither hopeless nor irrational are candidates for being non-truth-indicatively justified beliefs; i.e. a belief in presuppositions of such a project has a chance of being justified independently from truth-indicative factors speaking in favor of the truth of the belief itself. (Thus, these beliefs constitute possible exceptions to (TI)). Please note that the candidates for non-truth-indicatively justified beliefs are restricted to beliefs in presuppositions of projects that are neither hopeless nor irrational; the presuppositions of any old cognitive project will not do. Note also that beliefs in presuppositions of such projects are only candidates of non-truth-indicatively justi-

fied beliefs. Actually to count as non-truth-indicatively justified, these beliefs have to satisfy further conditions, as explained below.

Question (2): In which sense are non-truth-indicatively justified beliefs epistemically justified, i.e. in which sense are they conducive to our epistemic aim of improving the balance of (interesting) true beliefs over false ones? The given characterization of cognitive projects has revealed that a cognitive project can be considered a systematic quest to achieve the epistemic goal of increasing the number of intersting true beliefs while at the same time avoiding false ones. In fact, engaging in cognitive projects seems to be one of the best means available to achieve this goal. Because beliefs in the presuppositions of cognitive projects are necessary to perform the projects—as the presuppositions constitute the structure and direction of these projects in the first place—and performing these projects in turn seem to be one of the best systematic means available to achieve the specified epistemic goal, beliefs in the presuppositions of cognitive projects are conducive to our epistemic goal.[35]

However, please note that this is only true from a first-person perspective. It is not guaranteed that performing a cognitive project, which was made possible by holding certain presuppositions to be true, actually leads to a greater balance of interesting true beliefs over false ones. However, subjects engaged in such projects expect and intend that this is the case. Indeed, one of the main reasons subjects are engaged in cognitive projects is that by performing these projects they intend to dismiss false answers and eventually find the complete true answer to a question in which they are interested. Thus, the envisaged veritistic consequentialist position that does not subscribe to the truth-indicative principle (TI) is a variant of subjective consequentialism insofar as not the actual consequences of holding a non-truth-indicatively justified belief, but rather the consequences intended and expected by the subject are relevant.

Question (3): Is there a way to spell out the conduciveness of non-truth-indicatively justified beliefs towards the specified epistemic goal that respects constraints (a) and (b)? The conduciveness of non-truth-indicatively justified beliefs towards the epistemic goal is spelled out in a way that meets the means-end relation (see constraint (a)). Believing the presuppositions of a cognitive project is a nec-

---

[35] This answer can also be considered an answer to an important challenge raised with respect to Wright's theory of entitlement, namely the challenge to specify in which sense "entitlement" is is an epistemic notion rather than a purely pragmatic one (cf. Pritchard 2007: 207; Jenkins 2007: 27). Wright's own answer to this challenge proceeds broadly along similar lines (cf. Wright 2014: 238–239).

essary means to perform such a cognitive project, and performing such a project, in turn, seems to be one of the best means available to achieve the specified epistemic goal. Thus, the means-end relation between holding a non-truth-indicatively justified belief in the presuppositions of cognitive projects and the specified epistemic aim is neither arbitrary nor remote.

What about the no-trade-off constraint (see constraint (b))? This constraint demands that it should not be allowed that we knowingly make epistemic sacrifices with respect to a belief in p to achieve a greater epistemic good with respect to beliefs in other propositions. The truth-fairy example vividly illustrates the importance of this constraint. By subscribing to (TI), epistemic consequentialists can ensure that this constraint is met. However, it is unclear whether the envisaged consequentialist position that rejects (TI) and allows that beliefs in presuppositions of cognitive projects are non-truth-indicatively justified satisfies the constraint as well. The easiest way to make sure that the envisaged position satisfies constraint (b) consists in adding further conditions for non-truth-indicatively justified beliefs. Thus, the envisaged account should be modified and extended along the following lines:

S's belief that p is non-truth-indicatively justified if and only if

(I) p is a presupposition of one of S's cognitive projects that is neither hopeless nor irrational;
(II) the body of evidence E available to S does not make it likely that not-p;
...

Condition (I) ensures that non-truth-indicatively justified beliefs are conducive to the epistemic aim in a way that satisfies the means-ends relation (a). Condition (II) ensures that the no-trade-off constraint (b) is met as well. Condition (II) ensures that one cannot gain a non-truth-indicatively justified belief by knowingly making epistemic sacrifices with respect to a belief in a certain proposition to achieve a greater epistemic good with respect to beliefs in other propositions. Thus, even though the proposed variant of veritistic epistemic consequentialism is not committed to (TI), it nevertheless satisfies constraints (a) and (b).

The dots in the definition indicate that the account could easily be extended by further conditions (III), (IV), etc. Conditions (I) and (II) already seem to suffice to circumvent all counter-examples against epistemic consequentialism put forward in the literature. However, conditions (I) and (II) by themselves still seem too permissive, insofar as they probably make it too easy to have a non-truth-indicatively justified belief. In order to respond to this problem, it might become necessary to extend the definition by further conditions.[36][37]

As far as the definition in its current form goes, a promising example of a non-truth-indicatively justified belief is the belief that my senses work reliably. The proposition that my senses are working reliably is unquestionably a presupposition of many of my cognitive projects that are neither hopeless nor irrational, and the body of evidence available to me does not make it likely that this proposition is false.[38]

In summary, the specified version of epistemic consequentialism has the following features. First, it is veritistic insofar as it claims that beliefs can be epistemically evaluated by recourse to the specified truth-goal. More precisely, it holds that, if a belief is epistemically justified, then holding the belief is conducive to the aim of increasing the number of interesting true beliefs and simultaneously avoiding false beliefs. Second, the position is non-truth-indicative insofar as it allows that at least some beliefs are justified independently of truth-indicative factors' speaking in favor of the truth of the beliefs themselves. Third, the position is subjective insofar as – at least with respect to non-truth-indicatively justified beliefs – not the actual consequences of holding the belief are epistemically relevant, but rather the consequences the subject intends or reasonably expects.[39] Engaging in a cognitive project does not guarentee that the balance of true over false beliefs is improved. However, epistemic agents expect that this is the case, the only reason why they engage in these kind of projects is because they intend to make headway with respect to the aim of increasing the number of interesting true beliefs while at the same time avoiding false ones. Fourth, even though the position rejects (TI) as a general principle, it neverthe-

---

36 Of course, the definition of "non-truth-indicative justification" cannot be extended by conditions demanding truth-indicative factors (i.e. evidence for the belief or the reliability of the belief-forming process). Otherwise, it would not be a definition of *non-truth-indicative* justification.
37 Building on Wright's theory of epistemic entitlement, we could, for example, add the following condition: (III) any attempt to justify *p* by evidence would be epistemically circular insofar as it would involve something of no more secure standing than *p* itself (cf. Wright 2004: 191–192).
38 Please note that, even if we add condition (III) to the definition of non-truth-indicative justification (see fn.36), the belief that my senses work reliably would still seem like a promising example of a non-truth-indicatively justified belief. It seems plausible that my belief that my senses work reliably cannot be justified *a priori*. However, any attempt to justify the belief by empirical evidence seems to be epistemically circular insofar as it would presuppose that my senses work reliably. Therefore, the belief in question seems to satisfy condition (III) as well.
39 Whether the same is true for truth-indicatively justified beliefs as well is left open by the suggested version of non-truth-indicative epistemic consequentialism.

less satisfies the means-end constraint (see constraint (a)) and the no-trade-off constraint (see constraint (b)).

5. Concluding Remarks

The results of the discussion can be summarized as follows: Veritistic epistemic consequentialism is structurally analogous to hedonistic consequentialism in ethics. Both variants of consequentialism explicate normative notions via recours to final values and ultimate goals in their respective domains. Furthermore, consequentialism in both domains can be spelled out in a direct or indirect and a subjective or objective version (see. Sect. 2).

Besides these similarities, there are also important dissimilarities. One difference consists in the fact that the former has to meet the means-end constraint (see constraint (a)) and the no-trade-off constraint (see constraint (b)), whereas the latter does not have to satisfy analogous constraints in the ethical domain. Epistemic consequentialists can ensure that their theory meets the specified constraints by incorporating the truth-indication principle (TI) into their consequentialist framework, i.e. by claiming that a belief is epistemically justified only if there are factors indicating the truth of the belief itself. This is why popular versions of epistemic consequentialism subscribe to (TI), whereas popular versions of ethical consequentialism do not subscribe to an analogous pleasure-indication principle (PI)* (see Sect. 3).

However, building on ideas suggested by Wittgenstein, Williams, and most explicitly by Wright, a version of veritistic epistemic consequentialism can be defended that rejects (TI) as a general principle, but is nevertheless able to satisfy constraints (a) and (b). The basic thought is roughly that beliefs in presuppositions of cognitive projects can be justified independently of factors speaking in favor of their truth. Nonetheless, these beliefs can be epistemically justified in the sense that they are conducive to our epistemic aim of improving the overall balance of (interesting) true beliefs over false ones – at least from a first-person perspective. Combining the idea that a cognitive project is an attempt to answer a question with the proposition-set theory allows one to specify this basic thought in more detail. Furthermore, this combination delivers the resources to spell out the conduciveness of non-truth-indicatively justified beliefs regarding the specified epistemic aim in a way that respects constraints (a) and (b) (see Sect. 4).

Thus, even though the truth-indication principle (TI) seems plausible for many beliefs, veritistic consequentialists can allow for exceptions to the principle without thereby violating constraints (a) and (b). Hence, just as hedonistic consequentialism in ethics is not committed to the pleasure-indication principle

(PI)*, so veritistic consequentialism in epistemology is not committed to the truth-indication principle (TI).[40]

References

Alston, W. P. (1989). *Epistemic Justification: Essays in the Theory of Knowledge*. Ithaca (NY): Cornell University Press.

Alston, W. P. (2005). *Beyond "Justification": Dimensions of Epistemic Evaluation*. Ithaca (NY): Cornell University Press.

Berker, S.(2013a). Epistemic Teleology and the Separateness of Propositions. *Philosophical Review* 122: 337–392.

Berker, S. (2013b). The Rejection of Epistemic Consequentialism. *Philosophical Issues* 23: 363–387.

BonJour, L. (1985). *The Structure of Empirical Knowledge*. Cambridge (MA): Harvard University Press.

BonJour, L. (2003). A Version of Internalist Foundationalism. In L. Bonjour and E. Sosa, *Epistemic Justification: Internalism vs. Externalism, Foundations vs. Virtues*. Malden (MA): Blackwell.

Conee, E. (1992). The Truth Connection. *Philosophy and Phenomenological Research* 52: 657–669.

Dewey, J. (1938). *Logic – The Theory of Inquiry*. New York: Holt, Rinehart and Winston.

Feldman, R. (2000). The Ethics of Belief. *Philosophy and Phenomenological Research* 92: 1–24.

Foley, R. (1987). *The Theory of Epistemic Rationality*. Cambridge (MA): Harvard University Press.

Foley, R. (1993). *Working without a Net: A Study in Egocentric Epistemology*. Oxford: Oxford University Press.

Fumerton, R. (2001). Epistemic Justification and Normativity. In M. Steup (ed.), *Knowledge, Truth, and Duty*. Oxford: Oxford University Press.

Goldman, A. (1979). What is Justified Belief? In G. Pappas (ed.), *Justification and Knowledge*. Dordrecht: Reidel.

Goldman, A. (1986). *Epistemology and Cognition*. Cambridge (MA): Harvard University Press.

Goldman, A. (2001). The Unity of the Epistemic Virtues. In A. Fairweather and L. Zagzebski (eds.), *Virtue Epistemology: Essays on Epistemic Virtue and Responsibility*. Oxford: Oxford University Press.

Grimm, S. (2008). Epistemic Goals and Epistemic Values. *Philosophy and Phenomenological Research* 77: 725–744

Grimm, S. (2009). Epistemic Normativity. In A. Haddock, A. Millar, and D. Pritchard (eds.), *Epistemic Value*. Oxford: Oxford University Press.

---

40 For their interesting, very helpful, and challenging comments, I want to thank John Allkemper, Arno Goebel, Brendan Balcerak Jackson, Selim Berker, Catherine Elgin, Dina Emundts, Amber Griffioen, Thorsten Helfer, Susanne Mantel, Jacob Rosenthal, Joshua Schechter, and Pedro Schmechtig.

Groenendijk, J. and Stokhof, M. (1982). Semantic Analysis of Wh-Complements. *Linguistics and Philosophy* 5: 1752–33.
Groenendijk, J. and Stokhof, M. (1984). On the Semantics of Questions and the Pragmatic of Answers. In F. Landman and F. Veltman (eds.), *Varieties of Formal Semantics*. Dordrecht: Foris.
Groenendijk, J. and Stokhof, M. (1997). Questions. In J. van Bentham and A. ter Meulen (eds.), *Handbook of Logic and Language*. Amsterdam: Elsevier.
Haddock, Adrian, Millar, Alan, and Pritchard, Duncan (ed.) (2009): *Epistemic Value*. Oxford: Oxford University Press.
Hamblin, C. L. (1958). Questions. *Australasian Journal of Philosophy* 36: 159–168.
Hamblin, C. L. (1973). Questions in Montague Grammar. *Foundations of Language* 10: 41–53.
Higginbotham, J. (1996). The Semantics of Questions. In S. Lappin (ed.), *The Handbook of Contemporary Semantic Theory*. Oxford: Blackwell.
Hookway, C. (1996). Questions of Context. *Proceedings of the Aristotelian Society*, 96: 1–16.
James, W. (1897). The Will to Believe. In *The Will to Believe and Other Essays in Popular Philosophy*. New York: Dover.
Jenkins, C. S. (2007). Entitlement and Rationality. *Synthese* 157: 25–45.
Karttunen, L. (1977). Syntax and Semantics of Questions. *Linguistics and Philosophy* 1: 3–44.
Kvanvig, J. (2005). Truth is not the Primary Epistemic Goal. In M. Steup and E. Sosa (eds.), *Contemporary Debates in Epistemology*. Malden (MA): Blackwell.
Lehrer, K. (1974). *Knowledge*. Oxford: Oxford University Press.
Leitgeb, H. and Pettigrew, R. (2010): An Objective Justification of Bayesianism I: Measuring Inaccuracy. *Philosophy of Science* 77: 201–235.
Littlejohn, C. (2012). *Justification and the Truth-Connection*. Cambridge: Cambridge University Press.
Pritchard, D. (2007). Wittgenstein's *On Certainty* and Contemporary Anti-Scepticism. In D. Moyal-Sharrock and W. Brenner (eds.): *Readings of Wittgenstein's On Certainty*. Basingstoke: Palgrave Macmillan.
Rawls, J. (1971). *A Theory of Justice*. Cambridge (MA): Harvard University Press.
Sinnott-Armstrong, W. (2014). Consequentialism. In E. N. Zalta (ed.), *The Stanford Encyclopedia of Philosophy* (Spring 2014 Edition), URL = <http://plato.stanford.edu/archives/spr2014/entries/consequentialism/>.
Stalnaker, R. (1970). Pragmatics. *Synthese* 22: 272–289.
Stalnaker, R. (1973). Presuppositions. *Journal of Philosophical Logic* 2: 447–457.
Thomson, J. J. (1976). Killing, Letting Die, and the Trolley Problem. *The Monist* 59: 204–217.
Williams, M. (1996). *Unnatural Doubts*. Princeton: Princeton University Press.
Williams, M. (2001). *Problems of Knowledge*. Oxford: Oxford University Press.
Wittgenstein, L. (1996). *On Certainty*. Oxford: Blackwell.
Wright, C. (2004). On Epistemic Entitlement: Warrant for Nothing (and Foundations for Free). *Aristotelian Society Supplementary* 78: 167–212.
Wright, C. (2014). On Epistemic Entitlement (II) – Welfare State Epistemology. In D. Dodd and E. Zardini (eds.), *Scepticism and Perceptual Justification*. Oxford: Oxford University Press.

Christian Piller
How to Overstretch the Ethics-Epistemology Analogy: Berker's Critique of Epistemic Consequentialism

1. Introduction

Should we punish the innocent? Some consequentialists answer, it depends. It depends on how much good may come from punishing the innocent and on much how much bad it may prevent. Anti-consequentialists disagree. They tell us not to punish the innocent. An innocent person has done nothing wrong. So we cannot punish her. The benefits others might receive from such punishment are simply irrelevant.

In this paper, I won't argue for this view. It is, I think, a most reasonable view. The question I will pursue is whether this view, anti-consequentialism in ethics, does teach us anything about epistemology.

Compare the following example. Start with some unreasonable view, like the belief that illness is punishment for one's sin. According to this view, if you have a headache, you suffer for your impure thoughts, and if you have AIDS you suffer for your unnatural inclinations. Should we believe that illness is punishment for one's sins? An epistemic consequentialist may answer, it depends. It depends on how much epistemic good may come from holding this view. And like above, many will disagree with such a consequentialist. Even if believing that illness is punishment for one's sins happens to be, for some reason, an entrance ticket to the discovery of important truths in some other domain, this epistemic benefit regarding other truths does not make holding the view reasonable. Like above, how the belief in question affects our other epistemic endeavours is simply irrelevant for whether it can be reasonably held.

We all agree, I assume, on the two normative facts in play. It is wrong to punish the innocent. And it is unreasonable to believe that illness is punishment for one's sins. Selim Berker has argued that these normative facts receive analogous explanations. The ethical consequentialist goes wrong when he claims that benefits to others can outweigh the harms inflicted on the innocent. As Rawls (1971, 26f.) has put it, such thinking would violate the separateness of persons. (I will say a bit more about how to understand this point later on.) The epistemic consequentialist goes wrong when he claims that epistemic benefits in one domain justify epistemic harms in another domain. As Berker has put it, epistemic consequentialism violates the separateness of propositions.

In this paper I will argue that the idea to appeal to 'the separateness of propositions' is misguided. Although there is a sense in which we should consider each proposition 'on its own merits', this has nothing to do with the reasons we find in the ethical realm to treat people 'as individuals'.

2. An Implausible Starting Point

If we want to draw a parallel between the separateness of persons and the separateness of propositions, we need to ask what is meant by those who demand that we treat people as individuals. It could mean that we need to be able to justify what we do to each affected person individually, i.e. by considering the effects our actions have on each person.[1] Let us assume that this is what anti-consequentialists have in mind when they urge us to treat people as individuals, i.e. separately and not as collective. Their claim is a claim about how we ought to relate to each other and, though, it may go beyond our species and encompass all agents, human or otherwise, it won't apply to other kinds of things. For example, we don't need to treat grains of sand or grains of sugar as individuals. Whatever it is that marks out humans as a source of obligations in whatever way – and different ethical theories will focus on very different aspects – we certainly won't find it in grains of any kind. Neither, I want to suggest, will we find what makes humans objects of legitimate moral concern in propositions. Propositions are nothing like people. They don't cry out to me or put me in some other way under the obligation to consider them, to believe or disbelieve them, whether separately or jointly. In contrast to people, who can hold me to account, propositions are not the kind of thing that could have any normative hold on me.[2]

Are we not, one might ask, sometimes obliged to think of or consider this or that? When, for example, I promise my friend Karl to read his paper, I ought to consider his ideas, i.e. the bunch of propositions that he endorses in his paper. In examples like these I ought to consider ideas with the required care because I owe it to Karl. I owe nothing, it seems to me, to the propositions he has asked me to think about.

---

1 For the development of this idea see Scanlon (1998).
2 For the purposes of this paper, we don't need to consider whether some normative propositions, namely true ones, are an exception to this general claim. Berker's analogy is not restricted to either normative propositions or to true ones.

To be fair, Berker's idea that we ought to respect the separateness of propositions doesn't entail that the source of this obligation are propositions. I have explained why such an idea would be implausible not in order to provide a master objection to his view, rather to urge for care when we try to find epistemological analogues of moral principles. In the ethical case, it is a reasonable view that each of us deserves our respect. Every person could raise legitimate complaints about what we do and these complaints matter. In the epistemic case, it is not a reasonable view that each proposition deserves our respect or would have a complaint about how we relate to it. So, initially, there is not much plausibility in such a parallel. Berker fails to consider the initial implausibility of the parallel he invokes. Let us look more closely at his ideas in order to find out whether he is able to undermine our initial scepticism.

3. Berker's Project

I will start my discussion by presenting Berker's general project. Consequentialism, in ethics, is a family of ethical theories to be distinguished from deontology on the one side and virtue theory on the other. A rough and ready first formulation of what distinguishes consequentialism from its alternatives is the following structural claim: the good, whatever it is, determines in some way or other what we ought to do. In other words, the evaluative determines the deontic.[3] Here is a simple example of a consequentialist view. Pain is bad, so we ought not to bring it about (neither in ourselves nor in others.) In general, we ought to do what makes the world as good as possible. Consequentialism, in epistemology, is likewise a family of theories about what we ought (or are allowed) to believe. It is called consequentialism because it incorporates the same structural idea. We start with an evaluative claim like that believing truly is a good thing and believing falsely is a bad thing. On this basis we argue that we ought to conduct our epistemic lives in ways such that we believe lots of (important) truths and try not to go wrong too often. As it stands this might sound innocent enough but, according to Berker, it is a devil in disguise and we know already why Berker thinks so: it violates the separateness of propositions.

Berker starts his paper 'Epistemic Teleology and the Separateness of Propositions' (Berker 2013a) by highlighting the common normative character of both

---

[3] I will stick with this rough and ready formulation because here is not the place to debate the nature of consequentialism. For a discussion of different ways to separate consequentialism form its rivals see, for example, Pettit (1997) or Brown (2011).

ethics and epistemology. 'What should I do?' and 'What should I believe?' are, he claims, analogous questions. He previews his paper as follows.

> I want to use this analogy between normative evaluations of actions and normative evaluations of beliefs to tease out, and then argue against, a certain strain of thought that seems to have become an article of faith in much recent epistemological theorizing. According to this strain of thought, what distinguishes epistemic norms from other sorts of norms [...] is that epistemic norms are guided by a distinctive set of 'epistemic' or 'cognitive' or 'intellectual' goals. [...]regardless of what the list of epistemic goals looks like, the guiding idea behind this strain of thought is that all other normative notions in epistemology are ultimately explicable in terms of how well the objects of assessment conduce toward, promote, or otherwise subserve these epistemic goals. (Berker 2013a, 339)

Here Berker talks about epistemic goals, later on he uses the notion of the epistemic good. The idea is the same: contemporary epistemology sees the aim of reaching truth and avoiding falsehood (or, alternatively, the idea that truly believing is a good thing and falsely believing a bad thing) as the basis on which to understand other epistemological notions. This priority of the evaluative over the deontic is what we identified as the defining feature of consequentialism. When it falls, much of contemporary epistemology, Berker suggests, will fall with it. 'I want to convince you', he says, 'that this consequentialist/teleological approach to normative epistemology is positively misguided' (Berker 2013a, 339) and later on he says that this 'teleological approach to normative epistemology is overwhelmingly the dominant view' (Berker 2013a, 351).

Consequentialism allows for trade-offs and some trade-offs are morally suspect. Think of trade-offs that would protect many people from some small harm by imposing a big burden on one person. By adding up the small harms which threaten the many we might cross the threshold set by the big burden. However, according to common-sense morality, it is usually no justification for imposing serious harm on someone that many people receive small benefits (by being protected from a small harm). If the many people were one person and so we would face a choice of imposing a big burden on one person or an even bigger burden on someone else, the lesser size of burden can be decisive. In the situation we face, however, in which there isn't one person who has to carry the whole sum of all the small harms, imposing the burden on the one to benefit the many is, according to commonly held views, impermissible. A utilitarian who thinks otherwise has made a mistake. He sees the situation as if the many could be treated as one big individual and thus he fails to respect the normative principle which Rawls has called 'the separateness of persons'.

At first sight, the example with which I started – namely that believing that illness is a punishment would open up truths in a different domain – seems to fit this bill. We sacrifice one belief for adopting many new ones. Berker's latest paper on this issue (Berker 2015) has 'Cutting up the One to Save the Five in Epistemology' in its title. He thinks that epistemologists of a consequentialist bend are committed to endorsing such sacrifices.

> [...] if the consequentialist/teleological approach to normative epistemology were the correct one, we'd expect that the correct theory of what we should believe would also countenance trade-offs between goods – in this case, trade-offs between epistemic goods. However, no one – not even those epistemologists who most willingly embrace the consequentialist/teleological framework – is willing to countenance all such trade-offs in the epistemic case. (Berker 2013a, 340)

Let us get clearer about the kind of argument Berker aims to put forward.

4. Two Ways of Pursuing Berker's Project

One kind of argument – for future reference I call it strategy 1 – would emphasise an unreasonable commitment on the part of the epistemic consequentialist. Everyone agrees that, given the evidence available, it would be unreasonable to believe that illness is punishment (even if it opens doors to new knowledge). However, on this line of argument, one tries to show that, regardless of their official denial, epistemic consequentialists are nevertheless committed to telling us that we ought to believe that illness is punishment on the basis of its epistemic benefits in other domains. This commitment, according to our strategy 1 argument, arises from the very nature of consequentialist thought. If we think about epistemic normativity in terms of how best to achieve our end of having a true picture of the world (at least in respect to the parts we are interested in), then, on these consequentialist lines, we should believe that illness is punishment because, by assumption, doing so would open our minds to new and important insights. We lose at one end, in our understanding of illness, but, by assumption, we gain much more in some other area. Overall our aim of understanding the world would be better achieved by adopting this unusual belief. Epistemic consequentialists want to be on our side, i.e. they want to say that seeing illness as punishment would be ridiculous, but the aim-directed nature of their approach commits them to saying what they do not want to say. This is the direction of what I call strategy 1. It could take its inspiration from familiar attempts to show that rule-utilitarianism has to collapse back into act-utilitarianism, or that it is a form of rule-fetishism that, thereby, is inconsistent with its outward commitment that only truth matters in the epistemic domain.[4]

Berker does not take this line. In order to understand the other line of argument, which is the one he actually takes and which I call strategy 2, we have to remember that consequentialism is a family of theories – just think about the differences between act-, rule-, and motive-utilitarianism. The epistemic analogue of act-utilitarianism has the implausible consequence of condoning our unreasonable illness-belief. This, for Berker, is why epistemic consequentialists have moved away from it. Berker says that examples of the kind illustrated here by the illness-belief and its epistemic benefits, is a counterexample only 'to extremely crude versions of epistemic consequentialism' (Berker 2015, 145). The epistemic consequentialist becomes more and more sophisticated and, thus, is not committed to thinking that the illness-belief is reasonable. Berker's project is to follow the development of consequentialism by adapting his counterexample to the ever new versions of consequentialism. In all these developments he has to focus on the structural features of epistemic consequentialism that allow the development and construction of counterexamples. In Berker (2013a) it is, as the title of the paper suggests, the violation of the separateness of propositions. In Berker (2013b, m8), he identifies 'epistemic-value conducivism' as the structural feature that makes consequentialism vulnerable to counterexamples. 'The problem with truth-conducivism', he says there, 'is that it is a form of epistemic-value conducivism, and conducivism of any sort is the wrong way to think about epistemic normativity.' I will clarify the idea of truth-conducivism in a moment. In Berker (2015), he explains his argumentative strategy as follows.

> The basic idea is to argue that all interesting forms of epistemic consequentialism condone (or mandate) the epistemic analogue of cutting up one innocent person in order to use the organs to save the lives of five people. The difficult part is figuring out exactly what the epistemic analogue of cutting up the one to save the five consists in. (Berker 2015, 145)

So we have to ask Berker, what is the objectionable structural feature of epistemic consequentialism? He reminds us that in (2013a) he thought it was the violation of the separateness of propositions and in (2013b) it was something more general, like truth-conducivism. He still has not reached a definitive answer. 'But', he says, 'that won't matter for the purposes of this note [which is to reject Goldman's views]: all the theories I will be considering flout the separateness of

---

[4] See Hooker (2000) for a discussion of such objections. Hooker's replies, for example his distinction between complying with a rule and accepting a rule, have not yet received much discussion in the epistemological literature.

propositions, so there will be no need to go beyond my initial diagnosis.' (Berker 2015, 146)

Berker's analysis of what goes wrong in epistemic consequentialism does not, at this point, look satisfactory. If only the most primitive forms of epistemic consequentialism are vulnerable to our counterexample and this example shows why it is important to respect the separateness of propositions, then more sophisticated forms of epistemic consequentialism, which won't be shaken by this example, need to fail for a different reason. There need to be a different structural feature of consequentialism which allows us to criticise its more sophisticated epistemic forms. The only principle Berker offers is what he calls truth-conducivism. I will follow his lead and explore this idea.

5. What Is Wrong With Truth-Conducivism?

Take an example of a self-fulfilling belief, i.e. a belief about something that is more likely to become true when so believed. If you wholeheartedly believe that you have the abilities that will bring you success, this very fact of believing makes it more likely that you will succeed. Success is, on this kind of view, often a matter of self-confidence. Berker (2013b, m18) gives an example in which an agent, he calls her Jane, believes that she will recover from an illness when this very believing makes what is believed more likely to be true. If you want to reach a true belief about some issue that concerns you, like whether you will recover, and one option – to believe that you will recover – has a tendency for self-fulfilment, could you adopt this belief on this basis? According to Berker, the epistemic consequentialist for whom only truth matters fundamentally – Berker calls this person a 'veritist' – needs to say, yes. But Berker insists that self-fulfilling beliefs are not justified by their potential for self-fulfilment.

> Now we are at the heart of the matter. Jane's belief makes it the case that she is more likely to have something which veritism deems to be epistemically good as an end in itself. But I take it to be obvious that her belief is not thereby epistemically justified. Thus the central problem with epistemic consequentialism is not that it neglects the separateness of propositions. Rather, the central problem is its focus on the promoting or conducing relation. (Berker 2013b, m18)

Let us investigate Berker's claim. Suppose you know more than I do and I ask you about some issue that concerns me. You say, 'Listen carefully. If you believe what I am about to tell you, you will, by thus believing, have brought it about that you believe the truth about what concerns you.' How will we expect me to react? Do I need to subscribe to some dubious doctrine of epistemic consequentialism in order to react correctly and believe what I am told? Realising that by forming a particular belief one would bring it about that one will have answered one's question correctly, amounts more or less to having formed this belief. As this example illustrates, adopting truth-conducivism, i.e. the maxim to bring it about that, by forming a particular belief, one has a true belief regarding a matter one is interested in, cannot, in general, be an objectionable feature of a belief-forming strategy.

What about the more particular cases of self-fulfilling beliefs? We have, I think, to distinguish between two kinds of cases. Sometimes the fact that having a belief tends to make true what is believed is not a salient consideration for assessing the truth of what the belief is about. Recovery beliefs in cases of serious and well understood illnesses are normally of this sort. When I get the news that the deadly virus has entered my bloodstream, my belief that confidence matters for recovery won't be salient. I don't believe that confidence can kill viruses and so it would indeed be irrational for me to believe in my recovery, even if recovery beliefs have in general some tendency of self-fulfilment. At other times, self-fulfilling beliefs are justified partly on the basis of their capacity for self-fulfilment. Beliefs that express one's future-directed intentions are of this latter sort. Some of my plans, I am confident, will be realised. My plan is to be in London tomorrow and I believe I will succeed, i.e. I believe that I will be in London tomorrow. Would I not believe this, I would, in this scenario, not really plan to go to London. Thus I will be in London partly because I reasonably believe that I will be in London. The belief that I will be in London plays a role in bringing about its own truth, and, it seems to me, can reasonably be held partly on this basis.

Berker said that 'now we are at the heart of the matter': what is really objectionable about epistemic consequentialism is that it focusses on bringing about what is epistemically desirable, namely to believe truly. So far I have argued that, in general, there is nothing objectionable about believing something in order to bring it about that one believes the truth. This view is supported by the close connection that holds between believing something and taking it to be true. Berker fails to engage with this general connection. He focusses instead on the special case of self-fulfilling beliefs. I have argued that self-fulfilling beliefs, like beliefs about what one is going to do, are sometimes justified partly on the basis that they are self-fulfilling. Some self-fulfilling beliefs, however, do not seem to be justified. The optimism expressed in one's belief in one's recovery, if not supported by appropriate evidence, will be unjustified even if, by some strange coincidence, it turns out to be true. Does this fact – some self-fulfilling beliefs are unjustified – refute a doctrine that is prevalent in contemporary epistemology? At the very least, more needs to be said on behalf of such a conjecture to capture the complexity of the situation. Why is conduciveness to truth generally acceptable when in some cases of self-fulfilling beliefs the fact that they are self-fulfilling does not determine their justificatory status?

There is a natural answer to this question. Some recovery beliefs are not justified, even if they turn out to be true. Given the way I see the world, recovery in a case where I have been infected by a deadly virus is, from my epistemic perspective, not up to me. Thus, any belief in the power of my optimism would be in tension with my way of seeing the world. Contrast this case with one's confidence that one will achieve what one intends to do. Given the way I see the world – with trains running on time that bring me to London in less than 2 hours – whether I will be in London is, from my perspective, up to me. If I believe that I will be in London, I will be. The self-fulfilling nature of this belief, within the setting of my plan of going to London, justifies my so believing.

I have drawn a distinction between problematic and unproblematic self-fulfilling beliefs and it remains unclear why an epistemic consequentialist, for whom reaching the truth is epistemically most important, could not subscribe to the explanation that I offered of why one's optimism in the problematic case would not be justified: it would be in tension with other things one believes and so doesn't promise that one reaches one's aim of believing truly. I conclude that self-fulfilling beliefs pose no special problem for epistemic consequentialism. Sometimes they are justified and sometimes not. The epistemic consequentialist is able to participate in the explanation of when they are and when they are not justified.

6. Is there an Epistemological Analogue of the Separateness-of-Persons Principle?

Let me probe again and ask what, in Berker's view, the objectionable feature of epistemic consequentialism is. It is, he has told us in his latest publication on this topic (Berker 2015), the epistemic analogue of cutting up the one to save or benefit the many. If you sacrifice one in order to save many, you treat the benefits to the many as if they were benefits to one individual and, thus, you violate the idea that we ought to treat persons as separate. Berker's thinking is driven by the thought that there must be people in epistemology who make an analogous mistake. As our example of the belief that illness is punishment for one's sins has illustrated, trade-offs between epistemic goods seem highly questionable and so there has to be some principle that such trade-offs would violate. I will approach the aim of finding such an analogue principle by looking more closely at the separateness-of-persons principle.[5]

Note first that the separateness-of-persons objection to act-utilitarianism does not condemn all trade-offs. We should not sacrifice one person for the good of the many – this is true. But if one person would be able to save another from significant harm by making a small sacrifice, then one ought to make this sacrifice. For example, even if busy, one should stop and see whether the person who fell down close to us is ok or, if not, one should call an ambulance. The minor loss of convenience for one person is justified by the prevention of a potentially big loss to the other person. The epistemic analogue would be that we are asked to make sacrifices in one domain in order to prevent an even bigger harm in some other domain. On this picture it would be acceptable to give up one epistemic good for another epistemic good which is more significant. For example, I give up my belief that there is milk in the fridge in order to gain some important philosophical or scientific insight. Note that such a transfer would not violate the separateness of persons: the separateness-of-persons principle forbids some forms of aggregation but allows interpersonal comparability. When it comes to morality, small sacrifices for big individual benefit are, often, required; when it comes to epistemology such sacrifices look as bad as the ones that are supposed to violate the epistemic analogue of the separateness-of-persons principle: no promise of a philosophical or scientific insight justifies my abandoning any belief regarding the content of my fridge. So an analogue to the separateness-of-persons principle that could capture all forbidden epistemic trade-offs would have to look rather different from its ethical cousin. This is my first observation: if the parallel between ethics and epistemology ran in the direction Berker takes it to run, one would expect an analogue for allowable transfers but there is no such thing in epistemology.[6]

Looking back at ethics, we can make a second observation. Within personal goodness sums of benefits can be weighed against big sacrifices. It is only when it comes to interpersonal transfers that ethics sets what its defenders would call limits of decency. In the intrapersonal case, the sum of the small benefits of, for

---

[5] For reasons I explained earlier, I am not entirely satisfied by his ambition to find 'the analogue of the separateness-of-persons principle', when he said earlier that 'only the most primitive form of epistemic consequentialism' violates it. One way to make progress here would be to understand what he is doing as an instance of strategy 1. This strategy, however, would require additional arguments about the collapse of reliabilism, which is a form of rule-consequentialism, to its act-consequentialist base form, which is not supported by anyone in the literature.

[6] It is open to Berker to say that this is simply a point where the analogy breaks down. There are permissible trade-offs in ethics, whereas there are no such trade-offs in epistemology.

example having a slightly cheaper energy bill each month, might justify the big sacrifice of investing in a new heating system. Berker will have to say that this is another point at which the analogy breaks down. Whereas there is a virtue, prudence, that covers trade-offs under the umbrella of what is good for a particular person, it is hard to imagine the epistemic analogue of such intrapersonal trade-offs. It would mean that benefits and harms can be traded-off in respect to one particular belief that p. I am not sure how best to illustrate this point. Consider the following case. Should one simply disregard one piece of evidence in order to gain access to many other pieces of evidence? Or rather, would the epistemic state that constitutes my disregarding one piece of evidence be justified by the epistemic benefits of being in this state? In the ethical realm I should normally be willing to give up one good thing for many others of the same value. This, however, does not transfer to the epistemic case.

Berker's analogy, I have argued, breaks down at two points. Neither normatively required interpersonal transfers nor normatively required intrapersonal transfers find a parallel on the side of epistemology. Whereas in the practical domain weighing, comparing and trading-off goods is an essential part of practical thought, epistemology has no room for such kind of reasoning. Non-consequentialist ethics forbids some trade-offs, epistemology, it seems, forbids all. That we find impermissible trade-offs in both domains is, I agree, some parallel. This parallel, however, cannot run very deep: the different attitudes towards trade-offs signify a substantial divide between ethical and epistemological accounts of reasoning and normativity.

7. Why Beliefs are Not Justified by their Epistemic Benefits

Many illnesses are well understood. The evidence is clear: illnesses are not punishment for one's sins. Anyone who believed otherwise would not be justified in so believing, even if, in some imagined scenario, such believing would bring important epistemic benefits. Such epistemic benefits are in general irrelevant for determining whether a belief is justified. Why is this so?

Berker says we would violate an epistemological principle which is related to the ethical separateness-of-persons principle. We have found that the epistemological principle which we are trying to explain has a normative shape different from that of its alleged ethical analogue: it simply says that epistemic benefits do not render a belief justified.

There is, I have already argued at the beginning, not much promise in the idea to let propositions play a role analogous to that which persons play in ethics. The mistake in ethics is to treat the many as one. If the many were indeed one, interpersonal sacrifices would be justified. In epistemology, by contrast, it does not matter whether there is one benefit to believing something or many. Neither many nor one benefit will justify any believing. Thus we have one principle – epistemic benefits do not justify beliefs – but the invoked parallel to ethics does little to offer an explanation of this principle.

Epistemic trade-offs don't justify beliefs. This fact, I want to argue, does not show us anything about the nature of epistemic values. When we bracket the question whether beliefs are justified and look at the ways in which we conduct our lives regarding epistemic matters we realize that trade-offs between epistemic goods are commonplace. Suppose I need to say a long number out aloud in order not to forget it. This activity and the concentration it requires are, in the imagined situation, necessary to retain one epistemic good – knowing the number. The same activity prevents me from achieving other epistemic goods. For example, you want to tell me something, but I can't concentrate on what you are saying because I am constantly repeating the number I want to remember. I have to make a comparative judgement about what is more important: knowing the number or knowing what you are trying to tell me. Once we recognise the structure of this example we realise that epistemic trade-offs are common place and, furthermore, that our epistemic concerns mesh naturally with non-epistemic concerns. Information gathering is part of our lives and its costs, epistemic or otherwise, will have to be weighed against its expected epistemic benefits.

We want to explain the following fact – epistemic benefits of believing do not settle the epistemic status of beliefs. I have just argued that the nature of epistemic values, which is by no means hostile to trade-offs, will offer no such explanation. I have argued earlier that pointing to anti-consequentialism in ethics has not resulted in any useful parallels that could help us in our explanatory task. Neither the normative landscape in which the ethical separateness-of-persons principle is set, nor the starting point – propositions exert some normative force on us to be treated separately – would support Berker's view of an analogous explanation of the respective epistemological and ethical points. Beliefs are not justified by their benefits – this will come out true on any ordinary conception of what may and what may not justify beliefs. Berker told us that his analysis will undermine much of contemporary epistemology. But who will deny the claim that beliefs are not justified by their benefits?[7]

Though Berker offers no explanation of the fact that beliefs are not justified by their epistemic benefits, an explanation is not hard to come by. Whereas actions can be justified via the benefits they promise to provide (be they epistemic or otherwise), beliefs cannot. In order to find an explanation, we need to focus on what it is to believe and on the intimate connection between belief and truth. A believing is, after all, a taking to be true. What I don't take to be true, I do not believe. Consequently, truth will always be an unnegotiable aspect in our assessment of beliefs. The fact that holding a belief offers epistemic benefits does not speak to its truth. Either we hold the belief, i.e. we take what we believe to be true, or we do not. Factors unrelated to truth, are unable to change this state, which, as I said, is the state of taking something to be true. If I don't think that holding a particular belief would be holding a true belief, I do not have this belief. No promise of benefits would be a consideration of the right kind to make me hold something true, when I take it that such promise does not affect in any way whether such believing would be true.[8]

Note that endorsing the connection between truth and believing does not carry any evaluative commitment with it. Even if we say that a belief is correct if and only if true, such a notion of correctness need not be normative. It would be, without doubt, a further step to argue that we (always) ought to have correct beliefs. The very nature of what believing is shows us that we cannot avoid assessing beliefs in terms of their truth. Thus, considerations unrelated to truth cannot get any grip when it comes to forming beliefs. It does not matter for this explanation of Berker's basic fact whether we say that believing truly is the aim of believing or whether we claim that believing truly is a good thing (though, in many cases, it will be).

Take the following example as an illustration of my point. Suppose I keep everything I own in a box. Sometimes I take out one item, some coins let's say, and put another item in my box. I trade one thing for another. My belief box is not like this. I cannot simply take out one thing and exchange it for another thing. What is in my belief box is in there in virtue of my believing it. As long as I believe it, it cannot be taken out. What are not in the box are the things I do not believe. I cannot simply put them into my belief box because believing is an entry ticket without which nothing will be admitted. This picture, naïve as it

---

[7] Roderick Firth (1981, 12), whom Berker often invokes as an ally, says that '... epistemological belief-utilitarianism is not a position that anyone is likely to advocate.'
[8] For a related argument to a similar conclusion, see Shah (2006).

may be, is sufficient to explain Berker's fact. If a belief's further epistemic benefits have no bearing on its truth, they have no bearing on our taking something to be true, which, we have said, is what believing is.

We can make the same point in another way. There is no notion of something being instrumentally true. A belief that leads to other true beliefs is a means to truth but that does not make it true in any sense: instrumental truth is not a kind of truth. Beliefs are, in virtue of their nature, assessable in terms of truth. Their capacity for bringing about truths is, without a notion of instrumental truth, irrelevant for this assessment. We can assess actions, including attempts to forget or attempts to keep something in mind, in terms of their epistemic and other benefits. The same goes for the employment of methods, the following of rules, and the involvement in or the endorsement of practises – all these things can be assessed in terms of how they further our epistemic interests. Beliefs can be assessed in many ways but their assessment in terms of truth is non-negotiable. That is why other forms of assessment will never be able to fully capture epistemic normativity.

8. Conclusion

I said at the beginning that the epistemic consequentialist might tell us that we ought to conduct our epistemic lives in ways such that we believe lots of (important) truths and try not to go wrong too often. I also said that this sounded innocent enough. We now know that it really is innocent. How to conduct one's life, including its epistemic aspects, is, at least to some extent, a matter of weighing goods.

Reading Berker has reminded me of the promise I mentioned earlier to read Karl's paper. Berker talks about 'the spectre that is haunting contemporary epistemology: the spectre of reliabilism' and, in sharp contrast to Karl, he describes his work as an attempt of exorcising this ghost (Berker, 2013b, 363). One of his commentators (Goldman 2015), the author of what we could call 'The Reliabilist Manifesto', has accused him of misunderstanding his opponents in epistemology. Goldman emphasises that adopting or endorsing a reliable method and, on this basis, its deliverances, is not a way of judging beliefs by their benefits. In this paper I have looked at Berker's attempt to learn from non-consequentialism in ethics. I have argued that there is hardly any parallel between the epistemologist's general adversity to allowing epistemic trade-offs for a certain purpose, namely for the purpose of determining the justificatory status of beliefs, and the non-consequentialist's claim that it would lead ethical thought astray if we simply summed up the good and the bad things and disregarded their distribution over individuals and groups. Berker is taken by the fact that when believing one thing leads to believing other true things this, by itself, does not determine the justificatory status of the belief. Berker, I have suggested, is mistaken in thinking that this thought, which I feel is generally agreed upon, has much leverage in the contemporary debate in epistemology. An uncontentious assumptions about the nature of belief – believing is a taking to be true – is able to explain this fact. This assumption is available to the epistemic consequentialist like to anyone else. Goldman (2015) looked at Berker's ideas from the reliabilist's perspective. I tried to look at the analogy which Berker appealed to from an ethical perspective. In our verdict we agree.

References

Berker, S. (2013a). Epistemic teleology and the separateness of propositions. *Philosophical Review, 122*(3), 337–393.
Berker, S. (2013b). The rejection of epistemic consequentialism. *Philosophical Issues, 23*(1), 363–387.
Berker, S. (2015). Reply to Goldman: Cutting Up the One to Save the Five in Epistemology. *Episteme, 12* (Special Issue 02), 145–153.
Brown, C. (2011). Consequentialize This. *Ethics, 121*(4), 749–771.
Firth, R. (1981). Epistemic merit, intrinsic and instrumental. *Proceedings and Addresses of the American Philosophical Association, 55,* 5–23.
Goldman, A. I. (2015). Reliabilism, veritism, and epistemic consequentialism. *Episteme, 12* (Special Issue 02), 131–143.
Pettit, P. (1997). The consequentialist perspective. In M. Baron, P. Pettit, and M. Slote (eds.), *Three Methods of Ethics.* Blackwell.
Rawls, J. (1971). *A Theory of Justice.* Harvard University Press.
Scanlon, T. (1998). *What We Owe to Each Other.* Harvard University Press.
Shah, N. (2006). A new argument for evidentialism. *The Philosophical Quarterly, 56,* 481–498.

IV Epistemic Goals and Values

Pedro Schmechtig
External Goals and Inherent Norms – A Cluster-Conception of Epistemic Normativity

1. Introduction

Teleological vocabulary is usually referred to when explaining epistemic norms and values. Thereby, however, two notions need to be distinguished. Aristotle used the nominal expression 'telos' to mean the *correct execution of an activity* (*energia*) as well as the *successful result* or *product* of a specific praxis (*ergon*). A very similar differentiation can be found in contemporary epistemology:

> And the evaluative aspect of epistemology involves an attempt to identify ways in which the *conduct* and the *products* of our cognitive activities can be better or worse vis-à-vis the goals of cognition. And what are those goals? Along with many other epistemologists I suggest that the primary function of cognition in human life is to acquire true beliefs rather than false beliefs about matters that are of interest or importance to us. (Alston 2005, 8 – my emphasis)

There are currently two separate discussions running parallel to this distinction. On the one hand, epistemic normativity is captured as the *inherent aim* of the conducts of our cognitive activities. According to this view, epistemic normativity arises from something like a goal, but a goal built into the nature of belief itself.[1] In this debate, it is often said in a metaphorical way that 'belief aims at truth'.

On the other hand, epistemic normativity is explained as the *external goal* of the product of our cognitive activities. According to this view, epistemologists think that the source of epistemic normativity is a goal that human beings have in terms of the results of our epistemic practices, such as the goal of believing what is true and not what is false.[2] In contrast to the inherent aim of the conduct of our cognitive activities, the external goal says nothing about the subjective pursuit of a person. Rather, the external goal defines how the product of the subjective pursuit can be successful as a part of a certain intellectual inquiry.

In both debates different questions play a role. While in the first case the *deontic* question "What should or what are we allowed to believe?" is central, the second case is primarily about an *axiological* question: "When is a cognitive con-

---

1 See, for example, Wedgwood (2002).
2 Cf. Alston (1985, 2005); David (2001); Lynch (2004); Goldman (2002).

dition epistemically good?". Consequently, at this point the classic Euthyphro dilemma surfaces: When it comes to epistemic normativity, should we take the good to be prior to the right or the right prior to the good? Which of the two targets has priority? The strict separation of both discussions implies that we are dealing with two competing response strategies:

Deontic Priority
One should believe something if and only if the respective belief is good (in an epistemic sense).

Axiological Priority
A belief is good if and only if it is correct (in an epistemic sense), i.e. if it should be believed.

By way of contrast, in this paper I would like to argue for an alternative way of thinking. According to my proposal, there is no priority in either of the two positions since both questions are inextricably linked to each other. In fact, an adequate teleological characterization of epistemic normativity must make obvious how the various applications of goals related to both questions are connected.

The reasoning of this proposal will be made in several stages. First and foremost I will show that the two above-named response strategies exhibit shortcomings due to the fact that certain relationships between deontic and axiological standardization have not been considered. For this purpose, in the first step, I will look at two variations of epistemic consequentialism which are considered common in a teleological standard position (section 2). All positions of this kind assume that there is a primary external source for the explanation of epistemic normativity—namely the increase of true beliefs—which is why the axiological question takes precedence. In the second step, I will then examine the reverse approach (section 3). In this reverse approach, the consequence is that doxastic norms take priority. Here various difficulties also occur. The focus is on the formulation and on the insufficient explanation of the regulatory force of such norms. Based on that, I will develop an alternative concept in the third step (section 4). According to this proposal, epistemic projects can be characterized as clusters, which are composed of one or more normative standards (the inherent doxastic aims) and the respective leading external goal of the intellectual inquiry. The fundamental assumptions advocate that according to the inquiry's kind of external epistemic goal, the corresponding doxastic standards under which the obtaining of a belief (relative to the leading external goal) is correct or appropriate then also change. Finally, I will highlight the principle advantages of this proposal in the last step (section 5).

2. Epistemic Consequentialism and the External Source of Epistemic Normativity

The overwhelming majority of contemporary epistemologists take our concept of epistemic justification to have a consequentialist structure. With such a view the *external* source of epistemic normativity lies in the value of appropriate epistemic goals that characterize our intellectual inquiry. From the epistemic point of view, justified beliefs acquire their normative force since they serve the goal of inquiry. According to this picture, there is a primary external goal, namely, maximizing truth and minimizing falsity in a large body of beliefs that is epistemically good for us to promote. The question of what we *should* believe is determined by how well our believing conduces to the fulfilling of this truth-goal.[3]

This standard approach to explaining epistemic normativity has one familiar problem. Sometimes cognitive activities have consequences which are conducive to the external truth-goal although the activity *itself* doesn't appear justified. The classic example for such a normativity trade-off can be seen with the following 'grant-seeking scientist case':[4]

John is a scientist seeking to get a grant from a religious organization. He is an atheist and the organization does not give grants to atheists. His research, however, would allow him to form a large number of new true beliefs and to revise a large number of false beliefs about a variety of matters. But John must recognize that his only chance of receiving funding from the organization is to believe in the existence of God.

In this situation, should John believe in the existence of God? Is this belief epistemically justified? Some philosophers hold the *radical* opinion that one should answer *both* questions in the affirmative.[5] The majority, however, favors a more *moderate* view in which the epistemic consequentialism has agreed that some-

---

[3] Normally, one would expect that authors who represent fully different positions in regards to the term of justification would also debate another concept of epistemic normativity. However, it's an interesting fact that this approach greatly appeals to externalists like Goldman (2002), internalists like Bonjour (1985) or Foley (1993), and also to representatives of a trade-off position like Alston (2005).

[4] The original case stems from Roderick Firth (1981, 261).

[5] My reason for calling this account radical is because for the majority of epistemologists, it is very counterintuitive that beliefs in such situations can be epistemically justified. Accepting that they can be would undermine the credibility one should give to epistemic intuitions.

one in this type of situation is not epistemically justified to believe something. Both positions can be differentiated as follows:[6]

Radical Epistemic Consequentialism (R-EC)
The epistemic status of a cognitive activity is directly determined by what this activity produces. A particular belief is epistemically justified if the consequences of the belief serve the epistemic goal of inquiry (i.e. true belief).

Moderate Epistemic Consequentialism (M-EC)
The epistemic status of a cognitive activity is indirectly determined by what this activity produces. A particular belief is justified if the belief is produced or well-based on the occurrence of process or reason-type which serves the epistemic goal of inquiry (i.e. true belief).[7]

In the following passages I will argue that both approaches—independent of the difference between them—have the same pitfalls. In both cases it cannot be satisfactorily explained wherein the *binding sense* of the external source of epistemic normativity exists.

2.1 Radical Epistemic Consequentialism and Non-Evidential Reason for Belief

Recently, Brain Talbot (2014) defended an internalistic version of radical consequentialism. According to his claim, John in the 'grant-seeking scientist case' is justified in believing that God exists since he has a "truth promoting non-evidential reason" (TPR, for short) for his belief. This kind of reasoning justifies a cognitive activity directly through what the activity produces. According to Talbot, S's belief that p is objectively supported by TPR if and only if S's having of a belief that p leads to having other beliefs whose contents are true and this fact is a reason that S believes that p. Talbot names three essential characteristics of his approach:

---

[6] In view of metaethics, this differentiation is generally known analog to the separation of "act consequentialist approaches" and "rule consequentialist approaches.
[7] Followers of the (M-EC) define epistemic justification in two steps. The first step identifies which types of entities (cognitive process types or reason types) produce epistemic value within a given domain. The second step attributes justification to those belief-tokens that are produced by (or well-based on) tokens of the entity-types that have been identified in the first step to produce epistemic value.

> What are the views that entail that we sometimes epistemically ought to believe on our TPR? They are these, in conjunction: epistemic oughts have a source, the source of epistemic oughts is an end in which true belief plays a necessary role, and epistemic oughts are normative. (Talbot 2014, 600)

There are a number of questions that arise in light of this characterization of (external) sources of epistemic oughts. These especially apply to the assertion that the characteristics of TPRs are of an epistemic nature.[8] However, I'd like to emphasize two other things. The first concerns the way such radical epistemic consequentialism refers to goals as external sources of epistemic normativity. The second refers to a specific conflict which then occurs between doxastic norms and reasons, provided one agrees that TPRs possess a normative force.

Talbot bases his position on two arguments. The first argument says: Given that (i) epistemic oughts have its source in an epistemic end, (ii) get their force from this end, and (iii) the epistemic end has true belief as a necessary component, then it is *prima facie* plausible that the epistemic end generates TPR.[9] Belief on one's TPR promotes true belief, and promoting true beliefs will promote things that have true belief as a necessary component. According to this, Talbot supposes there are no accounts of any epistemic end that endorse the three claims while not generating TPR. But how convincing is this argument?

To begin with, it can be doubted as to whether it's prima facie plausible under the given conditions that external epistemic goals really generate TPRs that possess a normative force. Talbot seems to accept the following: Even when it's unclear whether a belief with content p is true or false, there is, prima facie, a compelling reason to believe that p when, as a result of p, the whole ratio of true and false belief improves. On this point it should be considered, however, that truth as a goal of the inquiry is a twofold target which is composed of two sub-conditions, namely, the maximizing of true belief and the minimizing of false belief. Balancing both sub-goals, however, can be associated with various epistemic normativities. Assume that the acquiring of even only a single false belief had extremely negative consequences. In this situation it seems rationally appropriate not to believe something false than to maximize the number of true beliefs. Likewise, it clearly seems appropriate not to believe

---

8 Talbot discusses three objections: (i) TPR cannot be epistemic reasons because then we would also have epistemic reasons to breathe, which is absurd; (ii) TPR cannot be epistemic reasons because one who believes p concerning TPR cannot thereby know that p; (iii) TPR cannot be epistemic reasons because, if they were, one could be epistemically justified in believing things that one has conclusive evidence for believing are false. I do not think that Talbot's replies to the three objections are convincing, but there is no room for discussion on this point here.
9 Cf. Talbot (2014, 603).

something false than to increase the number of trivial or totally uninteresting true beliefs. Under these kinds of conditions it is not prima facie plausible that TPRs possess a normative force—not even when one concedes that true belief is a necessary component of a leading goal of the inquiry.

Talbot not only assumes that his argument is prima facie plausible, but he is also convinced that his characterization of TPRs is compatible with the usual notion of external epistemic goals. However, at this point an additional problem surfaces: It is a common assumption among epistemologists that epistemic justification is an evaluative notion that is either *synchronic*, as in the case of evidentialist approaches to epistemic justification,[10] or *backward-looking* as in the case of process reliabilist approaches to epistemic justification. But in contrast to this, external epistemic sources that generate TPR seem to presuppose that the epistemic goal is *diachronic* or *forward-looking*. This is why radical consequentialists have to accept epistemic trade-offs. In the case of TPR, it is not the belief itself which implies an appropriate response to the actual situation although it leads to good consequences in the future. But if epistemic evaluation is fundamentally synchronic or backward-looking, then future epistemic benefits are irrelevant for the fulfillment of epistemic goals.

Nevertheless, Talbot argues that synchronic ends *can* generate TPR. His argument is based on the following assumption:[11]

> An agent's beliefs at a moment can depend on one another, so that, for example, if Jennifer did not believe *p* now, then Jennifer would not believe *q*, *r*, and *z* now. We can imagine either supernatural explanations or quite plausible psychological explanations for this dependence. If having q, r, and z were endorsed by the epistemic end – if q, r, and z were true beliefs, or pieces of knowledge, wisdom, or understanding – then Jennifer's belief that p would put her at this moment closer to achieving the epistemic end than she would be if she lacked that belief. Jennifer would thus have TPR to believe p relative to even synchronic epistemic ends. (Talbot 2014, 605)

This response, however, is not plausible in two ways. The present example merely makes it clear that there are sometimes psychological or causal dependencies between synchronous beliefs. But even when, psychologically seen, the present having of beliefs with the contents of q, r, and z is dependent on Jennifer believing p at the same time, it doesn't mean that the epistemic justification of this belief is a sheer consequence of the having of p. The psychological or causal explanation of the dependency of beliefs (at the same time) shouldn't be confused with the question of whether Jennifer, as a result of p, is *epistemically*

---

10 See, for example, Feldman (2000), Foley (1987, 1993).
11 In this connection, Talbot refers to Fumerton (2001).

justified at the current moment to believe that q, r and z are beneficial to the (external) epistemic goal. Even if p is definitely wrong at the current moment, the psychological or causal dependency would remain, albeit Jennifer—through the acquiring of a belief with these contents—doesn't approach the epistemic truth-goal. In order to fulfill the synchronous epistemic goal, either the beliefs q, r and z have to be directly justified or it must be guaranteed that they do not originate from an inferential dependency on an unjustified (wrong) belief.

Furthermore, Talbot seems to assume that each only generates conceivable candidates for an external epistemic goal (knowledge, wisdom, understanding, etc.) in the same way as the TPRs truth-goal. This assumption is also highly questionable. Especially in connection with objective epistemic understanding—and also for specific forms of wisdom—it's assumed that a true belief is not an essential component for the fulfillment of such goals.[12] And that's not all. In specific circumstances, like in the case of knowledge, it's argued that out of an inferential dependency to a false belief, knowledge sometimes follows. If such cases of "knowledge as a result of falsity" are significantly epistemic, then Talbot's argument for TPR cannot be transferred to knowledge as an external goal of the inquiry.[13] Hence, the proposed position becomes even less attractive.

Talbot's second argument is based on the following consideration: If the epistemic end generates TPRs, then TPRs have *enough normative force* to generate epistemic oughts. In regards to this assumption, another difficulty arises concerning the distinction between epistemic reasons and norms. As Talbot very properly states, what one epistemically ought to believe is a function of reasons and norms.[14] But if we look at how goals generate reasons that have normative force, we would see that the epistemic end *does* generate norms forbidding belief of a TPR. Here is the best example for such a conflicting norm:

Evidential Norm of Belief (EN$_B$)
For any S, p: S should believe that p if and only if S has sufficient evidence for p.

If S is guided in the process of rational deliberation of beliefs by a subjective accessible norm such as (EN$_B$), then S reaches a belief which is compatible with the external source of epistemic normativity (maximizing truth and minimizing falsity). But it is very hard to see how an external epistemic goal that is promoted by belief of a TPR can be compatible with such a norm for belief.

---

12 Catherine Elgin (2004) and Linda Zagzebski (2001) have noted that understanding in this form is possible even in the absence of truth.
13 See for this discussion, among others, Klein (2008) and Warfield (2005).
14 See Talbot (2014, 607).

How can a radical consequentialist respond to this objection? Talbot's proposal is this: After following (EN_B) for sometime, a person will be much worse off relative to the epistemic end. This shows that norms prohibiting belief on TPR are only "rules-of-thumb". Such rules don't generate absolute duty because they can be undermined given we have strong enough reason. At least in situations where we have strong enough reason to undermine (EN_B), it is possible that one should believe anything if one has TPR.

It's correct that external epistemic goals unfold a normative force only in cooperation with corresponding doxastic norms. I will more thoroughly explain this, in my opinion, very basic assertion later. Nevertheless, this response raises the question: In what circumstances is a reason strong enough to override a doxastic norm like (EN_B)? Talbot's basal example is the following: Fred has the unusual choice to either believe any proposition p—for which he has absolutely no evidence—or else to die (for whatever reason). According to Talbot, because of the dramatic consequence in this situation, Fred has an undermined reason for (EN_B).

Is this response to the present objection convincing? I don't think so. Of course Fred has a good reason to ignore (EN_B). Talbot is correct when he claims that epistemic obligations, as they're expressed in (EN_B), are *not absolute*. Sometimes doxastic norms lose their normative force because the epistemic regard in which they prove significant doesn't count. Fred's wish to live provides an undermining reason for (EN_B). But it's clear that the source of the normativity of this reason is purely practical nature and not epistemic. The normative force of this reason doesn't result out of the fulfillment of the truth-goal but out of the practical requirement to protect human life. Fred has *no* compelling reason to undermine (EN_B) in an *epistemic regard*. If the external source of this reason was really epistemic in nature, then the avoidance of (EN_B) would have to directly serve the goal of maximizing true belief. This is clearly not the case. The undermining of (EN_B) serves the practical purpose of preserving Fred's life. In other words, it is a mistake to believe that external source of normativity, which underlies the undermining of (EN_B) through TPRs is the *same* as in the initial conflict. Therefore, radical consequentialism doesn't have a satisfactory explanation for why one may ignore a norm like (EN_B) in an *epistemic* regard as a result of TPRs.[15]

---

15 Talbot seems to acknowledge this problem. For this reason, he offers a special "trump" argument: He will show that, even if it were inappropriate to call the ought in light of TPR an epistemic ought, such an ought should replace the epistemic in our evaluation of beliefs. Why? Talbot suggests that there is almost no context in which it would make any sense to follow epistemic oughts over oughts due to TPR because both kinds of oughts are generated by the same end (this is true belief); and this is why we cannot explain our interest in one over the

2.2 Moderate Epistemic Consequentialism and Structural Trade-offs

Selim Berker (2013a/b) provides an argumentative strategy that leads to a strong rejection of epistemic consequentialism. He is convinced that the consequentialist approach to normative epistemology is misguided because we should not proceed by first identifying certain external epistemic goods and then constructing a theory of epistemic justification in terms of what promotes those goods. However, Berker recognizes that there are moderate forms of the epistemic consequentialism (M-EC) which are not affected by the original 'grant-seeking scientist cases'. Hence, he pursues a complex incremental strategy: First, he considers certain counterexamples to extremely crude versions of radical epistemic consequentialism[16] because this is the hallmark of consequentialist theories, namely their proclivity for trade-offs. Second, he tries to reveal the structural features that characterize such cases. Here Berker writes that even moderate epistemic consequentialism (M-EC), which disputes that you are justified in original trade-off situations, have a *structural* problem. This being the promotion of epistemic good with regard to one proposition which is then sacrificed in order to greatly benefit the promotion of epistemic good with regard to many other propositions; this means such a theory ignores 'the separateness of propositions'. Third, he tries to show that there is a general recipe for generating counterexamples for even very sophisticated forms of epistemic consequentialism. At this time, Berker admits that he has slightly changed his position to the following: Although the structural feature of ignoring the separateness of propositions suffices to generate problems for many consequentialist theories in epistemology, there is a *more general structural feature* that allows us to also generate problem cases for moderate consequentialist epistemic theories which adhere to the separateness of propositions.

Why this third step? Perhaps the most prominent variant of moderate (M-EC) is the process reliabilism.[17] But adherents of this approach have successfully argued that you can see, by inspecting actual examples, that there is nothing like

---

other with an interest in different ends. But this is wrong if we realize that we have other external epistemic goals besides true belief.

16 This 'grant seeking-scientist case' is originally credited to Roderick Firth (1981, 1998).

17 As Ahlstrom-Vij & Dunn (2014, 2) correctly highlight, there are two reasons for focusing on reliabilism here: First, it is one of Berker's explicit targets. Second, by showing that the *most prominent* version of epistemic consequentialism is unscathed by Berker's examples, it will make clear that a commitment to such consequentialism is by no means the death sentence for a theory that Berker thinks it is.

the structural problem for such forms of moderate epistemic consequentialism.[18] Berker (2015) admits that the 'grant-seeking scientist case' and other examples like the 'sick mathematician case' are not counterexamples to process reliabilism. However, he thinks that process reliabilists are not off the hook so easily. For moderate consequentialist theories, such as the process reliabilism which note the separateness of propositions, one can generate other kinds of counterexamples. In such cases the same underlying structure is not directly applied to particular belief-tokens (as in case of R-EC), but to the occurrence of an entity-type, namely to a process of the formation of a belief, which serves the epistemic goal of inquiry (i.e. maximizing truth and minimizing falsity).[19]

The third step is especially significant for Berker's overall strategy. Therefore, it begs the question of whether the argumentation is successful or not. In that which follows I will argue that Berker's argumentation is only partially successful. Nonetheless, this discussion will make it clear that even a moderate approach to epistemic consequentialism has difficulties explaining the "binding sense" of the external source of epistemic normativity.

In the original 'grant-seeking case' the item doing the foregoing and promoting is a particular belief. However, Berker believes the same strategy can also apply to a moderate epistemic consequentialism (M-EC). If this is right, the process reliabilism is at least sometimes affected by the normative problem at work in trade-off cases. The main example for this third step of his strategy is the following 'prime numbers' example:

> Suppose the following is true of me: whenever I contemplate whether a given natural number is prime, I form a belief that it is not. "Is 25 prime? No, it is not." "Is 604 prime? No, it is not." "Is 7 prime? No, it is not." Let us also stipulate that this is the *only* cognitive process by which I form beliefs about the primeness of natural numbers. (I'm a simpleminded kind of guy.) Since the ratio of prime to composite numbers less than n approaches 0 as n approaches infinity, my belief-forming process tends to yield a ratio of true to false beliefs that approaches 1. Therefore process reliabilists are forced to say that, because my belief-forming process is almost perfectly reliable, any belief formed on its basis is justified. But that's crazy! When I form a belief that 7 is not prime, it is simply not correct to say that, although that belief is false, it is epistemically redeemed by the truth of the other beliefs which would be formed via the process that led to it. (Berker 2013, 374–5, my emphasis)

---

18 See Ahlstrom-Vij & Dunn (2014), Goldman (2015), likewise Hamid and Wrenn (both in this collection).
19 As Berker (2013) emphasizes, this is a great benefit for his account: "This recipe makes my style of argument particularly versatile: Even if fault is found with the specific examples I have offered in this essay, my recipe allows me to find other examples of a structurally similar sort that suffice to make the same point."

The 'belief-forming process' quoted here is highly reliable. Accordingly, this process appears to be correct in the framework of moderate epistemic consequentialism. Beliefs that come about on the basis of this process serve the goal of the inquiry with a higher probability (i.e. they maximize truth and minimize falsity). Still, intuitively, we would say that a belief that "7 is not a prime number" is *not* justified in an epistemic regard.

But what does this mean for the process reliabilism? The answers to this question are very contradictory. Some defenders (Ahlstrom-Vij & Dunn 2014) have argued as follows: If there is a process dedicated to generating beliefs about primehood and this process generates the output "7 is not prime", then the reliabilism must say that this belief *is* justified. According to this, the reliabilism generates the correct verdict at this place: It is *not* counter-intuitive to say that the belief "7 is not prime" is epistemically justified under these assumptions.

In contrast to this view, Alvin Goldman (2015) proposes a completely different kind of defense. He doubts that the type of the belief-forming process specified in the example above has an *epistemic value* or significance at all. If this defense is true, we are not justified in believing that "7 is not prime" in the example above because it is counter-intuitive to say that this belief serves the epistemic goal of inquiry. But this is odd. How can it be that a defense of reliabilism leads to such different results? A coherent theory should not be based on such contradictory value-intuitions.

However, perhaps Goldman's response can be interpreted differently. Another way to defend process reliabilism against the 'prime-number case' is as follows: The type of process cited in the example is indeed reliable somehow, yet it's insignificant in an epistemic regard since there's a *better* belief-forming process-type because, one in which a person can attain reliable beliefs about prime numbers and it's *not* implied that 7 isn't a prime number. According to these modified strategies, 'belief-forming processes' are not reliable in an absolute sense ("not reliable full stop"), but rather, only *relative* to a specific area. This area is given by the interrogative information demands of the inquiry. Therefore, not all beliefs which come about through reliable processes are equally epistemically valuable. On the contrary, only those whose contents deliver an adequate *answer to the leading question of inquiry* possess an epistemic value.

With that said, the problem at hand can be solved as follows: The cited belief-forming process in the example is indeed reliable, but insignificant in an epistemic regard since that process type doesn't fulfill the interrogative information demand of the inquiry due to such beliefs being formed; this means that at least sometimes, no adequate answer can be supplied to the question of whether a number is a prime number.

I sympathize with the idea that the assessment of cognitive activities must be relativized in regards to the leading question of the inquiry. Nevertheless, in my view, this proposal as defense of the reliabilistic position seems inadequate for at least two reasons. For one, this proposal ignores a particular assumption about the cited example. Berker describes the underlying situation in that there is only a *single* cognitive process in which the belief in question can be achieved ("I'm a simpleminded kind of guy"). It's debatable whether this assumption is valid. It's obvious, however, that the proposed explanation doesn't work in a world where there is no better process type.

The second point, however, seems more important. A relativization of the epistemic significance on a specific area of information interest implies a crucial *modification* in the way one understands the external goals of the inquiry. It is not only a matter of maximizing truth and minimizing falsity ("in a large body of beliefs"). Instead, the external source now consists in satisfying the interrogative information demand of the inquiry. In doing so, it is quite obviously a matter of a *generic* goal, namely of the general fact of getting a satisfying answer to the leading question of inquiry. This generic goal, however, can be individualized in a variety of ways. Depending on the kind of information interest that is paramount (knowledge, understanding, wisdom, etc.), the conditions under which the content of a cognitive activity delivers a satisfying answer to the leading question of inquiry differ.[20]

The dialectic of the present discussion makes two things clear. On the one hand, it shows that without additional modification, even a moderate epistemic consequentialism cannot explain the "binding sense" of the external source of epistemic normativity. On the other hand, a central weakness in Berker's rebuttal of the teleological approach also incidentally becomes apparent. Berker (2013) asks himself what the scope of his argument is. He admits that in some respect the target of his argument is very *narrow*. What he has argued is only that epistemic normativity cannot be reduced to a set of epistemic appraisals which is purely defined by the goal of maximizing truth and minimizing falsity in a large body of belief. Regarding such a limited understanding of the external source of the epistemic normativity, it is quite right to say that belief-forming practices don't have the central sort of positive normative status we associate with epistemic norms. However, of course this doesn't mean that the teleological approach has to be completely dismissed. Based on the narrow scope, Berker's strategy is determined by a very particular form, namely, by the consequentialist

---

20 This connection will be more precisely addressed later as part of the explanation of my proposed cluster conception (section 4).

standard explanation. Such proposals, as a rule, assume two things: They consider the acquiring of true beliefs as the sole (primary) external goal of inquiry; and they assume that such norms that correlate with these external truth-goals in epistemic regards are exclusively significant. Both assumptions, however, are, in the broad sense, not essential for a teleological approach. The fact that Berker's argumentative strategy can be easily bypassed by dropping the stated requirements does not consequentially argue against a teleological explanation of epistemic normativity, but at best against a very particular "pure" externalist version, namely the *veritistic* consequentialist framework.

The problem of the missing "binding sense" of external epistemic goals makes it clear that an adequate theory of epistemic normativity not only needs to answer the question of when it's epistemically justified to believe, but that it must explain, in a comprehensive way, why we *should* believe something in an epistemic regard. As emphasized in the beginning, this outcome could be used as an opportunity to argue in the other direction, that inherent doxastic aims take priority. Thusly, a belief would be good in an epistemic regard if and only if it should be believed. In the following, I will more precisely consider if it's possible to progress with this strategy.

3. Deontic Correctness and the Inherent Source of Epistemic Normativity

According to many philosophers, epistemology deals particularly with finding out when a belief is epistemically correct. Mostly it's accepted that there are conditions which specify whether one *should* believe something. Such a purely deontic explanation of epistemic normativity follows a general schema:

The Global Template for Doxastic Normativity
S should believe that p under condition C.

In order to animate this schema, more about the condition C needs to be said. The most common form in which to do this is based on the idea that beliefs aim at truth.[21] How this general metaphor should be understood, however, is controversial. Epistemic normativists assume that the fulfillment of the condition

---

21 The classic source of this claim comes from Williams (1973, 148).

C requires that we strive to acquire only those beliefs which comply with the following truth norm:[22]

(TN$_O$) For any S, p: S should believe that p if and only if p is true.

According to this point of view, it doesn't depend on wherein the external goal of the inquiry exists and whether there even are such epistemic goals; more importantly is the question of whether we are striving for beliefs which comply with (TN$_O$).

It's known that the acceptance of such a truth norm has many problems. I will only partially elaborate on this point.[23] For my purposes, the only question that's interesting is that of whether norms like (TN$_O$) have a *normative force* which exists independently of the external epistemic goal leading the inquiry. In the following I will consider two objections which doubt that the prescriptive character of doxastic norms independent of external sources can be explained. The first objective deals with the formulation of norms like (TN$_O$). The second pertains to the related 'guiding function of our belief formation'.

3.1 Strong versus Weak Prescriptive Account

According to an established argument, not every true proposition that can be taken into consideration by one person is compatible with (TN$_O$). There appear to be propositions that, although they're true, we cannot believe without becoming false as a consequence. The most common example for such psychologically, seemingly impossible propositions is the following (Bykvist & Hattiangadi 2007):

Blindspot-Propositions (BP): It is raining but nobody believes it.

According to (TN$_O$), we should believe the true proposition. If, however, a (BP) is true and I believe it, then there appears to be at least one person who believes

---

[22] The most common proposal is that belief is essentially subject to a norm of truth (Boghossian 2008; Gibbons 2014, Lynch 2004, Littlejohn 2010; Shah and Velleman 2005; Weiner 2005, Whiting 2010). Alternative proposals include that belief is governed by a knowledge norm (Bird 2007, Engel 2013; Smithies 2012; Sutton 2007, Williamson 2000), an evidential norm (Conee and Feldman 1984), or norms of rationality (Zangwill 2010). Some authors adopt an inclusive position. Wedgwood (2002), for example, suggests that the fundamental norm is truth and takes norms of rationality and knowledge as a consequence.

[23] An overview of the central problems can be found in Chan (2013).

that it's raining.[24] In this case, the proposition in question would be false. This makes Blindspot-Propositions puzzling for (TN$_O$) since such norms are connected to the prescriptive claim that all true propositions—which are taken into consideration—should be believed.

In view of this difficulty, Daniel Whiting (2010) proposes a weak prescriptive approach to the explanation of epistemic norms, and many other authors pursue this approach as well.[25] Thusly, the strict deontic "should" in (TN$_O$) can be replaced by a weaker "may" in the sense of the following *permissive* truth norms (TN-P):

(TN-P) For any S, p: S *may* (believe that p) if and only if it is true that p.

Depending on whether (TN-P) is understood as a necessary principle (TN-P$_N$) or a sufficient principle (TN-P$_S$) (right-to-left interpretation or left-to-right interpretation of the biconditional), we're dealing with two variations of norms:

(TN-P$_N$) For any S, p: If it is true that p, then S *may* (believe that p).

(TN-P$_S$) For any S, p: If S *may* (believe that p), then it is true that p.

According to Whiting, on the basis of both principles it can be made clear why Blindspot-Propositions aren't puzzling for the permissive approach. In his view the basic problem is that a norms conflict arises in the application of (TN$_O$), whereby one believes and doesn't believe (BP). This conflict doesn't seem to appear in the case of (TN-P). Indeed the second principle (TN-P$_S$) indirectly demands that one isn't allowed to believe (BP) when such a proposition is false. However, this demand does *not* strictly conflict with the first principle (TN-P$_N$) because this principle doesn't imply that one *should* believe (BP); it only implies that one can believe (BP) when it's true. Therefore, both principles appear to be mutually compatible.[26]

But even this approach is problematic in my opinion. According to Whiting, one can say that a norm like (TN-P) is justified even in the application of (BP) since, based on the second principle, (TN-P$_S$) demands that one may not believe such propositions because they are then false when one believes them. But this is strange somehow. (BP) are not false *per se*. The actual puzzle is that such a

---

24 This assumes that the following principle applies for a rational person S: When S believes that p & q, then S believes p as well as q.
25 See for example Papineau (2013, 66).
26 Cf. Whiting (2010).

proposition is first rendered false *when* they are believed by someone. In view of the general question of whether one may or may not believe a true (BP), (TN-P$_S$) doesn't seem to make the claim that it is not allowed to believe such propositions. Consequentially, it's not clear in what way (BP) is less puzzling in the case of (TN-P).

Moreover, another problem arises here: Why should it be assumed that a norm like (TN-P) is justified in the application of (BP) when we regard this norm as a *necessary* principle in terms of (TN-P$_N$)? This principle doesn't demand that one may not believe (BP) when such propositions are false. It only implies that one may believe true (BP). So when it's correct that a norm like (TN-P) is justified because one may not believe (BP), the question at this point is, why does (TN-P$_N$) play no role in the application of (BP)? Whiting doesn't seem to be able to explain why the second principle, particularly in the application of (BP), is seen as dominant.

What could speak in favor of the supposition that in the application of (BP), the first principle (TN-P$_N$) exerts no normative force? The obvious answer is that truth as an external epistemic goal is normative in two ways. It is not so that the general norm (TN-P) only contains the permission to increase true beliefs; no more is it allowed to acquire false beliefs. As a result, it could be argued that the balancing of the different normative demands in the case of (BP) leads to the fact that a principle like (TN-P$_S$) plays a dominant role. In such cases, the permission to believe a true proposition through the command to believe false propositions is undermined. This explanation, however, makes clear that a general norm like (TN-P) doesn't possess a "binding sense" *simpliciter*. The "normative force" of (TN-P) is not given in an absolute sense. Rather, it seems the question is in *what* regard (TN-P) possesses a normative force to be dependent wherein the external epistemic goal exists. Depending on wherein this external goal exists, the balancing of the various regards under those (TN-P) of a normative force turn out differently. This shows, however, that a fulfillment of the inherent goal of epistemic normativity is not possible without a previous determination of the external goal of the inquiry.

3.2 The No-guidance Argument Against the Truth Norm of Belief

Independent of formulation, the alleged prescriptive character of (TN$_O$) creates another general problem. It's commonly accepted that norms have a guiding function in one form or other. However, it can be doubted whether doxastic norms possess such a guiding function for our belief formation. Notably, Kathrin

Glüer & Asa Wikforss (2009, 2010, 2013) have argued on various points that (TNO)—and all other candidates of a truth norm—cannot acquire "the role of a norm guiding our belief formation". There arguments are abbreviated as such:

(P_1) In accordance to the 'global template for doxastic normativity', norms have the following conditional structure: If the condition C is fulfilled, then S should believe that p.
(P_2) (TN_O) has a guiding function for the belief of S only if S believes that the condition C is fulfilled.
(P_3) S only believes that the condition C is fulfilled if S previously believed that p is true.
(P_4) If, however, the question of whether S, because of (TN_O), should believe that p is *identical* with the question of whether p is true—*or* that the previous question of whether p is true already *implies* that s believes that p is true—then a norm like (TN_O) has no guiding function for the belief formation by S.
(P_5) A norm that does not exert a guiding function on the belief formation does not possess a prescriptive force.

On the basis of (P_4) and (P_5)

(C) The objective truth norm (TN_O) is not prescriptive.

With this argument it shouldn't be disputed that there is a strong link between the correct formation of beliefs and the (true) contents of the position at hand. Glüer & Wikforrs don't explain that beliefs with false contents are epistemically correct.[27] Instead, their point is to show that it is generally problematic to speak about a *prescriptive form of correctness* in the realms of epistemic normativity. According to this view, even a weak prescriptive approach is affected by this argument.

What can be said in defense of (TN_O)? The central premise of the argument is (P_4). One can doubt in at least two ways whether (P_4) is true.[28] The first part of this premise is based on the following claim: An answer to the question of whether one should believe that p is only then epistemically correct if this an-

---

[27] Cf. Glüer & Wikforss (2013, 84).
[28] Furthermore, there's the possibility of avoiding the existing argument by pursuing a purely *evaluative* approach to the the usual deontic strategies for the explanation of doxastic norms (McHugh 2012). In this case, the normative force of such norms would not be understood in the sense of the guiding motivation under discussion here. I'll come back to this thought later.

swer is identical to the answers to the question of whether p is true. But this is not quite right. As Steglich-Petersen (2013) points out, it is quite possible to try to answer the question of whether to believe that p without regarding the question of whether p is true as relevant to the issue. Here is an example: You can think that the correctness of believing p depends on understanding why p rather than the truth of p. This means, however, if we followed the truth norm rather than the norm based on understanding why, we would end up in any case with a different belief. For this reason the truth norm makes a difference about what one should believe.

A similar difficulty arises in the second part of premise (P_4). According to this part, what the argument points out is that the guidance of (TN_O) comes 'too late' to influence one's beliefs.[29] In order to go by a norm like (TN_O), one must know when this norm is applicable. The only possibility of ascertaining this consists of investigating whether the content p of the relevant belief is true or not. But then the application of (TN_O) seems to imply that one believes that p is true. However, even here one could argue that through the following of other (epistemic) norms of truth, independent criteria exists for which it's appropriate to apply a norm like (TN_O) in certain circumstances.

According to these considerations, it is not clear whether Glüer & Wikforrs's argument works. The crucial question at this point is whether the previously acquired belief that the condition C is fulfilled actually prevents (TN_O) from having a normative force. In order to clarify this point, it's useful to differentiate the two views of the explanation of the guiding function of doxastic norms:[30]

Narrow conception of the guiding belief formation
A truth norm as "(TNO)" can influence S's cognitive activity ϕ if it is possible that "(TNO)" can make a difference to S's ϕ-ing compared to S's ϕ-ing after having determined whether C is fulfilled.

Broad conception of the guiding belief formation
A truth norm as (TN_O) can influence S's cognitive activity ϕ if it possible that (TN_O) can make a difference to S's ϕ-ing compared to S's ϕ-ing determined to what one comes to believe as a consequence of following other epistemic norms.

---

[29] Cf. Glüer & Wikforss (2013, 84).
[30] This differentiation harks back to Steglich-Petersen (2013). As Steglich-Petersen accurately noticed, for a minimal determination of the 'guiding belief formation', it's completely sufficient to explain how the compliance of the norm accomplishes a *significant difference in the cognitive behavior* of the person concerned.

Implying a narrow conception—as Glüer & Wikforss evidently do—seems to actually make it difficult to explain how (TN_O) has influence on the formation of beliefs. By contrast, with regard to a broad conception, it looks totally different. In the context of this notion, it's namely debated that the guiding function is explained through the application of the norm *itself*. Instead, for this explanation it's assumed that a *comparison to other doxastic norms* must be established. Thus, the guiding function is not explained through mere application of (TN_O), but through the fact that, compared to the compliance of other norms, a difference in cognitive behavior exists which we epistemically appraise. Whether someone correctly forms a belief that complies with (TN_O), it's clear that there are other external goals of inquiry relative to those where it's not (epistemically) correct to acquire a belief of this kind. In other words, for an explanation in the sense of broad conception, it's constitutive that there are also other epistemic norms besides (TN_O) in comparison to those of the specific character of normative force which first emerge from (TN_O).

What follows from this discussion of the question of whether the compliance of a norm like (TN_O) has a priority in relation to all other inherent or external epistemic goals? The 'no-guidance argument' makes it clear that such a claim is inaccurate since the prescriptive force of (TN_O)—with regard to the formation of correct beliefs—is thereby not explained out of the mere application of this norm. Still, this doesn't mean that it's principally impossible to follow such inherent goals. The proposed broad conception offers an alternative explanation of the guiding function of doxastic norms. This explanation is connected with a *change in the consideration* of such inherent goals. The particular prescriptive character of (TN_O) does *not directly* arise from the norm but *relative* to the application of other norms. In what circumstance a doxastic norm is given the priority, consequently doesn't depend on on the norm alone, but also on the external conditions (meaning the epistemic goals) which are directive for a particular inquiry. In the next section I will more precisely illustrate how to understand this connection.

4. The Relationship between Inherent Doxastic and External Epistemic Goals

The previous discussion shows that a close connection exists between inherent doxastic goals and external epistemic goals. In the following, I'd like to develop an approach to the explanation of epistemic normativity which accounts for this fact. My proposal is based on two basic ideas: First, a "broad conception of the guiding belief formation" of doxastic norms needs to be connected with the pluralistic conjecture that there are various kinds of external epistemic goals, from which it depends under what conditions inherent goals develop a prescriptive force. The general claim here is this: It can be said whether the compliance of a doxastic norm is binding for the cognitive activities at hand only *relative* to a particular kind of external goal of the inquiry.

The second basic idea proves that the fulfillment of a norm like (TN_O) is not a primary inherent goal with an overriding epistemic value. Instead of a hierarchical model, the proposed conception of a "linear" connection between prescriptive and axiological elements attempts to establish an explanation of epistemic normativity. Thusly, epistemic projects are to be understood as normative *clusters* which combine out of one or more *external epistemic goals* and the *corresponding doxastic norm (inherent doxastic goal)*. A cognitive activity is correct in epistemic regards if it is formed in accordance with the doxastic norm that is epistemically significant in the sense of the leading (external) goal of the inquiry. Both will be more closely explained in the following.

(a) The Axiological Component of Epistemic Normativity

In order to answer the question of when a norm is epistemically significant (i.e. when they have a normative force) it must be more closely observed under which conditions a cognitive activity acquires an epistemic value. Interestingly, at this point we can find an obvious connection between epistemic accuracy and the so-called fitting attitude theories (FAT) of value. Fitting attitude theories propose to analyze values in terms of weak normative evaluative attitudes endorsed as fitting, appropriate, or correct. There are many ways to spell out this view in more detail, but we can start as general as possible and base this discussion on the following FAT-style definition of (propositional) value:[31]

---

[31] Different sorts of fitting attitude theories have been discussed in the literature, for instance the *sensibility theory* proposed by McDowell (1998) and Wiggins (1987), *sentimentalism* proposed by D'Arms and Jacobson (2000, 2006), and the so-called *buck-passing account* proposed by Scanlon (1998). It can be disputed whether all of these views would wholeheartedly accept the two claims of fitting attitude theories. Scanlon's buck-passing account, for instance, relies more strongly on normative reduction and could possibly be spelled out without the attitude dependency thesis. Some forms of sentimentalism, on the other hand, rely more on attitude dependency and don't explicitly discuss normative reduction.

Fitting attitude theory of value
It is valuable that p if and only if it is appropriate to have a pro-attitude towards p.

This definition accepts both main claims of fitting attitude theories, i.e. the attitude-dependency of value claims and the weakly normative reduction of values. Such an account, however, only gives us a very broad framework for an explanation of various sorts of values. In order to explain what is meant not only by 'valuable' but by 'epistemically valuable', we must explain what the appropriateness of the expressed approval of an epistemic ascription consists in. In regards to a teleological framework, I argue that the reason for epistemically admiring a cognitive stance is that it serves or satisfies our epistemic goals or interests:

Definition of epistemic value
It is epistemically valuable that p if and only if p serves our epistemic interests or the epistemic goals of our inquiry.

According to this account, the remaining question is, what is really an epistemic interest or external goal for that matter? I think the straightforward answer of this question is this: An epistemic interest or epistemic goal, generally speaking, can be characterized (similar to Sosa 2007) as an "ultimate explainer". This means two things: External goals represent those normative sources which we appoint when we want to explain what distinguishes a particular area of esteem from another. One can define various areas of esteem (aesthetic, moral, political, etc.) from one another by identifying the basis (external) goal which consistently constitutes a particular area of esteem. The reference to external epistemic goals enables an explanation of what it means in *epistemic regards* (i.e. viewed from an epistemic standpoint) that a cognitive activity has value.

Furthermore, my represented pluralistic concept implies, in terms of epistemic esteems, that there isn't just one single basic external goal but more such goals (truth, knowledge, understanding, wisdom, etc.). Each of these goals is capable of generating a *particular* epistemic regard. *Relative* to this regard, it is correct or appropriate (for the given context) to esteem a cognitive activity. This, of course, takes place within the framework of the inquiry at hand.

Which of the various external epistemic goals is leading in a given context, however, depends on a broader aspect, namely on the issue that invokes our interest in information within the framework of the current inquiry.[32] This second

---

[32] In accordance to the prevalent viewpoint, our interest in truth information is to be analysed on the basis of human curiosity (cf. Brady 2009, Grimm 2008, Kvanvig 2009, 2013; Whitcomb

aspect refers to the following relationship: When we consider something from an epistemic point of view, we see it as something which satisfies (or is intended to satisfy) a certain information demand, and the general and most common model of an information demand is a *question we ask*. You can say, therefore, that asking a question is an explicit expression of epistemic interest (but possibly not the only one). Or more directly, asking a question is something which individualizes the current goal of inquiry because it satisfies our information demand and helps to answer the question which is invoked by our epistemic inquiry.[33]

In addition to the aforesaid, the claim is linked to the fact that the various external goals—which are generated through the prevailing interest in the question—correlate with different doxastic conditions in which, as a result, it is appropriate or correct in an epistemic regard to assess the formation of a belief. This approach contains an additional prescriptive aspect.

(b) The Prescriptive Component of Epistemic Normativity

The cluster-conception assumes the basic idea that, with a change of the leading external epistemic goal—caused by a different information demand—even the inherent doxastic goals change according to those one should or may believe from an epistemic standpoint. Schematically, this connection can be represented as follows:

The Normative Template of the Cluster-Conception
If Z is the leading (external) goal of the inquiry, then the application of a doxastic norm NB has a normative-binding force in epistemic regard if the following of NB satisfies the actual interest in the question that Z has generated.

2010). Thus, the following general connection exists between the contents of a cognitive activity and the kind of curiosity that's invoked in a person with regard to the open question of an inquiry: A proposition p is significant for S if and only if p delivers an answer to the question that's invoked by S's curiosity within the framework of a specific inquiry. According to this approach, for an epistemological inquiry, influential curiosity refers to a relation (S-F) that's invoked within the framework of such an inquiry. For the definition of epistemic value indicated above, this means it is appropriate to esteem a doxastic attitude with content p if the content p delivers an answer to the question that's invoked by S's curiosity. Provided S bears a relation to F which is significant in epistemic regards, then the content p of cognitive activity must give an answer to F that only then is adequate if p plays a crucial role in the explanation of why S's curiosity is satisfied.

33 For further details of this analysis see Braeuer & Schmechtig (Ms.).

This schema makes it clear that one can no longer suggest, in an absolute sense, that a doxastic norm is significant in an epistemic regard. What "binding sense" the following of a doxastic norm has is much more dependent on what can be used for Z (truth, knowledge, understanding, wisdom, etc.). For this purpose, we'll consider the case that knowledge is the leading (external) goal of the inquiry. Here, the application of a doxastic norm like (TN_O) doesn't seem to possess a normative power since the following of (TN_O), in the case of a incidental true belief, is not successful when observed from an epistemic standpoint. To say that a belief is correct whose content is incidentally true, doesn't correspond with the leading (external) goal of the inquiry. The actual interest in the question that knowledge, as a leading external goal, invokes our attempts to gain knowledge would not be satisfied in the case of a mere incidentally true belief. The leading interrogative impulse of inquiry would continue to exist despite an application of this norm. To be really successful, the inquiry must be pursued. Consequentially, the fulfillment of (TN_O) doesn't represent an inherent goal that correlates with the actual leading (external) goal of the inquiry, i.e. knowledge.

Of course this doesn't mean that the following of (TN_O) is never significant. When we assume that the acquiring of true beliefs is the leading (external) goal of the inquiry, then nothing objects that (TN_O)—at least in an indirect form—possesses a normative force. Then the actual interest in the question actually corresponding with the (TN_O) would also be satisfied by a incidentally true belief in this case.

The same also applies to the other (external) epistemic goals. By way of example, let's assume that our actual interest in the question entails finding out whether S *understands why* p is the case. In this situation it can be that even the application of a knowledge norm—standardly expressed in the form of S should believe that p if S knows that p—is not normatively-bound. How is that possible? Sometimes, due to testimonial sources, we get to knowledge *without* a following of the connected knowledge norm being compatible with the (external) goal of the epistemic understanding. In such situations, it's typical that S should believe that p because S knows that p although the content of this belief is not significantly relative to the leading goal of the inquiry. This is because the actual interest in the question—understanding-why—is not satisfied. As in the previous case, the inquiry must be pursued.

At this point, this question naturally arises: How can it be explained, in the framework of such a pluralistic cluster-conception, that doxastic norms acquire a normative-binding force dependent on the leading external goal of the inquiry? An obvious answer is that external epistemic goals generate, virtually by themselves, prescriptive doxastic standards which, in the form of a *direct ought*, declare under what circumstances a cognitive activity is epistemically correct. However, such an approach—analog to the discussion of the abstract truth norm (TN_O)—would have the basic problem of not being able to explain how such a direct epistemic ought is sedimented in cognitive behavior.

By way of contrast, the cluster-conception tries to give another explanation. In doing so, three considerations play a central role. In relation to the discussion of radical consequentialism, it's already been highlighted that epistemic accuracy is a function of norms and reasons. These can be clarified in the existing framework as follows: If a norm is correct in an epistemic regard, then the fact that a belief complies with this norm supplies a sufficiently good reason that the content of this belief serves the leading (external) goal of the inquiry, meaning the interrogative information demand is satisfied. Under this idea, the leading (external) goal of the inquiry lends the corresponding doxastic norms something like a 'reason-giving force'. The following of the norms, which turn out to be significant in view of the actual information demand, supply a good reason that the inquiry can be successfully completed through the acquiring of the appropriate belief. For this reason, it is not helpful to say that doxastic standards generate the external goals by themselves because normative standards do not provide reasons for their compliance. They function more like fashion trends that impose something (f.i. what one should wear) but they themselves don't supply good reason for accepting these trends.

The second aspect concerns the way in which the leading (external) goal of the inquiry transmits the just mentioned 'reason-giving force'. The cluster-conception relies on an *indirect* explanation of this transformation. If S is guided in the process of rational deliberation of beliefs by a subjectively accessible norm N_B which corresponds with the guiding goal of inquiry Z—because N_B is an appropriate means for the successful accomplishment of Z—then S reaches a belief which is compatible with an external source of epistemic normativity.[34] According to this approach, the idea of a direct deontic ought—which should virtually be given by itself due to the application of an abstract norm like (TN_O)—is denied and replaced by the prescriptive term of the normative reason.[35] Doxastic norms that correspond with the leading external goal acquire a normative-binding force because their following supplies a good reason that, through a belief

---

[34] Such an indirect explanation is represented in a different form by Shah & Velleman (2005) and Wedgwood (2007). With respect to the indirect approach, different objections arise (cf. Glüer & Wikforss 2013, 85 ff.). However, without being able to elaborate on this point here, I think that these objections can be avoided in the framework of the cluster-conception.

[35] See, for example, Cuneo (2007), Millar (2004), Mitova (in this collection), Scanlon (1998), Skorupski (2007).

which complies with such norms, the actual inquiry can be successfully completed.

The third aspect ultimately refers to the kind of prescriptive character of the reason at hand. The 'reason-giving force' of the corresponding doxastic norms can be understood in two different forms: Either as a strong act-motivation prescription or in terms of a weak *evaluative* normalization of the appropriate cognitive attitude. A strong prescription exists if G is a normative reason, so that it's appropriate for S, due to G, *to do something*—namely to accept or to reject a belief—that's in accordance with the corresponding doxastic norm N_B. In contrast, the present cluster-conception assumes that the epistemic term 'reason-giving force' is to be used in a weaker *evaluative* sense. Thusly, a normative reason G is (weak) prescriptive if it is, in an epistemic regard, appropriate or correct for S, due to G, to possess a pro-attitude (approval) or contra-attitude (disapproval) as opposed to a belief that's in accordance with N_B. The latter states that the "reason-giving force" of doxastic norms therein is not established to give reasons which motivate the act of generating a belief, but it has influence on how we will epistemically *appraise* cognitive attitudes. With an evaluative approach of the explanation of doxastic norms (cf. McHugh 2012), I share the view that a strong prescriptive term of the regulation of beliefs—whether it's in the form of an immediate deontic ought or in the sense of a direct action-guiding control of doxastic behavior—is inappropriate. Within the framework of the cluster-conception, it can be more precisely explained what is meant by such a weak prescription of the 'reason-giving force' of doxastic norms:

Weak prescriptive reason giving force
If S acquires a belief with content p as a result of being in accordance with a doxastic norm N_B and thereby serves the leading (external) goal of the inquiry Z, then p supplies a good reason why a pro-attitude towards belief is appropriate in regards to the attainment of Z.

According to this broad characterization of "reason-giving force" (subjective) of doxastic norms, the prescriptive character of the reason refers to the conditions of *appropriateness of pro- and contra-attitudes*. Only those beliefs whose contents justify an approval or disapproval of such beliefs in light of the leading (external) goal of the inquiry are significant in epistemic regards.

5. Conclusions

The cluster approach at hand assumes that cognitive activities are epistemically valuable as long as the contents of these activities serve the external goal of the inquiry. A particular external goal, however, is only then leading if it has a "binding sense" within the framework of the actual inquiry. In addition to that, the cognitive activities have to be in accordance with those doxastic norms which are connected with the respective external goal. By the same token, the corresponding doxastic norms only have a "normative force" *relative* to the actual (interrogative) information demands which generate the leading external goal of the inquiry. Since a closer connection between the inherent doxastic and external epistemic goals exists, the deontic question "What should or may we believe?" cannot be separated from the axiological question "When is a cognitive activity good or significant in epistemic regard?".

Against the backdrop of this connection, an array of the previously addressed problems can be avoided in the framework of the cluster-conception:

(1) The teleological standard position (epistemic consequentialism) cannot explain wherein the "binding sense" of the external source of epistemic normativity exists. The mentioned radical approach must assume that external epistemic goals are not synchronous nature and conflict with subjective accessible norms like (EN_B). Neither of the two problems is a consequence of the proposed conception. On the contrary. According to the cluster approach, this is valid: As long as truth is the external goal of the inquiry, a belief, precisely as a consequence, possesses an epistemic value because it is thereby (synchronously) justified as a result of being indirectly formed in accordance with a subjective norm like (EN_B).

Furthermore, within the scope of radical consequentialism, it's claimed that 'epistemic ought' is a function of norms and reasons. Although this assumption is true, it remains open as to what is meant by this. The cluster-conception supplies an explanation. It clarifies that the following of doxastic norms contains a 'reason-giving force' as long as the norm at hand corresponds with the leading external goal of the inquiry.

(2) Compared to the moderate variation of epistemic consequentialism, it's objected that there is a particular kind of example which argues against such an approach. I argued that perhaps the best strategy for avoiding such examples is based on the assumption that the external sources of epistemic normativity is a *generic* goal, namely the satisfaction of the interrogative information demand which is decisive in the area of actual inquiry. The cluster-conception takes up these thoughts. However, it does so in a way that avoids the problem of not

being able to explain how such a generic goal gets along with the typical consequentialist assertion that truth is the primary goal of all intellectual inquiries. The cluster-conception avoids the monistic assumption that the acquiring of true beliefs has an absolute epistemic value that overrides all other goals. Instead, it's claimed that the connection can be pluralistically conceived from generic interests in the question and in the leading external goal of the inquiry.

(3) The dialect of this discussion has also made clear that the focus of the standard explanation of epistemic normativity is too narrow. In epistemic consequentialism, the link between truth and justification is exclusively considered. An adequate theory of epistemic normativity should not only answer the question of whether it is epistemically justified to believe something; it must explain, in a broader sense, when a belief is appropriate or correct in an epistemic regard. If one admits that there are also other external epistemic goals besides truth—although even the corresponding doxastic norms could change with these goals—then the focus of the standard explanation must be expanded. In this regard, the cluster-conception supplies a *comprehensive* explanation of epistemic normativity.

(4) The discussion of the question of whether there is possibly, conversely, a priority of the explanation of doxastic normativity has unearthed the problem of the so-called belief blindspots. Thusly, there is a particular class of propositions that—although true—do not agree that an objective truth norm like (TN_O) possesses a normative force. Even a weakening in the formulation of the prescriptive force of such norms could not avoid this problem because norms like (TN-P) don't possess a normative force *simpliciter*. The cluster-conception avoids this trouble since it's not assumed that an abstract norm like (TN_O) or (TN-P) possess a prescriptive force independent of the leading external goal of the inquiry. This enables the following simple observation of 'belief blindspots': In contexts where it's useful to ask whether one should or shouldn't believe a (BP), the interrogative information demand doesn't seem to be to figure out whether those propositions are true. For this reason, norms like (TN_O) are not significant in such contexts since they don't correlate with the leading external goal in regards to that the cognitive attitudes concerned are epistemically appraised. Nevertheless, it can still be epistemically correct to believe (BP) if, for example, the context of the question is that understanding-why is the leading external goal of the inquiry with regard to that such an attitude appears valuable.[36]

---

[36] This approach, of course, assumes that there are (interrogative) forms of epistemic understanding which correlate with doxastic norms that are not dependent on (TN_O). In addition to that, Pascal Engel (2007) proposes a different strategy. This results in the problem of the Blindspot-Proposition not really being relevant since, from an epistemic regard, one should believe

(5) The second central issue within the scope of this discussion concerns the addressed 'no-guidance' argument. Doxastic norms should have a regulating influence of some form. According to the 'no-guidance' argument, it is impossible to explain the guiding function of a norm like (TN_O) directly from the application of such a norm. In contrast, the cluster-conception proposes a "broad conception of the guiding belief formation". According to this, the regulating influence can be derived from the *prescriptive difference*, which has the following of a particular doxastic norm *compared* to the application with other norms. This proposal, however, requires that there are also other doxastic norms besides (TN_O) which are significant in epistemic regard and can, consequentially, be linked with various external epistemic goals.

(6) The cluster-conception rules out that epistemic correctness is explained as a direct following of an abstract norm like (TN_O). Rather, it's claimed that the doxastic norm, which is connected with the external goal, is prescriptive in an *indirect* form. The advantage of this indirect explanation is apparent when, for example, one observes in what form the acquiring of true beliefs can be an external goal of the inquiry. In contrast to the problematic assumption that an abstract norm like (TN_O) implies a direct epistemic ought, within the scope of the cluster-conception, it's assumed that truth indirectly—mediated as an external goal of the inquiry by subjective, accessible norms like (EN_B)—exerts a regulatory function on the formation of beliefs. Thus, the following of (EN_B) supplies a sufficiently good reason that a belief, which is formed in accordance with this norm, will serve the external truth-goal. With this, one avoids the 'no-guidance' argument discussed above. The question of whether one should believe that p is obviously *not identical* with the question of whether p is true, meaning it is not identical with the fulfillment of the antecedent-attitudes of (TN_O).[37]

(7) The following objection can be raised against such an indirect approach of the explanation of the prescriptive force of doxastic norms: The indirect approach appears to assume that doxastic norms play a prescriptive role only with-

---

that which one actually understands. It should be clear that this deflationist strategy is not to be confused with the solution proposed here. As Bykvist & Hattiangadi (2007, 2013) make clear, the problem does not exist in the question of whether one can understand (BP). Obviously, we can understand (BP)'s. To a greater degree, the problem affects the doxastic claim which is linked with norms like (TN_o). The "should-implies-can" principle is not subject to negotiation here, but the assumption that the prescriptive demand is raised with (TN_O) is justified.

37 Nor is it implied, through the question of whether p is true, that S should believe that p is true under the application of (EN_B). For, the conditions under which it is epistemically correct to believe something in terms of (EN_B) are obviously not the same under which one believes that p is true. S can believe that p is true without having sufficient evidence for p, with the result that S —with the correct application of (EN_B)—shouldn't believe that p.

in concrete acts which lead an agent to conscious assumptions or the avoidance of beliefs. According to this approach, reasons for beliefs are viewed as a kind of consideration in which agents move to carry out particular doxastic acts. This kind of direct action-leading control of beliefs, however, is extremely disputed under epistemic points of view. The cluster-conception takes this fact into account in that it doesn't understand the 'reason-giving force' of doxastic norms in a strictly action-leading sense. Thus, the reasons that emerge from the following of doxastic norms don't speak for the execution of a doxastic action in the strict sense, but for the appropriateness of the epistemic appraisal of the cognitive attitude at hand. According to this notion, reasons which speak for the approval or disapproval of a belief in regards to the external goal of the inquiry could appear appropriate although they don't motivate an action-leading control for this attitude. The cluster-conception is thusly compatible in that doxastic norms possess a regulatory function even beyond a deliberative product of strict reasons for actions.

In conclusion, I would like to emphasize that it seems to be completely clear, that in terms of single problems which have been addressed throughout this paper, there is still further need for clarification. Nevertheless, the advantages just discussed seem to show that the proposed cluster-conception is a promising candidate for being able to adequately explain wherein the close connection between both core questions of epistemic normativity exists. Lastly, within such a comprehensive consideration of this topic, one should no longer be able to suggest that either of the two questions takes priority over the other.

References

Ahlstrom-Vij, K. & Dunn, J. (2014). A Defence of Epistemic Consequentialism. *The Philosophical Quarterly* 64, 541–551.
Alston, W. P. (1989). *Epistemic Justification: Essays in the Theory of Knowledge*. Ithaca, NY: Cornell University Press.
Alston, W. P. (2005). *Beyond "Justification": Dimensions of Epistemic Evaluation*. Ithaca, NY: Cornell University Press.
Berker, S. (2013a). Epistemic Teleology and the Separateness of Propositions. *Philosophical Review* 122, 337–392.
Berker, S. (2013b). The Rejection of Epistemic Consequentialism. *Philosophical Issues*, 23, 363–387.
Berker, S. (2015). Reply to Goldman: Cutting Up the One to Save the Five in Epistemology. *Episteme* 12, 145–53.
Bird, A. (2007). Justified Judging. *Philosophy and Phenomenological Research* 74, 81–100.
Boghossian, P. (2008). *Content and Justification*. Oxford: OPU.

BonJour, L. (1985). *The Structure of Empirical Knowledge*. Cambridge, MA: Harvard University Press.
Brady, M. (2009). Curiosity and the Value of Truth. In A. Haddock, A. Millar and D. Pritchard (eds.), *Epistemic Value*. Oxford: OPU.
Braeuer, H. and P. Schmechtig (Manuscript). Epistemic Expressivism and the Value of Epistemic Goods, 1–23.
Bykvist and Hattiangadi (2007). Does Thought Imply Ought?. *Analysis* 67, 277–285.
Bykvist, K. and Hattiangadi, A. (2013). Belief, Truth, and Blindspots. In T. Chan (ed.), *The Aim of Belief*. Oxford: OUP.
Conee, E. and Feldman, F. (1984). *Evidentialism*, Oxford: OUP.
Cuneo, T. (2007). *The Normative Web*. Oxford: OUP.
D'Arms, J. and Jacobson, D. (2000). Sentiment and value. *Ethics* 110, 722–748.
D'Arms, J. and Jacobson, D. (2006). Anthropocentric Constraints on Human Value. In R. Shafer-Landau (ed.), *Oxford Studies in Metaethics* (Vol. 1). Oxford: Clarendon Press.
David, M. (2001). Truth as the Epistemic Goal. In M. Steup (ed.), *Knowledge, Truth, and Duty: Essays on Epistemic Justification, Virtue, and Responsibility*. Oxford: OUP.
Engel, P. (2007). Belief and Normativity? *Disputatio* 2 (23), 153–77.
Engel, P. (2013). In Defence of Normativism About the Aim of Belief. In T. Chan (ed.), *The Aim of Belief*. Oxford: OUP.
Elgin, C. (2004). True Enough. *Philosophical Issues* 14, 113–31.
Elgin, C. (2007). Understanding and the Facts. *Philosophical Studies* 132, 33–42.
Firth, R. (1981). Epistemic Merit, Intrinsic and Instrumental. *Proceedings and Addresses of the American Philosophical Association*, 5–23.
Feldman, F. (2000). The Ethics of Belief. *Philosophy and Phenomenological Research* 60, 667–695.
Foley, R. (1987). *The Theory of Epistemic Rationality*. Cambridge, MA: Harvard University Press.
Foley, R. (1992). *Working Without a Net*. Oxford: OUP.
Fumerton, R. (2001). Epistemic Justification and Normativity. In M. Steup (ed.), *Knowledge, Truth, and Duty: Essays on Epistemic Justification, Responsibility and Virtue*. Oxford: OUP.
Gibbons, J. (2014). Knowledge versus Truth. In C. Littlejohn and J. Turri (eds.), *Epistemic Norms*. Oxford: OUP.
Grimm, St. (2008). Epistemic Goals and Epistemic Values. *Philosophy and Phenomenological Research* 77, 725–744.
Glüer, K. and A. Wikforss (2009). Against Content Normativity. *Mind* 18, 31–70.
Glüer, K. and A. Wikforss (2010). The Truth Norm and Guidance: A Relpy to Steglich-Petersen. *Mind* 119, 757–61.
Glüer, K. and A. Wikforss (2013). Against Belief Normativity. In T. Chan (ed.), *The Aim of Belief*. Oxford: OUP.
Goldman, A. (2002). *The Unity of the Epistemic Virtues, in his Pathways to Knowledge*. New York: OUP.
Goldman, A. (2015). Reliabilism, Veritism, and Epistemic Consequentialism. *Episteme* 12, 131–143.
Klein, P. (2004). Useful Falsehoods. In: Q. Smith (ed.), *New Essays in Epistemology*. Oxford: OUP.

Kvanvig, J. (2003). *The Value of Knowledge and the Pursuit of Understanding*, New York: Cambridge University Press.
Kvanvig, J. (2013). Curiosity and the Response-Dependent Special Value of Understanding. In T. Henning and D. Schweikard (eds.), *Knowledge, Virtue, and Action*. Boston: Routledge.
Littlejohn, C. (2012). *Justification and the Truth-Connection*. Cambridge: Cambridge UP.
Lynch, D. (2004). *True to Life*. MIT Press.
McDowell, J. (1998). *Mind, Value, and Reality*. Cambridge, Mass: Harvard University Press.
McHugh, C. (2012). The Truth Norm of Belief. *Pacific Philosophical Quarterly* 93, 8–30.
Millar, A. (1994). *Understanding People*. Oxford: OUP.
Papineau, D. (2013). There Are No Norms of Belief. In T. Chan (ed.), *The Aim of Belief*. Oxford: OUP.
Scanlon (1998). *What We Owe to Each Other*. Harvard University Press.
Shah, N. and J. D. Velleman (2005). Doxastic Deliberation. *Philosophical Review* 114, 497–534.
Skorupski, J. (2007). Buck-Passing about Goodness. In Hommage à Wlodek (online source), URL = http://www.fil.lu.se/hommageawlodek/site/papper/SkorupskiJohn.pdf
Smithies, D. (2012). The Normative Role of Knowledge. *Noûs* 46, 265–288.
Sosa, E. (2007). *A Virtue Epistemology*. Oxford: OUP.
Steglich-Petersen, A. (2013). The No Guidance Argument. *Theoria* 79, 279–283.
Sutton, J (2007). *Without Justification*. Cambridge: CUP.
Talbot, B. (2014). Truth Promoting Non-Evidential Reasons for Belief. *Philosophical Studies* 168, 3, 599–618.
Warfield, T. (2005). Knowledge from Falsehood. *Philosophical Perspectives* 19, 405–16.
Weiner, M. (2005). Must We Know What We Say?. *Philosophical Review* 114, 227–251.
Wedgwood, R. (2002). The Aim of Belief. *Philosophical Perspectives* 16, 267–297.
Wedgwood, R. (2007). *The Nature of Normativity*. Oxford: OUP.
Whitcomb, D. (2010). Curiosity was Framed. *Philosophy and Phenomenological Research* 81, 664–687.
Whiting, D. (2010). Should I Believe the Truth. *dialectica* 64, 213–224.
Wiggins, D. (1987). A Sensible Subjectivism?. In his *Needs, values, truth: essays in the philosophy of value*. Oxford: Blackwell.
Williams, B. (1973). Deciding to Believe. In his *Problems of the Self*. Cambridge: CUP.
Williamson, T. (2000). *Knowledge and its Limits*. Oxford: OUP.
Zagzebski, L. (2001). Recovering Understanding. In M. Steup (ed.), *Knowledge, Truth, and Duty: Essays on Epistemic Justification, Responsibility, and Virtue*. New York: OUP.
Zangwill, N. (2010). The Normativity and the Metaphysics of Mind. *Australasion Journal of Philosophy* 88, 21–39.

Matthew Chrisman
The Aim of Belief and the Goal of Truth: Reflections on Rosenberg[1]

"What makes us cognitive beings at all is our capacity for belief, and the goal of our distinctively cognitive endeavors is truth...the basic role of justification is that of a means to truth, a more directly attainable mediating link between our subjective starting point and our objective goal" (BonJour, 1985: 7-8).

"Naturalization of epistemology does not jettison the normative...For me, normative epistemology is a branch of engineering. It is the technology of truth-seeking...it is a matter of efficacy for an ulterior end, truth" (Quine, 1986: 664).

*

"[Truth] is not what common sense would call a goal. For it is neither something we might realize we had reached, nor something to which we might get closer" (Rorty, 1995: 39).

"We know many things, and will learn more; what we will never know for certain is which of the things we believe is true. Since it is neither a visible target, nor recognizable when achieved, there is no point in calling truth a goal" (Davidson, 2000: 67).

"The upshot seems to be that no notion of truth, neither a transcendent notion of objective truth nor a minimalist notion of immanent truth, can play any determinative role at all in our epistemic activities...it begins to look as if we would do well to stop talking about truth altogether and just identify the goal of our cognitive-epistemic activities per se as justified belief" (Rosenberg 2002: 229).

1. Introduction

At the beginning of *Thinking about Knowing*, Rosenberg advertises his argumentative aim with characteristic panache: "The leading thesis developed in this book...is that knowledge is simply adequately justified belief" (2002: 1). With this, he doesn't mean to deny that knowledge is factive: one who is committed to S's knowing that p is committed to p's being true. However, as he explains, "Since from any one epistemic perspective the judgements that S has done every-

---

[1] The original version of this essay appeared in *Self, Language, and World: Problems from Kant, Sellars, and Rosenberg*, edited by James R. O'Shea and Eric M. Rubenstein (Ridgeview Publishing Company, www.ridgeviewpublishing.com, 2010). In what follows, the text has been lightly edited and a substantive postscript added.

thing requisite to be entitled confidently to believe that p and that S has done everything requisite to establish the truth of p stand or fall together, a further 'truth requirement' is vacuous and idle. Truth may arguably be an outcome of enquiry, but it can function neither as enquiry's goal nor as a constraining condition on any de facto epistemic policy or procedure" (ibid.: 2). Since reading this, I've found his idea both enticing and confusing. Ultimately, I think it is mistaken, but, as is often the case with philosophers we respect, appreciating why one of their central claims is mistaken teaches us as much or more than appreciating why many of their other claims are correct. I think a lot of what Rosenberg claims, both in that book and elsewhere is correct, so I hope it will be particularly instructive to appreciate why his idea that truth can function neither as enquiry's goal nor as a constraining condition on any de facto epistemic policy or procedure is mistaken.

Understanding why Rosenberg claims that truth cannot function as a goal of enquiry or a constraining condition on any de facto epistemic policy or procedure requires discussing some dialectical preliminaries, after which I shall first state and then explain Rosenberg's argument for the claim. This will involve pointing out several places where one might want to object to Rosenberg, but, in each case, I'll argue that doing so misses his point. Finally, I shall say where and why I object to the argumnt. This will involve sketching a way that truth can be usefully thought of as the "aim of belief", even if it's not properly called a "goal of enquiry", so that it can, pace Rosenberg, constrain epistemic policies and procedures.

2. Dialectical Preliminaries

In the course of attempting to explain epistemic normativity, it is common to treat truth as the definitive epistemic end. The idea is that there may be many different kinds of reasons to believe some proposition – e.g., prudential, moral, epistemic, etc., but what epistemology is concerned with, when it seeks to explain epistemic normativity, is what makes some consideration a good or bad epistemic reason to believe some proposition. Moreover, many have thought we might give a teleological explanation of something's being an epistemic reason if we take truth to be the definitive epistemic end. A distinctively epistemic reason for believing some proposition is some consideration, the following of which conduces to the end of having true beliefs, rather than, say, beliefs that make you happy, are interesting, or save the world. As the quotes above from BonJour and Quine indicate, this is a prominent view; it is also popular for the way that it makes epistemic normativity seem relatively un-mysterious because it treats epistemic reasons as a species of goal-directed reasons.²

Some philosophers deny that truth is the definitive epistemic end because they think there is no one end that can be used to distinguish epistemic normativity from other sorts of normativity. This is because they think there are several distinctively epistemic ends.³ As far as they are concerned, truth may be an epistemic end, but we have competing ends such as falsehood avoidance, epistemic responsibility, explanatory coherence, understanding, knowledge, and wisdom; and one might think these cannot be reduced to or understood in terms of the goal of truth. Depending on what we mean by "epistemic end", I'm inclined towards something like this pluralist position. However, the crux of the issue regarding Rosenberg's leading thesis is, I think, precisely what we should mean by "epistemic end". So it will prove useful, even for the debate between epistemic monists and pluralists, to consider the more radical argument against the idea that truth is the definitive epistemic end. We find the beginnings of this in some suggestive passages from Rorty and Davidson (quoted above), who understand the proposal to be about our cognitive-epistemic goals. They argue, roughly, that in order for truth to be a genuine goal, we'd have to be able to tell when we achieve it, but, since we are always fallible in our beliefs and only ever have other beliefs to go on, this is impossible. Ergo truth cannot be a goal and ipso facto is not the definitive epistemic end.

3. Rosenberg's Argument

This argument is suggestive but not rigorous. I think it is Rosenberg who has worked it out most thoroughly in ch. 6 of Thinking about Knowing. He claims that those who think that truth is the definitive epistemic end might be thinking of truth in one of two ways. First, they might be thinking of truth in a "realist" or enquiry-transcendent way, in that truth is not epistemically defined but something that could always in principle go beyond what we might discover. The putative goal then would be to believe that p iff p is objectively true. Second, he suggests they might be thinking of truth in a "minimalist" or enquiry-immanent way, in that truth is more or less a matter of mere disquotation. In this case, the putative goal is to believe p if and only if p.

---

2 Other writers defending something like this idea include Foley (1987), Alston (1989), Sartwell (1992), Haack (1998: 203), Beckermann (2001), Lynch (2009, 2013), Hofmann (2005).
3 Kvanvig (2003), Riggs (2002, 2003), Pritchard (2010).

To a first approximation, then, Rosenberg's argument is this: If one is thinking of truth along enquiry-transcendent lines, then truth transcends our beliefs in that there is "no epistemically accessible truth-determinative feature of beliefs" (ibid.: 214). This is because we can never "get outside" of our belief-system to check in a non-question-begging way, whether believing for the reasons that we do brings us closer or farther away from believing what is objectively true. On the other hand, if one is thinking of truth along enquiry-immanent lines, then truth is immanent to any given belief system in that "whatever we currently believe, we hold true" (ibid.: 228). So, there is nothing more to the pursuit of the putative goal of truth about a particular proposition p than the pursuit of belief as to whether p, which means that "…the ostensible goal of immanent truth is … a goal in name only, [since] it does not exert any constraints on the actual concrete conduct of our enquiries"(ibid.: 228–229).

Here is that argument more explicitly:

(1) There is no epistemically accessible feature of beliefs about the world that determines whether they are objectively true. (ibid.: 214)
(2) If there is no epistemically accessible feature of beliefs about the world that determines whether they are objectively true, then there is no way to ascertain whether our belief-forming methods result reliably in our having objectively true beliefs about the world. (ibid.)
(3) If there is no way to ascertain whether our belief-forming methods result reliably in our having objectively true beliefs, then there is no reasonable way to evaluate the efficacy of these methods for achieving the end of our having objectively true beliefs about the world.

First lemma: There is no reasonable way to evaluate the efficacy of our belief-forming methods for achieving the end of our having objectively true beliefs about the world. (ibid.: 218)

(4) We accept each of our beliefs to be true. (ibid.: 228)
(5) If we accept each of our beliefs to be true, then we take each of our belief-forming methods to generate beliefs we accept to be true. (ibid.)
(6) If we take each of our belief-forming methods to generate beliefs we accept to be true, then there is no reasonable way to evaluate the efficacy of these methods for achieving the end of our having beliefs which we accept to be true. (ibid.)

Second lemma: There is no reasonable way to evaluate the efficacy of our belief-forming methods for achieving the end of our having beliefs which we accept to be true. (ibid.)

(7) Some end E can be a genuine goal or capable of constraining our policies or procedures only if there is a reasonable way to evaluate the efficacy of our methods for achieving E. (ibid.: 206–07)

Thus,

(8) Neither our having objectively true beliefs about the world nor our having beliefs that we accept to be true can be a genuine goal or capable of constraining our epistemic policies or procedures. (ibid.: 229)

3.1 The Argument Explained

I shall now explain in a bit more detail each premise and why I think some reasons for objecting to several of them are misguided.

Premise (1) says that there is no epistemically accessible feature of beliefs about the world that determines whether they are objectively true. I think this should be understood as denying two things. First, it denies that there are self-evident beliefs about the world. Perhaps there are self-evident beliefs in tautologies or about the contents of one's own mind. That's debatable (Rosenberg would deny the latter sort of self-evidence for complicated Sellarsian reasons having to do with the 'myth of the given'; I'm not sure what he'd say about the former). But set these aside. When we form a belief about the world, according to premise (1), this belief never comes with an infallible marker of its truth. Second, one of the features of our beliefs may be our reasons for holding them, and, if so, (1) also denies that these reasons can ever guarantee the truth of the beliefs they support. These two denials embody a commitment to a sort of epistemic fallibilism. Rosenberg characterizes a "fallibilist understanding of the notion of justification or warrant" as "one which allows that a person may be justified or warranted in believing a proposition which is nevertheless false"(ibid: 136). Many philosophers take fallibilism to be a reflection of the in principle mind-independence of the world, or the idea that how we take things to be in the world and our reasons for doing so must always be distinguished from how the world really is. Rosenberg suggests that fallibility is "the epistemic reflection of objectivity", i.e., "that the fact that someone believes that p, or even the fact that everyone believes that p, does not imply that it is true that p"(ibid.: 217). To fail to recognize this distinction, many think, is to commit to a crude form of idealism.

However, even while avoiding the crude idealism which rejects the in principle mind-independence of the world, other philosophers will object to fallibilism (and premise (1) of Rosenberg's argument) based on a certain view of what our reasons for belief can be. They will say that sometimes you believe that p because you see that p or you hear that p or you figure out that p or etc., and you cannot see, hear, figure out, etc. that p unless p is true.[4] This means that beliefs formed for these reasons are not fallible. If one's reason for believing that p is that one sees that p, that reason does guarantee the truth of the belief.

If you're sympathetic to this idea, then you may want to reject premise (1) of Rosenberg's argument. However, before doing so, notice that philosophers more sympathetic to Rosenberg will worry that, even if there is a sense in which seeing, hearing, figuring out, etc. that p are genuine reasons for believing that p, they are not reasons that are epistemically accessible features of the beliefs that they support, since we often think that we have seen, heard, or figured out that p only later to discover that we were mistaken. In the cases where we were mistaken, it's natural to think that our reason for believing that p was that we thought that we saw, heard, or figured out that p, but this thought turned out to be false. But why then shouldn't that be the story about reasons in the good cases as well?

One way to diffuse this dispute in the present dialectical context is to distinguish between the reason for believing that p and one's reason for believing that p. We can view the former as facts about the subject's relationship to the fact that p, and the later as facts about what the subject takes her relationship to the ostensible fact that p to be. Then, if p is false, the reasons to believe that p are nonexistent, since there is no fact that p for one to stand in some relation to. However, in such a case, one's reasons to believe that p may nonetheless be things such as one's (unfortunately false) belief that one saw, heard, or figured out that p.

Given this distinction, deep and perennial philosophical controversy hangs on whether we think the primary focus of normative epistemology should be the reasons for belief or one's reasons for belief. However, without being too dismissive of the seriousness of this dispute, I think we should recognize that both proponents and opponents to the idea that truth is the definitive epistemic end, in the sense outlined above, must be committed to focusing on – in the terminology of the distinction I just made – one's reasons for belief rather than the reasons for belief. This is because these philosophers take the claim that truth is the de-

---

4 Compare McDowell (1982, 1986), Martin (2002, 2004).

finitive epistemic end to provide not only a way of distinguishing epistemic reasons from nonepistemic reasons, but also a way of distinguishing good epistemic reasons from bad epistemic reasons. What I'm calling the reasons for belief cannot by their very nature be bad epistemic reasons, so all parties to this debate must instead be after an account of one's reasons for belief. But, if that's right, then parties to this debate cannot reject (1) on the basis of rejecting the fallibilism about reasons it embodies. And, if that's right then I don't presently see any other reason to reject (1) short of a commitment to the crude sort of idealism that rejects the in principle mind-independence of the world.

Premise (2) says that, if there is no epistemically accessible feature of beliefs about the world that determines whether they are objectively true, then there is no way to ascertain whether our belief-forming methods result reliably in our having objectively true beliefs about the world. Rosenberg's idea is not, I think, to deny that we can use one belief-forming method to check the results of another. For, surely, it is commonplace to discover that, relative to an assumed background method, some candidate belief-forming methods are more reliable than others. If, for instance, we come to doubt the veracity of the reporting on the propaganda channel and so check it against the independent news channel, we may find out that forming beliefs based on what is reported on the propaganda channel is not a very reliable way to form true beliefs, at least as judged by the reporting on the independent news channel. Instead, the idea behind (2) must be that in relying on one method to check another, we have to simply assume that the former is reliable. This means that when we check the reliability of a particular belief-forming method, we are not checking whether it is absolutely reliable but merely whether it is reliable relative to the outputs of some other method. After all, if we had instead started by doubting the veracity of the reporting on the independent news channel and then checked it against the propaganda channel, perhaps we would have reached exactly the opposite verdict. And if we checked both against our actually witnessing the events they reported on, we may discover that the independent news channel is more reliable than the propaganda channel, but only relative to the outputs of our actually witnessing the events.

What we seem to need in order to tell whether a belief-forming method is absolutely reliable is a way to compare its results directly to the objective facts. But, given (1), we are only ever able to compare the results of one belief-forming method to the results of some other belief-forming method, which means that we can never tell if we have objectively true beliefs about the facts. This is why Davidson writes, "Truths do not come with a 'mark', like the date in the corner of some photographs, which distinguishes them from falsehoods. The best we can do is test, experiment, keep an open mind. Since it is neither a visible target, nor recognizable when achieved, there is no point in calling truth a goal" (op. cit.).

Lynch objects to Davidson's thought here, and this is another place where you may want to object to the argument I've attributed to Rosenberg. Lynch suggests claims like (2) trade on the false assumption that "we can't recognize whether a belief is true or false unless we can compare it to the naked facts"(2004: 25). Lynch thinks that the idea of comparing a belief to the naked facts is a strange sort of requirement and there is a more natural sense of recognizing when a belief is true, on which it should be a truism that we can and often do recognize when a belief is true. He writes, "The most natural interpretation of what it means to 'recognize when a belief is true' is that to recognize a belief as true or false is either to confirm that it is based on adequate grounds or note that it is not…In this sense of 'recognize' I clearly can recognize when my beliefs are true or false – it amounts to noticing whether or not they are justified" (ibid.: 26).

However, unless Lynch means to reject premise (1) by following those philosophers who claim that there are some ways of noticing a belief to be justified which guarantee to us that the belief is true, I can't see how confirming that a belief is based on adequate grounds or noting that it is not can count as a way of "recognizing that it is true or false". After all, even beliefs based on adequate grounds can turn out to be false.

Indeed, I think the fallibilism embodied in (1) is animated by the idea that an adequately grounded belief may nevertheless be false and a poorly grounded belief may nevertheless be true. If we accept that, then, although Lynch is of course right that when we doubt some belief we can check on its grounds or justification, this won't provide a way to check the absolute reliability of any belief forming method. It will provide only a way to check one method against another – like checking the propaganda channel against the independent news channel. This will produce beliefs that we take to be true – in the immanent sense of truth – because we take all of our beliefs to be true; but it won't ever put us in a position to recognize the objective truth of our beliefs. I believe this is precisely Rorty's point in writing: "If I have concrete, specific doubts about whether one of my beliefs is true, I can resolve those doubts only by asking whether it is adequately justified – by finding and assessing additional reasons pro and con. I cannot bypass justification and confine my attention to truth: assessment of truth and assessment of justification are, when the question is about what I should believe now, the same activity" (1998: 19).

Premise (3) says that, if there is no way to ascertain whether our belief-forming methods result reliably in our having objectively true beliefs, then there is no reasonable way to evaluate the efficacy of these methods for achieving the end of our having objectively true beliefs about the world. I take this to be the least controvertible premise of the argument. If there is no way to tell when we have achieved a particular end, then surely there is no way to tell which means are best for achieving it. And, likewise, if there is no way to tell whether a candidate means for achieving an end like having objectively true beliefs about the world results reliably in this end, then surely there is no way to evaluate the efficacy of that means. That's the simple idea behind premise (3). If you want to get off board here, I'm not sure what else I can say to convince you.

Premises (1)-(3) entail the first lemma. So, if I've convinced you to stay on board with them, you're committed to acknowledging that there is no reasonable way to evaluate the efficacy of candidate belief-forming methods for achieving the end of objective truth. It's worth pausing to notice how radical this conclusion will at first appear from the point of view of commonsense realism. Can we really accept that it's impossible to reasonably evaluate our attempts to hone and improve the ways we form beliefs? If that's what the first lemma of Rosenberg's argument comes to, agreeing to it may seem to involve avoiding crude idealism at the steep cost of pointless skepticism.

I think this clash with commonsense realism can be avoided. Recall the idea that Lynch and Rorty apparently agree on, viz., that trying to determine whether one of our beliefs is true or false amounts to nothing more than trying to determine whether or not it is based on adequate grounds. If we accept this, then we may think Rosenberg's talk of "objective truth" imputes a much stronger position to proponents of truth as the definitive epistemic end than they really need. Perhaps, believing truly doesn't have to be equated with infallible contact with the naked facts in order for the goal of believing truly to structure our epistemic policies and procedures. Maybe all we need is a less lofty idea of truth in interpreting Lynch's suggestion that "recogniz[ing] when my beliefs are true or false... amounts to noticing whether or not they are justified"(ibid.: 26).

It is in these terms that I think we should understand Rosenberg's claim at (4), that we accept each of our beliefs to be true. For, there is of course a sense in which we accept as true each of our beliefs that we take to be based on adequate grounds. This follows from the fact that believing that p entails accepting that p is true. So, to interpret truth in this way is, in effect, to transition to the second horn of Rosenberg's original dilemma, on which truth is disquotationally understood and so "enquiry-immanent".

In light of this, premise (5) may seem uncontroversial. It says that, if we accept each of our beliefs to be true, then we take each of our belief-forming methods to generate beliefs we accept to be true. This links a platitude about beliefs to a correlative conceptual fact about our belief-forming methods. If it's part of believing that we take each of our beliefs to be true, then it's part of something's being one of our belief-forming methods that we take it to generate something, i.e. beliefs, which we take to be true. In spite of this, I think (5) is problematic; however, I'll postpone discussion of my worry until later.

Premise (6) says that, if we take each of our belief-forming methods to generate beliefs we accept to be true, then there is no reasonable way to evaluate the efficacy of these methods for achieving the end of truth. I think the idea is that, since it's part of their being belief-forming methods that these methods lead to our accepting some proposition as true, there is no meaningful sense in which we can evaluate them as more or less reliable for achieving this end. Insofar as they are methods that form beliefs, they will always achieve this end, so there is no way that they can serve as constraints on actual epistemic policies and procedures. As Rosenberg puts the point, "...the ostensible goal of immanent truth is a goal in name only...[For] nothing can count as a reason to believe that we have failed to reach or realize the putative goal"(ibid.: 228).

However, premises (4)-(6) entail the second lemma. So, if we accept them, we're committed to acknowledging that there is no reasonable way to evaluate the efficacy of our belief-forming methods for achieving the end of our having beliefs which we accept to be true.

That leaves premise (7), which says that some end E can be a genuine goal or capable of constraining our policies or procedures only if there is a reasonable way to evaluate the efficacy of our methods for achieving E. As I said above, I think that a lot rides on how we're to think of the ostensible end of truth, which means that a lot rides on premise (7). I suspect it is false as stated. However, I'll postpone criticism until I've finished explaining the argument. For, even if we're thinking of the end of truth as a goal, premise (7) then states a necessary condition on being a genuine goal which some have objected to.

In his review of Rosenberg 2002, Fantl objects to the idea that for something to be a genuine goal, it must be possible to check whether we've achieved it. He writes "Why buy into the premise that the only thing that can count as [an epistemic] goal is something that can constrain our epistemic practices or that we can confirm we've reached?"(2007: 231). As a counterexample, Fantl asks us to consider his goal that his children thrive after his death. He writes, "Regardless of whether my life goes worse if that goal is not achieved, there is a clear sense in which I have it as a goal and a clear sense in which I have failed to achieve that goal if they do not thrive after I am dead"(ibid.). However, I think this misses the point of premise (7) in the argument.

The point is not to deny that some of our goals are for ends that we will not, as a matter of fact, be able to confirm whether they have been achieved. The point is rather that the allegedly definitively epistemic goal of truth is one for which it would be either impossible to tell that we have achieved it or impossible to tell that we have not achieved it. It's quite clear how Fantl could tell whether he has achieved his goal that his children thrive after he is dead. He'd just have to wait a sufficient amount of time after his death and then check on how his children are doing. To be sure, that isn't humanly possible, but it's pretty clear what it would take for us to check whether the goal had been achieved. By contrast, opponents of the putative goal of truth think it's unclear what it would take for us to check that we had achieved the goal of having objectively true beliefs and utterly pointless to check that we had achieved the goal of having beliefs that we take to be true.

Nevertheless, we might still worry about premise (7) for related reasons. For it may seem that it is enough, in order for something to be one of my goals, that I take it that some means are better than others. Consider, for example, the ostensible goal of getting into heaven, which, for the sake of argument, suppose we cannot even in principle ascertain whether we have achieved it since heaven is pure bliss and devoid of unified consciousnesses. In this case, (7) implies that getting into heaven cannot be a genuine goal; however, it seems clearly possible to have this as one of our goals and let it prescribe particular conducts, e.g., praying, going to church, etc. insofar as we take these practices to be encouraged by having that goal.

I think Rosenberg's initial answer to this objection comes in the distinction he draws between a motive and a goal:

> ... a motive is whatever in fact moves someone, and there's no in-principle limit to the sorts of mental goings-on that might in fact give rise to activities that we'd recognize as enquiry – a desire for money or fame or respect...In this sense, a desire for objective truth might indeed motivate enquiry. But it doesn't follow that objective truth can function as the goal of enquiry, and that becomes clear when we observe that, unlike such other potential motivating desires as those for money or fame or respect, a desire for objective truth is one that we can't ever determine has been satisfied.(ibid.: 219fn.)

If a motive is whatever in fact moves one to act, then what is a goal? The causal-psychological description of a motive suggests that the contrasting notion of a goal could be understood in terms of the distinction between motivating and validating practical reasons. A motivating reason is part of the best psychological explanation of why an agent acts as she does, and a validating reason is whatever would validate a particular action (whether or not the agent actually performs it or performs it for that reason). On this reading, Rosenberg's claim is that a desire for truth can provide a motivating reason for particular actions, but truth cannot provide a validating reason, and thus is not a goal, because it's impossible to tell whether it has been achieved. So, a goal is distinguished from a mere motive in that it validates, i.e. provides a validating reason for, the relevant action.

But in order to evaluate this idea and to see how it supports (7), we need an account of "validating reasons" in the context of the question of whether truth is the distinctive epistemic goal. What are the relevant actions that may or may not be validated in this case? To begin, Rosenberg proposes the following:

The specification or formulation of a goal...is characteristically the first step in a process of means-ends reasoning. In traditional terms, it yields the major premise of a practical syllogism:

(P1) I/We shall achieve E
(P2) The only/best means for achieving E are M
(P3) So, I/we shall adopt M. (ibid.: 206)

The idea here is that since the practical syllogism is the traditional formulation of instrumental reasoning per se, we can define the sense of "goal" that is relevant to the argument by means of the functional role of goals in practical syllogisms. With respect to the activity of enquiry, Rosenberg is specific about what he thinks it would take for truth to be the relevant goal. He writes:

What we need, to make sense of the idea that true belief is the goal of enquiry...is an instantiation of this general practical syllogistic form which establishes a connection between a commitment to that goal and the actual conduct of enquiry; that is, which shows how our having the goal of truth can structure our actual concrete cognitive-epistemic practices (ibid.: 207).

The general idea seems to be that some end E can provide a validating reason for doing M only if we can produce an instantiation of the practical syllogistic form which establishes a connection between doing M and achieving E. Whether this supports (7), however, will depend on what it means to produce an instantiation of the practical syllogistic form which establishes a connection between doing M and achieving E. For in one sense, it has to be trivial that, if some of our belief forming methods are indeed objectively reliable, then it is logically, physically, and epistemically possible that we can produce an instantiation of the practical syllogistic form where the minor premise is objectively true. And this instantiation would, in a sense, establish a connection between these methods and attaining the goal of objective truth. The problem with this, however, is that we cannot ever tell that we have produced this. That is to say, even if we have done this, since the fallibilism of (1) committed us to the idea that the truth of our beliefs transcends our reasons for believing them, we cannot distinguish a validating practical syllogism from indefinitely many others which do not validate any particular action. So, in stronger sense, we would not have established the necessary connection unless there is a reasonably way to evaluate whether candidate means for achieving x are more or less likely to succeed. So, I think Rosenberg means that, in order for an end E to be a genuine goal or capable of constraining policies or procedures, it must be possible for us to produce an instantiation of the practical syllogistic form which we can tell to establish a connection between doing particular conducts M and achieving E. If that's right, then (7) appears to successfully state a necessary condition on being a goal. Moreover, with the first and second lemmas, it entails Rosenberg's leading negative thesis, viz. (8): Neither our having objectively true beliefs about the world nor our having beliefs that we accept to be true can be a genuine goal or capable of constraining our epistemic policies or procedures.

This completes my explanation of the argument suggested by Davidson and Rorty and developed most thoroughly by Rosenberg against the idea that truth is an epistemic end. I've attempted to motivate each of its premises, though I've already said that I think there's a problem with premises (5) and (7). I want to turn now to spelling out these problems. I'll start with premise (5) because the objection I have to it is more easily stated, but the real insight Rosenberg's argument promises, is in forcing us to rethink his conception of epistemic ends as goals, which is basically what funds my objection to premise (7).

4. Two Objections

Recall that premises (5) is a conditional linking the platitude about accepting each of our beliefs to be true to the idea that we take each of our belief-forming methods to generate beliefs we accept to be true. Here it is again:

(5) If we accept each of our beliefs to be true, then we take each of our belief-forming methods to generate beliefs we accept to be true.

The problem I see with this stems from an ambiguity in the term "our belief-forming methods". Premise (5) is trivially true if this means "each of our actually and currently deployed belief-forming methods"; for part of what it is to be an actually and currently deployed belief-forming method is to be a method which generates a mental state in the person who deploys it that this person currently accepts as true. However, if we separate belief-forming methods across members of a population or across time-slices of an individual person, we can generate a different reading of the term "our belief-forming methods" that makes premise (5) much less plausible. For instance, if that term means "the candidate belief-forming methods that might be deployed by one of us" then surely we don't take each of our belief-forming methods to generate beliefs that we all accept as true. After all, some of us form beliefs by watching the propaganda channel, and, as we have already seen, this generates beliefs that those of us who are viewers of the independent news channel will not accept as true, and vice versa. Likewise, a single individual may have formed beliefs in the past by watching the propaganda channel, which she then accepted as true, but, after she has become a devotee of the independent news channel, she will not take it that forming beliefs by watching the propaganda channel is a reliable way to generate beliefs that she now accepts to be true.

So far, all this suggests is that Rosenberg needs the reading of "our belief-forming methods" on which it means "each of our actually and currently deployed belief-forming methods", in order for premise (5) of his argument to be plausible. However, recall that (5) is a premise in Rosenberg's argument along the second horn of his original dilemma for the conclusion that immanent truth, i.e. believing p iff p, cannot be a genuine goal of our cognitive-epistemic practices. Someone who thinks that immanent truth is a goal of our cognitive-epistemic practices might reasonably insist that they don't mean for us to use this goal to evaluate the efficacy of our actually and currently deployed belief-forming methods but rather for us to use this goal to evaluate candidate belief-forming methods, such as those used by others, those we used to use in the past, and those we might use in the future. And it is not in general true that the belief-forming methods used by others, our past selves, or our future possible selves are ones that generate beliefs that we now accept as true.

What this means is that although Rosenberg is of course right that we accept each of our own beliefs as true, he's wrong that this implies that there is no reasonable way for us use the ostensible goal of immanent truth to evaluate candidate belief-forming methods. To be sure, as long as we have accepted premises (1) and (2), such evaluations will always transpire relative to an assumed background of belief-forming methods and so will never get at the absolute reliability of candidate belief-forming methods for achieving the end of objective truth. However, the second horn of Rosenberg's dilemma is not concerned with such objective truth. And it does seem that, relative to a background method, a method like the propaganda channel can be judged to be less reliable than another method, such as the independent news channel, for forming true beliefs. If that's right, however, then Rosenberg's premise (5) is acceptable only on a reading which his opponents could reasonably reject.

I turn now to premise (7). In effect, I object to premise (7) because of the univocal conception of ends on which it rests. As we have seen, it rests on a conception of ends as goals that can serve as the first premise in a practical syllogism. I think this is misguided in the present dialectical context because it assumes that one who thinks that some end, such as truth, may help to distinguish epistemic reasons from other sorts of reasons must be conceiving of epistemic reasons as fundamentally reasons for some action, i.e. practical reasons for some epistemic-cognitive conduct.

I doubt, however, that the primary objects of epistemic evaluations are epistemic-cognitive actions or conducts. Rather the primary objects of epistemic evaluations seem to me to be states of belief. After all, we evaluate whether someone's belief that p is justified in determining whether she knows that p, and normative epistemology is concerned with what count as good and bad reasons for a particular kind of mental state: belief. To see those evaluations as deriving from evaluations of some implicit cognitive conducts strikes me as backwards.

At the very least, this suggests a worrying disconnect between premise (7) of Rosenberg's argument and attempts to use the putative goal of truth to distinguish good epistemic reasons for belief from other sorts of reasons. Yet, it may not seem like a very deep worry if we could come up with a cognitive action or conduct which is conceptually very close to the cognitive state of belief and the reasons we may have for such states. In a way, this is what Rosenberg suggests as part of his own positive theory. He appeals to Sellars' (1963) "forward-looking" and "proceduralist" conception of justification, according to which

> justification is itself in the first instance a cognitive-epistemic activity – giving reasons, citing evidence, enumerating grounds – and being in a position to engage in such activities can and often will itself be a consequence of having engaged in other, preparatory and enabling, cognitive-epistemic conducts – seeking reasons, evidence, or grounds for what one in fact believes, however one in fact has come to believe it. (ibid.: 212)

This is ultimately why he thinks, "the relevant executable epistemic conducts can be specified only generically, as whatever is necessary to put one into a position to justify one's beliefs if they are legitimately challenged" (ibid., p. 213).

However, there's a much simpler way to reconcile the fact that the primary object of epistemic evaluations are cognitive states of belief with a teleological conception of such evaluation. This is by appealing to something active that is conceptually very close to the state of belief: the formation of beliefs. Rosenberg would probably object that although forming beliefs is undoubtedly active rather than stative, and surely also a central element of our cognitive activities, it is not properly speaking what he calls an "executable conduct" – it is active but not something we freely choose to do (at least not in normal cases), rather like digesting one's dinner or falling asleep. What that means is that, while forming beliefs – like digesting dinner or falling asleep – is, broadly speaking, something that we do, it cannot cogently serve in the conclusion of a practical syllogism meant to represent (even if only schematically and ideally) the way truth is the goal of belief-formation. And that means that it cannot comprise the epistemic policies and procedures that are supposed to be constrained by the ostensible goal of truth.

That objection, however, exemplifies the way in which I think premise (7) is misguided. Why must we think that reasons for forming beliefs must ultimately be capable of being characterized as practical reasons that justify performing some "executable conduct"? Rosenberg might respond: "Well, how else do you propose to characterize them?" So, let me quickly sketch a provisional proposal.

Indeed, I think it is Sellars who provides the distinction crucial for developing an alternative. In a different context, he distinguishes between "rules of criticism" and "rules of action", i.e. between rules that articulate how something ought to be and rules that articulate what agents ought to do. (1969: 508) For instance, a car ought to be disposed to start when the key is turned and my mechanic ought to do what is necessary to make my car be disposed to start when the key is turned. These ought-statements express two different kinds of norms. Although, as this example indicates, they can be logically related: that my car ought to be disposed to start when the key is turned implies ceteris paribus and where possible that my mechanic ought to do whatever is necessary to make my car disposed to start when the key is turned.

What I like about Sellars' distinction in the present context is that it opens up conceptual space for a mixed account of normative epistemic principles, according to which the genuine executable conducts of agents are subject to rules of action, while cognitive states and all of the other mere activities and performances that make up our cognitive lives are only subject to rules of criticism.[5] And this means that we can ask what beliefs we ought to form, and understand this question in terms of what beliefs we have reasons to form, without assuming that these reasons must be reasons for performing some action conceived of on the model of the practical syllogism validating some "executable conduct". Instead, they are conceived of as a distinctive kind of reasons: reasons for being in a particular state.

It is because of the availability of this sort of account of reasons for belief and the fact that proponents of the idea that truth is the definitive epistemic end or goal have been concerned to develop an account of epistemic normativity that distinguishes reasons for belief from other sorts of reasons that I think premise (7) of Rosenberg's argument is misguided. The way that it presupposes that

---

[5] I developed a similar idea in more detail in my (2008), whose central thesis is that 'ought-to-believe's should be thought of as rules of criticism; this allowed me to diffuse the debate between doxastic involuntarists, who think belief formation is not voluntary, and epistemic deontologists, who think that beliefs can be the proper subjects of epistemic obligations.

all reasons are essentially practical reasons obscures the fact that epistemic reasons for belief are not practical reasons but something fundamentally different: reasons for being a particular way.

Someone might want to defend Rosenberg here by arguing that whether or not epistemic reasons for forming beliefs are fundamentally different from practical reasons, those philosophers who seek to distinguish epistemic reasons from other sorts of reasons in terms of the putatively definitive epistemic end of truth are committed to following Rosenberg in his conception of the relevant reasons as being essentially practical reasons. This is because an end just is something we pursue, and we pursue it by performing particular actions, i.e. engaging in particular "executable conducts".

To begin to see why this is wrong and why premise (7) is false, notice that the logical form of (7) appears to be a conditional that embeds a disjunction in its antecedent. The two disjuncts are

(a) Some end E can be a genuine goal,
and
(b) Some end E can be capable of constraining our policies or procedures.

The premise then says, in effect, that if (a) or (b) is true, then there will be a reasonable way to evaluate the efficacy of our methods of achieving E. However, to put my objection bluntly, I think Rosenberg has illicitly assumed that (a) and (b) come to the same thing. That is, what a goal is, on his conception, is an end capable of constraining our policies and procedures; and an end capable of constraining our policies and procedures just is, on his conception, a goal. However, I want to argue that, even if a goal must be capable of constraining our policies and procedures, it's not the case that all ends, which are capable of constraining our policies and procedures are goals. If that's right, then it's possible that there are ways for ends to constrain our policies and procedures other than by structuring a practical syllogism that validates particular actions or concrete conducts.

In particular, I want to suggest that there are two ways an end can be related to some active performance. First, as we have seen, an end can be a regulative goal of that performance; regulative goals can be used to evaluate various means in terms of their efficacy at attaining the goal. Second, an end may also be a constitutive aim of a particular performance; appeal to constitutive aims can be used to determine whether or not one is engaged in some specific type of performance. For example, the legal liability of a doctor when her patient dies may depend on whether the doctor was treating illness (however poorly) or murdering someone (however skilfully). Relative to the goals, respectively, of preserving life and of terminating life, we can evaluate how skilful the doctor's conduct was; this is an evaluation of a performance in terms of its regulative goal. But skill is beside the point in deciding whether the doctor should be charged with malpractice or murder. In order to answer this question, presumably we need to form an opinion about which type of performance she was engaged in, which we can do if we have an opinion about what its constitutive aim was. This is an evaluation of a performance in terms of its constitutive aim.

Importantly, as I just stated the distinction between regulative goals and constitutive aims, it applies first and foremost to ways of evaluating performances. Now, some performances may be genuine actions, i.e. what Rosenberg thinks of as the executable conducts that can be referred to in the conclusion of a practical syllogism, but, as we've already seen, not all active performances are executable conducts, some are mere performances, like digesting one's dinner or falling asleep. And, as I've already said, forming beliefs seems to be a mere performance rather than a genuine action (at least in most cases). That may mean that it is incoherent to speak of the regulative goal of this performance. In forming beliefs, one is not, strictly speaking, trying to attain some goal. This is because one isn't trying to do anything; forming beliefs isn't (typically) an "executable conduct". However, that doesn't mean that this performance doesn't have a constitutive aim. Digesting one's dinner and falling asleep are both end-directed performances, even though they are not goal-promoting actions. We can evaluate whether some performance is one of these specific types of performances in terms of whether it is aimed at the relevant end. Likewise, I think this opens a new route to understanding the claim that truth is an epistemic end, usable in an account of what distinguishes good epistemic reasons for belief from other sorts of reasons. We could treat truth as a constitutive aim of the performance of forming beliefs rather than as the regulative goal of some action or cognitive conduct. The idea would be to say that what constitutes a performance's being the performance of forming beliefs is (at least in part) that it is aimed at the truth. But what does that mean?

I admit that it's not entirely clear to me, but in what follows, I'll provisionally suggest an answer that I think is plausible and undermines premise (7) of Rosenberg's argument. In order to do so, it's helpful to note two things about rules of criticism. First, they seem to divide into intrinsic and extrinsic rules. Second, their logical grammar seems to allow for an 'in order to E' operator. Let me explain.

The rules of criticism applying to something seem to divide into those which are intrinsic to what that thing is and those which are extrinsic to what that thing is. For example, the rules governing the bishop in chess seem to include: (i) The bishop ought to be moved only diagonally, and (ii) The bishop ought not to be sacrificed for a pawn. The first of these 'ought-to-be's is intrinsic in that it partially defines what it is for something to count as a bishop; if this rule is broken with respect to a particular thing, it calls into question whether that thing is a bishop. By contrast, the second of these 'ought-to-be's is extrinsic in that it is not partially definitive of what it is for something to be a bishop; if this rule is broken with respect to a particular thing, it does not call into question whether that thing is a bishop, only whether the owner of the bishop is a good chess player.

Moreover, all rules – both 'ought-to-do's and 'ought-to-be's – seem to admit of modification with an 'in order to E' operator. That is to say that, if they aren't already so modified, we can make the full logical form of statements deploying the concept 'ought' more explicit by adding 'in order to E', where E is a variable that can be filled in by various ends. We can refer to this as the end-relativity of 'ought'.[6] For example, it may be the case that one ought to give to charity in order to develop the character trait of being charitable or in order to assuage one's guilty conscience, or perhaps both. Depending on what the relevant end is, we get logically distinct readings of "A ought to give to charity". Likewise with rules of criticism: It may be the case that one ought to be charitable in order to help the world or in order to impress one's mother, or perhaps both. Again, we get logically distinct readings of "A ought to be charitable" depending on the relevant end. The end-relativity of 'ought' shows up with the rules of criticism governing belief-formation as well. For example, it may be the case that someone ought to be disposed to form the belief that she can jump across certain crevices, in order to believe what's true, but it may also be the case that she ought to be disposed to form this belief in order to have the confidence to jump far enough to make it, or perhaps both.

In light of the distinction between intrinsic and extrinsic rules of criticism and the general end-relativity of 'ought', I think we can make better sense of the idea that truth is the constitutive aim of the formation of beliefs. To a first approximation, the idea would be to say some 'ought-to-be's governing beliefs are intrinsic to belief and belief formation while others are extrinsic, and we can tell the difference by the end to which the oughts are explicitly or implicitly relative. More specifically, it's the 'ought-to-believe's which are implicitly or explicitly modified by 'in order to believe truly' that are intrinsic rules of criticism for beliefs, whereas those 'ought-to-believe's that are explicitly or implicitly modified by some other end are extrinsic rules of criticism for beliefs.

---

[6] Compare Finlay (2009).

So, for example, consider the claim "You ought to believe that you are reading this paper." One thing this could mean is that you ought to believe that you are reading this paper in order to believe truly. Another thing this could mean is that you ought to believe that you are reading this paper in order to make me happy. The current interpretation of the idea that truth is the definitive epistemic end would treat the former but not the latter as constitutive rules of criticism applying to that belief. That is to say that violations call into question something's being a belief.

That's suggestive, but it won't work as it stands. A false belief that p is one that would violate the rule "S ought to believe that p, in order to believe truly"; so, if this rule really is constitutive of something's counting as a belief that p, it'd be impossible to believe falsely without calling into question the status of one's belief, as a belief. A helpful modification of the proposal can be gleaned from Velleman, who argues that an important difference between belief and desire is that for a propositional attitude to be a belief it must (at least) involve regarding its propositional object as true, whereas for a propositional attitude to be a desire it must (at least) involve regarding its propositional object as to be made true. But, although this so-called "difference in direction of fit" distinguishes belief from desire, Velleman argues that more is needed to distinguish belief from other cognitive attitudes such as imagining or assuming. This is because these too involve regarding a proposition as true, just not seriously or in earnest. However, according to him "what distinguishes a proposition's being believed from its being assumed or imagined is the spirit in which it is regarded as true, whether tentatively or hypothetically, as in the case of assumption; fancifully, as in the case of imagination; or seriously, as in the case of belief"(2000: 183). This suggests the following modification of the proposal from the previous paragraph. We could say that it's the 'ought-to-believe's which are implicitly or explicitly modified by 'in order to have a propositional attitude we seriously regard as true' that are intrinsic rules of criticism for beliefs, whereas those 'ought-to-believe's that are explicitly or implicitly modified by some other end are extrinsic rules of criticism for beliefs. This, I think, provides a more plausible interpretation of the idea that truth is the definitive epistemic end.

As I said above, I myself suspect that truth is not the definitive epistemic end because I'm sympathetic to the pluralist position that there are other distinctively epistemic ends, which are not reducible to the end of truth. However, the present point is that by understanding the idea as a claim about constitutive aims rather than regulative goals we seem to block any conflation of (a) and (b), the two disjuncts of the antecedent of premise (7) of Rosenberg's argument. And by doing so, we open up conceptual space for the possibility that truth is an end capable of constraining epistemic policies and procedures even if it is not a goal, in the sense of being a possible first premise in a practical syllogism which turns on the efficacy of certain actions vis-à-vis that goal. It does so just like the end of moving diagonally constrains the movements of the bishop in chess. If the rule of criticism, "Bishops ought to be moved diagonally in order to conform to the rules of chess," is violated, that violation calls into question whether the relevant thing counts as a bishop. Likewise, if the rule of criticism, "Beliefs ought to be held in order to have a propositional attitude we seriously regard as true" is violated, that violation calls into question whether the relevant thing counts as a belief. And this provides a sense in which truth is an end constraining epistemic policies and procedures but not a genuine goal, which is capable of serving cogently as the first premise of a practical syllogism that validates particular cognitive actions or executable epistemic conducts.

5. Conclusion

So, in the end, although Rosenberg may be right that objective truth cannot be a goal constraining our actual epistemic policies and practices, there are, as far as I can tell, two cogent responses defenders of the idea that truth is a distinctively epistemic end may make to his argument. First, they may reject his imputation to them of a conception of truth as enquiry-transcendent and yet reject premise (5) along the enquiry-immanent horn of his original dilemma. I challenged this premise based on different readings of "our belief-forming methods". Second, they may reject the conception of epistemic ends as goals capable of serving as the first premise of a valid practical syllogism, which was the idea behind (7). We saw this to be questionable based on possible conflation of the first and second disjuncts of the antecedent of (7); and I've tentatively sketched an alternative way of conceiving of truth as an epistemic end that doesn't involve seeing it as a regulative goal but as a constitutive aim of belief.

6. Postscript

Since I wrote this paper, an interesting literature on "normativism" about belief has flourished.[7] As I understand it, this is the view that an essential part of what it is for something to be a belief is for it to be governed by certain kinds of norms;

---

7 See McHugh and Whiting (2014) for a useful survey of the recent literature and some of the key issues.

or similarly, being governed by an identifiable kind of norm is partially constitutive of being a belief. This is usually conceived as a central part of the explanation of which sorts of normative evaluations of a belief count as "epistemic".

The most widely discussed form of normativism seems to be the view that belief is essentially governed by a "truth norm". It's controversial how exactly to state this norm, but the basic idea is that an essential part of what it is for a state to be a belief is for its truth value to determine whether the state is correct/incorrect, right/wrong, permissible/impermissible.[8] This idea is, I think, related to but not exactly the same as the idea I sketched in this paper that truth might be usefully thought of as a constitutive aim of the performance of forming beliefs. So, I suspect it will be useful to identify similarities and differences.

We can come at this by considering some criticisms of both ideas. The critical argument from Rorty-Davidson-Rosenberg that I attempt to reconstruct in the main text of the paper is similar to one of the prominent criticisms of belief normativism due to Glüer and Wikforss (2009, 2013a). Working from the assumptions that norms are supposed to be prescriptive or at least be capable of guiding us, they argue that a truth-norm could never do that directly, since we'd have to already believe p in order to follow a rule such as "You ought to believe p, only if p!" Although supported differently, this is very much in line with Rosenberg's conclusion that a supposed goal of truth cannot "play a determinative role at all in our epistemic activities"(2002: 229) because there is no way to evaluate candidate means of achieving it, which don't depend on one's having already done everything one could know to do to achieved it.

What should the truth normativist say in response to Glüer and Wikforss? I take it they should (and sometimes do) say something similar to what I said in response to Rosenberg: There is more than one way that the end of truth could be related to belief. Being what Rosenberg refers to as a regulative goal that could fund a prescription or rule capable of being followed in concrete executable conduct is not the only way for truth to be an end. It might also be a constitutive aim, an end the relation to which constitutes something as the formation of a belief rather than something else.

In the main text of the paper, I tried to make good on this suggestion by appealing to a distinction Sellars makes in connection to linguistic rules between "rules of action" and "rules of criticism". The former say how someone ought to act, while the latter say how something ought to be (which implies, ceteris paribus and in some complicated way, that someone ought to act in some way). For

---

8 Defended in one form or another by Millar (1994), Shah and Velleman (2005), Boghossian (2008), Littlejohn (2012), Wedgwood (2002), and Whiting (2010).

example, that an eighteen-month-old child ought to be disposed, ceteris paribus, to say "red" when queried about the color of red things is not plausibly thought to be a rule that guides that child's linguistic behavior. And this rule of criticism is only indirectly prescriptive for the behavior of the child's caregivers in that it implies that, when they are trying to teach the child words for colors, they ought ceteris paribus to take whatever concrete means are at their disposal to inculcate, encourage, and stiffen the child's disposition to say "red" when queried about the color of red things.

As far as that goes, however, a rule of criticism needn't be constitutive of anything. The previous example illustrates this: the fact that one ought to be disposed to say "red" when queried about the color of red things isn't constitutive of being an eighteen-month-old child.

Nevertheless, I think we could get a version of the normativist position out of rules of criticism by accepting that the following rule of criticism is constitutive of belief: beliefs ought to be true. If you find a propositional attitude that is not true, then either it is liable to a kind of criticism as not true or it is not a belief. A normativist might say that this is a necessary condition on something's being a belief. Adhering to Sellars's distinction then provides materials for a response to Glüer and Wikforss: We needn't think this rule (the "truth norm") is a rule that directly guides people's actions, in particular the agent's actions that result her having a belief. For it could be a constitutive rule of criticism, only related to rules of action in some complicated way. Hence, I think rules of criticism, when they are thought to be constitutive of belief, provide a way to work out the normativist position about belief in a way that is immune to the objection that these norms cannot guide action.

This is an interesting position. I'm sometimes attracted to it, but I think it is stronger than the view I sketched in the main text of the paper and I harbor worries about it. As I indicated in the main text of the paper, I'm sympathetic with a pluralist view, which would find room for some sort of plurality of definitive epistemic ends. So even if it is essential to something's being a belief that it ought to be true, I doubt that is the only thing that determines which evaluations of belief are epistemic. If that's right, then truth normativism would only be part of the story about which norms constitutively govern belief.

But more to the point, I now suspect there are several ways philosophers and ordinary people use the term 'belief', which makes me skeptical that there is one unified kind of thing properly thought of as belief, whose essence could be normative in the way suggested in the previous paragraph. Just to name a few: there are the rationally formed conclusions of careful deliberation, the pieces of common sense inculcated by nature and culture, the things we accept on faith, the mere opinions (or doxa) about some matter of the non-experts, the information tacitly possessed by normal people, the ways our pets conceptualize and track reality, the representational states attributed to intentional systems (including corporations, animals, computers, and ecosystems) as part of a particular kind of explanation and prediction.

Perhaps there is some common essence to all of the things on this list, but I doubt it's being governed by anything usefully thought of as a norm, even a "rule of criticism". The normativist could, of course, maintain that not all of these are properly called "belief" or even just stipulatively limit the focus of his account of belief to a subset of this list.

I suspect, however, that there is a way the things on this list are unified in their relation to the end of truth, even if this isn't normative in the sense that seems to be assumed by the normativist. This comes into sharper relief when we remember that it's a metaphor when we say that belief aims at truth. Since belief is stative rather than active, on the standard categorization deriving from Aristotle, Vendler, and Ryle,[9] it doesn't even fall into the metaphysical category of things whose telicity (or relation to an end) helps to define them. So, if anything belief aims at truth in a sense derivative of the fact that belief formation is a telic process. The proximal end of this process is having a belief, but plausibly one isn't engaged in belief-formation unless the result when this process completes is something that can be evaluated as correct/incorrect in terms of being true/false. Does that mean that all such states ought to be true (in the way of a "rule of criticism")? If we accept panoply of kinds of belief alluded to above, the affirmative answer to this question seems implausible. There may be many systems for which it is usefully to describe them functionally as believing p but where it would be rather odd to think that anyone ought, even ceteris paribus, to do anything to ensure that such beliefs are true.

If we shift attention from the beliefs of our colleagues, friends, and children to those of corporations, animals, computers, and ecosystems, even weak normativism developed with the concept of a rule of criticism begins to seem to strong. If we shift attention in this way, the force of any normative epistemic evaluations also weakens considerably. Hence, the lesson I draw is that some kind of constitutive norm might apply to the beliefs of people whose cognitive efforts we evaluate as epistemically justified/unjustified, good/bad, permissible/impermissible, etc. But if so that is not constitutive of the relevant states being beliefs but rather of the sort of epistemic community within which the normative evaluation of beliefs and believers makes sense.

---

9 See Chrisman (2012) for more discussion of this categorization and why it's important for normative epistemology that belief is a state rather than a process.

References

Alston, W. (1989). *Epistemic Justification*. Ithaca (NY): Cornell University Press.
Beckermann, A. (2001). Wissen and Wahre Meinung. In: W. Lenzen (ed.), *Das weite Spektrum der Analytischen Philosophie: Festschrift für Franz von Kutschera*. Berlin: Walter de Gruyter.
BonJour, L. (1985). *The Structure of Empirical Knowledge*. Cambridge (MA): Harvard University Press.
Chrisman, M. (2008). Ought to Believe. In: *Journal of Philosophy* 105: 346–370.
Chrisman, M. (2012). The Normative Evaluation of Belief and the Aspectual Classification of Belief and Knowledge Attributions. In: *Journal of Philosophy* 109: 588–612
Davidson, D. (2000). Truth Rehabilitated. In: R. Brandom (ed.), *Rorty and His Critics*. Malden (MA): Blackwell Publishing.
Fantl, J. (2007). Review of Thinking About Knowing. In: *Philosophy and Phenomenological Research* 17.
Finlay, S. (2009). Oughts and Ends. In: *Philosophical Studies* 143: 315–340.
Foley, R. (1987). *The Theory of Rationality*. Cambridge (MA): Harvard University Press.
Haack, S. (1998). *Manifesto of a Passionate Moderate*. Chicago: University of Chicago Press.
Hofmann, F. (2005). Epistemic Means and Ends: In Defense of Some Sartwellian Insights. In: *Synthese* 146: 357–369.
Kvanvig, J. (2003). *The Value of Knowledge and the Pursuit of Understanding*. Cambridge: Cambridge University Press.
Lynch, M. (2009). Truth, Value and Epistemic Expressivism. In: *Philosophy and Phenomenological Research* 79: 76–97.
Lynch, M. (2013). The Truth of Values and the Values of Truth. In: D. Pritchard (ed.), *Epistemic Value*. Oxford; New York: Oxford University Press.
McDowell, J. (1982). Criteria, Defeasibility, and Knowledge. In: *Proceedings of the British Academy* 68: 455–479.
McDowell, J. (1986). Singular Thought and the Extent of Inner Space. In J. McDowell and P. Petit (eds.), *Subject, Thought, and Context*. Oxford: Clarendon Press.
Martin, M. G. F. (2002). The Transparency of Experience. In: *Mind and Language* 17: 476–425.
Martin, M. G. F. (2004). The Limits of Self-Awareness. In: *Philosophical Studies* 120: 37–89.
Pritchard, D. (2010). The Value of Knowledge. In: A. Haddock, A. Millar and D. Pritchard, *The Nature and Value of Knowledge*. Oxford, New York: Oxford University Press.
Quine, W. V. O. (1986). Reply to Morton White. In: P. Schilpp and L. Hahn (eds.), *The Philosophy of W. V. Quine*. La Salle, Ill: Open Court.
Riggs, W. (2003). Balancing Our Epistemic Ends. In: *Noûs* 37: 342–352.
Riggs, W. (2002). Beyond Truth and Falsehood: The Real Value of Knowing That P. In: *Philosophical Studies* 107: 87–108.
Rorty, R. (1995). Is Truth a Goal of Enquiry? Davidson Vs. Wright. In: *Philosophical Quarterly* 45: 281–300.
Rosenberg, J. (2002). *Thinking About Knowing*. New York: Oxford University Press.
Sartwell, C. (1992). Why Knowledge Is Merely True Belief. In: *Journal of Philosophy* 89: 167–180.
Sellars, W. (1969). Language as Thought and as Communication. In: *Philosophy and Phenomenological Research* 29: 506–527.
Velleman, D. J. (2000). *The Possibility of Practical Reason*. Oxford: Oxford University Press.

Christos Kyriacou
Ought to Believe, Evidential Understanding and the Pursuit of Wisdom

1. Introduction

The working hypothesis of many epistemologists is that the standard (epistemic) goal of inquiry is to simultaneously pursue truth-acquisition and falsity-avoidance.[1] But further reflection on this dual goal of inquiry reveals that the two (sub)goals are in tension because they are inversely proportionate: the more we satisfy the one (sub)goal the less we satisfy the other (and vice versa). The point is sometimes acknowledged in the literature but mostly in passing and its puzzling implications for epistemic normativity have been rather underappreciated.[2] In this paper, I revisit the inverse proportionality point in order to ameliorate this unfortunate predicament.

To this effect, I elaborate the inverse proportionality point in some detail and bring out its puzzling implications about the normative question of what one ought to believe. As I argue, given the tension between the two (sub)goals, the problem of the correct regulation of belief-fixation pops to the surface. That is, what the correct policy of belief-fixation is in light of the fact that we cannot satisfy the two individually valuable (sub)goals to the same extent simultaneously.

---

[1] See, for example, Foley (1987), Alston (1988), Sosa (2003) and Elgin (2004). For a list of epistemologists that rather unreflectively subscribe to the standard conception see Piller (2009).
[2] See Foley (1987), Alston (1988), Kelly (2003), Wedgwood (2008) and Zagzebski (2009) for brief airings of the James insight. For notable exceptions that do discuss the James insight at some length see Riggs (2003) and Piller (2009). As Piller (2009:193–5) notes, the standard goal of inquiry may be formally represented in terms of the biconditional desire to (Bp if and only if p). This breaks up into two conditionals that reveal the dual nature of the standard goal: (a) desire that (if p to believe that p) and (b) desire to (believe p if p). The first world-to-mind conditional reveals our interest in getting at the truth and the second mind-to-world conditional reveals our interest in being right about our beliefs and avoiding falsity. As Piller argues, it is the first conditional that lies at the heart of rational cognitive endeavors and not the latter. The latter only reflects our dogmatic proclivities in being right, in bending the world to our will, which is of course epistemically culpable. This, of course, leaves open the question of the James problem, something that Piller (2009) is sensitive to.

Call this *'the James problem'* in tribute to William James (1896) who first drew attention the point.³

A natural approach to the James problem is to surmise that we can resolve the tension if we weigh the relative epistemic value of the two (sub)goals and adjudicate which goal is primary and which secondary. I argue, however, that this approach ushers us into the horns of a 'weighing value dilemma': either the value of the one (sub)goal completely trumps the value of the other (sub) goal and, therefore, we should solely strive to satisfy one (sub)goal at the complete expense of the other; or we can balance the relative satisfaction of the two (sub)goals on the basis of the relative individual value of the two (sub)goals.⁴

The first horn of the dilemma does not take us very far because two very implausible and contrasting policies of belief-fixation emerge on the basis of how we evaluate and weigh these (sub)goals. I call the first policy *epistemic licentiousness* and the second *epistemic asceticism*. The second horn of the dilemma, in essence, restates the initial problem because it is unclear in virtue of what external criterion we can strike the right kind of balance between the two (sub) goals.

As a response to the problem, I follow the second horn of the dilemma and explain that in virtue of the goal of eudaimonia (or good life) we can strike the right kind of balance between the two (sub)goals. Accordingly, I offer a sketch of a solution to the problem that involves the rather neglected epistemic concepts of understanding and wisdom and links these concepts to the Aristotelian goal of eudaimonia. The sketched picture amounts to a novel theory of epistemic nor-

---

3 Compare James (1896/2008: 109): 'There are two ways of looking at our duty in the matter of opinion- ways entirely different, and yet ways about whose difference the theory of knowledge seems hitherto to have shown very little concern. *We must know the truth*; and *we must avoid error*- these are our first and great commandments as would-be knowers; but they are not two ways of stating an identical commandment, they are two separable laws' (James' own emphasis).

4 Some may harbour legitimate worries about how much we can control and influence our belief-fixation processes, habits etc. given that they are largely, directly involuntary (cf. Alston (1988), Feldman (2001)). For the purposes of this article I set aside questions of doxastic (in) voluntarism, control and responsibility and I assume that there is at least some doxastic control that suffices to rescue doxastic responsibility. For one thing, if we had no control (direct or indirect) whatsoever on belief-fixation, we would not be in the business of doing normative epistemology because the whole cognitive endeavour would have been useless and worthless. We would simply be victims of our belief-fixation processes without being able to do anything to enhance our cognitive condition. But, of course, normative epistemology is not useless and worthless. Be that as it may, this is a question for another day.

2. Unpacking the James Problem: Inverse Proportionality and Ought to Believe

It is widely thought that the epistemic goal of inquiry is Janus-faced: acquiring the truth and avoiding falsity. That is, when we inquire about a certain p we simultaneously aim at the truth about p and avoiding falsity about p, say, about who killed the butler or where I have left my keys. This is the standard and almost platitudinous conception of the epistemic goal of inquiry and one can easily see why: it is an intuitive conception that comports well with the commonplace idea that the epistemic goal of inquiry is acquiring truth and, consequently, avoiding falsity. If, say, I am Poirot investigating the murder of the poor butler, I aim at the truth about the matter and, consequently, aim at avoiding false belief about the matter.

Aiming at the truth implicates aiming at avoiding falsity because aiming at the truth entails aiming at avoiding falsity. If I aim at the truth about the murderer of the butler, then it is logically impossible that I do not aim at avoiding falsity. But the reverse does not hold because it does seem logically possible to aim at avoiding falsity without aiming at the truth. In cases of suspense of judgement, if I suspend judgement that p I avoid the falsity of p but I do not thereby aim at the truth of p.[6]

---

5 Zagzebski (2009:141–2) suggests that different historical periods of philosophy were driven by different epistemic goals. Some periods were driven by the threat of skepticism and focused on goals like knowledge and certainty, while other periods were driven by the quest for explanation and focused on understanding. According to Zagzebski, Descartes is an example of the former drive and Plato of the latter. Even if Zagzebski is right, however, there is little doubt that modern epistemology has been determinately Cartesian and preoccupied with knowledge and the menace of skepticism.

6 Without being anything close to an expert in Jamesian exegesis, here is one possible reading of James (1896\2008). He is criticizing Clifford (1877/2008) and his famous paper as being too epistemically reluctant or passive because he prioritizes the goal of falsity-avoidance over the goal of truth-acquisition. That is, epistemically passive in the sense that he is not willing to believe anything without 'sufficient evidence'. There is nothing wrong with having 'sufficient evidence', says James, but this would leave us with very few beliefs and this cannot be made to work. We cannot just live our lives in the fear of being duped. We also have to pursue the truth and have a workable web of belief to rely on. For this reason, we should relax a bit (but not of course abandon) our notion of sufficiency of evidence. Believing is not just about falsi-

Now, the James problem consists in the fact that the Janus-faced character of the standard epistemic goal of inquiry induces tension between the two (sub) goals because the two (sub)goals are in implicit, albeit direct competition.[7] The reason is that the two (sub)goals are inversely proportionate : the more we satisfy the one (sub)goal the less we satisfy the other and vice versa. This was James' original insight.

To grasp the James insight, think of the cognitive mean for truth-acquisition \falsity-avoidance, namely, epistemic justification. Epistemic justification is gradable, comes in degrees and setting the exact threshold of the standards of justification regulates the exact satisfaction of the two (sub)goals. If we set the epistemic standards for justification pretty high [(sub) $p(b\backslash e)=0.9$][8], then we promote the satisfaction of falsity-avoidance over truth-acquisition because it will be much more demanding and much harder for a belief to count as justified and likely to be true.[9] As a result few beliefs will be considered justified and be endorsed as likely to be true. Accordingly, few false beliefs would be endorsed as justified and likely to be true because of the demandingness of the justification standards.

Instead, if we set the epistemic standards for justification relatively low [(sub) $p(b\backslash e)=0.51$], then we inversely promote the satisfaction of truth-acquisition over falsity-avoidance because it will be much less demanding and much easier for a belief to count as justified and likely to be true. This occurs because the less demanding epistemic standards of justification are set, the easier is to endorse propositions as justified and likely to be true. And the easier is to endorse propositions as justified and likely to be true, the more likely it is that you acquire more true beliefs, but also more false beliefs; at least in normal, demon-proof worlds that involve no radical cognitive illusion of sorts.[10]

---

ty-avoidance but also about truth-acquisition for clearly practical reasons. Hence, we arrive at the James problem about how to regulate belief-fixation. This evidentialist construal of James contrasts with the nonevidentialist that takes James to be arguing for the justification of belief even in the absence of sufficient evidence in its favor. The nonevidentialist reading of James is quite popular and can be found, for instance, in Blackburn (2005).

7 See Riggs (2003), Kelly (2003) and Wedgwood (2008) for airing the point.
8 This reads as 'subjective probability of belief on the given evidence'. For some discussion of the subjective interpretation of probability see Mellor (2005).
9 I understand justification as truth-conducive, which can be spelled out in terms of increase of the likelihood for truth. This is a quite common idea about justification. See Fumerton (1995) for example.
10 This is so because if we are the victims of an evil demon scenario (or some such skeptical scenario), then obviously in spite of our best cognitive efforts we may have almost no true beliefs.

Alternatively, the basic Jamesian insight can be illustrated in vivid terms through a suggestive analogy of another (though, merely conventional) norm-governed activity: football (i.e. soccer for Americans).[11] In football, the proximate practical goal is victory and to achieve this you need to score more goals than the conceding goals. But the two (sub)goals are again in tension : the more you play offence than defence, the more likely is to score goals but also to concede goals. Inversely, the more you play defence than offence the less likely is to score goals but also to concede goals. It is, obviously, a matter of offensive \defensive football tactics. It is also a matter of offensive\defensive doxastic tactics in the epistemic game. If you play more for scoring truths you play more offensively (and lower your standards of justification) and if you play more for avoiding false beliefs you play more defensively (and raise up your standards of justification).

This much concludes an outline of the James problem. But at this point some may have worries about the epistemological seriousness of the James problem, so let us present and quickly set aside this objection. Some may object that it is a spurious problem because belief-fixation is quite balanced between the two (sub)goals on its own accord, anyway. So why bother and think that this makes for a philosophically interesting problem?

This worry, however, entirely misses the normative aspect of the James insight, which is the quintessence of the insight. The James insight is not about descriptive epistemic psychology that plausibly for evolutionary reasons is prone to be struck somewhere in-between the continuum of the two (sub)goals.[12] That is, the question is not about how we actually balance and reconcile these two epistemic (sub)goals in our cognitive lives. This is, obviously, a very interesting question on its own right, but one for cognitive psychologists and experimental philosophers and not for epistemologists.

---

[11] I clarify that football is merely conventional because the epistemic game may very well not be just a conventional game or activity. Epistemic realists who insist on the mind-independence of epistemic facts would deny this, for example, and insist that the epistemic game in not merely an activity regulated by socially constructed epistemic facts. See for example Boghossian (2007).
[12] See Papineau (2003) and Griffiths and Wilkins (forthcoming) for the fast-and-frugal adaptive pressures on cognition that may have shaped our suboptimal but good enough for survival and reproduction cognitive abilities, processes etc.. Intuitively, the epistemic tradeoff between truth-acquisition and falsity-avoidance would have been (and probably has been) necessary for the survival and reproduction of the species. As will become obvious in a moment, humanoids with -what I shall call- 'dominant goals' of either truth-acquisition or falsity-avoidance would have dim chances of survival and reproduction. So, given the evolutionary pedigree of cognition, cognition operates as it should be.

Rather, the philosophical point is about inescapable epistemic normativity and about how we ought to form beliefs in light of the fact that the two goals are in implicit, albeit direct competition. Thus, the problem can be stipulated in these simple terms: if both (sub)goals are epistemically valuable and we cannot equally satisfy both simultaneously, how ought we to regulate belief-fixation? That is the James problem.[13]

Once we set aside worries about the epistemological seriousness of the problem, the natural approach to the puzzle is to surmise that we can resolve the tension if we weigh the relative epistemic value of the two (sub)goals and adjudicate which goal is primary and which secondary. Besides, this is the usual procedure we follow when we have two conflicting practical goals that we cannot equally satisfy simultaneously. If I want ice cream and want to control the glucose levels in my bloodstream, then I weigh the relative value of the two goals. Depending on how the weighing goes, I may decide to refrain from ice cream and defy my ice cream desire, or imprudently decide to have my ice cream and defy my desire for healthy living or balance the two desires and have only some ice cream or have some sugar-free ice cream etc. So, it is completely unsurprising that we should follow the same 'weighing value approach' in the epistemic goals case.

The weighing value approach, though, ushers us into the horns of a thorny dilemma: either the weighing shows that the value of the one (sub)goal completely trumps the value of the other (sub)goal and, therefore, we ought to promote the exclusive satisfaction of only one (sub)goal; or the weighing shows that we can somehow balance and compromise the relative satisfaction of the two (sub)goals on the basis of the individual value of the two (sub)goals. Call it *'the weighing value dilemma'*. As I explain below, the first horn is outright implausible while the second horn, as it stands, fails to make any progress against the James problem. I go on to tentatively suggest a way to make progress against the James problem via the second horn by appealing to the Aristotelian notion of eudaimonia. But for now let us turn to the implausible first horn of the dilemma.

---

[13] Compare Zagzebski (2009:18): 'We want to avoid both ignorance about important matters and error about such matters. It is not at all obvious how to balance the two strategies'. Note that she speaks in terms of avoiding ignorance instead of truth-acquisition, but this is entirely innocuous because avoiding ignorance entails truth-acquisition and vice versa.

3. Weighing Epistemic Value\Goals: Truth-Acquisition or Falsity-Avoidance?

In light of the first horn of the weighing value dilemma, two rival policies of belief-fixation emerge: either we assume that truth-acquisition completely trumps falsity-avoidance or the opposite. Depending on how we weigh and prioritize the value of these epistemic (sub)goals, we get different normative incentives about how we ought to proceed with belief-fixation.

The problem, however, is that no matter how we weigh between the two (sub)goals, it turns out that it is implausible to prioritize one (sub)goal at the complete expense of the other because in both cases we end up with very implausible pictures of belief-fixation.[14] In effect, as we shall see in a moment, the first horn of the dilemma is so implausible that seems hopeless as a possible way of addressing the James problem. For the sake of ease of exposition, let us call the goal that is prioritized at the complete expense of the other goal '*dominant*'.

If we consider truth-acquisition as the dominant goal, then the best policy in promoting this goal would be to lower so much epistemic standards of justification so that they virtually become nonexistent and we believe just anything on the basis of no evidence at all, even considered outright contradictions [(sub) $p(b\backslash e)=0$]. If we believe all propositions we come across, then we would have as many true beliefs as possible, but also as many false beliefs as possible. But given that truth-acquisition is the dominant goal, the implication of having many false beliefs would be entirely epistemically innocuous because the sole epistemic value\goal is truth-acquisition.[15] For obvious reasons, call this picture of belief-fixation '*epistemic licentiousness*'.

Unfortunately, epistemic licentiousness is implausible. Very briefly, here are some reasons that suggest its implausibility. First, if we assume that true belief is the norm of practical reasoning, epistemic licentiousness would entail a cognitive clutter of sorts in terms of practical reasoning. If all beliefs are considered true, it is unclear how we can have practical reasoning at all because all relevant

---

[14] See Alston (1988) and Piller (2009) for brief airings of the same point.
[15] There is a subtle relationship between something being a goal and being valuable. Given that (a) intentional action is goal-orientated and that (b) if we are rational we opt for intentional action that appears to us under-the-guise-of-the-good, it follows that the goals that orientate our under-the-guise-of-the-good intentional action should be taken to be valuable. This is why I place epistemic value and goal side by side.

beliefs would seem equally good in promoting the satisfaction of our practical goals.

Suppose that I would like to go for a stroll and I have many -considered- true beliefs about which places are suitable for a nice stroll and I also have many -considered- true beliefs about how to decide between these many suitable locations. On the face of it, it seems that I would be at a loss about how to deliberate about the matter because all my relevant beliefs are considered justified and true, even contradictory ones. Like Buridan's ass, practical paralysis seems to ensue in such a bizarre scenario, which also explains why Darwinian evolution has not designed our cognitive faculties in such a hopeless way. We wouldn't survive, reproduce and perpetuate the species.

Second, the picture of belief-fixation that epistemic licentiousness portrays seems entirely psychologically unrealistic, plausibly again for evolutionary reasons. Psychologically speaking, it is very hard to envisage that we could just believe anything at will, especially if we take into consideration that belief-fixation is not usually under our direct voluntary control. So, even if we ought to believe just anything, we cannot really do so.[16]

Third, it seems clearly irrational to believe on the basis of [(sub) p(b\e)≤0.51], or even plain contradictions [(sub) [p(b\e)=0], and surely we would like to pursue policies of belief-fixation that satisfy such basic constraints of epistemic rationality (i.e. logical and probabilistic coherence). Yet epistemic licentiousness licenses believing just anything and breaches even such basic constraints of rationality. This is so because if the [(sub) pr (b)= 0.7], then rationally the [(sub) pr(-b)=0.3] and we would believe both of these according to epistemic licentiousness, even considered contradictions with [(sub) pr (b)=0], which is clearly irrational by any plausible standard of rationality.[17] I conclude that epistemic licentiousness is an implausible picture of belief-fixation.

But we could still set as a dominant goal the alternative goal of falsity-avoidance. That is, if we inversely consider falsity-avoidance as the dominant goal,

---

[16] This result would seem to breach the plausible normative principle that 'rational ought implies can'. The principle, roughly, suggests that to rationally ought to exhibit a certain kind of conduct (epistemic or practical) you must be able to exhibit such conduct. By contraposition, if you can't exhibit such conduct for whatever reasons, then you are not rationally bound to act accordingly.

[17] This point is slightly exaggerated because there may be exceptions to even such basic constraints of rationality. If, for example, the concept of truth is indispensable for a web of belief and this concept is necessarily incoherent because of self-referential semantic paradoxes (like the liar), we would still have good reasons to employ the concept of truth. Thus, the principles may be only defeasible and hold for the most part. See Harman (1986:15 – 7) for some discussion.

then the best policy in promoting this goal would be to raise epistemic standards of justification to the ultimate point of deduction\indefeasibility and believe just what is considered deductively proved [(sub) p(b\e)=1]. If we believe only deductively proved propositions, then we would have as few false beliefs as possible, but also very few true beliefs.[18]

A fortiori, we could even suggest that because our deductive reasoning sometimes slips and is fallacious\fallible and, inevitably, this would bestow us with some false beliefs that perhaps we should believe nothing at all! Given that falsity-avoidance is the dominant goal, the implication of having no (true) beliefs would be entirely epistemically innocuous because the sole epistemic value \goal is falsity-avoidance. For obvious reasons, call this picture of belief fixation *'epistemic asceticism'*.

Unfortunately, again, epistemic asceticism is very implausible. Very briefly, here are three reasons that support its implausibility. First, epistemic asceticism entails some form of very radical scepticism because we would be licensed to believe very, very few propositions, if any at all. Perhaps we would be licensed to believe some logical, mathematical, modal beliefs and some other classes of beliefs that may exemplify the very demanding property of indefeasible justification. At any rate, this class of beliefs would represent only a very small portion of what sort of beliefs we hold in our everyday doxastic life (perceptual, memorial, inductive, introspective, testimonial etc.). Note also that this is a very strong form of scepticism because it is scepticism not just about knowledge but about justified belief.[19]

Second, again, this picture of belief-fixation is psychologically unrealistic, plausibly for evolutionary reasons. Psychologically speaking, it is very hard to envisage that we could just restrain belief to the minimum of deductive proof, or even completely withhold belief. Many of our cognitive faculties, processes or abilities have evolved to produce belief-output in a spontaneous and unreflective way (perceptual, memorial, introspective etc.) and of course this belief-out-

---

18 Assuming here that our subjective credences are reliably tracking deductive relations, of course. Of note, is that there have been philosophers who have endorsed such a demanding conception of justification for knowledge, such as Fogelin (1994). More recently, Kyriacou (forthcoming) has argued for what he calls 'Bifurcated Sceptical Invariantism'. The theory accepts that knowledge requires justification that deductively entails truth. This move is supposed to help address various problems for fallibilism, such as the Gettier problem, the dogmatism paradox and concessive knowledge attributions. The account is also supposed to pay some tribute to ordinary knowledge appearances.

19 See Fumerton (1995: Ch. 1) for some discussion of why skepticism about justified belief is much more radical than skepticism about knowledge.

put is often quite reliable, something that lends some intuitive support to externalist theories of justification\knowledge.[20]

Third, suppose that epistemic asceticism is right in spite of its psychological extravagance and implausibility. This would mean, again, that practical paralysis would ensue because we would have very few beliefs to rely on for our everyday practical deliberations. Deductive reasoning is mostly applicable to a priori beliefs (logic, mathematics, modality etc.), and it is very hard to envisage how we could rely on just a priori beliefs for our everyday practical deliberations. Thus, epistemic asceticism also seems implausible.

I hasten to conclude that we cannot resolve the James problem via the first horn of the weighing value approach, be it via epistemic licentiousness or epistemic asceticism. Weighing and prioritizing the promotion of one dominant (sub) goal over the other will not tackle the problem. But we still have the option of the second horn at our disposal. Besides, why think that weighing the two goals should be an all-or-nothing affair? We may reasonably surmise that we need not prioritize the one (sub)goal at the complete expense of the other and that a (sub)goal need not be dominant. We could, in principle, strike just the right kind of balance between the two (sub)goals.

Moreover, the second horn bears some intuitive appeal because compromising goals is what we often try to do when we have conflicting practical goals of individual value that we cannot both satisfy to the same extent at the same time. Think of the ice cream example again. One way to reconcile the two conflicting desires is to have an ice cream of low sugars. So we both satisfy the desire for ice-cream and the desire for a healthy diet.

Or think of the football analogy. One way to reconcile offensive\defensive tactics is to try to strike some kind of right balance between the two, so that we reconcile the two goals. Instead of playing the more defensive formation of 5-3-2 or the more offensive 4-3-3 you could play the more balanced 4-4-2. So if we want to balance our footballing practical goals, we change the tactical formation of our team. Now, the train of thought is that given that both practical and epistemic goals share structural similarities, the same reconciliation strategy could in principle carry over from practical to epistemic goals.[21] The obvious question is how should *principled* balancing go in the epistemic case?[22]

---

20 Again, this seems to breach the plausible normative principle that 'rational ought implies can'.

21 For one thing, they both seem to be normative goals in the sense that they should guide our practical and epistemic lives correctly, whatever correctness might mean. For the idea that the moral and the epistemic domain share important structural similarities see Zagzebski (1996) and Cuneo (2007). It is surely not accidental that expressivism has recently been transposed

4. Aristotelian Eudaimonia and Evidential Understanding

Thus far we have argued that the two (sub)goals are in tension and taking one (sub)goal as dominant delivers very implausible policies of belief-fixation. As a result we are forced into the second horn of the dilemma and we are in essence stuck with the initial puzzle. How are we to correctly regulate belief-fixation given that the two (sub)goals are in competition?

Thinking about the football analogy might give us some hints about how to address the question. In the case of the football analogy, we shift the tactical formation of the team in virtue of an overarching goal, namely, the goal of winning matches. So, the ultimate goal of final value, at least in professional football, is winning matches (and consequently trophies) and constitutes the external criterion that guides our balancing between offensive\epistemic tactics.[23]

The parallel line of thought in the epistemic case would be that to strike the right kind of balance between the two (sub)goals, we also need some sort of external criterion in virtue of which we could non-arbitrarily balance the relative satisfaction of the two (sub)goals. Given that what we weigh here are goals of epistemic value, one may suspect that we should approach the problem from the perspective of more general (epistemic) value considerations. After all, this is what we do in the football game that seems sufficiently analogous to the epistemic game, namely, we appeal to the overarching goal\value of winning matches. By parity of reasoning, if there is an ultimate (epistemic) goal of greater value, then we can perhaps appeal to that goal and use it as an external criterion for a judicious adjudication of the matter.

This intuitive, teleological line of reasoning is broadly Aristotelian in origin. Famously, Aristotle thought that there is an ultimately final goal (or 'telos') about

---

from metaethics to metaepistemology. For the transposition see Chrisman (2007) about knowledge and Kyriacou (2012) about epistemic justification. For a defense of Cuneo's structural parity claim about the moral and the epistemic see Cuneo and Kyriacou (forthcoming).

22 Of note, is that the same kind of question, namely, how to balance inversely proportionate goals is found in debates of military strategy. For example, Wellington is typically considered a master of defensive strategy and Napoleon of offensive strategy and opinions about who was the better commander diverge. Perhaps opinions diverge partly because some prioritize defensive strategy while others offensive strategy.

23 Ideally, athletic values like fair play and sportsmanship should also be goals but for the sake of the analogy I ignore such complications.

human life, namely, eudaimonia (living well or flourishing)[24] and that this goal can shed light in value questions.[25] This is so because eudaimonia is the goal determining how we should lead our lives, tout court, and our epistemic lives are no exception to this. Due to lack of space, I will not argue for the Aristotelian position here but take it for granted for the sake of the argument.[26] I will be assuming that eudaimonia is our ultimately final[27] goal and, hence, to the extent that we are rational agents we should be aiming at living well and be doing what we can to live well (morally, epistemically, aesthetically, politically or otherwise).

Once this Aristotelian, teleological assumption is in place we can revisit the problem of balancing the two (sub)goals of inquiry with some perspective. This is so because if eudaimonia is the ultimately final goal any other interim (epistemic or non-epistemic) goal must be to some extent instrumental to the promotion of eudaimonia.[28] So, we could appeal to eudaimonia in order to balance the

---

24 See *Nicomachean Ethics* (1094a-5a). There is some interpretive dispute about how to exactly gloss the classical Greek notion of eudaimonia. Some translate it as human flourishing, success, well-being or happiness but none of these really captures the exact meaning of the Classical Greek for reasons we need not dwell on here. Perhaps what comes close is 'good life' or 'living well'. For this reason many commentators insist on the transliterated usage of the Classical Greek word. This is the policy I will also follow in the text. For some discussion of the notion of eudaimonia see Shields (2007: 310–6).

25 Of note, is that eudaimonia should not be identified as a distinctively and exclusively moral goal (at least by my lights). It might be a broad practical goal that involves moral, political, epistemic, aesthetic etc. (sub)goals. On this way of construing eudaimonia, the proposal should not be mistaken as aiming at reducing the epistemic to the moral, although the two domains bear obvious normative inter-connections (cf. Clifford (1877); Zagzebski (1996); Cuneo (2007); Baehr (2012)).

26 For a defense of the application of the teleological, Aristotelian position on questions of (moral\political) value see Sandel (2010: Chs 8,9, 10). Sandel's (2010) case could be extended to the case of epistemic value in pretty much the spirit of the current work, but this is something that will have to wait for another occasion.

27 I specify that eudaimonia is the 'ultimately final' goal because, as Aristotle (*Nicomachean Ethics (?)*) himself pointed out, there are also *interim* final goals like friendship and love. Friendship might be valuable for its own sake, but it is also a constitutive part of eudaimonia and thereby promotes it. I had some difficulties in pinning down this reference in Aristotle's work, though I am relatively confident that there is such a reference in his work.

28 For the idea that epistemic values (or goods) should promote eudaimonia see also Zagzebski (2003). Talk of 'promotion' should not invite a consequentialist reading but, in true Aristotelian spirit, a primarily constitutive reading. Positive consequences might tend to follow from epistemic values but this is not to identify epistemic values with those consequences. The distinction is subtle but important. See Sandel (2010) for a similar point.

two (sub)goals of inquiry and indicate that the right way to balance the two (sub) goals is the way that best promotes good living.

Obviously, this is not much of progress yet because we have not answered the question about what kind of balancing would best promote eudaimonia. Both (sub)goals are valuable and therefore should both be taken into consideration. Besides, as we have seen, if we set a dominant goal and belief-fixation is driven solely either by truth-acquisition or by falsity-avoidance we end up with bizarre and implausible pictures of belief-fixation. The obvious question now is how we can take both valuable (sub)goals into consideration in the right way in order to promote the final goal of eudaimonia.

Given that the individual value of both (sub)goals should be taken into relative consideration, some theoretical space might open if we drop the assumption that belief-fixation should be regulated by an atomistic epistemic goal.[29] An *atomistic* epistemic goal is a goal that sets a goal for individual beliefs, not for whole sets of beliefs. Call this latter epistemic goal *holistic*.[30] [31]

The idea is that theoretical space might open if we shift from atomistic to holistic epistemic goals because holistic goals are goals for whole sets of beliefs and this allows for balancing the two (sub)goals in a way that atomistic goals do not. Atomistic goals simply set goals for individual beliefs and it is hard to see how the two (sub)goals can be balanced if we are solely considering the goals

---

29 See Riggs (2003) for a similar idea. Piller (2009), although argues that truth-acquisition and not falsity-avoidance should be our primary goal, he is also sensitive to the challenge posed by the James problem. As a response to the challenge, he suggests that we have (and should have) a desire to avoid inconsistencies. One could see that both Riggs and Piller's responses to the James problem converge towards the line I pursue here. In fact, I think the account proposed here complements and improves on their proposals on a number of counts. I can't really engage in contrastive discussion here with these two theories but, for one thing, these two theories do not appeal to the notions of minimal wisdom and eudaimonia as the account on offer here does.
30 Holistic goals have been generally ignored in the history of epistemology. For some discussion of the point see Zagzebski (1996: Part I).
31 One might object here that by appealing to holistic and not atomistic goals, we are in essence, changing the initial Jamesian question of how to balance the two competing subgoals. In response, this worry is unfounded because, although we might be appealing to extraneous third goals, we do so in order to address the initial Jamesian problem. Note also that the problem seems insoluble, unless we appeal to some other goal in virtue of which we can balance them. Indeed, this is a broadly Sellarsian\Hegelian 'semantic holism' insight. Individual beliefs can never be understood and evaluated atomistically but always holistically in light of background beliefs. If this is the case, then epistemic goals should also be holistic in tandem. Brandom (2000; 2010) typically defends such holistic ideas and, of course, Quine (1953; 1992) has also propounded them. Such ideas can be traced back to Hegel (1910\2003) and Sellars (1956\1997).

for an individual belief. For either you go for the truth of an individual belief or for avoiding its falsity and no balancing is involved. In contrast, if we are considering the goals for whole sets of beliefs, we can in principle balance the two (sub)goals because whole sets of beliefs allow for taking into consideration different (sub)goals at the same time.

Now, in response to the puzzle, we could propose that a holistic epistemic goal could be suggested as an overarching goal that can strike the right kind of balance between the two (sub)goals because it promotes the ultimate goal of eudaimonia. A goal that could play this role is what I shall call *'evidential understanding'*. I will fist introduce the rudiments of the holistic goal of evidential understanding and afterwards undertake to explain how it can take both (sub) goals into consideration in a balanced way that promotes eudaimonia.

Roughly, evidential understanding is the view that the final goal of inquiry is holistic, not atomistic, and should offer an evidence-based conception of the wider and more comprehensive picture of how (sets of) beliefs probabilistically inter-support each other. Broadly construed, it is to be understood in terms of evidentialist and coherentist lines.[32] We should form beliefs in a way that is sensitive to relevant and available evidence and in a way that promotes the explanatory coherence links between the agent's beliefs, where these links are to be understood in terms of inferential and probabilistic inter-support.[33]

Admittedly, I cannot even begin to delineate the basics of evidentialist understanding because this would require lengthy excursions into the intricate notions of evidence, coherence and probability (and even more!) and due to space restrictions this will have to wait. All I can afford to describe here are some of the basic contours of evidentialist understanding which are the following:

First, evidential understanding is a species of understanding-why in the sense that the probabilistic and inferential inter-support of the beliefs help us explain phenomena and answer relevant why-questions. For example, a coherent set of beliefs about economic theory might help explain why many western capitalist economies are currently experiencing difficulties (recession, deflation, unemployment etc.). The economic theory in play might be Marxist, Keynesian

---

[32] Feldman's and Connee's evidentialism (2004) seems to bear important similarities with the account outlined here. But there are also important differences that I cannot now really pursue. For one thing, the account here need not subscribe to their mentalist internalist account of justification. Clifford (1877) was also an evidentialist of sorts. At any rate, this is a story for another occasion. Also, for some sympathetic discussion of the notion of explanatory coherence see Harman (1986: Ch.7).

[33] See Fumerton (1995:146–7) about why the coherence relation should not be understood in terms of the austere, deductive material implication.

or Classical but the important thing is that it should be evidentially supported. Of course, these coherent economic beliefs, even if they are evidentially supported, they need not be true. This leads to the second point.

Second, evidential understanding is also to be distinguished from factive conceptions of understanding.[34] Evidential understanding need not entail truth. For all the relevant evidence at our disposal, even if we correctly grasp what this evidence rationally supports, it may fail to lead to the truth. That is, even if we believe as we rationally ought to believe in the circumstances, given the evidence, we may fail to get at the truth. But evidential understanding does imply that in non-demonically-skeptical worlds we should, in principle, be in better contact with reality.[35] If we weigh the evidence correctly and grasp what it rationally supports, it is likely that a fair number of our beliefs will be true and inter-supporting and therefore improve our understanding of reality, even if strict truth on the matter remains as elusive as ever. This is because rational belief is, ceteris paribus, truth-conducive.[36]

Third, talk of evidential understanding should not mistake it for an inevitably internalist conception of understanding, no matter how internalism is to be glossed.[37] True enough, notions like evidence, probability and coherence are often (and perhaps more naturally) explicated along internalist lines but an internalist construal is not inescapable.[38] It could well be the case that evidentialist understanding relies on an externalist conception of evidence, probability and coherence.[39] For current purposes, I cannot dwell on the murky internalism\externalism contention and I will leave it open about what sort of metaepistemological interpretation is the most plausible.

In the same vein, the coherentist framework of evidential understanding comports well with the Quinean idea that one's web of belief should be under continuous revision and reconstruction in light of what new evidence supports

---

[34] Recently there has been a lot of discussion about the nature of understanding that I have to skip here. See Zagzebski (1996, 2009), Kvanvig (2003), Elgin (2004), Grim (2010) and Pritchard (2010).

[35] The idea that understanding is in this way truth-conducive is supported by philosophers like Riggs (2003) and Elgin (2004).

[36] It is truth-conducive in 'normal', demon-proof worlds. I employ the concept of 'normal worlds' here. Normal worlds are worlds pretty much close and thereby similar to the actual world (that is commonsensically assumed to be real).

[37] That is, be it in terms of accessibility internalism, mentalist internalism, or even other. For the various takes on epistemic internalism see Pappas (2014).

[38] See Fumerton (1995: Ch.5), Pollock and Cruz (1999: Ch.3)) and Olson (2007) for the concept of coherence and its intricacies.

[39] See for example how Greco (2010) develops an externalist account of such notions.

(or even new and improved assessments of what old evidence may support).⁴⁰ This continuous reworking could be carried out either along internalist or externalist (or even hybrid) lines that, unfortunately, we don't have the space now to spell out in much detail, not to mention arbitrate which one is our favourite.

It could, for example, be carried out along deontological lines or reliabilist lines. On the one hand, it could be carried out in line with internalist contours and in terms of rational epistemic duties about what one ought to believe, given the available and relevant evidence. On the other hand, it could be carried out in line with externalist contours and in terms of reliable virtuous dispositions for belief-fixation. It could even build on both internalist and externalist insights in order to construct a kind of hybrid theoretical framework.⁴¹

Fourth, to repeat, evidential understanding is an attainable, final epistemic goal in regard to interim, instrumental epistemic goals like atomistic truth-acquisition\falsity-avoidance. However, in the ascending ladder of value hierarchy, it is again an instrumental goal in regard to the ultimately final goal of eudaimonia (or human flourishing). Further, one may ponder about the value of the Big Truth (and Knowledge) and their place in this hierarchy. Suffice it to say here that they are nothing but elusive, unattainable goals. Given the often fragmentary (and sometimes even tempered with) character of evidence, the difficulty of the subjects of inquiry and human cognitive frailty (e.g. confirmation biases and other irrationalities like the affect heuristic or the halo effect, deep-seated vicious character traits like narrow-mindedness, social and situational pressures etc.) it is rather unlikely that we will find the truth about all the matters that really interest us.⁴²

Fifth, it should not be assumed that we can somehow set up a certain fixed and rigid (perhaps even quantified) balance between the (sub)goals of truth-acquisition\falsity-avoidance that best promotes evidential understanding, which in its own turn promotes eudaimonia. The balance between the two goals may be context-sensitive and flexible enough to fluctuate in certain contexts of inquiry. Epistemic life is messy and in some epistemic contexts the best way to pro-

---

40 See Quine (1953; 1992).
41 Such a hybrid account has been developed, for example, by Sosa (1991, 2007). Sosa distinguishes between virtue-theoretic reliable knowledge that is merely 'apt' and reflective knowledge that is also coherent. Reflective knowledge is the distinctively human kind of knowledge, while apt knowledge the merely animal kind of knowledge.
42 For some fascinating empirical work on the psychology of judgment that illustrates our cognitive frailty see Kahneman (2011). Of course, as Kahneman (2011) underlines, human cognition is not just capable of 'flaws' but also of 'marvels'.

mote evidential understanding may be to confer some relative priority to truth-acquisition over falsity avoidance and vice versa.

In some contexts, inquiry might be sensitive to practical interests, needs and stakes and these may affect how the exact balancing of the two (sub)goals should go. We may, for instance, give some relative priority to avoiding falsity in contexts where falsity might incur disastrous practical repercussions (e.g. when battling steep economic recession) and we may give some relative priority to acquiring truth in contexts where the truth would incur beneficent practical repercussions (e.g. when battling cancer or Ebola).[43]

The same happens in the case of the football game. In certain football contexts where you have to play away with a gifted, technically superior team you should adapt your tactics in order to promote the practical goal of winning matches. For instance, you could opt for a more defensive formation that looks for the opportunity to strike in the counterattack, knowing that a more offensive tactic will expose the team to a humiliating defeat. Equally, in a different occasion you could opt for a more offensive formation that intends to dominate the game, knowing that a more defensive tactic will grant gratuitous freedom of offensive action to a team that is less gifted than your team.

Sixth, obviously, not all infinity of propositions are, or should be, or could be, of equal interest to us and of equal value to know.[44] There are pointless propositions that one, ceteris paribus, ought not to care about like how many blades of grass there are in the backyard or how many grains of sand there are on a sandy beach. This brings forth the interesting question of what propositions one ought to be interested in. We can afford the brief note that at least one ought to be interested in propositions bearing on the ultimate goal of living well. So, one should have some interest in political philosophy, for example, about the right way to structure a political community (and key political concepts like social justice, liberty, equality etc.) because the question of how to structure a political community directly bears on the question of living well.

With this basic outline of how eudaimonia could be invoked as the external criterion in virtue of which we can balance the two (sub)goals (by means of intermediate reference to evidential understanding), let us now turn to the question of how exactly evidential understanding promotes eudaimonia. As I argue in a moment, it does so by promoting what I shall call *'theoretical minimal wisdom'*.

---

43 Like knowledge attributions (cf. DeRose (1996) and Cohen (1998)), the exact balancing of the two (sub)goals may fluctuate because it is sensitive to contextual factors.
44 As Harman (1986:15) notes, as rational and cognitively finite believers we should aim at cognitive clutter-avoidance.

5. Evidential Understanding and Theoretical Minimal Wisdom

Evidential understanding is an interim final goal, though, instrumental goal in regard to eudaimonia because it promotes the satisfaction of the ultimate goal of eudaimonia. If you satisfy the goal of evidential understanding you inevitably promote the goal of eudaimonia because it promotes theoretical minimal wisdom that seems a necessary condition for eudaimonia. Let us explain a bit what theoretical minimal wisdom is, how evidential understanding promotes it and how theoretical minimal wisdom promotes eudaimonia.

With theoretical minimal wisdom I stipulate the cognitive state (or condition) in which (a) an agent forms a certain evidence-based and coherent understanding of the bigger picture of things about all that should interest her as a rational agent (a Weltanschauung, if you like) and (b) the agent is humble, reflective and open-minded enough to be aware of the fact that her Weltanschauung is just one out of many evidence-based and coherent ones and, therefore, is possible, if not likely, not to be true, at least not true in all respects.[45] I call it 'theoretical minimal wisdom' because it specifies a minimal necessary condition of being (theoretically) wise.[46]

Satisfying these two necessary conditions does not imply full wisdom per se, whatever this might mean, but solely implies a minimal state of wisdom.[47] Evidential understanding promotes theoretical minimal wisdom because we expect

---

[45] The (b) condition bears out the intuition well-known from the epistemology of disagreement debates that disagreement with respected and reliable peers should somewhat mitigate one's confidence in one's (web of) belief and invite reflection and reconsideration of the reasons we have for this (web of) belief. This is not to imply that mere peer disagreement should usher an agent to fall back to anything so radical as suspense of judgment or abandoning the belief. We may esteem and trust our peers and take seriously their argued views but we should also esteem and trust ourselves and our own argued views. Anyway, this goes far beyond the scope of this essay.

[46] From Aristotle onwards (cf. Zagzebski (1996), Whitcomb (2011)), we tend to distinguish between theoretical and practical wisdom. I set aside here the distinction and the relation between the two according to the present account.

[47] Ryan (2013) calls this general conception of wisdom 'the epistemic humility theory of wisdom'. Note also that my take on theoretical minimal wisdom is very different from Ryan's (2013) exposition of humility accounts. It is rather more akin to Zagzebski's (1996: 49–50) 'grasping the whole structure of reality' understanding of wisdom and Whitcomb's 'deep understanding' version of theoretical wisdom, though, very important differences remain that I cannot delve into here. See also Whitcomb (2011) for some useful discussion of the complexities besetting the concept of wisdom.

minimally wise agents to have a certain evidence-based and coherent understanding of the bigger picture of things and a humbling sense of their fallibility. That is, a systematic, comprehensive, explanatory, evidence-based and coherent worldview that helps agents find their place in the world by reflecting on core life-changing questions like 'How should I live?', 'What am I?', 'What do I owe to others, if anything?', 'What should I believe?' etc.[48]

To illustrate the fact that evidential understanding promotes theoretical minimal wisdom consider the following simple thought experiment. Suppose a possible world very close and thereby very similar to our actual world. Agents in this world have the same biology, psychology, linguistic and cognitive abilities, social life settings etc. with us humans. Now, in such a world would you consider someone (theoretically) wise at all if he lacked a certain evidence-based and coherent understanding of the bigger picture of things that includes such life-changing matters as politics, morality, art, science, religion etc.? I think that most of us would consider such a person (theoretically) unwise because of his unreflective naivety.

Suppose now that in the same possible world we do have an agent with a certain evidence-based and coherent understanding of the bigger picture of things that includes such life-changing matters as politics, morality, art, science, religion etc. Would this agent display (theoretical minimal) wisdom? I think not necessarily because there could be cases where such an agent is dogmatic, arrogant and complacent enough to consider her own Weltanschauung the Truth. Think, for example, of the occasional Marxist, Freudian, libertarian etc. who complacently believes that her Weltanschauung is the Truth. In that case, I think most people would not attribute (theoretical) wisdom because it seems incongruent with dogmatism, arrogance and complacency.[49] This need not imply that a person who satisfies the two proposed conditions enjoys the exalted status of being fully wise but s\he at least satisfies necessary conditions for wisdom that we have dubbed the conditions of theoretical minimal wisdom.

---

48 It should not be assumed that theoretical minimal wisdom is overly intellectualistic in the sense that only philosophers, intellectuals, artists, scientists etc. can be minimally wise. Laypeople can in principle also be philosophically refined to some extent and therefore minimally wise. It sometimes can be surprising how sensitive laypeople are to fundamental philosophical questions that remain questions for all (e.g. the moral question of the right thing to do, God's existence, social justice, aesthetic value, even composition and identity etc.).
49 Of note is that intellectual vices (naivety, arrogance, complacency etc.) seem to appear in an explanation of our intuitions in these thought experiments. This might be indicative that a theory of (theoretical) wisdom should involve virtue-theoretic considerations. For discussion of intellectual character virtue-theoretic epistemology and its place in the field, see Baehr (2012).

This simple duo of thought experiments indicates that evidential understanding and a humbling sense of our fallibility are necessary conditions for theoretical minimal wisdom and promote it. An analogous duo of thought experiments can also be run to indicate that theoretical minimal wisdom is a necessary condition for eudaimonia (or a good life) and promotes it.

Suppose, again, a possible world very close and thereby very similar to our actual world. Agents have the same biology, psychology, linguistic and cognitive abilities, social life settings etc. with us humans. Now, in such a world would you consider someone having a good life at all if he lacked (a) a certain evidence-based and coherent understanding of the bigger picture of things that includes such life-changing matters as politics, morality, art, science, religion etc., and (b) a humbling sense of her fallibility that jointly confer (theoretical minimal) wisdom?[50] I think that most of us would consider such an unreflective and naive person, not only unwise, but a person that does not enjoy a really good life.[51]

As Socrates would have it, 'the unexamined life is not worth living' in the sense that it is a life that does not rise up to the level of reflective scrutiny and theoretical minimal wisdom.[52] It is not a life lived in thorough examination as it could and should be. Of course, this need not imply that the minimally reflective person enjoys a fully good life, whatever this might exactly mean.[53]

Suppose now that in the same possible world we do have an agent with a certain evidence-based and coherent understanding of the bigger picture of

---

50 The agent could fail the desideratum of evidential understanding for theoretical minimal wisdom in various ways. She might fail to base her beliefs on relevant evidence, or fail to probabilistically inter-connect the various sets of her beliefs, or fail to reflect on life-changing questions.

51 I refrain from the term happy because common usage, unfortunately, bears utilitarian\hedonistic connotations. These connotations are of course philosophically dubious because some happiness\well-being theorists could question if happiness need involve pleasure and avoidance of pain. Stoics would be a historical example of such a position, I think.

52 See Plato's *Apology* (38a) for the famous retort of the Socratic character.

53 Some may have skeptical worries about whether being epistemically virtuous (or 'in the right') really promotes eudaimonia. They may even cite empirical work supporting the idea. For example, some may question whether epistemic virtue, like moral virtue, does promote eudaimonia. They may suggest that virtue, be it moral or epistemic, only incurs suffering and misery because it is better to do and believe what promotes your self-interest and not what is virtuous. They may also continue to press the skeptical question of why be moral, epistemically in the right, or plain virtuous, anyway. These are legitimate hard questions that exercise philosophers since Plato's *Republic* but unfortunately I cannot pursue them here. Suffice it to say that, like Plato, I find reasonable the idea that virtue is at least necessary for eudaimonia and that we ought to be virtuous, be it morally or epistemically.

things that includes such life-changing matters as politics, morality, art, science, religion etc. Would this agent have a good life at all? I think not necessarily because there could be cases where such an agent is dogmatic, arrogant and complacent enough to consider her own Weltanschauung the Truth. Think again of the occasional Marxist, Freudian, libertarian etc. who complacently believes that her Weltanschauung is the Truth. In that case, I think most people would not attribute having a good life to the agent because a good life seems incongruent with dogmatism, arrogance and complacency. A life lived in dogmatic certainties, complacency and, inevitably, accompanied with arrogance and perhaps even utter disrespect for other evidence-based, coherent systems of belief is intuitively lacking in value.

What is more, evidential understanding and a humbling sense of our fallibility seem to cultivate exactly the wisdom-conducive virtues of epistemic humility, tolerance and open-mindedness that are the opposites of vices like arrogance, intolerance and narrow-mindedness that dogmatic, arrogant and complacent agents tend to exhibit.[54] It does so because it eschews dogmatic insistence on truth, certainty and knowledge but on having a rational, evidential understanding while conceding that we may don't have, and may not ever be able to have, the elusive and perhaps unattainable Big Truth (and Knowledge) about all the things that should interest us.[55]

I conclude that evidential understanding and a humbling sense of our fallibility are necessary conditions for theoretical minimal wisdom and promote it and theoretical minimal wisdom is a necessary condition for eudaimonia and promotes it. This is how evidential understanding balances the Janus-faced goal of truth-acquisition and falsity-avoidance in light of the ultimate goal of having a good life.

---

54 See Ryan (2013) for some discussion of a related point.
55 Compare Quine (1992:101–2): 'Limited to our terms and devices, we grasp the world variously. I think of the disparate ways of getting at the diameter of an impenetrable sphere: we may pinion the sphere in calipers or we may girdle it with a tape measure and divide by pi, but there is no getting inside...[W]hat the empirical under-determination of global science shows is that there are various defensible ways of conceiving the world.' Of course, for Quine (1992:95–102) not all conceptions are equally good\useful for our purposes. Pragmatic criteria like prediction, simplicity, economy, consilience etc. help us opt for the best conception of the world.

6. Conclusion

I have presented a puzzle about epistemic normativity, the so-called James problem. The James problem indicates that the standard conception of the goal of inquiry as the pursuit of truth-acquisition and falsity-avoidance induces tension between the two (sub)goals because they are inversely proportionate: the more we satisfy the one the less we satisfy the other and vice versa. I suggested that we could follow a weighing value approach to the James problem, namely, that we weigh the relative epistemic value of each (sub)goal and accordingly regulate belief-fixation.

The weighing value approach then ushered us into the horns of a dilemma: either the value of one of the two (sub)goals completely trumps the value of the other (sub)goal; or we can somehow balance and reconcile the value of the two (sub)goals without either of the two becoming dominant. The first horn of the dilemma was found very implausible. Whether we go solely for truth-acquisition or for falsity-avoidance, we end up with respective policies of belief-fixation (epistemic licentiousness\epistemic asceticism) that are bizarre and implausible.

The second horn of the dilemma was found more promising as we invoked an external criterion in virtue of which we can indicate a principled way to balance and reconcile the satisfaction of the two (sub)goals. I suggested that this external criterion is the ultimate goal of eudaimonia and that eudaimonic considerations imply that a more holistic epistemic goal may help open theoretical space for balancing the two (sub)goals. This more holistic goal is what I have called evidential understanding. Evidential understanding promotes eudaimonia because it promotes what I have called theoretical minimal wisdom, which is a necessary condition for eudaimonia and promotes it. [56]

References

Alston, W. (1988). The Deontological Conception of Epistemic Justification. *Philosophical Perspectives* 2: 115–152.
Aristotle (2003). *Nicomachean Ethics*. Cambridge (MA): Harvard University Press.
Baehr, J. (2012). *The Inquiring Mind*. Oxford: Oxford University Press.

---

[56] I am indebted to Christian Piller, the editors Martin Grajner and Pedro Schmechtig and an anonymous referee for valuable feedback. I have presented earlier versions of the paper at a workshop at the University of Cyprus and at the European Epistemology Network Meeting, 2014, in Madrid. I am also indebted to the audiences of these two venues for their helpful comments and suggestions.

Blackburn, S. (2006). *Truth*. London: Penguin Books.
Boghossian, P. (2007). *Fear of Knowledge*. Oxford: Oxford University Press.
Brandom, R. (2000). *Articulating Reasons*. Cambridge (MA): Harvard University Press.
Brandom, R. (2010). *Between Saying and Doing*. Oxford: Oxford University Press.
Chrisman, M. (2007). From Epistemic Contextualism to Epistemic Expresivism. *Philosophical Studies* 135: 225–254.
Clifford ,W. (1877/2008). The Ethics of Belief. In J. Feinberg and R. Shafer-Landau (eds.), *Reason and Responsibility*. Belmont (CA): Thompson.
Cohen, S. (1998). Contextualist Solutions to Epistemological Problems: Scepticism, Gettier and the Lottery. *Australasian Journal of Philosophy* 74: 549–567.
Conee, E. and Feldman, R. (2004). *Evidentialism*. Oxford: Oxford University Press.
Cuneo, T. (2007). *The Normative Web*. Oxford: Oxford University Press.
Cuneo, T. and Kyriacou, C. (forthcoming). Defending the Moral/Epistemic Parity.
In C. McHugh, J. Way and D. Whiting, *Metaepistemology*. Oxford: Oxford University Press.
DeRose, K. (1995). Solving the Skeptical Problem. *The Philosophical Review* 104: 1–52.
Elgin, C. (2004). True Enough. *Philosophical Issues* 14: 113–131.
Feldman R. (2001). Voluntary Belief and Epistemic Evalutation. In M. Steup (ed.), *Knowledge, Truth and Duty*. Oxford: Oxford University Press.
Fumerton, R. (1995). *Metaepistemology and Skepticism*. London: Rowman and Littlefield.
Fogelin, R. (1994). *Pyrrhonian Reflections on Knowledge and Justification*. Oxford: Oxford University Press.
Greco, J. (2010). *Achieving Knowledge*. Oxford: Oxford University Press.
Griffiths, P. and Wilkins, J. (forthcoming). When Do Evolutionary Explanations of Belief Debunk Belief? *Darwin in the 21st Century*.
Grimm, S. (2010). Understanding. In S. Bernecker and D. Pritchard (eds.), *The Routledge Companion to Epistemology*. New York: Routledge.
Harman, G. (1986). *Change in View*. Cambridge (MA): MIT Press.
Hegel, G. W. F. (1910/2003). *The Phenomenology of Mind*. Mineola: Dover Publications.
James, W. (1896/2008). The Will to Believe. In J. Feinberg and R. Shafer-Landau (eds.), *Reason and Responsibility*. Belmont (CA): Thomson.
Kahneman, D. (2011). *Thinking, Fast and Slow*. London: Penguin Books.
Kelly, T. (2003). Epistemic Rationality as Instrumental Rationality: A Critique. *Philosophy and Phenomenological Research* 66: 612–40.
Kvanvig, J. (2003). *The Value of Knowledge and the Pursuit of Understanding*. Cambridge: Cambridge University Press.
Kyriacou, C.. (2012). Habits-Expressivism about Epistemic Justification. *Philosophical Papers* 41: 209–237.
Kyriacou, C. (2013). How Not to Solve the Wrong Kind of Reasons Problem. *The Journal of Value Inquiry*. Vol.47, Nos. 1–2: 101–110.
Kyriacou, C. (2015). Critical Discussion of Foundations for Moral Relativism, David Velleman. UK: Open Book Publishers. 2013. *Ethical Theory and Moral Practice* 18(1): 209–214.
Kyriacou, C. (2016). Metaepistemology. In *Internet Encyclopedia of Philosophy*. Eds. J. Fieser and B. Dowden. URL= http://www.iep.utm.edu/meta-epi/
Kyriacou, C. (forthcoming). Bifurcated Sceptical Invariantism: Between Gettier Cases and Saving Epistemic Appearances. *Journal of Philosophical Research*.
Mellor, H. (2005). *Probability: A Philosophical Introduction*. London: Routledge.

Olson, E. (2007). The Place of Coherence in Epistemology. In V. Hendriks and D. Pritchard (eds.), *New Waves in Epistemology*. London: Palgrave Macmillan

Papas, G. (2014). Internalist vs Externalist Conceptions of Epistemic Justification. In E. Zalta (ed.), *Stanford Encyclopedia of Philosophy*. URL= http://plato.stanford.edu/entries/justep-intext/

Papineau, D. (2003). The Evolution of Knowledge. In D. Papineau, *The Roots of Reason*. Oxford: Oxford University Press.

Piller, C. (2009). Desiring the Truth and Nothing But the Truth. *Noûs* 43: 192–213/

Plato (2005). *Euthyphro, Apology, Crito, Phaedo, Phaedrus*. Cambridge MA : Harvard University Press.

Pritchard, D., Millar, A. and A. Haddock (2010). *The Nature and Value of Knowledge*. Oxford: Oxford University Press.

Quine, W.V.O. (1953). Two Dogmas of Empiricism. In Quine, W. V. O., *From A Logical Point of View*. Cambridge, MA: Harvard University Press. 20–46.

Quine, W.V.O. (1992). *Pursuit of Truth*. Cambridge (MA): Harvard University Press

Riggs, W. (2003). Balancing Our Epistemic Goals. *Noûs* 37(2), 342–252.

Ryan, S. (2013). Wisdom. In E. Zalta (ed.), *Stanford Encyclopedia of Philosophy*. URL : http://plato.stanford.edu/entries/wisdom/

Sandel, M. (2010). *Justice*. London: Penguin Books.

Sellars, W. (1956/1997). *Empiricism and the Philosophy of Mind*. Cambridge (MA): Harvard University Press.

Sosa, E. (1991). *Knowledge in Perspective*. Cambridge: Cambridge University Press.

Sosa, E. (2003). The Place of Truth in Epistemology. In M. DePaul and L. Zagzebski (eds.), *Intellectual Virtue*. Oxford: Oxford University Press.

Sosa, E. (2007). *A Virtue Epistemology*. Oxford: Oxford University Press.

Zagzebski, L. (1996). *Virtues of the Mind*. Cambridge: Cambridge University Press.

Zagzebski, L. (2003). The Search for the Source of the Epistemic Good. *Metaphilosophy* 34: 12–28.

Zagzebski, L. (2009). *On Epistemology*. Belmont (CA): Wadsworth.

Wedgwood, R. (2008). Contextualism About Justified Belief. *Philosopher's Imprint* 8: 1–20.

Whitcomb, D. (2011). Wisdom. In S. Bernecker and D. Pritchard. (eds.), *The Routledge Companion to Epistemology*. New York: Routledge.

Duncan Pritchard
Epistemic Axiology

1.

I want to treat the question of what defines the epistemic, and what is the nature of epistemic value, as tightly interconnected. This is because once we understand what the epistemic is, we will have thereby delineated a certain specifically epistemic domain of evaluation. Thus, any account of the epistemic is thereby also an account of epistemic goodness. I grant that this might not be immediately obvious, but as we go along we will see that the reasons why it might initially look suspect are based on muddled thinking. Once we have clarified the terrain we are exploring here, the plausibility of this thesis about the nature and value of the epistemic should become apparent.

At first blush at least, it can seem as if there is a plurality of epistemic goods, with no straightforward hierarchy in play. Truth, knowledge, understanding, wisdom, justification, reliability, cognitive agency, explanatory power, and so on, all seem to be epistemically desirable, in ways that are sometimes similar and sometimes quite distinct. Faced with such a smorgasbord of epistemic goodness, one can be tempted to embrace a radical pluralism about both the nature of the epistemic and about epistemic value. On this view, there is no base-level account of the epistemic available, and nor is there a fundamental epistemic good—i.e., fundamental in the sense that the epistemic value of other epistemic goods is reducible to the fundamental epistemic good.

Alternatively, one might opt for a monistic approach to the nature of the epistemic and to epistemic goodness, but fixate on what one takes to be the most elevated epistemic standing in the list (understanding, for example). One rationale for this approach is that one can then account for the goodness of the other epistemic standings in terms of how they approximate to, or otherwise open a pathway towards, this higher epistemic good. The nature of the epistemic is thus understood in terms of this elevated epistemic standing.

An even more radical response to the apparent plurality of epistemic goods is to give up on the project of offering any overall account of either the epistemic or of epistemic goodness. Perhaps we should treat the notion of the epistemic as simply a term of art that doesn't latch onto any distinction that is rooted in our everyday practices. If that's right, then there is little to be gained by becoming fixated on offering an account of the epistemic, much less an overarching account of epistemic value. Rather, we should only be concerned with whether the items our list of 'epistemic goods' have any general value (where this value is not a specifically epistemic value).[1]

While I can see the temptation to head in these directions, I think it is a temptation that we should resist. Indeed, I want to suggest that the right way to think about the axiology of the epistemic is to adopt a straightforward account which was common currency in epistemology until relatively recently. This is the idea that we should understand the nature of the epistemic in truth-directed terms, such that the fundamental epistemic good is concerned with grasping the truth.[2] For ease of expression, I will focus in this regard on believing the truth, though the reader should bear in mind that I think the notion of 'grasping' in play is broader than just belief. There is, for example, a kind of cognitive contact with reality that one gains in first-person observation which I think represents an epistemic good in virtue of the grasping of the truth involved, but which need not issue in beliefs, specifically.[3] But we will be settling such complications to one side in what follows.[4]

Construed as a thesis about epistemic value, I have elsewhere called this view *epistemic value truth monism*, where this view stands opposed to, for example, epistemic value pluralisms of various stripes, and also epistemic value monisms which don't treat truth as the fundamental epistemic good.[5] Since we are

---

[1] This is view that Stewart Cohen has urged on me in discussion. See also Alston (2005) for a related highly pluralist conception of epistemic *desiderata*, particularly with regard to epistemic justification.

[2] See David (2001, 151–2) for a long list of quotations illustrating how widely held this view once was in epistemology. The list of contemporary epistemologists that he quotes includes William Alston, Laurence Bonjour, Roderick Chisholm, Richard Foley, Alvin Goldman, Keith Lehrer, Paul Moser, Alvin Plantinga, and Ernest Sosa. Note that often this proposal isn't about our grasping the truth as such, but simply about the value of truth and its fundamentality when it comes to the nature of the epistemic. My view—although I won't be arguing for this here—is that we value true beliefs because we value the truth. I further explore this contrast between truth, as opposed to grasping the truth, as the fundamental epistemic good in Pritchard (2014).

[3] Put another way, I think there is an epistemic goodness involved in directly seeing things for oneself. For further discussion of this idea, see Pritchard (forthcoming c).

[4] Note that one advantage of focusing on belief in this regard could be that one could then appeal to the familiar idea that there is a close conceptual relationship between belief and truth (i.e., in the sense that, broadly speaking, the former is in some significant way directed at the latter). For reasons of space, I will not be considering this issue here. I briefly discuss its relevance to questions of epistemic value in Pritchard (2011, §1). For more on the idea that belief is in some sense 'aimed' at truth, see Wedgwood (2002), Shah (2003), and Shah & Velleman (2005).

[5] See, for example, Pritchard, Millar & Haddock (2010, ch. 1) and Pritchard (2011; forthcoming d).

here concerned with the project of offering a thesis that is simultaneously an account of the nature and of the value of the epistemic, we will need a more generic description. I propose the *traditional account*, to reflect the fact that this thesis was widely held in epistemology until relatively recently.

2.

One attraction of the traditional account is that it offers us the most straightforward way of understanding why we might demarcate a particular epistemic domain of evaluation in the first place. It is often noted that 'epistemology' is a term that was only invented—by the Scottish philosopher, James Frederick Ferrier—in the middle of the 19th Century. One can thus see why certain philosophers might regard the notion of the epistemic as somewhat artificial, in the sense that it doesn't answer to any underlying distinction that one draws in everyday life. This line of reasoning is much too quick, however, at least if one treats the traditional account as a viable proposal. For even though the everyday folk might not employ the terminology of epistemology—in contrast, for example, to how they will readily use terms like 'ethics' or 'aesthetics'—it is clear that they mark a distinction between the epistemic and the non-epistemic insofar as this concerns a grasping of the truth. The folk would surely recognise, for example, the important difference between believing that a person charged with murder is guilty because of the overwhelming evidence available to support that verdict, as opposed to believing that he is guilty because of some feature of the defendant (his skin colour, say) which one is prejudiced against. Thus, if the epistemic is concerned with our grasp of the truth, then we can plausibly contend that it picks out a certain kind of evaluative domain which is rooted in our everyday practices, such that it isn't merely a term of art. The epistemic is thus more akin to the ethical and the aesthetic than we might have hitherto supposed.

In contrast, if one opts for a pluralistic conception of the epistemic good, then it will obviously become more difficult to find this conception rooted in our everyday practices. The idea that there might be a more elevated epistemic good which is fundamental fares better on this score, since as we will see it is widely held that some higher epistemic standings, such as understanding, are distinctively valuable. As we will also see, however, the problem with this proposal is that it is hard to make out why the kind of distinctive value in play as regards these higher epistemic standings should be regarded as specifically epistemic. (More carefully, the problem is that insofar as we can discern a specifically epistemic kind of value that is in play with regard to these higher epistemic standings, we can comfortably account for this epistemic value within the rubric of the traditional account).

3.

A few clarificatory remarks are in order regarding the traditional account, at least as I am understanding this thesis. The first thing to note that is that it doesn't follow from the fact that there is a distinctive kind of goodness that is epistemic that epistemic standings are good *simpliciter*. I suspect that part of the initial opposition one might have to the idea that an account of the epistemic can thereby be an account of epistemic value is rooted in the thought that there is a genuine entailment here. One might think, after all, that the epistemic good must be good *simpliciter*, and then one might worry about how an account of what the epistemic is could all by itself introduce a new kind of unqualified goodness into the world.

That there is no such entailment in play here can be brought out by considering Peter Geach's (1956) distinction between predicative and attributive adjectives. From 'x is a red flea', one can infer that 'x is a flea' and 'x is red'. This is what Geach has in mind when he talks about predicative adjectives. Contrast this expression with 'x is a big flea', which employs an attributive adjective. Clearly one cannot now infer both that 'x is a flea' and that 'x is big', since all that is meant by this expression is that x is big *for a flea*, and not that x is big *simpliciter*.

In the same vein, we cannot simply infer from the fact that something is epistemically good—i.e., that it is good when assessed along some distinctively epistemic axis of evaluation, one that is concerned, on the traditional account, with grasping of the truth—that it is thereby good *simpliciter*. That's not to say that the epistemic good *isn't* good *simpliciter*—perhaps it is—only that the former doesn't entail the latter.

There is a related point that we need to make in this regard, which concerns an ambiguity in the very notion of epistemic value or goodness. Properly understood, this notion concerns a particular kind of value or goodness which is distinctively epistemic, just as ethical goodness concerns a particular kind of value which is distinctively ethical, and aesthetic goodness concerns a particular kind of value which is distinctively aesthetical. There is another way of using this notion, however, which is as describing what we might call the *value of the epistemic*. That is, commentators often use the notion of epistemic value or epistemic goodness to describe a kind of goodness that attaches to epistemic standings, regardless of whether that goodness is specifically epistemic. So, for example, one finds virtue-theoretic proposals regarding 'epistemic value' in the literature that account for that value by appealing to the *ethical* value of epistemic standings like knowledge and understanding.⁶

Clearly, however, we should be keeping these two notions apart, and henceforth we will do so by explicitly referring to the second construal of 'epistemic value' specifically as 'the value of the epistemic'. Note that this distinction between epistemic value and the value of the epistemic does not quite square up with the previous point about predicative and attributive adjectives. After all, the fact that an epistemic standing has worth in the value of epistemic sense needn't entail that it is good *simpliciter*, though it will often entail that the epistemic standing has a value that isn't exclusively epistemic. That said, typically when epistemologists appeal to the value of the epistemic they do so because they have in mind a kind of value that attaches to the epistemic which is in the relevant sense predicative. So, for example, it is widely held that if something is ethically good then it is good *simpliciter*. Thus, if a certain epistemic standing is ethically valuable, then it will also be good *simpliciter*.

The traditional account as I am construing it takes no stand on whether the epistemic good is good *simpliciter*. It follows that we should keep questions about epistemic value and questions about the value of the epistemic entirely distinct when evaluating this proposal. Relatedly, it is no objection to the traditional account that the elucidation of the epistemic that it offers cannot also be an account of epistemic goodness which explains how the epistemic is good *simpliciter* as it is no part of the traditional account to offer such a thesis.⁷

4.

Having this distinction between epistemic value and the value of the epistemic in mind can help us to see why at least one *prima facie* difficulty that has been lev-

---

6 See, for example, Greco (2009).
7 I explore this distinction between what I am here calling epistemic value as opposed to the value of the epistemic in a number of places. See, for example, Pritchard (2014b; forthcoming a; forthcoming d). Note that I also defend the claim that there are epistemic standings that are valuable *simpliciter*, such as understanding—see Pritchard (2009; 2014a), and Pritchard, Millar & Haddock (2010, chs. 1–4). My point is just that this value is not a specifically epistemic value, and hence this claim is not entailed by the traditional account. For more the topic of epistemic value more generally, see Pritchard (2007b) and Pritchard & Turri (2011).

elled against the traditional account, at least when construed as an account of epistemic value, doesn't hold water. This is the so-called *swamping problem*.[8]

We noted earlier that when construed as a thesis specifically about epistemic value, the traditional account is committed to epistemic value truth monism—*viz.*, that there is one fundamental epistemic good, and that good concerns grasping the truth. As I've argued elsewhere, the swamping problem is best understood as a putative *reductio* argument against epistemic value truth monism and hence, thereby, against the traditional account.[9]

In order to get a handle on the swamping problem, consider the following analogy.[10] Imagine two cups of coffee that are identical in every respect: taste, quantity, smell, quality, and so on. It would seem to follow that one should value them equally to the extent that, for example, one should be indifferent about which of the two cups of coffee one is given. The twist in the tale is that while one of the cups of coffee was produced by a coffee machine that regularly produces good coffee, the other cup was produced by a coffee machine that usually produces terrible coffee (but which happened to produce a good cup of coffee on this occasion). Now we value good coffee machines, but only instrumentally as a means to good coffee. In particular, once the good coffee is present it doesn't seem to matter anymore how it was produced. The moral of the story thus seems to be that once we have the good coffee available to us, it shouldn't matter to us whether it was the result of a good coffee machine or a bad coffee machine. As we might put the point, whatever value is generated by a cup of coffee being the product of a good coffee machine, that value is 'swamped' by the fact that it is good cup of coffee.

The relevance of this example for our purposes is that it seems we can run exactly the same kind of reasoning with regard to true beliefs, at least if epistemic value truth monism is correct. After all, on this view while we epistemically value how a belief is produced—i.e., whether it is produced in a way that is truth-conducive—it should no longer matter how the belief is produced once we have a true belief in hand. In particular, faced with the prospect of two identical true beliefs, one formed in a truth-conducive way (via a reliable belief-forming method, say) and one formed in a non-truth-conducive way (e.g., via guesswork), we

---

[8] For some of the key statements of the swamping problem, see Jones (1997), Swinburne (1999), Riggs (2002a; 2002b), Kvanvig (2003; 2010), and Zagzebski (2003).

[9] Note that the swamping argument wasn't always understood this way. Zagzebski (2003), for example, explicitly treats it as an argument against reliabilist epistemologies. See Pritchard (2011) for an account of the swamping problem as specifically directed at epistemic value truth monism.

[10] This analogy is due to Zagzebski (2003).

should value both true beliefs equally, just as we value the two identical cups of coffee equally. But on the face of it that is wrong, in that from an epistemic point of view the true belief that is formed in an epistemically appropriate fashion—which is an instance of knowledge, say—appears to be more valuable than an identical mere true belief that is formed in an epistemically inappropriate fashion.

Faced with this argument, one might be tempted to reject epistemic value truth monism, and hence the traditional account, and opt instead for some sort of revisionary option, such as a kind of epistemic value pluralism or non-truth epistemic value monism described above. That would be premature, however, since this argument is not the devastating *reductio* for epistemic value truth monism that it first appears.

There is a very subtle sleight of hand in play in this argument, which in effect trades on the distinction between the value of the epistemic and epistemic value that we noted earlier. In particular, notice that the conclusion of the argument is *not* that two identical true beliefs are equally valuable regardless of how they are produced. Instead the conclusion of the argument is the more specific claim that two identical true beliefs are equally *epistemically* valuable regardless of how they are produced. This second claim, notice, is entirely compatible with the idea that, for example, a true belief that amounts to knowledge might be more valuable than a mere true belief. After all, the difference in value might have nothing essentially to do with the epistemic. (Perhaps, for example, one of the arguments offered by virtue epistemologists for the ethical value of knowledge, which we noted above, is successful). So the question we need to ask ourselves is whether there is anything particularly counterintuitive about the idea that two identical true beliefs could be equally epistemically valuable. The point is that once we recognise that this claim is entirely compatible with the idea that these true beliefs could nonetheless differ in value, then it is no longer straightforward that there is anything especially problematic about this contention. Put another way, far from being a *reductio* of epistemic value truth monism, this claim seems more like an expected consequence of the view.

There is a further point we need to make in this regard, which further undermines this putative *reductio* for epistemic value truth monism. For while the epistemic value truth monist is committed to treating these two beliefs as identical in terms of epistemic value, she is not thereby committed to holding that there is no further epistemic value that is relevant here. In the standard case, for example, the reason why one agent has a mere true belief while the other agent has, say, a true belief that amounts to knowledge, will be because of some ignorance on the part of the first agent. Viewed from the perspective of epistemic value truth monism, then, the knowing subject will potentially exhibit an epistemic goodness that is lacking in the agent who has a mere true belief.[11] Again, then, we find that the epistemic value monist has a way of axiologically differentiating between these two scenarios—in this case in terms of specifically epistemic value—without thereby giving up on their commitment to the contested account of epistemic value.

5.

One difficulty that the traditional account has faced is that it seems to lead to a kind of epistemic consequentialism, whereby we evaluate sets of beliefs by simply counting the number of true beliefs present. One could well interpret the remarks I just made about how the proponent of epistemic value truth monism could account for a potential disanalogy between the two sets of beliefs at issue in the swamping problem as indicating just such a picture. That is, one might think that there is a straightforward way of 'weighing' epistemic value in play here, such that where the agent who has a mere true belief lacks some further true beliefs that his knowing counterpart possesses, then it immediately follows that the beliefs of these two agents are not on a par from the perspective of epistemic value.

In fact, however, the claim I was making was far more cautious. Indeed, note that I only went so far as to say that there is a *potential* difference. Part of the issue here is that we don't know enough about the other beliefs possessed by these agents to be able to determine whether these sets of beliefs are substantially different with regard to the extent to which they are true. Perhaps, that is, errors in one set of beliefs are counterweighted by additional true beliefs elsewhere. Thus, even if one does subscribe to a view according to which epistemic value is gauged by counting the number of true beliefs in play, then it might still follow that these two agents are on an epistemic par in this regard.

My qualification of this claim was not primarily concerned with this particular issue, however, even though I do think that it is salient here. Instead, it reflected the fact that I don't think we can simply weigh epistemic value by counting true beliefs. Indeed, I think it is simply a mistake to think that epistemic value truth monism, and thus the traditional account, is wedded to such a picture. The worry here is not simply a concern about the very viability of counting true beliefs, though there is a genuine concern in this direction (exactly how

---

[11] For a discussion of the notion of ignorance in the context of epistemic value, see Pritchard (forthcoming b).

does one individuate one belief from another in its general vicinity?). The source of my concern is rather that I don't think this consequentialist way of thinking about epistemic value is really what the proponent of the traditional account ought to have in mind.

In order to see this, we first need to note that understanding the fundamental epistemic good as grasping the truth does not entail thinking that we should gauge success in this regard in terms of the number of true propositions believed. There is a very intuitive sense in which a scientist with a well-developed theory about a certain domain might well have a better grasp of the truth than someone who is forming a massive amount of trivial true beliefs about the office phone numbers of his colleagues by looking them up online.

Interestingly, this is a point that is often completely overlooked in the literature. Indeed, it is often said that those committed to the traditional account (or some view in the general vicinity of the traditional account at any rate) *must* be committed to supposing that even the most trivial truths (e.g., about the phone numbers of one's colleagues) are on a par, from the perspective of epistemic value, with even the weightiest scientific truth. After all, on the traditional account all one cares about is acquiring the truth, and the truth is present in both cases. So on what principled basis could the proponent of the traditional account distinguish between the two? Put another way, insofar as the proponent of the traditional account does distinguish between the two, and so favours the weighty scientific truth, then must be because she is implicitly supposing that there is more to epistemic value than just grasping the truth.[12]

Fortunately for the traditional account, this line of reasoning rests on a mistake. One can see the error in the reasoning here by appeal to an analogy which has been very usefully offered by Nick Treanor (2013; 2014). Gold miners obviously care about acquiring gold—the acquisition of gold is, we might say, the fundamental good of the 'goal mining' evaluative domain. But suppose one argued that if they *really* cared about the acquisition of gold, then they would care about all pieces of gold equally, whether a small nugget or a large seam. After all, if it's just gold that they are after, then both would constitute the acquisition of gold, and hence there would be nothing, from the perspective of caring about the acquisition of gold, that could distinguish the two. But clearly gold miners do care more about finding rich seams of gold than finding small nuggets. So does

---

[12] Versions of this general line of argument abound in the contemporary epistemological literature. For a sample of high-profile endorsements of this reasoning, see DePaul (2001), Sosa (2001), and Goldman (2002).

that mean that there is something that they care about *in addition to finding gold* that enables them to distinguish between the nuggets and the rich seams?

I think it is clear that the reasoning in the goal mining case has obviously gone awry. The gold miners care about the acquisition of gold, and that's precisely why they want to find a rich seam of it rather than a small nugget. In the same way, in desiring the truth as we do, in line with the traditional account, we desire grasping as much of the truth as possible. This means that grasping a weighty scientific truth, like the gold miner finding the rich seam, can be of more epistemic value than coming across a trivial truth, the counterpart of a small nugget of gold. Once we understand this point, we realise that there is no hope of weighing two sets of beliefs purely in terms of the extent to which each set of beliefs is true. In particular, a set of beliefs could be true but involve very little by way of grasping the truth because of the banal nature of the beliefs in question.

6.

There is another common objection to the traditional account that we should consider, and which reflects a popular set of positions in contemporary epistemology that run counter to that account. This is the idea that since merely forming a true belief does not legitimately close inquiry—and since the nature of the epistemic is closely tied to the notion of a well-conducted inquiry—hence grasping the truth cannot possibly be thought of as the mark of the epistemic, much less as the fundamental epistemic good.

It is undeniably true that merely acquiring a true belief does not suffice to legitimately close inquiry, at least where the propriety at issue is of a broadly epistemic nature. It is also plausible to suppose that the mark of the epistemic ought to have something essentially to do with well-conducted inquiry. But I think that one can grant both claims while nonetheless retaining the traditional account.

Let's begin with the first claim—*viz.*, that true belief does not suffice to legitimately close inquiry. Suppose that I want to find out about a certain subject matter—say, what the capital of France is. Now imagine that on a whim I decide that the answer to this question is 'Paris', perhaps because I have a vague recollection that Paris is the capital of some country or other. This belief is, of course, true. Nonetheless, it would clearly be remiss of me to end my inquiry the moment I form a belief in this regard if that belief has no epistemic standing at all, as is the case in this instance. But what would close inquiry? Well, often at least, *knowledge* of the answer would suffice, at least where this is knowledge that involves a rational grounding.¹³ So if, for example, one looked up France in what one knows to be an authoritative reference work, and saw that Paris was there listed as its capital, such that one thereby came to know that this is the case, then that would ordinarily be sufficient to legitimately close this inquiry.¹⁴

Now consider the second claim—*viz.*, that the mark of the epistemic is revealed by well-conducted inquiries. As noted above, I accept this claim too, though as a defender of the traditional account I will obviously argue that well-conducted inquiries are geared towards the acquisition of truth. In any case, when this second claim is added to the last, it can seem as if it follows that the mark of the epistemic must be something to do with epistemic standings more elevated than mere true belief, such as knowledge.¹⁵ I think the reasoning in play here is faulty. In particular, I think that there is a way of squaring these two claims with the traditional account.

In order to see this, imagine that one is engaged in a project to produce a perfect cup of coffee. So one goes to great lengths to select beans, source suppliers, test coffee-making equipment, and so forth. Eventually one produces what one hopes to be a perfect cup of coffee. Let's suppose for the sake of argument that one has succeeded. Should one conclude that one's project is complete? Clearly not, for this is a further stage that is required—*viz.*, the tasting of the coffee, in order to determine that it really is the perfect cup of coffee that one is seeking.¹⁶ But does that mean that the goal of this project wasn't actually producing the perfect cup of coffee after all, but rather the tasting of the said cup of coffee? Of course not. The point about tasting the coffee is just to ascertain that the goal of this project has been met; it is not itself part of the goal of the project.

---

13 Of course, some epistemologists of an externalist bent will allow that knowledge can be possessed even in the absence of supporting reasons, but it's not so clear that knowledge of this variety, if it is *bona fide* at all, would suffice to legitimately close inquiry.

14 Note that I am not making a general claim here about the sufficiency of knowledge to legitimately close inquiry. Indeed, my own view, which I will not be exploring here, is that often what legitimately closes inquiry is understanding rather than knowledge. (Note that I have also argued elsewhere that knowledge and understanding are distinct epistemic standings, in that one can have understanding without the corresponding knowledge, and *vice versa*). On both points, see Pritchard (2009; 2014b) and Pritchard, Millar & Haddock (2010, ch. 4).

15 For a particularly clear and recent statement of the idea that knowledge, as opposed to truth, is the goal of inquiry, see Millar (2011), to which Kvanvig (2011) is a response. See also Kappel (2010), Gelfert (2011), and Kelp (2011).

16 Note that it needn't be you who tastes the coffee; indeed, it might be preferable to get a coffee expert to taste it. The point is just that tasting it is required to properly complete the project.

What goes for this coffee-making project applies to truth and inquiry. That only knowledge (say) might legitimately close a particular inquiry does not entail that this inquiry was *really* aimed at knowledge rather than true belief. Rather, the inquiry is aimed at the truth, but we insist on knowing the truth because, as with tasting the coffee, we want to ascertain that the goal of the project has been attained. At the very least, then, there is an alternative explanation available for why an epistemic standing higher than mere true belief might be required to legitimately close an inquiry that is entirely compatible with the traditional account.[17]

7.

This last point about the goal of inquiry dovetails with the previous point about the inherent dangers of weighing truth by simply counting true propositions. If the goal of acquiring truth were weighed purely in terms of counting true propositions, then the good inquirer would be someone who initiates lots of easy inquiries—e. g., to settle questions like how many items are on the menu in front of him, how many of them start with the letter 'S', and so on. Clearly, however, this is not what a good inquirer would do. But that is because good inquirers are not concerned with simply maximising the number of true beliefs, but rather with getting as much truth as possible, and the latter is not reducible to the former. For good inquirers, one inquiry will lead to another as they seek out a deep and comprehensive understanding of the nature of things. In doing so, they will be led to more by way of the truth than would be available simply by maximising true beliefs through a focus on the kind of easy inquiries noted above.

I think that comprehending this point can help us to see how the traditional account need not be in tension with the idea that certain elevated epistemic standings might have a special kind of epistemic importance. Take understanding, for example. In understanding a certain phenomena—such as the motion of the tides—one does not merely have lots of true beliefs about that phenomena, but one instead gets to see how these various parts fit together, and this usually leads to a greater degree of grasp of the truth. Understanding why the tides function as they do is thus typically epistemically better than merely knowing lots of truths about the tides without the corresponding understanding (e. g., as when

---

[17] For further development of this point, see Pritchard (2014b).

one simply defers to an expert).[18] In particular, it is epistemically better even from the perspective of the traditional account, since it involves a deeper and more comprehensive grasp of the truth.

That said, we should also bear in mind the distinction we raised earlier regarding epistemic value and the value of the epistemic. After all, some of the value of these higher epistemic standings may not be specifically epistemic at all. Understanding, for instance, is a good candidate for being an epistemic standing that has some broadly ethical value, and it will certainly often be practically valuable. Thus we shouldn't expect an account of epistemic value to *entirely* capture what is good about epistemic standings, but only their specifically *epistemic* goodness.[19] If we keep this distinction in mind, we will thus be on guard to only evaluate the traditional account in terms of what it promises, and not in terms of further claims which the traditional account does not entail.

8.

We have seen that the traditional account of the nature and value of the epistemic is far more defensible than many have supposed. In particular, many of the objections to this account have been shown to rest on faulty reasoning and on failures to make important distinctions (e.g., between the value of the epistemic and epistemic value). I conclude that we should resist the contemporary rejection of the traditional account and revert back to our previous widespread endorsement of this account of epistemic axiology.

---

18 Note that some commentators have denied that understanding does involve having lots of true beliefs, though I think it is fair to say that this proposal is controversial. See, for example, Elgin (1996; 2004; 2009) and Zagzebski (2001).

19 For example, I have argued elsewhere for a conception of knowledge—known as *anti-luck virtue epistemology*—which gives due weight both to the manifestation of relevant cognitive agency and also to the exclusion of epistemic luck/risk. Whereas I'm inclined to think that the value that attaches to a true belief which is free of significant levels of epistemic luck/risk is likely to be largely an epistemic value, it is at least plausible to suppose that some of the value that attaches to a true belief that involves the significant manifestation of relevant cognitive agency might not be specifically epistemic. In particular, if one supposes that achievements (roughly, successes that are due to one's agency) have a distinctive kind of broadly ethical value, then the kind of cognitive achievements that tend to go hand-in-hand with knowledge may well inherit that value. For more on anti-luck virtue epistemology, see Pritchard, Millar & Haddock (2010, ch. 3) and Pritchard (2012). For further discussion of epistemic luck and the related notion of epistemic risk, see Pritchard (2005; 2007a; 2015a; 2015b). For a general examination of the putative value of achievements, see Pritchard (2010).

References

Alston, W. P. (2005). *Beyond "Justification": Dimensions of Epistemic Evaluation.* Ithaca, NY: Cornell University Press.
Brady, M. S., and Pritchard, D. H. (eds.) (2003). *Moral and Epistemic Virtues.* Oxford: Blackwell.
David, M. (2001). Truth as the Epistemic Goal. In M. Steup (ed.), *Knowledge, Truth, and Duty: Essays on Epistemic Justification, Virtue, and Responsibility.* Oxford: Oxford University Press, 151–69.
DePaul, M. (2001). Value Monism in Epistemology. In M. Steup (ed.), *Knowledge, Truth, and Duty: Essays on Epistemic Justification, Virtue, and Responsibility.* Oxford: Oxford University Press, 170–86.
Elgin, C. (1996). *Considered Judgement.* Princeton, NJ: Princeton University Press.
Elgin, C. (2004). True Enough. *Philosophical Issues* 14, 113–31.
Elgin, C. (2009). Is Understanding Factive? In A. Haddock, A. Millar and D. H. Pritchard (eds.), *Epistemic Value.* Oxford: Oxford University Press, 322–30.
Geach, P. T. (1956). Good and Evil. *Analysis* 17, 32–42.
Gelfert, A. (2011). Expertise, Argumentation, and the End of Inquiry. *Argumentation* 25, 297–312.
Goldman, A. (1999). *Knowledge in a Social World.* Oxford: Oxford University Press.
Goldman, A. (2002). The Unity of the Epistemic Virtues. In his *Pathways to Knowledge: Private and Public.* Oxford: Oxford University Press, 51–72.
Goldman, A., and Olsson, E. J. (2009). Reliabilism and the Value of Knowledge. In A. Haddock, A. Millar and D. H. Pritchard (eds.), *Epistemic Value.* Oxford: Oxford University Press, 19–41.
Greco, J. (2009). The Value Problem. In A. Haddock, A. Millar and D. H. Pritchard (eds.), *Epistemic Value.* Oxford: Oxford University Press, 313–21.
Jones, W. (1997). Why Do We Value Knowledge? *American Philosophical Quarterly* 34, 423–40.
Kappel, K. (2010). On Saying that Someone Knows: Themes from Craig. In A. Haddock, A. Millar and D. Pritchard (eds.), *Social Epistemology.* Oxford: Oxford University Press, 69–88.
Kelp, C. (2011). What's the Point of 'Knowledge' Anyway? *Episteme* 8, 53–66.
Kvanvig, J. (2003). *The Value of Knowledge and the Pursuit of Understanding.* Cambridge: Cambridge University Press.
Kvanvig, J. (2010). The Swamping Problem Redux: Pith and Gist. In A. Haddock, A. Millar and D. H. Pritchard (eds.), *Social Epistemology.* Oxford: Oxford University Press, 89–111.
Kvanvig, J. (2011). Millar on the Value of Knowledge. *Proceedings of the Aristotelian Society (suppl. vol.)* 85, 83–99.
Millar, A. (2011). Why Knowledge Matters. *Proceedings of the Aristotelian Society (suppl. vol.)* 85, 63–81.
Pritchard, D. H. (2005). *Epistemic Luck.* Oxford: Oxford University Press.
Pritchard, D. H. (2007a). Anti-Luck Epistemology, *Synthese* 158, 277–97.
Pritchard, D. H. (2007b). Recent Work on Epistemic Value. *American Philosophical Quarterly* 44, 85–110.

Pritchard, D. H. (2009). Knowledge, Understanding and Epistemic Value. In: A. O'Hear (ed.), *Epistemology (Royal Institute of Philosophy Lectures)*. Cambridge: Cambridge University Press, 19–43.
Pritchard, D. H. (2010). Achievements, Luck and Value. *Think* 25, 1–12.
Pritchard, D. H. (2011). What is the Swamping Problem? In A. Reisner and A. Steglich-Petersen (eds.), *Reasons for Belief.* Cambridge: Cambridge University Press, 244–59.
Pritchard, D. H. (2012). Anti-Luck Virtue Epistemology. *Journal of Philosophy* 109, 247–79.
Pritchard, D. H. (2014a). Knowledge and Understanding. In A. Fairweather (ed.), *Virtue Scientia: Bridges Between Virtue Epistemology and Philosophy of Science*. Dordrecht, Holland: Springer, 315–28.
Pritchard, D. H. (2014b). Truth as the Fundamental Epistemic Good. In J. Matheson and R. Vitz (eds.), *The Ethics of Belief: Individual and Social*. Oxford: Oxford University Press, 112–29.
Pritchard, D. H. (2015a). Anti-Luck Epistemology and the Gettier Problem. *Philosophical Studies* 172, 93–111.
Pritchard, D. H. (2015b). Epistemic Risk. *unpublished manuscript.*
Pritchard, D. H. (forthcoming a). Engel on Pragmatic Encroachment and Epistemic Value. *Synthese.*
Pritchard, D. H. (forthcoming b). Ignorance and Epistemic Value. In M. Blaauw and R. Peels (eds.), *The Epistemic Dimensions of Ignorance*. Cambridge: Cambridge University Press.
Pritchard, D. H. (forthcoming c). Seeing It For Oneself: Perceptual Knowledge, Understanding, and Intellectual Autonomy. *Episteme.*
Pritchard, D. H. (forthcoming d). Veritism and Epistemic Value. In H. Kornblith and B. McLaughlin (eds.), *Alvin Goldman and His Critics*. Oxford: Blackwell.
Pritchard, D. H., Millar, A., and Haddock, A. (2010). *The Nature and Value of Knowledge: Three Investigation*. Oxford: Oxford University Press.
Pritchard, D. H., and Smith, M. (2004). The Psychology and Philosophy of Luck. *New Ideas in Psychology* 22, 1–28.
Pritchard, D. H., and Turri, J. (2011). The Value of Knowledge. In E. Zalta (ed.), *Stanford Encyclopædia of Philosophy*, URL = http://plato.stanford.edu/entries/knowledge-value/.
Riggs, W. (2002a). Beyond Truth and Falsehood: The *Real* Value of Knowing that *P.* *Philosophical Studies* 107, 87–108.
Riggs, W. (2002b). Reliability and the Value of Knowledge. *Philosophy and Phenomenological Research* 64, 79–96.
Shah, N. (2003). How Truth Governs Belief. *Philosophical Review* 112, 447–83.
Shah, N., and Velleman, D. (2005). Doxastic Deliberation. *Philosophical Review* 114, 497–534.
Sosa, E. (2001). For the Love of Truth? In A. Fairweather & L. Zagzebski (eds.), *Virtue Epistemology: Essays on Epistemic Virtue and Responsibility*. Oxford: Oxford University Press, 49–62.
Swinburne, R. (1999). *Providence and the Problem of Evil*. Oxford: Oxford University Press.
Treanor, N. (2013). The Measure of Knowledge. *Noûs* 47, 577–601.
Treanor, N. (2014). Trivial Truths and the Aim of Inquiry. *Philosophy and Phenomenological Research* 89, 552–59.
Wedgwood, R. (2002). The Aim of Belief. *Philosophical Perspectives* 16, 268–97.

Zagzebski, L. (2001). Recovering Understanding. In M. Steup (ed.) *Knowledge, Truth, and Obligation: Essays on Epistemic Justification, Virtue, and Responsibility.* Oxford: Oxford University Press, 235–52.

Zagzebski, L. (2003). The Search for the Source of the Epistemic Good. *Metaphilosophy* 34, 12–28.

J. Adam Carter and Emma C. Gordon
Objectual Understanding, Factivity and Belief

1. Introduction

Objectual understanding—*viz.*, the sort of understanding one has when one understands a subject matter or body of information—is often thought to be *factive*, in a way that (for example) mere coherent delusions are not. In short, understanding a subject matter demands we have at least *some* true beliefs about the subject matter in question[1]. That being said, it is ubiquitous to claim that we understand some false subject matters or theories. For example, most high-school students have some understanding of Ptolemy's earth-centred view of the universe, even though the Ptolemaic view is premised on a false conception of what revolves around what. One very natural way to reconcile the kind of factivity demanded of understanding with the datum that we can plausibly count as understanding false theories, models or subject matters is to point out a relevant fact about *the way* we regard ourselves as understanding (for instance) the Ptolemaic view: we understand it *as* false, which is to say, we see how the view holds together while at the same time appreciating *that* the view does not accurately represent what it purports to.

After outlining a rationale for this kind of reply with reference to a particular —and we suggest, very plausible—model on which to think of objectual understanding as factive, our primary aim in the paper is to engage with the comparatively more complicated issue of what objectual understanding demands in the *inverse sort of case*. Specifically, our focus will be cases where the central claims of the theory *itself* are true, an individual sees how the theory fits together (in a way that would ordinarily suffice for understanding), and yet does not appreciate the theory's central claims *as* true. For example, should we regard Lackey's (2007) 'Creationist Teacher' as *understanding* evolution, even though she does not, given her religious convictions, *believe* it? We think this question raises a range of important and unexplored questions about the relationship between understanding, factivity and belief. Our aim will be to diagnose this case in a

---

[1] The term 'objectual understanding' owes to Kvanvig (2003), who distinguishes objectual understanding from understanding-why (where the complement clause is a proposition–viz., 'S understands why *p*), and propositional understanding (e.g. S understands that *p*).

principled way, and in doing so, to make some progress toward appreciating what objectual understanding demands of us.

Here is the plan. §2 outlines and motivates a plausible working model—*moderate factivity*—for characterising the sense in which objectual understanding should be regarded as factive. §3 shows how the datum that we can understand false theories can, despite initial suggestions to the contrary, be assimilated straightforwardly within the moderate factivity model. §4 highlights how the *inverse* kind of case to that explored in §3—viz., a variant of Lackey's creationist teacher case—poses special problems for moderate factivity. With reference to recent work on moral understanding by Hills (2009), §5 proposes a solution to the problem, and §6 attempts to diagnose why it is that we might originally have been led to draw the wrong conclusion.

2. Objectual Understanding and Factivity

It is generally assumed that propositional knowledge is factive (*cf.* Hazlett (2010)) in the sense that S fails to know that p if p is false. However, there is more room for disagreement about whether objectual understanding is factive, where the object of objectual understanding is not a proposition, but rather, is (or can be treated as) a body of information (e.g. S understands Australian rules football; S understands organic chemistry)[2]. While it seems sensible to suppose that some kind of factivity constraint would feature as a necessary condition on objectual understanding, we might wonder just *how* strong a link there must be between the beliefs an agent has about subject matter φ and the propositions that are true of φ. We shall briefly explore three different strengths that a factivity constraint on objectual understanding might take, and in the course of doing so will make a case for thinking the moderate of the three models is far and away the most plausible[3]. The relevance of motivating moderate factivity will be to contextualise the puzzles raised in the next two sections, which are perplexing only in so far as they seem to suggest that moderate factivity would (counterintuitively) have to be rejected.

On one end of the factivity spectrum, we can imagine a maximally inclusive account—call this 'weak factivity'—according to which one can count as understanding a subject matter φ even if *none* of one's beliefs about φ are true. Zagzebski (2001) is tacitly committed to this proposal in virtue of allowing that at

---

[2] See Kvanvig (2003, chapter 8) for discussion.
[3] See Gordon (forthcoming) for a fuller discussion of this topic.

least some cases of understanding do not require any true beliefs; similarly, Elgin (2007), in discussing the role the ideal gas law plays in the acquisition of scientific understanding, allows that at least some items of understanding might be (entirely) non-factive.

There are, we want to emphasise, several very serious problems with this type of view. Firstly, this kind of proposal lacks (entirely) the resources to explain certain elements of our linguistic practices of attributing understanding. For one thing, the weak view has trouble explaining why individuals take facts to be *relevant* at all to adjudicating disagreements about understanding. For example, if A attributes understanding of quantum mechanics to B, and C believes that the books B has read on quantum mechanics were in fact sham books with false information, C will be inclined to disagree with A's attribution of understanding to B. However, if understanding is compatible with all false beliefs, as the weak view under consideration suggests, this disagreement would make no sense. Relatedly, the weak view can't account for our willingness to retract former attributions of understanding, as when we find out that some of our φ-beliefs were false. Even more, and perhaps most problematically, the weak view allows cases of internally coherent delusions (e.g. made up stories that fit together) to count as cases of understanding, no matter how wide the cognitive gap between truths about φ and the delusional agent's beliefs about φ[4].

More generally, in light of these consequences, a weak, non-factive account seems out of step with the common intuition that understanding is an especially valuable cognitive achievement[5]. For example, as Kvanvig (2003, 206) points out, 'we have an ordinary conception that understanding is a milestone to be achieved by long and sustained efforts at knowledge acquisition' (see e.g. Whitcomb 2012 for agreement, who observes that understanding is often thought of a "higher" epistemic good)[6].

In response to the apparent failings of the weak view, we might instead move entirely in the opposite direction and embrace a maximally strong view of objec-

---

[4] It's also worth noting that such a weak factivity constraint allows two people who deny all of each other's beliefs about some subject matter X might nevertheless be attributed an equally good understanding of the subject matter in question.

[5] See Pritchard (2014) and Carter & Pritchard (2014; 2015) for discussion.

[6] Perhaps part of the potential draw of a weak factivity constraint on understanding might be explained by the fact that there are closely related epistemic states that (while similar to understanding) does not involve a factivity constraint. The primary example might be intelligibility (Riggs, 2003) or subjective understanding (Grimm, 2011), which merely requires a grasp of connections between a coherent group of beliefs and lacks a need for truth. We consider this point in more detail in §6.

tual understanding's factivity—one on which understanding φ requires that *all* of one's beliefs about φ be true—and as such tolerates no false beliefs about the subject matter in question. This approach has two advantages over the non-factive account: firstly, it accounts for the apparent epistemic desirability of understanding (e.g. understanding would certainly be epistemically valuable if permitted no error) and, secondly, a strictly factive view could easily explain disagreement and retraction data in the kinds of cases considered. Problematically, though, the strong view renders understanding very rare indeed. Experts who merely happen to have one false belief about a minor area of their subject fail to count as understanding on a strictly factive view. Even if such a view can explain some cases of disagreement and retraction better than the non-factive view, the strictly factive view does not square more generally with our practices of attributing understanding, as we are generally happy to attribute understanding of a subject matter φ to individuals who have some false beliefs about φ; this is reflected in our tendency to view understanding as a matter of *degree*, with some agents having poorer understanding of a subject that others (who nonetheless we also think of as *having* understanding).

Consequently, it seems like we should reject both of these extremes and embrace something in between—a *moderate* factivity constraint. After all, we have seen that not every belief relevant to an agent's understanding of φ needs to be true, even though there are obviously cases in which false beliefs about φ *will* undermine a potential case of understanding. Kvanvig (2003; 2009) advocates this type of position (as does Wilkenfeld (2015), under the name 'quasi-factivity'[7]). On Kvanvig's view, one can understand subject matter φ provided all of one's *central beliefs* about φ are true, thereby leaving room for degrees of understanding and for attributions of understanding when the agent has false *peripheral* beliefs (without leaving so much room that internally consistent delusions creep in as cases of understanding, as they would on the weak factivity constraint discussed at the beginning of this section). Of course, a moderate factivity constraint invites a range of interesting further questions, which remain underexplored. In particular, we might ask what it is in virtue of which a belief should attain the status of a 'central belief.' Similarly, a plausible substantive moderate factivity account will need to have some principled way to distinguish peripheral beliefs from central beliefs as well as from beliefs which fall outside the subject matter in question entirely. It is beyond the scope of what we can do

---

[7] Wilkenfeld (2015) defends what he calls 'The Contextual Quasi-Factivity (CQF) of objectual understanding' according to which one understands object o only if one's central beliefs about o are true, where a belief's centrality is pragmatically determined.

here to answer these more specific questions about how a moderate factivity view would go. Our aim in this section is rather to show that something *like* the moderate view (suitably embellished) will surely be a necessary condition on understanding.

3. False Theories and Moderate Factivity

Consider the following two cases.

GEOCENTRISM: Helena, along with the other students in her Astronomy class, learns about Ptolemy's geocentric model of the cosmos, according to which the planet Earth is the orbital centre of the solar system—that around which other stars and planets revolves. Moved by the model's simplicity and elegance, Helena goes above and beyond, reading the entire *Almagsest* and laboriously drawing out maps of the Ptolemaic epicycles of the planets. On the exam, Helena gets a perfect score.

WESTEROS: Having read (10 times) each of George R.R. Martin's books in the *A Song of Ice and Fire* series, Mark has a deep and extensive appreciation of the inter-familial dynamics of the leading families of Westeros, their lineage and the more general geopolitical climate within which each family is vying for control of the Iron Throne of the Seven Kingdoms.

On the face of things, it would seem as though GEOCENTRISM and WESTEROS are going to pose some obvious problems for a proponent of the kind of moderate factivity account put forward in the previous section. This is for the reason that it *looks* very much like:

(i) both GEOCENTRISM and WESTEROS are cases where genuine objectual understanding is present; and yet,
(ii) in light of the falsehood of the central propositions constituting each subject matter, moderate factivity is satisfied in neither case.

In support of claim (i), consider that that it would be very odd to simply deny that Helena actually understands Ptolemy's geocentrism or that Mark understands the geopolitics of Westeros given that, by most any standard of assessment, each has not merely become acquainted with, but has mastered, the subject matter in question. By attributing understanding, rather than something less, in these cases, we are able to mark an important kind of cognitive achievement that Helena and Mark have attained but which is *not* attained by individuals who (unlike Helena and Mark) merely memorised bits of the relevant subject matter without seeing how the pieces fit together (e.g. as might one who, in WESTEROS, learns *that* the Starks don't trust the Lannisters and commits this to memory, but has no conception of why this is so). Nor for that matter is this cognitive achievement attained by individuals who have mere coherent delusions about the subject matter in question (e.g. as might one who, in GEOCENTRISM, believes the Ptolemaic view postulates the moon, rather than the earth, as the orbital centre of all celestial bodies, and then forms an elaborate, coherent but misguided picture around this false 'moon-centric' belief). So biting the bullet and denying (i) doesn't look like a very promising way out.

Likewise, there is strong *prima facie* support for (ii). After all, with respect to GEOCENTRISM, Ptolemy's view is almost entirely false—certainly, the central claims underwriting the Ptolemaic model are false (e.g. the claim that the earth does not move). Meanwhile, in WESTEROS, unqualified geopolitical claims about the place are categorically false because Westeros does not exist. It looks very much like the propositions which Mark pieces together in such sophistication are propositions of the form 'The Lannisters did X' and 'The Starks did Y', and these are, strictly speaking, false propositions, given that there were no Lannisters and there were no Starks.

Obviously, if (i) and (ii) really *are* true, then it simply follows that moderate factivity cannot, despite what was suggested in the previous section, capture a plausible necessary condition on understanding. And so it looks initially like GEOCENTRISM and WESTEROS generate a kind of puzzle: moderate factivity is by far more plausible than the weak and strong alternatives, and yet, if we grant (i) and (ii), we have to reject moderate factivity as a necessary condition on objectual understanding. So *which* of (i) or (ii) must be rejected?

Perhaps there are various ways a proponent of moderate factivity could convincingly explain away the apparent tension posed by cases like GEOCENTRISM and WESTEROS. For our purposes, we submit that a sufficient and appealing way to reconcile these cases with moderate factivity is to accept (i) and then reject (ii).

Rejecting (ii), *via* the kind of rationale we suggest, brings with it the benefit of making it evident why false theories, as such, needn't be *de facto* ruled out as potential objects of objectual understanding, which is a pleasing result.

To a first approximation, what we want to suggest in the case of false theories is that, for an agent S and some subject matter F whose *central* claims are strictly false, S understands F *only if* S understands F *as* (strictly) false. Correspondingly, we suggest S understands F *as* (strictly) false *only if* S has a belief (either occurrent or dispositional) *that* the theory's central claims are false.

Such a belief is important, as it *de facto* qualifies the *mode* under which the agent is grasping the relationship between the propositions that constitute the subject matter (a point we'll unpack shortly). To make this point concrete, consider briefly two variations in GEOCENTRISM:

GEOCENTRISM-Variation 1: Helena, along with the other students in her Astronomy class, learns about Ptolemy's geocentric model of the cosmos, according to which the planet Earth is the orbital centre the solar system, that around which other stars and planets revolves. Moved by the model's simplicity and elegance, Helena goes above and beyond, reading the entire *Almagsest* and laboriously drawing out maps of the Ptolemaic epicycles of the planets. On the exam, Helena gets a perfect score. Despite her fascination with the geocentric model, Helena is aware that the earth does not stand still, but in fact (as she appreciates that Copernicus showed with the help of Kelper in the 17th century) revolves around the sun[8].

GEOCENTRISM-Variation 2: Helena, along with the other students in her Astronomy class, learns about Ptolemy's geocentric model of the cosmos, according to which the planet Earth is the orbital centre the solar system, that around which other stars and planets revolves. Moved by the model's simplicity and elegance, Helena goes above and beyond, reading the entire *Almagsest* and laboriously drawing out maps of the Ptolemaic epicycles of the planets. On the exam,

---

8 We could envision a variant on this case, one that is a kind of 'middle ground' between GEOCENTRISM-1 and GEOCENTRISM-2. In this middle-ground variant, let's suppose Helena neither believes nor disbelieves the view's central claims, but withholds judgment. Perhaps, we can suppose, Helena is in the process of comparing the Ptolemaic model with other models, and is waiting for more evidence to come in before making an endorsement. In this case, Helena would satisfy moderate factivity trivially given that she has no false central *beliefs* (i.e., she does not, like Helena in GEOCENTRISM-2 believe the theory's claims accurately represent the Solar System.) However, she would satisfy moderate factivity in a way that differs importantly from the way in which one might satisfy moderate factivity by never entertaining the propositions in the first place. We think the appropriate way to articulate Helena's position, in such a middle-ground case, is as having what we can call *dispositional understanding*; as with dispositional beliefs, where a condition—namely, occurrent endorsement—activates the belief, likewise, actively taking a correct doxastic stand (rather than withholding) with respect to the central propositions about which one was previously agnostic activates the understanding. Given that the variations with GEOCENTRISM involved a subject matter the central claims of which are false, this will mean that Helena (in the envisioned middle-ground case) activates her dispositional understanding upon believing (rather than withholding) of the central claims, that they are false—something she fails to do when withholding judgment. Thanks to Heather Battaly for raising this kind of case.

Helena gets a perfect score. Helena's fascination with the geocentric model leaves her blinded to the Copernican evidence against it, and she believes that the theory's claims accurately represent the structure of our Solar System.

On the rationale for rejecting (ii) which we want to propose, Helena satisfies moderate factivity in Variation-1 but *not* in Variation-2. Given that, on Variation-1, Helena *believes* that the central claims characterising the Ptolemaic view are false, the unqualified claims such as:

The earth is the orbital centre of the solar system
and
The sun revolves around the earth

which are false claims, do not accurately characterise the propositions Helena (in Variation 1) actually believes, and the relationships between which she competently grasps.

Rather, and to draw analogy from Sebastian Kletzl's (2011) work on assertion and testimony, the deeper structure of Helena's beliefs in Varation-1 are (in light of her belief in Copernicanism) to be read as qualified in the same sense that— for example, and to use Kletzl's case—a teacher leading a discussion on Plato's *Parmenedies* might baldly assert 'X' where the content of the teacher's assertion should be best understood as *indirect* testimony to the effect that:

According to Plato in the Parmenides, X[9].

Analogously, in light of Helena's belief in Variation-1 *that* the central claims of Ptolemy's geocentric model are false, the particular propositions Helena believes are best understood as *not* the false unqualified propositions (the corresponding beliefs of which would be in conflict with moderate factivity), but rather, *true qualified propositions* (the belief-analogues of Kletzl-style indirect assertions) to the effect that:

According to Ptolemy, the earth is the orbital centre of the solar system
and
According to Ptolemy, the sun revolves around the earth

---

9 See Carter & Nickel (2014) for further discussion on these kinds of cases.

Understood as qualified in this respect, the original tension—premised upon the idea that Helena's understanding of geocentrism must involve false beliefs on Helena's part, given the falsehood of the theory, is dissolved.

Of course, an implication of our escaping the puzzle by rejecting (ii) on the basis of the rationale we've suggested is that someone who pieces together the Ptolemaic view of the heavens, *while believing as the Ptolemaic view says that the earth is the centre of the universe*, lacks understanding of the Ptolemaic view. (And, likewise, one fails to understand the geopolitics of the seven kingdoms of Westeros if one actually thinks that these kingdoms really existed, as might one who was utterly clueless that this was a work of fiction by George R.R. Martin, and thought instead the structure of the actual world includes supernatural White Walkers, etc.[10]) But this, we think, is just as it should be.

It's plausible to suppose that understanding, in the special case where the object of the understanding is a false theory, simply can *not permit* a false meta-belief (as Helena has in Variation 2 of GEOCENTRISM) *about* the subject matter to the effect that the subject matter's central claims are correct (when these claims are false), even if we grant that the false meta-belief, itself, is not *part* of the subject matter in question (and so wouldn't itself violate moderate factivity, which applies to central beliefs *of* the subject matter). The reasoning here is that such a false meta-belief will entail that the agent's first-order beliefs (in Helena's case in Variation-2, beliefs about the cosmos) are not *merely* qualified propositions of the form (according to theory the Ptolemaic view, X....) which are *true*, but *also* false propositions of the form 'X' (where these are unqualified claims about the structure of the cosmos, which are false). And false propositions of *this* form fail to satisfy moderate factivity.

4. Creationist Teacher Case

Consider now, the following case:

CREATIONIST TEACHER: Stella is a devoutly Christian fourth-grade teacher, and her religious beliefs are grounded in a deep faith that she has had since she was a very young child. Part of this faith includes a belief in the truth of creationism and, accordingly, a belief in the falsity of evolutionary theory. Despite

---

[10] And, correspondingly in WESTEROS: Mark understands the geopolitics of Westeros provided he is aware the work is in fact a fiction (in which case the propositions the relationships between which he grasps are best understood as true propositions of the form According to Martin's novels... [X] and not false propositions of the form The Lannisters ... [X].

this, she fully recognizes that there is an overwhelming amount of scientific evidence against both of these beliefs. Indeed, she readily admits that she is not basing her own commitment to creationism on evidence at all but, rather, on the personal faith that she has in an all-powerful Creator. Because of this, Stella does not think that religion is something that she should impose on those around her, and this is especially true with respect to her fourth-grade students. Instead, she regards her duty as a teacher to involve presenting material that is best supported by the available evidence, which clearly includes the truth of evolutionary theory. As a result, after consulting reliable sources in the library and developing reliable lecture notes, Stella asserts to her students, "Modern-day Homo sapiens evolved from Homo erectus," while presenting her biology lesson today. Though Stella herself neither believes nor knows this proposition, she never shares her own personal faith-based views with her students, and so they form the corresponding true belief solely on the basis of her reliable testimony. (Lackey 2008: 48).

Lackey's case has been used to argue, among other things[11], that the following principle concerning the transmission of epistemic properties is false:

TEP-N: For every speaker, S, and hearer, A, A knows (believes with justification/ warrant) that p on the basis of S's testimony that p only if S knows (believes with justification/ warrant) that p. (Lackey 2008: 39–40).

Lackey's key point in adverting to CREATIONIST TEACHER[12] in the service of challenging TEP-N is that Stella's failing to believe evolutionary theory is not, contrary to what TEP-N says, a barrier to students' coming to acquire knowledge of the theory on the basis of Stella's testimony. While Lackey's much-discussed case has been (unsurprisingly) controversial among social epistemologists as a counterexample against TEP-N[13], it is usually taken for granted by both sides that Stella herself would not know evolutionary theory *if* she believed it was false[14] (and so this is taken for granted apart from the more contentious issue

---

[11] Lackey (2007) has also used the case to argue against the knowledge norm of assertion (e.g. Williamson 2000). See Carter & Gordon (2011) and Lackey (2011) for related discussion. Cf. Benton (2014).
[12] For related cases, see DISTRAUGHT DOCTOR and RACIST JUROR.
[13] See Carter & Nickel (2014) for a defence of this kind of counterexample against TEP-N against recent attempts to defend TEP-N. Cf. however Wright (forthcoming) for a reply to Carter & Nickel.
[14] For a heterodox position on this point, see Myers-Schultz & Schwitzgebel (2013).

of whether Stella's students could gain knowledge of Stella's testimony *despite* Stella's failing to believe it).

Things with objectual understanding are quite a bit more complex, however: that is, it's less clear that the analogue to the point about knowledge accepted on both sides of the TEP-N debate would also hold equally for (objectual) understanding. And this is because it seems Stella might very well be a candidate for understanding evolution, in CREATIONIST TEACHER, even if we grant that she fails to know the proposition 'Modern-day *Homo sapiens* evolved from *Homo erectus*' because she doesn't believe it.

But in order to make this point, it will be helpful to make an amendment to CREATIONIST TEACHER, so that features typically associated with objectual understanding are made more explicit, and then we'll hold fixed that Stella, due to her Christian faith, fails to believe that evolution is true. Consider now the following abridged version of the case (in which we promote her to university professor, with a stronger pedigree in the subject matter than we'd attribute to a fourth grade teacher), focusing only on Stella's own epistemic situation with respect to evolutionary theory.

CREATIONIST TEACHER*: Stella is a devoutly Christian university professor, and her religious beliefs are grounded in a deep faith that she has had since she was a very young child. Part of this faith includes a belief in the truth of creationism and, accordingly, a belief in the falsity of evolutionary theory. Despite this, she fully recognizes that there is an overwhelming amount of scientific evidence against both of these beliefs. Stella, in fact, reads contemporary scientific journals and regularly teaches advanced graduate seminars on evolution, where students and colleagues alike admire the deep appreciation Stella has of how the theory holds together. Moreover, Stella readily admits that she is not basing her own commitment to creationism on evidence at all but, rather, on the personal faith that she has in an all-powerful Creator.

Here's a structural explanation of how CREATIONIST TEACHER* seems to pose a problem for moderate factivity—in short, it seems very much like both of the following claims are true:

(i) CREATIONIST TEACHER* is a case where genuine objectual understanding is present; and yet,
(ii) moderate factivity is not satisfied, even though the propositions constituting evolutionary theory are themselves true

And if (i) and (ii) are right, then we have to reject moderate factivity. Because rejecting moderate factivity is tantamount to embracing the very implausible weak factivity account (one which fails to save the difference between understanding and coherent delusions), the question is: should we reject (i), (ii), or both?

We've already suggested that it's at least *prima facie* very intuitive to attribute understanding of evolution to Stella. It's tempting to say that Stella's demonstration of her competence (in teaching and in her scholarship) *retroindicates* understanding—*viz.*, one cannot plausibly get to the point Stella has got without understanding evolution.

On the matter of (ii): Support for this claim can be made with reference to two kinds of doxastic claims—a *negative* doxastic claim, about what Stella does not believe, and a *positive* doxastic claim, about what she does believe. (The relationship between these points involves some delicacy). The negative doxastic claim is that Stella *does not* believe various propositions that are themselves true and central to the subject matter. For instance, Stella does not believe that modern-day *Homo sapiens* evolved from *Homo erectus*. (Compare: someone plausibly does not understand the geography of the Great Lakes if that individual does *not* believe that these lakes are located in the North American continent).

One retort to the negative doxastic claim is that Stella does possess a range of true beliefs which, drawing from Kletzl's indirect testimony analogy discussed in the previous section, take the form:

According to evolutionary theory, [X]

where 'X' represents such propositions as *Modern-day Homo sapiens evolved from Homo erectus*. As the retort goes, since qualified propositions of these sort are good enough for Helena to satisfy moderate factivity in GEOCENTRISM (Variation-1) in virtue of believing, then surely they'd have to be good enough for Stella to satisfy moderate factivity in virtue of believing, in CREATIONIST TEACHER*.

We think this retort is misguided. The Kletzl line was useful in showing how, in the cases of false subject matters, the central beliefs the agents (e.g. Helena and Mark) actually have are best described not as false unqualified beliefs but as true qualified beliefs. *Merely* showing that Stella has some true qualified beliefs about the subject matter in question (e.g. such as *According to evolutionary theory, X, Y, Z ...*) does not suffice for demonstrating that Stella *thereby does not have any false central beliefs*.

But at this point we can imagine a rejoinder. Suppose the proponent of the retort considered were to argue: "Okay, so even if we grant that there are true central propositions (unqualified claims such as *Modern-day Homo sapiens evolved from Homo erectus*) which Stella does not believe, it wouldn't follow from moderate factivity that Stella doesn't understand evolution. Moderate factivity says understanding is incompatible with *false central beliefs*, where as Stella's attitude with respect to the true unqualified propositions is just that she *does not believe* them."

In response to this retort, it will be helpful to compare CREATIONIST TEACHER* with THEORETICALLY NIHILISTIC TEACHER*:

THEORETICALLY NIHILISTIC TEACHER*: Bella desires above all financial security and a comfortable life. While she recognises that she lacks many practical and entrepreneurial skills that would be useful in the service of achieving these aims, she comes to recognise (on the basis of theoretical aptitude scores) that she has a natural proclivity for appreciating the nuances of evolutionary theory—something which does not in itself interest her in the slightest. Her desire for financial security and a comfortable life leads her to publish extensively on evolutionary theory and to receive an endowed professorship, which affords her the financial security and comfort she desired. Bella has never cared whether the theory is *true* and has not stopped to contemplate whether it's *actually* the case that *Modern-day Homo sapiens evolved from Homo erectus*.

We want to remain non-committal on the matter of whether Bella counts as understanding evolutionary theory, in virtue of simply *not* believing the central true propositions of evolutionary theory. We may suppose that Bella's beliefs in THEORETICALLY NIHILISTIC TEACHER* are best understood as *qualified*, just like the true beliefs we can attribute to Stella, which take the form

According to evolutionary theory, [X].

Importantly, though—and this connects with the *positive doxastic claim* in support of (ii)—Stella is actually *not* like Bella in one very important respect. Stella not *only* (like Bella) is such that she fails to believe various true (unqualified) central propositions about evolutionary theory (e.g. *Modern-day Homo sapiens evolved from Homo erectus*), but moreover, Stella *positively* holds central unqualified propositions to be false. After all, Stella, due to her deeply held Christian faith, while believing *According to evoluationary theory, Modern-day Homo sapiens evolved from Homo erectus* is true, believes *Modern-day Homo sapiens evolved from Homo erectus* is false. And so, in support of (ii), *regardless of whether* failing to believe true propositions central to a subject matter violates moderate factivity, positively believing (as Stella does) that propositions central to the subject matter in question are false, would be in violation with moderate factivity, understood as a constraint to the effect that understanding is incompatible with any central false beliefs.

Putting this all together, it should be clear now why CREATIONIST TEACHER* looks like a much more difficult challenge for one wishing to uphold moderate factivity than do the inverse sort of cases involving understanding of false theories (GEOCENTRISM and WESTEROS). And so the remaining question is: in light of the support we've seen for both (i) and (ii), and given that (i) and (ii) entail that moderate factivity must be rejected as a necessary condition on understanding, *which* should we give up, (i) or (ii)?

What we want to now suggest is that the way out of the puzzle is to deny (i) and thus, contrary to what is admittedly plausible, to deny that Stella (in CREATIONIST TEACHER*) does understand evolutionary theory. A satisfactory answer will of course require a residual explanation for why it is nonetheless attempting to attribute to Stella understanding in CREATIONIST TEACHER* despite the fact that, as we'll argue, this attribution would be mistaken.

5. Diagnosis

Of course, one kind of argument for why we should refrain from attributing understanding evolutionary theory to Stella in CREATIONIST TEACHER* is very simple. The argument proceeds as follows: moderate factivity is a necessary condition on understanding; Stella (as suggested in the previous section, in the support of claim (ii)) violates moderate factivity, and so therefore Stella doesn't understand evolutionary theory.

This kind of argument, however, would be *dialectically ineffective* in the context of the puzzle raised in the previous section. The puzzle took the following form: two prima facie claims (e. g. that understanding is present in CREATIONIST TEACHER* and that moderate factivity is violated in CREATIONIST TEACHER*) imply that moderate factivity is false; and so as the puzzle went, because we don't want to reject moderate factivity (given that it fails to save the difference between understanding and coherent delusion), we need to show *which one* is false. An explanation for why either (i) or (ii) is false should thus be *neutral* with respect to the truth of moderate factivity in the sense that any such explanation must not appeal to the truth of moderate factivity. And so this simple argument is off limits in the present context.

What is needed is an *independent* reason, one which does not *rely* on the truth of moderate factivity, to suggest that Stella fails to understand in CREATIONIST TEACHER*. We now turn to providing such an independent reason, one which draws some inspiration from recent work on understanding by Hills (2009).

Firstly, Hills' (2009) discussion of understanding is situated within the context of *moral* understanding, though the lessons that can be learned form her discussion can be *applied mutatis mutandis* to understanding more generally. Hills' particular interest is to suggest why moral *knowledge* should be thought of as different from moral understanding, the latter of which she takes to be more valuable; in drawing this distinction, Hills highlights a range of abilities the possession of which she regards as distinctive of understanding but not knowledge.

While Hills' discussion of understanding and abilities is situated specifically within the framework of understanding-why, rather than objectual understanding, we can very plausibly generalise from these conditions. Of understanding-why, Hills (2009, 102) writes:

> The grasp of the reasons why p that is essential to understanding involves a number of abilities: to understand why p, you need to be able to *treat* q as the reason why p, not merely *believe* or *know that* q is the reason why p. If you understand why p (and q is why p), then in the right sort of circumstances you can successfully:
>
> (i) follow an explanation of why p given by someone else
> (ii) explain why p in your own words
> (iii) draw the conclusion that p (or that probably p) from the information that q
> (iv) draw the conclusion that p' (or that probably p') from the information that q' (where p' and q' are similar to but not identical to p and q)
> (v) given the information that p, give the right explanation, q;
> (vi) given the information that p', give the right explanation, q'

For Hills, possessing the abilities in (i)–(vii) is part of what is required to treat p as the reason why q, something one must be able to do in order to understand why p.

With reference to Hills' criteria, we can straightforwardly show why Stella would fail to count as understand-*why* evolutionary theory explains the presence of modern day *Homo sapiens*, and from this, we want to suggest why an analogous move suggests Stella doesn't understand (in the objectual sense) evolutionary theory.

With reference to Hills' criteria, Stella (in CREATIONIST TEACHER*) satisfies (i) and (ii) but fails (iii) and (iv). She fails (iii) because she is not disposed to draw the conclusion that *that evolutionary theory is true* (or that probably, evolutionary theory is true) from the information about the presence of modern day *Homo sapiens*. Likewise, where p' and q' are similar to but not identical to 'evolutionary theory' and 'facts about the presence of modern day homo sapiens' respectively, Stella is not disposed to draw the conclusion that p' (or that probably p') from the information that q'. In light of the facts about present day homo sapiens, Stella in fact has drawn a strikingly different conclusion from evolutionary theory, one involving an all-powerful god[15].

Putting this altogether, on Hills' model, Stella doesn't understand why evolution explains the presence of modern-day *Homo sapiens* because Stella (in virtue of failing (iii) and (iv)) lacks certain dispositions needed to treat evolution as a reason for the presence of modern-day Homo sapiens.

Let's now transpose this kind of philosophical point to the arena of *objectual understanding*. One helpful way to do so will be to consider Hills' (2009, 102–3) remarks, shortly after noting these various abilities, of what they—but not mere propositional knowledge—afford an individual.

> But I think that having these abilities is not the same as having extra pieces of knowledge. Gaining this extra knowledge may help you acquire the requisite abilities, but you might have the extra pieces of knowledge without having the kind of good judgement that enables you to *generate new true moral beliefs yourself.* Surely no extra piece or pieces of knowledge guarantee that you have these abilities.[16] (Hills 2009, 103).

Transposing now the relevant context to *evolutionary* beliefs (rather than moral beliefs). Is Stella (in light of her epistemic position with respect to the subject matter of evolution and the corresponding abilities plausibly attributed to her) able to generate *new true evolutionary beliefs?* We want to consider the case

---

15 Consider, though, the following potential 'contextualist'-style objection: that Stella could potentially meet all of Hills' conditions, if Stella was *presupposing* evolutionary theory within the context of teaching. If she presupposes evolutionary theory, then she is in the position to draw the relevant inferences, satisfying (iii) and (iv). However, when Stella is not in that context and isn't presupposing evolutionary theory, she won't draw those inferences. On this kind of rationale, (iii) and (iv) are failed outside of the classroom but satisfied within it. And so, contrary to the line we suggest, Stella does understand, by Hills criteria, evolutionary theory, at least when it is being presupposed. While we aren't in principle opposed to a contextualist-style treatment of understanding (though see Carter 2014 for some reservations), we have two reasons to resist the above diagnosis. Firstly, if being disposed to draw the relevant inferences is something that would simply follow from (genuinely or properly) presupposing evolutionary theory, then it seems unclear that Stella is presupposing evolutionary theory in the classroom. *Ex hypothesi*, Stella is not disposed to treat evolution as a reason for the presence of modern-day Homo sapiens, even if she is disposed, in the classroom, to teach what the theory says. If, by contrast, presupposing the theory in the classroom does *not* entail having the disposition to draw the relevant (i.e., to (iii) and (iv)) inferences, then it's hard to see what work the inclusion of presupposing in Stella's narrative would do in the service of undermining the suggestion that Stella fails (iii) and (iv) in the context of the classroom. Thanks to Heather Battaly for pressing us on this point.
16 Our italics.

for 'yes' and then to show why this case is problematic (and, in doing so, we'll offer some initial suggestions for why individuals might be *tempted* to attribute Stella understanding even though she lacks it).

The case for thinking Stella *can* generate new true evolutionary beliefs (in light of the situation described in CREATIONIST TEACHER*) is, firstly, that Stella seems to be clearly in a better position to form new true evolutionary beliefs than would be, say, a teacher who has merely memorised a teaching book but has failed (as Stella does) to appreciate the intricate way the pieces of the theory fit together. Following from Hills', we might think such an individual (provided she holds the relevant beliefs in question) would be a candidate for items of evolutionary *knowledge* but not understanding, as we'd be inclined to attribute Stella. The second part of the 'yes' case insists that Stella (despite not believing evolutionary theory) has the ability to draw new true evolutionary beliefs *because* she can (in virtue of the coherent picture of evolution she possesses) draw new true beliefs of the form:

According to evolutionary theory, [X].

and further that these *are* new, true, evolutionary beliefs. It strikes us as a trap to get bogged down in the semantic point of whether beliefs of the form *According to evolutionary theory, [X] is itself* a 'new true evolutionary belief' (in the sense that is relevant to Hills' point about what understanding affords us) or whether only learning new unqualified propositions about evolution would qualify.

For our purposes, we want to highlight a very important *limit* on Stella's abilities to acquire new true evolutionary beliefs, a limit in place specifically *because* Stella believes *Not-[X]* for most all the beliefs she has which take the form *According to evolutionary theory, [X]*. Consider that a full description of most of Stella's evolutionary-related doxastic attitudes takes the following conjunctive form:

According to evolutionary theory, [X] and Not-[X]

For example:

According to evolutionary theory, Homo sapiens evolved from Homo erectus AND It's not the case that Homo sapiens evolved from Homo erectus.

Because for every 'X' claim (where X is a claim of evolutionary theory) Stella believes this conjunction, Stella is deeply limited in the new true evolutionary beliefs she can *learn* via her competence with the theory. For every unqualified proposition which she could learn about evolutionary theory (e.g. by applying what she grasps to new cases and new information) she fails to do so. She merely acquires new beliefs in qualified propositions. Even if these new beliefs in qualified propositions 'count' as new beliefs about evolutionary theory, there is in each case, exactly one corresponding belief (expressed by the unqualified proposition) which Stella lacks the ability to learn, and this precisely because she believes evolutionary theory is false.

To summarise the reasoning just put forward: to the extent that (*a la* Hills) understanding *involves* the ability to learn new (relevant) propositions, Stella is profoundly limited in what she is able to learn, and on the basis of this, we think there is good cause to place an important wedge between Stella and individuals who (unencumbered with her mistaken belief that evolutionary theory is false) are able to learn *unrestrictedly* in light of the grasp they have on evolutionary theory. To the extent that this is right, we have a principled explanation for how we can escape the puzzle, without (illicitly) *relying* on the truth of moderate factivity to make the point.

Moderate factivity, recall, looked to be in trouble because the following two claims seemed very plausible:

(i) CREATIONIST TEACHER* is a case where genuine objectual understanding is present; and yet,
(ii) moderate factivity is not satisfied, even though the propositions constituting evolutionary theory are themselves true

We've suggested that the best way to vitiate the threat to moderate factivity posed by CREATIONIST TEACHER* is to deny (i), and so to say, contrary to what might have seemed originally compelling, that Stella in fact does not understand evolutionary theory.

6. Concluding Remarks

We want to conclude with two final points, both aimed at diagnosing why we might originally be inclined to attribute understanding in CREATIONIST TEACHER* even though this is a mistake. The first point is that, at least in her capacity as a teacher and academic, Stella is *acting* as if evolutionary theory is true, by carrying on her intellectual activities as though the view is true. To the extent that she does this, we naturally get the sense that evolutionary theory is something Stella uses regularly as a premise in practical reasoning and deliberations (as these deliberations and reasoning would play out in the classroom). But then, given the tight connection between practical deliberation and belief, it becomes hard to see how Stella doesn't (contrary to her protestations) simply *believe* the theory. Of course, and setting aside the psychological plausibility, it is stipulated in the case that she does not believe the theory. The point here is to suggest that one reason we might be inclined to attribute to her something she'd have only if she actually believed the theory (i.e. understanding) is that she is (in light of the details of the case) one we easily imagine as possessing all the trappings of one who did believe the theory.

The second concluding remark is that we might be mistakenly tempted to attribute to Stella understanding because Stella seems to attain a kind of cognitive achievement which is lacked by individuals who (for example) merely believe the key propositions of evolutionary theory on the basis of testimony but fail to see how they fit together, or for that matter people who have a coherent grasp on what they *take* to be evolutionary theory while (and unlike Stella) confused about what evolutionary theory actually says. Stella's epistemic situation is defective in neither of these ways, and so this might lead us to think that understanding rather than something less would rightly mark Stella's achievement not shared in the other two kinds of contrast cases.

Following Riggs' (2004) terminology—particularly his distinction between understanding and *intelligibility*—we think the explanation for the attractiveness of the line of thinking just stated is best accounted for by the fact that Stella has achieved a kind of intelligibility that is plausibly a necessary (but not sufficient) condition for understanding. Intelligibility is attained when one pieces together or grasps the items of information in a subject matter but regardless of whether the agent has *any* true beliefs. For example, a defense attorney might offer a tightly spun and very believable account of a series of events surrounding a murder in 'Case X' which helps the individuals of the jury to make sense very nicely of all the evidence shown in a courtroom over the course of Case X. By appreciating the way the defense attorney's story fits together, a juror might well attain a kind of intelligibility she lacked previously, when confused about how the evidence fit together. And this is so even if the defense attorney is clever but deceitful, and so even if the story told is one that was simply made up. Such an ability to grasp the relationships between the propositions is widely taken to be a hallmark of objectual understanding[17], and so the presence of intelligibility attained by Stella in CREATIONIST TEACHER* might plausibly explain part of the initial pull to think Stella can understand EVOLUTIONARY THEORY* without believing it: because she has attained a certain thing that one understands only if one attains.

---

17 See for example Grimm (2011) and Kvanvig (2004, Chapter 8).

In conclusion, while 'CREATIONIST TEACHER'-style cases pose a much more difficult kind of problem for a moderate factivity constraint on understanding than did the false-understanding style cases canvassed in §3, ultimately, moderate factivity remains unscathed.[18]

References

Carter, J. A. (2014). Relativism, Knowledge and Understanding. *Episteme* 11 (1): 35–52.
Carter, J. A. and Gordon, E. C. (2011). Norms of Assertion: The Quantity and Quality of Epistemic Support. *Philosophia* 39 (4):615–635.
Carter, J. A. and Nickel, P. J. (2014). On Testimony and Transmission. *Episteme* 11 (02):145–155.
Grimm, S. (2014). Understanding as Knowledge of Causes. In A. Fairweather (ed.), *Virtue Epistemology Naturalized: Bridges Between Virtue Epistemology and Philosophy of Science*. Dordrecht: Springer.
Hazlett, A. (2010). The Myth of Factive Verbs. *Philosophy and Phenomenological Research* 80 (3): 497–522.
Hills, A. (2009). Moral Testimony and Moral Epistemology. *Ethics* 120 (1): 94–127.
Kletzl, S. (2011). Somebody Has to Know: Jennifer Lackey on the Transmission of Epistemic Properties. In C. Löffler and W. Jäger (eds), *Erkenntnistheorie: Kontexte, Werte, Dissens*.
Kvanvig, J. (2003). *The Value of Knowledge and the Pursuit of Understanding*. New York: Cambridge University Press.
Kvanvig, J. (2009). The Value of Understanding. In D. Pritchard, A. Haddock and A. Millar (eds.), *Epistemic Value*. Oxford: Oxford University Press.
Lackey, J.(2007). Norms of Assertion. *Noûs* 41 (4):594–626.
Lackey, J. (2008). *Learning From Words: Testimony as a Source of Knowledge*. Oxford: Oxford University Press.
Myers-Schulz, B. and Schwitzgebel, E. (2013). Knowing That P without Believing That P. *Noûs* 47 (2):371–384.
Pritchard, D. (2009). Knowledge, Understanding and Epistemic Value. *Royal Institute of Philosophy Supplement* 64, 19–43.
Riggs, W. (2003). Understanding Virtue and the Virtue of Understanding. In M. DePaul and L. Zagzebski (eds.), *Intellectual Virtue: Perspectives from Ethics and Epistemology*. Oxford: Oxford University Press.
Whitcomb, D. (2012). Epistemic Value. In A. Cullison (ed.), *The Continuum Companion to Epistemology*. London: Continuum.
Wilkenfeld, D. (2015). The Contextual Quasi-Factivity of Objectual Understanding. Manuscript.
Zagzebski, L. (2001). Recovering Understanding. In M. Steup (ed.), *Knowledge, Truth and Duty*. Oxford: Oxford University Press.

---

[18] The authors would like to thank the volume's editors and Heather Battaly for helpful feedback.

Contributors

Jochen Briesen, University of Konstanz

Adam J. Carter, University of Edinburgh

Matthew Chrisman, University of Edinburgh

Terence Cuneo, University of Vermont

Davide Fassio, University of Geneva

Emma Gordon, University of Edinburgh

Martin Grajner, Dresden University of Technology

Christos Kyriakou, University of Cyprus

Veli Mitova, University of Johannesburg

Christian Piller, University of York

Duncan Pritchard, University of Edinburgh

Andrew Reisner, Uppsala University

Pedro Schmechtig, Dresden University of Technology

Mona Simion, KU Leuven Center for Logic and Analytic Philosophy

Erik Stei, University of Bonn

Nicholas Unwin, Lancaster University

Hamid Vahid, Institute for Fundamental Sciences Teheran

Chase Wrenn, University of Alabama

Author Index

Achinstein, P. 19
Adler, J. 139
Ahlstrom-Vij, K. 13, 245, 258, 260, 262, 267f., 333–335
Allkemper, J. 304
Alston, W. P. 3, 159, 228, 269, 283, 325, 327, 383f., 389, 408
Alvarez, M. 1, 52, 63
Anscombe, G. E. M. 176
Aristotle 24, 149, 325, 393f., 400
Arnold, Alex 51, 53, 55, 67
Austin, J.L. 122, 158

Baehr, J. 205, 394, 401
Balcerak Jackson, B. 304
Ballantyne, N. 95
Battaly, H. 429, 438, 442
Beaver, D. I. 39
Becker, K. 246
Beckermann, A. 3
Bennett, J. 127
Benton, M. 7, 432
Berker, S. 11, 13, 16, 25, 229, 240–246, 250, 252–262, 264f., 267–269, 278, 288–290, 304, 307–321, 333f., 336f.
Bird, A. 66, 338
Bishop, M. A. 21, 266f.
Blackburn, S. 73, 386
Blome-Tillmann, M. 194f.
Boghossian, P. 22, 100, 338, 387
BonJour, L. 1f., 228, 252, 283
Brady, M. S., 345
Braeuer, H. 346
Brandom, R. 395
Bratman, M. 124f., 128, 213
Brendel, E. 185
Broome, J. 5, 77, 96–100
Brown, C. 309f.
Brown, J. 165, 167f., 171–175, 181
Brunero, J. 97, 102
Bykvist 338, 352

Carter, J. A 19f., 28, 423, 425, 430, 432, 438
Cherniak, C. 96
Chisholm, R. 210, 251, 408
Chrisman, M. 1, 16, 24, 26, 393
Christensen, D. 105
Chudnoff, E. 33
Clifford, W. K. 199, 205, 385, 394, 396
Coffman, E. J. 51, 53, 95
Cohen, L. J. 43, 105, 113, 124, 142, 186–188, 190–192, 194–196, 399, 408
Cohen, S. 43, 105, 113, 124, 142, 186–188, 190–192, 194–196, 399, 408
Comesaña, J. 34, 47f.
Conee, E. 34, 67, 283, 338
Copp, D. 85
Cowie, C. 94
Cuneo, T. 6, 21, 71, 73, 77, 85, 348, 392–394
Cuoto, A. 221

Dancy, J. 1, 102, 202
D'Arms, J. 344
David, M. 9, 22f., 85, 120, 131, 134, 165, 188, 200, 221, 325, 408
Davidson, D. 1, 3, 7f., 13, 15f., 22, 26, 210
de Ridder, J. 95, 103
DePaul, M. 415
DeRose, K. 7f., 137, 148, 185–188, 190–192, 195f., 399
Descartes, R. 251, 385
Dewey, J. 293
Doggett, T. 94
Dougherty, T. 68
Douven, I. 8, 137–147, 150, 152, 156–158, 160f.
Dummett, M. 131
Dunn, J. 13, 245, 258, 260, 262, 267f., 333–335

Elgin, C. 19, 304, 331, 383, 397, 419, 425
Ellis, B. 131
Emundts, D. 304

Engel, P. 338, 351
Enoch, D. 72, 95

Fantl, J. 10, 67, 167, 170, 256
Fassio, D. 9, 22, 165, 176
Feldman, R. 34, 67, 252, 283, 330, 338, 384, 396
Finlay, S. 19
Firth, R. 257, 319, 327, 333
Fitelson, B. 51, 104
FitzPatrick, W. 72
Fogelin, R. 391
Foley, R. 3, 227, 283, 327, 330, 383, 408
Frankfurt, H. 149, 210 f.
Freitag, W. 185
Fumerton, R. 68, 229, 257, 287, 330, 386, 391, 396 f.

Gao, J. 183
Gaultier, B. 222
Geach, P. T. 410
Gelfert, A. 417
Gerken, M. 165, 167–169, 171, 173, 175, 179, 181
Geurts, B. 39
Gibbons, J. 142, 338
Gigerenzer, G. 272
Glüer, K. 22 f., 341–343, 348
Goebel, A. 304
Goldman, A. 13 f., 230, 246, 252, 255, 258, 260, 283, 312, 320 f., 325, 327, 334 f., 408, 415
Goldstein, D. G. 272
Goodman, N. 118
Gordon, E. C. 19 f., 28, 62, 423 f., 432
Gordon, R. 19 f., 28, 62, 423 f., 432
Grajner, M. 1, 3, 20, 33, 198, 206, 220 f., 404
Greco, J. 68, 397, 411
Green, M. 153, 158
Grice, P. 144
Griffioen, A. 304
Griffiths, P. 387
Grimm, S. 19, 206, 215, 278, 345, 425, 441
Groenendijk, J.
Gunnarrsson, L.

Haack, S. 3
Haddock, A. 278, 408, 411, 417, 419
Haji, I. 148 f.
Hamblin, C. L. 294
Hanisch, C. 221
Harman, G. 84, 100, 390, 396, 399
Hattiangadi 338, 352
Hawthorne, J. 7, 137, 165, 167, 170, 172, 186
Hazlett, A. 237, 424
Hegel, G. W. F. 395
Heil, J. 199, 205
Helfer, T. 304
Heuer, U. 231
Higginbotham, J. 295
Hills, A. 28, 424, 437–440
Hilpinen, R. 54
Hofmann, F. 3
Hookway, C. 293
Hornsby, J. 63
Horwich, P. 125
Huemer, M. 33 f., 46
Humberstone, I. L. 176
Hume, D. 129
Hyman, J. 52

Ichikawa, J. 188, 286

Jacobson, D. 344
James, W. 1, 27, 36, 251, 280, 383–387, 409
Jenkins, C. S. 286, 288, 290, 300
Jones, W. 201, 412
Joyce, R. 75, 92

Kagan, S. 254
Kahneman, D. 398
Kalderon, M. 73
Kant, I. 1, 131, 133 f.
Kantin, H. 51
Kappel, K. 417
Karttunen, L. 294
Kearns, S. 97
Kelly, T. 2, 10, 95, 105, 199, 383, 386
Kelp, C. 53, 140 f., 159, 417, 429
Kenny, A. 61
Kitcher, P. 19
Klein, Peter 51, 53, 55, 57, 63, 331

Kletzl, S.   430, 434
Kolodny, N.   77, 96
Kornblith, H.   199, 201, 205f., 246, 252
Korsgaard, C. M.   202, 254
Kusch, M.   204, 221
Kvanvig, J.   3, 19, 153f., 216, 278, 345, 397, 412, 417, 423–426, 441
Kyriacou, C.   18, 27, 383, 391, 393

Lackey, J.   28, 137, 141, 147, 150–152, 160, 423f., 432
Lamb, D.   134
Lang, G.   230
Lehrer, K.   43, 141, 283, 408
Leite, A.   68
Leitgeb, H.   286
Lewis, D.   75, 185f., 188–190, 194–196
Lipton, P.   19
Littlejohn, C   2, 4, 20, 22, 34f., 51–54, 63, 68, 147, 167, 170, 172, 235, 284, 338
Locke, D.   131, 167
Luzzi, F.   51f.
Lycan, W. G.   205
Lynch, M.   3, 8f., 204, 325, 338

MacFarlane, J.   111
Mantel, S.   94, 304
Martin, M. G. F.   1, 3, 6, 20, 33, 198, 206, 220f., 404, 427, 431
McCain, K.   3, 34
McDowell, J.   6, 344
McHugh, C.   21, 341, 349
McKenna, R.   174, 178
McKinnon, R.   174, 181
Mellor, H.   386
Millar, A.   22, 348, 408, 411, 417, 419
Mitova, V.   2, 9f., 23, 34, 53, 199, 202, 204, 348
Montminy, M.   174, 197
Myers-Schulz, B.   432f.

Nagel, T.   241, 269f.
Nickel, P. J.   430, 432
Noordhof, P.   127
Nozick, R.   187, 232

Olson, E.   6, 21, 71, 75–82, 84–87, 93f., 230, 397
Olson, J.   6, 21, 71, 75–82, 84–87, 93f., 230, 397

Palmira, M.   95, 113
Papineau, D.   131, 339, 387
Parfit, D.   96f., 102, 231f.
Pauer-Studer, H.   221
Pedersen, N.   237
Peirce, C.S.   123, 131, 133
Pettigrew, R.   286
Pettit, P.   309
Piller, C.   11, 13, 25, 231, 307, 383, 389, 395, 404
Plato   134, 385, 402, 430
Platts, M.   176
Pritchard, D. H.   3, 14f., 27, 199, 300, 397, 407f., 411f., 414, 417–419, 425
Pryor, J.   33f., 36f.
Putnam, H.   131f.

Quine, W. V. O.   1f., 119, 134, 252, 395, 398, 403

Rabinowicz. D.   230f., 231f.
Rachels, S.   274
Railton, P.   199, 207
Rawls, J.   241, 307, 310
Raz, J.   231
Reisner, A.   5, 21, 95f., 102, 106, 232
Reynolds, S.   159
Riggs, W.   3, 227, 383, 386, 395, 397, 412, 425, 441
Rizzieri, A.   51, 67
Rønnow-Rasmussen, T.   230f., 231f.
Rorty, R.   1, 3, 8f., 13, 15f., 22, 26
Rosenberg, J.   1–18, 20–22, 26
Rosenkoetter, T.   94
Rosenthal, J.   304
Russell, B.   71
Ryan, S.   400, 403

Sandel, M.   394
Sartwell, C.   3
Scanlon, T. M.   4, 201, 203, 308, 344, 348
Schaffer, J.   7f., 186, 191f.

Schechter, J. 304
Schellenberg, S. 46
Schmechtig, P. 1, 13f., 17, 26, 198, 206, 220f., 304, 325, 346, 404
Schnee, Ian 34f., 44–49, 51
Schroeder, M. 4, 35, 232f.
Schwitzgebel, E. 432
Searle, J. R. 176, 178
Sebald, W. 217–219
Sellars, W. 1, 15f., 22f., 395
Shackel, N. 97
Shafer-Landau, R. 73
Shaffer, M. 54–56
Shah, N. 22, 201, 205f., 319, 338, 348, 408
Siegel, S. 274
Silins, N. 48
Skorupski, J. 97, 232, 348
Smith, M. 192–196, 203
Smithies, D. 165, 168, 174, 338
Sosa, E. 35, 45f., 52, 205, 345, 383, 398, 408, 415
Stalnaker, R. 296
Stanley, J. 165, 167, 170, 172, 186
Star, D 97
Steglich-Petersen, A. 95, 205, 208, 342
Stich, S. 199, 204
Stokhof, M. 294, 297
Strawson, P.F. 134
Sutton, J. 52, 338
Swinburne, R. 412
Sylvan, K. 35, 45f.

Talbot, B. 230, 234f., 239f., 328–332
Thomson, J. 291
Tiercelin, C. 222
Tomayko, J.E. 110
Treanor, N. 15, 415
Trout, D. 266f.
Tucker, Ch. 33f., 46
Turri, J. 2, 4, 33–35, 42, 48, 137, 147, 178, 411

Unger, P. 62, 68
Unwin, N. 8f., 21, 117, 119, 133, 135

Van Fraassen, B. C. 119
Van Inwagen, P. 71
Velleman, D. 20, 22f., 120, 176, 200, 205, 207–213, 218, 221, 338, 348, 408
Vollet, J. 183

Wallace, R. J. 203, 212
Warfield, T. 51, 53, 331
Way, J. 77, 203, 311
Wedgwood, R. 22, 96, 99, 199, 205, 325, 338, 348, 383, 386, 408
Weiner, M. 7, 137, 338
Whitcomb, D. 345, 400, 425
White, R. 95, 431
Whiting, D. 21f., 94, 338–340
Wiggins, D. 344
Wikforss, A. 22f., 341–343, 348
Wilkenfeld, D. 426
Wilkins, J. 387
Williams, B. 120, 126–128, 130, 186, 202, 206, 292, 303, 337
Williams, M. 120, 126–128, 130, 186, 202, 206, 292, 303, 337
Williamson, T. 3, 7, 35, 46, 52–54, 68, 103, 137, 139, 142, 144, 147, 152, 157, 165, 167f., 170, 172, 185, 338, 432
Wittgenstein, L. 25, 279, 292, 303
Woodward, J. B. 19
Worsnip, A. 107
Wrenn, C. B. 13, 16, 24, 249, 252, 272, 334
Wright, C. 25, 185, 279, 292f., 300, 302f., 432

Zagzebski, L. 19, 199, 205, 331, 383, 385, 388, 392, 394f., 397, 400, 412, 419, 424
Zangwill, N. 176, 338
Zimmerman, M. 148f.

Subject Index

acceptance 9, 21f., 117f., 120, 124–126, 128f., 286, 292, 338
act consequentialism 140
act utilitarianism 140, 234, 252f.
agency 10, 23, 200, 207–214, 216, 220f., 407, 419
aim
– aiming at truth 22, 117, 127, 130, 208, 220
– constitutive 7, 9f., 15–24, 26, 92, 120f., 123, 137, 177–182, 200, 205–208, 210, 212–214, 220f., 269, 343, 394
– inherent 325, 337, 340, 343f., 347
– intensional 122f.
– of belief 15,16, 26, 358, 377
anti-luck virtue epistemology 419

belief
– centered epistemology 272
– dispositional 428f.
– enkrasia 102, 106, 112f.
– evidential norm of 331
– first-order 211, 241f., 431
– fixation 27, 383f., 386–391, 393, 395, 398, 404
– higher-order 106, 241f.
– impermissible 22, 24, 66, 138, 149, 151, 310, 317
– non-truth-indicatively justified 292f., 297, 299–303
– peripheral 19, 426
– permissible 9, 22, 24, 66, 120f., 137, 149, 161, 168, 254, 316
– self-fulfilling 313–315
– true evolutionary 438f.
– truth-determinative feature of 4
– unjustified 20, 24, 51, 69, 72, 82, 150, 175, 199, 230, 237, 240, 242f., 246, 250, 254, 260–262, 267, 270, 272f., 277, 282, 284, 287–290, 314, 331
– utilitarianism 233, 311f., 316, 319
blameless 147–152, 154, 156f., 172
blameworthy 148–151, 154, 156, 172

cognitive achievement 419, 425, 428, 441
cognitive conduct 15, 18
cognitive projects 292f., 297, 299–303
commonality thesis 9, 165
– horizontal approach to 174, 182
– vertical approach to 166, 174f.
consequentialism 11–13, 25f., 233f., 239–243, 249, 264, 277–288, 290–293, 300, 303f., 307, 309f., 312f., 318, 320, 328f., 332–336, 348, 350
– ethical 11, 25, 277–285, 287, 290f., 303, 307–309, 316–318, 320f., 409–411, 413, 419
– hedonistic 25, 280–282, 286f., 291, 303, 402
– objective 282–285, 303
– subjective 300
– veritistic 12, 16f., 24f., 256, 278, 280, 283f., 291f., 297, 299–304, 337
constructive empiricism 21, 119, 128, 130f.
context
– conversational 8, 169, 172f., 191
– deliberative 169f., 173, 177–180, 353
– dependent standards 188
creationist teacher case 28, 424, 431

deliberation
– practical 213, 263, 392, 440
– theoretical 213, 263
deontic correctness 337
direction of fit 9, 20, 127, 176–180
disagreement 5, 9, 19, 21, 88, 95, 101–107, 109–113, 119, 122f., 176, 251, 400, 424–426
– improbable 109f.
– probable 109f.
– radical 8, 22, 117, 119, 134
doxastic
– abundance 256, 268, 273
– norms 17, 325f., 329, 331f., 336–344, 347–353
– voluntarism 272, 384

epistemic
- antinomy 258–260
- anti-realism 6, 131
- asceticism 384, 391f., 404
- axiology 27, 407f., 419
- cognitivism 6
- curiosity 345f.
- duties 148, 150, 154, 273, 398
- error theory 6, 21, 71–82, 84–86, 88f., 92f.
- evaluations 11, 14f., 22–24, 26, 265, 269, 280f., 310
- externalism 102f., 203, 209, 284, 397
- goals 1, 14, 16f. 24, 158, 227, 245, 251–253, 263, 272f, 286, 310, 327, 329–333, 336–338, 343–348, 350–352, 383–390, 392–396, 398f., 404
- internalism 46, 102f., 202f., 209, 284, 397
- normativity 1–3, 9f., 23f., 27, 137f., 200, 214f., 221f., 227, 252, 263, 311f., 320, 325–329, 331, 334, 336f., 340f, 343–346, 351, 353, 358, 359, 372, 283, 404
- norms 1, 7, 9–11, 16f., 23, 142, 158f, 162, 166–168, 173–175, 179, 182, 199–203, 205–209, 213–216, 219–221, 310, 336, 339, 342f, 352
- oughts 19, 97f., 100, 235, 329, 331f.
- peers 95f., 101f., 108–112, 400
- reasons 1–9, 11f., 20f., 24, 26f., 33–43, 46, 50, 206, 214, 227, 229–235, 329, 331, 359, 363, 372–374
- reductionism 6, 21, 71, 74–76, 79–82, 84–88, 91–93
- self-promotion 24, 250f., 260, 264, 268, 273
- standards 8, 22–24, 168–172, 174, 177–182, 185–192, 194–197, 227, 386f., 389, 391
- teleology 24, 249–251, 253–256, 260–265, 268–273, 309
- utility 139, 158, 286
epistemic consequentialism 1, 10–14, 16, 24–26, 225, 227–230, 233–236, 238–246, 264, 277, 279, 281, 284–291, 297, 299, 301–303, 307f., 312–316, 326f., 333f., 350f., 414

- direct 242, 282
- indirect 13, 282, 284
- moderate 328, 333–336
- radical 328f., 333
ethics-epistemology analogy 11
eudaimonia 18, 27, 384, 388, 393–396, 398–400, 402–404
evidence norm 201, 205, 217, 219f.
evidential externalism 101–103
evidential internalism 101f., 108
evidentialism 5, 269, 396
evidentialist reliabilism 47
explanation 2, 7f., 10f., 13, 17, 19, 22, 24, 37, 41, 63, 76, 98, 138f., 143–147, 156, 158, 161, 165f., 169, 171, 173–175, 181–183, 202f., 219, 228, 245f., 290, 307, 315, 318f., 326, 330, 332, 336f., 339–346, 348–352, 385, 401, 418, 433, 436f., 440f.

factive conceptions of understanding 397
factivity 19, 28, 37, 144, 146, 185, 188, 423–431, 433–436, 440, 442
- contextual 181, 189, 399, 426
- moderate 19, 28, 424, 426–431, 433–436, 440, 442
- quasi 426
- weak 424–426, 434
factualism about reasons 3f.
fitting attitude theory of value 345
foundationalism 68f.

goal
- atomistic epistemic 395
- extrinsic 18–20, 48
- final 235, 238f., 393–396, 398, 400
- generic 336, 350f.
- holistic epistemic 395f., 404
- inherent doxastic 326, 337, 343f., 346, 350
- instrumental 398, 400
- inversely proportionate 27, 383, 386, 393, 404
- primary 1, 17, 351, 395
- regulative 16–18, 20–22

human flourishing 394, 398

Subject Index — 451

inquiry   14–18, 26–28, 54, 131f., 235, 249, 251, 263, 267, 271, 273, 325–331, 334–338, 340, 343–353, 383, 385f., 394–396, 398f., 404, 416–418

James problem   27, 383–389, 392, 395, 404
justification   1f., 5, 8, 10, 12, 15, 17f., 20f., 24, 33, 39, 46–48, 51f., 55, 57–60, 64, 66–69, 79, 85, 95, 121, 123, 137, 140–142, 153f., 157, 159, 174, 177, 182, 199, 222, 227–229, 233–235, 239, 245f., 250, 255f., 260–265, 268, 270, 273, 277f., 280f., 284, 302, 310, 327f., 330, 333, 351, 386f., 389, 391, 393, 396, 407f., 432
– as truth-conducive   386
– counter-closure of   51–53, 57f.
– inferential   66–69
– moral   280
– non-inferential   39, 45, 47, 59, 66f., 69
– pragmatic   277

knowledge   1, 3f., 7f., 14f., 17–20, 22f., 27f., 51f., 54f., 58–62, 64–69, 71, 89, 103, 118, 121, 131f., 137f., 140–146, 149–152, 157–161, 165, 167–170, 172, 174, 177–183, 185–189, 191–194, 197, 199, 234, 237–239, 241, 251, 261, 265, 311, 330f., 336, 338, 345, 347, 384f., 391–393, 398f., 403, 407, 411, 413, 416–419, 424f., 432f., 437–439
– account of assertion   8, 137, 140
– first epistemology   20, 68
– from falsehood   4, 7, 20, 51
– norm of assertion   7f., 137f., 140f., 143, 145f., 148, 153, 158, 161, 172, 174, 432

metaethical externalism   203
Moorean statements   143–146, 156f., 161

no-guidance argument   340, 343
normative
– authority   73–75, 77, 81, 83, 85, 87–90, 92f., 199–201, 205, 208, 210, 215f., 220f.
– demands   17, 28, 123, 301, 335, 339f., 350, 423f.
– force   2, 15, 17, 23f., 74, 200, 206f., 213f., 218, 227, 318, 327, 329–332, 338, 340–344, 347–351
normativity   1–3, 9f., 23f., 27, 76f., 95–97, 100, 135, 137f., 141, 147, 156f., 161, 199f., 205, 207, 214f., 221f., 227, 252, 263, 311f., 317, 320, 325–327, 332, 336f., 341, 351, 383, 388, 404
– of action   1, 16, 22f., 85, 138, 147, 150, 153, 156–159, 210, 213, 271, 310
– of assertion   7f., 132, 137, 139, 147, 151, 153, 156–161, 165, 174, 179, 181f.
norm
– of assertion   7f., 137f., 140–146, 153, 158–161, 172, 174, 432
– of belief   8, 20, 51f., 69, 168, 174, 331, 340
– of social commitment   149f.

peer disagreement   101, 109f., 112
perceptual experience   36, 47
practical reasoning   7, 9, 22f., 165–175, 177, 179, 181–183, 205, 211, 389, 440
presupposition   39, 84, 176–179, 292f., 295–303
– pragmatic   295–299
– semantic   295, 297f.
priority   11, 16f., 26, 310, 326, 337, 343, 351, 353, 399
– axiological   326
– deontic   326
propositionalism about reasons   35
proposition-set theory   293, 297, 303
psychological facts   35, 45f.
psychologism   2f., 20, 33–37, 43, 49
– about reasons   3, 20, 33f.
– factive   33–35, 43
– non-factive   33–35
– truthy   33f., 43

radical disagreement   8, 21f., 117, 119, 134
rational credibility   8, 22, 137, 140–142, 144f., 150, 159–161
rationality   2, 4f., 21, 47, 95–97, 99f., 103, 112f., 139, 177, 232, 243, 269, 271, 277f., 390
rational requirements   5, 21, 95f., 100, 102f., 105–107, 112f.

narrow scope 5, 99, 336
wide scope 5
realism 6, 9, 22, 72, 75, 85, 119, 131–133, 135
– anti-realism 2, 6, 25, 33, 68, 105, 123, 131, 307 f., 318
– internal 22, 131–133, 135,
reason-giving force of epistemic norms 201–203, 205–207, 216, 221, 348–350, 353
reasoning 7, 12, 20 f., 51 f., 55–59, 64 f., 68 f., 96–98, 100 f., 104, 111, 144, 170, 173, 177–181, 206, 235, 237, 243 f., 251, 258, 269 f., 272, 326, 391 f., 415–417, 419, 431, 440
– conjectural 177–179, 181
– deliberative 178–180
– practical 7, 9, 22 f., 165–175, 177, 179, 181–183, 205, 211, 389, 440
– theoretical 100, 269 f.
reasons
– and bad cases 43
– and rationality 47, 277 f.
– motivational 1, 23, 98, 200, 202–204, 206, 208 f.
– normative 1, 2, 4, 95–98, 112
– object-given 231–233
– state-given 231–233
– truth promoting non-evidential 234, 328
– validating 368
reliabilism
– process 12 f., 244–246, 255, 333–335
– strategic 266
requirements
– direct evidential 103, 109
– higher order evidential 104
– of reasoning 95, 101, 112
rule-consequentialism 11 f., 282, 284, 316
rules
– of action 16, 372, 378, 379
– of attention 189
– of criticism 16, 18–24, 174, 235
rule utilitarianism 234, 244

sensitivity condition 243
separateness-of-persons principle 25, 316–318
separateness of propositions 241, 259, 261, 264, 267, 308 f., 312 f., 333 f.

source
– of epistemic normativity 10 f., 16 f., 26, 227, 325–329, 331, 334, 336 f., 340 f., 343 f., 346, 348, 350 f., 353, 385
– of epistemic norms 1, 10, 15, 23, 26, 199–210, 213–216, 220 f., 339
– of epistemic oughts 235, 329
structural rationality 4
subject-sensitive invariantism 185
swamping problem 27, 412, 414

teleological account
– of norms 7, 10, 16, 21, 310, 338 f., 348, 350
– of values 345
testimony 105, 150, 152, 160, 243, 430, 432–434, 441
thetic representation 180–183
trade-offs 12 f., 240 f., 245, 289–291, 310 f., 315–318, 320, 330, 333
– cross-propositional 24, 245, 250 f., 258 f., 261, 264 f., 268, 273
– propositional 13, 245
– structural 333 f.
transcendental idealism 22, 132–135
truth 1–27, 44, 54, 63, 74, 92, 117 f., 120–133, 135, 137, 140, 142, 150, 160 f., 165, 174, 178, 186, 188, 199, 205–207, 216, 220, 227–229, 231, 233–246, 249–251, 255, 257, 259 f., 262 f., 271 f., 277–280, 283, 285 f., 288–293, 297–304, 307, 309 f., 312–315, 319 f., 325, 327, 329, 331 f., 334–342, 345, 347 f., 350–352, 383–389, 391, 395–399, 401, 403 f., 407–410, 412–419, 425, 431–433, 436, 440
– conducivism 312–314
– indication principle 11, 25, 277, 279, 285 f., 291, 303 f.
– indicative factors 289, 292, 299, 302

understanding 2 f., 5, 14, 17–20, 26–28, 73, 77, 91, 101, 133, 135, 183, 200, 212, 238, 250, 269, 293, 311, 330 f., 336, 342, 345, 347, 351, 383–385, 393, 396–404, 407, 409–411, 415, 417–419, 423–429, 431, 433–442
– dispositional 428 f.

– evidential   393, 396–404
– moral   28, 424, 428
– of false theories   428, 436
– propositional 423
– scientific   425
– subjective 425
– why   19, 342, 347, 351, 396, 418, 423, 437

value
– ethical 411, 413, 419
– fundamental   228, 239, 252
– monism   408, 412–414
– of the epistemic   15, 28, 407–411, 413, 419

– overall   241, 253–258, 263f., 266
– primitive   253f.
– ultimate   252, 258
veritistic value monism   14–16

weighing value approach   388, 392, 404
weighing value dilemma   18, 384, 388f.
Weltanschauung   400f., 403
wisdom   3, 14, 18, 27, 330f., 336, 345, 347, 383f., 395, 399–404, 407
– conducive virtues   403
– epistemic humility theory of   400
– theoretical minimal   399–404
wrong kind of reason problem   229–232

www.ingramcontent.com/pod-product-compliance
Lightning Source LLC
Chambersburg PA
CBHW022103290426
44112CB00008B/526